HAMMOND'S
NEW SUPREME
WORLD ATLAS

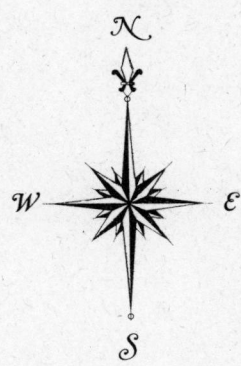

GARDEN CITY BOOKS
GARDEN CITY   NEW YORK

Contents

HISTORICAL MAPS

List of Maps

HAMMOND'S
WORLD ATLAS AND GAZETTEER

Copyright MCMLIV by C. S. Hammond & Co., New York. Printed in U.S.A.

GAZETTEER-INDEX OF THE WORLD

This alphabetical list of grand divisions, countries, states, colonial possessions, etc., gives area, population, capital, seat of government or chief town, and index references and numbers of plates on which they are shown on the largest scale. The mother country of colonial possessions is indicated by abbreviations in parentheses. The index reference shows the square on the respective map in which the name of the country, state or colonial possession is located.

ABBREVIATIONS

Aust. = Australian.	I. = Island.	Pak. = Pakistan.	Trust. = Trust Territory.
Belg. = Belgian or Belgium.	Is. = Islands.	pen. = peninsula.	U. S. A. = United States of America.
Br. = British Commonwealth of Nations.	It. = Italian or Italy.	Port. = Portugal or Portuguese.	U. S. Adm. = U. S. Administration.
	Jap. = Japan or Japanese.	Rep. = Republic.	U. S. S. R. = Union of Soviet Socialist Republics.
Dan. = Danish or Denmark.	Mand. = Mandate.	So. = South.	U. of So. Africa = Union of South Africa.
E. = East.	N. = North.	Sp. = Spain or Spanish.	
Fr. = France or French.	Neth. = Netherlands.	sq. mi. = square miles.	W. = West.
Gr. = Greece or Greek.	N. Z. = New Zealand.	S. S. R. = Soviet Socialist Republic.	

Country	Area (Sq. Miles)	Population	Capital or Chief Town	Index Ref.	Plate No.
Aden (incl. Protectorate) (Br.)	112,000	650,000	Aden	E 7	26
Aden Colony	75	80,516	Aden	E 7	26
Admiralty Is. (Aust. Tr.)	820	13,000	Lorengau	E 6	37
Afghanistan	250,000	12,000,000	Kabul	J 3	26
Africa	11,850,000	190,000,000			34, 35
Alabama, U.S.A.	51,078	3,061,743	Montgomery	M 6	43
Alaska (U.S.A.)	571,065	128,643	Juneau	C 3	38
Albania	11,096	1,112,355	Tiranë	E 5	21
Alberta, Canada	248,800	939,501	Edmonton	G 4	40
Aleutian Islands (U.S.A.)	6,800	5,600		F 3	6
Algeria (Fr.)	851,284	8,681,785	Alger (Algiers)	G 5	34
Andaman Is. (India)	2,508	21,316	Port Blair	G 1	29
Andorra	191	5,265	Andorra la Vieja	F 3	17
Anglo-Egyptian Sudan	967,500	8,309,663	Khartoum	M 9	34
Angola (Port.)	481,351	4,094,000	Loanda	K14	35
Antarctica	5,500,000				8
Antigua (Br.) (incl. Barbuda and Redonda)	171	41,757	St. Johns	G 3	45
				E 3	45
Antilles, Greater, Lesser					
Arabia	1,000,000	10,700,000		D 5	26
Arctic Ocean					8
Argentina	1,078,266	16,108,573	Buenos Aires	H10	47
Arizona, U.S.A.	113,580	749,587	Phoenix	E 6	42
Arkansas, U.S.A.	52,725	1,909,511	Little Rock	K 6	43
Armenian S.S.R. (U.S.S.R.)	11,500	1,345,000	Yerevan (Erivan)	F 5	22
Ascension Island (Br.)	34	159	Georgetown	D13	35
Asia	16,500,000	1,301,000,000			25
Australia, Commonwealth of (Br.)	2,974,581	7,579,358	Canberra		36
Australian Capital Territory	939	16,905	Canberra	J 7	36
Austria	32,369	6,918,959	Wien (Vienna)	B-C 3	20
Azerbaidzhan S.S.R. (U.S.S.R.)	33,100	3,100,000	Baku	F 5	22
Azores Islands (Port.)	890	287,091	Ponta Delgada	B 4	34
Bahama Islands (Br.)	4,404	79,000	Nassau	C 1	45
Bahrein Islands (Br.)	213	109,650	Manama	F 4	26
Balearic Islands (Sp.)	1,936	422,127	Palma	H 3	17
Baluchistan (Pak.)	134,002	530,000	Quetta	A 3	29
Barbados (Br.)	166	192,800	Bridgetown	G 4	45
Barbuda and Redonda Is. (Br.)	63	979	Codrington	F-G 3	45
Basutoland (Br.)	11,716	563,854	Maseru	M17	35
Bechuanaland Prot. (Br.)	275,000	294,232	Mafeking	L16	35
Belgian Congo	902,274	11,121,463	Léopoldville	L12	35
Belgium	11,775	8,512,195	Bruxelles (Brussels)	E 7	15
Bermuda (Br.)	21	37,000	Hamilton	G 2	45
Bhutan	18,000	300,000	Bumthang	F 3	29
Bismarck Archipelago (Aust. Trust.)	19,660	145,000	Rabaul	E 6	37
Bolivia	412,777	3,019,031	La Paz, Sucre	G 7	46
Bonin Is. (U.S. Adm.)	76			E 3	37
Borneo	208,286			E 5	31
Brazil	3,286,170	52,645,479	Rio de Janeiro	K 6	46
British Columbia, Canada	359,279	1,165,210	Victoria	F 4	40
British Honduras	8,867	59,220	Belize	C 2	39
Brunei (Br.)	2,226	40,657	Brunei	E 5	31
Bulgaria	42,796	7,022,206	Sofiya	G 4	21
Burma	261,610	18,489,000	Rangoon	C 2	30
Byelorussian S.S.R. (White Russian S.S.R.) (U.S.S.R.)	80,100	7,220,000	Minsk	D 4	22
California, U.S.A.	156,803	10,586,223	Sacramento	C 5	42
Cambodia	69,884	3,748,000	Phnom Penh	E 4	30
Cameroons (Br. Trust.)	34,081	1,027,100	Lagos	J10	34
Cameroun (Fr. Trust.)	161,787	3,065,800	Yaoundé	J10	34
Canada	3,621,616	14,009,429	Ottawa		40, 41
Canal Zone (U.S.A.)	362	52,822	Balboa Heights	G 6	39
Canary Islands (Sp.)	2,894	776,912	Las Palmas, Santa Cruz	B 4	17
Cape of Good Hope, U. of So. Africa	277,169	4,053,848	Capetown	M18	35
Cape Verde Islands (Port.)	1,557	147,328	Praia	N 5	6
Caroline Islands (U.S. Trust.)	525	36,980	Truk	E 5	37
Cayman Is., Jamaica (Br.)	104	6,670	Georgetown	B 3	45
Celebes	72,986	5,500,000	Makassar	G 6	31
Central America	217,813	8,918,547			39
Ceylon	25,332	6,657,339	Colombo	D 7	29
Channel Islands (Br.)	75	102,776	St. Helier	E 8	10
Chatham Islands (N.Z.)	372	505		J10	37
Chile	286,396	5,809,000	Santiago	F10	47
China	3,724,273	461,006,285	Peiping, Taipei		32
Christmas Island (Br.)	60	866		O11	25
Colombia	439,828	11,260,000	Bogotá	F 3	46
Colorado, U.S.A.	103,967	1,325,089	Denver	G 5	42
Comoro Is. (Is. Comores), (Fr.)	849	156,150	Dzaoudzi	P14	35
Connecticut, U.S.A.	4,899	2,007,280	Hartford	P 4	43
Cook Islands (N.Z.)	99	14,088	Avarua	K 7	37
Corsica (Corse), (Fr.)	3,367	267,873	Ajaccio	G 6	16
Costa Rica	19,238	800,875	San José	E 5	39
Cuba	42,857	5,348,000	Habana	48 & B 2	45
Curaçao (Neth. Antilles)	173	95,195	Willemstad	E 4	45
Cyprus (Br.)	3,572	450,114	Nicosia	E 5	28
Czechoslovakia	49,356	12,090,164	Praha (Prague)	D 2	20
Dahomey (Fr.)	42,471	1,476,000	Porto Novo	G10	34
Daito Is. (U.S. Adm.)	18	2,691		M 6	32
Damão (Port.)	213	63,521		B 4	29
Delaware, U.S.A.	1,978	318,085	Dover	P 5	43
Denmark	16,556	4,279,151	København (Copenhagen)	E 9	13
District of Columbia, U.S.A.	61	802,178	Washington	O 5	43
Diu (Port.)	12	19,731		B 4	29
Dominica (Br.)	305	53,900	Roseau	G 4	45
Dominican Republic	19,129	2,121,083	Ciudad Trujillo	D 6 48 & D 3	45
Ecuador ... approx.	115,000	3,076,933	Quito	E 4	46
Egypt	386,000	19,087,304	Cairo	M 6	34
England and Wales	58,340	43,744,924	London		10
Eritrea	15,754	1,086,000	Asmara	O 8	34
Estonia (Estonian S.S.R.), (U.S.S.R.)	17,400	1,000,000	Tallin (Tallinn)	D 4	22
Ethiopia (excl. Eritrea)	350,000	10,000,000	Addis Ababa	O 9	34
Europe	4,129,908	551,000,000			9
Faeröe Islands (Dan.)	540	29,178	Thorshavn	D 2	9
Falkland Islands (Br.) (incl. S. Georgia)	5,618	2,239	Port Stanley	H14	47
Fernando Póo (island), (Sp. Guinea)	800	17,249	Santa Isabel	H11	34
Fiji (Br.)	7,036	259,638	Suva	H 7	37
Finland	130,500	4,028,910	Helsinki	P 4	13
Florida, U.S.A.	54,262	2,771,305	Tallahassee	N 7	43
Formosa (Taiwan), (China)	13,885	6,126,000	Taipei	K 7	32
France	212,736	40,502,513	Paris		16
Franz Josef Land (Zemlya Frantsa Iosifa)				F 1	22
French Equatorial Africa	961,392	4,168,910	Brazzaville	K10	34
French Sudan	584,942	3,137,000	Bamako	F 8	34
French West Africa	1,814,852	16,377,000	Dakar	G 8	34

Country	Area (Sq. Miles)	Population	Capital or Chief Town	Index Ref.	Plate No.
Gabon (Fr.)	90,733	423,904	Libreville	J12	35
Galápagos Islands, Ecuador	3,042	1,346	El Progreso	D 7	46
Gambia (Br.)	4,033	278,858	Bathurst	C 9	34
Georgia, U.S.A.	58,518	3,444,578	Atlanta	N 6	43
Georgian S.S.R. (U.S.S.R.)	29,400	3,555,000	Tbilisi (Tiflis)	F 5	22
Germany, East (German Democratic Rep.)	41,535	18,488,316	Berlin	....	14
Germany, West (Federal Republic of) (excl. Saar)	94,926	49,728,263	Bonn		14
Gibraltar (Br.)	2	23,232	....	D 4	17
Gilbert, Ellice and Phoenix Islands	196	32,311	Tarawa	H 6	37
Gôa (Port.)	1,313	540,925	Pangim	B 5	29
Gold Coast (Br.)	78,803	3,735,682	Accra	F10	34
Great Britain and Northern Ireland	94,279	50,210,472	London	E 3	9
Greece	51,182	7,856,000	Athenai (Athens)	F 6	21
Greenland (Dan.)	839,999	21,412	Godthaab	D22	8
Grenada (Br.)	133	72,387	St. George's	G 4	45
Guadeloupe and Dependencies (Fr.)	688	278,864	Basse Terre	F 3	45
Guam (U.S.A.)	203	59,498	Agaña	E 4	37
Guatemala	45,452	2,787,030	Guatemala	B 3	39
Guiana, British	89,480	375,701	Georgetown	J 2	46
Guiana, French	35,135	25,499	Cayenne	K 3	46
Guiana, Netherlands (Surinam)	54,300	219,000	Paramaribo	J 3	46
Guinea, French	96,525	2,130,000	Conakry	D 9	34
Guinea, Portuguese	13,948	510,736	Bissau	C 9	34
Guinea, Spanish	10,830	161,032	Santa Isabel	J11	35
Haiti	10,714	3,111,973	Port-au-Prince	C 5 48 & D 3	45
Hawaii (U.S.A.)	6,420	499,794	Honolulu	L 3	37
Holland (Netherlands).land	12,883	9,625,499	's Gravenhage, Amsterdam	F 4	15
Honduras	45,000	1,505,465	Tegucigalpa	D 3	39
Honduras, British	8,867	59,220	Belize	C 2	39
Hong Kong (Br.)	391	1,857,000	Victoria	J 7	32
Hungary	35,875	9,204,799	Budapest	E 3	20
Iceland	39,709	144,263	Reykjavík	C 2	9
Idaho, U.S.A.	82,808	588,637	Boise	E 3	42
Ifni (Sp.)	676	45,852	Sidi Ifni	D 6	34
Illinois, U.S.A.	55,947	8,712,176	Springfield	L 4	43
India	1,059,342	356,755,978	New Delhi	....	29
Indiana, U.S.A.	36,205	3,934,224	Indianapolis	M 5	43
Indochina (Fr.)	285,927	26,876,510	....	E 3	30
Indonesia (East Indies)	735,286	79,260,000	Djakarta (Batavia)	F 7	31
Iowa, U.S.A.	55,986	2,621,073	Des Moines	K 4	43
Iran (Persia)	628,000	19,000,000	Tehran	H 4	27
Iraq (Mesopotamia)	116,600	4,799,500	Baghdad	C 4	27
Ireland (Eire)	26,601	2,958,878	Dublin (Baile Átha Cliath)		12
Ireland, Northern	5,238	1,369,579	Belfast	H 2	12
Isle of Man (Br.)	221	55,213	Douglas	C 3	10
Israel	7,978	1,554,000	Jerusalem		24
Italy	116,000	47,020,536	Roma (Rome)	....	18
Ivory Coast (Fr.)	183,397	2,066,000	Abidjan	E10	34
Jamaica (Br.)	4,411	1,237,391	Kingston	48 & C 3	45
Japan	142,272	83,199,637	Tokyo	....	33
Java and Madura	51,032	52,000,000	Djakarta	K 2	31
Jordan (Trans-Jordan)	34,750	1,250,000	Amman	D 4	24
Kansas, U.S.A.	82,113	1,905,299	Topeka	J 5	42
Karelo-Finnish S.S.R. (U.S.S.R.)	68,900	600,000	Petrozavodsk	E 3	22
Karikal, India (Fr.)	52	70,541	Karikal	D 6	29
Kazakh S.S.R. (U.S.S.R.)	1,061,600	6,000,000	Alma-Ata	H 5	22
Kentucky, U.S.A.	40,109	2,944,806	Frankfort	M 5	43
Kenya (Br.)	219,730	5,377,393	Nairobi	O11	35
Kerguelen Arch. (Fr.)			....	T 8	6
Kirghiz S.S.R. (U.S.S.R.)	76,100	1,490,000	Frunze	J 5	22
Korea	85,228	29,291,000	Seoul, P'yongyang	C 4	33
Krētē (Crete), Greece	3,232	441,687	Erákleion	G 8	21
Kuria Muria Is. (Br.)		70		G 6	26
Kuril Is. (Chishima), (U.S.S.R.)	5,700	15,000	Severo-Kuril'sk	R 5	23
Kuwait	8,000	170,000	Al Kuwait	E 4	26
Laccadive Islands (India)	746	18,393	....	B 6	29
Laos	89,343	1,200,000	Vientiane	E 3	30
Latvia (Latvian S.S.R.), (U.S.S.R.)	24,600	1,800,000	Riga	D 4	22
Lebanon	3,475	1,165,208	Beirut	F 6	28
Leeward Islands (Br.)	423	108,838	St. Johns	G 3	45
Liberia	43,000	1,600,000	Monrovia	E10	34
Libya	679,358	1,100,000	Tripoli, Bengasi	K 6	34
Liechtenstein	65	13,757	Vaduz	J 2	19
Lithuania (Lithuanian S.S.R.), (U.S.S.R.)	31,200	2,700,000	Vil'nyus (Vilna)	D 4	22
Louisiana, U.S.A.	45,177	2,683,516	Baton Rouge	K 7	43
Loyalty Islands (Fr.)	800	11,854	Chépénéhé	G 8	37
Luxembourg	999	290,992	Luxembourg	J 9	15

Country	Area (Sq. Miles)	Population	Capital or Chief Town	Index Ref.	Plate No.
Macao (Port.)	6	389,000	Macao	H 7	32
Madagascar (Fr.)	241,094	4,294,985	Tananarive	R15	35
Madeira Islands (Port.)	308	269,179	Funchal	A 2	17
Madura I.	1,752	2,444,000	Pamekasan	K 2	31
Mahé, India	23	18,293	Mahé	C 6	29
Maine, U.S.A.	31,040	913,777	Augusta	R 3	43
Malayan Federation (Br.)	50,690	4,908,086	Kuala Lumpur	E 6	30
Maldive Islands (Br.)	115	82,068	Malé	L 9	25
Malta (Br.)	122	305,991	Valletta	E 7	18
Manchuria (China)	412,801	36,903,000	Shenyang (Mukden)	K 2	32
Manitoba, Canada	219,723	776,541	Winnipeg	L 3	40
Mariana Islands (U.S. Trust.)	142	6,286	Saipan	E 4	37
Marquesas Is. (Fr.)	480	2,976	Taiohae	N 6	37
Marshall Islands (U.S. Trust.)	61	11,033	Kwajalein	H 4	37
Martinique (Fr.)	425	261,595	Fort de France	G 4	45
Maryland, U.S.A.	9,887	2,343,001	Annapolis	O 5	43
Massachusetts, U.S.A.	7,907	4,690,514	Boston	P 4	43
Mauritania (Fr.)	328,185	523,900	St.-Louis	D 8	34
Mauritius (Br.)	720	432,468	Port Louis	S19	35
Mesopotamia (See Iraq)	....	....	....	D 4	27
Mexico	760,373	25,581,250	México	....	44
Michigan, U.S.A.	57,022	6,371,766	Lansing	M 3	43
Midway Islands (U.S.A.)	2	437	....	J 3	37
Minnesota, U.S.A.	80,009	2,982,483	St. Paul	K 3	43
Mississippi, U.S.A.	47,420	2,178,914	Jackson	L 6	43
Missouri, U.S.A.	69,270	3,954,653	Jefferson City	K 5	43
Moldavian S.S.R. (U.S.S.R.)	13,100	2,660,000	Kishinev	D 5	22
Molucca Islands	30,168	544,302	Ternate	C 6	37
Monaco	370 Acres	19,242	Monaco	G 6	16
Mongolian Republic	625,946	2,000,000	Ulan Bator	F 2	32
Montana, U.S.A.	146,316	591,024	Helena	F 3	42
Montserrat (Br.)	32	14,333	Plymouth	G 3	45
Morocco, French Zone	153,870	8,617,387	Rabat	E 5	34
Morocco, Sp. Northern Zone	7,674	1,180,000	Tetuán	F 5	34
Morocco, Sp. Southern Zone	10,039	12,000	Villa Bens (Tarfaia)	D 6	34
Moyen Congo (Fr.)	175,676	675,400	Pointe Noire	J12	35
Mozambique (Port.)	297,731	5,730,930	Lourenço Marques	O15	35
Natal, U. of So. Africa	35,284	2,202,392	Pietermaritzburg	N17	35
Nauru (Austr.-N.Z.—Br. Tr. Terr.)	8	2,855	....	G 6	37
Nebraska, U.S.A.	76,653	1,325,510	Lincoln	H 4	42
Nepal	54,000	6,910,000	Katmandu	D 3	29
Netherlands (Holland).land	12,883	9,625,499	Amsterdam, 's Gravenhage	F 4	15
Netherlands Antilles	383	154,914	Willemstad	E 4	45
Nevada, U.S.A.	109,802	160,083	Carson City	D 5	42
New Britain (island), (Aust. Trust.)	14,600	105,000	Rabaul	F 6	37
New Brunswick, Canada	27,473	515,697	Fredericton	G 4	41
New Caledonia (Fr.)	7,201	61,250	Nouméa	G 8	37
Newfoundland, Canada	42,734	361,416	St. John's	J 4	41
New Guinea, Netherlands	161,514	1,000,000	Hollandia	K 6	31
New Guinea, Territory of (Aust. Trust.)	93,000	1,100,023	Port Moresby	B 7	31
New Hampshire, U.S.A.	9,024	533,242	Concord	R 3	43
New Hebrides Islands (Br. and Fr.)	5,700	48,538	Vila	G 7	37
New Ireland (island), (Aust. Trust.)	3,800	33,960	Kavieng	F 6	37
New Jersey, U.S.A.	7,522	4,835,329	Trenton	P 5	43
New Mexico, U.S.A.	121,511	681,187	Santa Fe	G 6	42
New South Wales, Australia	309,432	2,984,838	Sydney	H 6	36
New York, U.S.A.	47,929	14,830,192	Albany	P 4	43
New Zealand, Dominion of (Br.)	103,934	1,702,298	Wellington	M 7	36
Nicaragua	57,143	1,053,189	Managua	E 4	39
Nicobar Islands (India)	635	12,452	Port Blair	F 7	29
Nigeria (Br.)	338,593	24,300,000	Lagos	H10	34
Niger Colony (Fr.)	501,930	2,168,000	Niamey	H 8	34
Niue I. (Br.)	100	4,253	Alofi	K 7	37
North America	9,124,000	216,400,000	....	....	38
North Borneo (Br.)	29,387	331,361	Jesselton	F 5	31
North Carolina, U.S.A.	49,142	4,061,929	Raleigh	O 6	43
North Dakota, U.S.A.	70,054	619,636	Bismarck	J 3	42
Northern Ireland (Br.)	5,238	1,369,579	Belfast	H 2	12
*Northern Rhodesia (Br.)	290,320	1,849,000	Lusaka	M14	35
Northern Territory, Algeria	80,117	7,864,792	Alger	G 4	34
Northern Territory, Aust.	523,620	10,868	Darwin	E 3	36
Northwest Territories, Canada	1,258,217	16,004	Ottawa	F 1	40
Norway	124,560	3,156,950	Oslo	F 6	13
Nova Scotia, Canada	20,743	642,584	Halifax	H 4	41
*Nyasaland Prot. (Br.)	36,829	2,178,013	Zomba	N14	35
Ohio, U.S.A.	41,122	7,946,627	Columbus	N 4	43
Oklahoma, U.S.A.	69,283	2,233,351	Oklahoma City	J 6	42
Oman, Sultanate of	82,000	830,000	Masqat	J 5	26
Ontario, Canada	363,282	4,597,542	Toronto	C 3	41

*Member of new Federation of Rhodesia and Nyasaland.

Country	Area (Sq. Miles)	Population	Capital or Chief Town	Index Ref.	Plate No.
Orange Free State, U. of South Africa	49,647	879,071	Bloemfontein	M17	35
Oregon, U.S.A.	96,350	1,521,341	Salem	C 4	42
Orkney Islands, Scotland	376	21,258	Kirkwall	J 1	11
Oubangui-Chari (Fr.)	239,382	1,068,400	Bangui	K10	34
Pacific Islands (excl. Australia)	262,718	4,313,654			37
Pakistan	364,218	75,843,000	Karachi	A 3 & F 4	29
Palau Islands (U.S. Trust.)	189	6,596	Koror	D 5	37
Palestine					20
Panama (excl. Canal Zone)	28,575	801,290	Panamá	G 6	39
Papua Territory (Aust.)	90,540	282,072	Port Moresby	B 7	31
Paraguay	150,518	1,251,517	Asunción	J 8	47
Pennsylvania, U.S.A.	45,045	10,498,012	Harrisburg	O 4	43
Persia (Iran)	628,000	19,000,000	Tehran	H 4	27
Peru ... approx.	513,000	8,405,000	Lima	E 5	46
Philippines, Republic of the	115,600	19,234,182	Quezon City	H 4	31
Phoenix Is. (U.S. and Br.)	16	984	Canton I.	J 6	37
Pitcairn Island (Br.)	2	138		O 8	37
Poland	119,734	24,976,926	Warszawa (Warsaw)		24
Pondichéry, India (Fr.)	112	222,566	Pondichéry	D 6	29
Portugal	35,413	8,490,455	Lisboa (Lisbon)	B 3	17
Prince Edward Island, Canada	2,184	98,429	Charlottetown	H 4	41
Principe and S. Tomé (Port.)	372	62,000	São Tomé	H11	35
Puerto Rico (U.S.A.)	3,423	2,210,703	San Juan	G 2	45
Qatar	5,000	31,000	Doha	F 4	26
Québec, Canada	523,860	4,055,681	Québec	G 3	41
Queensland, Australia	670,500	1,106,269	Brisbane	G 4	36
Réunion (Fr.)	970	242,067	St. Denis	R20	35
Rhode Island, U.S.A.	1,058	791,896	Providence	R 4	43
Rio de Oro (Sp.)	71,583	24,000	Villa Cisneros	D 7	34
Rio Muni (continental Sp. Guinea)	10,040	142,237	Bata	J11	35
Ruanda-Urundi (Belg. Tr.)	20,309	3,889,051	Usumbura	M12	35
Rumania	91,671	15,872,624	Bucureşti	G 3	21
Russian S.F.S.R. (U.S.S.R.)	6,501,500	111,000,000	Moskva (Moscow)	E 4	22
Ryukyu Islands (U.S. Adm.)	921	914,462	Naha	L 7	33
Saar	988	851,615	Saarbrücken	B 4	14
Saguia el Hamra (Sp.)	31,660	14,298	Aiún	D 6	34
St. Croix, Virgin Is. (U.S.A.)	80	12,103	Christiansted	H 2	45
St. Helena I. (Br.)	47	4,748	Jamestown	E15	35
St. John, Virgin Is. (U.S.A.)	20	749		H 1	45
St. Lucia (Br.)	233	70,113	Castries	G 4	45
St. Pierre and Miquelon Is. (Fr.)	93	4,354	St. Pierre	J 4	41
St. Thomas, Virgin Is. (U.S.A.)	32	13,813	Charlotte Amalie	G 1	45
St. Vincent (Br.)	150	61,647	Kingstown	G 4	45
Sakhalin (U.S.S.R.)	35,400	300,000	Yuzhno-Sakhalinsk	R 5	23
Salvador, El	13,176	1,858,656	San Salvador	C 4	39
Samoa, Western (N.Z. Tr.)	1,133	78,155	Apia	J 7	37
Samoa (U.S.A.)	76	18,937	Pago Pago	J 7	37
San Marino	38	12,100	San Marino	D 2	18
Sarawak (Br.)	47,071	546,385	Kuching	E 5	31
Sardinia (Sardegna), (It.)	9,301	1,273,714	Cagliari	B 4	18
Saskatchewan, Canada	237,975	831,728	Regina	J 4	40
Saudi Arabia, Kingdom of	350,000	5,500,000	Riyadh, Mecca	D 4	26
Scotland	30,405	5,095,969	Edinburgh		11
Senegal (Fr.)	77,401	1,720,000	St. Louis	D 9	34
Seychelles (Br.)	157	34,637	Victoria	T 6	6
Shetland Islands, Scotland	550	19,343	Lerwick	L 3	11
Siam (Thailand)	200,148	17,324,581	Krung Thep (Bangkok)	D 3	30
Sicily (It.)	9,926	4,452,773	Palermo	D 6	18
Sierra Leone (Br.)	27,925	1,858,275	Freetown	D10	34
Sikkim	2,745	129,000	Gangtok	E 3	29
Singapore (Br.)	220	940,824	Singapore	F 6	30
Sinkiang, China	660,977	4,012,330	Tihwa (Urumchi)	C 3	32
Society Islands (Fr.)	650	41,798	Papeete	L 7	37
Socotra (Br.)	1,400	12,000	Tamrida	J 8	25
Solomon Islands (Aust. Tr.)	4,070	49,067	Sohano	F 6	37
Solomon Islands Prot. (Br.)	14,600	94,965	Honiara	F 6	37
Somaliland, French	8,492	44,800	Djibouti	P 9	34
Somaliland, (Italian Tr.)	194,000	916,300	Mogadiscio	R10	34
Somaliland Prot. (Br.)	68,000	700,000	Hargeisa	R10	34
South America	6,894,000	109,500,000			46, 47
South Australia, Australia	280,070	646,073	Adelaide	E 5	36
South Carolina, U.S.A.	30,594	2,117,027	Columbia	N 6	43
South Dakota, U.S.A.	76,536	652,740	Pierre	J 3	42
*Southern Rhodesia (Br.)	150,333	1,794,000	Salisbury	M15	35
Southern Territories, Algeria	767,435	816,993	Alger	G 6	34
South West Africa (U. of South Africa Mand.)	317,725	350,037	Windhoek	K16	35

*Member of new Federation of Rhodesia and Nyasaland.

Country	Area (Sq. Miles)	Population	Capital or Chief Town	Index Ref.	Plate No.
Spain	195,258	27,909,009	Madrid		17
Spanish Sahara	103,243	38,298	Aiún	D 6	34
Spanish West Africa	113,958	96,150	Sidi Ifni	D 6	34
Sumatra	164,148	12,000,000	Padang	C 6	31
Surinam (Netherlands Guiana)	54,300	219,000	Paramaribo	J 3	46
Svalbard, Norway (Spitsbergen)	24,294	1,539	Longyearbyen	C 2	13
Swaziland (Br.)	6,704	185,215	Mbabane	N17	35
Sweden	173,394	7,046,920	Stockholm	J 6	13
Switzerland	15,944	4,714,992	Bern		19
Syria	72,587	3,135,000	Dimishq (Damascus)	H 5	28
Tadzhik S.S.R. (U.S.S.R.)	54,900	1,455,000	Stalinabad	J 6	22
Tahiti (island), (Fr.)	600	29,684	Papeete	M 7	37
Tanganyika Territory (Br. Trust.)	342,706	7,408,096	Dar es Salaam	N13	35
Tangier, International Zone	225	152,000	Tangier	E 4	34
Tasmania, Australia	26,215	257,078	Hobart	J 8	36
Tchad (Fr.)	455,598	2,052,469	Fort Lamy	K 8	34
Tennessee, U.S.A.	41,961	3,291,718	Nashville	M 6	43
Texas, U.S.A.	263,644	7,711,194	Austin	J 7	42
Thailand (Siam)	200,148	17,324,581	Krung Thep	D 3	30
Tibet, China	469,413	2,000,000	Lhasa	C 5	32
Timor (Port.)	7,332	424,132	Dili	H 7	31
Timor Archipelago (Indon.)	24,450	1,657,376	Kupang	G 8	31
Togo (Fr. Trust.)	20,733	923,000	Lomé	G10	34
Togoland (Br. Trust.)	13,041	382,768	Accra	G10	34
Tokelau (Union Group) (N.Z. and U.S.)	4	1,388	Fakaofo	J 6	37
Tonga (Friendly) Is. (Br.)	269	46,870	Nukualofa	J 7	37
Transvaal, Union of South Africa	110,450	4,283,038	Pretoria	N17	35
Trieste, Free Territory of	285	383,000	Trieste	A 3	21
Trinidad and Tobago (Br.)	1,980	557,970	Port of Spain	G 5	45
Tristan da Cunha (Br.)	38	230		N 7	6
Trucial Oman	12,000	95,000	Sharja	F 5	26
Tuamotu (Low) Arch. (Fr.)	332	5,127	Apataki	M 7	37
Tunisia (Fr.)	48,300	2,230,952	Tunis	H 5	34
Turkey	296,185	20,934,670	Ankara		28
Turkmen S.S.R. (U.S.S.R.)	187,200	1,170,000	Ashkhabad	G 6	22
Turks and Caicos Is., Jamaica (Br.)	202	6,138	Grand Turk	D 2	45
Uganda Protectorate (Br.)	80,301	4,959,196	Entebbe	N11	35
Ukrainian S.S.R. (U.S.S.R.)	220,600	40,500,000	Kiev	E 5	22
Union of South Africa	472,494	11,418,349	Capetown, Pretoria	L18	35
Union of Soviet Socialist Republics	8,570,600	191,595,000	Moskva (Moscow)		22, 23
United Kingdom	94,279	50,210,472	London	D 3	9
United States of America — land	2,977,128	150,697,361	Washington		42, 43
land and water	3,022,387				
Upper (Haute) Volta (Fr.)		3,070,000	Ouagadougou	F 9	34
Uruguay	72,172	2,353,000	Montevideo	J10	47
Utah, U.S.A.	82,346	688,862	Salt Lake City	F 5	42
Uzbek S.S.R. (U.S.S.R.)	157,400	6,000,000	Tashkent	H 5	22
Vatican City	109 Acres	1,010		B 6	18
Venezuela	352,143	4,985,716	Caracas	G 2	46
Vermont, U.S.A.	9,278	377,747	Montpelier	P 4	43
Victoria, Australia	87,884	2,054,701	Melbourne	G 7	36
Vietnam	126,700	21,928,510	Saigon	E 3	30
Virgin Islands (Br.)	58	6,508	Road Town	H 1	45
Virgin Islands (U.S.A.)	132	26,665	Charlotte Amalie	H 1	45
Virginia, U.S.A.	39,899	3,318,680	Richmond	O 5	43
Volcano Is. (U.S. Adm.)	29			E 3	37
Wake Island (U.S.A.)	3			G 4	37
Wales (excluding Monmouthshire)	7,466	2,172,339	Cardiff	D 5	10
Walvis Bay (Br.)	430	2,263		J16	35
Washington, U.S.A.	66,977	2,378,963	Olympia	C 3	42
Western Australia, Australia	975,920	502,480	Perth	C 4	36
West Indies	90,000	27,000,000			45
West Virginia, U.S.A.	24,090	2,005,552	Charleston	N 5	43
White Russian S.S.R. (Byelorussian S.S.R.), (U.S.S.R.)	80,100	7,220,000	Minsk	D 4	22
Windward Islands	821	251,771	St. George's	G 4	45
Wisconsin, U.S.A.	54,715	3,434,575	Madison	L 3	43
World ... land area	57,500,000	2,200,000,000			6, 7
Wyoming, U.S.A.	97,506	290,529	Cheyenne	G 4	42
Yanaon, India (Fr.)	6½	5,833	Yanaon	D 5	29
Yap (U.S. Trust.)	87	2,560	Yap	D 5	37
Yemen	75,000	3,500,000	San'a	D 7	26
Yugoslavia	99,079	15,751,935	Beograd (Belgrade)	C 3	21
Yukon Territory, Canada	205,346	9,096	White Horse	C 1	40
Zanzibar Prot. (Br.)	1,020	264,162	Zanzibar	P13	35

This alphabetical list of cities gives statistics of population based on the latest official reports. Each line begins with the name of a place, followed by the name of the country or state, the population, the index reference and the plate number. Different forms of names have been included to a large extent, in the index.

Capitals are designated by asterisks * † Including suburbs.

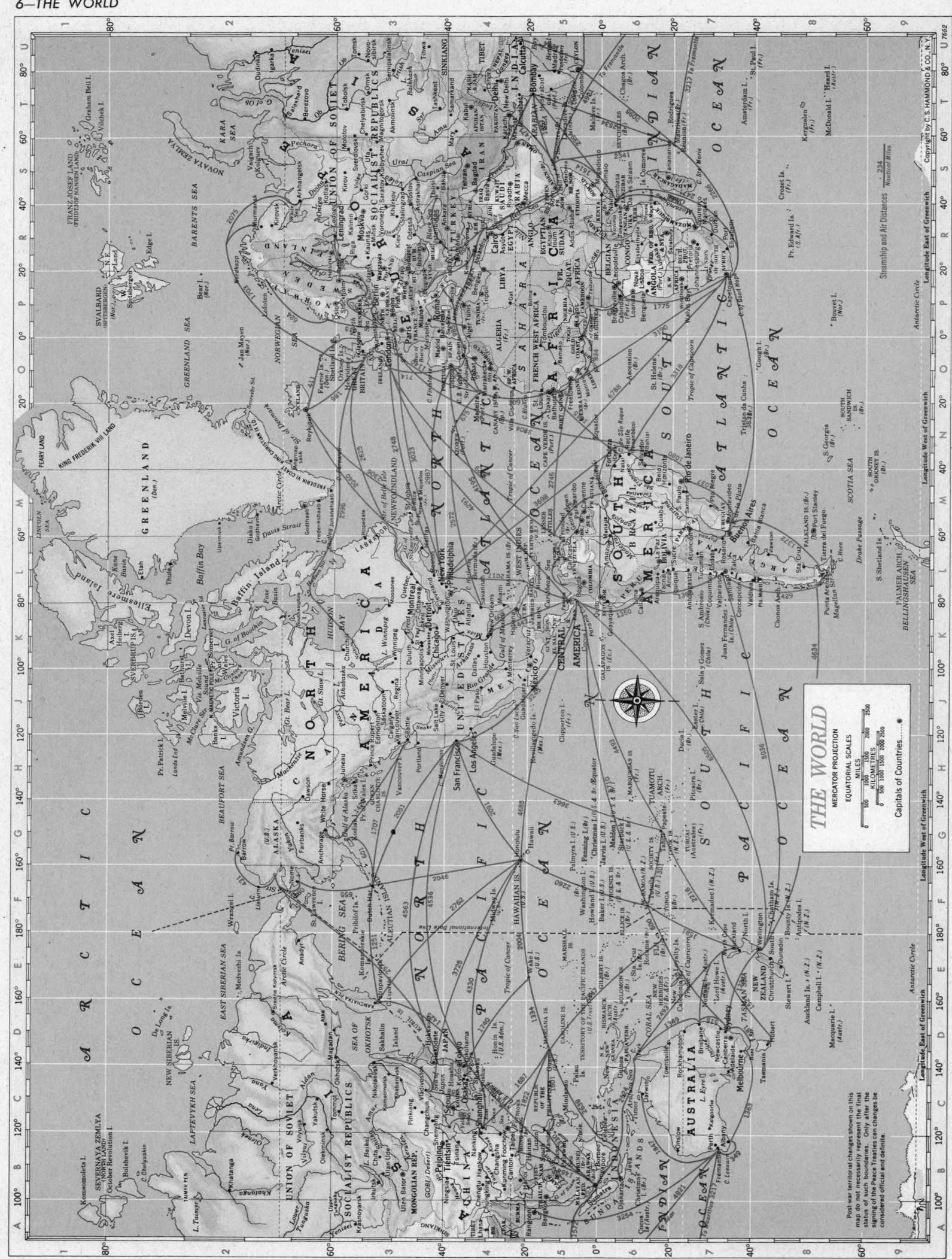

THE WORLD
MERCATOR PROJECTION
EQUATORIAL SCALES

MILES

KILOMETRES

Capitals of Countries........●

Steamship and Air Distances

234
Nautical Miles

Post war territorial changes shown on this map do not necessarily represent the final status of such boundaries. Only after the signing of the Peace Treaties can changes be considered official and definite.

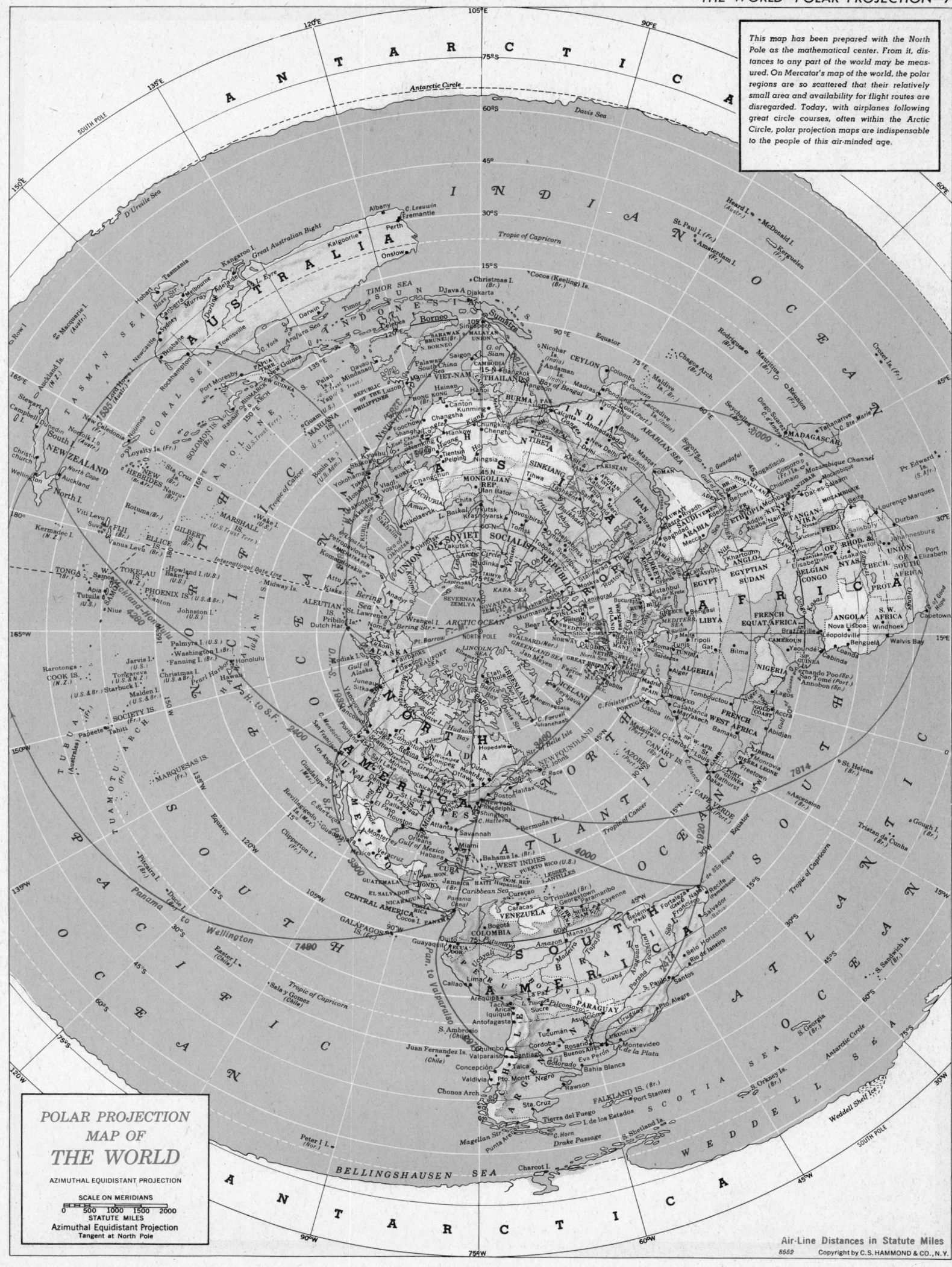

This map has been prepared with the North Pole as the mathematical center. From it, distances to any part of the world may be measured. On Mercator's map of the world, the polar regions are so scattered that their relatively small area and availability for flight routes are disregarded. Today, with airplanes following great circle courses, often within the Arctic Circle, polar projection maps are indispensable to the people of this air-minded age.

POLAR PROJECTION
MAP OF
THE WORLD

AZIMUTHAL EQUIDISTANT PROJECTION

SCALE ON MERIDIANS

0   500   1000   1500   2000
STATUTE MILES
Azimuthal Equidistant Projection
Tangent at North Pole

Air-Line Distances in Statute Miles

8552
Copyright by C.S. HAMMOND & CO., N.Y.

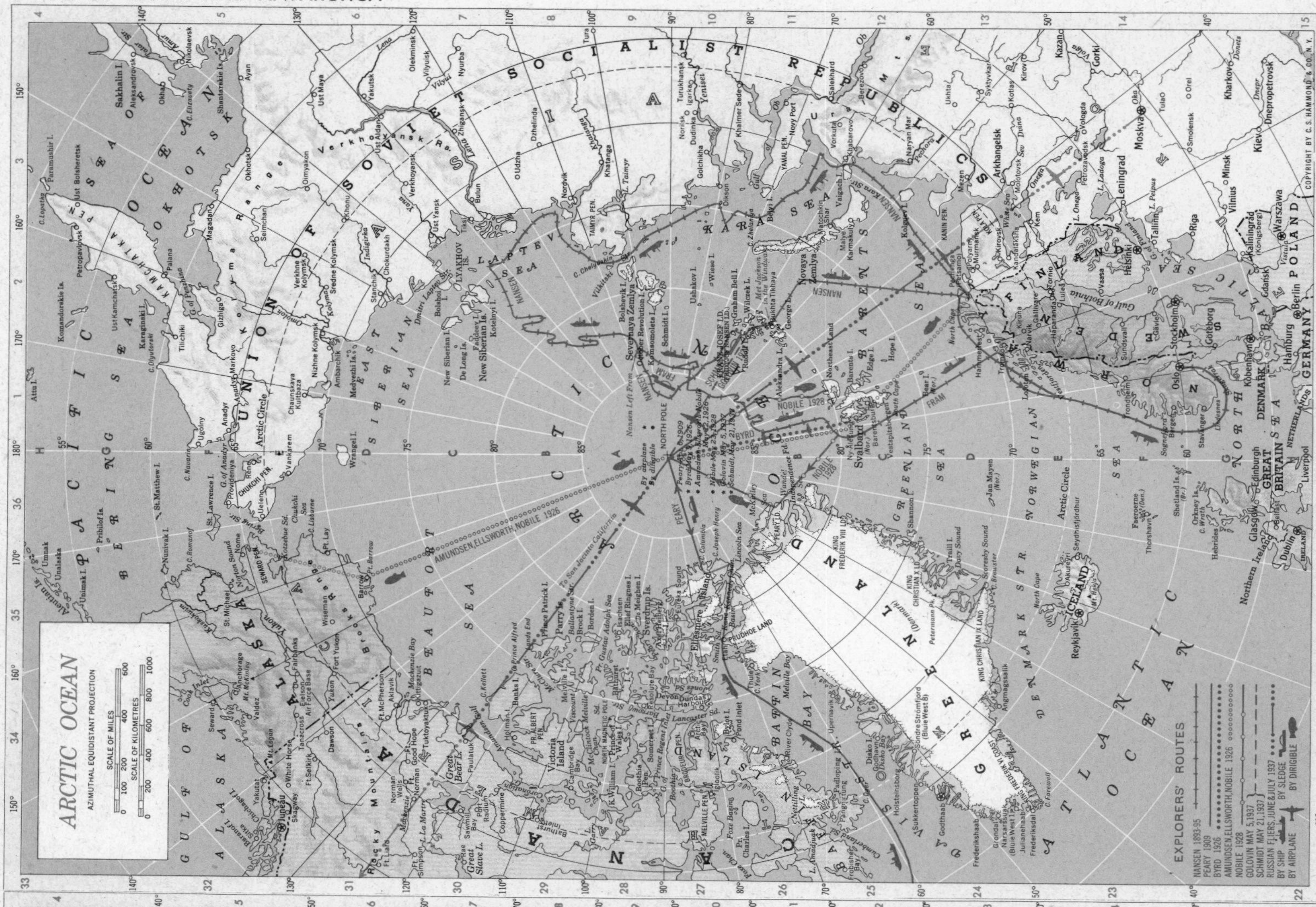

ARCTIC OCEAN
AZIMUTHAL EQUIDISTANT PROJECTION
SCALE OF MILES
SCALE OF KILOMETRES
EXPLORERS' ROUTES
NANSEN 1893-95
PEARY 1909
BYRD 1926
AMUNDSEN, ELLSWORTH, NOBILE 1926
NOBILE 1928
GOLOVIN MAY 5, 1937
SCHMIDT MAY 21, 1937
RUSSIAN FLIERS, JUNE & JULY 1937
BY SHIP
BY SLEDGE
BY AIRPLANE
BY DIRIGIBLE
COPYRIGHT BY C. S. HAMMOND & CO., N. Y.

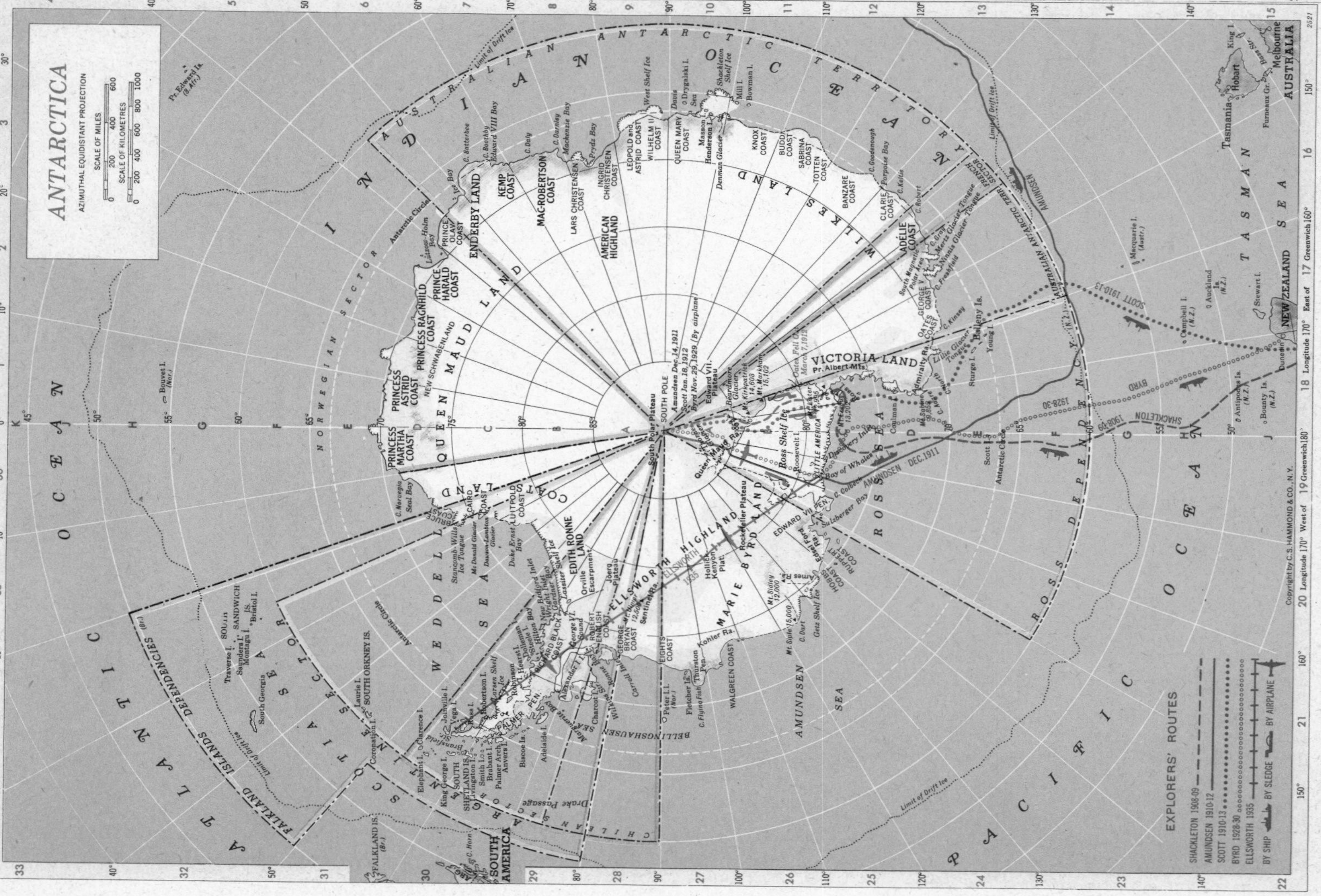

ANTARCTICA
AZIMUTHAL EQUIDISTANT PROJECTION
SCALE OF MILES
SCALE OF KILOMETRES
EXPLORERS' ROUTES
SHACKLETON 1908-09
AMUNDSEN 1910-12
SCOTT 1910-13
BYRD 1928-30
ELLSWORTH 1935
BY SHIP
BY SLEDGE
BY AIRPLANE
Copyright by C. S. HAMMOND & CO., N. Y.

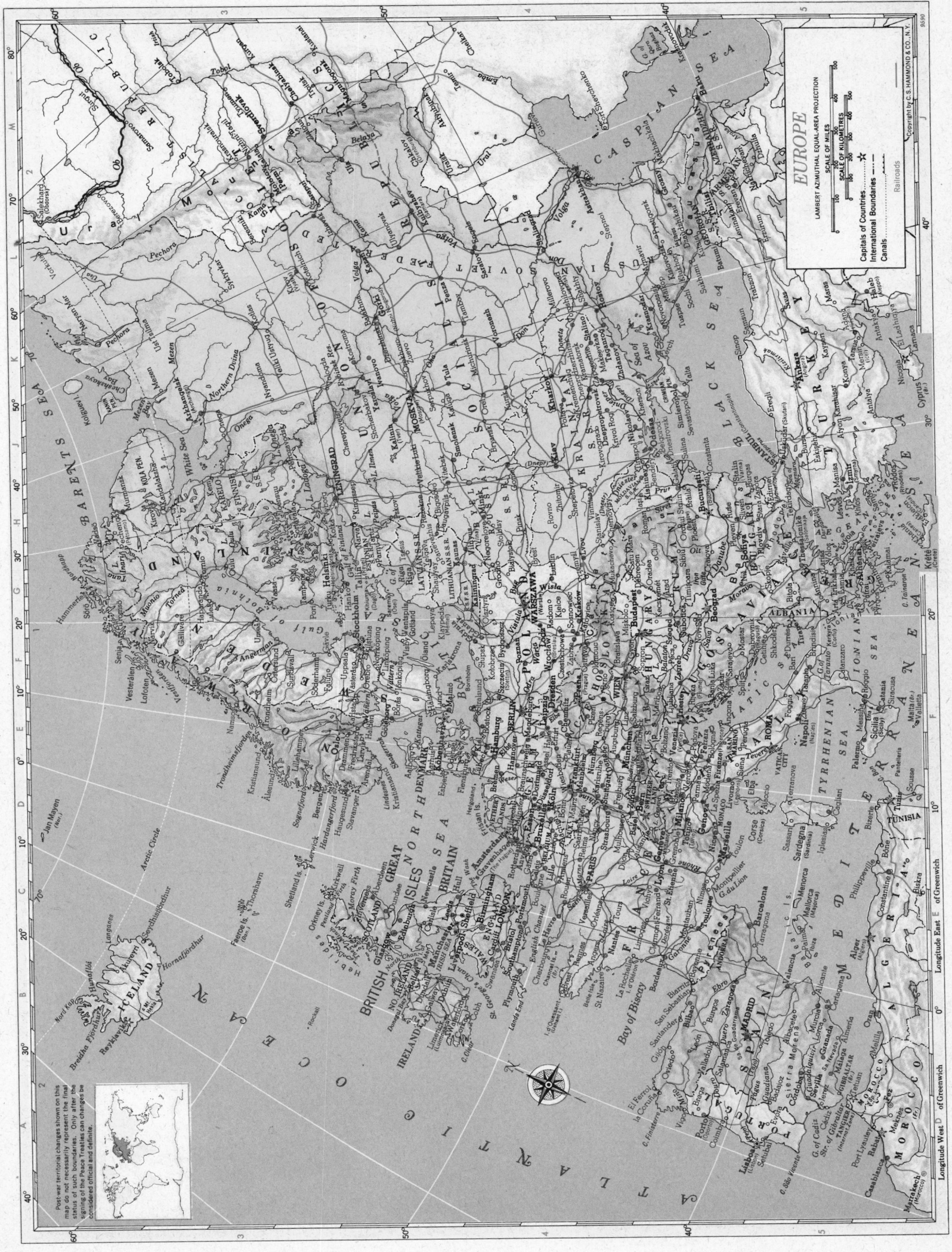

EUROPE

LAMBERT AZIMUTHAL EQUAL-AREA PROJECTION

SCALE OF MILES

SCALE OF KILOMETRES

Capitals of Countries .... ☆
International Boundaries .... ─ ─ ─
Canals ....
Railroads ....

Copyright by C.S. HAMMOND & CO., N.Y.

Post-war territorial changes shown on this
map do not necessarily represent the final
status of such boundaries. Only after the
signing of the peace treaties can changes be
considered official and definite.

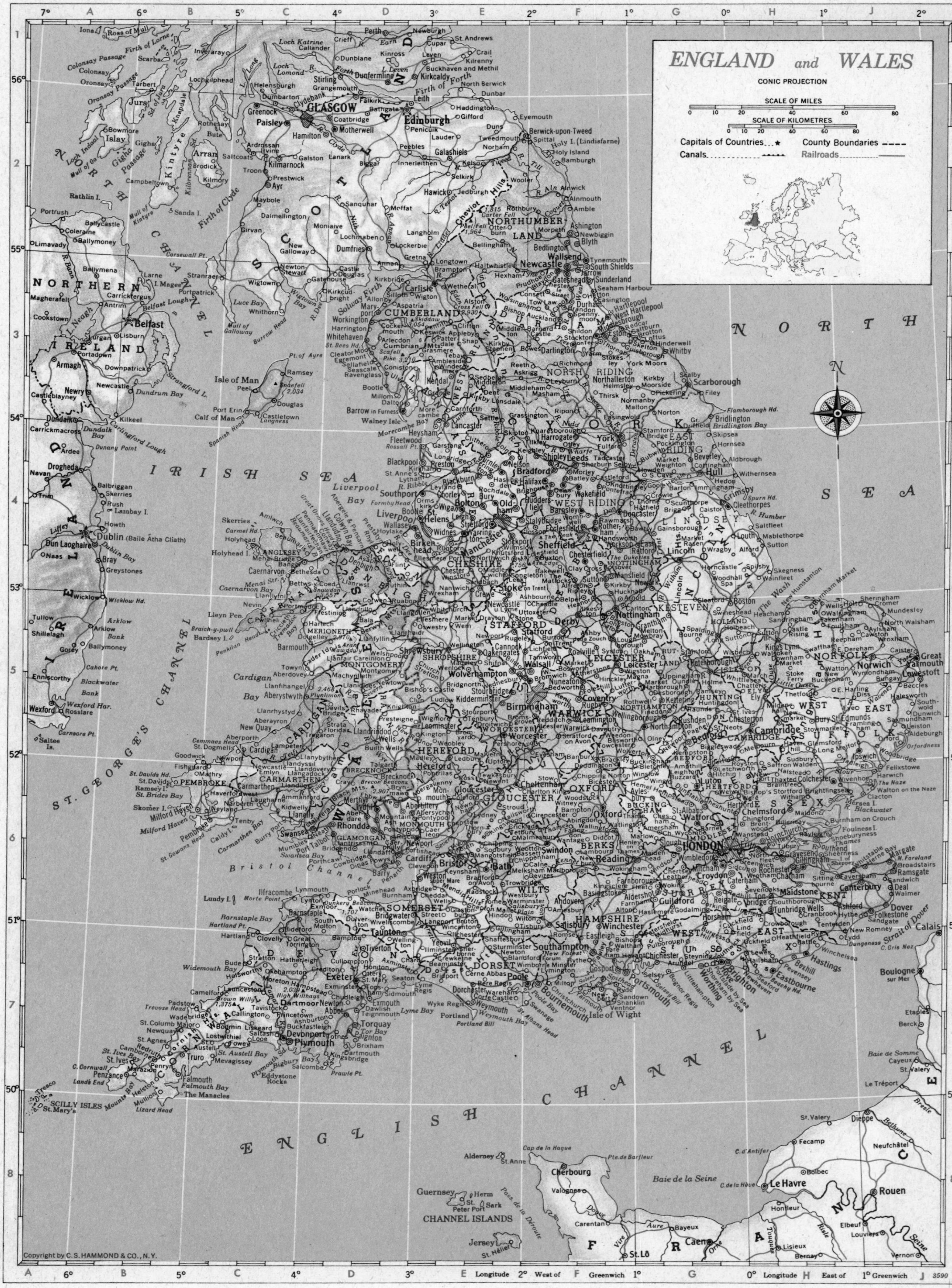

ENGLAND and WALES

CONIC PROJECTION

SCALE OF MILES

SCALE OF KILOMETRES

Capitals of Countries......★   County Boundaries -----

Canals.................   Railroads _____

NORTH SEA

IRISH SEA

NORTHERN IRELAND

ST. GEORGE'S CHANNEL

ENGLISH CHANNEL

Bristol Channel

CHANNEL ISLANDS

GLASGOW   Edinburgh   Belfast   Dublin (Baile Átha Cliath)

LONDON

NORTHUMBERLAND   CUMBERLAND   NORTH RIDING   WEST RIDING   EAST RIDING   LINCOLN   NORFOLK   SUFFOLK   ESSEX   KENT   SUSSEX   HAMPSHIRE   DORSET   DEVON   CORNWALL   SOMERSET   WILTS   GLOUCESTER   WARWICK   WORCESTER   HEREFORD   SHROPSHIRE   STAFFORD   CHESHIRE   DERBY   NOTTINGHAM   LEICESTER   NORTHAMPTON   BEDFORD   CAMBRIDGE   HERTFORD   BUCKINGHAM   OXFORD   BERKS   SURREY   MIDDLESEX

ANGLESEY   CAERNARVON   MERIONETH   MONTGOMERY   CARDIGAN   PEMBROKE   CARMARTHEN   BRECKNOCK   RADNOR   GLAMORGAN   MONMOUTH

Longitude 2° West of Greenwich 1°   Longitude East of 1° Greenwich

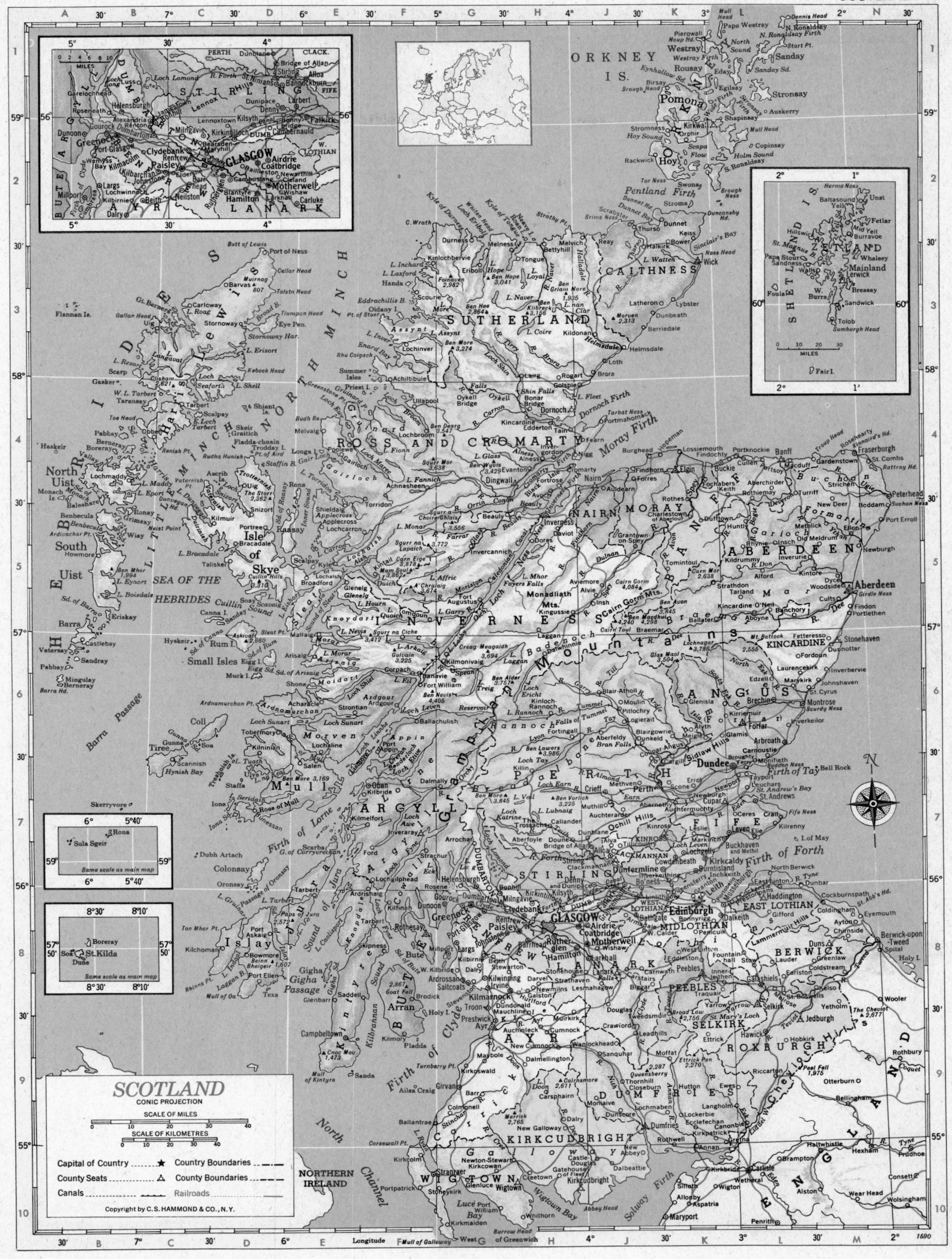

SCOTLAND

CONIC PROJECTION

SCALE OF MILES

SCALE OF KILOMETRES

Capital of Country .... ★   Country Boundaries _____

County Seats .... △   County Boundaries _ _ _ _

Canals ....   Railroads

Copyright by C.S. HAMMOND & CO., N.Y.

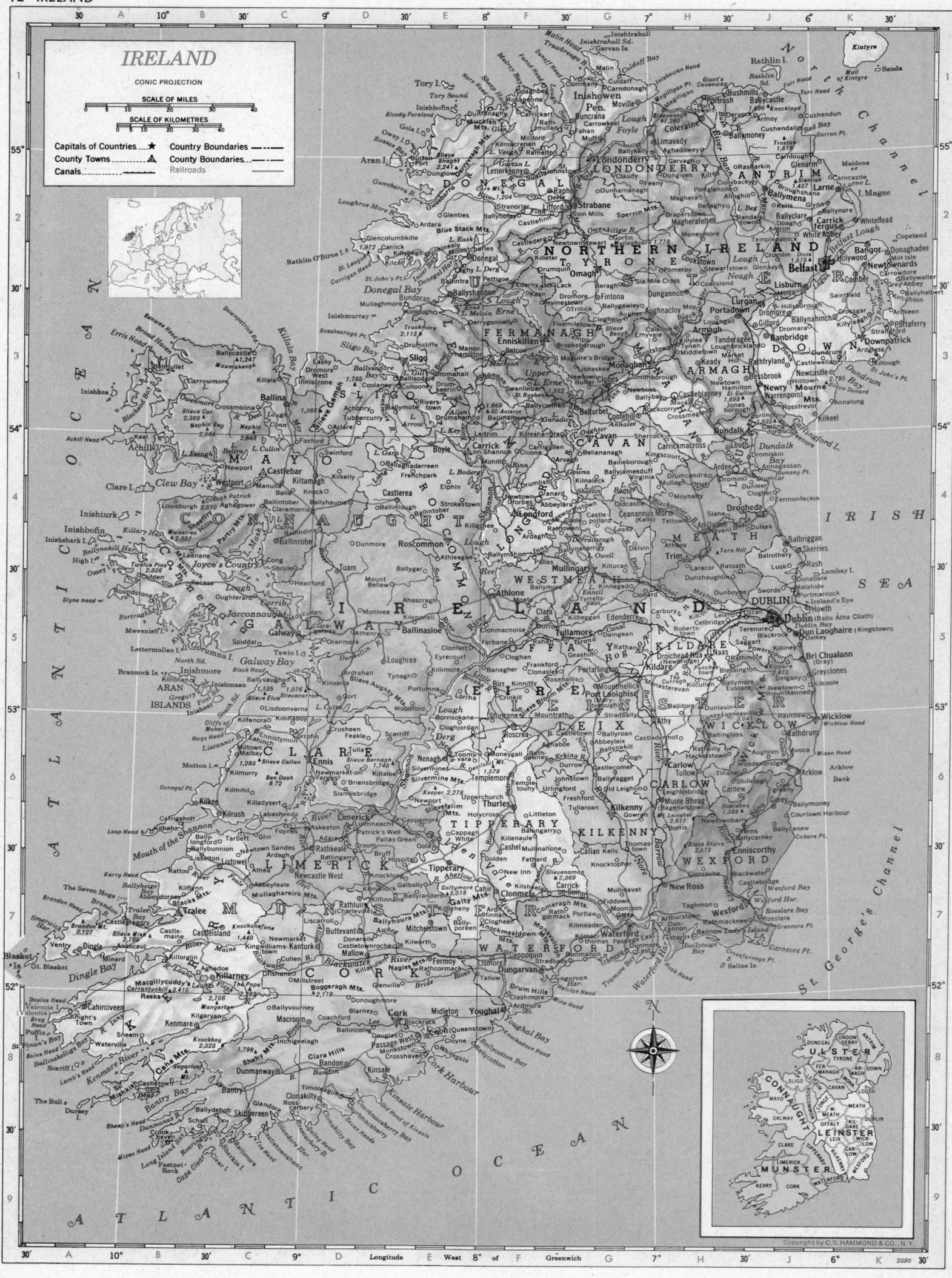

IRELAND

CONIC PROJECTION

SCALE OF MILES

SCALE OF KILOMETRES

Capitals of Countries .... ★
County Towns .... ▲
Canals ....
Country Boundaries ——·——·
County Boundaries ...—··—··
Railroads ————————

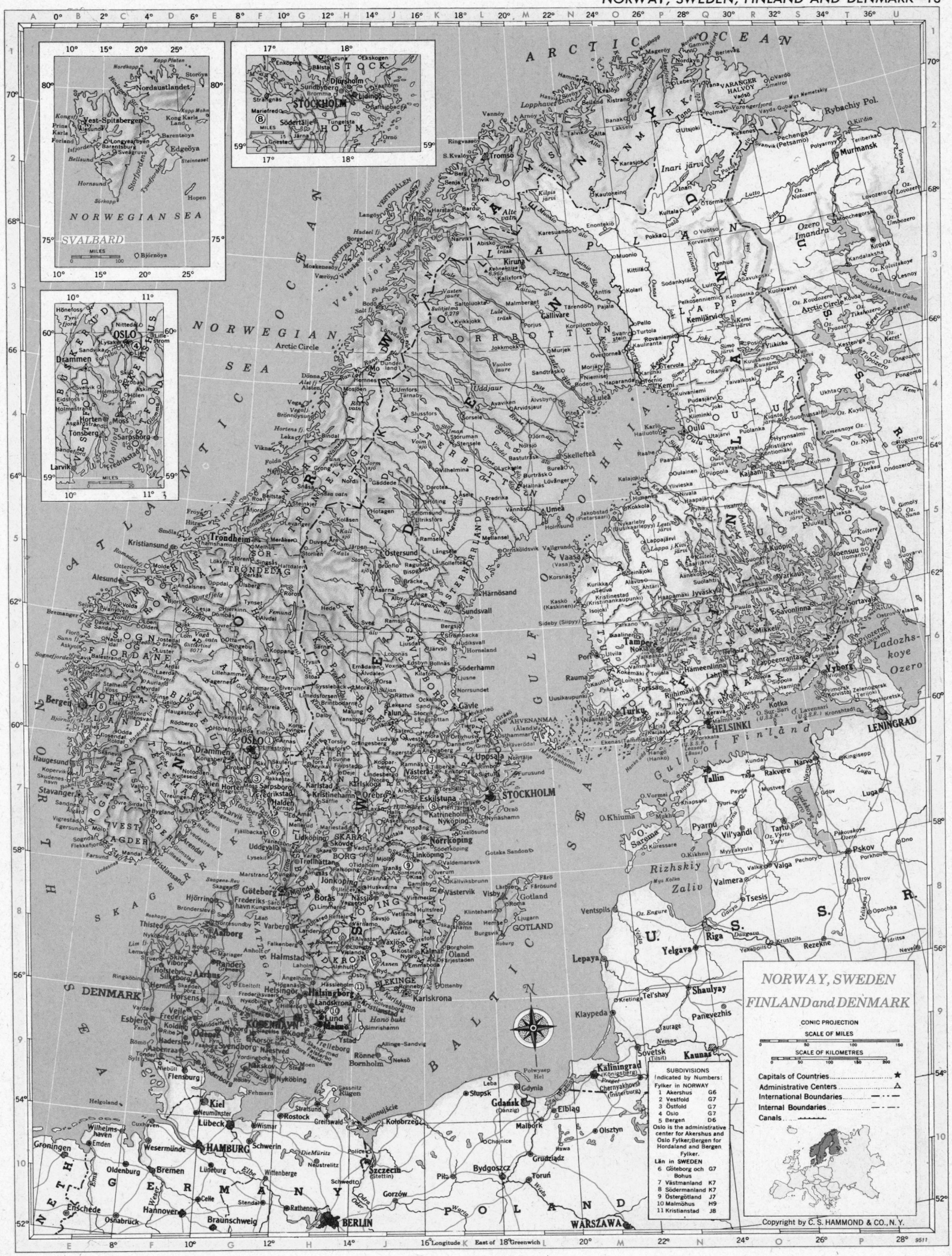

SVALBARD

NORWEGIAN SEA

NORWEGIAN SEA

STOCK-HOLM

STOCKHOLM

NORWAY, SWEDEN FINLAND and DENMARK

CONIC PROJECTION

SCALE OF MILES

SCALE OF KILOMETRES

Capitals of Countries............★
Administrative Centers..........△
International Boundaries........
Internal Boundaries.............
Canals.........................

SUBDIVISIONS
Indicated by Numbers:
Fylker in NORWAY
1 Akershus G6
2 Vestfold G7
3 Østfold G7
4 Oslo G7
5 Bergen D6
Oslo is the administrative
center for Akershus and
Oslo Fylker; Bergen for
Hordaland and Bergen
Fylker.
Län in SWEDEN
6 Göteborg och G7
   Bohus
7 Västmanland K7
8 Södermanland K7
9 Östergötland J7
10 Malmöhus H9
11 Kristianstad J8

Copyright by C. S. HAMMOND & CO., N.Y.

9511

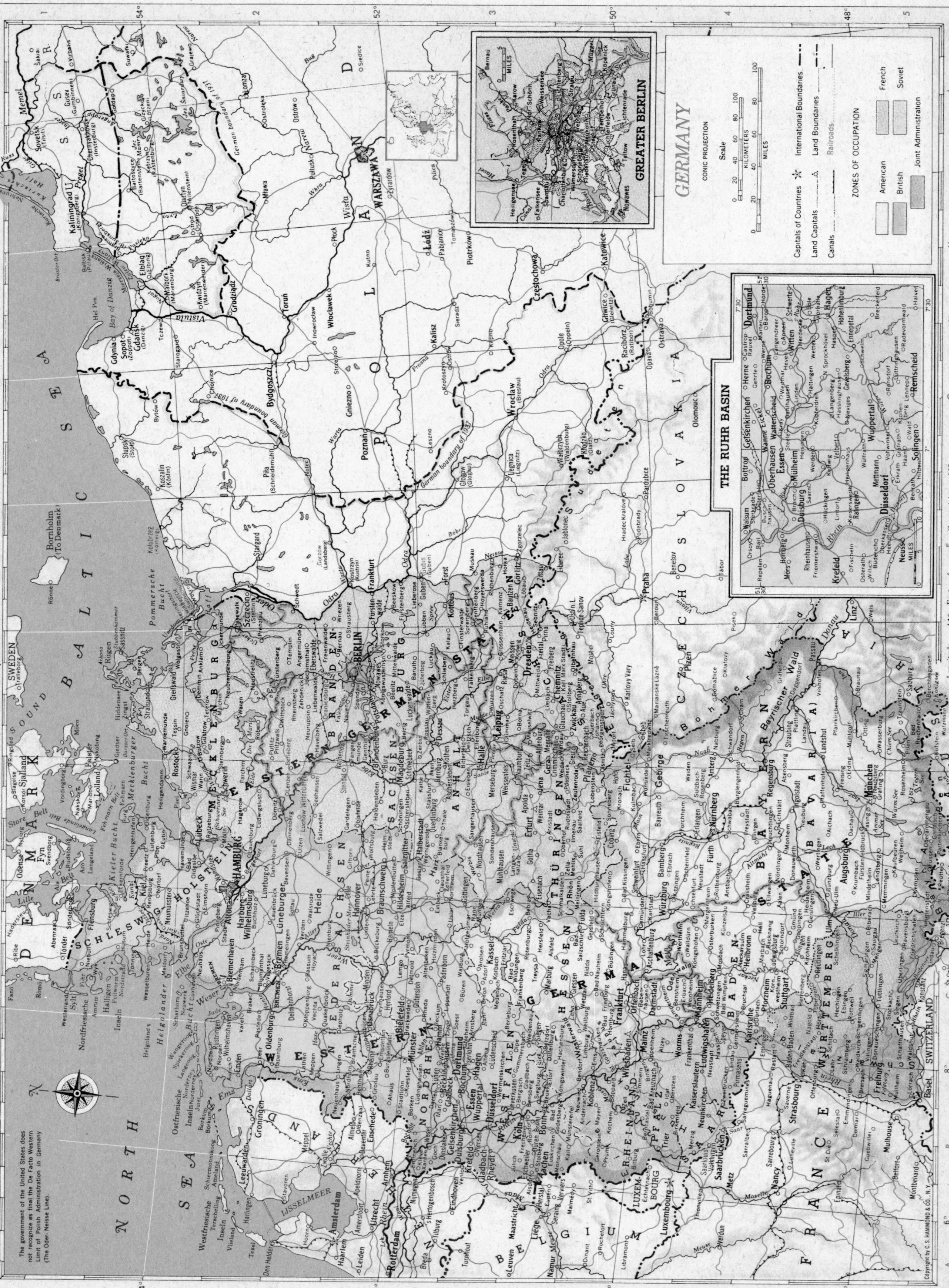

GERMANY

CONIC PROJECTION

Scale

KILOMETERS
0 20 40 60 80 100

MILES
0 20 40 60 80 100

Capitals of Countries ✪
Land Capitals △

International Boundaries
Land Boundaries
Canals   Railroads

ZONES OF OCCUPATION

American
British
French
Soviet
Joint Administration

GREATER BERLIN

THE RUHR BASIN

The government of the United States does not recognize as final the De Facto Western Limit of Polish Administration in Germany (The Oder-Neisse Line).

NORTH SEA

BALTIC SEA

DENMARK

SWEDEN

POLAND

CZECHOSLOVAKIA

FRANCE

SWITZERLAND

BELGIUM

LUXEMBOURG

NETHERLANDS

U.S.S.R.

SCHLESWIG-HOLSTEIN

MECKLENBURG

HAMBURG

NIEDERSACHSEN

WESTFALEN

NORDRHEIN

RHEINLAND-PFALZ

HESSEN

THÜRINGEN

SACHSEN

SACHSEN-ANHALT

BRANDENBURG

EASTERN GERMAN STATES

BADEN

WÜRTTEMBERG

BAYERN

BERLIN

WARSZAWA

Łódź

Poznań

Wrocław (Breslau)

Gdańsk (Danzig)

Bydgoszcz

Praha

München

Nürnberg

Stuttgart

Frankfurt

Köln

Dortmund

Düsseldorf

Essen

Hannover

Bremen

Kiel

Lübeck

Rostock

Stettin (Szczecin)

Leipzig

Dresden

Halle

Erfurt

Magdeburg

Kassel

Mannheim

Karlsruhe

Freiburg

Basel

Strasbourg

Amsterdam

Rotterdam

Luxembourg

Bay of Danzig

Pommersche Bucht

Kieler Bucht

Bornholm (To Denmark)

German boundary of 1937

German boundary of 1937

Copyright by C. S. Hammond & Co., N.Y.

Longitude 14° East of F Greenwich 16°

NETHERLANDS, BELGIUM
and LUXEMBOURG

CONIC PROJECTION

SCALE OF MILES

SCALE OF KILOMETRES

Capitals of Countries .... ★
Provincial Capitals .... ⌖
International Boundaries ....
Provincial Boundaries ....
Canals ....
Railroads ....

Elevations in Feet

AMSTERDAM

BRUXELLES (Brussel)

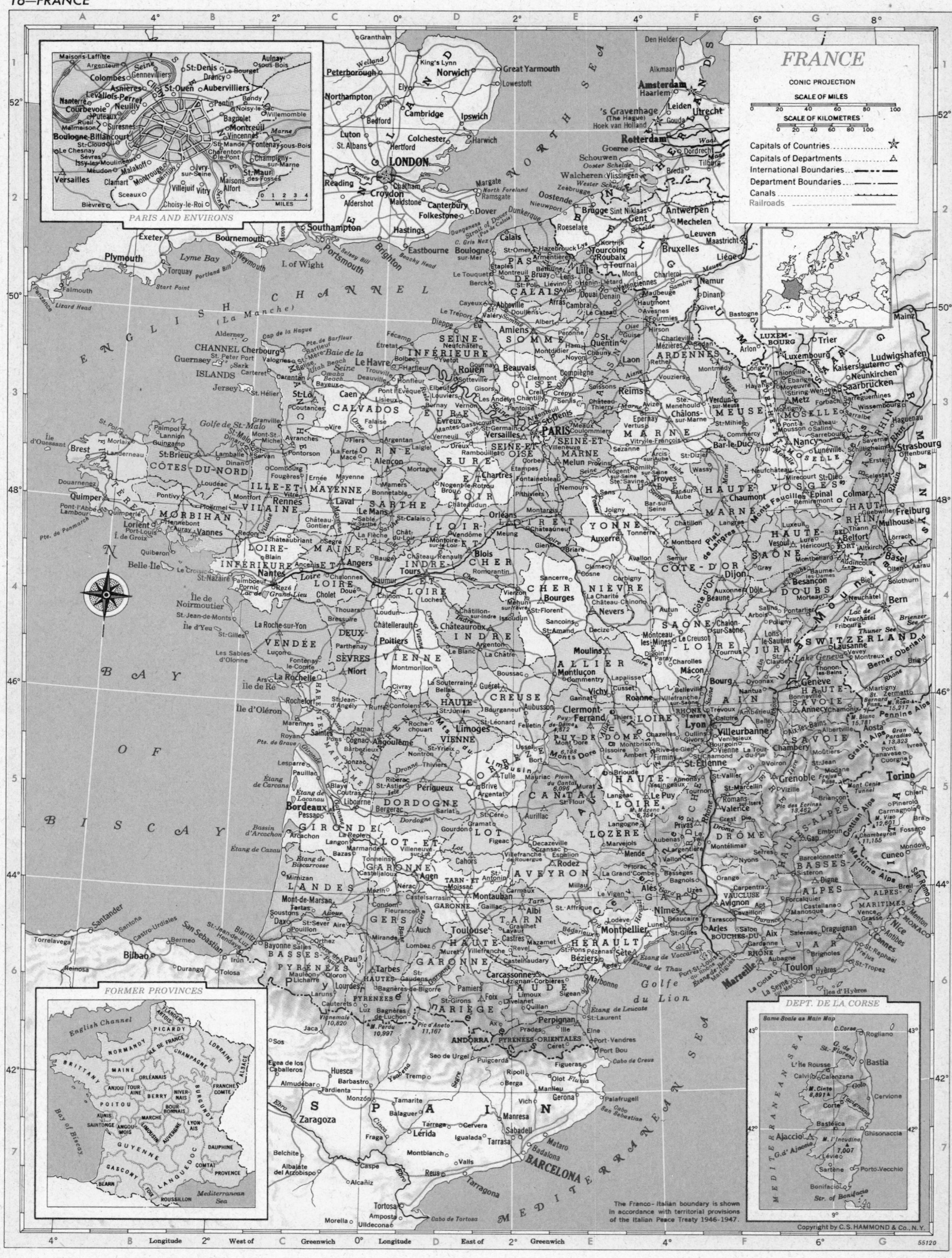

PARIS AND ENVIRONS

FRANCE

CONIC PROJECTION

SCALE OF MILES

SCALE OF KILOMETRES

Capitals of Countries .... ☆
Capitals of Departments .... △
International Boundaries .... — ·· —
Department Boundaries ..... — · —
Canals
Railroads

FORMER PROVINCES

DEPT. DE LA CORSE

The Franco-Italian boundary is shown
in accordance with territorial provisions
of the Italian Peace Treaty 1946-1947.

Copyright by C.S. HAMMOND & Co., N.Y.

55120

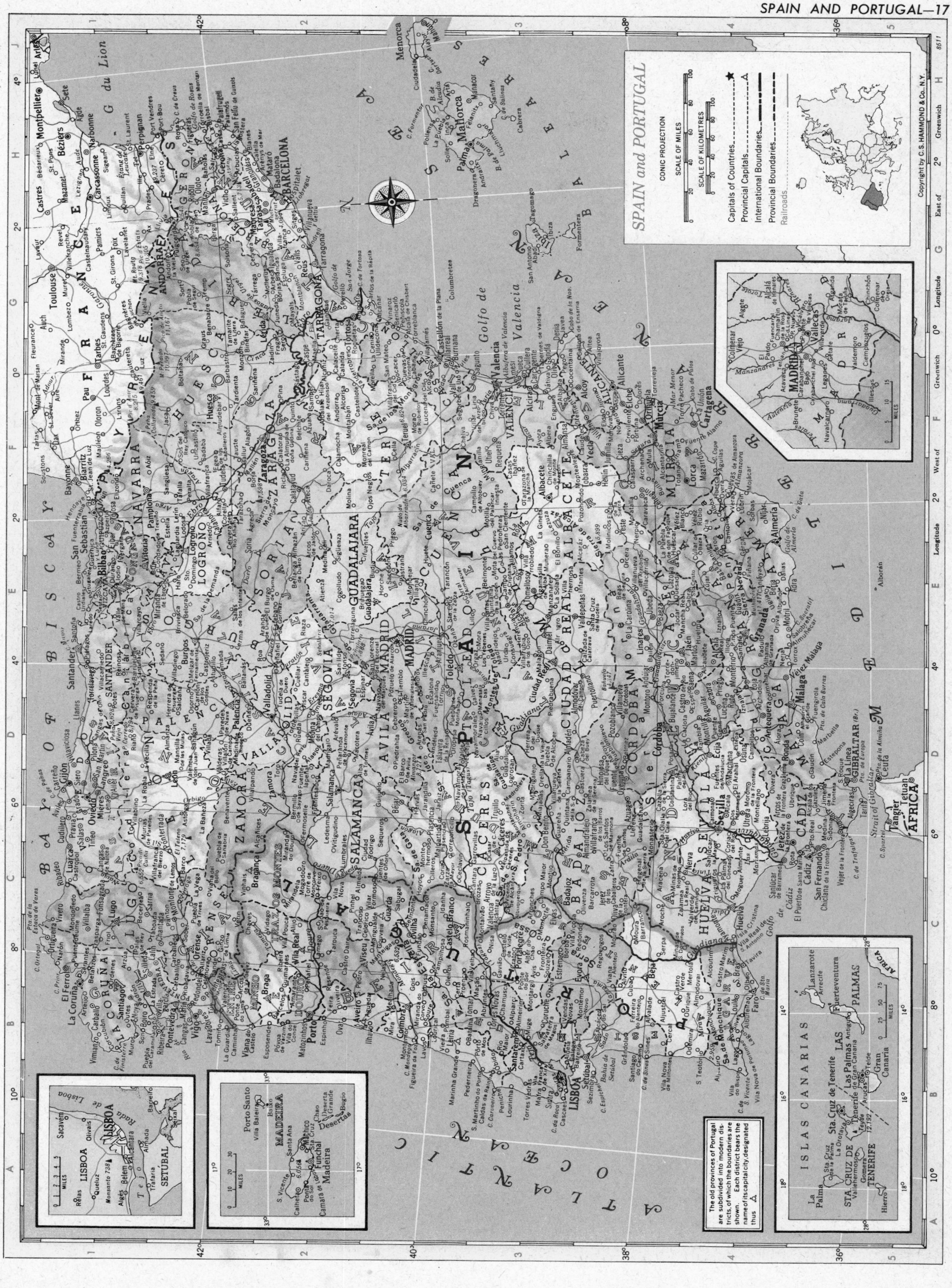

SPAIN and PORTUGAL

CONIC PROJECTION

SCALE OF MILES

SCALE OF KILOMETRES

Capitals of Countries........★
Provincial Capitals............⊛
International Boundaries.....
Provincial Boundaries........
Railroads.........................

Copyright by C.S. HAMMOND & Co. N.Y.

The old provinces of Portugal are subdivided into modern districts, of which the boundaries are shown. Each district bears the name of its capital city, designated thus ⊛

MADRID

SETUBAL
LISBOA

MADEIRA
Porto Santo
Funchal
Desertas

ISLAS CANARIAS
STA. CRUZ DE TENERIFE
LAS PALMAS
Gran Canaria
Lanzarote
Fuerteventura
La Palma
Gomera
Hierro

ATLANTIC OCEAN

B A Y   O F   B I S C A Y

Gulf of Lion

BALEARES

MEDITERRANEAN SEA

AFRICA

ITALY

CONIC PROJECTION

SCALE OF MILES

SCALE OF KILOMETERS

Capitals of Countries .... ★
Regional Capitals .... ⊞
Provincial Capitals .... △
International Boundaries ___.___.___
Regional Boundaries ___ ___ ___
Railroads

ITALY is divided for administrative purposes into
19 regions, shown on the map in separate colors.
The regions of Friuli-Venezia Giulia, Sardegna, Sicilia,
Trentino - Alto Adige and Valle d'Aosta enjoy special
autonomy.
The regions are subdivided into provinces bearing
the same names as their respective capitals, except:

PROVINCE	CAPITAL
IONIO	Taranto
MASSA E CARRARA	Massa
PESARO E URBINO	Pesaro

CITTÀ DEL VATICANO

PROVINCIA DI LATINA

Copyright by C.S. HAMMOND & Co., N.Y.

Longitude East of Greenwich

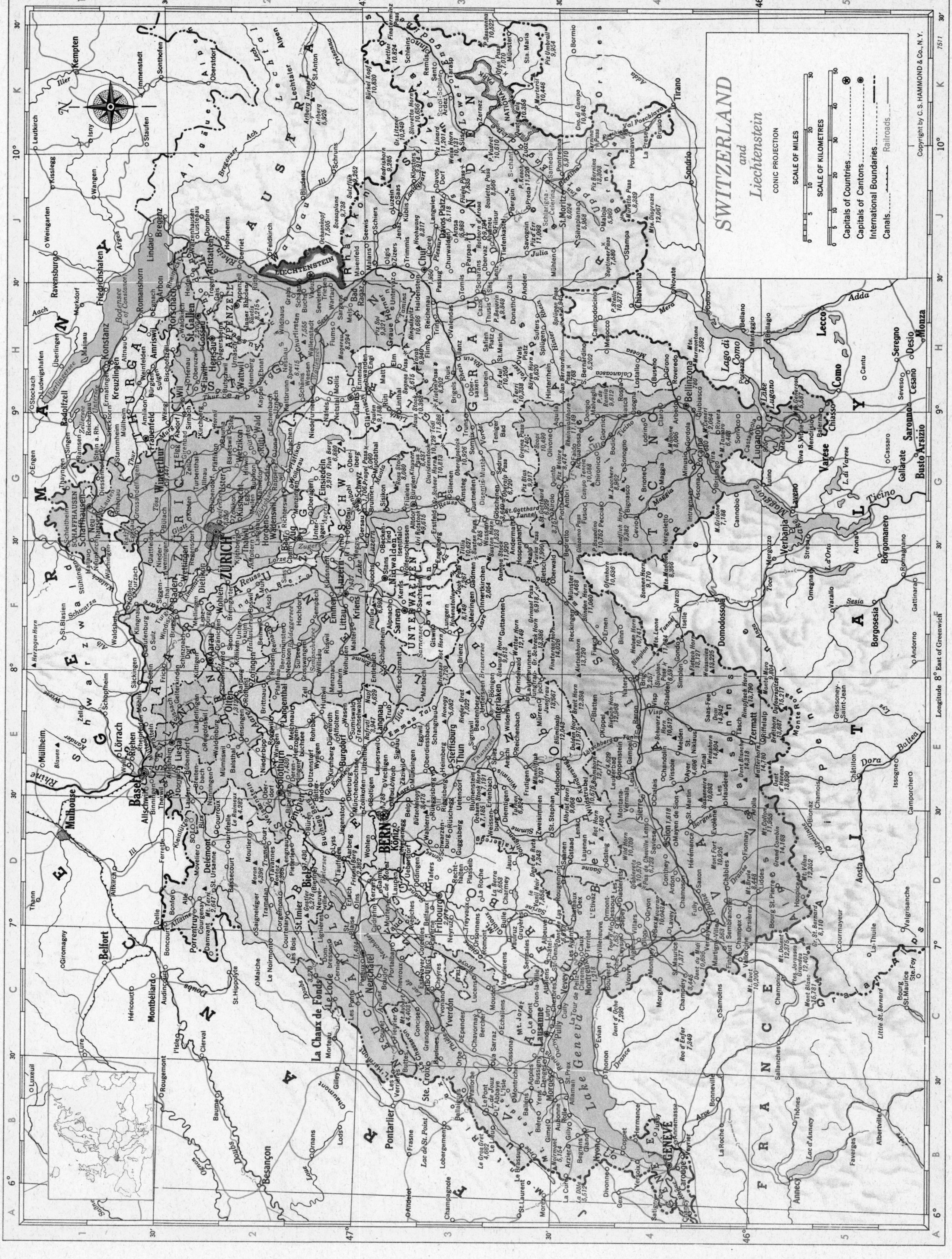

SWITZERLAND
and
Liechtenstein

CONIC PROJECTION

SCALE OF MILES

SCALE OF KILOMETRES

⊛ Capitals of Countries
⊙ Capitals of Cantons
International Boundaries
Canals
Railroads

AUSTRIA

FRANCE

ITALY

BADEN

WÜRTEMBERG

BAVARIA

THURGAU

ZÜRICH

SCHWYZ

GRAUBÜNDEN

TICINO

VALAIS

BERN

LUZERN

UNTERWALDEN

APPENZELL

ST. GALLEN

LIECHTENSTEIN

Bodensee (L. of Constance)

Lake Geneva

Lago di Como

Lake Lugano

Lago Maggiore

ZURICH

BERN

GENÈVE

BASEL

Lausanne

Winterthur

Schaffhausen

La Chaux de Fonds

Neuchâtel

Fribourg

Chur

St. Moritz

Bellinzona

Zermatt

Mont Blanc 15,781

Monte Rosa 15,217

Matterhorn 14,804

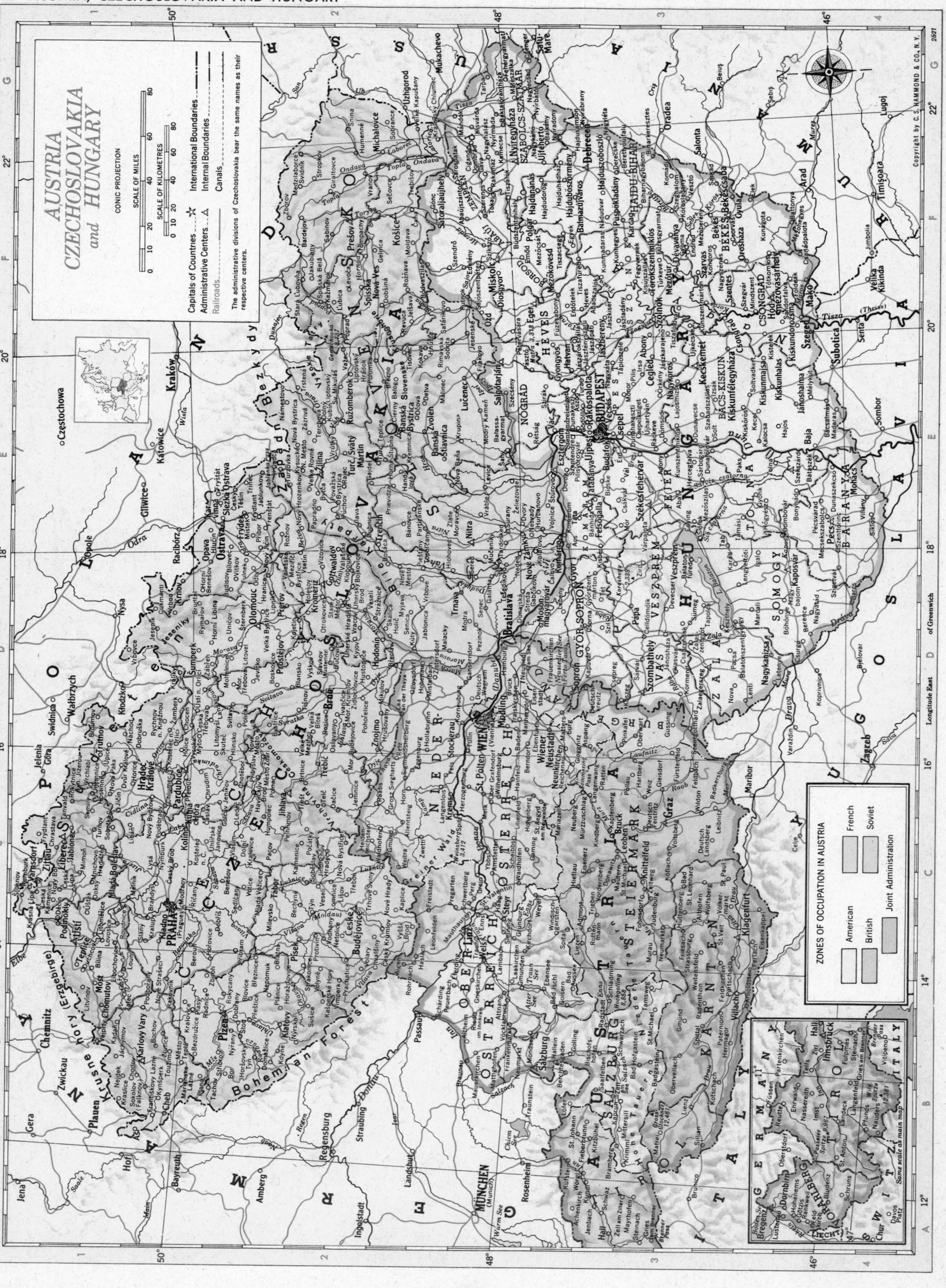

AUSTRIA CZECHOSLOVAKIA and HUNGARY

CONIC PROJECTION

SCALE OF MILES

SCALE OF KILOMETRES

Capitals of Countries ..... ☆
Administrative Centers ..... △
Railroads

International Boundaries ----
Internal Boundaries ----
Canals

The administrative divisions of Czechoslovakia bear the same names as their respective centers.

ZONES OF OCCUPATION IN AUSTRIA

American
British
French
Soviet
Joint Administration

Copyright by C. S. HAMMOND & CO., N. Y.

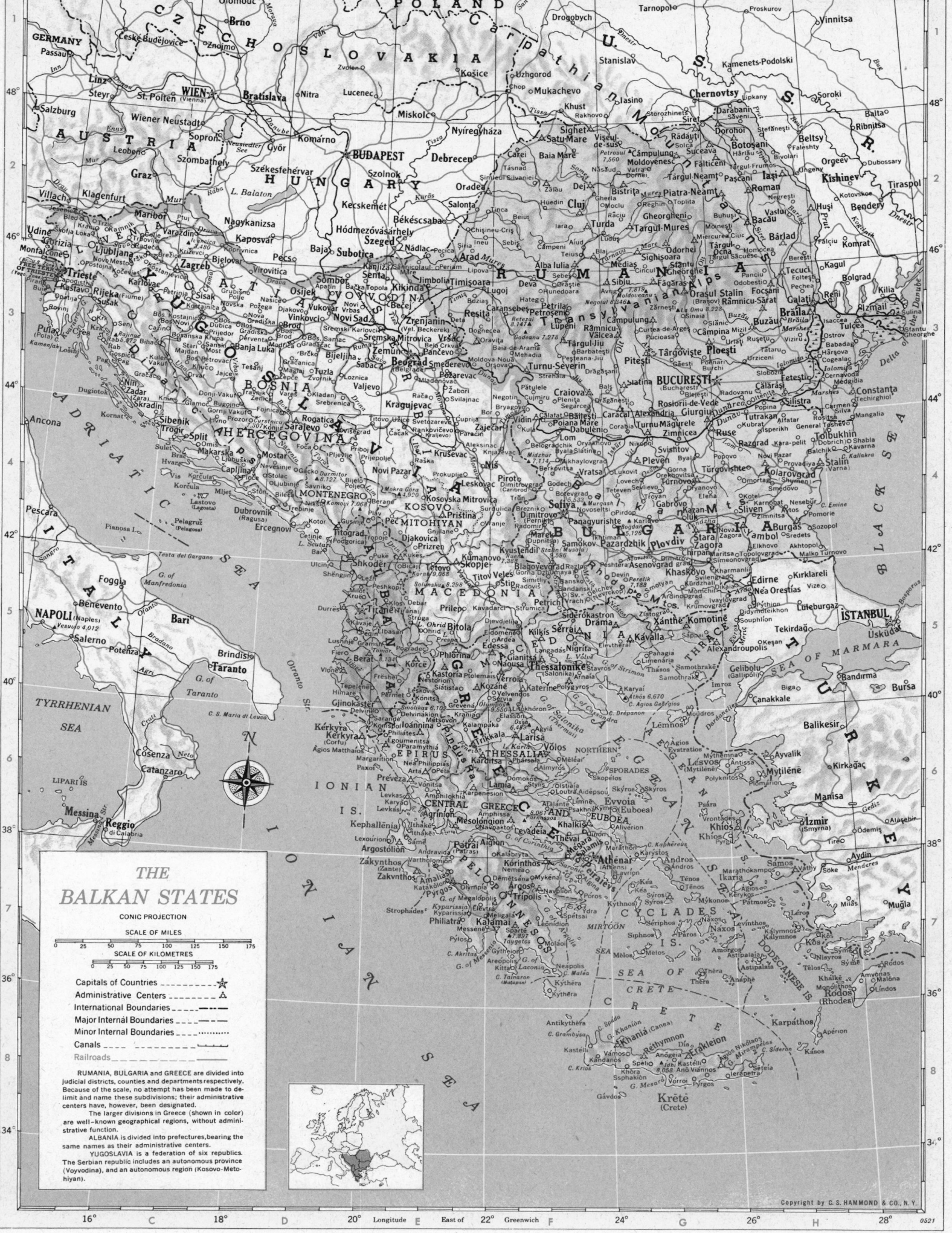

THE BALKAN STATES

CONIC PROJECTION

SCALE OF MILES

0 25 50 75 100 125 150 175

SCALE OF KILOMETRES

0 25 50 75 100 125 150 175

Capitals of Countries _____ ★
Administrative Centers _____ △
International Boundaries _____
Major Internal Boundaries _ _ _ _ _
Minor Internal Boundaries ....
Canals ____ _ _ _ _ _ _ _ _
Railroads _____

RUMANIA, BULGARIA and GREECE are divided into judicial districts, counties and departments respectively. Because of the scale, no attempt has been made to delimit and name these subdivisions; their administrative centers have, however, been designated.

The larger divisions in Greece (shown in color) are well-known geographical regions, without administrative function.

ALBANIA is divided into prefectures, bearing the same names as their administrative centers.

YUGOSLAVIA is a federation of six republics. The Serbian republic includes an autonomous province (Voyvodina), and an autonomous region (Kosovo-Metohiyan).

0521

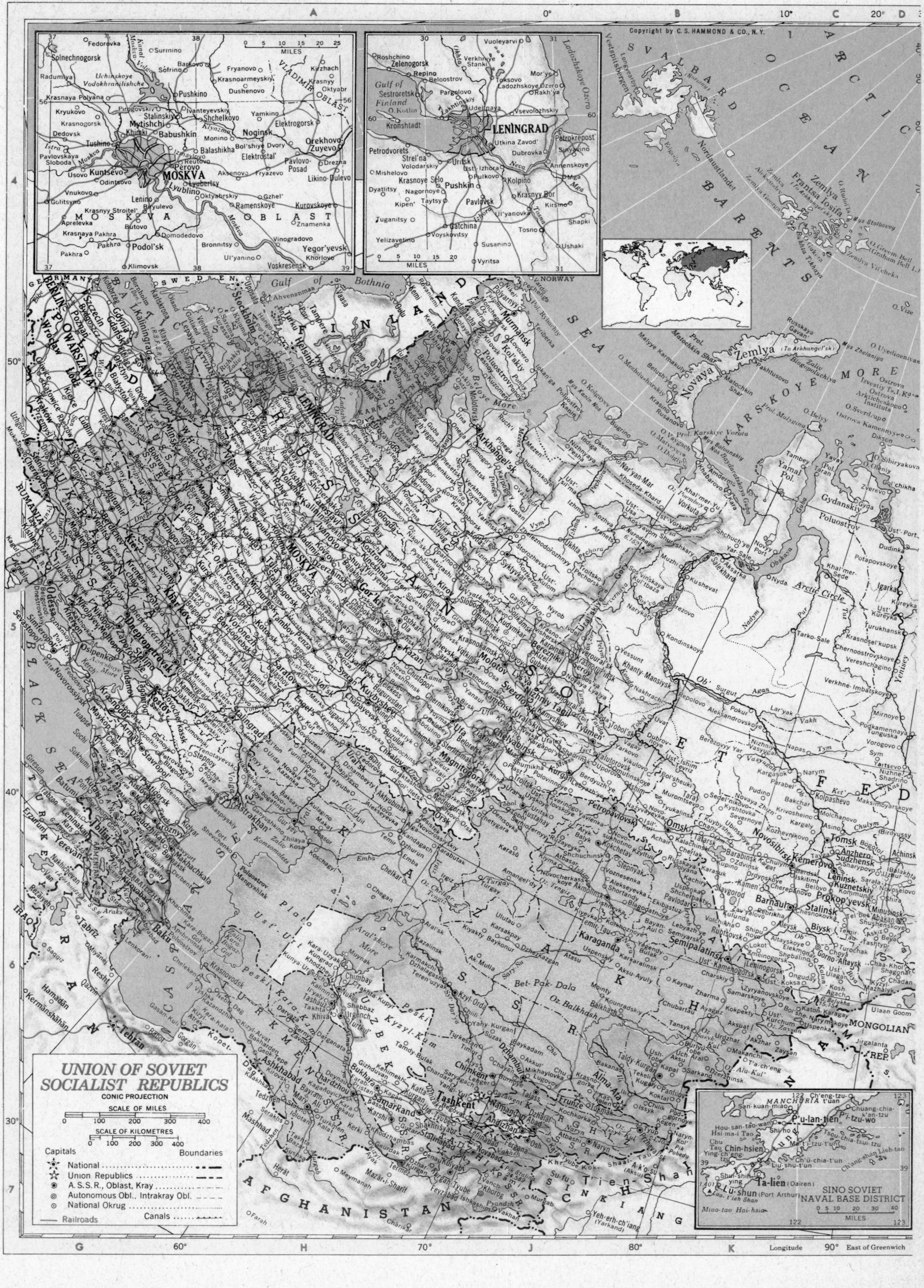

Copyright by C.S. HAMMOND & CO., N.Y.

MOSKVA

MOSKVA OBLAST

LENINGRAD

UNION OF SOVIET SOCIALIST REPUBLICS

CONIC PROJECTION

SCALE OF MILES
0 100 200 300 400

SCALE OF KILOMETRES
0 100 200 300 400

Capitals   Boundaries
★ National ....
☆ Union Republics .... —·—·—·
◉ A.S.S.R., Oblast, Kray .... —··—··—
◎ Autonomous Obl., Intrakray Obl. ......
○ National Okrug
▬ Railroads   Canals ....

SINO SOVIET
NAVAL BASE DISTRICT

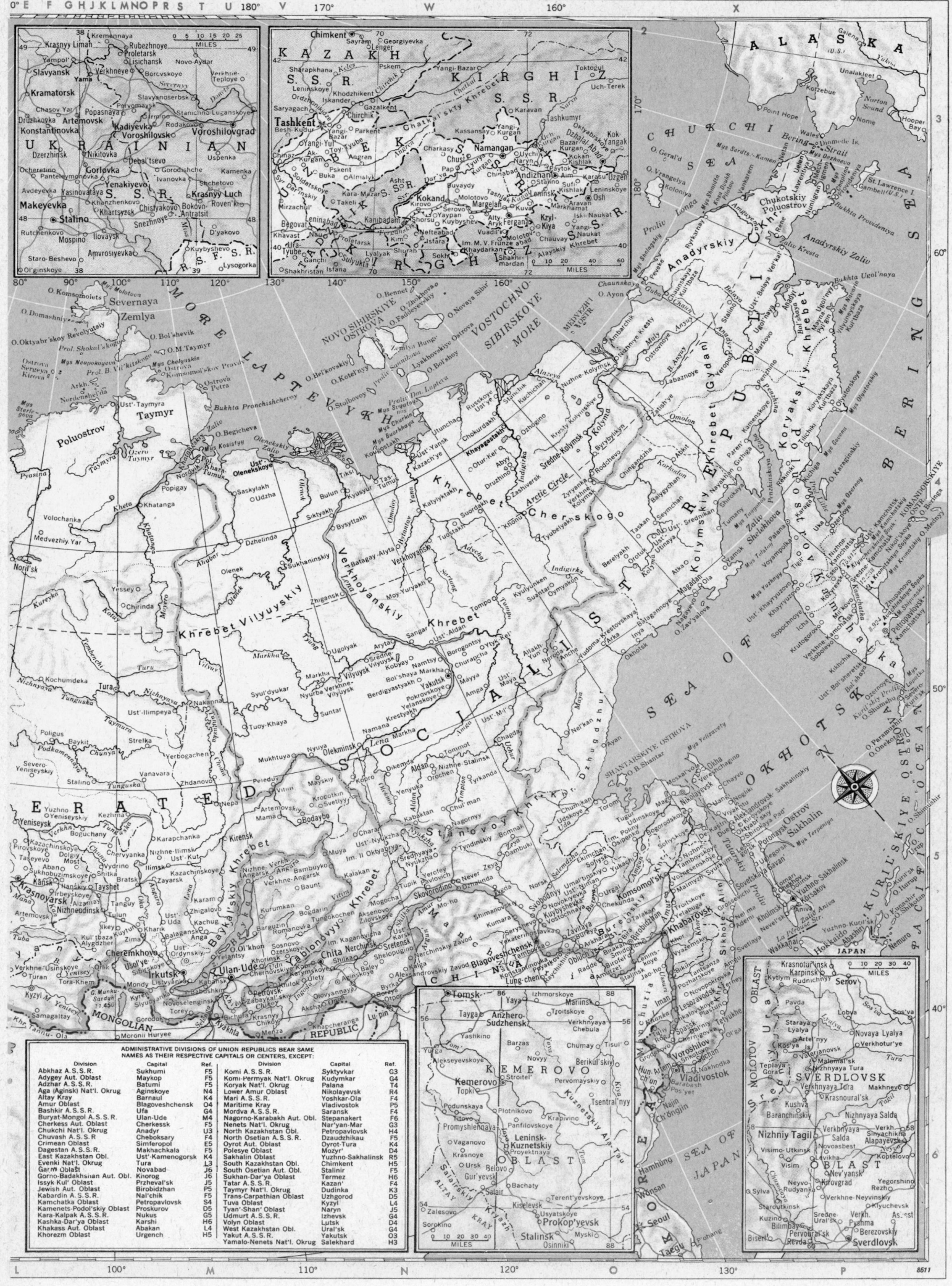

ADMINISTRATIVE DIVISIONS OF UNION REPUBLICS BEAR SAME NAMES AS THEIR RESPECTIVE CAPITALS OR CENTERS, EXCEPT:

Division	Capital	Ref.	Division	Capital	Ref.
Abkhaz A.S.S.R.	Sukhumi	F5	Komi A.S.S.R.	Syktyvkar	G3
Adygey Aut. Oblast	Maykop	F5	Komi-Permyak Nat'l. Okrug	Kudymkar	G4
Adzhar A.S.S.R.	Batumi	F5	Koryak Nat'l. Okrug	Palana	T4
Aga Aginski Nat'l. Okrug	Aginskoye	N4	Lower Amur Oblast	Nikolayevsk	R4
Altay Kray	Barnaul	K4	Mari A.S.S.R.	Yoshkar-Ola	F4
Amur Oblast	Blagoveshchensk	O4	Maritime Kray	Vladivostok	P5
Bashkir A.S.S.R.	Ufa	G4	Mordva A.S.S.R.	Saransk	F4
Buryat-Mongol A.S.S.R.	Ulan-Ude	M4	Nagorno-Karabakh Aut. Obl.	Stepanakert	F6
Cherkess Aut. Oblast	Cherkessk	F5	Nenets Nat'l. Okrug	Nar'yan-Mar	G3
Chuvash A.S.S.R.	Cheboksary	F4	North Kazakhstan Obl.	Petropavlovsk	H4
Chukchi Nat'l. Okrug	Anadyr	U3	North Osetian A.S.S.R.	Dzaudzhikau	F5
Crimean Oblast	Simferopol	E5	Oyrot Aut. Oblast	Oyrot-Tura	K4
Dagestan A.S.S.R.	Makhachkala	F5	Polesye Oblast	Mozyr'	D4
East Kazakhstan Obl.	Ust'-Kamenogorsk	K4	Sakhalin Oblast	Yuzhno-Sakhalinsk	R5
Evenki Nat'l. Okrug	Tura	L3	South Kazakhstan Obl.	Chimkent	H5
Garm Oblast	Novabad	J6	South Osetian Aut. Obl.	Stalinir	F5
Gorno-Badakhshan Aut. Obl.	Knorog	J6	Sukhan-Dar'ya Oblast	Termez	H6
Issyk Kul' Oblast	Przheval'sk	J5	Tatar A.S.S.R.	Kazan'	F4
Jewish Aut. Oblast	Birobidzhan	P5	Taymyr Nat'l. Okrug	Dudinka	K3
Kabardin A.S.S.R.	Nal'chik	F5	Trans-Carpathian Oblast	Uzhgorod	D5
Kamchatka Oblast	Petropavlovsk	S4	Tuva A.S.S.R.	Kyzyl	L4
Kamenets-Podol'skiy Oblast	Proskurov	D5	Tyan'-Shan' Oblast	Naryn	J5
Kara-Kalpak A.S.S.R.	Nukus	G5	Udmurt A.S.S.R.	Izhevsk	G4
Kashka-Dar'ya Oblast	Karshi	H6	Volyn Oblast	Lutsk	D4
Khakass Aut. Oblast	Abakan	L4	West Kazakhstan Obl.	Ural'sk	G4
Khorezm Oblast	Urgench	H5	Yakut A.S.S.R.	Yakutsk	O3
			Yamalo-Nenets Nat'l. Okrug	Salekhard	H3

8511

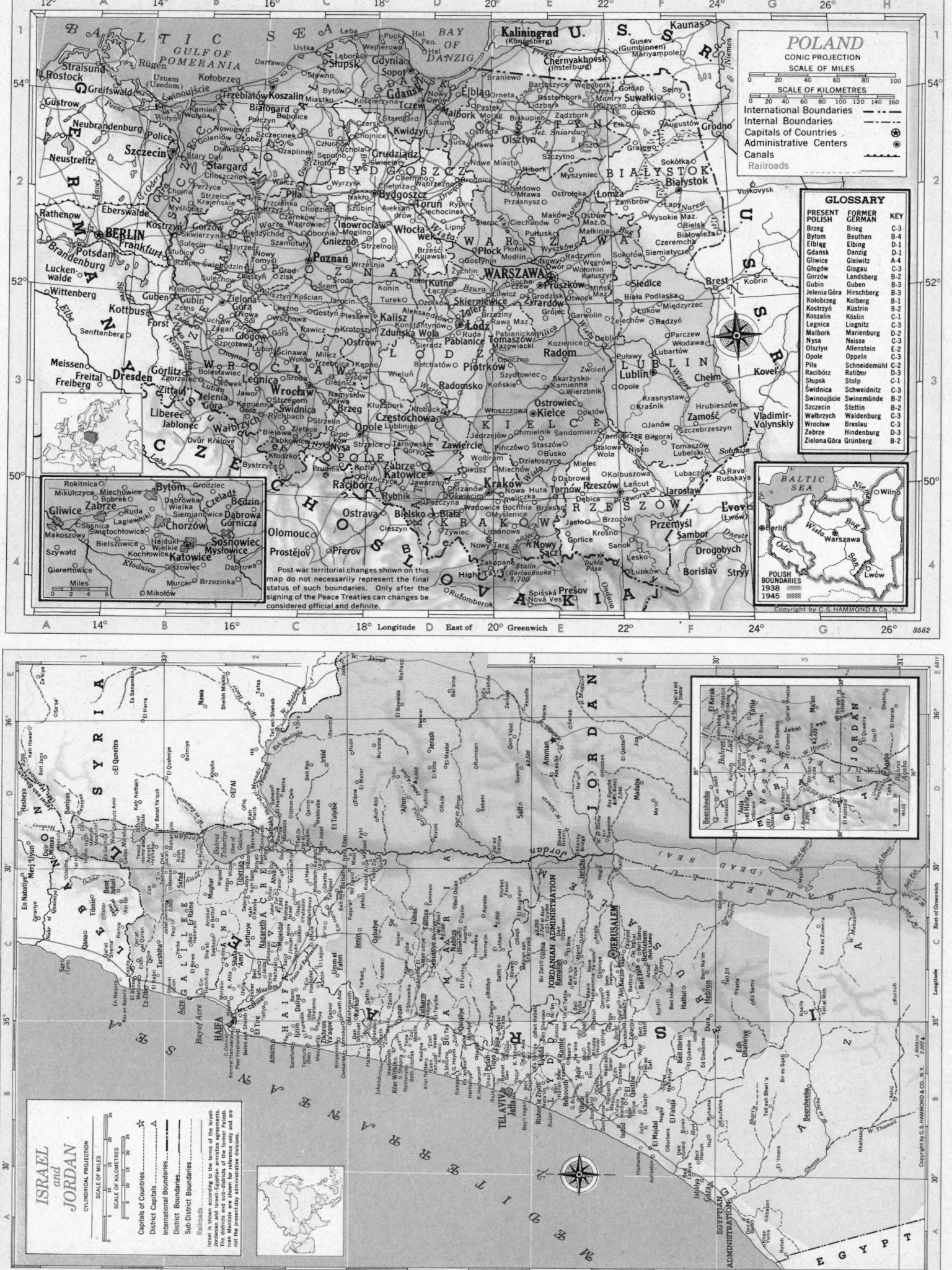

Post-war territorial changes shown on this map do not necessarily represent the final status of such boundaries. Only after the signing of the Peace Treaties can changes be considered official and definite.

POLAND
CONIC PROJECTION
SCALE OF MILES
SCALE OF KILOMETRES

International Boundaries
Internal Boundaries
Capitals of Countries
Administrative Centers
Canals
Railroads

GLOSSARY

PRESENT POLISH	FORMER GERMAN	KEY
Brzeg	Brieg	C-3
Bytom	Beuthen	B-4
Elbląg	Elbing	D-1
Gdańsk	Danzig	D-1
Gliwice	Gleiwitz	A-4
Głogów	Glogau	C-3
Gorzów	Landsberg	B-2
Gubin	Guben	B-2
Jelenia Góra	Hirschberg	B-3
Kołobrzeg	Kolberg	B-1
Kostrzyn	Küstrin	B-2
Koszalin	Köslin	C-1
Legnica	Liegnitz	C-3
Malbork	Marienburg	D-2
Nysa	Neisse	C-3
Olsztyn	Allenstein	E-2
Opole	Oppeln	C-3
Piła	Schneidemühl	C-2
Racibórz	Ratibor	D-3
Słupsk	Stolp	C-1
Świdnica	Schweidnitz	C-3
Świnoujście	Swinemünde	B-2
Szczecin	Stettin	B-2
Wałbrzych	Waldenburg	C-3
Wrocław	Breslau	C-3
Zabrze	Hindenburg	D-3
Zielona Góra	Grünberg	B-2

POLISH BOUNDARIES
1938
1945

Copyright by C.S. HAMMOND & CO., N.Y.

ISRAEL and JORDAN
CYLINDRICAL PROJECTION
SCALE OF MILES
SCALE OF KILOMETRES

Capitals of Countries
District Capitals
International Boundaries
District Boundaries
Sub-District Boundaries
Railroads

Israel is shown according to the terms of the Israeli-Jordanian and Israeli-Egyptian armistice agreements. The districts and sub-districts of the former Palestinian Mandate are shown for reference only and are not the present day administrative divisions.

Copyright by C.S. HAMMOND & CO., N.Y.

ASIA

LAMBERT AZIMUTHAL EQUAL-AREA PROJECTION

SCALE OF MILES

0   150   300   600   900   1200

SCALE OF KILOMETRES

0   300   600   900   1200

Capitals of Countries .... ★   Canals
International Boundaries _____   Railroads _____
Elevations in Feet

Copyright by C.S. HAMMOND & CO., N.Y.

6552

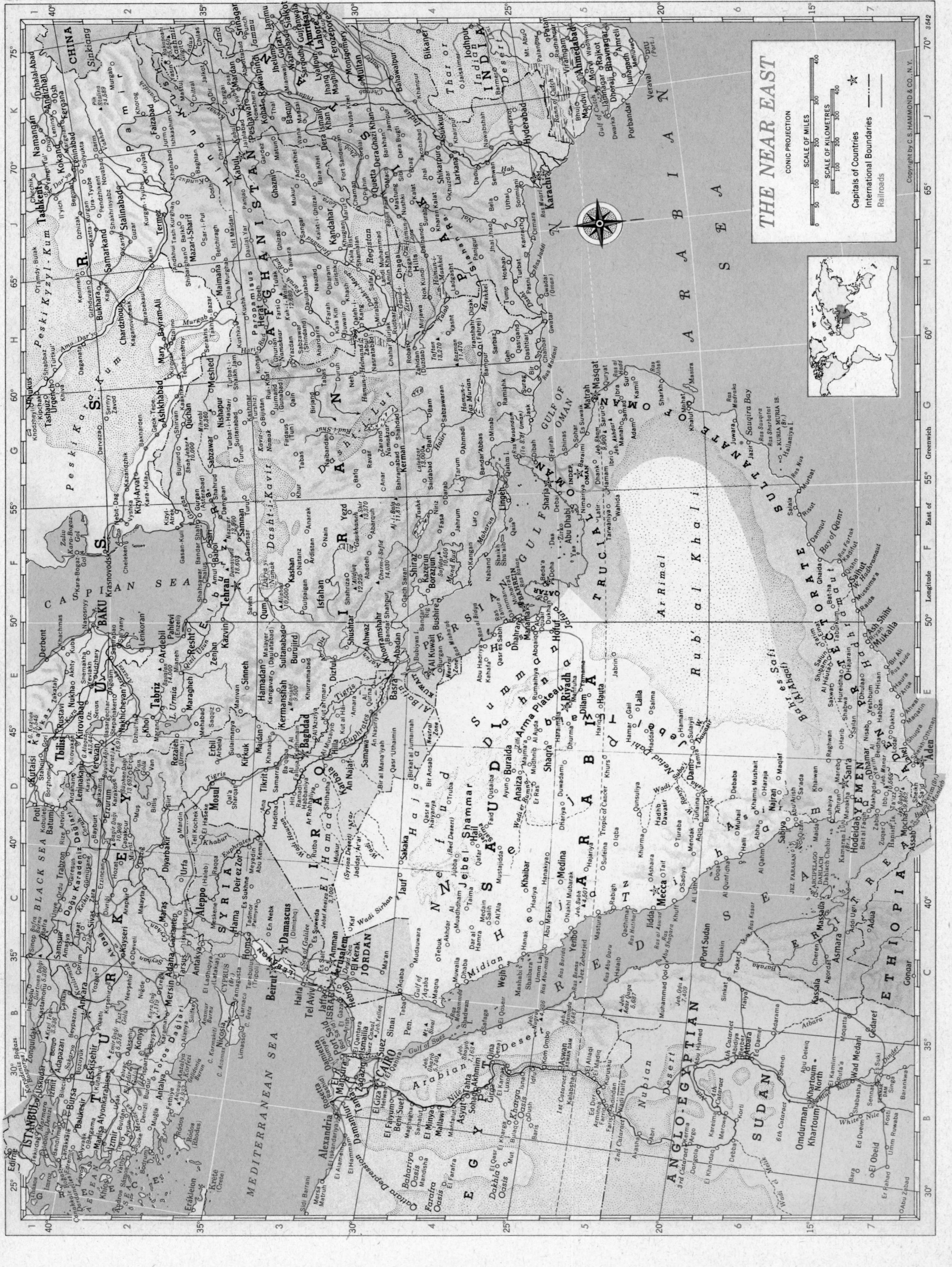

THE NEAR EAST

CONIC PROJECTION

SCALE OF MILES

SCALE OF KILOMETRES

Capitals of Countries ✶
International Boundaries ------
Railroads ————

Copyright by C. S. HAMMOND & CO., N.Y.

(Map of the Near East showing regions including: TURKEY, SYRIA, IRAQ, IRAN, SAUDI ARABIA, AFGHANISTAN, WEST PAKISTAN, INDIA, EGYPT, ANGLO-EGYPTIAN SUDAN, ETHIOPIA, ERITREA, YEMEN, JORDAN, ISRAEL, LEBANON, CYPRUS, KUWAIT, QATAR, TRUCIAL OMAN, MUSCAT AND OMAN SULTANATE, U.S.S.R., CHINA. Bodies of water labeled: MEDITERRANEAN SEA, BLACK SEA, CASPIAN SEA, RED SEA, ARABIAN SEA, PERSIAN GULF, GULF OF OMAN, GULF OF ADEN, AEGEAN SEA. Major cities include CAIRO, Baghdad, Tehran, Mecca, Medina, Riyadh, Damascus, Beirut, Jerusalem, Amman, Aden, Karachi, Kabul, Kandahar, Kerman, Isfahan, Shiraz, Tabriz, Mosul, Basra, Aleppo, Ankara, Istanbul, Khartoum, Asmara.)

IRAN and IRAQ

CONIC PROJECTION

SCALE OF MILES

SCALE OF KILOMETRES

Capitals of Countries ....
International Boundaries......
Railroads.....................
Elevations in Feet

Copyright by C. S. HAMMOND & CO., N.Y.

Countries and regions: TURKEY, SYRIA, SAUDI ARABIA, KUWAIT, IRAQ, IRAN, AFGHANISTAN, PAKISTAN, OMAN, TRUCIAL OMAN, QATAR, BAHREIN, U.S.S.R., U.S.S.R., MAKRAN, KERMAN, LARISTAN, KHUZISTAN, BAKHTIARI, LURISTAN, KURDISTAN, KHURASAN, MAZANDERAN, MESOPOTAMIA, Syrian Desert, Al Hajara, Al Jazira, Zagros Range, Elburz Range, Dasht-i-Lut, Dasht-i-Kavir, Kara Kum, Belwuda Kuh

Seas and gulfs: CASPIAN SEA, PERSIAN GULF, GULF OF OMAN, Lake Urmia, Gulf of Cheleken Pen.

Cities: BAKU, ERIVAN, TABRIZ, TEHRAN, BAGHDAD, Mesbed, Kerman, Shiraz, Isfahan, Hamadan, Kermanshah, Mosul, Basra, Al Kuwait, Kuwait, Kashan, Qum, Kazvin, Resht, Reza, Zahidano, Herat, Bushire, Bandar Abbas, Sharja, Doha, Manama, Muharraq, Hofuf, Dhahran, An Najaf, Karbala, Hilla, Kut al Imara, An Nasiriya, Samawa, Diwaniya, Tikrit, Samarra, Kirkuk, Erbil, Sulaimaniya, Diyarbakir, Malatya, Urfa, Mardin, Deir ez Zor, Raqqa

TURKEY, SYRIA, LEBANON AND CYPRUS

Copyright by C.S. HAMMOND & CO., N.Y.

SCALE OF MILES
0   25   50   75   100   125   150

SCALE OF KILOMETRES
0   25   50   75   100   125   150

★ Capitals of Countries   Provincial Boundaries
☆ Provincial Capitals   Railroads

Turkey is divided into provinces bearing the same names as their capital towns, except:

Province	Capital
AĞRI	Karaköse	K3
BİNGÖL	Çapakçur	J3
ÇORUH	Artvin	J2
HAKKÂRİ	Çölemerik	K4
HATAY	Antakya	G4
İÇEL	Mersin	F4
KOCAELİ	İzmit	C2
SEYHAN	Adana	F4
TUNCELİ	Çemişgezek	H3

ISTANBUL (inset map)

BLACK SEA

MARMARA DENİZİ

MILES 0 5 10

MILES 0 5 10 15 20

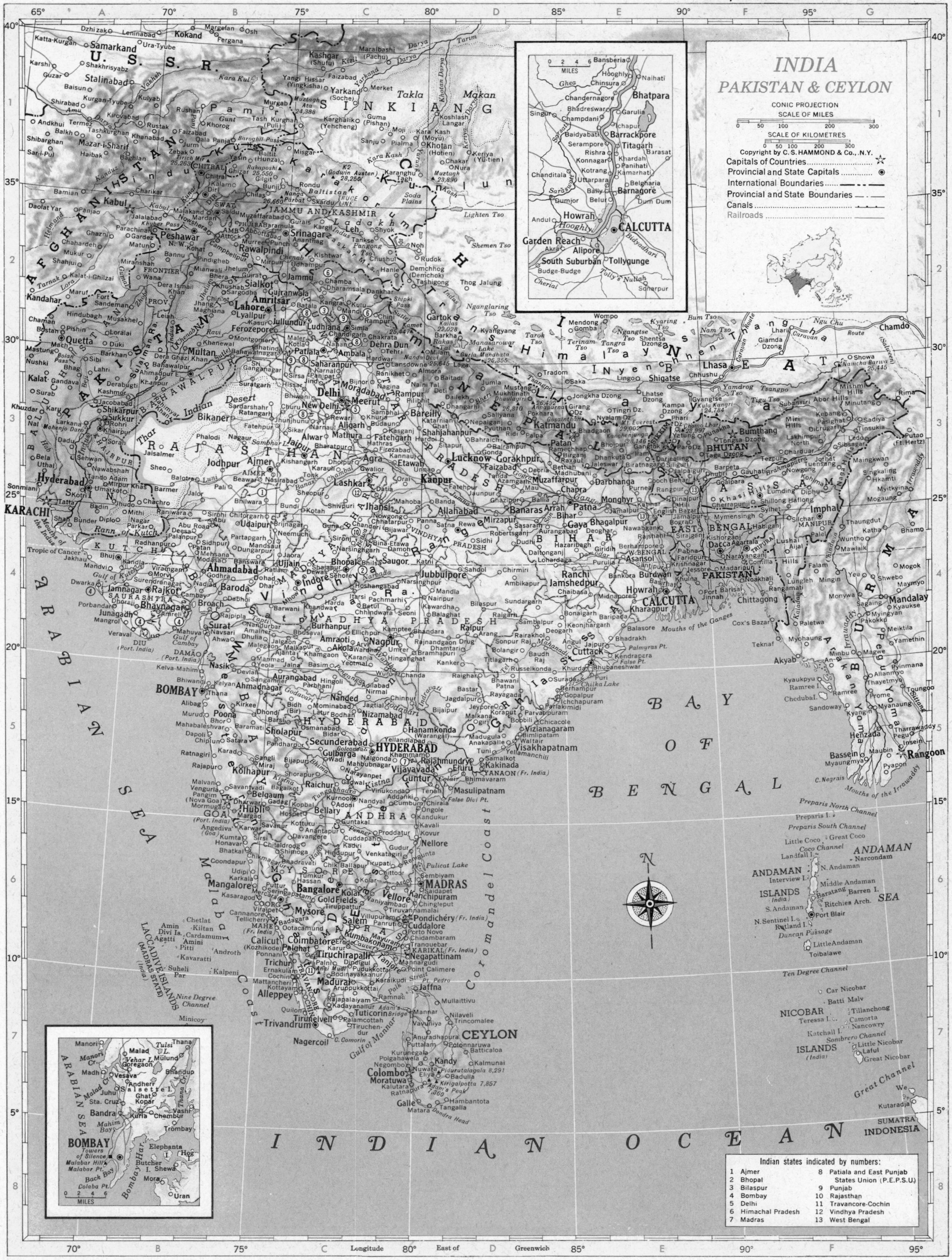

INDIA
PAKISTAN & CEYLON

CONIC PROJECTION

SCALE OF MILES

SCALE OF KILOMETERS
0 50 100 200 300

Copyright by C. S. HAMMOND & Co., N.Y.

Capitals of Countries .... ☆
Provincial and State Capitals .... ◉
International Boundaries .... ———
Provincial and State Boundaries —·—·—
Canals .... ————
Railroads ———————

Indian states indicated by numbers:

1	Ajmer	8	Patiala and East Punjab
2	Bhopal		States Union (P.E.P.S.U.)
3	Bilaspur	9	Punjab
4	Bombay	10	Rajasthan
5	Delhi	11	Travancore-Cochin
6	Himachal Pradesh	12	Vindhya Pradesh
7	Madras	13	West Bengal

CALCUTTA

MILES

BOMBAY

MILES

ARABIAN SEA

BAY OF BENGAL

INDIAN OCEAN

AFGHANISTAN

U. S. S. R.

SINKIANG

PAKISTAN

RAJASTHAN

HYDERABAD

MYSORE

MADRAS

CEYLON

ANDAMAN ISLANDS (India)

NICOBAR ISLANDS (India)

BURMA

Longitude East of Greenwich

BURMA, THAILAND, INDOCHINA AND MALAYAN FEDERATION

CONIC PROJECTION

SCALE OF MILES

0 50 100 150 200

SCALE OF KILOMETRES

0 50 100 200 300

International Boundaries .... _ _ _ _
Capitals of Countries .... ⊛
Administrative Centers .... ⊙
Railroads ....

Copyright by C. S. HAMMOND & CO., N.Y.

Longitude 100° East of Greenwich

Countries and major regions: PAKISTAN, INDIA, BURMA, CHINA, THAILAND (SIAM), LAOS, TONKIN, ANNAM, CAMBODIA, COCHIN CHINA, MALAYAN FEDERATION, SUMATRA, INDONESIA, JOHORE, PAHANG, TRENGGANU, KEDAH, PERAK, SELANGOR

Seas and waters: BAY OF BENGAL, ANDAMAN SEA, GULF OF MARTABAN, GULF OF SIAM, SOUTH CHINA SEA, GULF OF TONKIN, Strait of Malacca

Capitals and major cities: Mandalay, Rangoon, Krung Thep (Bangkok), Vientiane, Luang Prabang, Hanoi, Haiphong, Hue, Tourane, Saigon, Phnom Penh, Kunming, Kuala Lumpur, Singapore, Johore Bahru, Penang (George Town)

Islands: ANDAMAN IS., NICOBAR IS. (India), HAINAN, North Andaman I., Middle Andaman I., South Andaman I., Little Andaman I., Great Nicobar, Little Nicobar, Car Nicobar, Paracel Is. and Reefs, Mergui Arch.

Inset: JOHORE / SINGAPORE

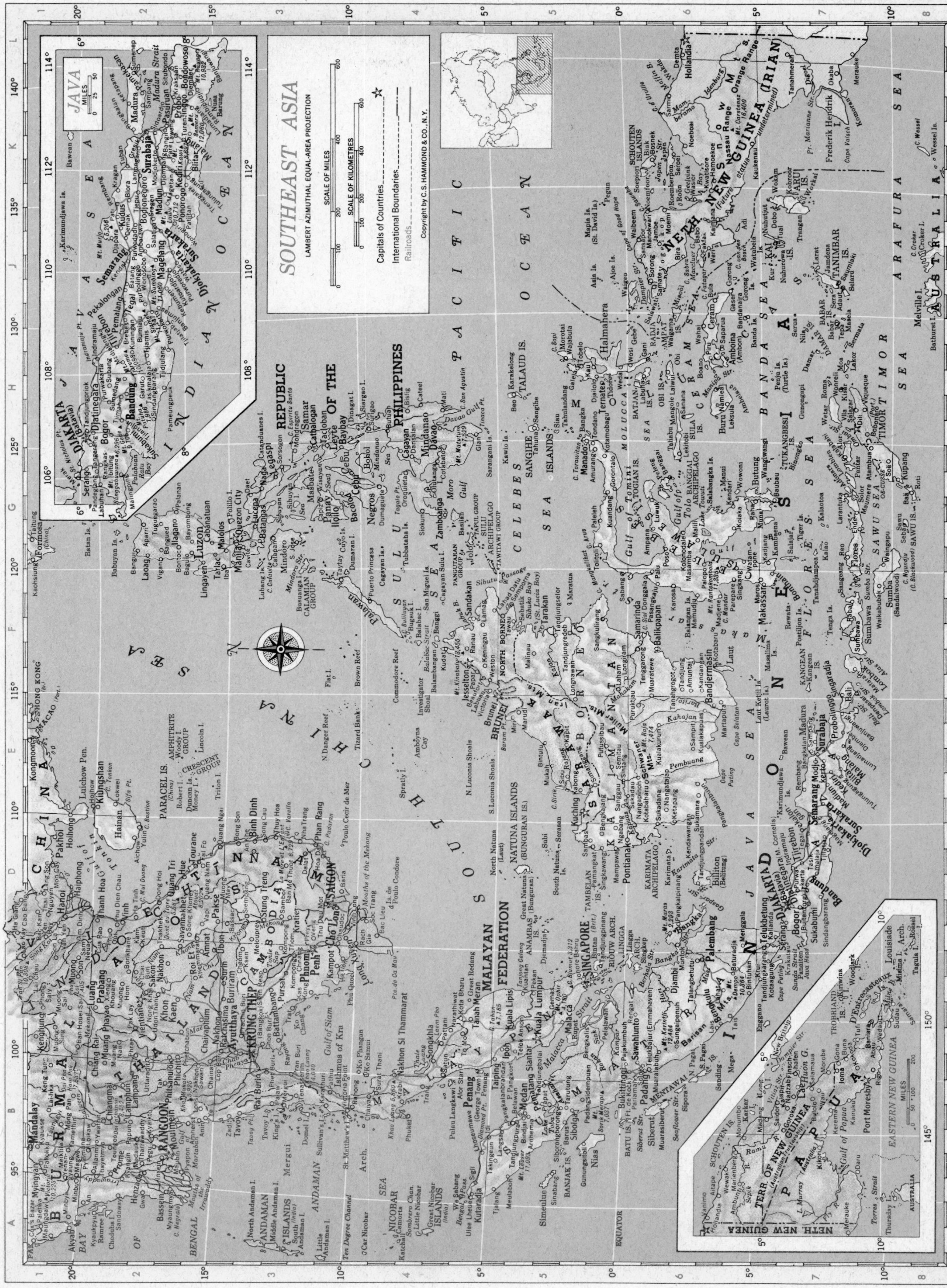

SOUTHEAST ASIA

LAMBERT AZIMUTHAL EQUAL-AREA PROJECTION

SCALE OF MILES

SCALE OF KILOMETRES

Capitals of Countries..........
International Boundaries.........
Railroads.....................

Copyright by C. S. HAMMOND & CO., N.Y.

JAVA
MILES
0   25   50

DJAKARTA (Batavia)
Bandung
Semarang
Surabaja
Surakarta
Djokjakarta

J A V A   S E A

I N D I A N   O C E A N

P A C I F I C   O C E A N

S O U T H   C H I N A   S E A

C H I N A

HONG KONG
MACAO (Port.)
Hainan

BURMA
Mandalay
RANGOON
Moulmein

THAILAND
KRUNG THEP (BANGKOK)

LAOS

CAMBODIA
Phnom Penh

VIETNAM
Hanoi
SAIGON

BAY OF BENGAL

ANDAMAN SEA

ANDAMAN ISLANDS

NICOBAR ISLANDS

Gulf of Siam

MALAYAN FEDERATION
Kuala Lumpur
Penang
SINGAPORE (Brit.)

REPUBLIC OF THE PHILIPPINES
Luzon
Manila
Quezon City
Mindoro
Samar
Panay
Negros
Cebu
Leyte
Bohol
Mindanao
Davao

SULU SEA

CELEBES SEA

B O R N E O

SARAWAK
BRUNEI
NORTH BORNEO
KALIMANTAN

Sumatra
Palembang
Medan

I N D O N E S I A

MOLUCCA SEA

CERAM SEA

BANDA SEA

FLORES SEA

Celebes
Makassar

Bali
Lombok
Sumbawa
Flores
Timor

TIMOR SEA

ARAFURA SEA

NETH. NEW GUINEA (IRIAN)
Hollandia

NETH NEW GUINEA
TERR. OF NEW GUINEA
PAPUA
Port Moresby
EASTERN NEW GUINEA

AUSTRALIA

EQUATOR

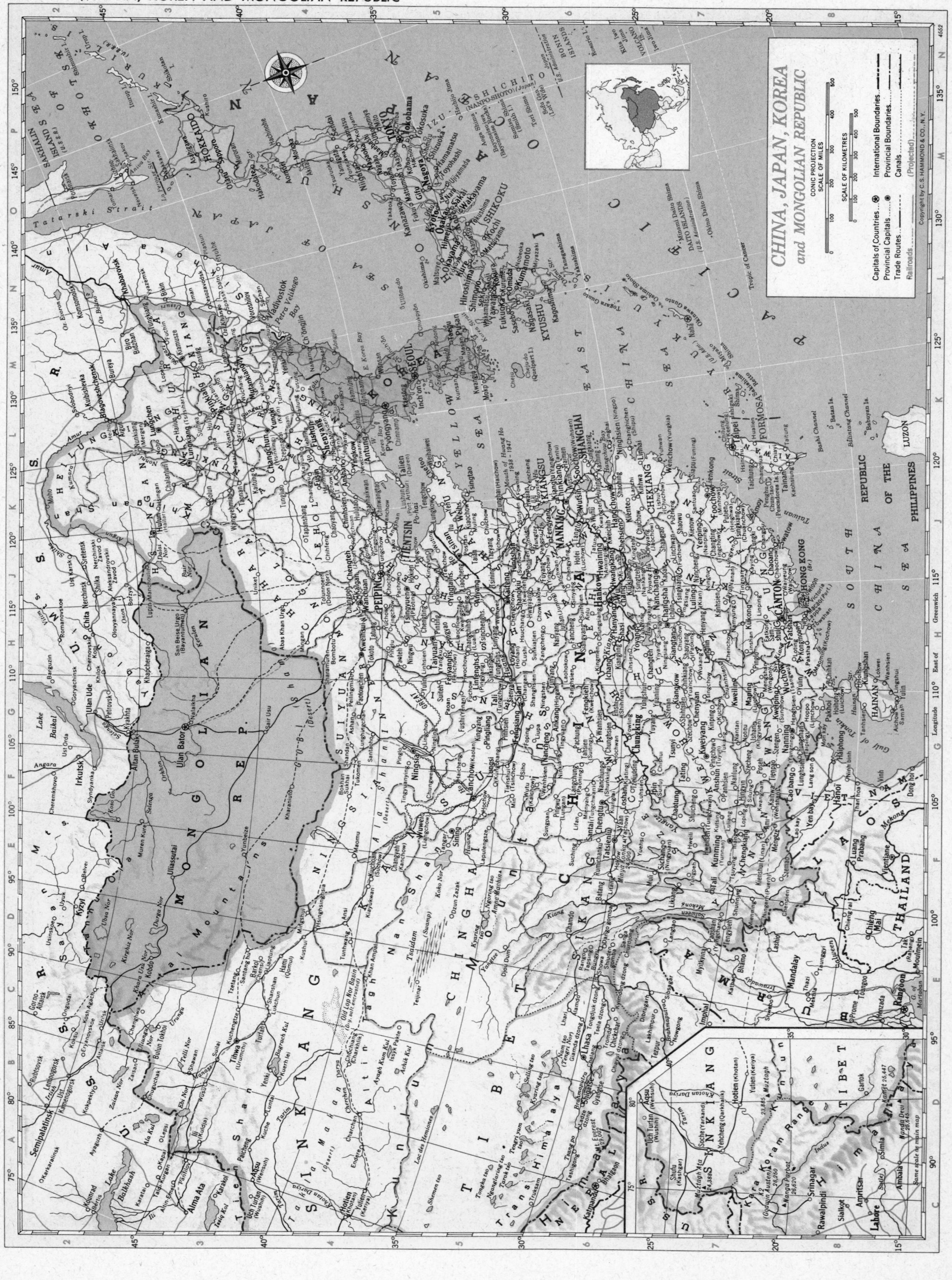

CHINA, JAPAN, KOREA and MONGOLIAN REPUBLIC

CONIC PROJECTION
SCALE OF KILOMETRES
SCALE OF MILES

Capitals of Countries..... ⊛
Provincial Capitals..... ⊙
Trade Routes.....
Railroads.....

International Boundaries.....
Provincial Boundaries.....
Canals.....
(Projected).....

Copyright by C. S. HAMMOND & CO., N.Y.

(Map of China, Japan, Korea and the Mongolian Republic with numerous place names, including: SAKHALIN ISLAND (U.S.S.R.), SEA OF OKHOTSK, HOKKAIDO, Sapporo, TOKYO, Yokohama, Kyoto, Osaka, Nagoya, SHIKOKU, KYUSHU, Nagasaki, Fukuoka, SEA OF JAPAN, KOREA, SEOUL, Pyongyang, Pusan, YELLOW SEA, SHANGHAI, NANKING, PEIPING, TIENTSIN, HANKOW, CANTON, HONG KONG, FORMOSA, Taipei, PACIFIC OCEAN, EAST CHINA SEA, SOUTH CHINA SEA, PHILIPPINES, LUZON, HAINAN, FRENCH INDO-CHINA, Hanoi, Haiphong, THAILAND, BURMA, Rangoon, Mandalay, TIBET, Lhasa, SINKIANG, CHINGHAI, KANSU, SZECHWAN, Chungking, Chengtu, Kunming, YUNNAN, MONGOLIAN REP., Ulan Bator, Altan Bulak, GOBI DESERT, MANCHURIA, HEILUNGKIANG, KIRIN, LIAONING, Mukden, Harbin, Changchun, U.S.S.R., Khabarovsk, Vladivostok, Lake Baikal, Irkutsk, Alma Ata, HIMALAYA, Everest, Srinagar, Lahore, Amritsar, TRANS-HIMALAYA).

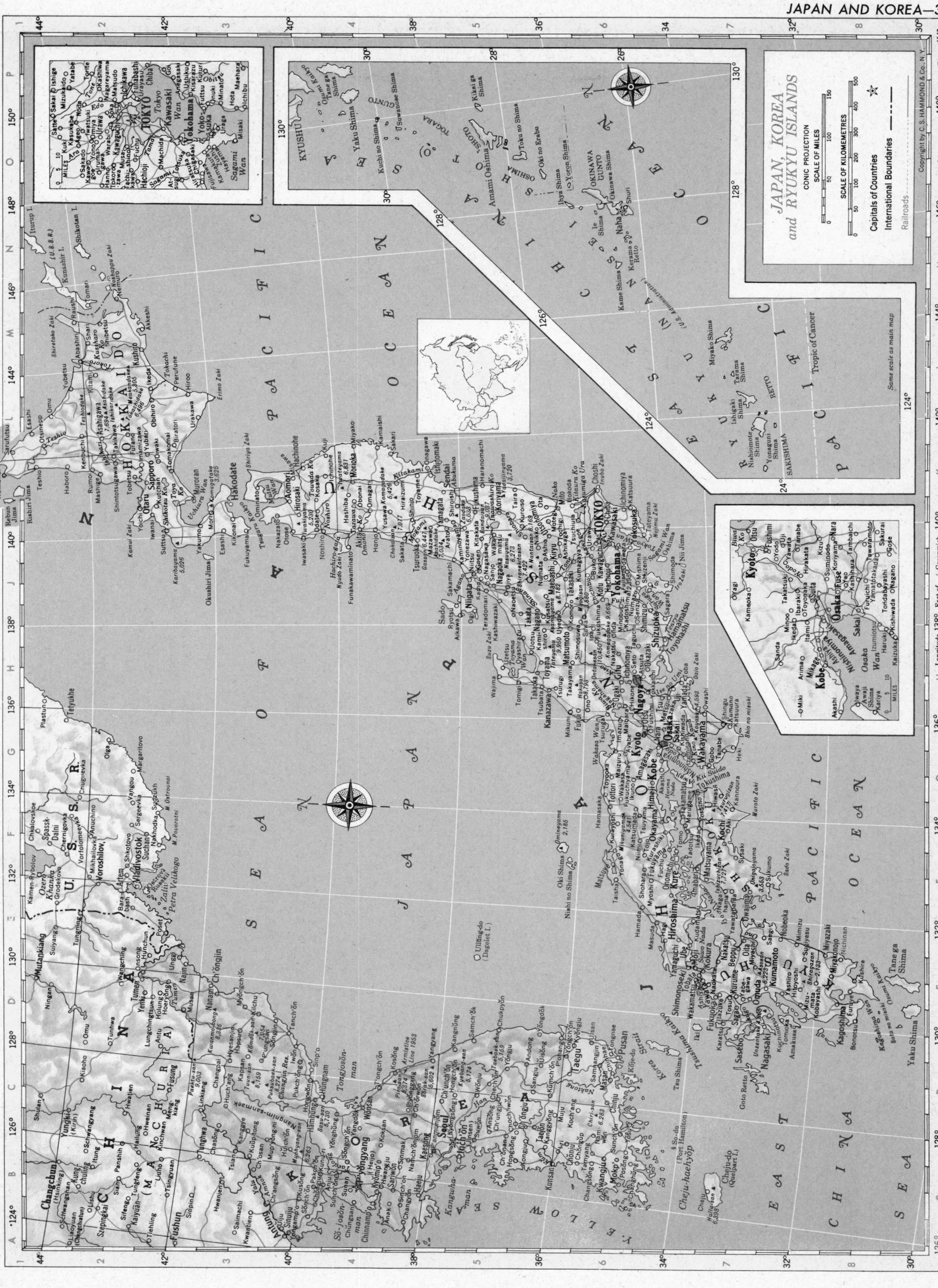

JAPAN, KOREA
and RYUKYU ISLANDS

CONIC PROJECTION

SCALE OF MILES

SCALE OF KILOMETRES

Capitals of Countries
International Boundaries
Railroads

Copyright by C.S. HAMMOND & Co., N.Y.

TOKYO

SEA OF JAPAN

PACIFIC OCEAN

EAST CHINA SEA

YELLOW SEA

NANSEI SHOTO

RYUKYU ISLANDS

Tropic of Cancer

H O K K A I D O

H O N S H U

K Y U S H U

S H I K O K U

C H I N A

M A N C H U R I A

K O R E A

U. S. S. R.

Changchun
Mutankiang
Vladivostok
Voroshilov

Seoul
Pyongyang
Pusan
Taegu
Taejon
Inchon
Wonsan
Hamhung
Chongjin

Sapporo
Hakodate
Aomori
Morioka
Sendai
Niigata
Nagano
TOKYO
Yokohama
Kawasaki
Chiba
Shizuoka
Nagoya
Kyoto
Osaka
Kobe
Himeji
Okayama
Hiroshima
Kure
Yamaguchi
Shimonoseki
Kokura
Fukuoka
Nagasaki
Kumamoto
Kagoshima
Matsuyama
Kochi
Takamatsu
Tokushima
Wakayama
Nara

KYUSHU

Amami Oshima
OKINAWA GUNTO
Naha
Shuri
Miyako Shima
Ishigaki Shima
SAKISHIMA

Yaku Shima
Tane ga Shima

Cheju-do (Quelpart I.)

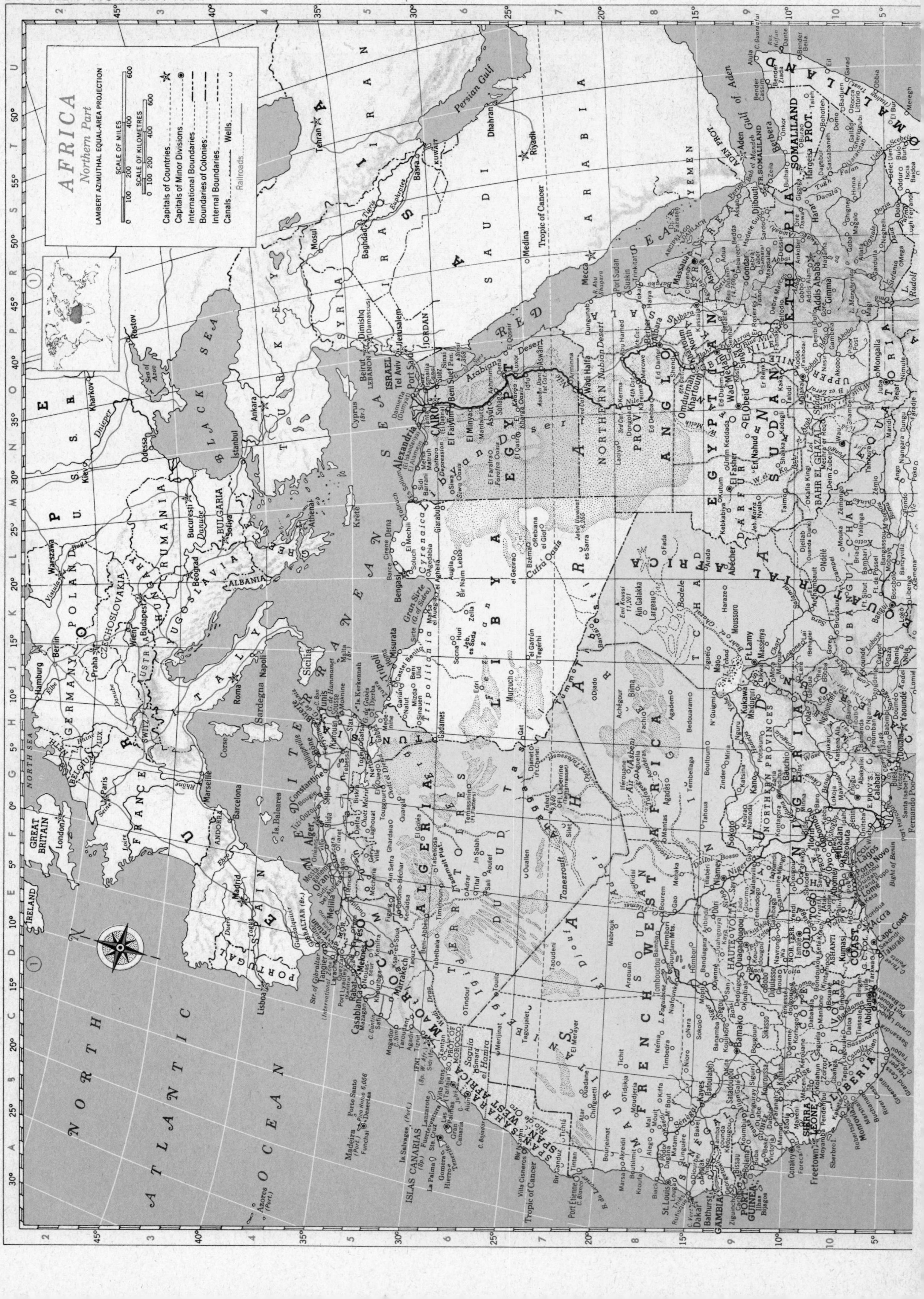

AFRICA
Northern Part
LAMBERT AZIMUTHAL EQUAL-AREA PROJECTION

SCALE OF MILES
0   100   200   400   600

SCALE OF KILOMETRES
0   100   200   400   600

Capitals of Countries..........✭
Capitals of Minor Divisions....◉
International Boundaries........
Boundaries of Colonies.........
Internal Boundaries............
Canals.........................
Wells..........................
Railroads......................

NORTH ATLANTIC OCEAN

MEDITERRANEAN SEA

BLACK SEA

RED SEA

Persian Gulf

GREAT BRITAIN
IRELAND
London
FRANCE
Paris
SPAIN
Madrid
PORTUGAL
Lisboa
GERMANY
Berlin
Hamburg
POLAND
Warszawa
CZECHOSLOVAKIA
Praha
AUSTRIA
Wien
HUNGARY
Budapest
RUMANIA
Bucureşti
YUGOSLAVIA
Beograd
BULGARIA
Sofiya
ALBANIA
GREECE
Athenai
ITALY
Roma
Napoli
Sicilia
Sardegna
Corse
ANDORRA
SWITZ.
BELGIUM
LUX.
HOLLAND

U. S. S. R.
Rostov
Kharkov
Kiev
Odessa
Istanbul
Ankara
TURKEY
SYRIA
IRAQ
Baghdad
Basra
Mosul
IRAN
Tehran
KUWAIT
SAUDI ARABIA
Riyadh
Mecca
Medina
Dhahran
YEMEN
ADEN PROT.
Aden

MOROCCO
Rabat
Casablanca
Marrakech
SPANISH MOROCCO
ALGERIA
Alger
Oran
Constantine
TUNIS
Tunis
Tripoli
LIBYA
Bengasi
Cyrenaica
Tripolitania
Fezzan
SPANISH SAHARA
RIO DE ORO
ISLAS CANARIAS
Madeira
Azores

EGYPT
CAIRO
Alexandria
Port Said
Suez
Aswan
Tropic of Cancer
Libyan Desert
Arabian Desert
Nubian Desert
ANGLO-EGYPTIAN SUDAN
Khartoum
Omdurman
Port Sudan
El Obeid
NORTHERN PROV.
KORDOFAN
DARFUR
BAHR EL GHAZAL
UPPER NILE
EQUATORIA
ERITREA
Asmara
Massaua
FRENCH SOMALILAND
Djibouti
BRITISH SOMALILAND
ITALIAN SOMALILAND
ETHIOPIA
Addis Ababa
Harar
Gondar

ISRAEL
Tel Aviv
Jerusalem
LEBANON
Beirut
JORDAN
Dimishq (Damascus)
Cyprus
Kriti

FRENCH WEST AFRICA
Dakar
St. Louis
GAMBIA
PORT. GUINEA
FRENCH GUINEA
Conakry
SIERRA LEONE
Freetown
LIBERIA
Monrovia
IVORY COAST
GOLD COAST
Accra
TOGO
NIGERIA
Lagos
Kano
Sokoto
CAMEROONS
FRENCH EQUATORIAL AFRICA
OUBANGUI-CHARI
TCHAD
Timbuktu
Niamey
Bamako
Kumasi
Ouagadougou
HAUTE VOLTA
NORTHERN PROVINCES
SPANISH SAHARA
FRENCH SUDAN
TERRITOIRES DU SUD
Tanezrouft
AIR

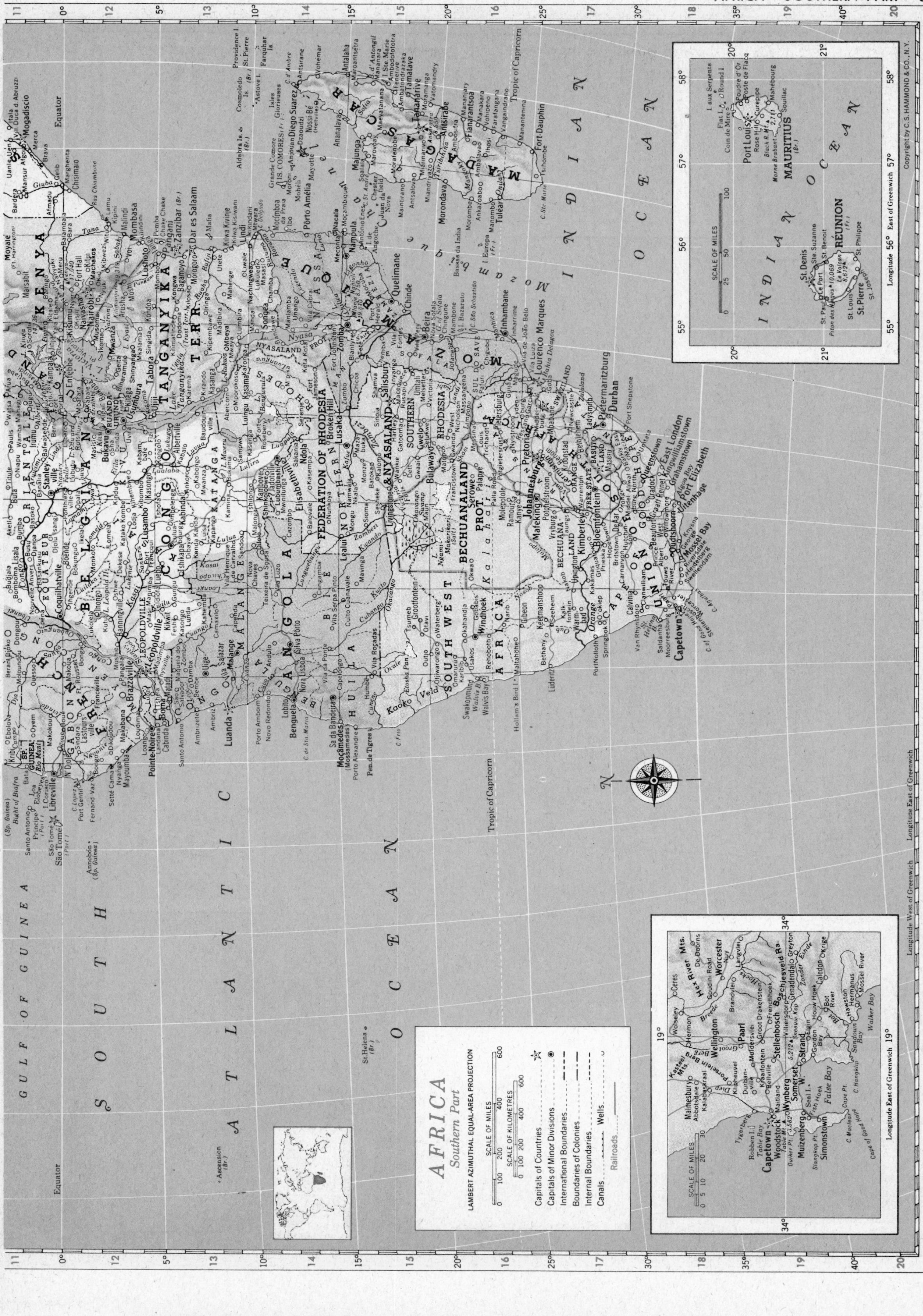

AFRICA
Southern Part

LAMBERT AZIMUTHAL EQUAL-AREA PROJECTION

SCALE OF MILES
0   100   200   400   600

SCALE OF KILOMETRES
0   100   200   400   600

Capitals of Countries	✦
Capitals of Minor Divisions	⊙
International Boundaries	— · · —
Boundaries of Colonies	— · —
Internal Boundaries	— — —
Canals	Wells ○
Railroads	————

MAURITIUS (Br.)

SCALE OF MILES
0   25   50   100

Longitude 56° East of Greenwich 57°

RÉUNION (Fr.)

INDIAN OCEAN

SCALE OF MILES
0   5   10   30

Longitude East of Greenwich 19°

Copyright by C. S. HAMMOND & CO., N.Y.

AUSTRALIA and NEW ZEALAND

BONNE PROJECTION

SCALE OF MILES

SCALE OF KILOMETRES

* Capital of Country
⊛ State and Territorial Capitals ▲
Railroads

New Zealand

NORTH ISLAND

SOUTH ISLAND

Auckland
Wellington
Christchurch
Dunedin
Invercargill

Same scale as main map

Main Map Labels

INDONESIA

ARAFURA SEA

TIMOR SEA

CORAL SEA

PACIFIC OCEAN

INDIAN OCEAN

GREAT AUSTRALIAN BIGHT

NORTHERN TERRITORY

WESTERN AUSTRALIA

SOUTH AUSTRALIA

QUEENSLAND

NEW SOUTH WALES

VICTORIA

TASMANIA

GULF OF CARPENTARIA

CAPE YORK PEN.

ARNHEM LAND

Gulf of Papua
Port Moresby

Darwin
Perth
Adelaide
MELBOURNE
SYDNEY
Brisbane
Hobart
BROKEN HILL
Kalgoorlie
Geelong

Tropic of Capricorn

Simpson Desert
Great Sandy Desert
Great Victoria Desert
Gibson Desert

AUSTRALIAN CAPITAL TERR.
Canberra

Inset Maps

MELBOURNE — PORT PHILLIP BAY

SYDNEY — PACIFIC
Parramatta
Wollongong

PERTH — INDIAN OCEAN
Fremantle

ADELAIDE — Gulf of St. Vincent
Port Adelaide
Glenelg

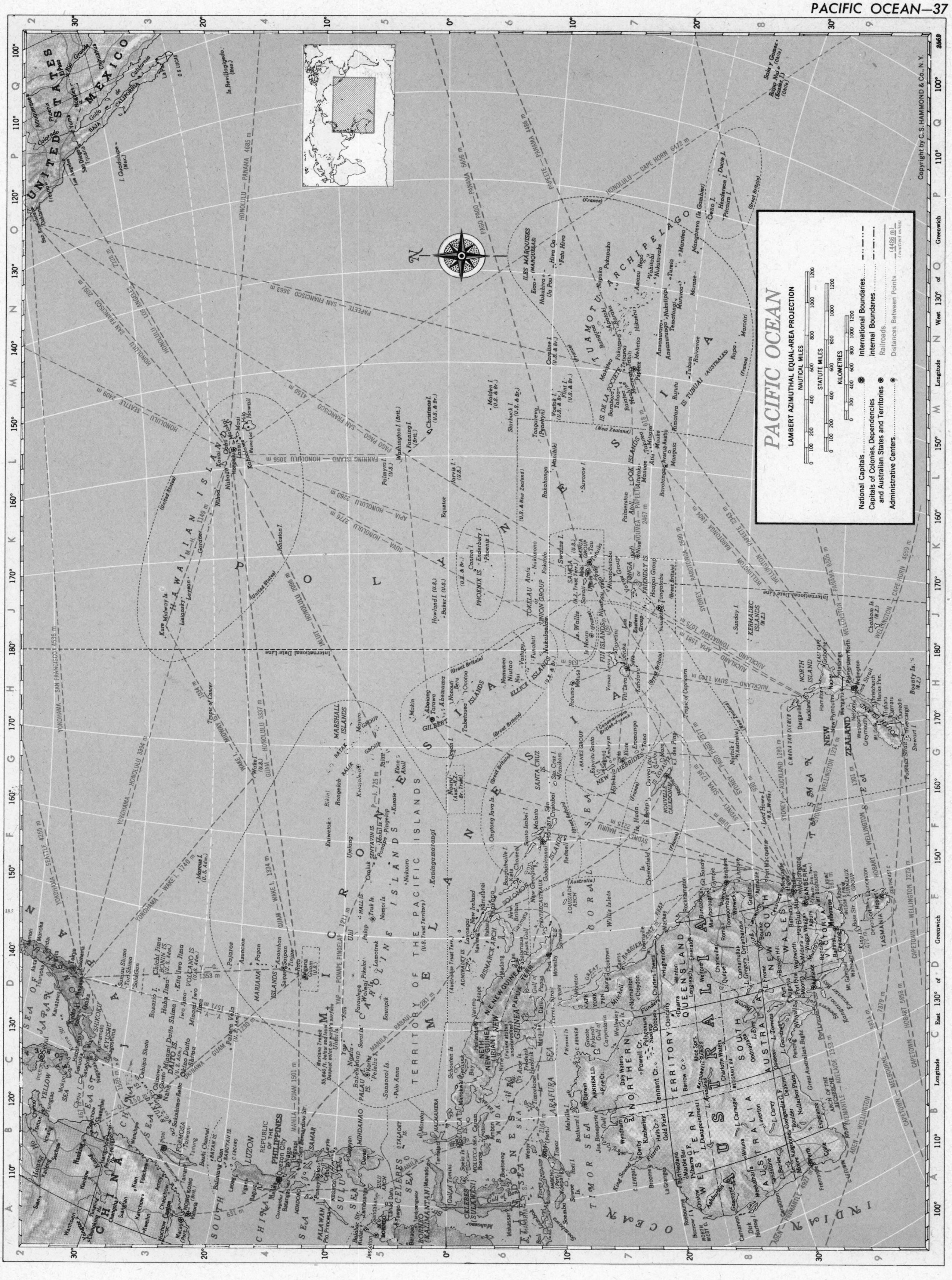

PACIFIC OCEAN
LAMBERT AZIMUTHAL EQUAL-AREA PROJECTION

NAUTICAL MILES

STATUTE MILES

KILOMETRES

National Capitals
Capitals of Colonies, Dependencies
Capitals of Colonies, Dependencies and Territories
Administrative Centers

International Boundaries
Internal Boundaries
Railroads
Distances Between Points

UNITED STATES

MEXICO

P O L Y N E S I A

M I C R O N E S I A

M E L A N E S I A

CAROLINE ISLANDS
TERRITORY OF THE PACIFIC ISLANDS
(U.S. Trust Territory)

MARSHALL ISLANDS

MARIANA ISLANDS

GILBERT

ELLICE ISLANDS

PHOENIX IS.

SAMOA

FIJI ISLANDS

TUAMOTU ARCHIPELAGO

ILES MARQUISES

IS. DE LA SOCIÉTÉ

COOK ISLANDS

IS. TUBUAI (AUSTRALES)

NEW ZEALAND

NORTH ISLAND

SOUTH ISLAND

AUSTRALIA

WESTERN AUSTRALIA

NORTHERN TERRITORY

QUEENSLAND

SOUTH AUSTRALIA

NEW SOUTH WALES

VICTORIA

TASMANIA

NEW GUINEA

CORAL SEA

TIMOR SEA

ARAFURA SEA

CELEBES SEA

SULU SEA

SOUTH CHINA SEA

CHINA

JAPAN

SEA OF JAPAN

YELLOW SEA

EAST CHINA SEA

PHILIPPINE SEA

REPUBLIC OF THE PHILIPPINES

LUZON

MINDANAO

SAMAR

BORNEO

CELEBES (SULAWESI)

INDONESIA

INDIAN OCEAN

HAWAIIAN ISLANDS

International Date Line

Equator

Tropic of Cancer

Tropic of Capricorn

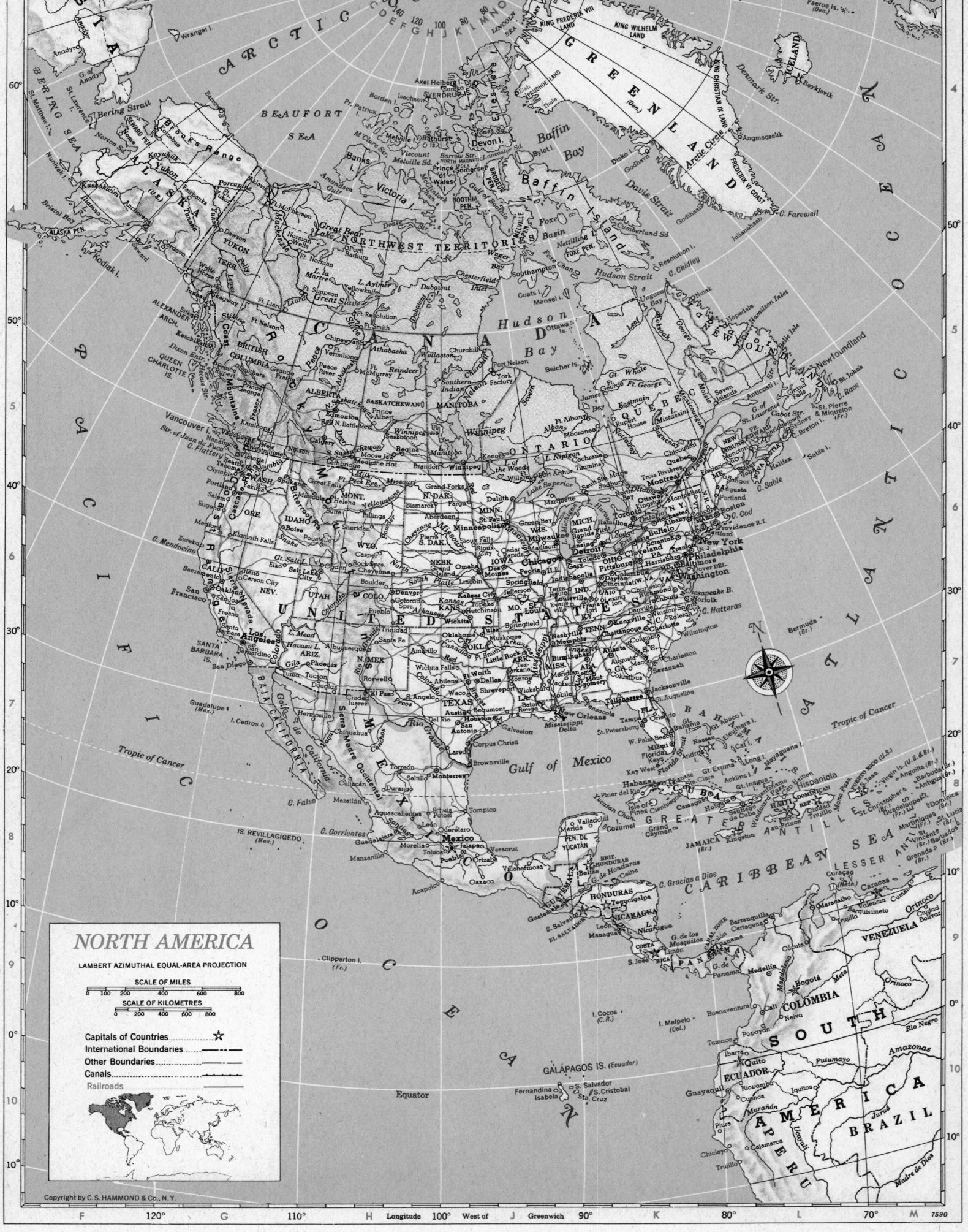

NORTH AMERICA

LAMBERT AZIMUTHAL EQUAL-AREA PROJECTION

SCALE OF MILES
0 100 200   400   600   800

SCALE OF KILOMETRES
0   200   400   600   800

Capitals of Countries .... ★
International Boundaries ....
Other Boundaries ....
Canals ....
Railroads ....

Copyright by C. S. Hammond & Co., N.Y.

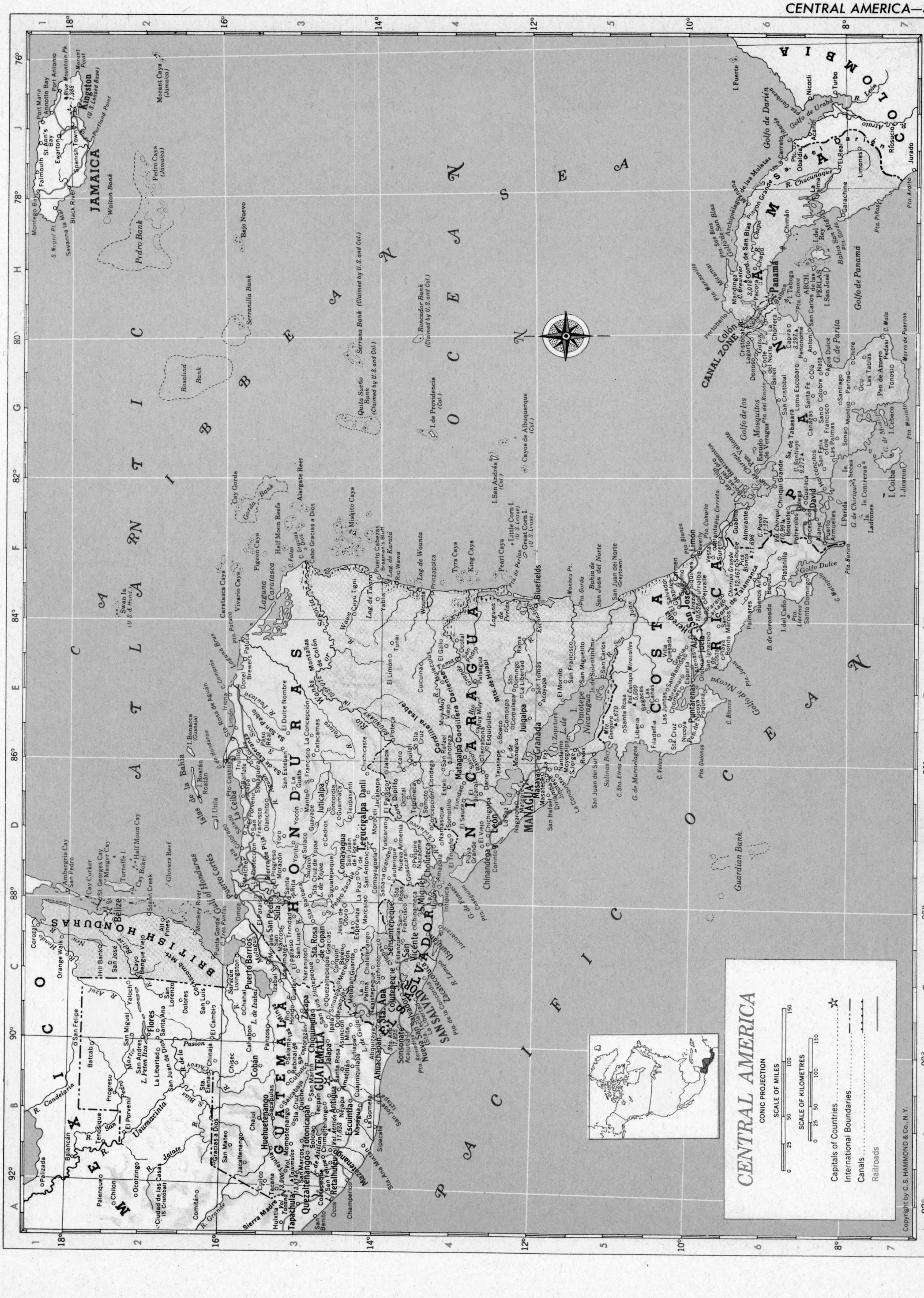

COLOMBIA

JAMAICA

Kingston *(U.S. Leased Base)*

C A R I B B E A N   S E A

A T L A N T I C   O C E A N

P A C I F I C   O C E A N

Golfo de Panamá

CANAL ZONE

Colón

Panamá

Golfo de Darién

Golfo de Uraba

P A N A M A

C O S T A   R I C A

San José

N I C A R A G U A

MANAGUA

Bluefields

H O N D U R A S

Tegucigalpa

Is. de la Bahía

EL SALVADOR

San Salvador

G U A T E M A L A

GUATEMALA

BRITISH HONDURAS

Belize

M E X I C O

Usumacinta

Gulf of Honduras

Mosquitos

Golfo de los Mosquitos

Roncador Bank *(Claimed by U.S. and Col.)*

Serrana Bank *(Claimed by U.S. and Col.)*

Serranilla Bank

Pedro Bank

Rosalind Bank

I. de Providencia *(Col.)*

I. San Andrés *(Col.)*

Little Corn I.

Great Corn I.

Cayos de Albuquerque *(Col.)*

CENTRAL AMERICA

CONIC PROJECTION

SCALE OF MILES

0   25   50   100   150

SCALE OF KILOMETRES

0   25   50   100   150

Capitals of Countries .... ★

International Boundaries ....

Canals ....

Railroads ....

Copyright by C. S. HAMMOND & Co., N.Y.

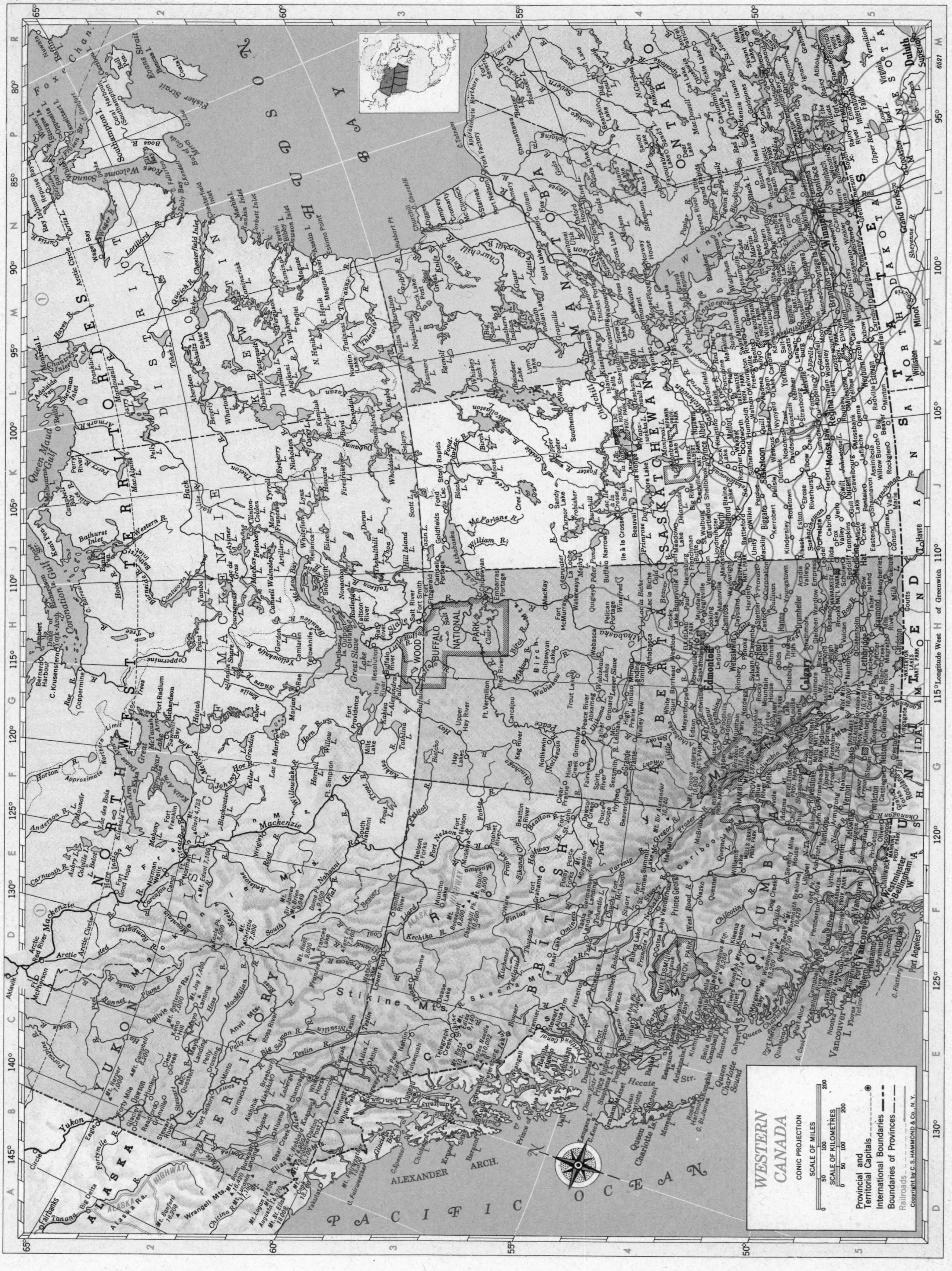

HUDSON BAY

NORTHWEST TERRITORIES

DISTRICT OF KEEWATIN

DISTRICT OF MACKENZIE

DISTRICT OF FRANKLIN

YUKON TERRITORY

ALASKA

BRITISH COLUMBIA

ALBERTA

SASKATCHEWAN

MANITOBA

ONTARIO

NORTH DAKOTA

SOUTH DAKOTA

MINNESOTA

MONTANA

IDAHO

WASHINGTON

PACIFIC OCEAN

ALEXANDER ARCH.

Queen Maud Gulf

Coronation Gulf

WOOD BUFFALO NATIONAL PARK

Stikine Mts.

Great Slave Lake

Great Bear Lake

Duluth

Superior

Winnipeg

Regina

Edmonton

Calgary

Saskatoon

Medicine Hat

Lethbridge

Moose Jaw

Brandon

Vancouver

Victoria

ALASKA HIGHWAY

Mt. Logan 19,850

Arctic Circle

Baffin L.

Foxe Chan.

Fisher Strait

Welcome Sound

Roes Welcome Sound

WESTERN CANADA
CONIC PROJECTION

SCALE OF MILES
0 50 100 200

SCALE OF KILOMETRES
0 50 100 200

Provincial and Territorial Capitals ●
International Boundaries
Boundaries of Provinces
Railroads

Copyright by C. S. HAMMOND & Co., N.Y.

115° Longitude West H of Greenwich 110°

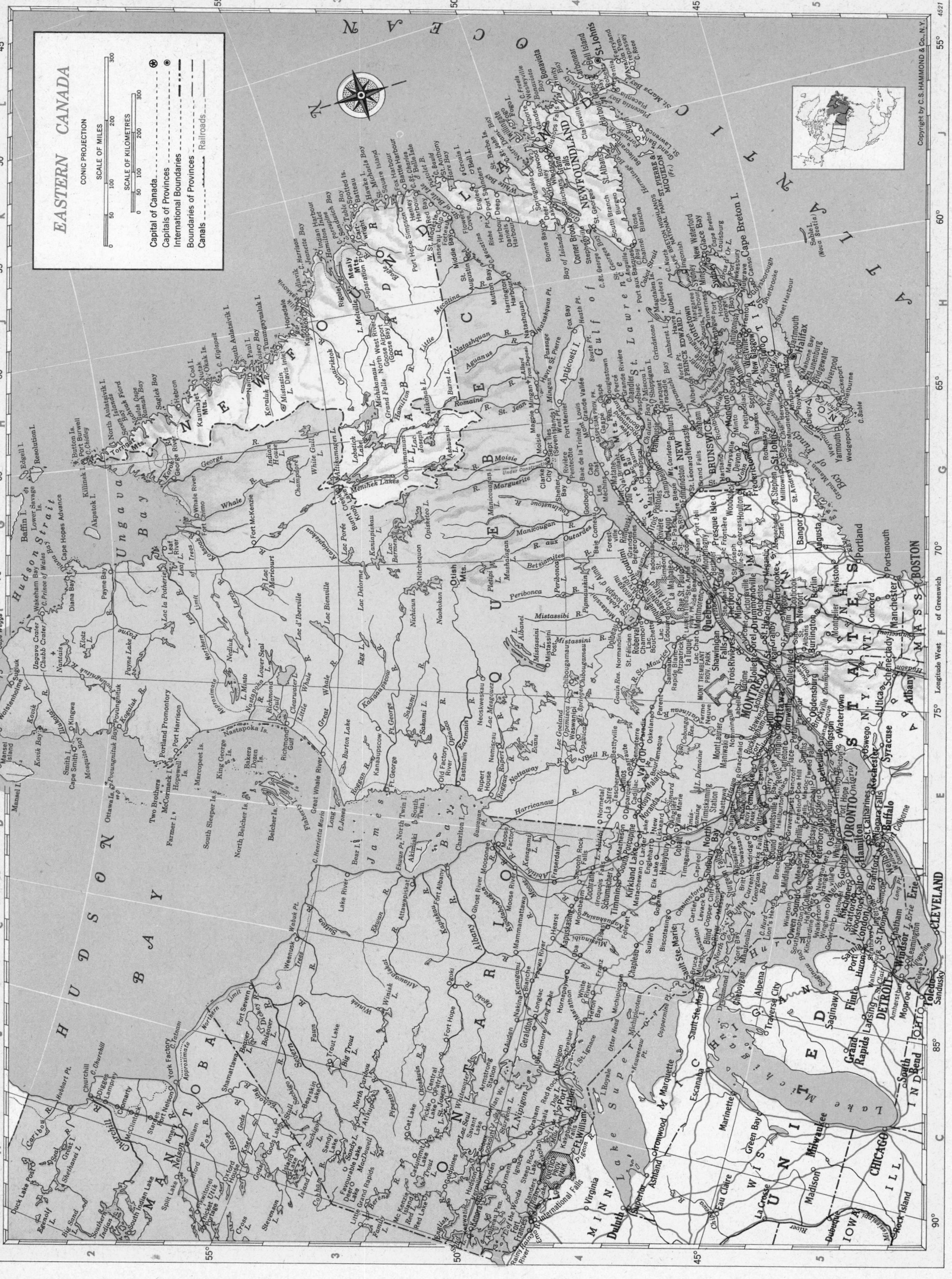

EASTERN CANADA
CONIC PROJECTION
SCALE OF MILES
0 50 100 200 300
SCALE OF KILOMETRES
0 50 100 200 300
Capital of Canada
Capitals of Provinces
International Boundaries
Boundaries of Provinces
Canals
Railroads
HUDSON BAY
James Bay
Ungava Bay
Hudson Strait
ATLANTIC OCEAN
Gulf of St. Lawrence
MANITOBA
ONTARIO
QUEBEC
NEWFOUNDLAND
LABRADOR
NEW BRUNSWICK
NOVA SCOTIA
PRINCE EDWARD ISLAND
UNITED STATES
Lake Superior
Lake Michigan
Lake Huron
Lake Erie
OTTAWA
MONTREAL
QUEBEC
TORONTO
HALIFAX
DETROIT
CHICAGO
CLEVELAND
BOSTON
Longitude West of Greenwich
4521
Copyright by C.S. HAMMOND & Co., N.Y.

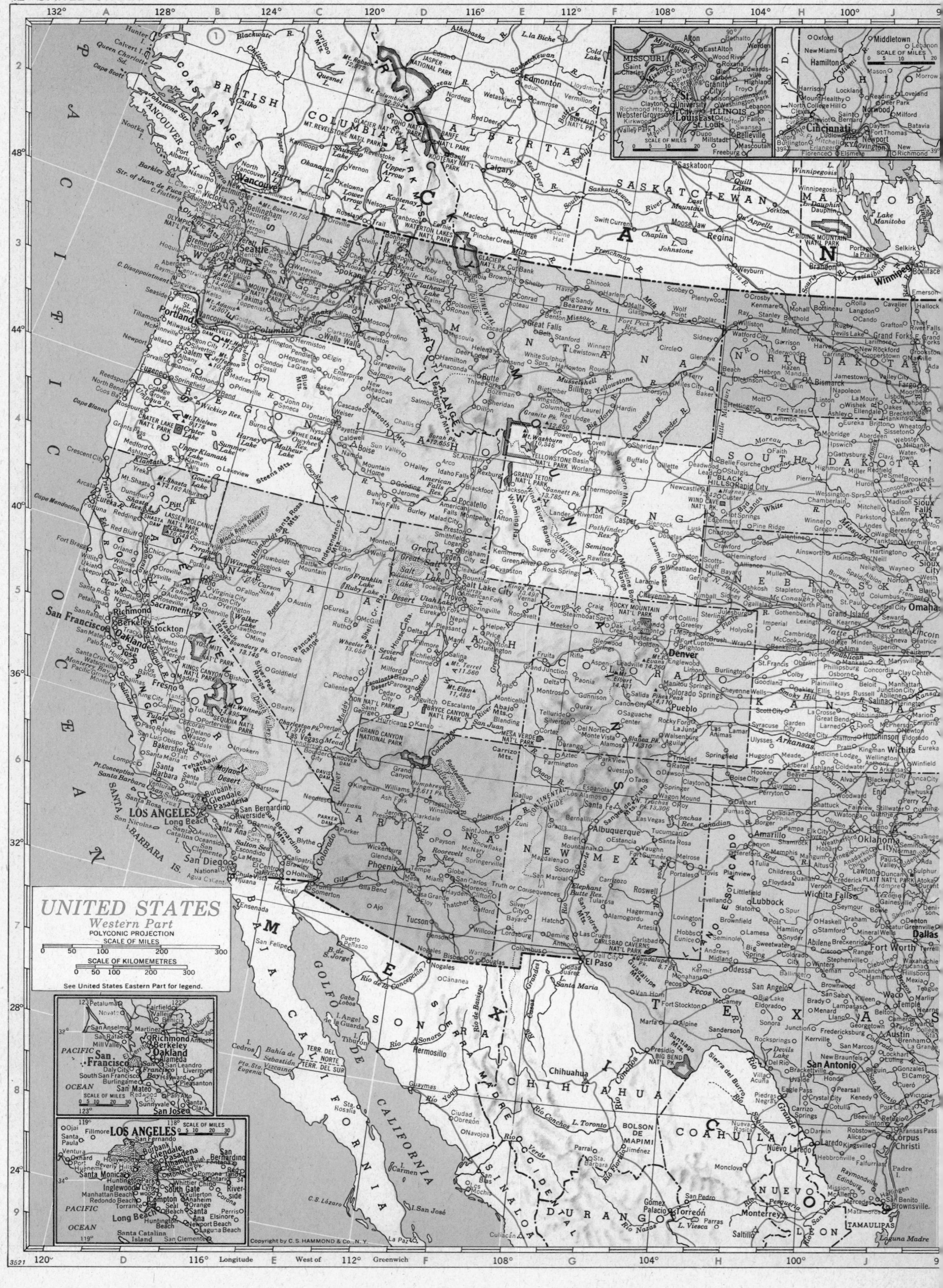

UNITED STATES
Western Part
POLYCONIC PROJECTION
SCALE OF MILES
0   50   100   300
SCALE OF KILOMETRES
0   50 100   200   300

See United States Eastern Part for legend.

LOS ANGELES

SAN FRANCISCO
PACIFIC OCEAN

Copyright by C. S. HAMMOND & Co., N.Y.

120°   116° Longitude   West of   112° Greenwich   108°   104°   100°

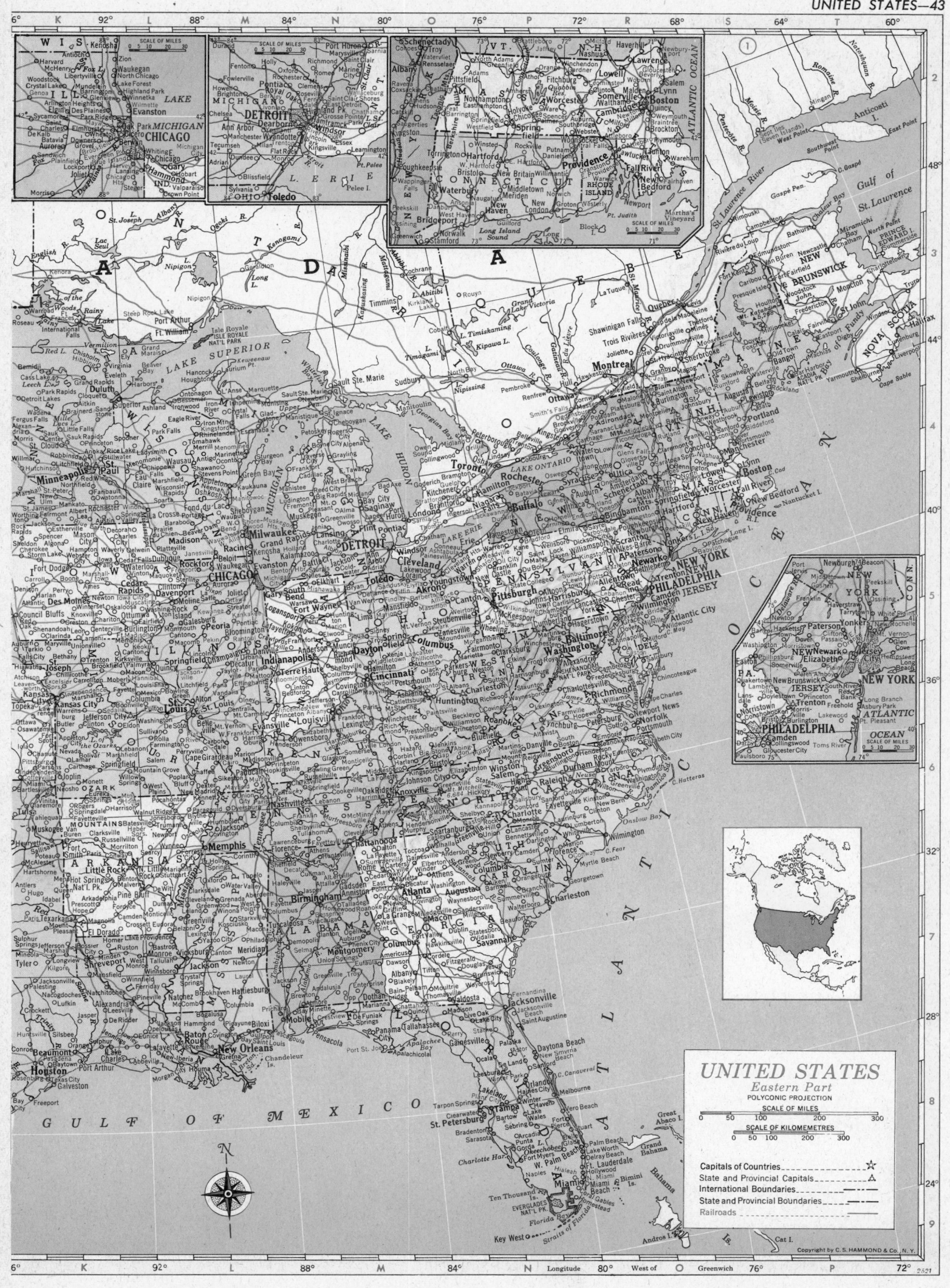

UNITED STATES
Eastern Part
POLYCONIC PROJECTION

SCALE OF MILES

SCALE OF KILOMETRES

Capitals of Countries .... ☆
State and Provincial Capitals .... △
International Boundaries ....
State and Provincial Boundaries ....
Railroads ....

Copyright by C. S. HAMMOND & Co. N. Y.

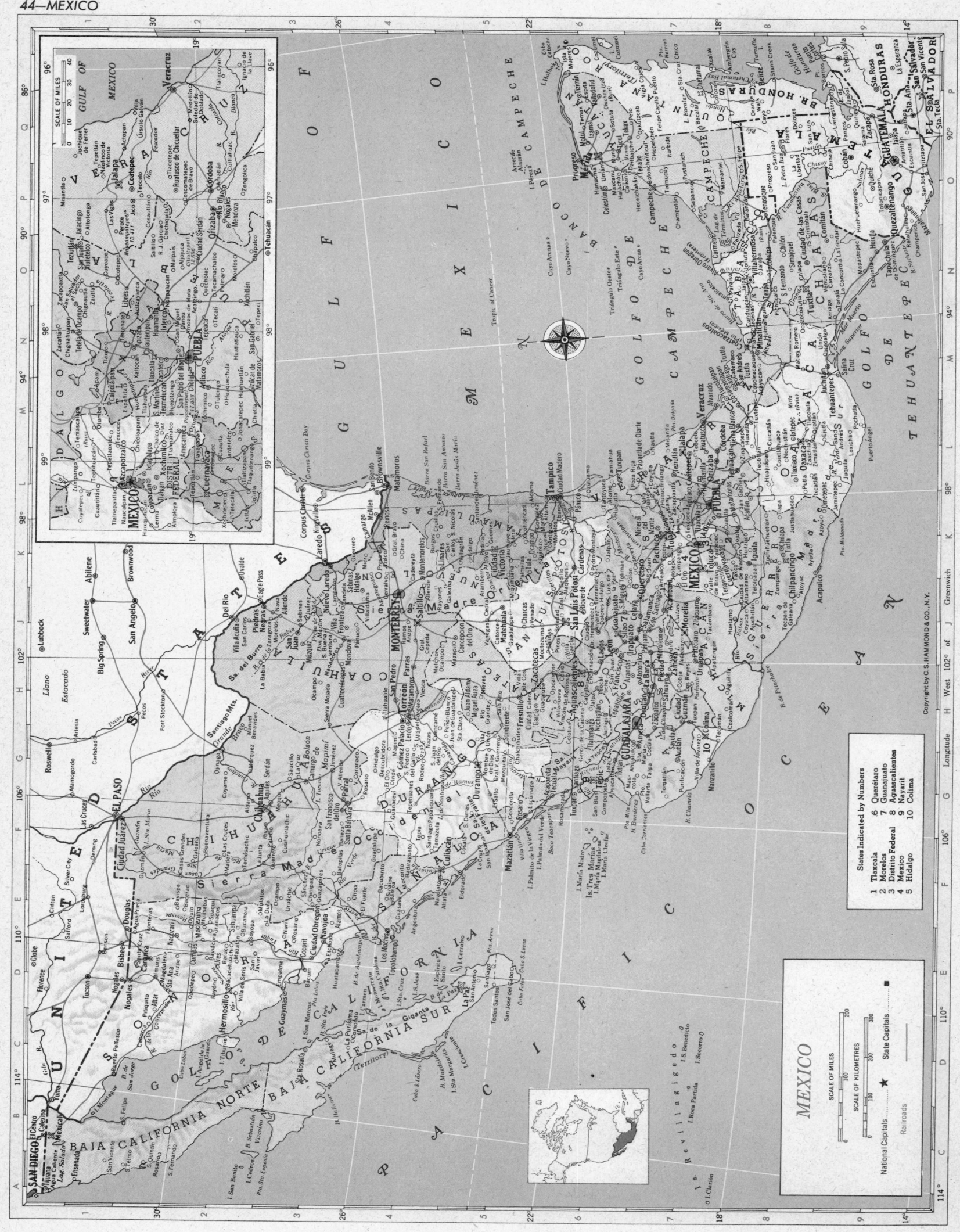

MEXICO

SCALE OF MILES

SCALE OF KILOMETRES

National Capitals ....★
State Capitals ....■

Railroads ....

States Indicated by Numbers

1 Tlaxcala   6 Querétaro
2 Morelos   7 Guanajuato
3 Distrito Federal 8 Aguascalientes
4 Mexico   9 Nayarit
5 Hidalgo   10 Colima

Copyright by C. S. HAMMOND & CO., N.Y.

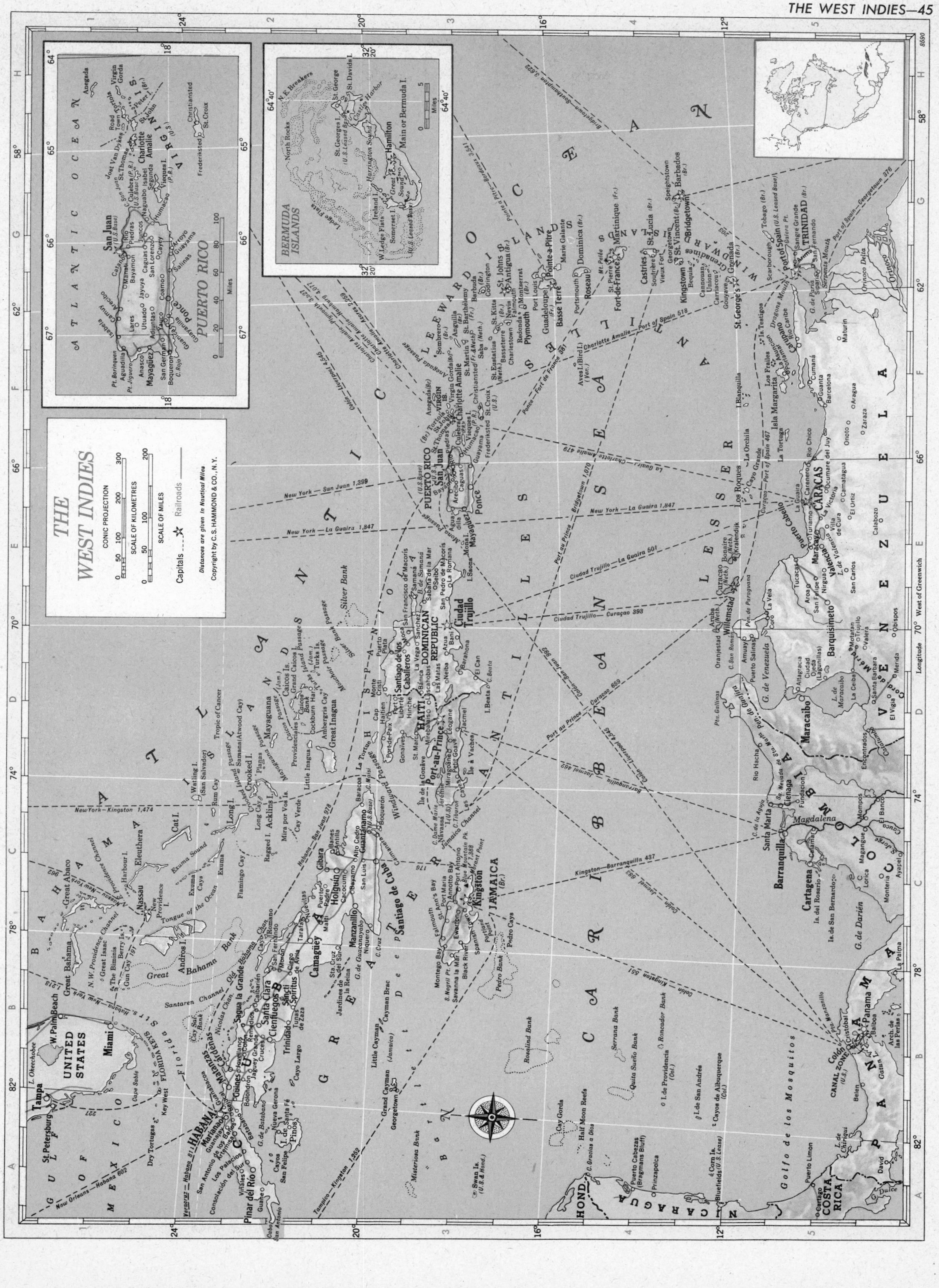

THE
WEST INDIES
CONIC PROJECTION

SCALE OF KILOMETRES
0 50 100 200 300

SCALE OF MILES
0 50 100 200

Capitals ---- ★
Railroads

Distances are given in Nautical Miles.
Copyright by C. S. HAMMOND & CO., N.Y.

PUERTO RICO (inset)

VIRGIN IS.
Anegada
Virgin Gorda
Jost Van Dykes
St. Thomas (U.S.)
Road Town
Tortola (Br.)
Charlotte Amalie (U.S.)
St. John
Culebra (P.R.)
Vieques (Isl.)
St. Croix (U.S.)
Christiansted
Frederiksted

San Juan
Bayamon
Rio Piedras
Caguas
Carolina
Fajardo
Humacao
Yabucoa
Guayama
Arroyo
Salinas
Coamo
Cayey
San Lorenzo
Juncos
Gurabo
Manati
Arecibo
Utuado
Adjuntas
Jayuya
Lares
Aguadilla
Pt. Borinquen
Aguada
Arecibo
Mayagüez
San Germán
Boquerón
Anasco
Pt. Jiguero
Sabana Grande
Yauco
Guanica
Ponce
C. Rojo

ATLANTIC OCEAN
PUERTO RICO
Miles

BERMUDA ISLANDS (inset)

N.E. Breakers
North Rocks
St. George I.
St. George
St. David's I.
Hamilton
Harrington Sound
Great Sound
Main or Bermuda I.
Ireland I.
Somerset I.
W. Ledge Flats
Ledge Flats
U.S. Leased Base
Miles

Main map labels

ATLANTIC OCEAN

WEST INDIES

BAHAMA IS.
Great Abaco
Great Bahama
W. Palm Beach
Miami
Nassau
New Providence
Eleuthera I.
Cat I.
Watling I. (San Salvador)
Rum Cay
Long I.
Crooked I.
Acklins
Mayaguana
Great Inagua
Little Inagua

UNITED STATES
Tampa
St. Petersburg
L. Okeechobee
Key West
Dry Tortugas
FLORIDA KEYS

GULF OF MEXICO

CUBA
HABANA
Matanzas
Cárdenas
Santa Clara
Cienfuegos
Trinidad
Sancti Spiritus
Camagüey
Holguín
Manzanillo
Santiago de Cuba
Guantánamo
Pinar del Río
Isle of Pines (I. de Pinos)

Grand Cayman
Little Cayman
Cayman Brac
Georgetown (Jamaica)

JAMAICA (Br.)
Kingston
Montego Bay
Port Antonio
Spanish Town

HISPANIOLA

HAITI
Port-au-Prince
Cap Haïtien
Gonaïves
Jérémie
Les Cayes
Tortuga I. (La Tortue)
Île de la Gonâve

DOMINICAN REPUBLIC
Ciudad Trujillo
Santiago de los Caballeros
La Vega
San Francisco de Macorís
San Pedro de Macorís
Puerto Plata
Monte Cristi
Barahona
I. Beata
I. Saona

PUERTO RICO (U.S.)
San Juan
Mayagüez
Ponce

VIRGIN IS.
Charlotte Amalie

LEEWARD ISLANDS
Anguilla (Br.)
St. Martin (Fr.)
St. Barthélemy
Saba (Neth.)
St. Eustatius
St. Kitts
Nevis
Antigua (Br.)
St. Johns
Barbuda (Br.)
Montserrat (Br.)
Redonda
Guadeloupe (Fr.)
Basse Terre
Pointe-à-Pitre
Marie Galante
Dominica (Br.)
Roseau

WINDWARD ISLANDS
Martinique (Fr.)
Fort-de-France
St. Lucia (Br.)
Castries
St. Vincent (Br.)
Kingstown
Grenadines
Grenada (Br.)
St. George's
Barbados (Br.)
Bridgetown

TRINIDAD (Br.)
Port of Spain
San Fernando
Tobago (Br.)
Scarborough

CARIBBEAN SEA

LESSER ANTILLES
GREATER ANTILLES

VENEZUELA
CARACAS
Maracaibo
L. de Maracaibo
Valencia
Barquisimeto
Cumaná
Barcelona
Maturín
Isla Margarita
Bonaire (Neth.)
Curaçao (Neth.)
Willemstad
Aruba (Neth.)
Oranjestad
Los Roques
La Orchila
La Tortuga
G. de Venezuela
Coro

COLOMBIA
Barranquilla
Cartagena
Santa Marta
Magdalena
Rio Hacha
G. de Darién

PANAMA
CANAL ZONE
Colón
Panamá

COSTA RICA
Cartago
David

NICARAGUA
Puerto Cabezas
Bluefields
Corn Is. (U.S. Lease)
Swan Is. (U.S. & Hond.)
C. Gracias a Dios

HONDURAS

Tropic of Cancer

Silver Bank
Mouchoir Bank
Navidad Bank
Caicos Is.
Turks Is.
Mona Passage
Anegada Passage
Windward Passage
Mona Pass.

New York — San Juan 1,399
New York — La Guaira 1,847
New York — Kingston 1,474
Ciudad Trujillo — La Guaira 501
Ciudad Trujillo — Curaçao 393
Kingston — Barranquilla 437
Port of Spain 518

Longitude West of Greenwich

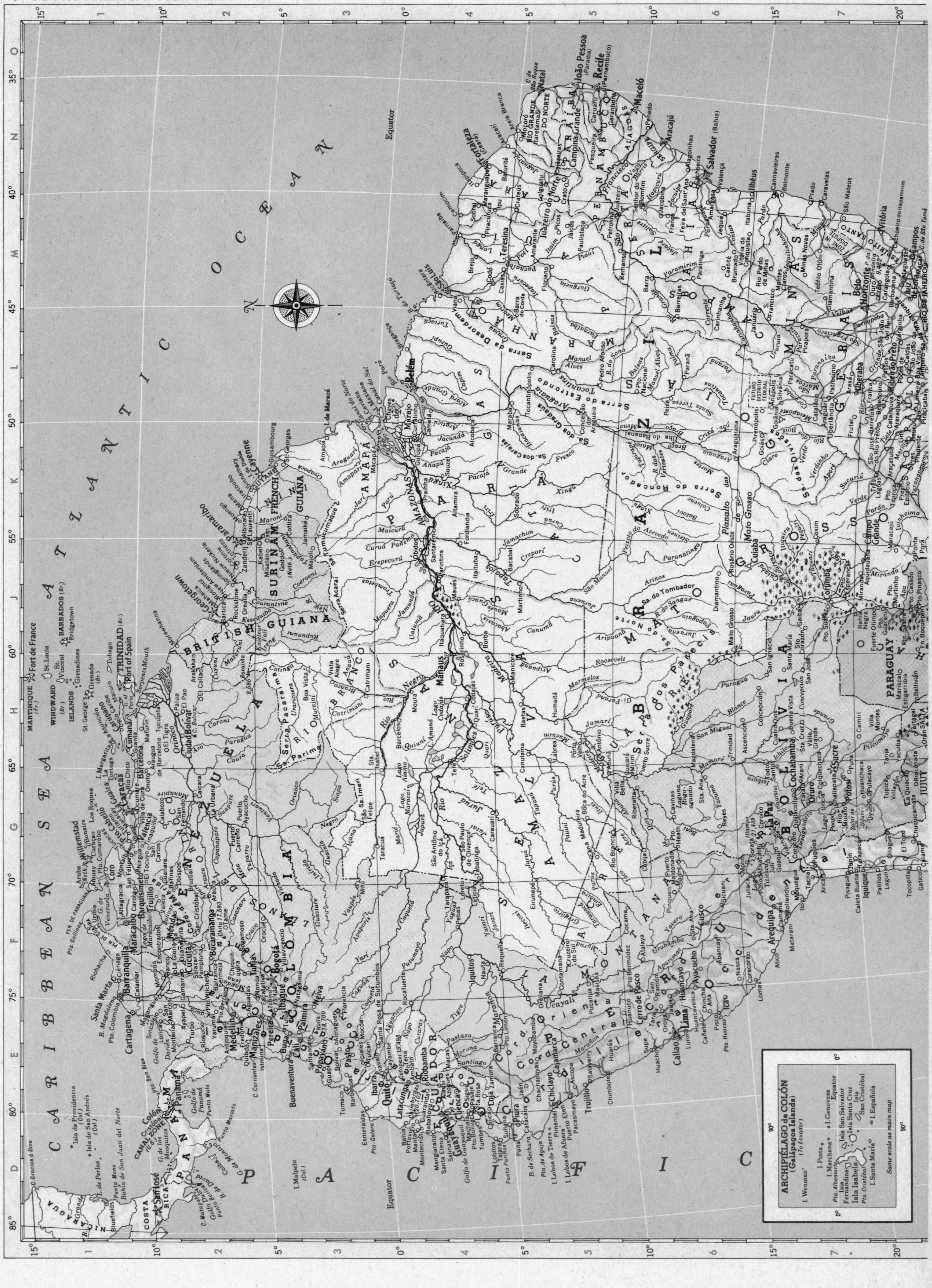

ATLANTIC OCEAN

CARIBBEAN SEA

PACIFIC

Equator

Countries and regions: VENEZUELA · COLOMBIA · ECUADOR · PERU · BOLIVIA · PARAGUAY · BRAZIL · BRITISH GUIANA · SURINAM (DUTCH GUIANA) · FRENCH GUIANA · PANAMA · COSTA RICA · NICARAGUA

States of Brazil: AMAZONAS · PARÁ · AMAPÁ · MARANHÃO · PIAUHY · CEARÁ · RIO GRANDE DO NORTE · PARAHYBA · PERNAMBUCO · ALAGOAS · SERGIPE · BAHIA · MINAS GERAES · ESPIRITO SANTO · RIO BRANCO · MATO GROSSO

Cities: Caracas · Maracaibo · Barranquilla · Cartagena · Santa Marta · Medellín · Bogotá · Cali · Quito · Guayaquil · Cuenca · Lima · Callao · Arequipa · La Paz · Cochabamba · Sucre · Potosí · Oruro · Belém · Fortaleza · Natal · Recife · Maceió · Salvador (Bahia) · João Pessoa · Teresina · Manáus · Cuiabá · Campo Grande · Corumbá · Cayenne · Paramaribo · Georgetown · Port of Spain · Fort de France · Bridgetown · Panamá · Colón

MARTINIQUE (Fr.) · St. Lucia (Br.) · St. Vincent · BARBADOS (Br.) · Grenadines · WINDWARD ISLANDS (Br.) · St. George's · TRINIDAD (Br.) · Tobago

ARCHIPIÉLAGO de COLÓN
(Galápagos Islands)
(To Ecuador)

I. Wenman · I. Pinta · I. Marchena · el Genovesa · Pta. Albemarle · Isla Fernandina · Isla Isabela · Isla San Salvador · Isla Santa Cruz · I. San Cristóbal · Pta. Española · I. Santa María

Same scale as main map

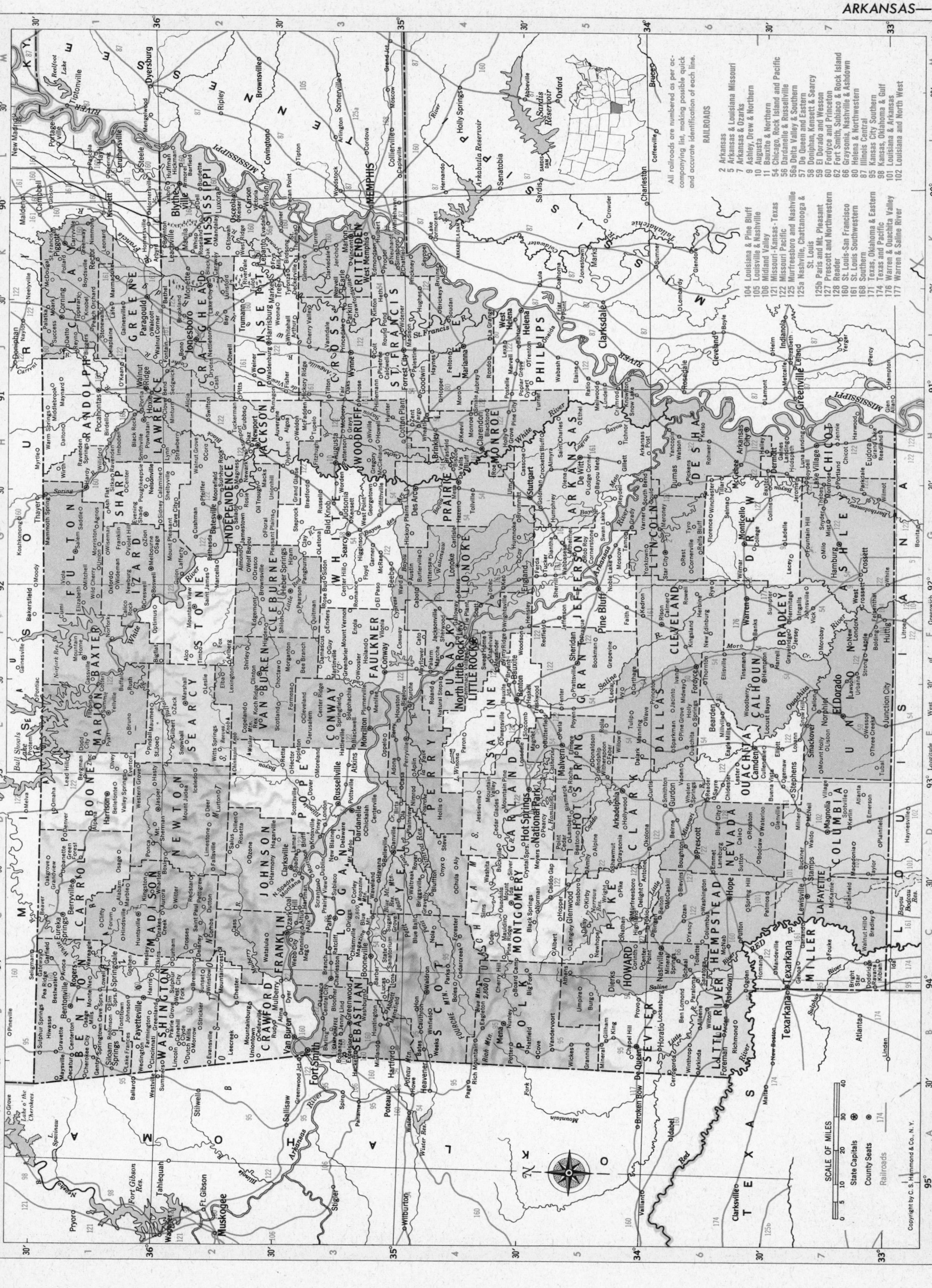

RAILROADS

All railroads are numbered as per accompanying list, making possible quick and accurate identification of each line.

No.	Railroad
2	Arkansas
5	Arkansas & Louisiana Missouri
7	Arkansas & Ozarks
8	Ashley, Drew & Northern
9	Augusta
11	Bauxite & Northern
54	Chicago, Rock Island and Pacific
56	Dardanelle & Russellville
56a	Delta Valley & Southern
57	De Queen and Eastern
58	Doniphan, Kensett & Searcy
59	El Dorado and Wesson
60	Fordyce and Princeton
62	Fort Smith, Subiaco & Rock Island
66	Graysonia, Nashville & Ashdown
80	Helena & Northwestern
87	Illinois Central
95	Kansas City Southern
98	Kansas, Oklahoma & Gulf
101	Louisiana & Arkansas
102	Louisiana and North West
104	Louisiana & Pine Bluff
105	Louisville & Nashville
106	Midland Valley
121	Missouri Pacific
122	Murfreesboro and Nashville
125a	Nashville, Chattanooga & St. Louis
125b	Paris and Mt. Pleasant
127	Prescott and Northwestern
128	Reader
160	St. Louis-San Francisco
161	St. Louis Southwestern
168	Southern
171	Texas, Oklahoma & Eastern
174	Texas-Kansas - Texas
176	Warren & Ouachita Valley
177	Warren & Saline River

SCALE OF MILES
0 10 20 30 40

State Capitals ⊛
County Seats ⊙
Railroads 174

All railroads are numbered as per accompanying list, making possible quick and accurate identification of each line.

RAILROADS

2 Almanor
3 Amador Central
4 Arcata & Mad River
7 Atchison, Topeka & Santa Fe
12 California Western
13 Camino, Placerville & Lake Tahoe
13a Eagle Mountain (Kaiser Steel Corp.)
14 Feather River
17 Great Northern
25 Holton Inter-Urban
38 McCloud River
88 Northwestern Pacific
89 Oregon, California & Eastern
90 Petaluma & Santa Rosa
91 Quincy
94 Sacramento Northern
95 San Diego & Arizona Eastern
98 Santa Maria Valley
99 Sierra
170 Southern Pacific
172 Stockton Terminal & Eastern
174 Tidewater Southern
176 Trona
180 Union Pacific
183 Western Pacific
189 Yreka Western

SAN FRANCISCO AND VICINITY
SCALE OF MILES

SCALE OF MILES
⊛ State Capitals
◉ County Seats
Canals
Railroads

SACRAMENTO AND VICINITY
SCALE OF MILES

LOS ANGELES AND VICINITY
SCALE OF MILES

Copyright by C. S. Hammond & Co., N.Y.

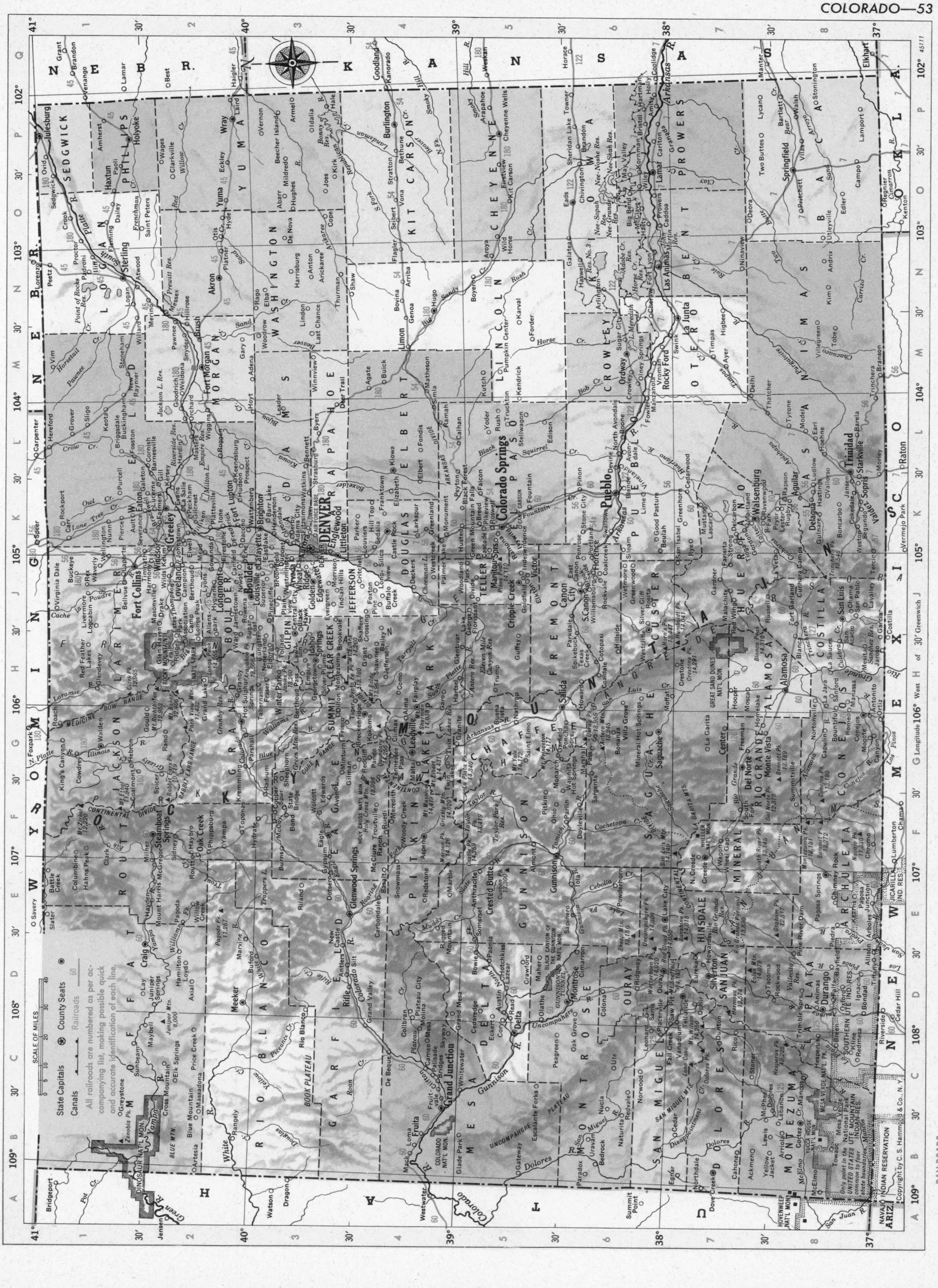

NEBR.

KANSAS

OKLA.

WYOMING

UTAH

NEW MEXICO

ARIZ.

Scale of Miles

State Capitals ⊛
County Seats ⊙
Railroads ——
Canals

All railroads are numbered as per accompanying list, making possible quick and accurate identification of each line.

Any point not in the National Park common to two or more states is named in UNITED STATES. State boundaries shown. INDIAN RESERVATION

Copyright by C. S. Hammond & Co., N.Y.

RAILROADS

7 Atchison, Topeka & Santa Fe
45 Chicago, Burlington & Quincy
54 Chicago, Rock Island & Pacific
54a Colorado
55 Colorado & South-Eastern
56 Colorado & Southern
57 Colorado & Wyoming
60 Denver & Rio Grande Western
64 Great Western
122 Missouri Pacific
125 Rio Grande Southern
126 San Luis Central
127 San Luis Valley Southern
180 Union Pacific

Major cities: DENVER, Colorado Springs, Pueblo, Fort Collins, Greeley, Boulder, Grand Junction, Durango, Trinidad, Sterling, Lamar, La Junta, Montrose, Gunnison, Leadville, Alamosa, Salida, Canon City, Walsenburg

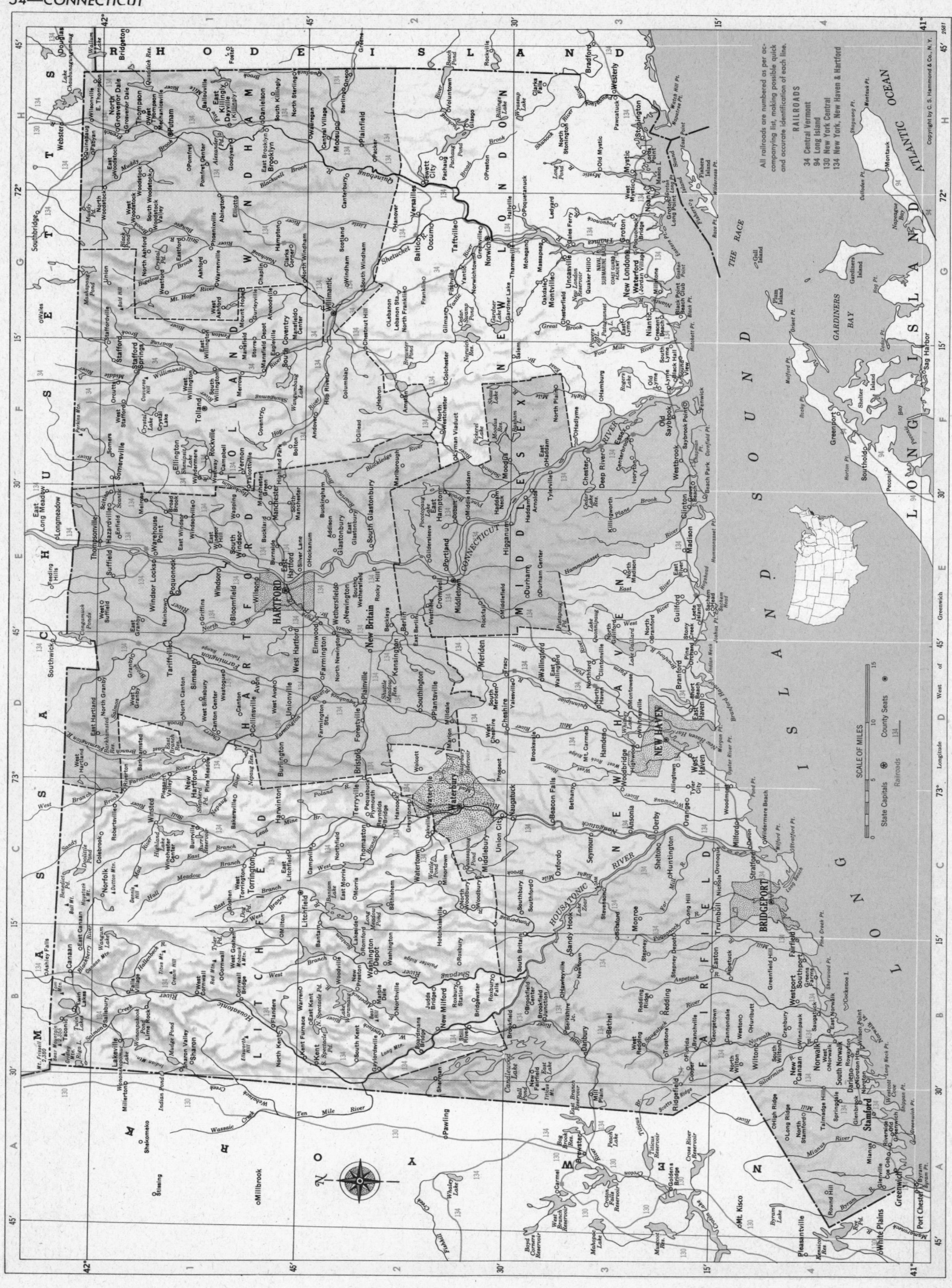

RAILROADS

All railroads are numbered as per accompanying list, making possible quick and accurate identification of each line.

34 Central Vermont
94 Long Island
130 New York Central
134 New York, New Haven & Hartford

SCALE OF MILES

State Capitals
County Seats
Railroads

Copyright by C. S. Hammond & Co., N.Y.

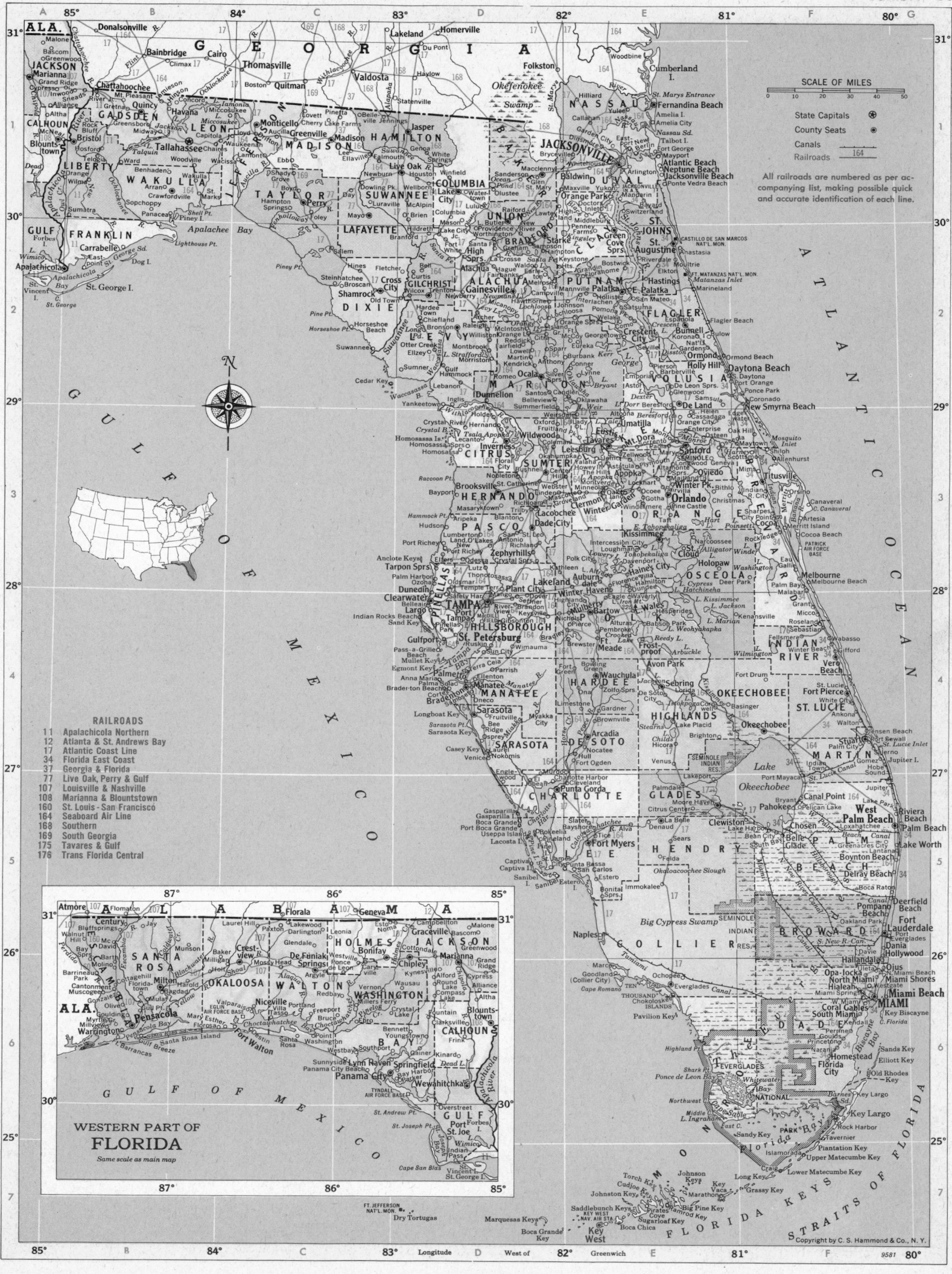

RAILROADS
11 Apalachicola Northern
12 Atlanta & St. Andrews Bay
17 Atlantic Coast Line
34 Florida East Coast
37 Georgia & Florida
77 Live Oak, Perry & Gulf
107 Louisville & Nashville
108 Marianna & Blountstown
160 St. Louis-San Francisco
164 Seaboard Air Line
168 Southern
169 South Georgia
175 Tavares & Gulf
176 Trans Florida Central

SCALE OF MILES
0 10 20 30 40 50

⊛ State Capitals
◉ County Seats
Canals ————
Railroads ——164——

All railroads are numbered as per accompanying list, making possible quick and accurate identification of each line.

WESTERN PART OF
FLORIDA
Same scale as main map

Copyright by C. S. Hammond & Co., N. Y.

9581

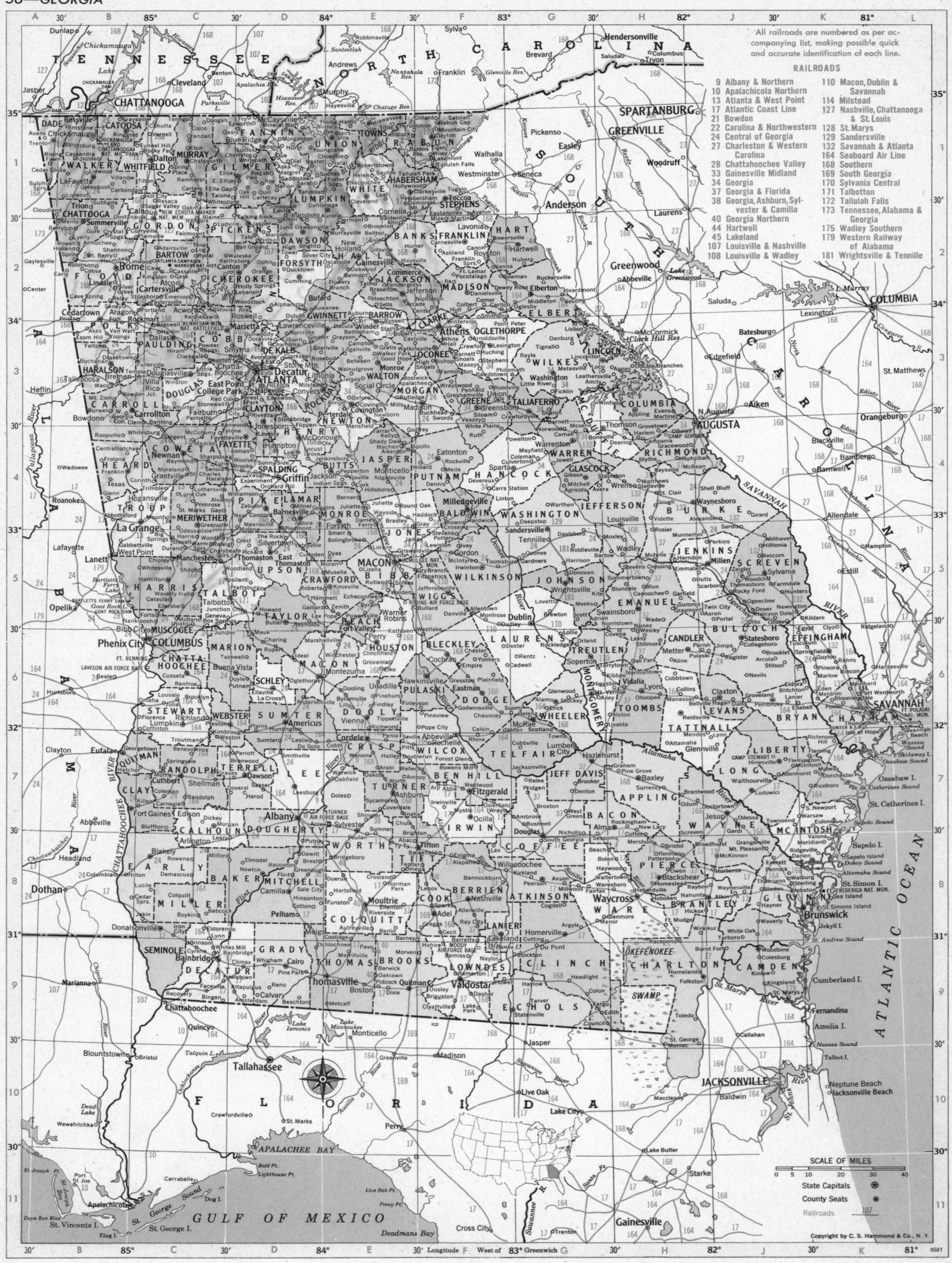

SCALE OF MILES

0 5 10 20 30 40

State Capitals ⊛
County Seats •
Railroads ——107——

Copyright by C. S. Hammond & Co., N. Y.

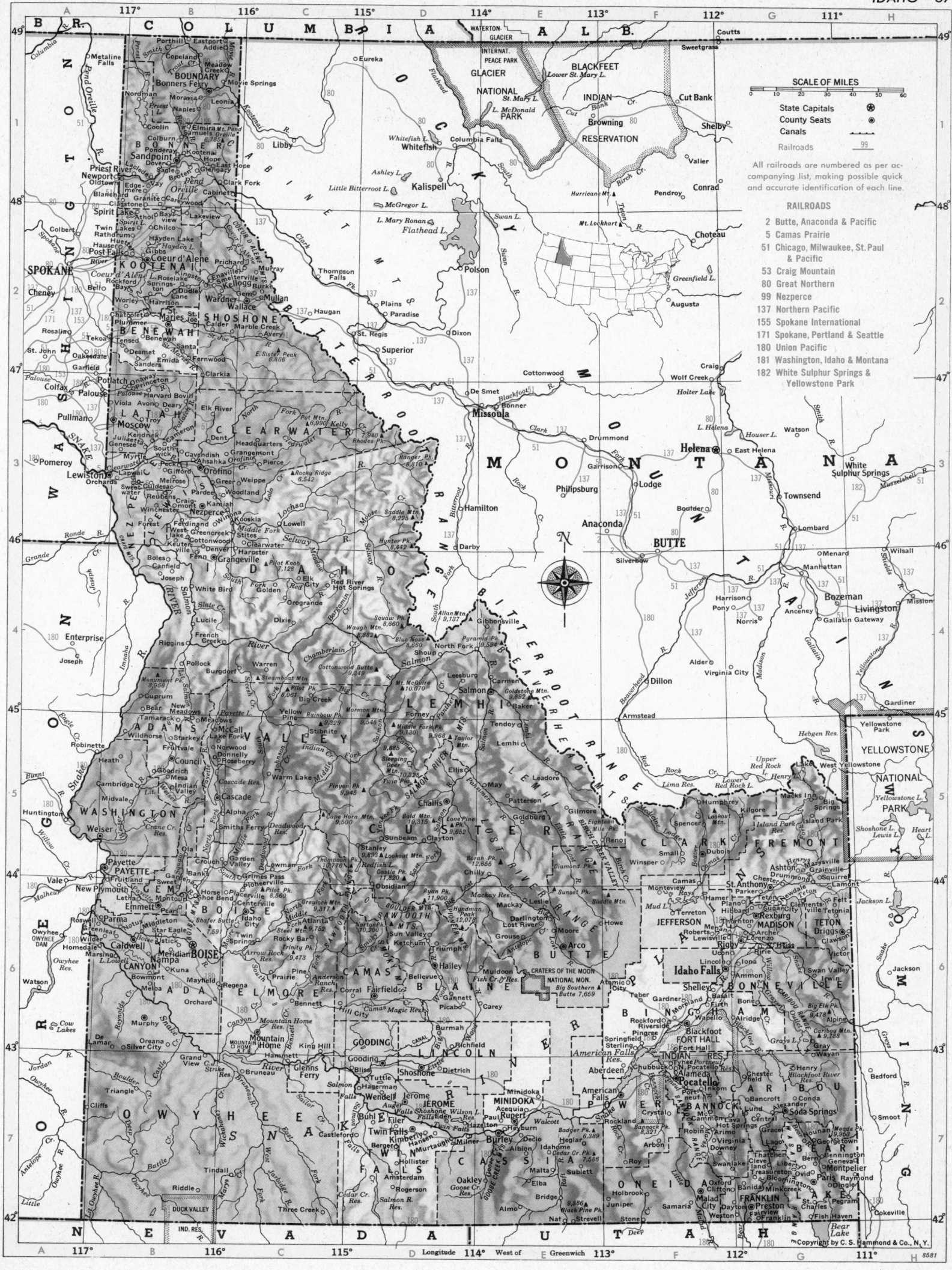

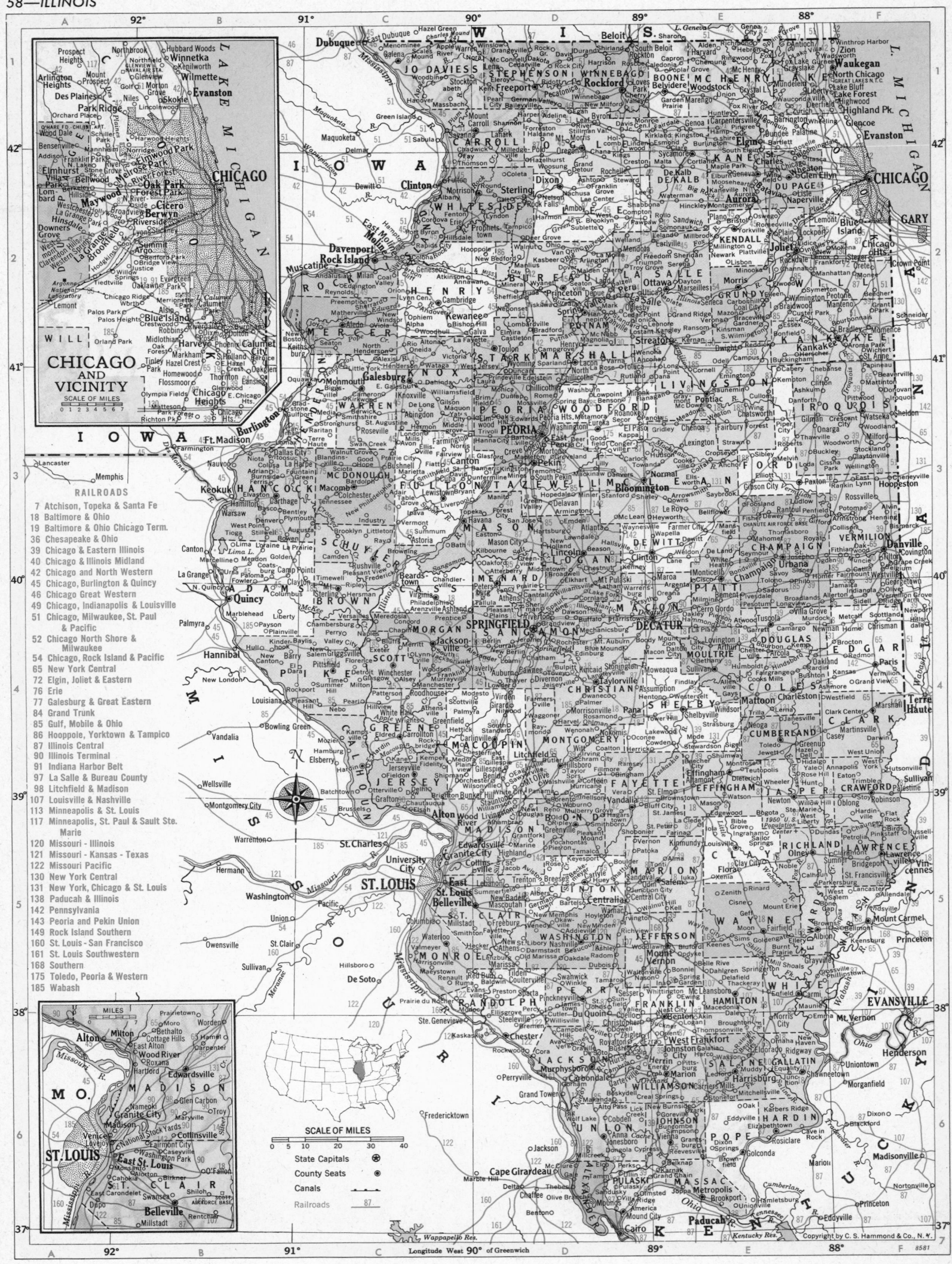

CHICAGO
AND
VICINITY

SCALE OF MILES
0 1 2 3 4 5 6 7

RAILROADS

7 Atchison, Topeka & Santa Fe
18 Baltimore & Ohio
19 Baltimore & Ohio Chicago Term.
36 Chesapeake & Ohio
39 Chicago & Eastern Illinois
40 Chicago & Illinois Midland
42 Chicago and North Western
45 Chicago, Burlington & Quincy
46 Chicago Great Western
49 Chicago, Indianapolis & Louisville
51 Chicago, Milwaukee, St. Paul
   & Pacific
52 Chicago North Shore &
   Milwaukee
54 Chicago, Rock Island & Pacific
65 New York Central
72 Elgin, Joliet & Eastern
76 Erie
77 Galesburg & Great Eastern
84 Grand Trunk
85 Gulf, Mobile & Ohio
86 Hooppole, Yorktown & Tampico
87 Illinois Central
90 Illinois Terminal
91 Indiana Harbor Belt
97 La Salle & Bureau County
98 Litchfield & Madison
107 Louisville & Nashville
113 Minneapolis & St. Louis
117 Minneapolis, St. Paul & Sault Ste.
    Marie
120 Missouri - Illinois
121 Missouri - Kansas - Texas
122 Missouri Pacific
130 New York Central
131 New York, Chicago & St. Louis
138 Paducah & Illinois
142 Pennsylvania
143 Peoria and Pekin Union
149 Rock Island Southern
160 St. Louis - San Francisco
161 St. Louis Southwestern
168 Southern
175 Toledo, Peoria & Western
185 Wabash

ST. LOUIS

SCALE OF MILES

State Capitals
County Seats
Canals
Railroads

Longitude West of Greenwich

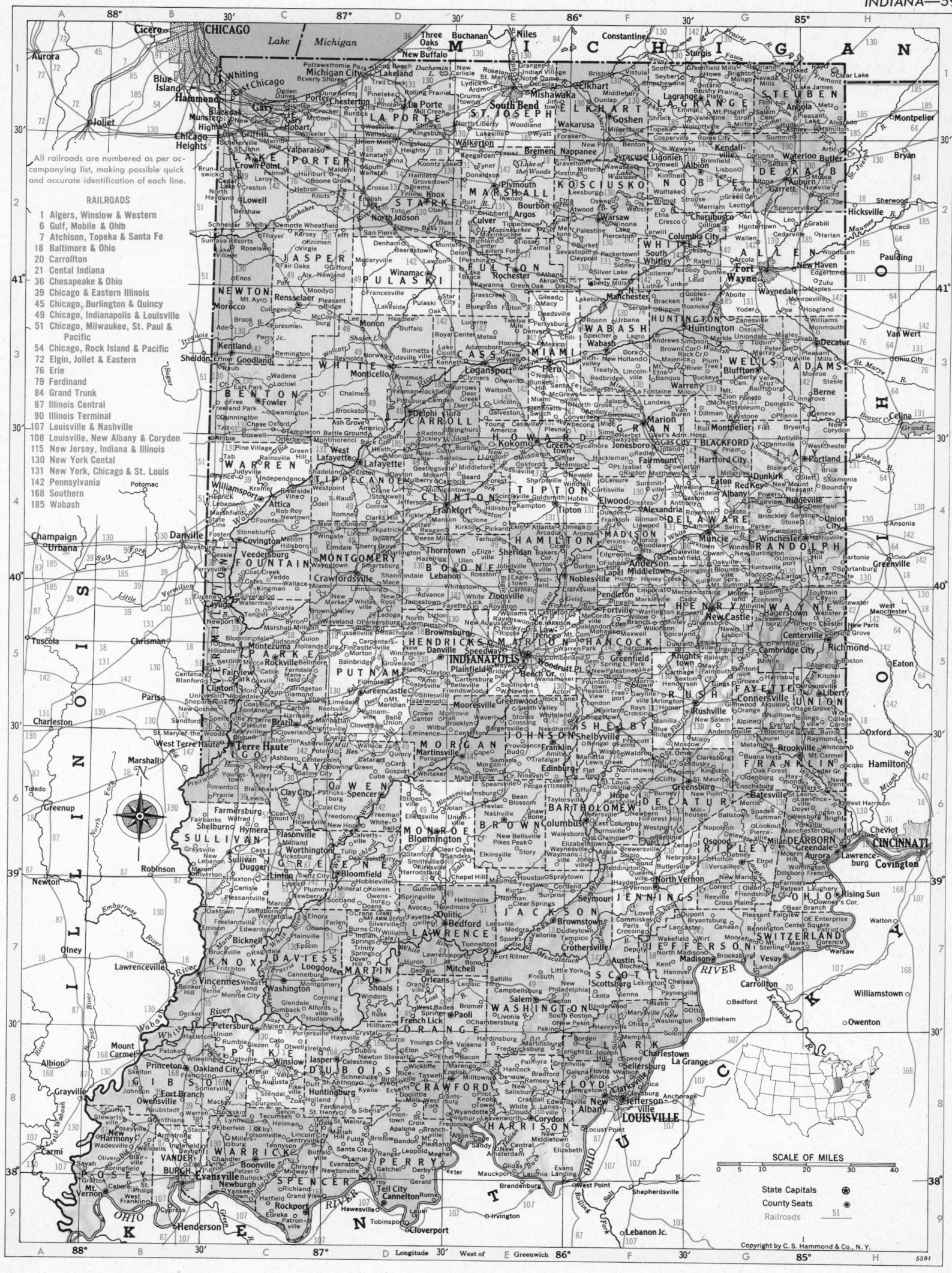

RAILROADS

1 Algers, Winslow & Western
6 Gulf, Mobile & Ohio
7 Atchison, Topeka & Santa Fe
18 Baltimore & Ohio
20 Carrollton
21 Cental Indiana
36 Chesapeake & Ohio
39 Chicago & Eastern Illinois
45 Chicago, Burlington & Quincy
49 Chicago, Indianapolis & Louisville
51 Chicago, Milwaukee, St. Paul &
    Pacific
54 Chicago, Rock Island & Pacific
72 Elgin, Joliet & Eastern
76 Erie
79 Ferdinand
84 Grand Trunk
87 Illinois Central
90 Illinois Terminal
107 Louisville & Nashville
108 Louisville, New Albany & Corydon
115 New Jersey, Indiana & Illinois
130 New York Central
131 New York, Chicago & St. Louis
142 Pennsylvania
168 Southern
185 Wabash

All railroads are numbered as per accompanying list, making possible quick
and accurate identification of each line.

SCALE OF MILES

0   5   10   20   30   40

State Capitals   ⊛
County Seats   ⊙
Railroads   ___51___

Copyright by C. S. Hammond & Co., N.Y.

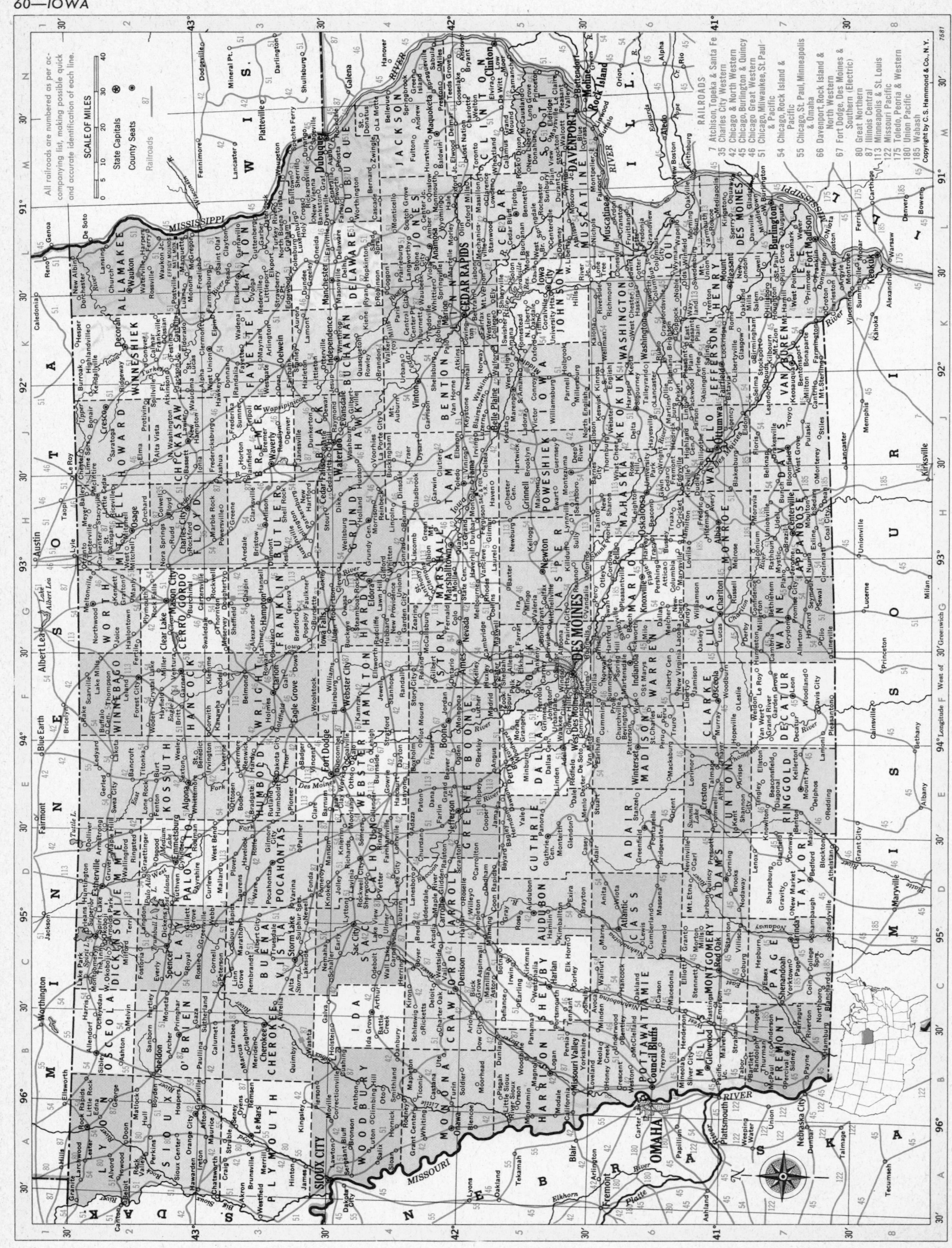

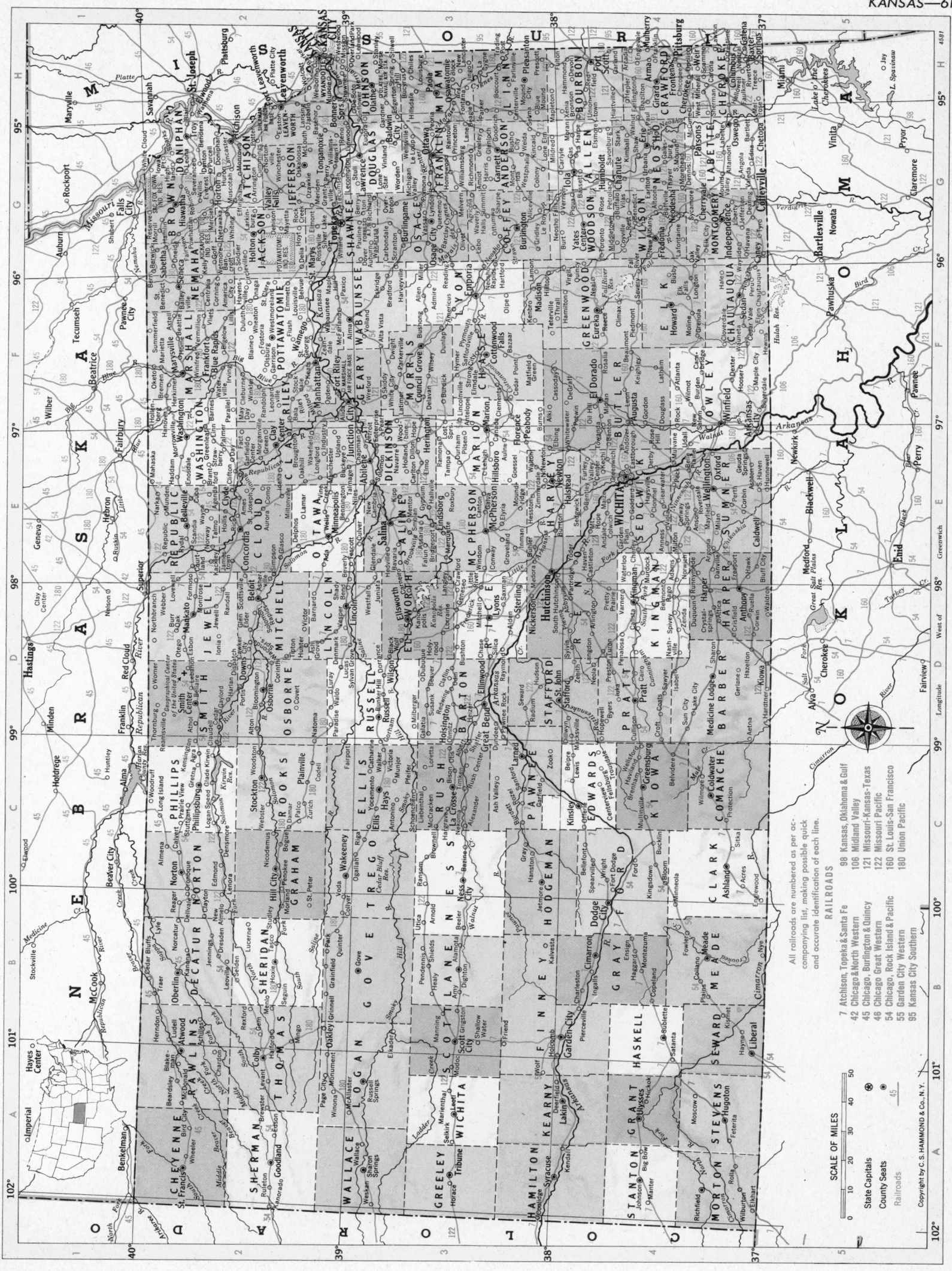

RAILROADS

All railroads are numbered as per accompanying list, making possible quick and accurate identification of each line.

7 Atchison, Topeka & Santa Fe	98 Kansas, Oklahoma & Gulf
42 Chicago & North Western	106 Midland Valley
45 Chicago, Burlington & Quincy	121 Missouri-Kansas-Texas
46 Chicago Great Western	122 Missouri Pacific
54 Chicago, Rock Island & Pacific	160 St. Louis-San Francisco
55 Garden City Western	180 Union Pacific
95 Kansas City Southern	

SCALE OF MILES

State Capitals

County Seats

Railroads

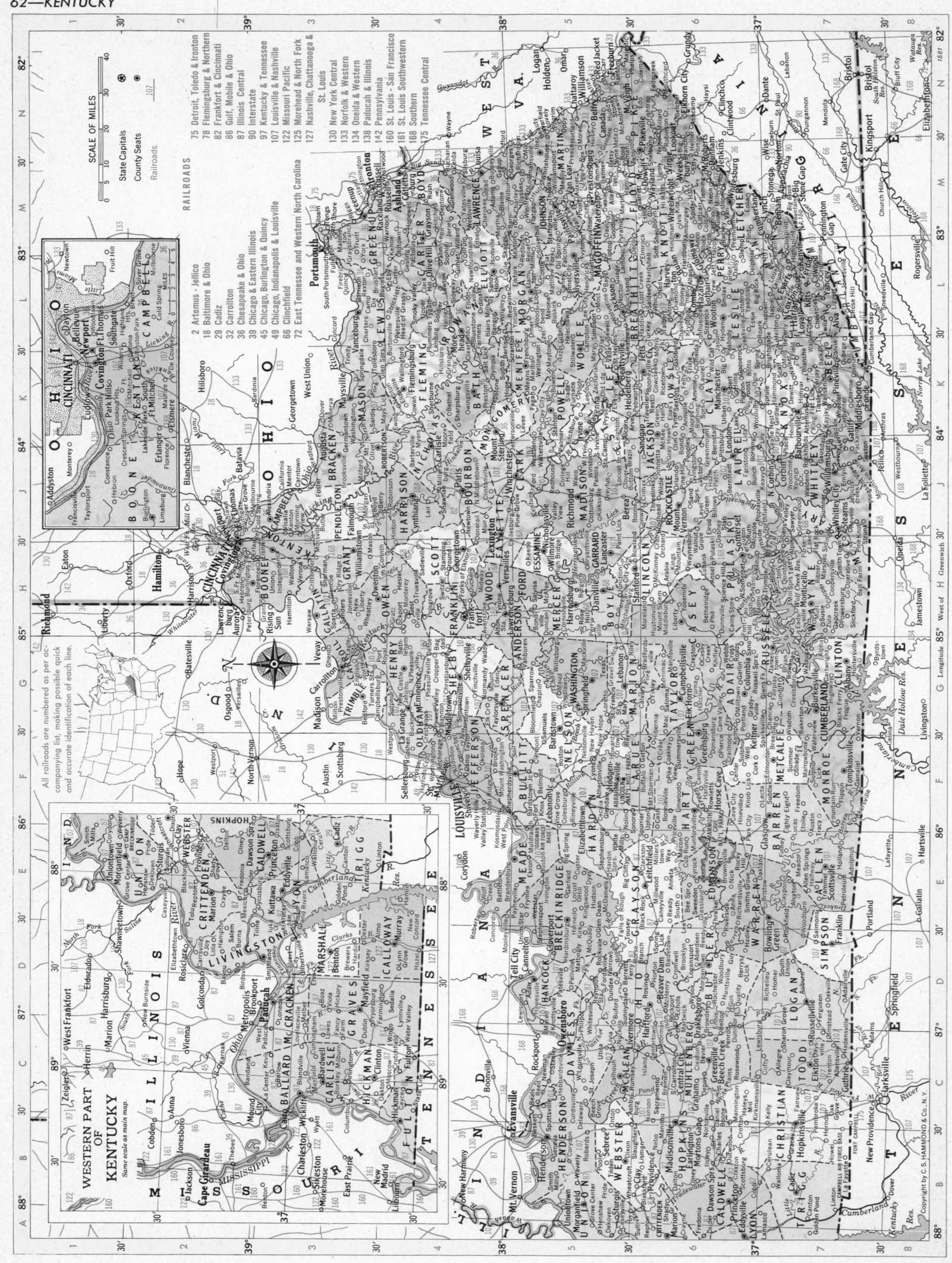

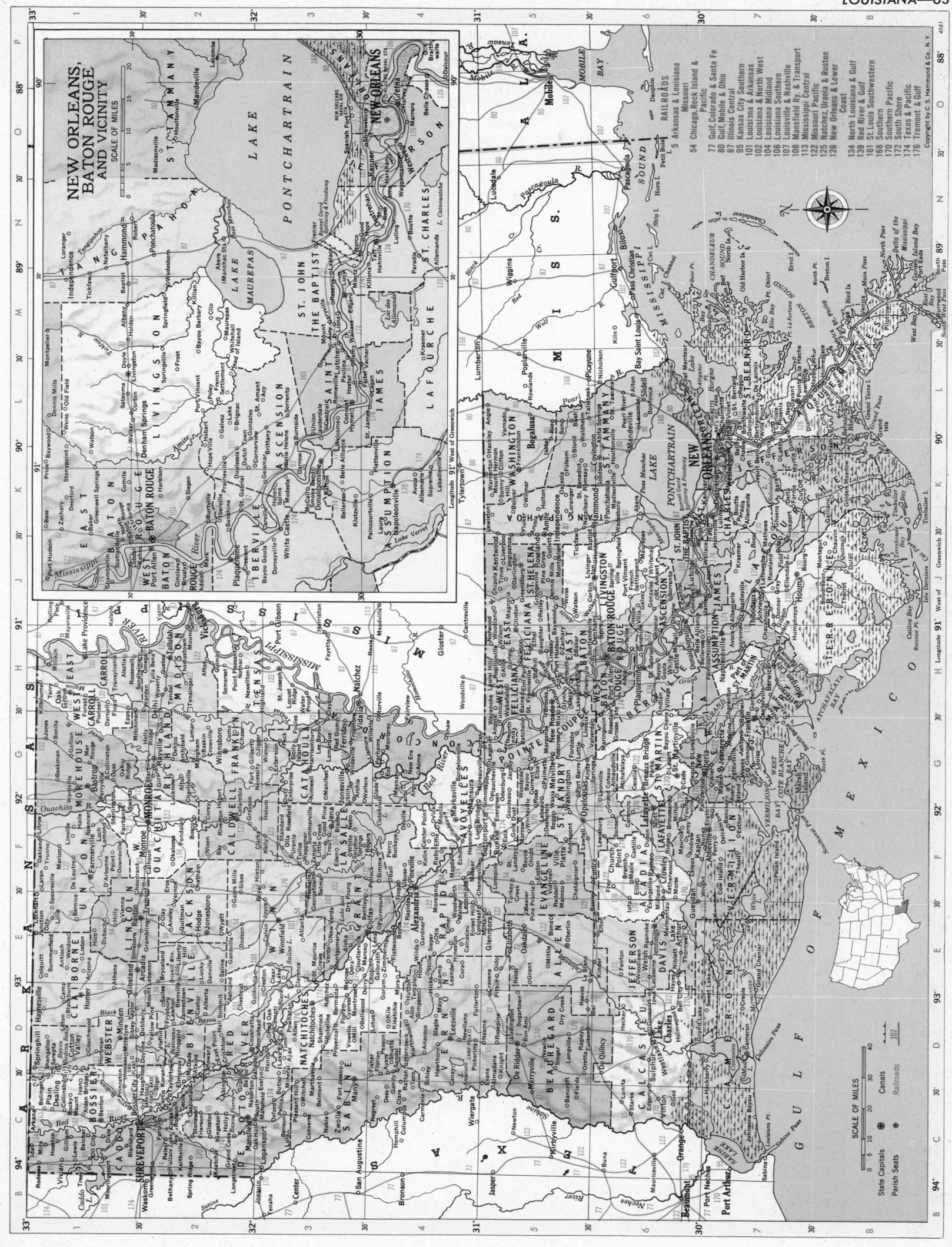

NEW ORLEANS, BATON ROUGE AND VICINITY

SCALE OF MILES

RAILROADS

5 Arkansas & Louisiana Missouri
54 Chicago, Rock Island & Pacific
77 Gulf, Colorado & Santa Fe
80 Gulf, Mobile & Ohio
87 Illinois Central
95 Kansas City Southern
101 Louisiana & Arkansas
104 Louisiana & North West
104 Louisiana Midland
106 Louisiana Southern
107 Louisville & Nashville
108 Mansfield Ry. & Transport
113 Mississippi Central
122 Missouri Pacific
125 Natchez, Urania & Ruston
126 New Orleans & Lower Coast
134 North Louisiana & Gulf
139 Red River & Gulf
161 St. Louis Southwestern
168 Southern
170 Southern Pacific
172 South Shore
176 Texas & Pacific
176 Tremont & Gulf

Copyright by C. S. Hammond & Co., N.Y.

SCALE OF MILES

● State Capitals
○ Parish Seats

Canals
Railroads

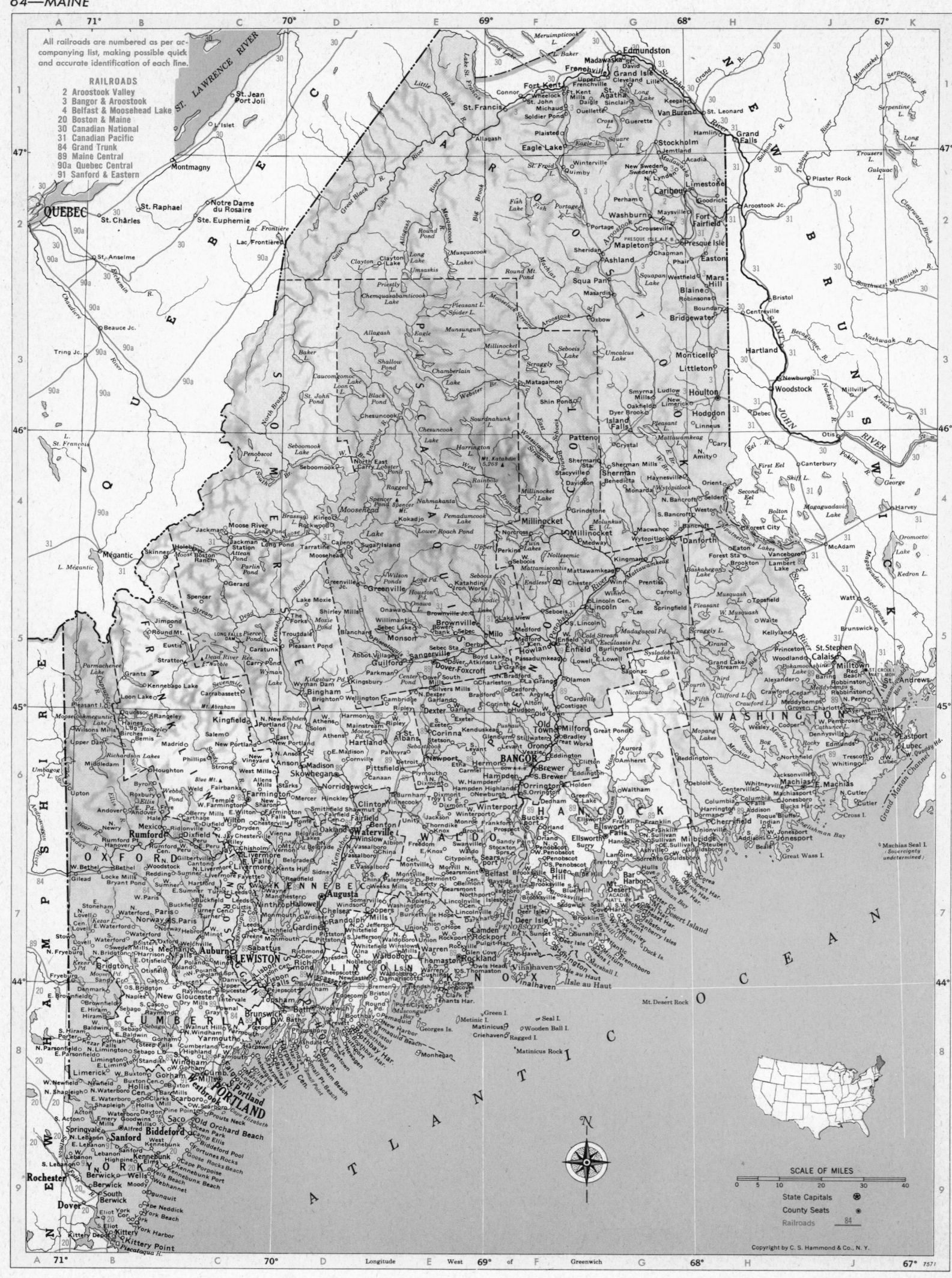

All railroads are numbered as per accompanying list, making possible quick and accurate identification of each line.

RAILROADS
2 Aroostook Valley
3 Bangor & Aroostook
4 Belfast & Moosehead Lake
20 Boston & Maine
30 Canadian National
31 Canadian Pacific
84 Grand Trunk
89 Maine Central
90a Quebec Central
91 Sanford & Eastern

SCALE OF MILES
0 5 10   20   30   40

⊛ State Capitals
⊙ County Seats
Railroads ──84──

Copyright by C. S. Hammond & Co., N.Y.

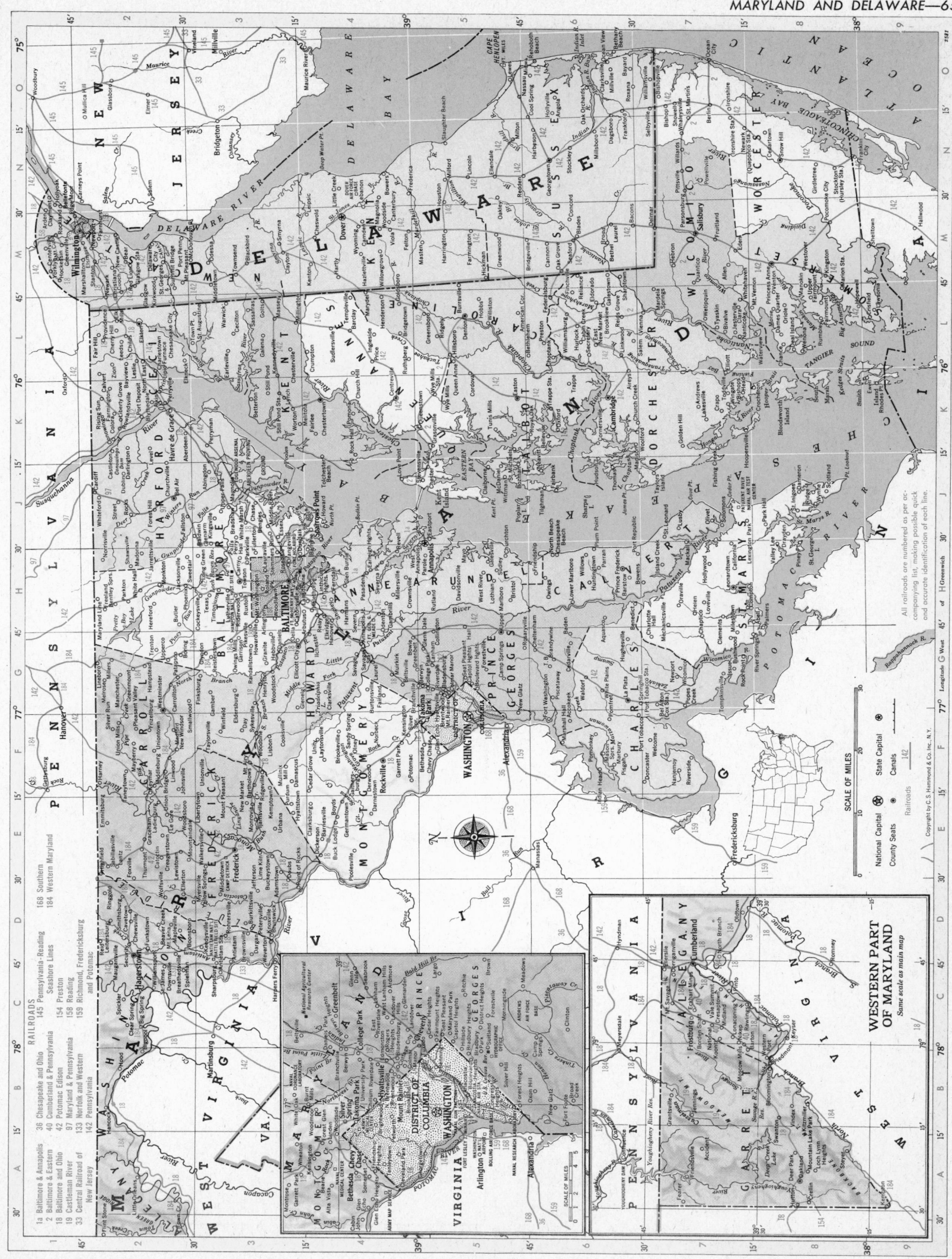

WESTERN PART
OF MARYLAND
Same scale as main map

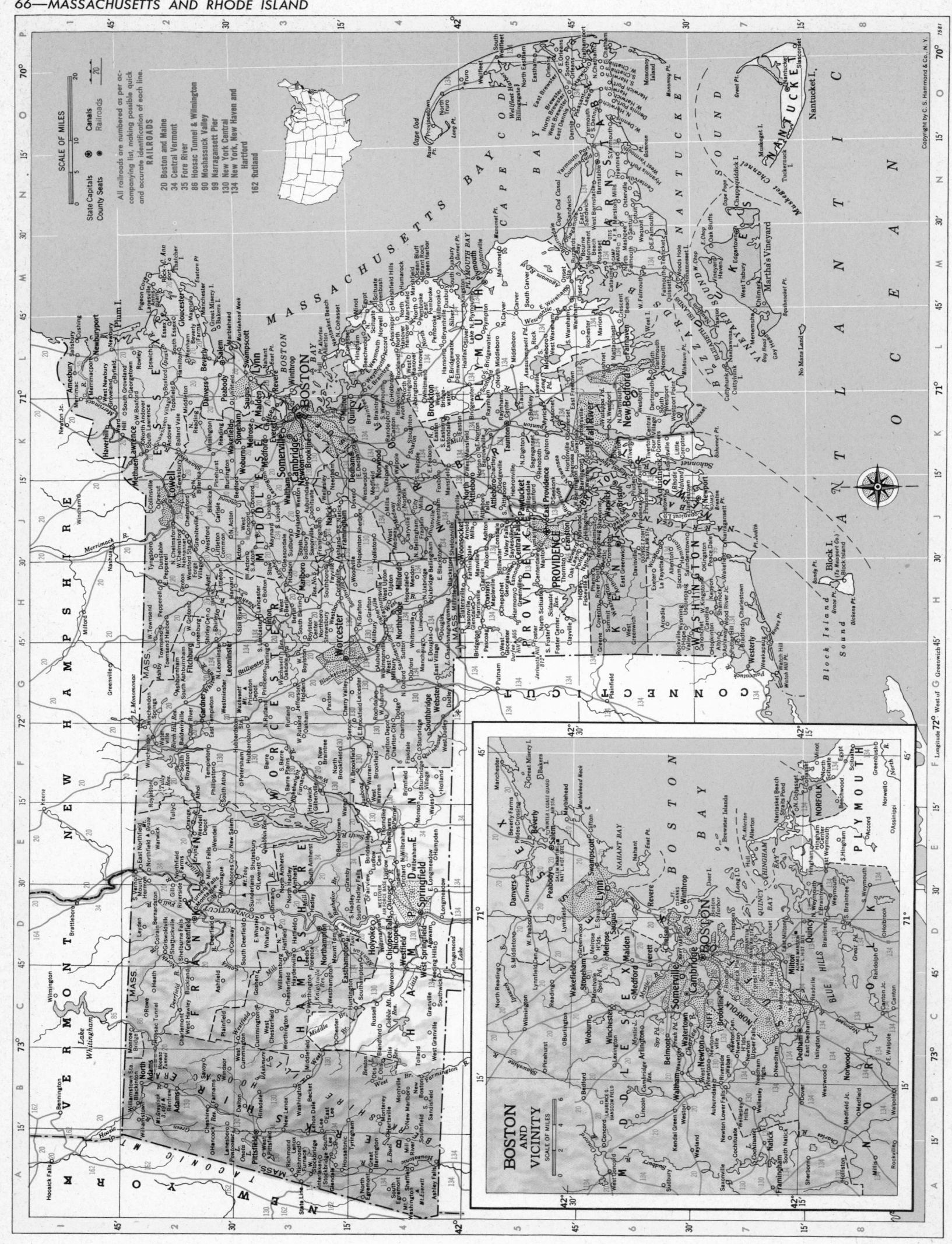

SCALE OF MILES

State Capitals
County Seats

RAILROADS

All railroads are numbered as per accompanying list, making possible quick and accurate identification of each line.

20 Boston and Maine
34 Central Vermont
35 Fore River
86 Hoosac Tunnel & Wilmington
90 Moshassuck Valley
99 Narragansett Pier
134 New York Central
134 New York, New Haven and Hartford
162 Rutland

Canals
Railroads

Copyright by C.S. Hammond & Co., N.Y.

BOSTON AND VICINITY
SCALE OF MILES

SCALE OF MILES

State Capitals
County Seats
Canals
Railroads

RAILROADS

4 Ann Arbor
6 Boyne City
18 Baltimore & Ohio
25 Canadian National
31 Canadian Pacific
36 Chesapeake & Ohio
42 Chicago & North Western
51 Chicago, Milwaukee, St. Paul &
   Pacific
66 Copper Range
69 Detroit & Mackinac
72 Detroit & Toledo Shore Line
73 Detroit, Caro & Sandusky
74 Detroit Terminal
75 Detroit, Toledo & Ironton
77 Duluth, South Shore and
   Atlantic
81 East Jordan & Southern
83 Escanaba & Lake Superior
84 Grand Trunk
85 Green Bay & Western
86 Lake Superior & Ishpeming
89 Ludington & Northern
90 Manistee & Northeastern
91 Manistique & Lake Superior
117 Minneapolis, St. Paul &
    Sault Ste. Marie
130 New York Central
131 New York, Chicago & St. Louis
142 Pennsylvania
147 Port Huron & Detroit
185 Wabash

9581

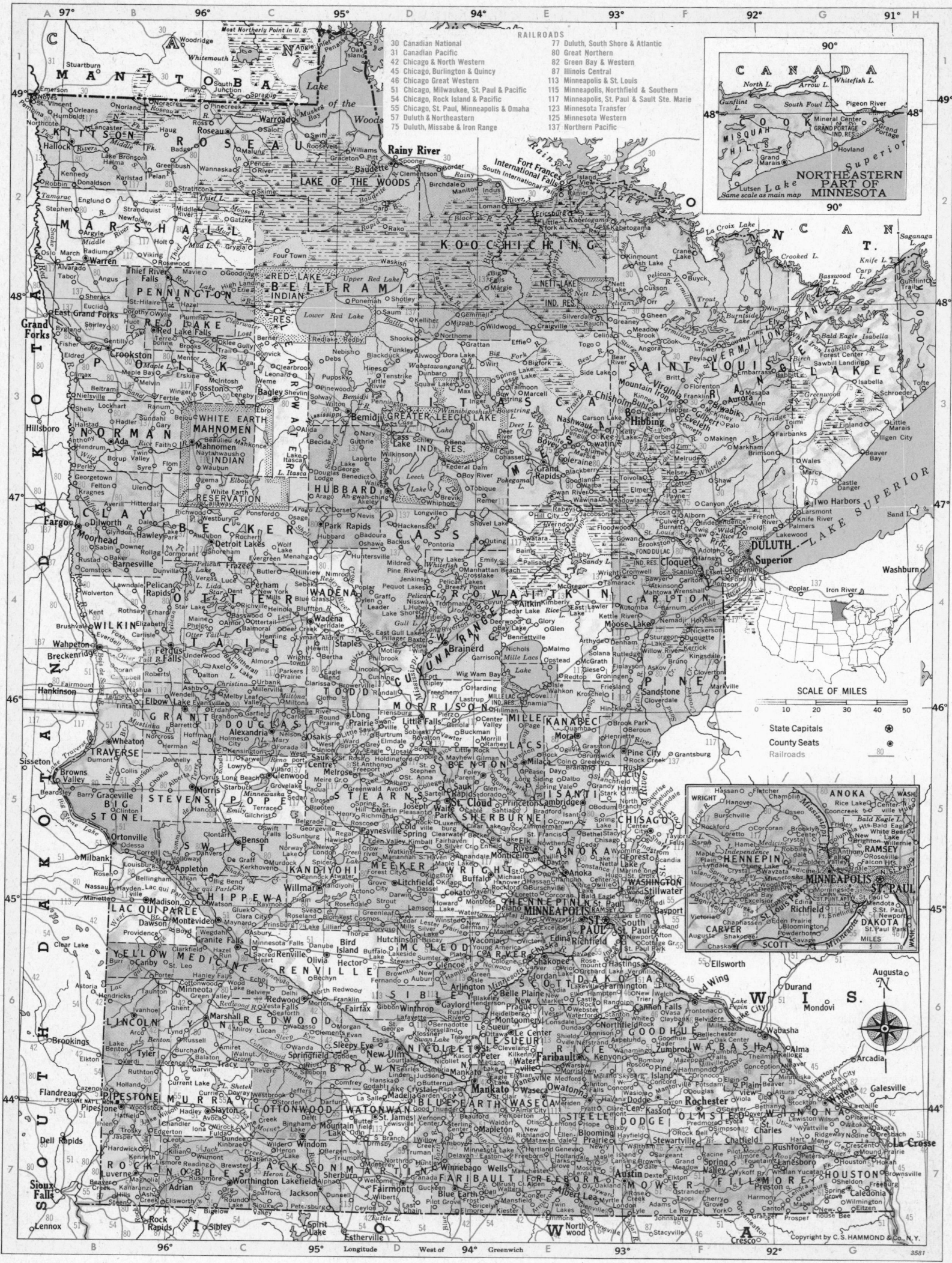

RAILROADS

30 Canadian National	77 Duluth, South Shore & Atlantic
31 Canadian Pacific	80 Great Northern
42 Chicago & North Western	82 Green Bay & Western
45 Chicago, Burlington & Quincy	87 Illinois Central
46 Chicago Great Western	113 Minneapolis & St. Louis
51 Chicago, Milwaukee, St. Paul & Pacific	115 Minneapolis, Northfield & Southern
54 Chicago, Rock Island & Pacific	117 Minneapolis, St. Paul & Sault Ste. Marie
55 Chicago, St. Paul, Minneapolis & Omaha	123 Minnesota Transfer
57 Duluth & Northeastern	125 Minnesota Western
75 Duluth, Missabe & Iron Range	137 Northern Pacific

NORTHEASTERN PART OF MINNESOTA
Same scale as main map

SCALE OF MILES

State Capitals
County Seats
Railroads

Copyright by C. S. HAMMOND & Co., N.Y.

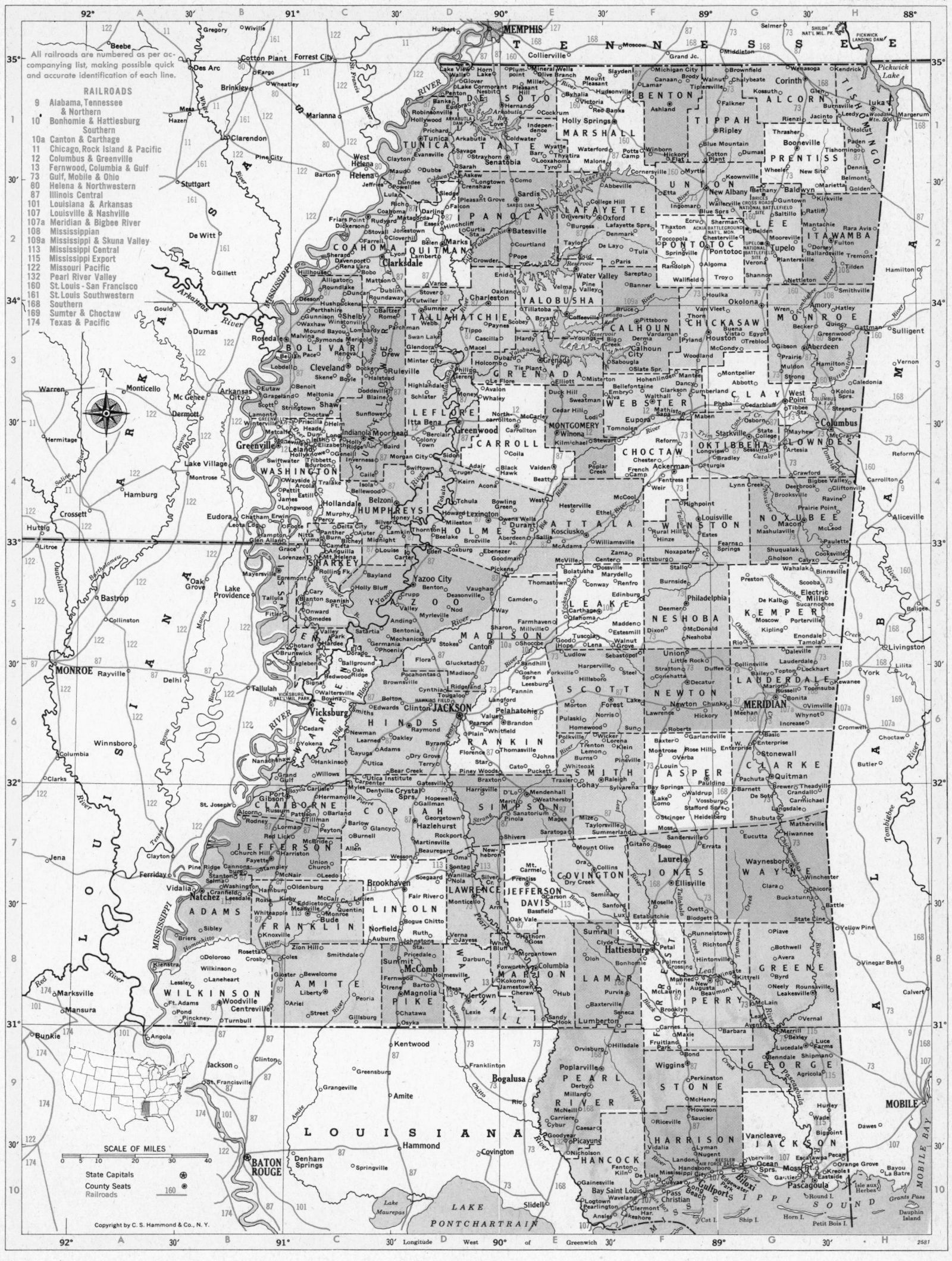

All railroads are numbered as per accompanying list, making possible quick and accurate identification of each line.

RAILROADS

9	Alabama, Tennessee & Northern
10	Bonhomie & Hattiesburg Southern
10a	Canton & Carthage
11	Chicago, Rock Island & Pacific
12	Columbus & Greenville
13	Fernwood, Columbia & Gulf
73	Gulf, Mobile & Ohio
80	Helena & Northwestern
87	Illinois Central
101	Louisiana & Arkansas
107	Louisville & Nashville
107a	Meridian & Bigbee River
108	Mississippian
109a	Mississippi & Skuna Valley
113	Mississippi Central
115	Mississippi Export
122	Missouri Pacific
132	Pearl River Valley
160	St. Louis-San Francisco
161	St. Louis Southwestern
168	Southern
169	Sumter & Choctaw
174	Texas & Pacific

SCALE OF MILES

State Capitals
County Seats
Railroads

Copyright by C. S. Hammond & Co., N.Y.

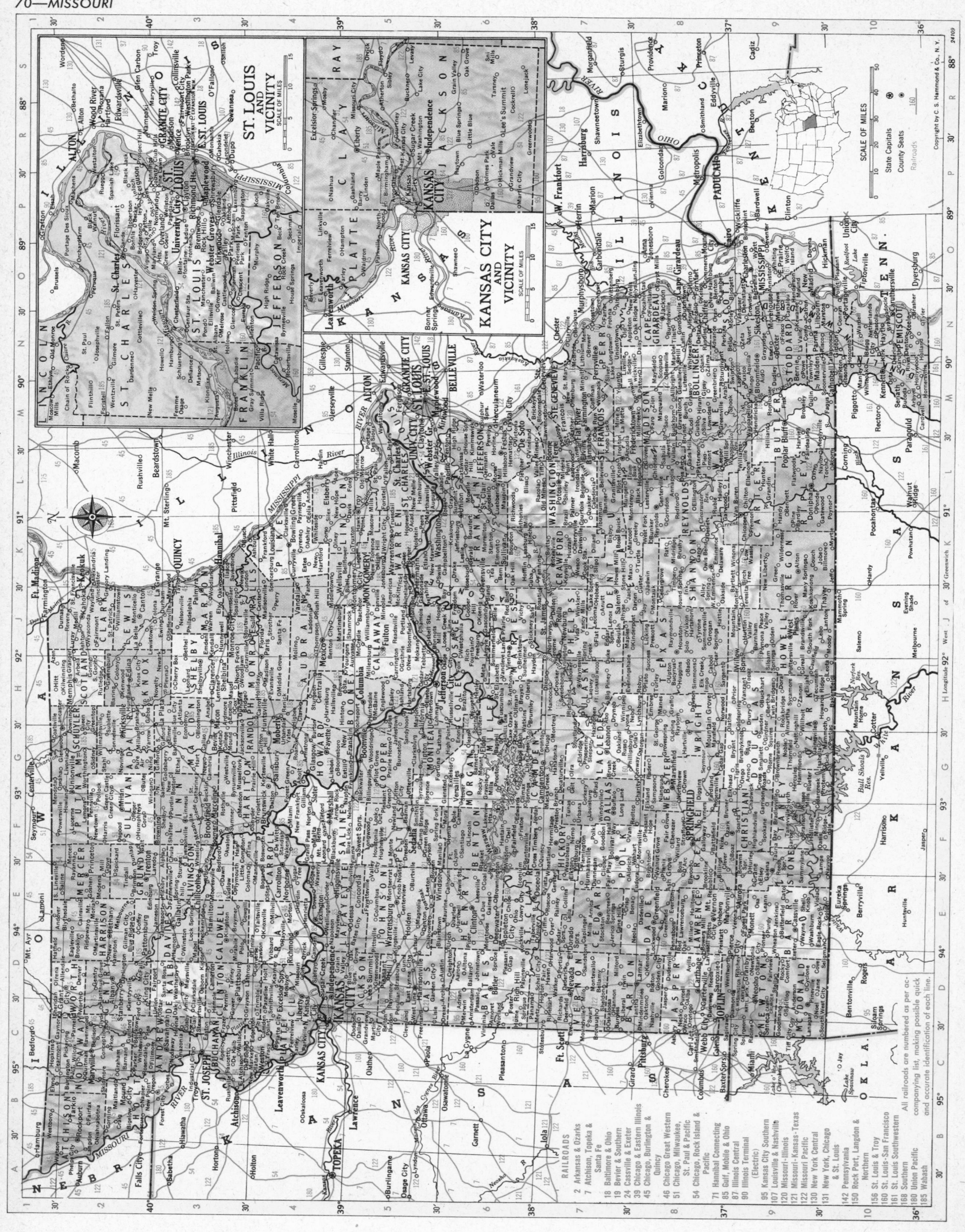

ST. LOUIS
AND
VICINITY
SCALE OF MILES

KANSAS CITY
AND
VICINITY
SCALE OF MILES

SCALE OF MILES

State Capitals
County Seats
Railroads

RAILROADS

2   Arkansas & Ozarks
7   Atchison, Topeka & Santa Fe
18 Baltimore & Ohio
24 Beyler & Southern
39 Cassville & Exeter
44 Chicago & Eastern Illinois
45 Chicago, Burlington & Quincy
46 Chicago Great Western
51 Chicago, Milwaukee, St. Paul & Pacific
54 Chicago, Rock Island & Pacific
71 Hannibal Connecting
85 Gulf, Mobile & Ohio
87 Illinois Central
90 Illinois Terminal (Electric)
95 Kansas City Southern
107 Louisville & Nashville
120 Missouri-Illinois
121 Missouri-Kansas-Texas
122 Missouri Pacific
130 New York Central
131 New York, Chicago & St. Louis
142 Pennsylvania
150 Rock Port, Langdon & Northern
156 St. Louis & Troy
160 St. Louis-San Francisco
161 St. Louis Southwestern
168 Southern
180 Union Pacific
185 Wabash

All railroads are numbered as per accompanying list, making possible quick and accurate identification of each line.

Copyright by C. S. Hammond & Co., N. Y.

24109

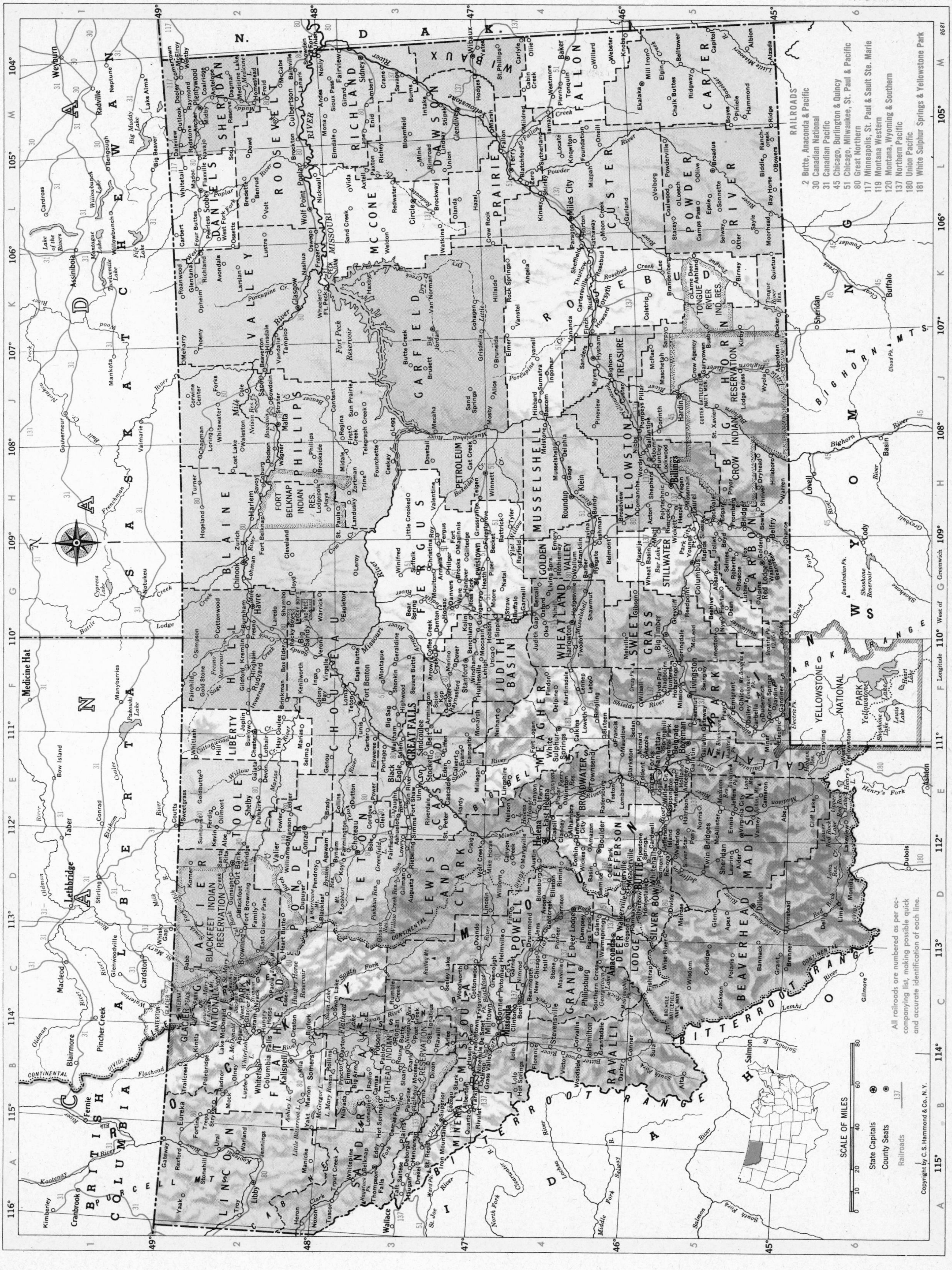

RAILROADS
2   Butte, Anaconda & Pacific
30 Canadian National
31 Canadian Pacific
45 Chicago, Burlington & Quincy
51 Chicago, Milwaukee, St. Paul & Pacific
80 Great Northern
117 Minneapolis, St. Paul & Sault Ste. Marie
119 Montana Western
120 Montana, Wyoming & Southern
137 Northern Pacific
180 Union Pacific
181 White Sulphur Springs & Yellowstone Park

All railroads are numbered as per accompanying list, making possible quick and accurate identification of each line.

SCALE OF MILES
0 10 20   40   60   80

State Capitals   ⊛
County Seats   ◉
Railroads   ——137——

Copyright by C. S. Hammond & Co., N.Y.

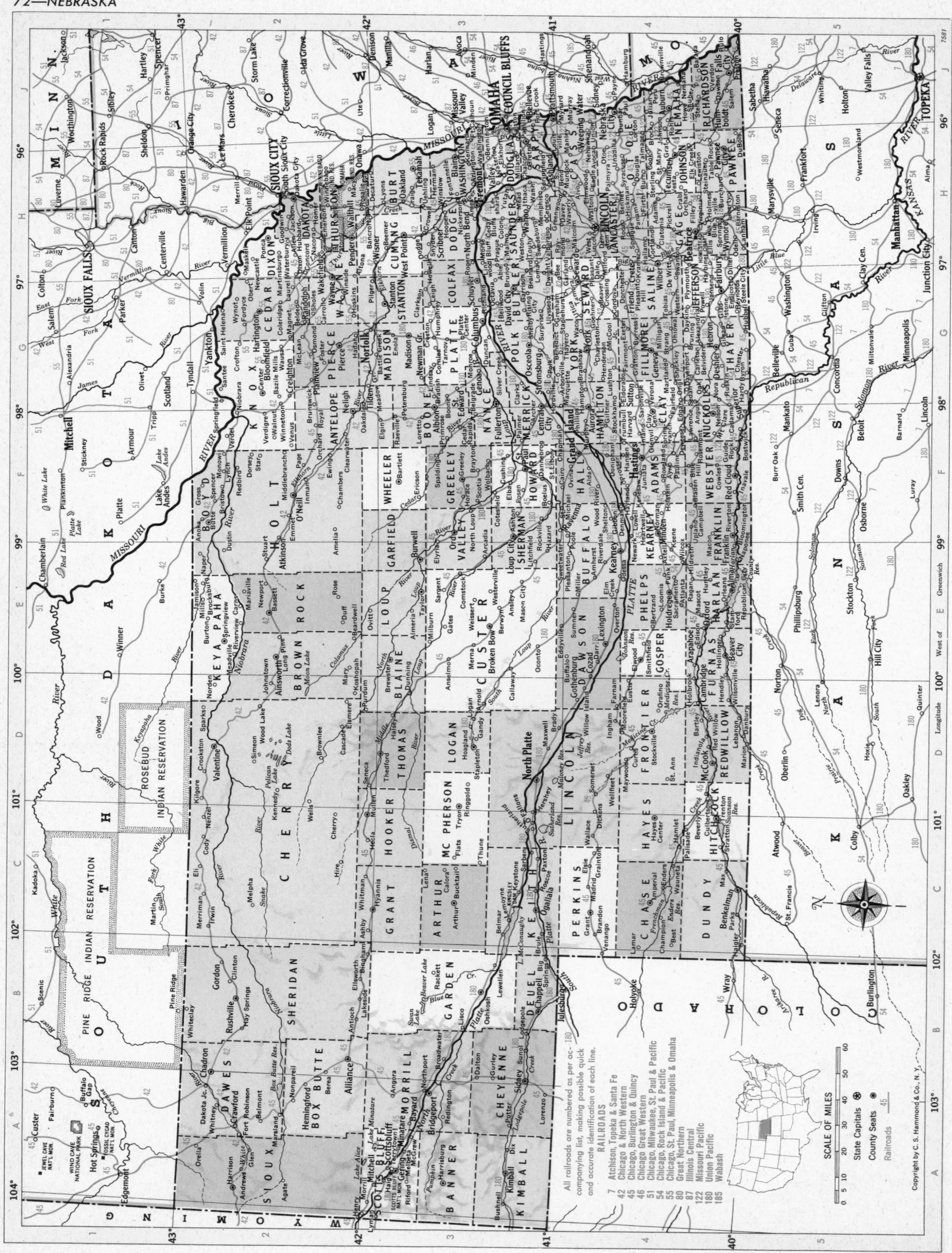

RAILROADS

All railroads are numbered as per accompanying list, making possible quick and accurate identification of each line.

7 Atchison, Topeka & Santa Fe
42 Chicago & North Western
45 Chicago, Burlington & Quincy
46 Chicago Great Western
51 Chicago, Milwaukee, St. Paul & Pacific
55 Chicago, Rock Island & Pacific
80 Chicago, St. Paul, Minneapolis & Omaha
87 Great Northern
122 Illinois Central
180 Missouri Pacific
180 Union Pacific
185 Wabash

SCALE OF MILES
0   10   20   30   40   50   60

⊗ State Capitals
⊙ County Seats
45 Railroads

Copyright by C. S. Hammond & Co., N. Y.

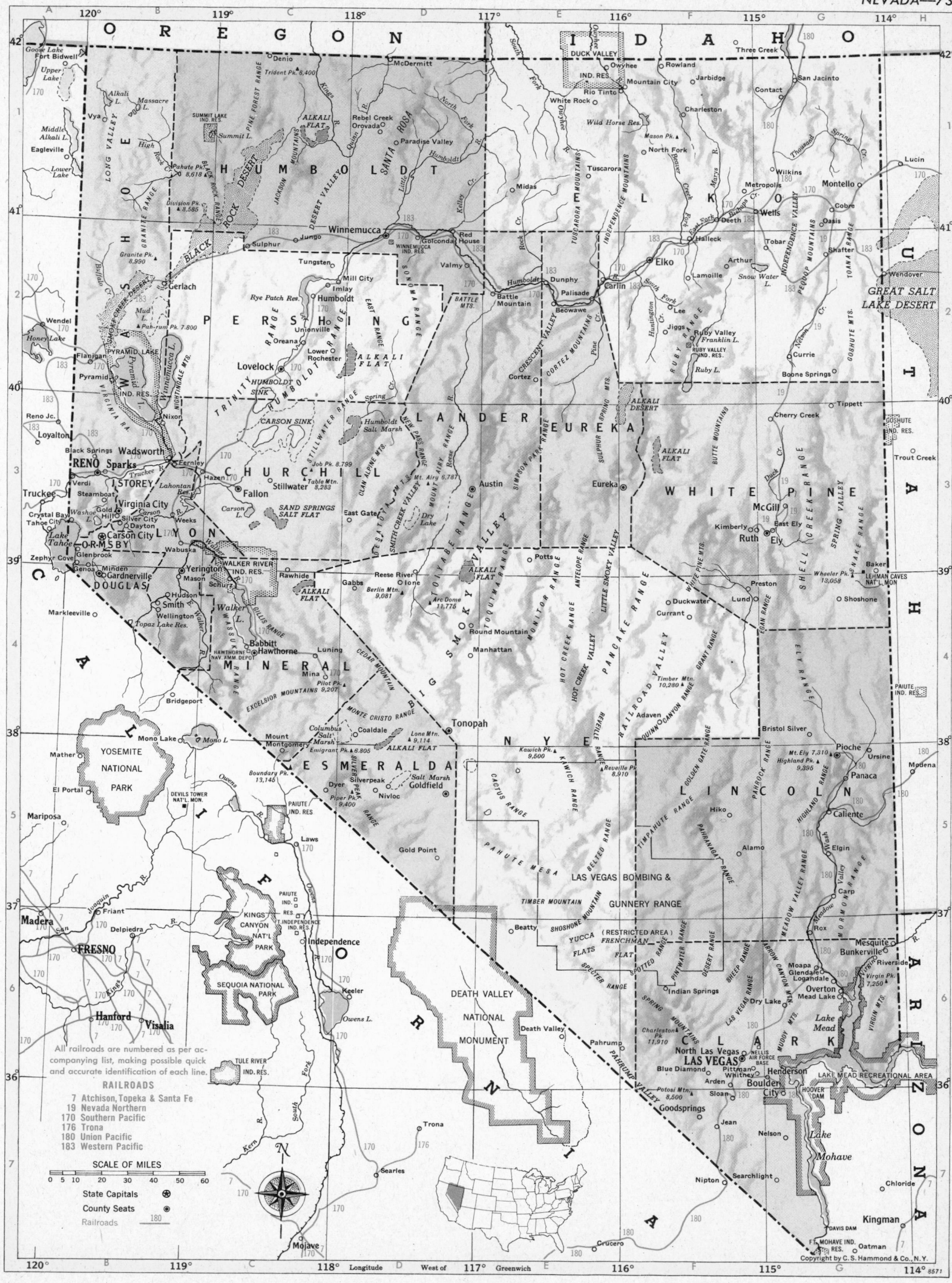

RAILROADS
7 Atchison, Topeka & Santa Fe
19 Nevada Northern
170 Southern Pacific
176 Trona
180 Union Pacific
183 Western Pacific

SCALE OF MILES
0 5 10 20 30 40 50 60

State Capitals ⊛
County Seats •
Railroads

All railroads are numbered as per accompanying list, making possible quick and accurate identification of each line.

Copyright by C. S. Hammond & Co., N. Y.

120° 119° 118° Longitude 117° West of Greenwich 116° 115° 114°

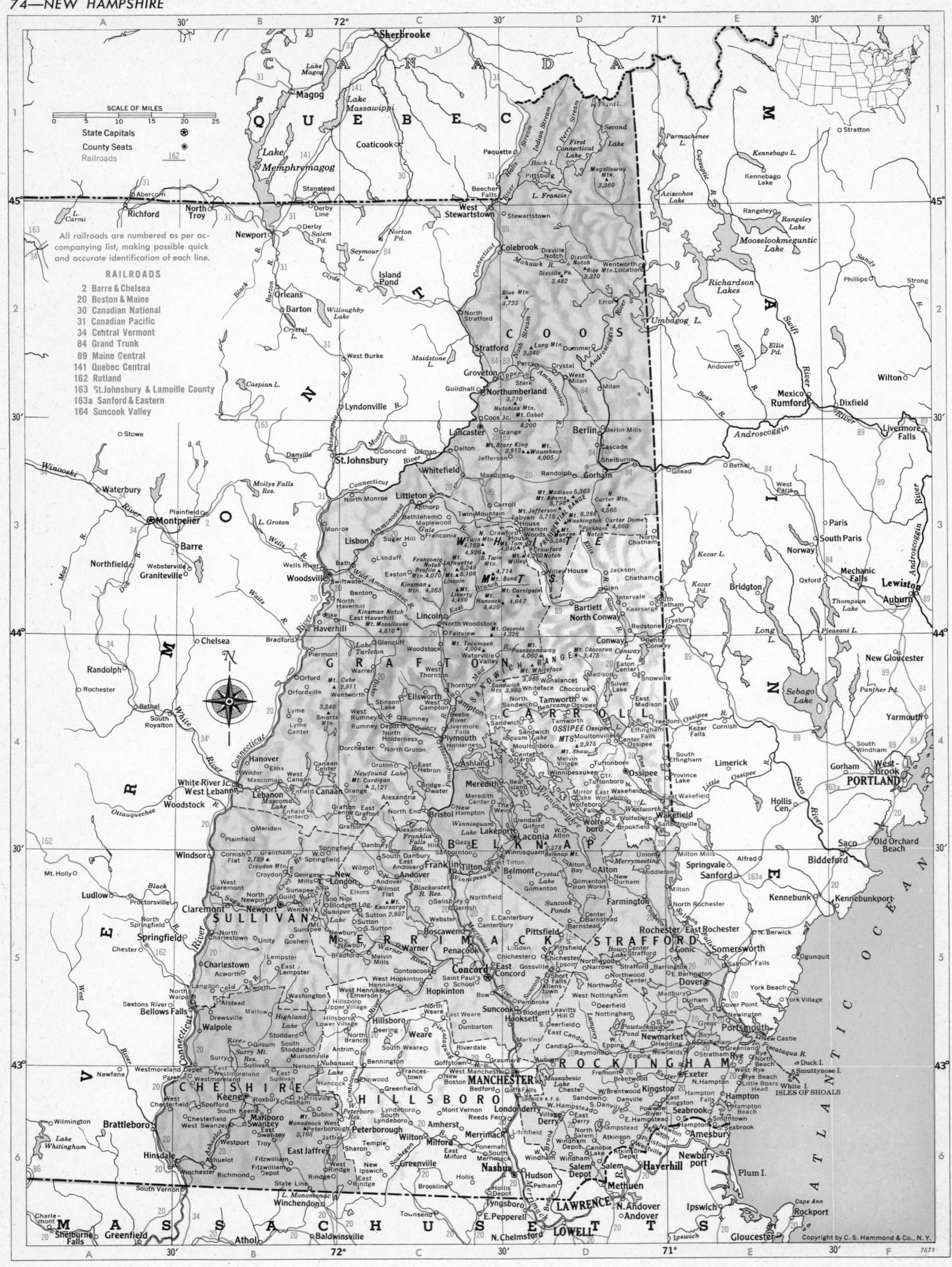

SCALE OF MILES

State Capitals
County Seats
Railroads

All railroads are numbered as per accompanying list, making possible quick and accurate identification of each line.

RAILROADS

2 Barre & Chelsea
20 Boston & Maine
30 Canadian National
31 Canadian Pacific
34 Central Vermont
84 Grand Trunk
89 Maine Central
141 Quebec Central
162 Rutland
163 St. Johnsbury & Lamoille County
163a Sanford & Eastern
164 Suncook Valley

Copyright by C. S. Hammond & Co., N.Y.

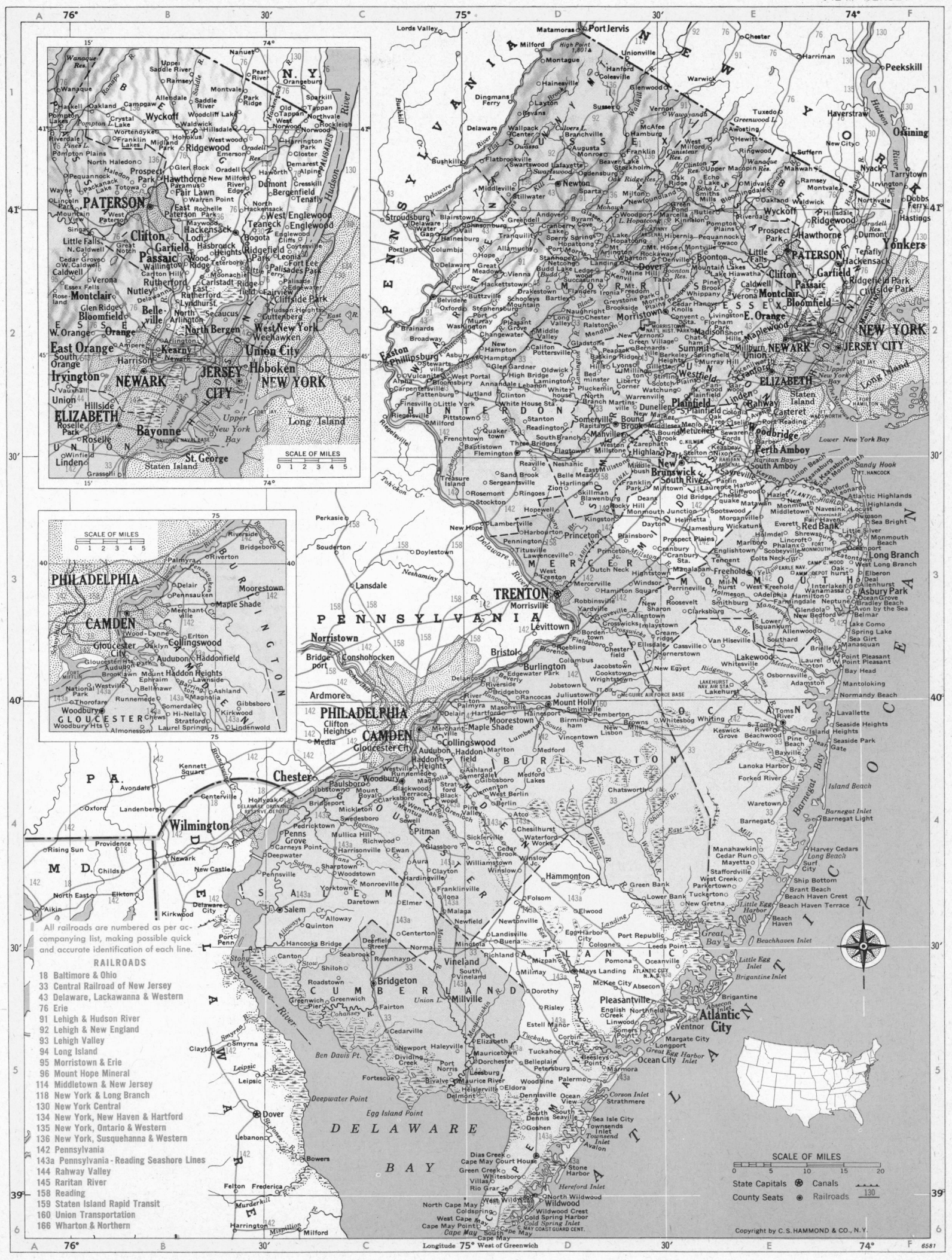

RAILROADS

18 Baltimore & Ohio
33 Central Railroad of New Jersey
43 Delaware, Lackawanna & Western
76 Erie
91 Lehigh & Hudson River
92 Lehigh & New England
93 Lehigh Valley
94 Long Island
95 Morristown & Erie
96 Mount Hope Mineral
114 Middletown & New Jersey
118 New York & Long Branch
130 New York Central
134 New York, New Haven & Hartford
135 New York, Ontario & Western
136 New York, Susquehanna & Western
142 Pennsylvania
143a Pennsylvania - Reading Seashore Lines
144 Rahway Valley
145 Raritan River
158 Reading
159 Staten Island Rapid Transit
160 Union Transportation
166 Wharton & Northern

All railroads are numbered as per accompanying list, making possible quick and accurate identification of each line.

SCALE OF MILES

State Capitals
County Seats
Canals
Railroads

6581

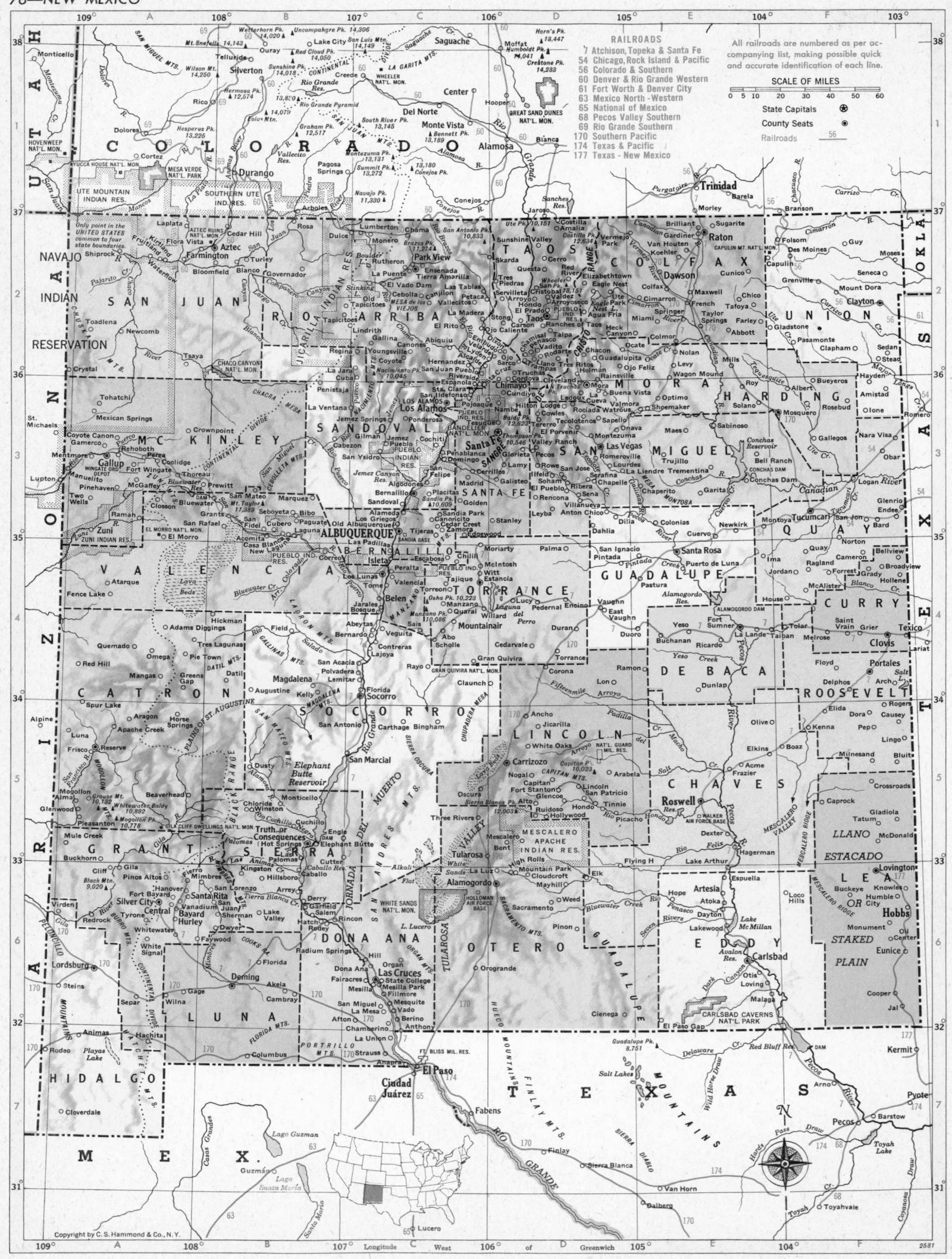

RAILROADS

All railroads are numbered as per accompanying list, making possible quick and accurate identification of each line.

7 Atchison, Topeka & Santa Fe
54 Chicago, Rock Island & Pacific
56 Colorado & Southern
60 Denver & Rio Grande Western
61 Fort Worth & Denver City
63 Mexico North-Western
65 National of Mexico
68 Pecos Valley Southern
69 Rio Grande Southern
170 Southern Pacific
174 Texas & Pacific
177 Texas-New Mexico

SCALE OF MILES

State Capitals ⊛
County Seats ⊙
Railroads

Copyright by C. S. Hammond & Co., N.Y.

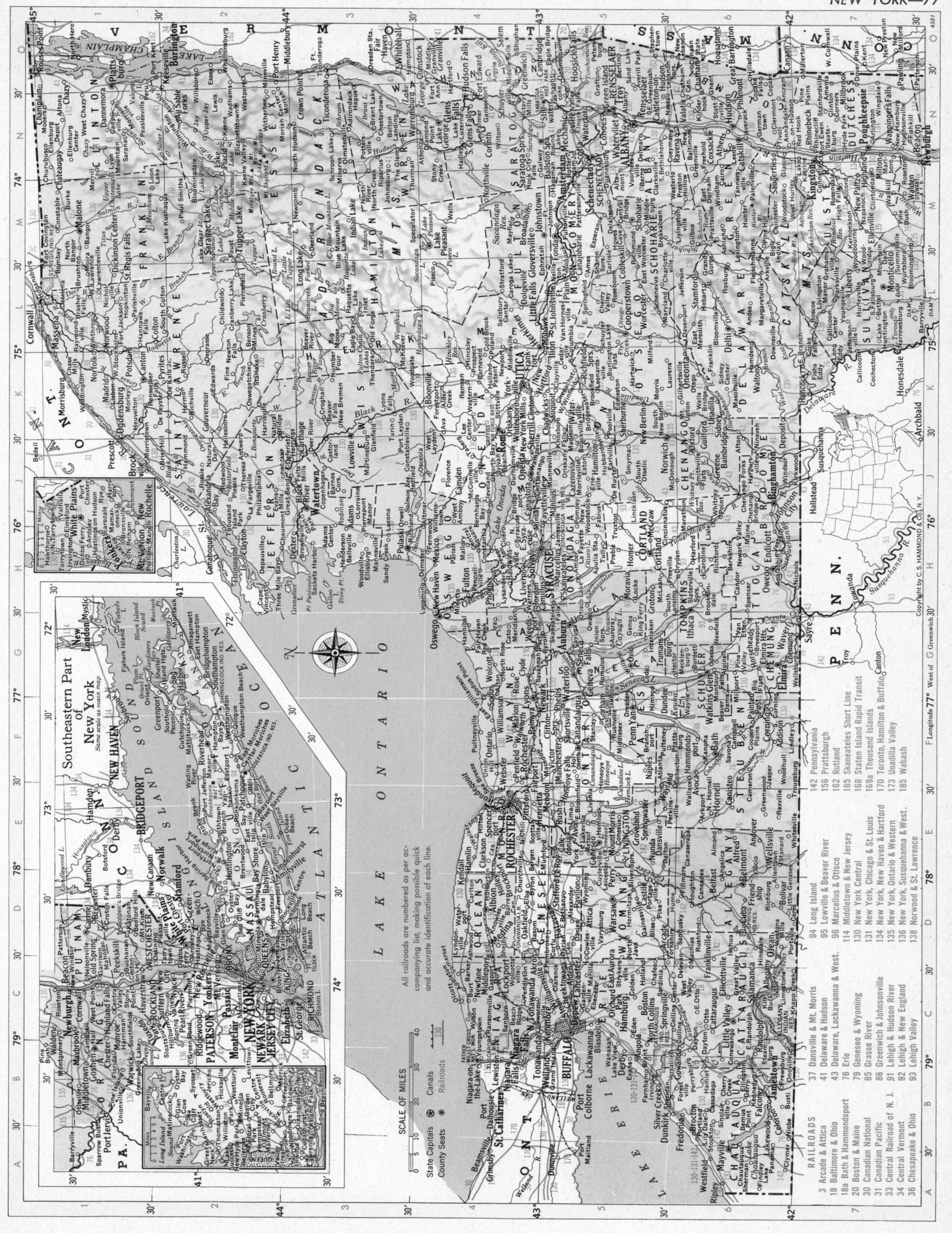

RAILROADS

3 Arcade & Attica	37 Dansville & Mt. Morris	94 Long Island	142 Pennsylvania
4 Baltimore & Ohio	41 Delaware & Hudson	95 Lowville & Beaver River	156 Prattsburg
18 Baltimore & Ohio	43 Delaware, Lackawanna & West.	96 Marcellus & Otisco	162 Rutland
18a Bath & Hammondsport	76 Erie	114 Middletown & New Jersey	165 Skaneateles Short Line
20 Boston & Maine	79 Genesee & Wyoming	130 New York, Chicago & St. Louis	168 Staten Island Rapid Transit
30 Canadian National	85 Grasse River	131 New York, Chicago & St. Louis	169a Thousand Islands
31 Canadian Pacific	86 Greenwich & Johnsonville	134 New York, New Haven & Hartford	170 Toronto, Hamilton & Buffalo
34 Central Railroad of N. J.	91 Lehigh & Hudson River	135 New York, Ontario & Western	173 Unadilla Valley
34 Central Vermont	92 Lehigh & New England	136 New York, Susquehanna & West.	185 Wabash
36 Chesapeake & Ohio	93 Lehigh Valley	138 Norwood & St. Lawrence	

SCALE OF MILES

Canals
Railroads

State Capitals
County Seats

All railroads are numbered as per accompanying list, making possible quick and accurate identification of each line.

Southeastern Part of New York
Same scale as main map

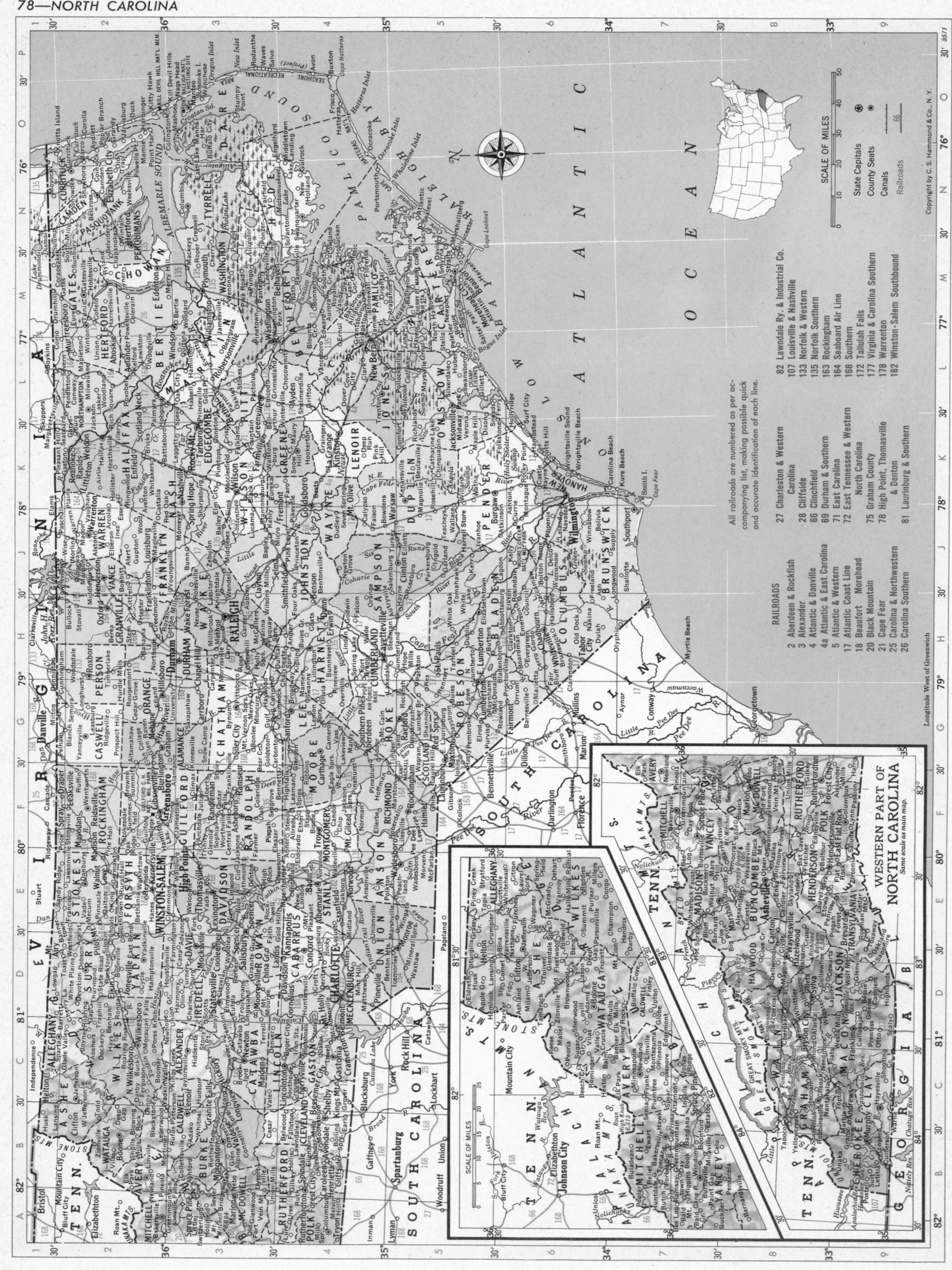

SCALE OF MILES

State Capitals
County Seats
Canals
Railroads

Copyright by C. S. Hammond & Co., N. Y.

RAILROADS

All railroads are numbered as per accompanying list, making possible quick and accurate identification of each line.

2 Aberdeen & Rockfish
4 Alexander
4 Atlantic & Danville
4a Atlantic & East Carolina
5 Atlantic & Western
17 Atlantic Coast Line
18 Beaufort Morehead
20 Black Mountain
21 Cape Fear
25 Carolina & Northwestern
26 Carolina Southern

27 Charleston & Western Carolina
28 Cliffside
66 Clinchfield
69 Durham & Southern
71 East Carolina
72 East Tennessee & Western North Carolina
75 Graham County
78 High Point, Thomasville & Denton
81 Laurinburg & Southern

82 Lawndale Ry. & Industrial Co.
107 Louisville & Nashville
133 Norfolk & Western
135 Norfolk Southern
163 Rockingham
168 Seaboard Air Line
168 Southern
172 Tallulah Falls
177 Virginia & Carolina Southern
178 Warrenton
182 Winston-Salem Southbound

WESTERN PART OF NORTH CAROLINA
Same scale as main map.

SCALE OF MILES

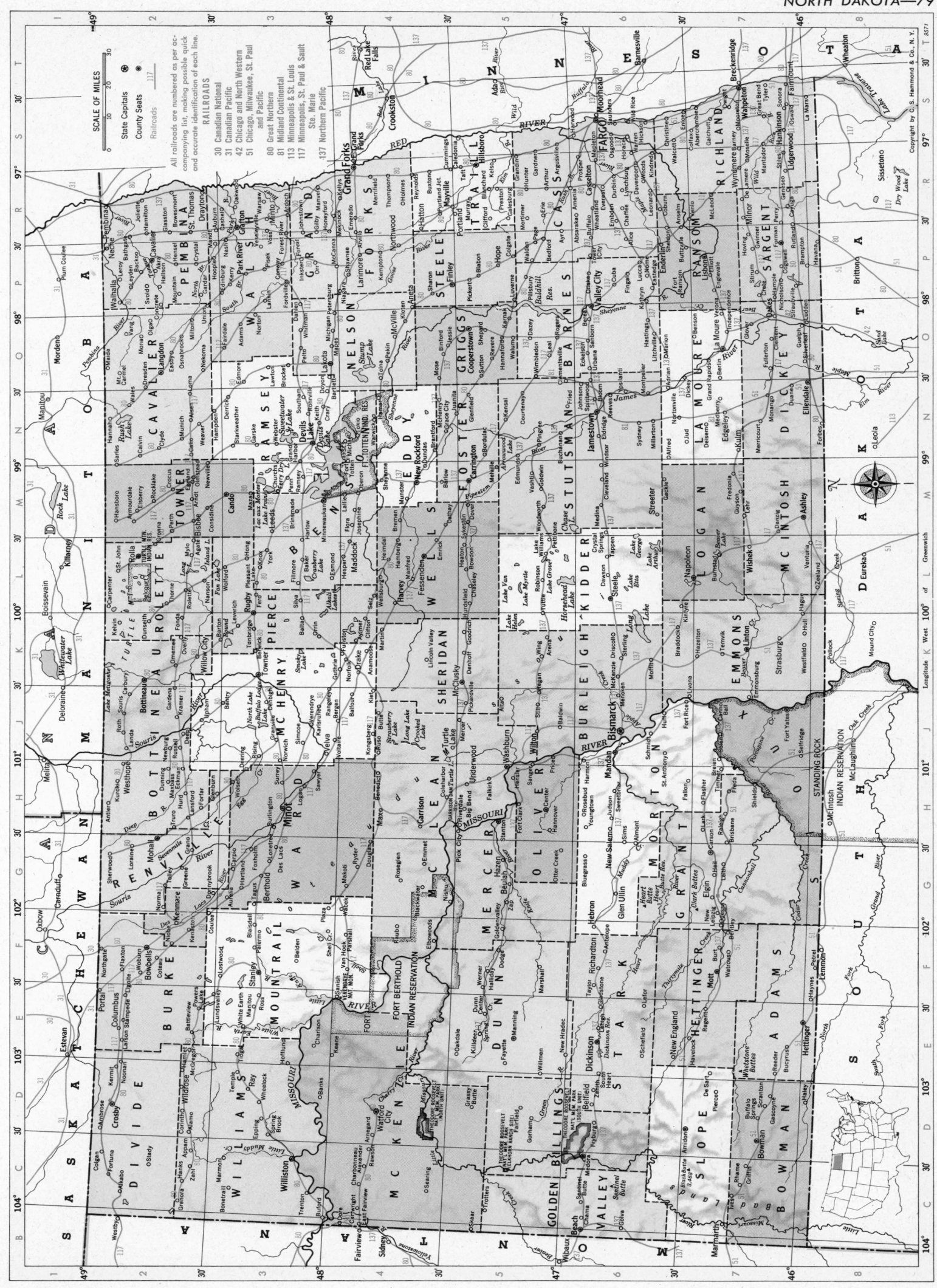

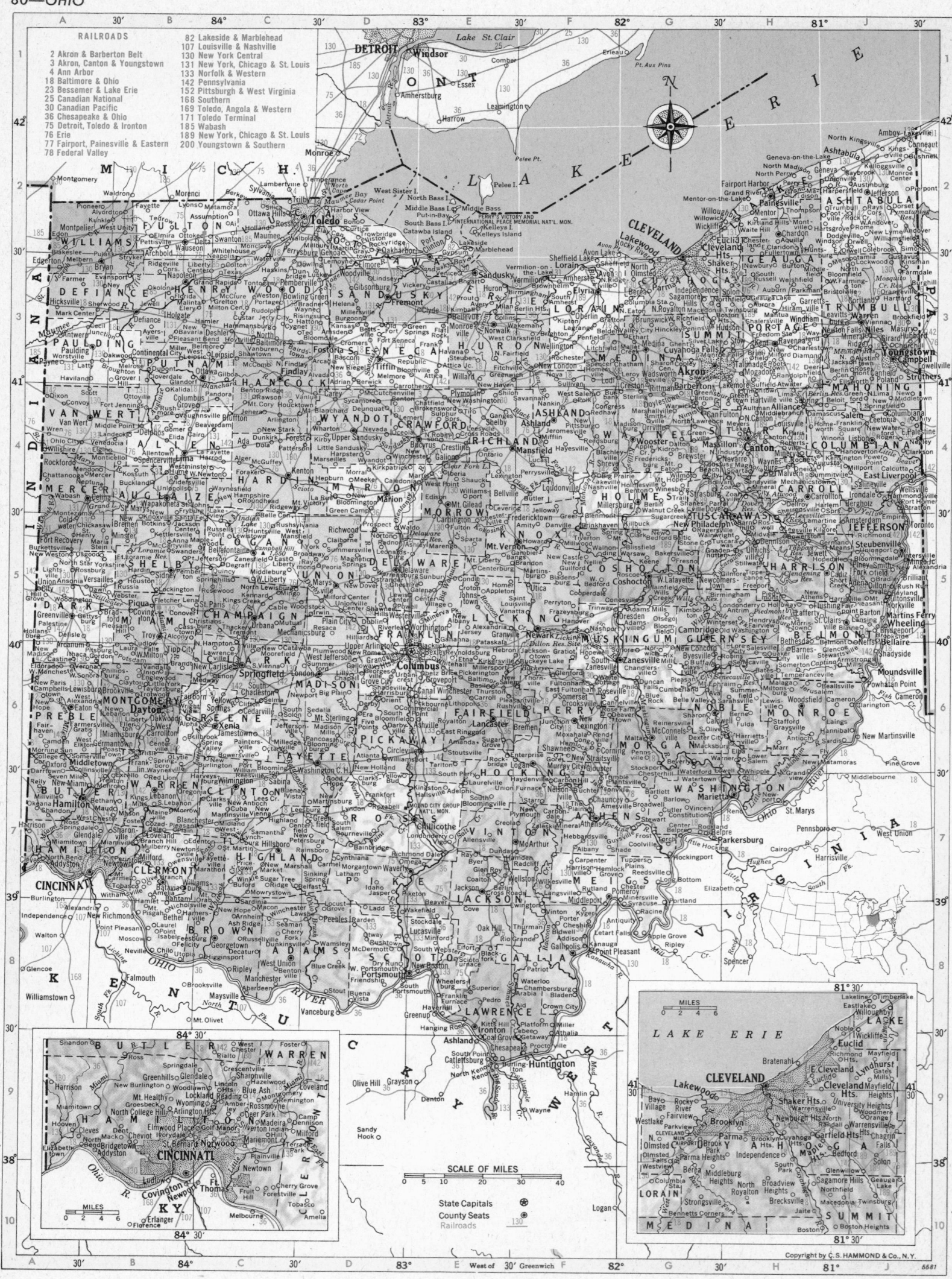

RAILROADS

2 Akron & Barberton Belt
3 Akron, Canton & Youngstown
4 Ann Arbor
18 Baltimore & Ohio
23 Bessemer & Lake Erie
25 Canadian National
30 Canadian Pacific
36 Chesapeake & Ohio
75 Detroit, Toledo & Ironton
76 Erie
77 Fairport, Painesville & Eastern
78 Federal Valley

82 Lakeside & Marblehead
107 Louisville & Nashville
130 New York Central
131 New York, Chicago & St. Louis
133 Norfolk & Western
142 Pennsylvania
152 Pittsburgh & West Virginia
168 Southern
169 Toledo, Angola & Western
171 Toledo Terminal
185 Wabash
189 New York, Chicago & St. Louis
200 Youngstown & Southern

SCALE OF MILES

State Capitals
County Seats
Railroads

Copyright by C.S. HAMMOND & Co., N.Y.

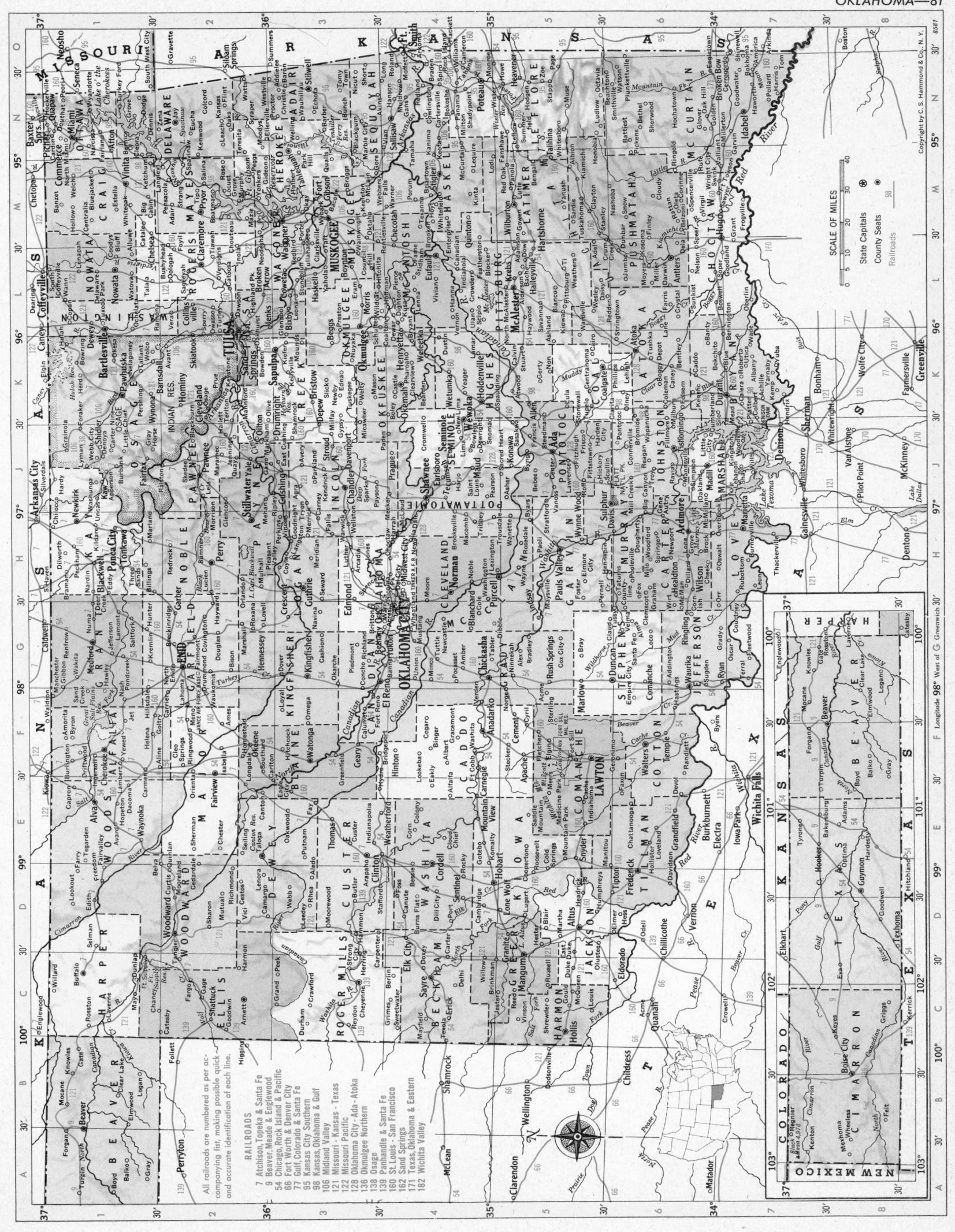

PORTLAND, SALEM
AND
VICINITY

SCALE OF MILES

All railroads are numbered as per accompanying list, making possible quick
and accurate identification of each line.

RAILROADS
1   Big Creek & Telocaset
5   City of Prineville
15   Condon, Kinzua & Southern
80   Great Northern
82   Mount Hood
137 Northern Pacific
138 Oregon & Northwestern
139 Oregon, California & Eastern
139a Oregon Electric
140 Oregon Pacific & Eastern
141 Oregon Trunk
142 Portland Traction
170 Southern Pacific
171 Spokane, Portland & Seattle
172 Sumpter Valley
180 Union Pacific
180a Union R. R. of Oregon
182 Valley and Siletz
190 Willamina & Grand Ronde

SCALE OF MILES

State Capitals ⊛
County Seats ⊚
Railroads

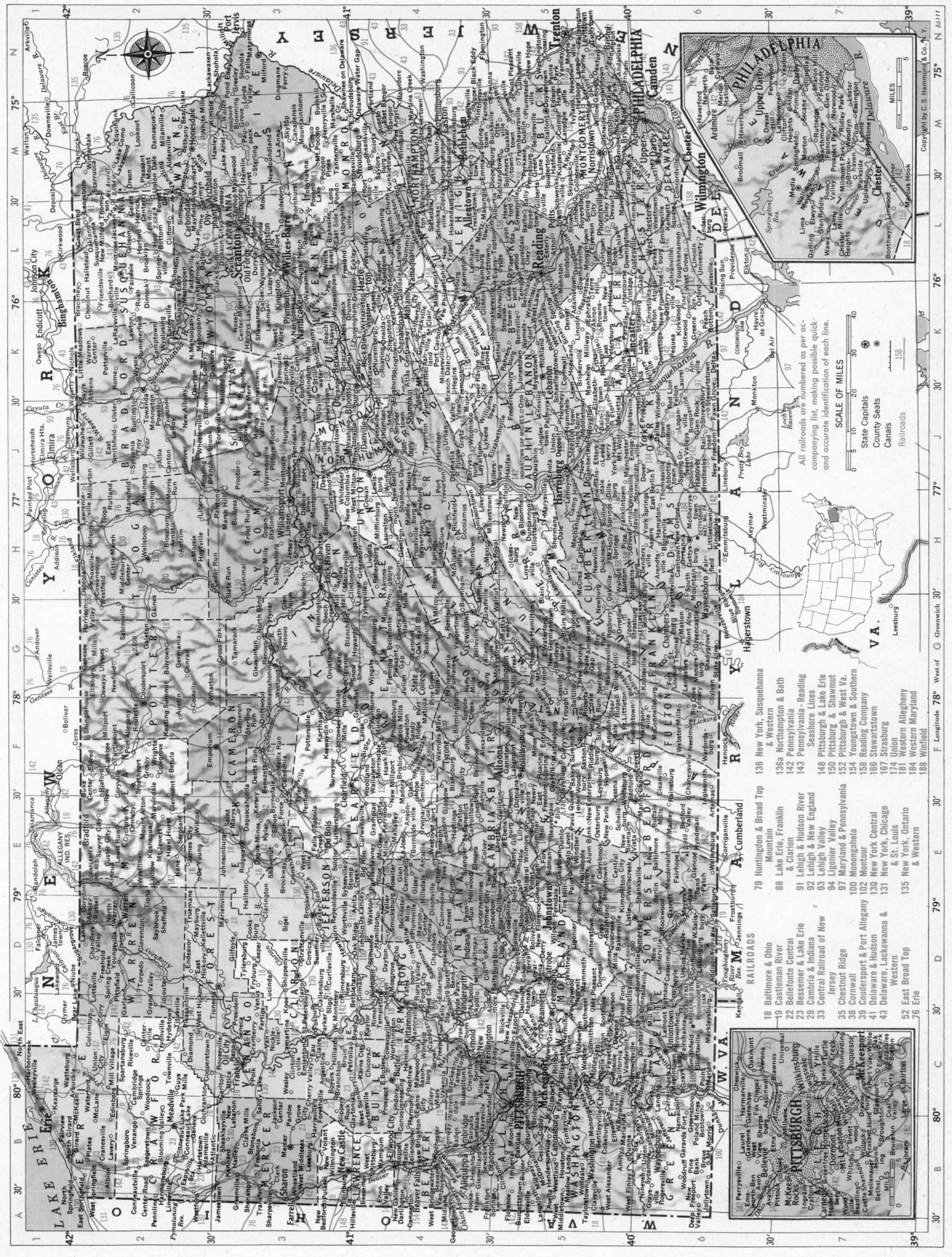

PHILADELPHIA

PITTSBURGH

SCALE OF MILES

All railroads are numbered as per accompanying list, making possible quick and accurate identification of each line.

State Capitals
County Seats
Canals
Railroads

RAILROADS

18	Baltimore & Ohio
19	Castleman River
22	Bellefonte Central
23	Bessemer & Lake Erie
29	Cambria & Indiana
33	Central Railroad of New Jersey
35	Chestnut Ridge
38	Cornwall
41	Coudersport & Port Allegany
43	Delaware & Hudson
43	Delaware, Lackawanna & Western
52	East Broad Top
76	Erie

79	Huntingdon & Broad Top Mountain
88	Lake Erie, Franklin & Clarion
91	Lehigh & Hudson River
92	Lehigh & New England
93	Lehigh Valley
94	Ligonier Valley
97	Maryland & Pennsylvania
100	Monongahela
102	New York Central
130	New York, Chicago & St. Louis
131	New York, Ontario & Western
135	New York, Susquehanna & Western

136	New York, Susquehanna & Western
136a	Northampton & Bath
142	Pennsylvania
143	Pennsylvania - Reading Seashore Lines
148	Pittsburgh & Lake Erie
150	Pittsburgh & Shawmut
152	Pittsburgh & West Va.
154	Youngstown & Southern
158	Reading Company
166	Montour
167	Strasburg
174	Union
181	Western Allegheny
184	Western Maryland
188	Winfield

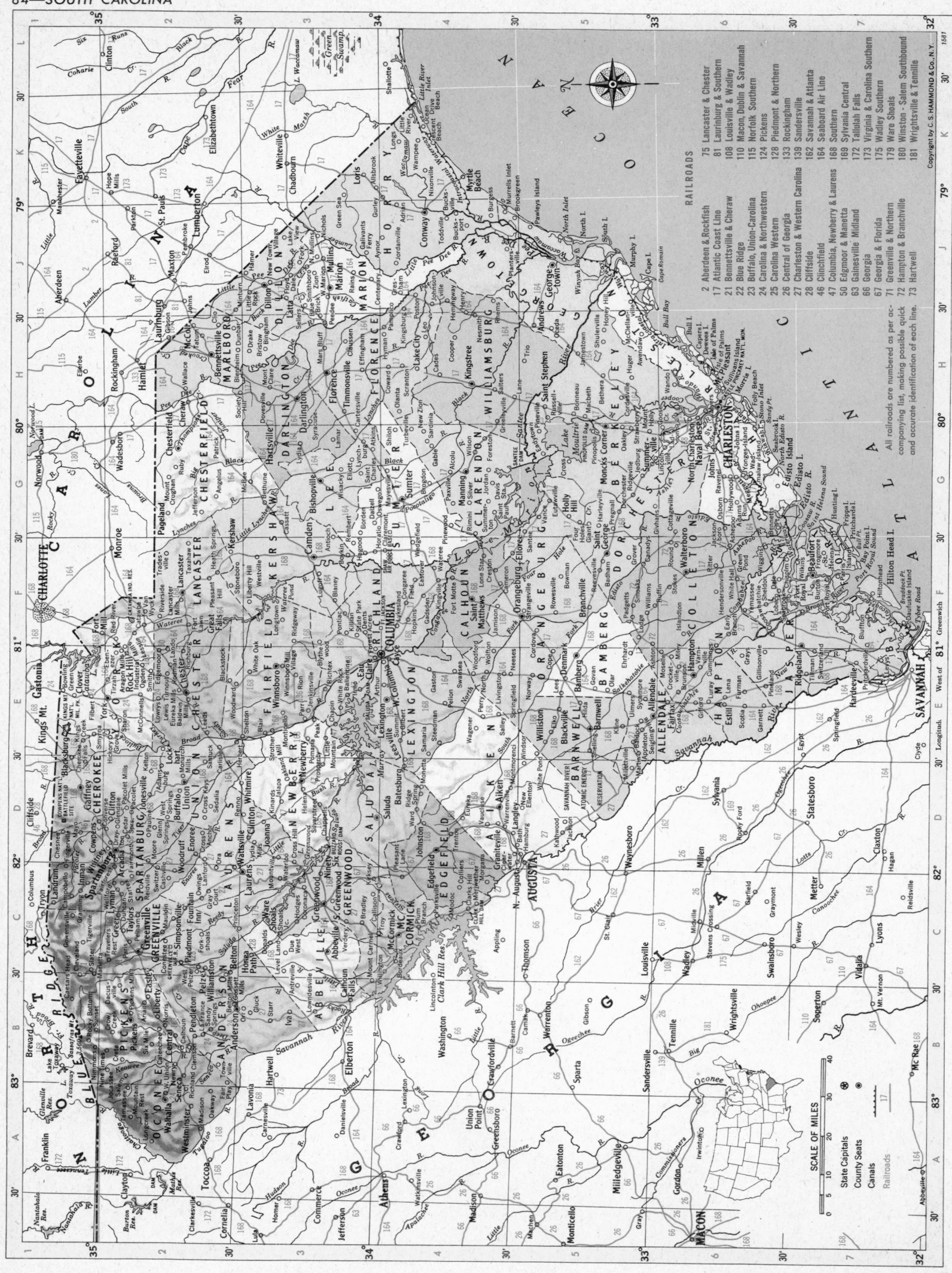

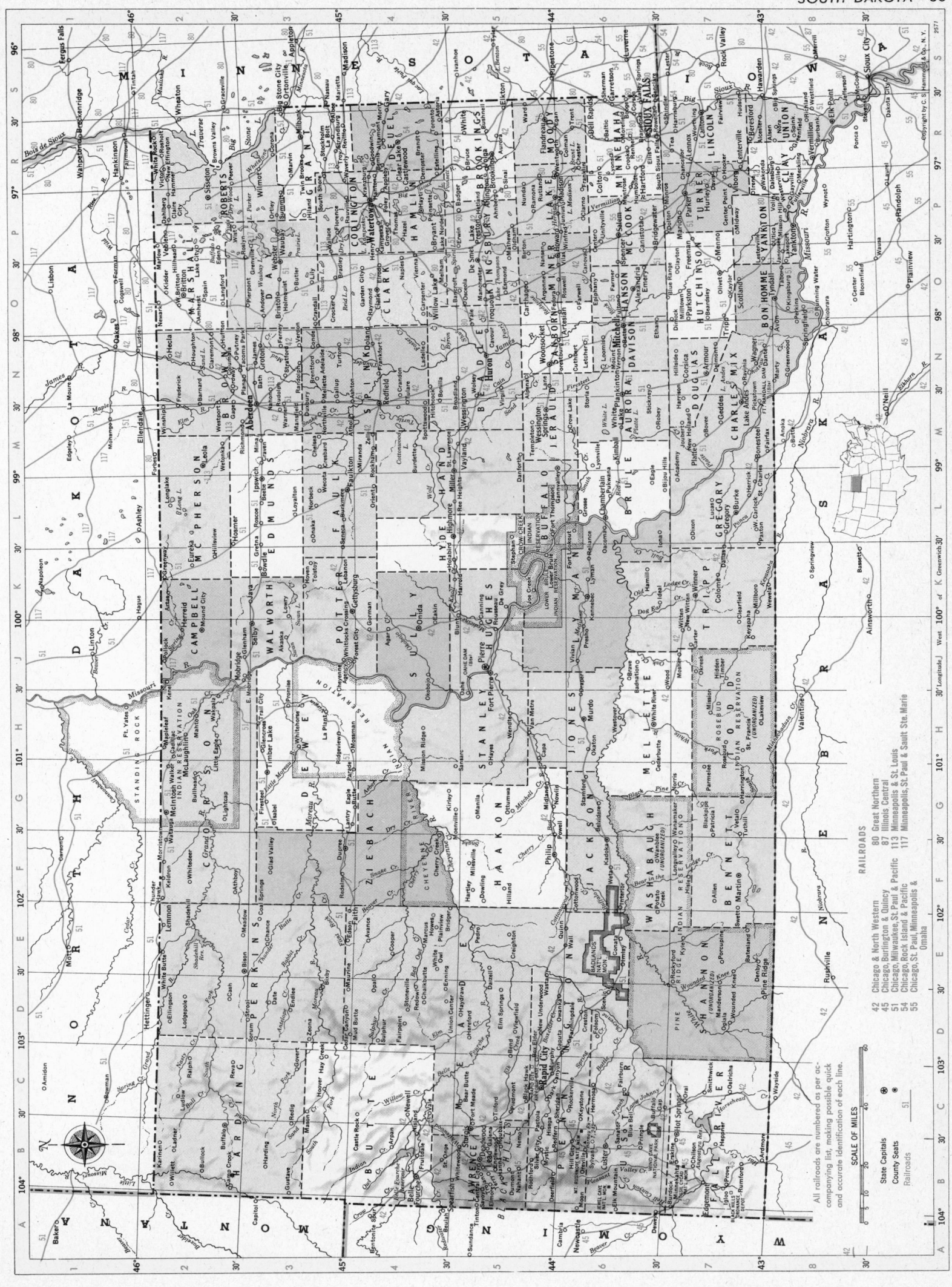

All railroads are numbered as per accompanying list, making possible quick and accurate identification of each line.

SCALE OF MILES

State Capitals ⊛
County Seats ◉
Railroads 51

RAILROADS
42 Chicago & North Western
45 Chicago, Burlington & Quincy
51 Chicago, Milwaukee, St Paul & Pacific
54 Chicago, Rock Island & Pacific
55 Chicago, St Paul, Minneapolis & Omaha
80 Great Northern
87 Illinois Central
113 Minneapolis & St Louis
117 Minneapolis, St Paul & Sault Ste. Marie

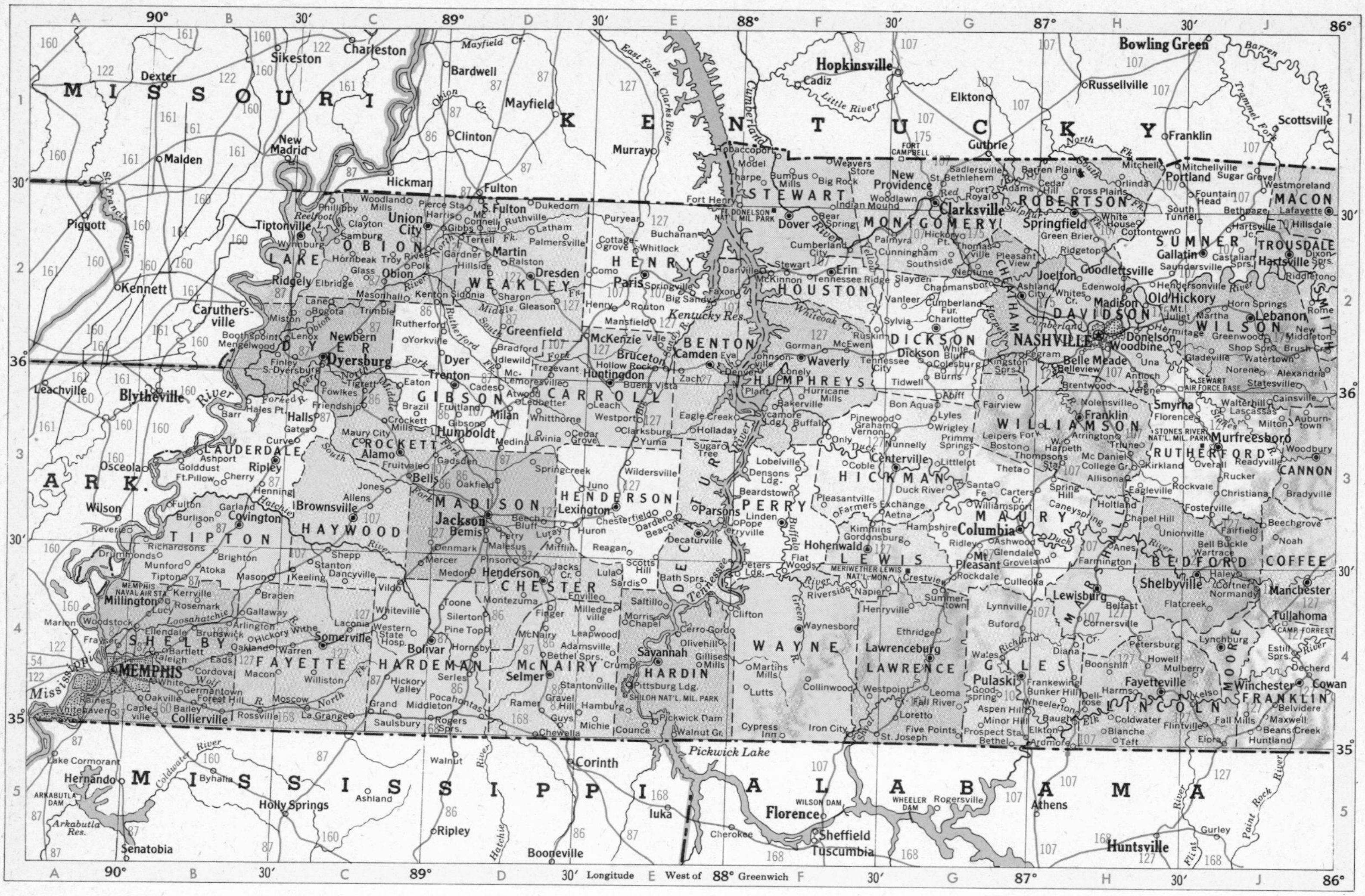
MISSOURI
KENTUCKY
ARK.
MISSISSIPPI
ALABAMA
Longitude West of 88° Greenwich
NASHVILLE
MEMPHIS
Jackson
Clarksville
Columbia
Bowling Green
Hopkinsville
Pickwick Lake
Kentucky Res.
SHILOH NAT'L. MIL. PARK
STONES RIVER NAT'L. MIL. PARK
SEWART AIR FORCE BASE
MEMPHIS NAVAL AIR STA.
CAMP FORREST
WILSON DAM
WHEELER DAM
MERIWETHER LEWIS NAT'L. MON.

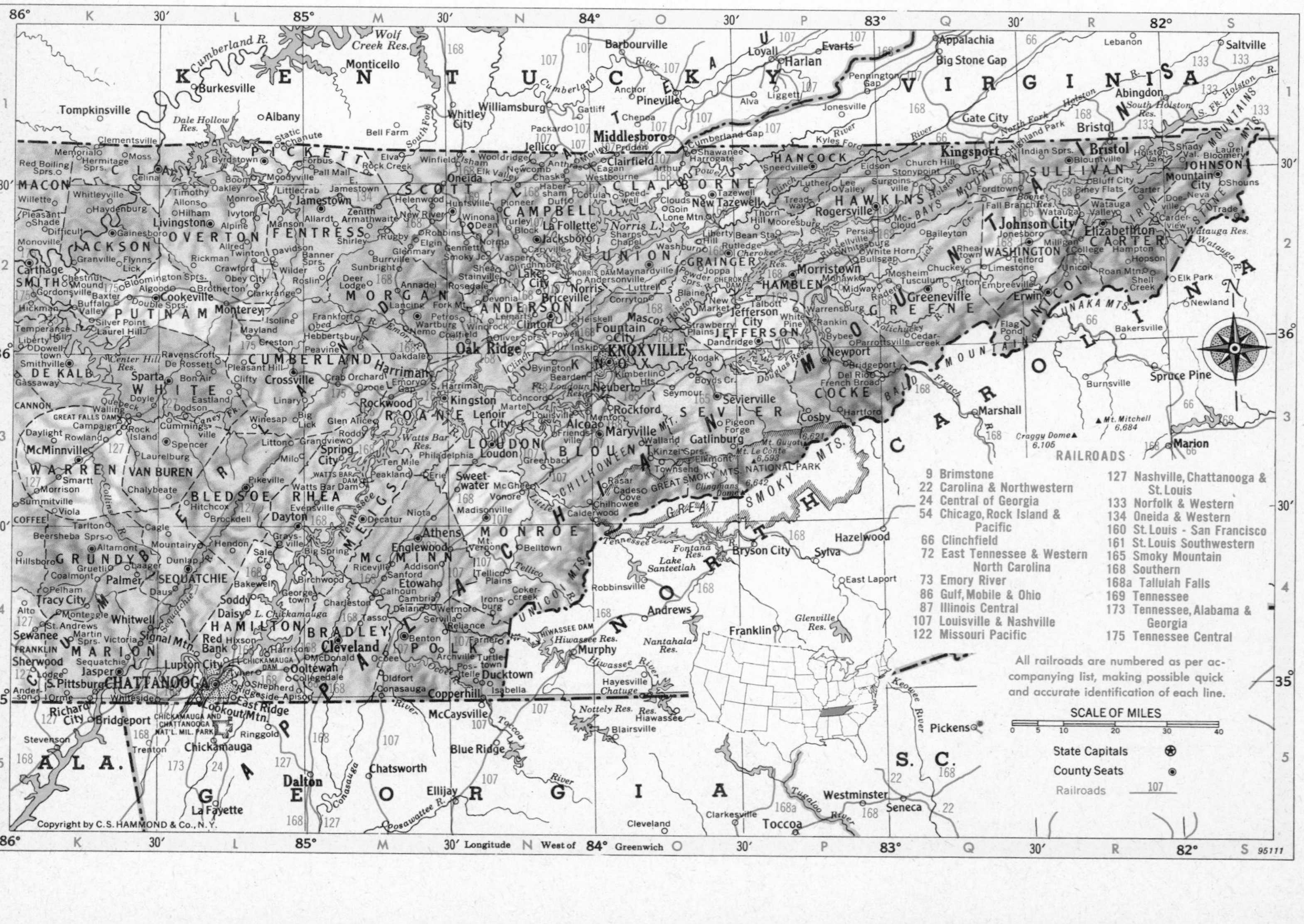
KENTUCKY
VIRGINIA
NORTH CAROLINA
GEORGIA
ALA.
S. C.
KNOXVILLE
CHATTANOOGA
Oak Ridge
Johnson City
Kingsport
Bristol
GREAT SMOKY MTS. NATIONAL PARK
CHICKAMAUGA AND CHATTANOOGA NAT'L. MIL. PARK
Longitude West of 84° Greenwich
RAILROADS
9 Brimstone
22 Carolina & Northwestern
24 Central of Georgia
54 Chicago, Rock Island & Pacific
66 Clinchfield
72 East Tennessee & Western North Carolina
73 Emory River
86 Gulf, Mobile & Ohio
87 Illinois Central
107 Louisville & Nashville
122 Missouri Pacific
127 Nashville, Chattanooga & St. Louis
133 Norfolk & Western
134 Oneida & Western
160 St. Louis - San Francisco
161 St. Louis Southwestern
165 Smoky Mountain
168 Southern
168a Tallulah Falls
169 Tennessee
173 Tennessee, Alabama & Georgia
175 Tennessee Central
All railroads are numbered as per accompanying list, making possible quick and accurate identification of each line.
SCALE OF MILES
0 5 10 20 30 40
State Capitals
County Seats
Railroads 107
Copyright by C.S. HAMMOND & Co., N.Y.
95111

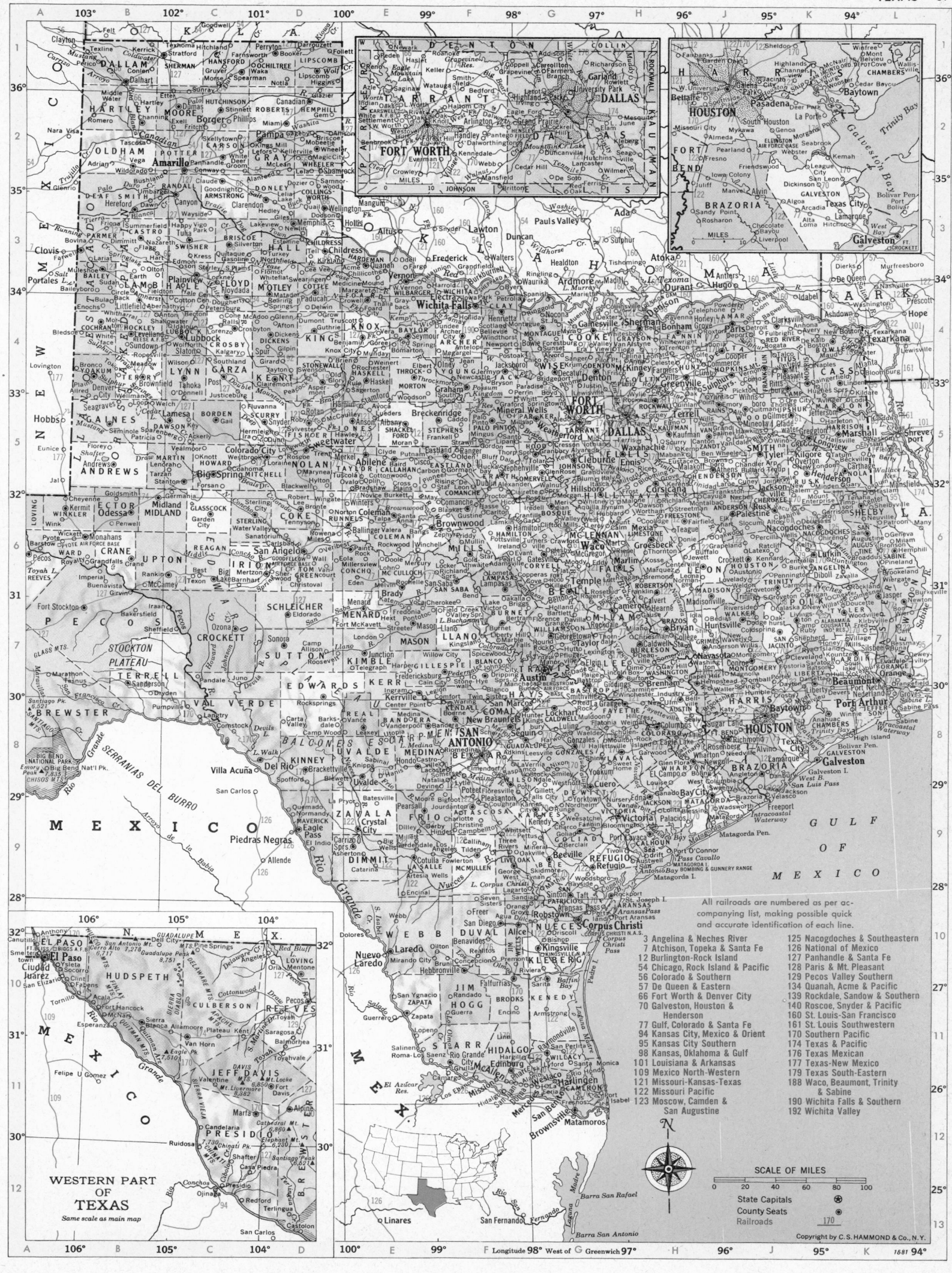

WESTERN PART OF TEXAS
Same scale as main map

All railroads are numbered as per accompanying list, making possible quick and accurate identification of each line.

3 Angelina & Neches River
7 Atchison, Topeka & Santa Fe
12 Burlington-Rock Island
54 Chicago, Rock Island & Pacific
56 Colorado & Southern
57 De Queen & Eastern
66 Fort Worth & Denver City
70 Galveston, Houston & Henderson
77 Gulf, Colorado & Santa Fe
94 Kansas City, Mexico & Orient
95 Kansas City Southern
98 Kansas, Oklahoma & Gulf
101 Louisiana & Arkansas
109 Mexico North-Western
121 Missouri-Kansas-Texas
122 Missouri Pacific
123 Moscow, Camden & San Augustine

125 Nacogdoches & Southeastern
126 National of Mexico
127 Panhandle & Santa Fe
128 Paris & Mt. Pleasant
129 Pecos Valley Southern
134 Quanah, Acme & Pacific
139 Rockdale, Sandow & Southern
140 Roscoe, Snyder & Pacific
160 St. Louis-San Francisco
161 St. Louis Southwestern
170 Southern Pacific
174 Texas & Pacific
176 Texas Mexican
177 Texas-New Mexico
179 Texas South-Eastern
188 Waco, Beaumont, Trinity & Sabine
190 Wichita Falls & Southern
192 Wichita Valley

SCALE OF MILES
0   20   40   60   80   100

⊛ State Capitals
⊙ County Seats
Railroads   170

Copyright by C. S. HAMMOND & Co., N.Y.

1681   94°

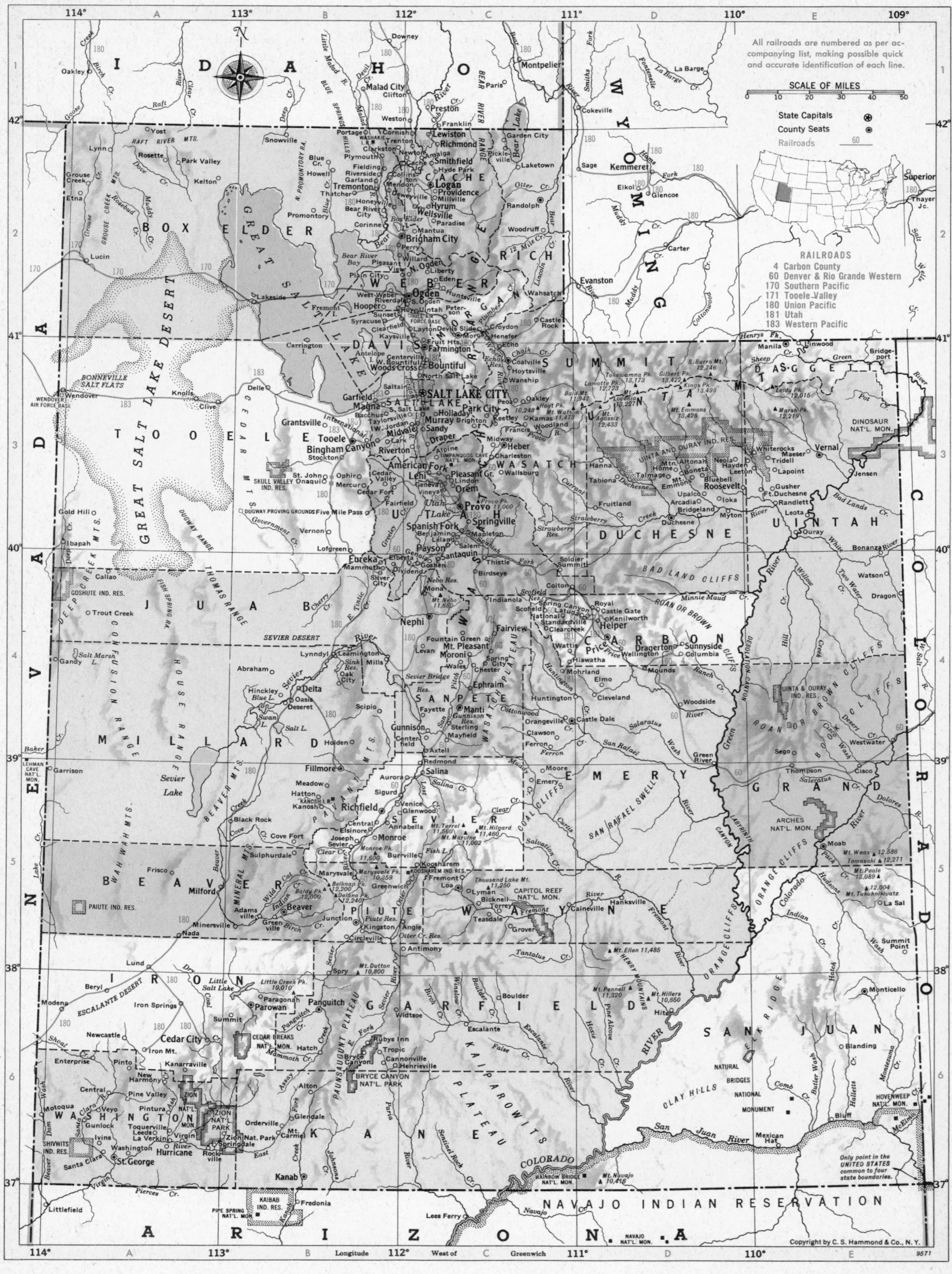

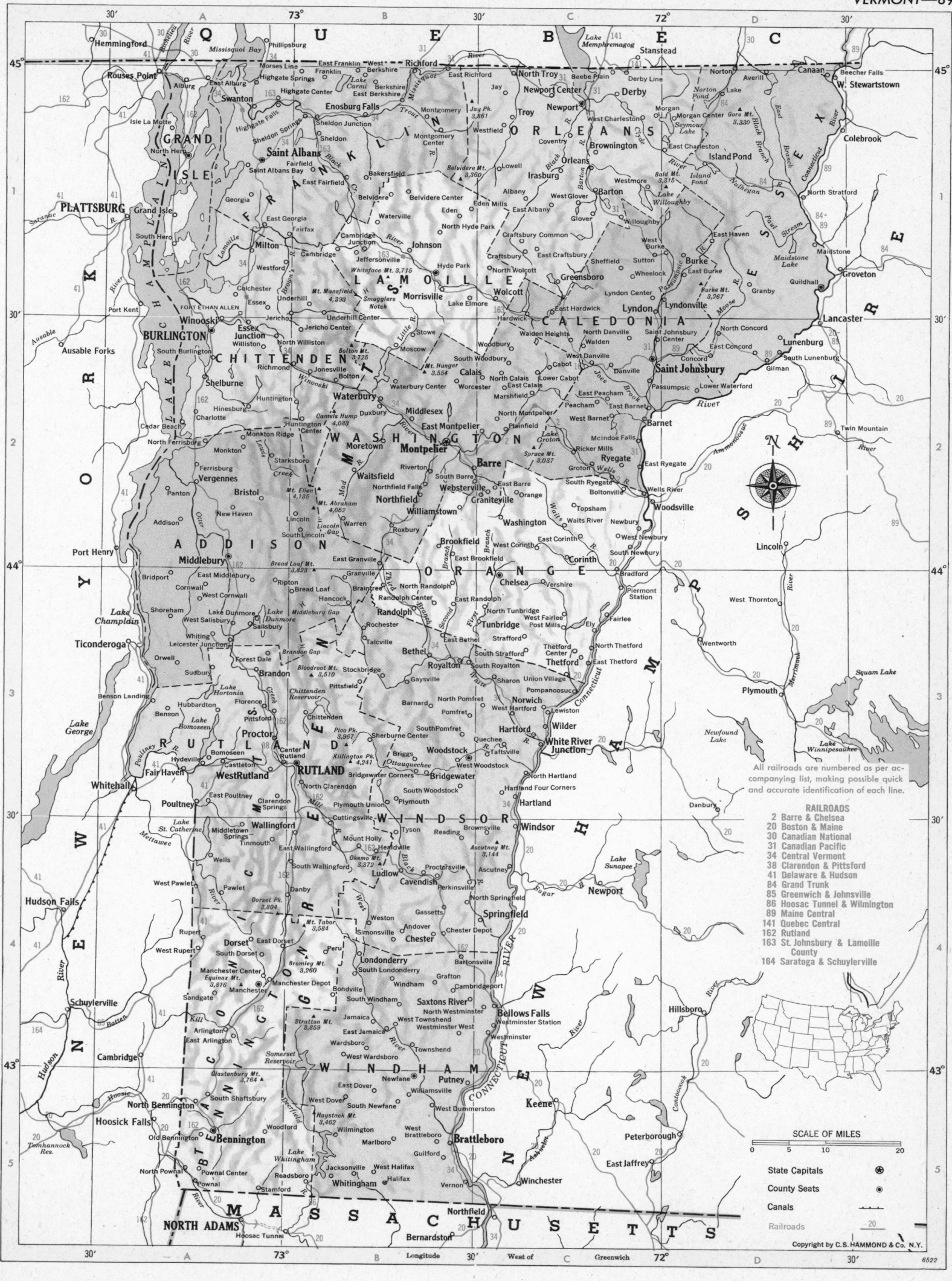

Map of Vermont

RAILROADS

2	Barre & Chelsea
20	Boston & Maine
30	Canadian National
31	Canadian Pacific
34	Central Vermont
38	Clarendon & Pittsford
41	Delaware & Hudson
84	Grand Trunk
85	Greenwich & Johnsville
86	Hoosac Tunnel & Wilmington
89	Maine Central
141	Quebec Central
162	Rutland
163	St. Johnsbury & Lamoille County
164	Saratoga & Schuylerville

All railroads are numbered as per accompanying list, making possible quick and accurate identification of each line.

SCALE OF MILES
0   20

State Capitals
County Seats
Canals
Railroads   20

6522

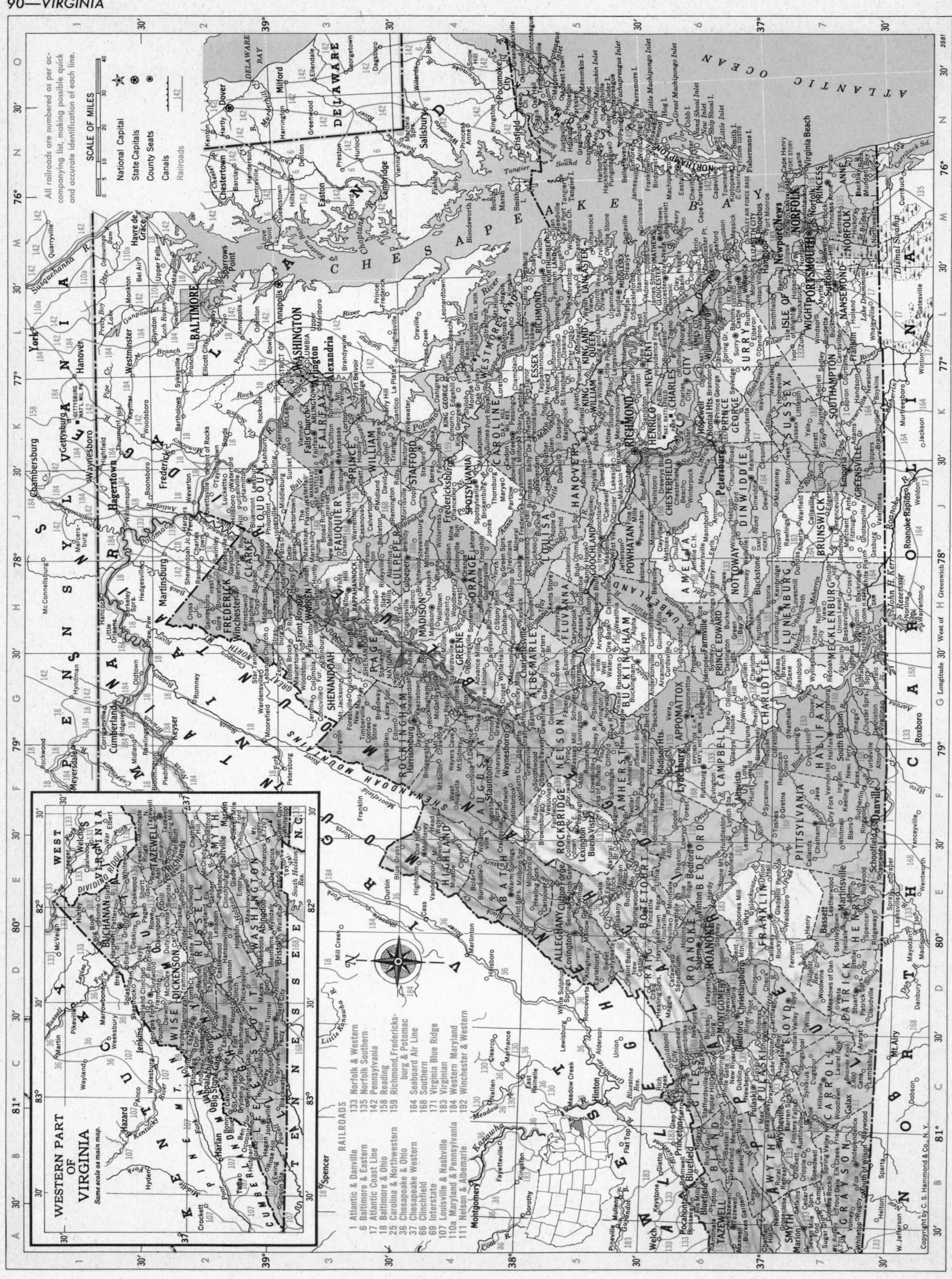

All railroads are numbered as per accompanying list, making possible quick and accurate identification of each line.

National Capital
State Capitals
County Seats
Canals
Railroads

SCALE OF MILES

WESTERN PART OF VIRGINIA
Same scale as main map.

RAILROADS
1 Atlantic & Danville
6 Baltimore & Eastern
17 Atlantic Coast Line
25 Baltimore & Ohio
36 Carolina & Northwestern
37 Chesapeake & Ohio
66 Clinchfield
69 Interstate
107 Louisville & Nashville
110a Maryland & Pennsylvania
111 Nelson & Albemarle

130 Montgomery
133 Norfolk & Western
135 Norfolk Southern
142 Pennsylvania
158 Reading
159 Richmond, Fredericksburg & Potomac
164 Seaboard Air Line
168 Southern
171 Virginia Blue Ridge
183 Virginian
184 Western Maryland
192 Winchester & Western

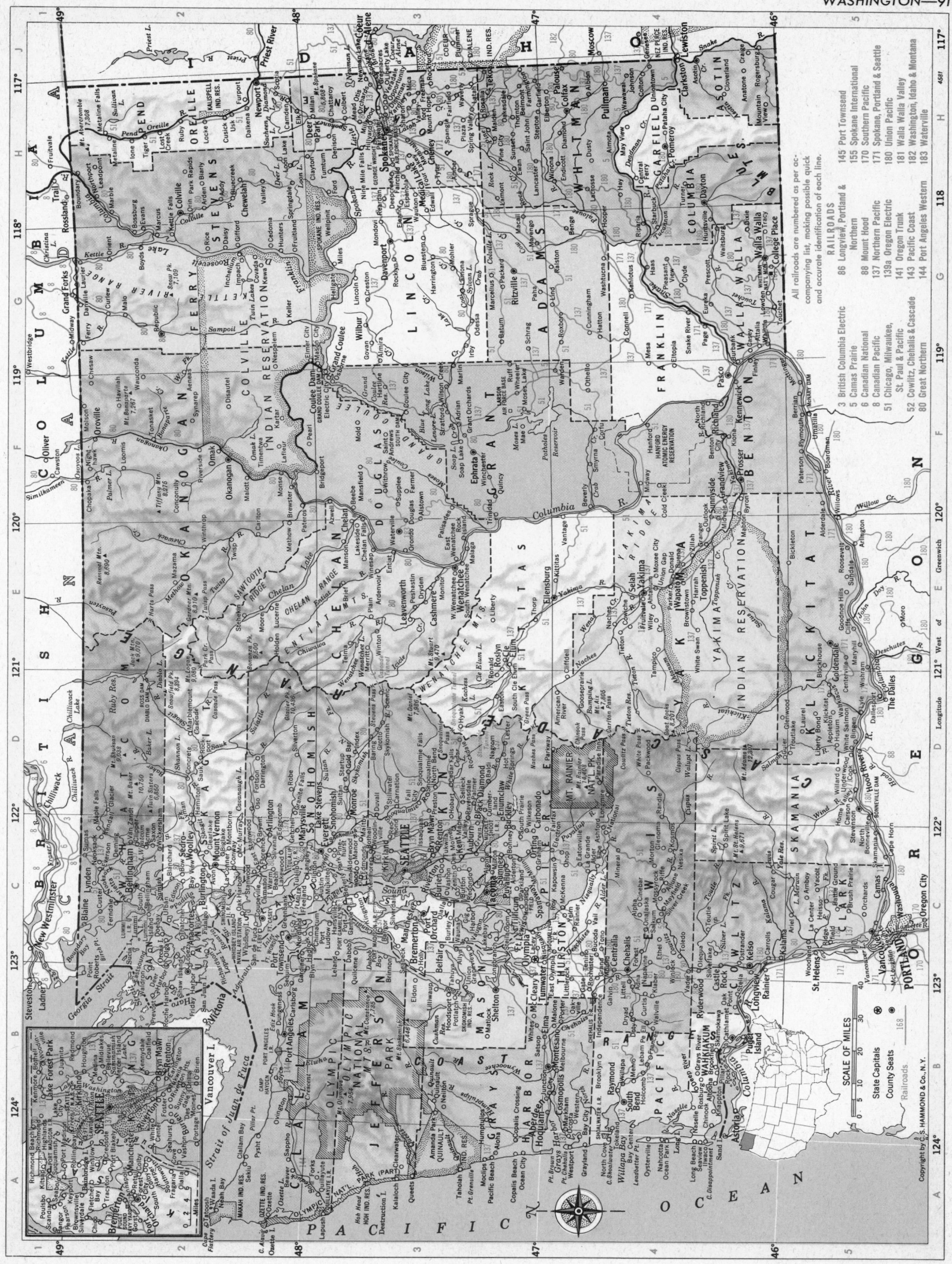

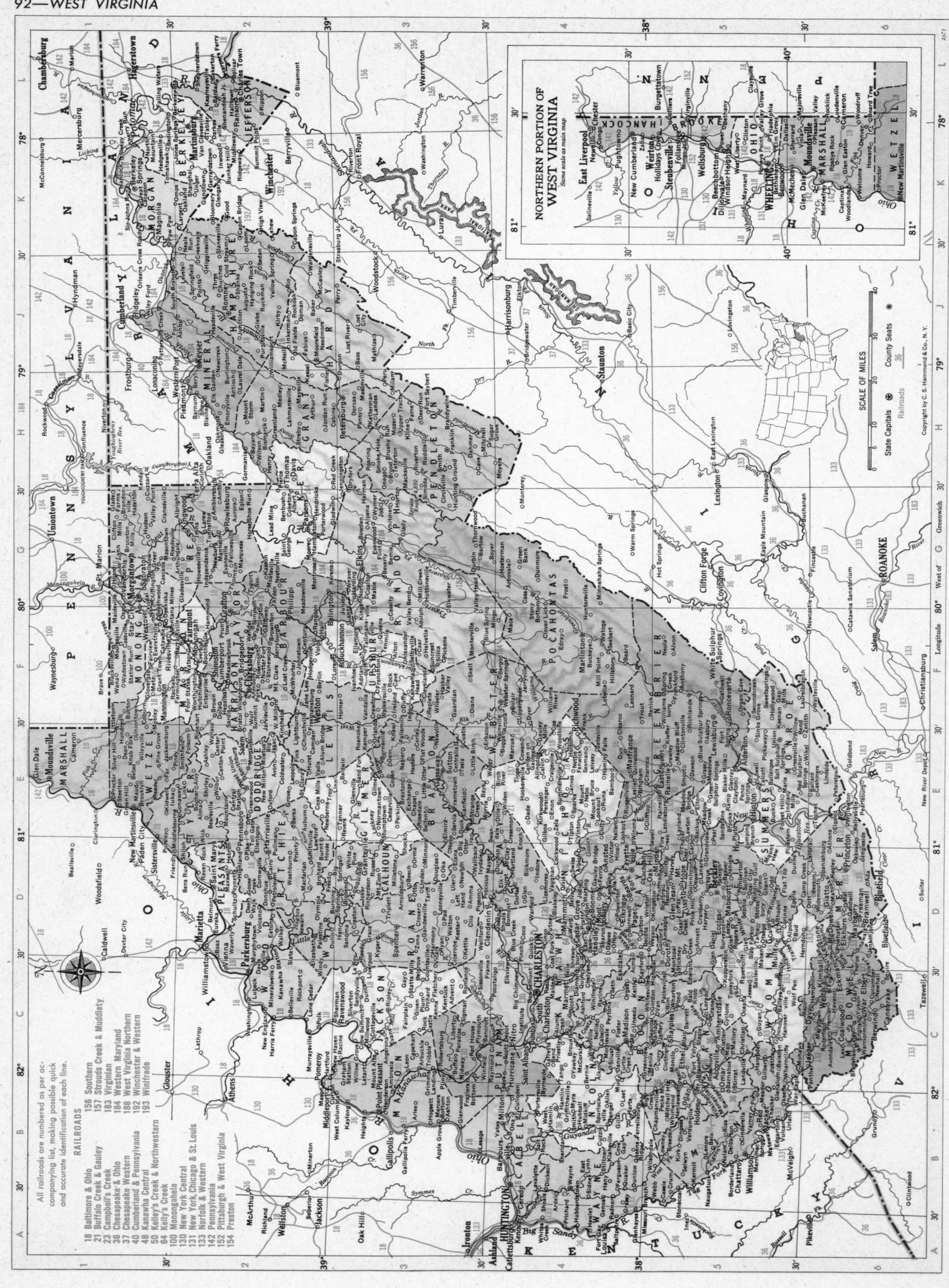

NORTHERN PORTION OF
WEST VIRGINIA
Same scale as main map

RAILROADS

18	Baltimore & Ohio	156	Southern
21	Buffalo Creek & Gauley	157	Strouds Creek & Muddlety
23	Campbell's Creek	183	Virginian
36	Chesapeake & Ohio	184	Western Maryland
37	Chesapeake Western	188	West Virginia Northern
40	Cumberland & Pennsylvania	192	Winchester & Western
48	Kanawha Central	193	Winifrede
50	Kelley's Creek & Northwestern		
64	Kelly's Creek		
100	Monongahela		
130	New York Central		
131	New York, Chicago & St. Louis		
133	Norfolk & Western		
142	Pennsylvania		
152	Pittsburgh & West Virginia		
154	Preston		

All railroads are numbered as per accompanying list, making possible quick and accurate identification of each line.

SCALE OF MILES

State Capitals ⊛
County Seats ●
Railroads

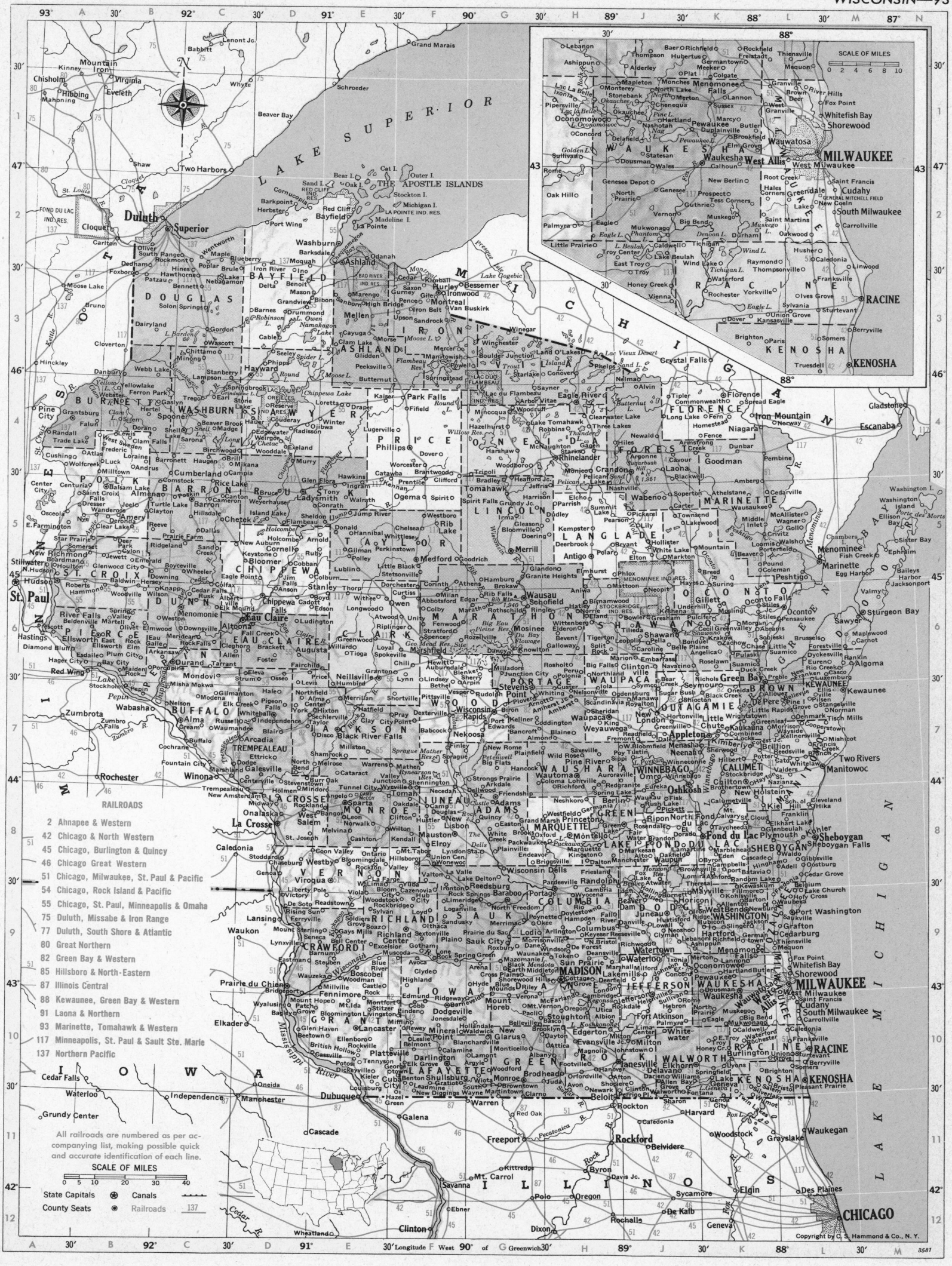

RAILROADS

2 Ahnapee & Western
42 Chicago & North Western
45 Chicago, Burlington & Quincy
46 Chicago Great Western
51 Chicago, Milwaukee, St. Paul & Pacific
54 Chicago, Rock Island & Pacific
55 Chicago, St. Paul, Minneapolis & Omaha
75 Duluth, Missabe & Iron Range
77 Duluth, South Shore & Atlantic
80 Great Northern
82 Green Bay & Western
85 Hillsboro & North-Eastern
87 Illinois Central
88 Kewaunee, Green Bay & Western
91 Laona & Northern
93 Marinette, Tomahawk & Western
117 Minneapolis, St. Paul & Sault Ste. Marie
137 Northern Pacific

All railroads are numbered as per accompanying list, making possible quick
and accurate identification of each line.

SCALE OF MILES

State Capitals ⊛ Canals
County Seats ⊙ Railroads 137

Copyright by C. S. Hammond & Co., N.Y.

3581

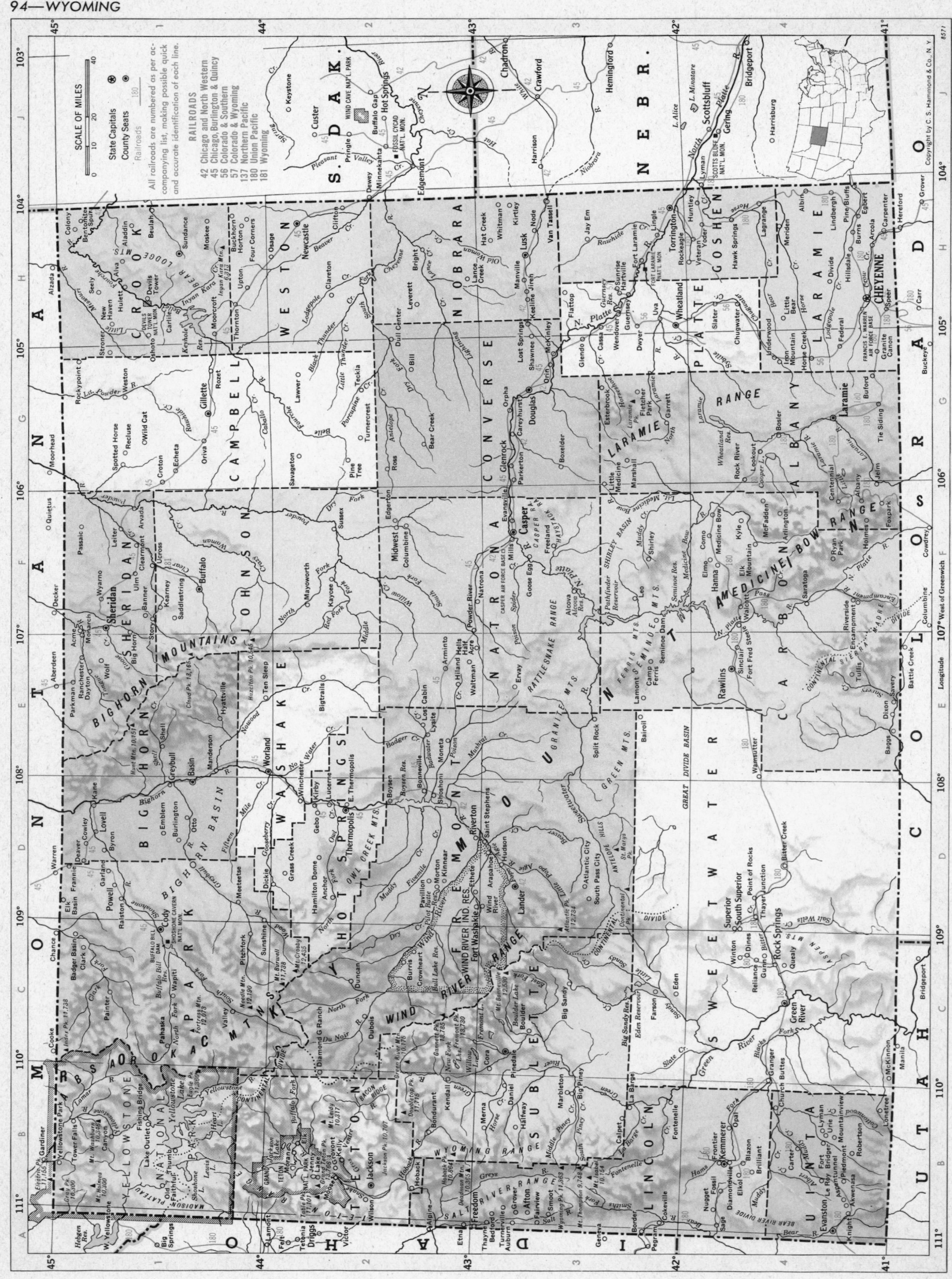

SCALE OF MILES

⊛ State Capitals
○ County Seats

RAILROADS

All railroads are numbered as per accompanying list, making possible quick and accurate identification of each line.

42 Chicago and North Western
45 Chicago, Burlington & Quincy
56 Colorado & Southern
57 Colorado & Wyoming
137 Northern Pacific
180 Union Pacific
181 Wyoming

Copyright by C. S. Hammond & Co., N.Y.

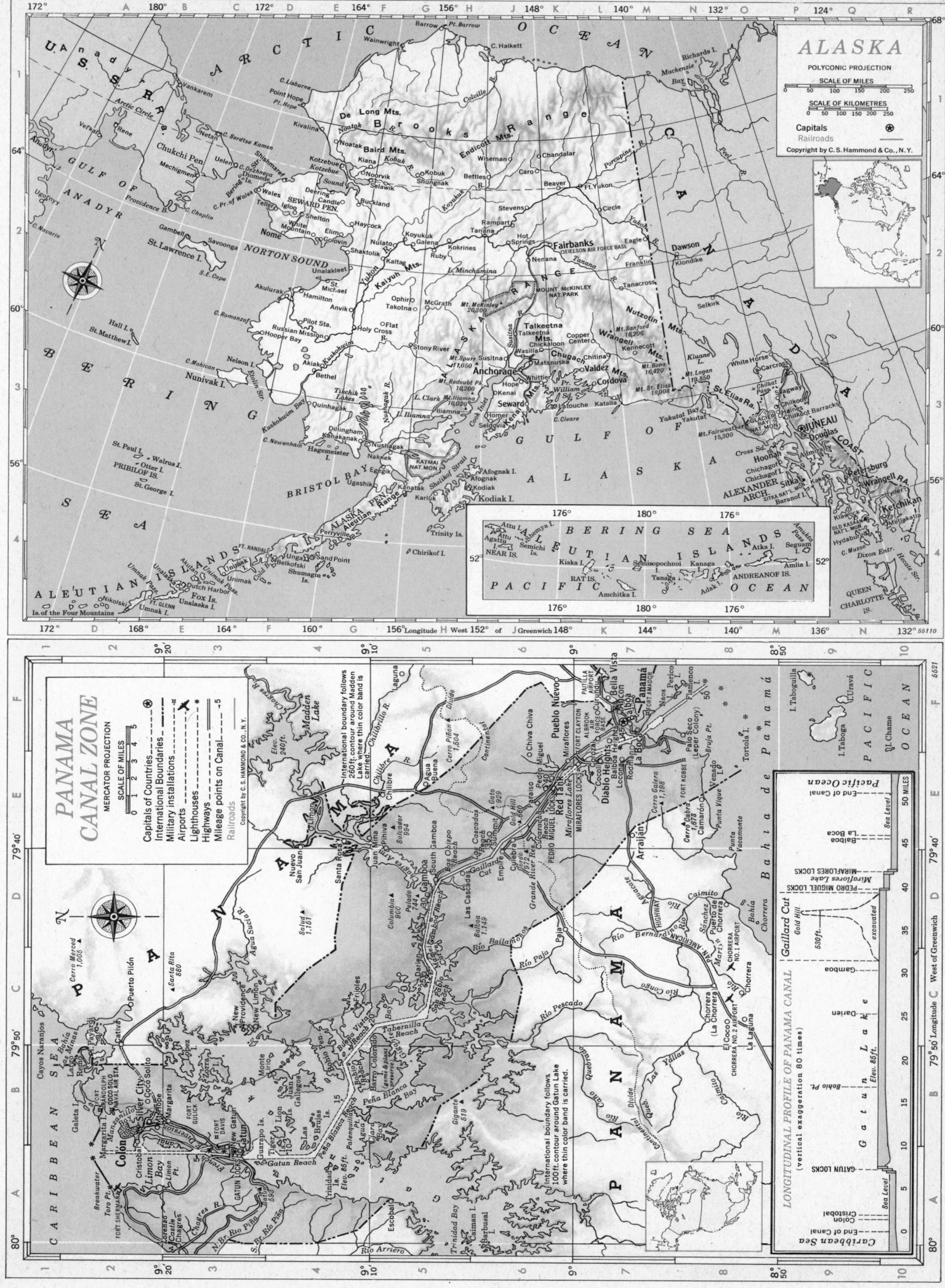

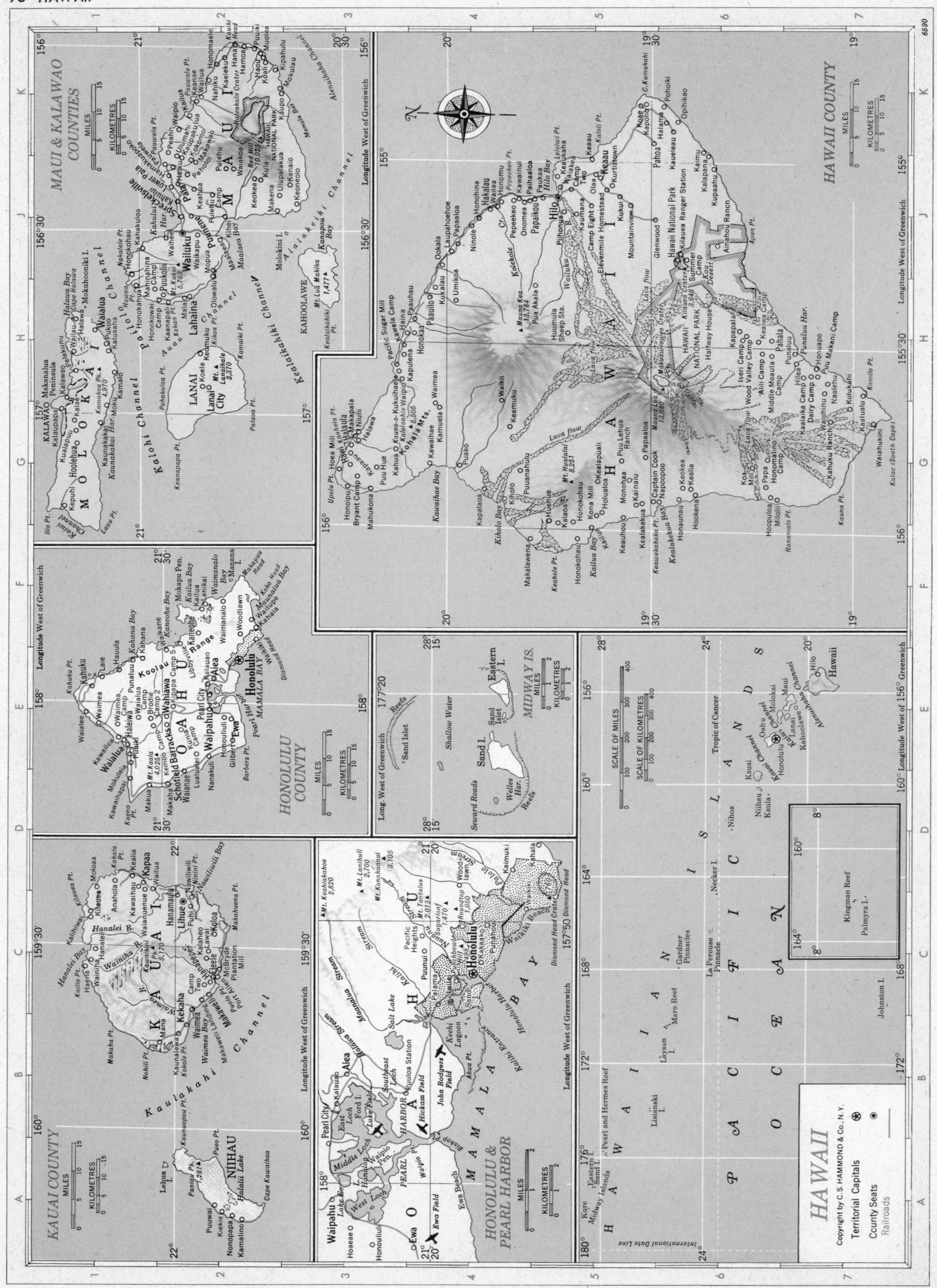

MAUI & KALAWAO COUNTIES

HAWAII COUNTY

KAUAI COUNTY

NIIHAU

HONOLULU COUNTY

MIDWAY IS.

HONOLULU & PEARL HARBOR

HAWAIIAN ISLANDS

PACIFIC OCEAN

HAWAII

Copyright by C. S. HAMMOND & CO., N.Y.

Territorial Capitals
County Seats
Railroads

Index of the
UNITED STATES

Introduction

$\mathcal{T}$HE INDEX OF CITIES AND TOWNS OF THE UNITED STATES gives the location and population statistics of all cities and towns appearing on the state maps in your atlas. The index entries are arranged alphabetically by states for easy reference and the proper state map page is given at the top of each state index. Each line begins with the name of the city or town, followed by the index reference and the population. The index reference gives the location of the city or town on the state map. The name is found within the square formed by the two lines of latitude and the two lines of longitude which enclose each of the index reference coordinates — i.e., the marginal letters and numbers.

The population figures are the most up-to-date statistics to be found in any reference work. The figures for all incorporated cities and villages are taken from the latest final Federal (1950) Census. The results of a special survey taken by the publishers are given for the population of unincorporated places which are not separately enumerated by the Census. This survey was taken at the same time as the Federal Census and constitutes a major population compilation in itself. Over 25,000 questionnaires were sent to the appropriate local township, county, state or federal authorities. The resulting answers provided the most reliable population statistics available today on unincorporated communities not covered by the Federal Census.

Places listed in the index without a population figure are largely points on the map without permanent inhabitants but which may be locally important as railroad shipping points, crossroad trading centers, or even post offices. In some cases they are communities with fluctuating populations such as resorts or military installations, as for example March Field Air Force Base in California.

A feature of the index especially valuable to the business man, sales manager and advertiser is the inclusion of "urban area" populations for the larger cities according to the 1950 Federal Census. The "urban areas" are defined as consisting of most central cities of over 50,000 inhabitants plus their surrounding built-up suburbs and urban fringes. In many cases the urban area figure gives a truer picture of the relative importance of a city than does the figure for the central municipality. This has become increasingly important with the accelerating movement of population to suburban areas. An example of this is Boston, Massachusetts, with 801,444 persons in the city itself and 2,218,893 in the urban area.

The photographs used throughout this index were used through the courtesy of the various state highway, conservation and publicity bureaus and the Standard Oil Company (N. J.).

160 YEARS OF URBAN AND RURAL POPULATIONS

State	POPULATION IN 1950		PER CENT URBAN				
	Urban	Rural	1950	1940	1890	1840	1790
Alabama	1,228,209	1,833,534	40.1	30.2	10.1	2.1	......
Arizona	273,794	475,793	36.5	34.8	9.4	......	......
Arkansas	617,153	1,292,358	32.3	22.2	6.5	*	......
California	7,099,166	3,487,057	67.1	71.0	48.6	......	......
Colorado	759,939	565,150	57.4	52.6	45.0	......	......
Connecticut	1,286,817	720,463	64.1	67.8	50.9	12.6	3.0
Delaware	147,890	170,195	46.5	52.3	42.2	10.7	*
Florida	1,566,788	1,204,517	56.5	55.1	19.8	*	......
Georgia	1,381,868	2,062,710	40.1	34.4	14.0	3.6	*
Idaho	234,138	354,499	39.8	33.7	*	......	......
Illinois	6,486,673	2,225,503	74.5	73.6	44.9	2.0	......
Indiana	2,217,468	1,716,756	56.4	55.1	26.9	1.6	......
Iowa	1,229,433	1,391,640	46.9	42.7	21.2	*	......
Kansas	903,468	1,001,831	47.4	41.9	18.9	......	......
Kentucky	985,739	1,959,067	33.5	29.8	19.2	4.0	*
Louisiana	1,363,789	1,319,727	50.8	41.5	25.4	29.9	......
Maine	374,507	539,267	41.0	40.5	28.1	7.8	*
Maryland	1,274,618	1,068,383	54.4	59.3	47.6	24.2	4.2
Massachusetts	4,122,138	568,376	87.9	89.4	82.0	37.9	13.5
Michigan	4,099,007	2,272,759	64.3	65.7	34.9	4.3	......
Minnesota	1,607,446	1,375,037	53.9	49.8	33.8	......	......
Mississippi	601,772	1,577,142	27.6	19.8	5.4	1.0	......
Missouri	2,290,149	1,664,504	57.9	51.8	32.0	4.3	......
Montana	252,906	338,118	42,8	37.8	27.1	......	......
Nebraska	606,530	718,980	45.8	39.1	27.4	......	......
Nevada	84,079	76,004	52.5	39.3	33.8	......	......
New Hampshire	301,249	231,993	56.5	57.6	39.3	10.0	3.3
New Jersey	3,847,771	987,558	79.6	81.6	62.6	10.6	*
New Mexico	314,636	366,551	46.2	33.2	6.2	......	......
New York	11,889,008	2,941,184	80.2	82.8	65.1	19.4	11.5
North Carolina	1,238,193	2,823,736	30.5	27.3	7.2	1.8	*
North Dakota	164,817	454,819	26.6	20.6	5.6	......	......
Ohio	5,273,206	2,673,421	66.4	66.8	41.1	5.5	......
Oklahoma	1,107,252	1,126,099	49.6	37.6	3.7	......	......
Oregon	732,247	789,094	48.1	48.8	27.9	......	......
Pennsylvania	6,906,993	3,591,019	65.8	66.5	48.6	17.9	10.2
Rhode Island	700,410	91,486	88.4	91.6	85.3	43.8	19.0
South Carolina	609,225	1,507,802	28.8	24.5	10.1	5.7	6.6
South Dakota	216,157	436,583	33.1	24.6	8.2	......	......
Tennessee	1,264,159	2,027,559	38.4	35.2	13.5	0.8	*
Texas	4,612,666	3,098,528	59.8	45.4	15.6	......	......
Utah	412,518	276,344	59.9	55.5	35.7	......	......
Vermont	137,612	240,135	36.4	34.3	15.2	*	*
Virginia	1,335,944	1,982,736	40.3	35.3	17.1	5.7	1.6
Washington	1,274,152	1,104,811	53.6	53.1	35.6	......	......
West Virginia	640,606	1,364,946	31.9	28.1	10.7	......	......
Wisconsin	1,906,363	1,528,212	55.5	53.5	33.2	*	......
Wyoming	144,618	145,911	49.8	37.3	34.3	......	......
U. S. A.	88,927,464	61,769,897	59.0	56.5	35.1	10.8	5.1

* — 100% Rural

POPULATION OF AMERICA'S LEADING CITIES*

City	1950	1940	1890	1840	1790
New York, N. Y.	7,891,957	7,454,995	2,507,414	391,114	49,401
Chicago, Ill.	3,620,962	3,396,808	1,099,850	4,470	....
Philadelphia, Pa.	2,071,605	1,931,334	1,046,964	93,665	28,522
Los Angeles, Calif.	1,970,358	1,504,277	50,395	....	....
Detroit, Mich.	1,849,568	1,623,452	205,876	9,012	....
Baltimore, Md.	949,708	859,100	434,439	102,313	13,503
Cleveland, Ohio	914,808	878,336	261,353	6,071	....
St. Louis, Mo.	856,796	816,048	451,770	16,469	....
Washington, D. C.	802,178	663,091	188,932	23,364	....
Boston, Mass.	801,444	770,816	448,477	93,383	18,320
San Francisco, Calif.	775,357	634,536	298,997	....	....
Pittsburgh, Pa.	676,806	671,659	343,904	31,204	....
Milwaukee, Wis.	637,392	587,472	204,468	1,712	....
Houston, Texas	596,163	384,514	27,557	....	....
Buffalo, N. Y.	580,132	575,901	255,664	18,213	....
New Orleans, La.	570,445	494,537	242,039	102,193	....
Minneapolis, Minn.	521,718	492,370	164,738	....	....
Cincinnati, Ohio	503,998	455,610	296,908	46,338	....
Seattle, Wash.	467,591	368,302	42,837	....	....
Kansas City, Mo.	456,622	399,178	132,716	....	....
Newark, N. J.	438,776	429,760	181,830	17,290	....
Dallas, Texas	434,462	294,734	38,067	....	....
Indianapolis, Ind.	427,173	386,972	105,436	2,692	....
Denver, Colo.	415,786	322,412	106,713	....	....
San Antonio, Texas	408,442	253,854	37,673	....	....
Memphis, Tenn.	396,000	292,942	64,495	....	....
Oakland, Calif.	384,575	302,163	48,682	....	....
Columbus, Ohio	375,901	306,087	88,150	6,048	....
Portland, Oreg.	373,628	305,394	46,385	....	....
Louisville, Ky.	369,129	319,077	161,129	21,210	200
San Diego, Calif.	334,387	203,341	16,159	....	....
Rochester, N. Y.	332,488	324,975	133,896	20,191	....
Atlanta, Ga.	331,314	302,288	65,533	....	....
Birmingham, Ala.	326,037	267,583	26,178	....	....
St. Paul, Minn.	311,349	287,736	133,156	....	....
Toledo, Ohio	303,616	282,349	81,434	1,222	....
Jersey City, N. J.	299,017	301,173	163,003	3,072	....
Fort Worth, Texas	278,778	177,662	23,076	....	....
Akron, Ohio	274,605	244,791	27,601	....	....
Omaha, Nebr.	251,117	223,844	140,452	....	....
Long Beach, Calif.	250,767	164,271	564	....	....
Miami, Fla.	249,276	172,172	....	....	....
Providence, R. I.	248,674	253,504	132,146	23,171	6,380
Dayton, Ohio	243,872	210,718	61,220	6,067	....
Oklahoma City, Okla.	243,504	204,424	4,151	....	....
Richmond, Va.	230,310	193,042	81,388	20,153	3,761
Syracuse, N. Y.	220,583	205,967	88,143	....	....
Norfolk, Va.	213,513	144,332	34,871	10,920	2,959
Jacksonville, Fla.	204,517	173,065	17,201	....	....
Worcester, Mass.	203,486	193,694	84,655	7,497	2,095
Tulsa, Okla.	182,740	142,157	....	....	....
Salt Lake City, Utah	182,121	149,934	44,843	....	....
Des Moines, Iowa	177,965	159,819	50,093	....	....
Hartford, Conn.	177,397	166,267	53,230	9,468	2,683
Grand Rapids, Mich.	176,515	164,292	60,278	....	....
Nashville, Tenn.	174,307	167,402	76,168	6,929	....
Youngstown, Ohio	168,330	167,720	33,220	....	....
Wichita, Kans.	168,279	114,966	23,853	....	....
New Haven, Conn.	164,443	160,605	86,045	12,960	4,487
Flint, Mich.	163,143	151,543	9,803	....	....
Springfield, Mass.	162,399	149,554	44,179	10,985	1,574
Spokane, Wash.	161,721	122,001	19,922	....	....
Bridgeport, Conn.	158,709	147,121	48,866	3,294	....
Yonkers, N. Y.	152,798	142,598	32,033	....	....
Tacoma, Wash.	143,673	109,408	36,006	....	....
Paterson, N. J.	139,336	139,656	78,347	....	....
Sacramento, Calif.	137,572	105,958	26,386	....	....
Albany, N. Y.	134,995	130,577	94,923	33,721	3,498
Charlotte, N. C.	134,042	100,899	11,557	....	....
Gary, Ind.	133,911	111,719	....	....	....
Fort Wayne, Ind.	133,607	118,410	35,393	....	....
Austin, Texas	132,459	87,930	14,575	....	....
Chattanooga, Tenn.	131,041	128,163	29,100	....	....
Erie, Pa.	130,803	116,955	40,634	3,412	....
El Paso, Texas	130,485	96,810	10,338	....	....
Kansas City, Kans.	129,583	121,458	38,316	....	....
Mobile, Ala.	129,009	78,720	31,076	12,672	....
Evansville, Ind.	128,636	97,062	50,756	....	....
Trenton, N. J.	128,009	124,697	57,458	4,035	....
Shreveport, La.	127,206	98,167	11,979	....	....
Baton Rouge, La.	125,629	34,719	10,478	2,269	....
Scranton, Pa.	125,536	140,404	75,215	....	....
Camden, N. J.	124,555	117,536	58,313	3,371	....
Knoxville, Tenn.	124,769	111,580	22,535	....	....
Tampa, Fla.	124,681	108,391	5,532	....	....
Cambridge, Mass.	120,740	110,879	70,028	8,409	2,115
Savannah, Ga.	119,638	95,996	43,139	18,214	....
Canton, Ohio	116,912	108,401	26,189	....	....
South Bend, Ind.	115,911	101,268	21,819	....	....
Berkeley, Calif.	113,805	85,547	5,101	....	....
Elizabeth, N. J.	112,817	109,912	37,764	4,184	....
Fall River, Mass.	111,963	115,428	74,398	6,738	....
Peoria, Ill.	111,856	105,087	41,024	1,467	....
Wilmington, Del.	110,356	112,504	61,431	8,367	....
Reading, Pa.	109,320	110,568	58,661	8,410	....
New Bedford, Mass.	109,189	110,341	40,733	12,087	3,313
Corpus Christi, Texas	108,287	57,301	....	....	....
Phoenix, Arizona	106,818	65,414	3,152	....	....
Allentown, Pa.	106,756	96,904	25,228	....	....
Montgomery, Ala.	106,525	78,084	21,883	2,179	....
Pasadena, Calif.	104,577	81,864	4,882	....	....
Duluth, Minn.	104,511	101,065	33,115	....	....
Waterbury, Conn.	104,477	99,314	28,646	....	....
Somerville, Mass.	102,351	102,177	40,152	....	....
Little Rock, Ark.	102,213	88,039	28,874	....	....
Utica, N. Y.	101,531	100,518	44,007	12,782	....

★ U. S. Census

A closer study of the geography of the United States does much to explain the growth of the nation. For example, the stony soil of New England discouraged farming and caused the early settlers to turn to manufacturing and commerce. The swift streams furnished water power and the jagged coastline provided bays for harboring the ships from Europe. Farther south, the coastal plains widen out into broad stretches of fertile land, and the rivers are short and deep. This led to the development of the large plantations in the deep south, where the climate is favorable to crops that require long hot summers. Here the coastal plain includes half of Georgia, all of Florida, and extends along the Gulf of Mexico. It reaches into the interior as far north as southern Illinois.

The lake and prairie region of the upper Mississippi Valley is one of the most fertile in the world, and is linked by waterways with the East and South through the Great Lakes and the Mississippi River system. The Great Plains region, depending upon the nature of the topsoil and amount of rainfall, is either grain or grazing country, with valuable deposits of oil in Texas and Oklahoma.

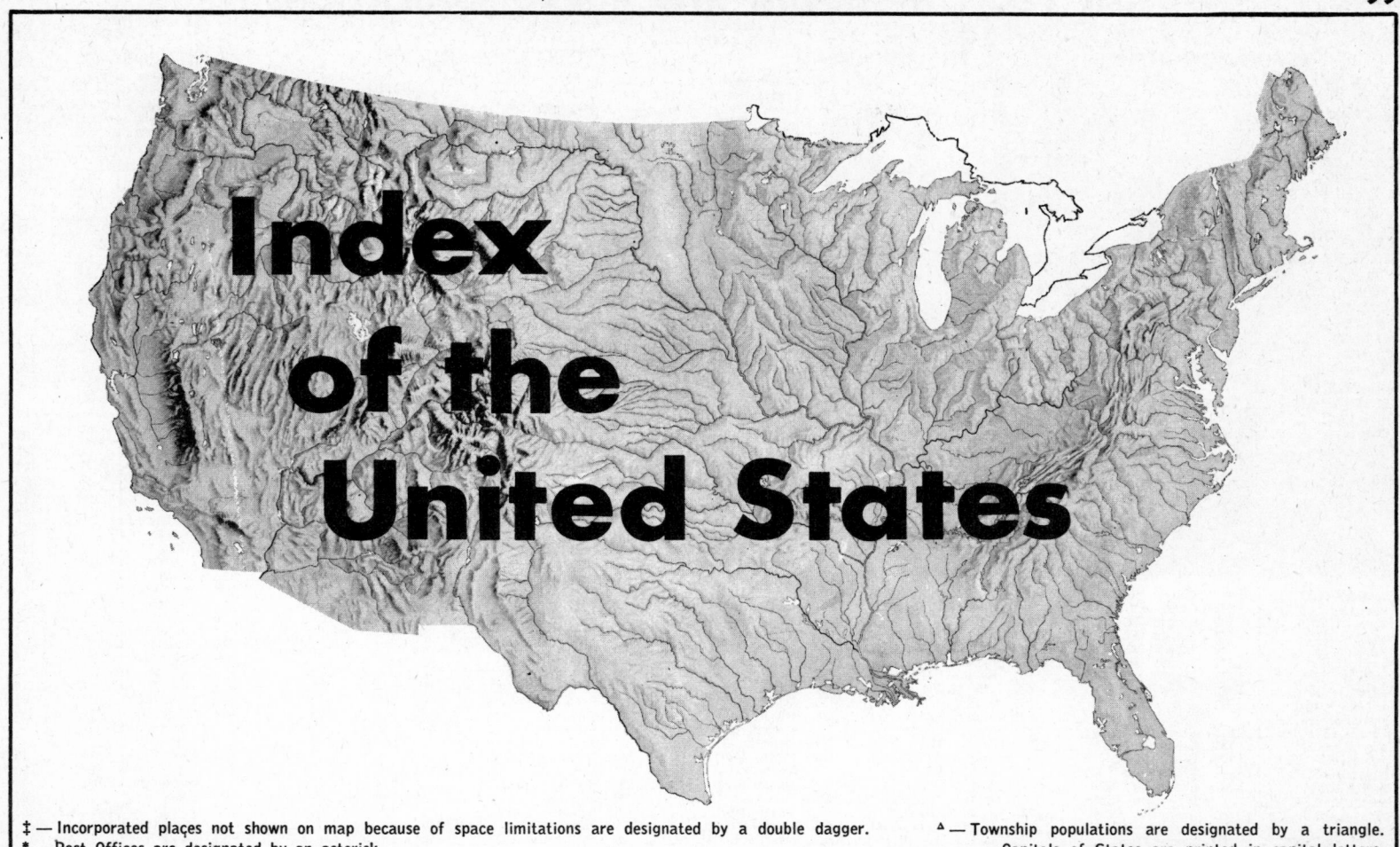

Index of the United States

‡ — Incorporated places not shown on map because of space limitations are designated by a double dagger.
* — Post Offices are designated by an asterisk.

△ — Township populations are designated by a triangle.
Capitals of States are printed in capital letters.

Map on Page 49   **ALABAMA**   *Total Population 3,061,743*

67 COUNTIES

Autauga (E5)	18,186
Baldwin (C9)	40,997
Barbour (H7)	28,892
Bibb (D5)	17,987
Blount (E2)	28,975
Bullock (G6)	16,054
Butler (E7)	29,228
Calhoun (G3)	79,539
Chambers (H5)	39,528
Cherokee (G2)	17,634
Chilton (E5)	26,922
Choctaw (B6)	19,152
Clarke (C7)	26,548
Clay (G4)	13,929
Cleburne (G3)	11,904
Coffee (G8)	30,720
Colbert (C1)	39,561
Conecuh (E8)	21,776
Coosa (F5)	11,766
Covington (F8)	40,373
Crenshaw (F7)	18,981
Cullman (E2)	49,046
Dale (G8)	20,828
Dallas (D6)	56,270
De Kalb (G2)	45,048
Elmore (G5)	31,649
Escambia (D8)	31,443
Etowah (F2)	93,892
Fayette (C3)	19,388
Franklin (C2)	25,705
Geneva (G8)	25,899
Greene (C5)	16,482
Hale (C5)	20,832
Henry (H8)	18,674
Houston (H8)	46,522
Jackson (F1)	38,998
Jefferson (E3)	558,928
Lamar (B3)	16,441
Lauderdale (C1)	54,179
Lawrence (D1)	27,128
Lee (H5)	45,073
Limestone (E1)	35,766
Lowndes (E1)	18,018
Macon (G6)	30,561
Madison (E1)	72,903
Marengo (C6)	29,494
Marion (C2)	27,264
Marshall (F2)	45,090
Mobile (B9)	231,105
Monroe (D7)	25,732
Montgomery (F6)	138,965
Morgan (E2)	52,924
Perry (D5)	20,439
Pickens (B4)	24,349
Pike (G7)	30,608
Randolph (H4)	22,513
Russell (H6)	40,364
Saint Clair (F3)	26,687
Shelby (E4)	30,362
Sumter (B5)	23,610
Talladega (F4)	63,639
Tallapoosa (G5)	35,074
Tuscaloosa (C4)	94,092
Walker (D3)	63,769
Washington (B8)	15,612
Wilcox (D7)	23,476
Winston (D2)	18,250

CITIES and TOWNS

Abanda (H4)*	125
Abbeville (H7)*	2,162
Abernant (D4)*	
Ackerville (E6)*	100
Acmar (E3)*	900
Adamsville (D3)*	1,531
Addison (D2)*	590
Adger (D4)*	500
Aimwell (C6)*	150
Akron (C5)*	684
Alabama City (F2)*	
Alberta (D6)*	200
Albertville (F2)*	5,397
Aldrich (E4)*	1,000
Alexander City (G5)*	6,430
Alexandria (G3)*	300
Aliceville (B4)*	3,170
Allen (C7)*	200
Allenton (E7)*	75
Allenville (C6)	
Allgood (F3)*	350
Allison (C5)	
Allsboro (B1)*	150
Alma (C8)*	50
Alpine (F4)*	
Alton (E3)*	500
Altoona (F2)*	860
America (D3)*	
Andalusia (E8)*	9,162
Anderson (D1)*	450
Angel (G3)	15
Annemanie (D6)*	100
Anniston (G3)*	31,066
Ansley (F7)*	
Arab (E2)*	1,592
Ararat (B7)	100
Ardmore (E1)*	408
Ariton (G7)*	620
Arkadelphia (E3)*	
Arley (D2)*	300
Arlington (C6)*	200
Asahel (D7)	
Ashby (E4)	75
Ashford (H8)*	1,400
Ashland (G4)*	1,593
Ashville (F3)*	494
Athens (E1)*	6,309
Atmore (C8)*	5,720

Attalla (F2)*	7,537
Atwood (C2)*	250
Auburn (H5)*	12,939
Austinville (D1)*	1,110
Autaugaville (E6)*	459
Axis (B9)*	130
Baileyton (E2)*	200
Bakerhill (H7)*	
Bamford (E4)*	12
Bangor (E3)*	
Banks (G7)*	222
Bankston (C3)*	350
Barlow Bend (C8)*	364
Barnwell (C10)	
Barton (C1)*	250
Bashi (C7)*	
Bass Station (G1)	125
Batesville (H6)	
Battles Wharf (C10)*	300
Bay Minette (C9)*	3,732
Bayou la Batre (B10)*	2,196
Bear Creek (C2)*	223
Beatrice (D7)*	375
Beaverton (B3)*	192
Bedford (B3)	
Belgreen (C2)*	255
Belk (C3)*	152
Bellamy (B6)*	
Belle Ellen (D4)*	400
Belle Mina (E1)*	
Belleville (D8)*	300
Bellview (D7)	50
Bellwood (G8)*	263
Belmont (C5)	153
Beloit (D6)*	250
Benson (G5)	
Benton (E6)*	
Bermuda (D8)*	240
Berry (C3)*	715
Bessemer (D4)*	28,445
Beulah (H5)	
Bevelle (G5)	
Bexar (B2)*	
Bigbee (B7)*	30
Billingsley (E5)*	158
Birmingham (D3)*	326,037
Birmingham (urban area)*	438,726
Bishop (B1)	75
Black (G8)*	239
Blacksher (C8)	
Bladon Springs (B7)*	375
Blalock (D6)	15
Blanche (G2)*	104
Blanton (H5)	
Bleecker (H5)*	250
Blocton (D4)*	1,500
Blount Springs (E3)*	
Blountsville (E2)*	695
Blue Mountain (G3)*	529
Blue Springs (G7)*	111

Bluffton (G2)	
Boaz (F2)*	3,078
Boligee (C5)*	168
Bolinger (B7)*	200
Bolling (E7)*	300
Bon Air (F4)*	360
Bon Secour (C10)*	180
Booth (E6)*	
Boothton (E4)*	814
Borden Springs (H3)*	100
Boston (C2)*	700
Boyd (B5)	300
Boylston (F6)*	500
Bradleyton (F7)*	107
Braggs (E6)*	300
Branchville (F3)*	
Brantley (F7)*	1,102
Bremen (E3)*	
Brent (D5)*	1,100
Brewton (D8)*	5,146
Brickyard (H6)	150
Bridgeport (G1)*	2,386
Bridgeton (E4)*	
Brierfield (E4)*	200
Brighton (E4)*	1,689
Brilliant (C2)*	600
Bromley (C9)	248
Brooklyn (E8)*	150
Brookside (E3)*	733
Brooksville (F2)*	
Brookwood (D4)*	500
Browns (D6)*	100
Brownsboro (F1)*	100
Brownville (C4)*	350
Brundidge (G7)*	2,605
Bucks (B8)*	60
Buena Vista (D7)*	200
Buffalo (H5)*	188
Buhl (C4)*	
Burbank (B8)*	
Burkville (E6)*	200
Burl (D7)*	100
Burnett (G2)	
Burnsville (E6)*	200
Burnt Corn (D7)*	250
Butler (B6)*	659
Butler Springs (E7)*	
Calcis (E4)*	
Caldwell (F3)	25
Caledonia (D7)	150
Calera (E4)*	1,361
Calhoun (F6)*	150
Calvert (B8)*	500
Camden (D7)*	931
Cameronsville (G1)*	100
Camp Hill (G5)*	1,296
Campbell (C7)*	126
Canoe (D8)*	
Canton Bend (D6)*	300
Capps (H8)*	110

Capshaw (E1)*	275
Carbon Hill (D3)*	2,179
Cardiff (E3)*	204
Carey (E1)	25
Carlowville (D6)*	400
Carlton (C8)*	
Carrollton (B4)*	710
Carrville (G5)*	760
Carson (C8)*	200
Castleberry (D8)*	667
Caswell (D10)*	33
Catherine (D6)*	200
Cecil (F6)*	150
Cedar Bluff (G2)*	563
Cedar Cove (D4)*	100
Central (F5)*	175
Central Mills (D6)	75
Centre (G2)*	1,672
Centreville (D5)*	1,160
Champion (F3)	
Chance (C7)*	
Chancellor (G8)*	125
Chandler Springs (F4)	
Chapman (E7)*	943
Chase (E1)*	750
Chastang (B8)*	
Chatom (B8)*	609
Chavies (G2)*	250
Chelsea (E4)*	300
Cherokee (C1)*	748
Chesson (G6)*	
Chestnut (D7)*	250
Chickasaw (B9)*	4,920
Childersburg (F4)*	4,023
China Grove (G7)	
Choccolocco (G3)*	267
Choctaw (B6)*	500
Choctaw Bluff (C8)*	500
Chrysler (C8)*	
Chunchula (B9)*	300
Citronelle (B8)*	1,350
Claiborne (D7)*	175
Clairmont Spgs. (G4)*	50
Clanton (E5)*	4,640
Clarence (F2)*	100
Claud (F5)*	80
Clayton (G7)*	1,583
Cleveland (E3)*	400
Clinton (C5)*	200
Clio (G7)*	840
Clopton (G7)*	140
Cloverdale (C1)*	250
Coal Bluff (D7)*	100
Coal Valley (D3)*	140
Coaling (D4)*	
Coatopa (B6)*	125
Cobb City (G3)*	20
Cochrane (B4)*	200
Coden (B10)*	
Coffee Springs (G8)*	173
Coffeeville (B7)*	211

Cohasset (E8)	
Coker (C4)*	325
Coleanor (E4)	25
Collbran (G2)*	109
Collinsville (G2)*	1,023
Collirene (E6)	
Columbia (H8)*	849
Columbiana (E4)*	1,761
Columbus City (F2)*	75
Comer (H6)*	150
Consul (C6)	
Cooks Springs (F3)*	300
Cooper (E5)*	300
Coosada (F5)*	207
Copeland (B7)*	
Cordova (D3)*	3,156
Corona (C3)*	225
Cortelyou (B8)*	
Cottage Grove (F5)*	400
Cotton Hill (H7)	
Cottondale (D4)*	
Cottonton (H6)*	125
Cottonville (F2)	60
Cottonwood (H8)*	864
Courtland (D1)*	507
Covin (C3)*	110
Cowarts (H8)*	300
Coy (D7)*	
Cragford (G4)*	200
Crane Hill (D2)*	
Crawford (H6)	100
Creek Stand (G6)	50
Creola (B9)*	25
Crews (B3)*	
Crichton (B9)*	
Cromwell (B6)*	200
Cropwell (F3)*	500
Crosby (H8)	50
Crossville (G2)*	609
Cuba (B6)*	525
Cullman (E2)*	7,523
Cullomburg (B7)*	350
Cusseta (H5)*	350
Cypress (C5)*	165
Dadeville (G5)*	2,354
Daleville (G8)*	300
Dallas Mills (E1)*	2,200
Dancy (B4)*	200
Danville (E2)*	350
Daphne (C9)*	1,041
Darlington (D7)*	150
Dauphin Island (B10)*	
Daviston (G4)*	110
Dawes (B9)	
Dawson (G2)*	
Dayton (C6)*	85
De Armanville (G3)*	260
Deatsville (F5)*	200
Decatur (D1)*	19,974
Deer Park (B8)*	200
Delmar (C2)*	350

Delta (G4)*	150
Demopolis (C6)*	5,004
Detroit (B2)*	250
Devenport (F6)	150
Dickinson (C7)*	250
Dixie (E8)	50
Dixons Mills (C6)*	350
Dixonville (E8)	
Dolomite (D4)*	4,500
Dora (D3)*	984
Dothan (H8)*	21,584
Double Springs (D2)*	524
Douglas (F2)*	200
Downing (F6)	47
Downs (G6)	
Dozier (F7)*	362
Drewry (D8)*	
Duke (G3)*	175
Dunavant (F4)*	300
Duncanville (D4)*	10
Dutton (G1)*	
Dyas (C9)	30
Easonville (F3)*	400
East Brewton (E8)*	2,173
East Florence (C1)*	
East Tallassee (G5)*	
Eastaboga (F3)*	700
Echo (G8)	100
Echola (C4)*	120
Eclectic (F5)*	715
Eden (F3)*	621
Edna (B6)*	500
Edwardsville (H3)*	179
Edwin (H7)	170
Eiler (B7)	25
Elamville (G7)*	155
Elba (F8)*	2,936
Elberta (C10)*	350
Eldridge (C3)*	500
Eleanor (D6)	20
Eliska (C8)	75
Elkmont (E1)*	179
Elkwood (E1)	50
Ellawhite (D6)	
Elmore (F5)*	350
Elon (F1)	42
Elrod (G4)*	500
Emelle (B5)*	
Empire (D3)*	
Enterprise (G8)*	7,288
Eoline (D4)*	250
Epes (B5)*	342
Equality (F5)*	176
Erin (G4)	50
Escatawpa (B8)*	90
Estillfork (F1)*	121
Ethelsville (B4)*	135
Eufaula (H7)*	6,906
Eunola (G8)	112
Eutaw (C5)*	2,348
Eva (E2)*	200

ALASKA

Map on Page 95 — *Total Population 128,643*

Adak (isl.) (L4)
Admiralty (isl.) (N3)
Afognak (J3)* 158
Afognak (isl.) (J3)
Aggattu (isl.) (J3)
Akiak (F2)* 168
Akulurak (E2) 197
Akutan (E4)* 86
Alaska (gulf) (JM3)
Alaska (mt. range) (HJ2)
Alaska (peninsula) (G3)
Aleution (isls.) (JN3) 5,600
Aleution (mt. range) (G3)
Alexander (arch.) (M3)
Amchitka (isl.) (K4)
Amlia (isl.) (M4)
Amukta (passage) (N4)
Anchorage (J2)* 11,254
Andreanof (isls.) (M4)
Anvik (F2)* 99
Atka (isl.) (M4)*
Attu (J3)
Attu (isl.) (J3)
Baird (mts.) (F1)
Baranof (isl.) (N3)
Barrow (G1)* 951
Barrow (point) (H1)
Beaver (K1)* 101
Belkofsky (F4)* 119
Bering (strait) (D1)
Bering (sea) (BE3)
Bethel (F2)* 651
Bettles (H1)* 47
Bona (mt.) (L2)
Bristol (bay) (FG3)
Brooks(mt. range)(GK1)
Buckland (G1)
Candle (F1)* 105
Cape Halkett (J1)
Caro (J1)
Chandalar (K1)
Chichagof (M3)*
Chichagof (isl.) (M3)
Chickaloon (J2)
Chilkoot Barracks (N3).
Chirikof (isl.) (H4)
Chitina (K2)* 92
Chugach (mts.) (K2)
Circle (L1)* 83
Clark (lake) (H2)
Cleare (cape) (K3)
Coast (mt. range) (N3)
Cold (bay) (F4)
Coleville (river) (H1)
Cook (inlet) (H3)
Copper Center (K2)* 90
Cordova (K2)* 6,165
Cross (sound) (M3)
De Long (mts.) (F1)
Deering (F1)* 174
Dillingham (G3)* 577
Diomede (isls.) (D1)
Dixon Entrance (channel) (N4)
Douglas (N3)* 699
Dutch Harbor (E4)
Eagle (L1)* 55
Egegik (G3)* 119
Eielson Air Force Base (K1)
Elim (F1)* 154
Endicott (mts.) (H1)
Etolin (strait) (E2)
Fairbanks (K1)* 5,771
Fairweather (mt.) (M3)
Flat (G2)* 95
Fort Glenn (E4)
Fort Randall (F4)
Fort Yukon (K1)* 446
Four Mountains (isls.) (D4)
Fox (isls.) (E4)
Franklin (L1)
Galena (G1)* 176
Gambell (C2)* 309
Glacier Bay Nat'l Mon. (M3)
Golovin (F1)* 94
Hagemeister (isl.) (F3).
Haines (N3)* 338
Hall (isl.) (C2)
Hamilton (F2)* 43
Haycock (F1)*
Holy Cross (G2) 157
Homer (J3)* 307
Hoonah (M3)* 563
Hooper Bay (E2)* 307
Hope (J2)* 63
Hope (point) (E1)
Hot Springs (J1)* 29
Hydaburg (N4)* 353
Hyder (O4)* 30
Igloo (E1)* 64
Iliamna (H3)* 44
Iliamna (lake) (H3)
Iliamna (mt.) (H2)
JUNEAU (N3)* 5,956
Kaiyuh (mts.) (G2)
Kake (N3)* 376
Kaltag (G1)* 121
Kanaga (isl.) (L4)
Kanakanak (G3) 54
Kanatak (H3)*
Karluk (H3)* 144
Katalla (K2)
Katmai Nat'l Mon. (H3)
Kenai (J2)* 321
Kenai (mts.) (J2)
Kennecott (L2)
Ketchikan (O4)* 5,305
Kiana (F1)* 181
Kiska (isl.) (K4)
Kivalina (E1)* 117
Klawock (N4)* 404
Kobuk (H1)* 38
Kobuk (river) (G1)
Kodiak (J3)* 1,710
Kodiak (isl.) (J3)
Kokrines (H1)* 68
Kotzebue (sound) (F1).
Kotzebue (F1)* 623
Koyukuk (G1)* 79
Koyukuk (river) (H1)
Kuskokwim (river) (F2)
Kuskokwim (bay) (F3)
Latouche (K2)*
Lisburne (cape) (E1)
Matanuska (K2) 41
Mc Grath (H2)* 175
Mc Kinley (mt.) (H2)
Metlakatla (O4)* 817
Minchumina (lake) (H1)
Mohican (cape) (D2)
Mount McKinley Nat'l Park (K2) 59
Muzon (cape) (N4)
Naknek (G3)* 174
Near (isls.) (J4)
Nelson (isl.) (E2)
Nenana (J1)* 242
Newenham (cape) (F3).
Nikolski (D4)* 64
Noatak (F1)* 326
Noatak (river) (F1)
Nome (E1)* 1,876
Noorvik (G1)* 248
Norton (sound) (E2)
Nulato (G1)* 176
Nunivak (isl.) (E3)
Nushagak (G3)
Nushagak (river) (G3)
Nutzotin (mts.) (L2)
Old Kasaan Nat'l Mon. (N4)
Ophir (G2)* 68
Otter (isl.) (D3)
Perryville (G3)
Petersburg (O3)* 1,619
Pilot Station (F2)* 52
Point Hope (D1)*
Porcupine (river) (L1)
Pribilof (isls.) (D3)
Prince of Wales (cape) (D1)
Prince William (sound) (K2)
Quinhagak (F3)* 194
Rampart (J1)* 94
Rat (isls.) (K4)
Redoubt (mt.) (H2)
Romanzof (cape) (E2)
Ruby (H1)* 132
Russian Mission (F2)* 55
St. Elias (mt.) (L2)
St. Elias (mt. range) (M3)
St. George (isl.) (D3)
St. Lawrence (isl.) (D2)
St. Matthew (isl.) (C2).
St. Michael (F2)* 157
St. Paul (isl.) (D3)*
Sand Point (G4)* 107
Sanford (mt.) (L2)
Savoonga (D2)* 249
Seguam (isl.) (M4)
Selawik (G1)* 273
Seldovia (J3)* 437
Semichi (isls.) (J4)
Semisopochnoi(isl.)(L4)
Seward (J2)* 2,114
Seward (peninsula)(E1)
Shaktoolik (F1)* 127
Shelikof (strait) (H3)
Shelton (F1)
Shemya (isl.) (J3)
Shishmaref (E1)* 194
Shumagin (isls.) (F4)
Shungnak (H1)* 141
Sitka (N3)* 1,985
Sitka Nat'l Mon. (M3)
Skagway (N3)* 758
South East (cape) (D2)
Spurr (mt.) (H2)
Stevens Village (J1)* 84
Stony River (H2)*
Susitna (J2)
Susitna (river) (J2)
Takotna (G2)* 42
Talkeetna (J2)* 106
Talkeetna (mts.) (J2)
Tanacross (L2)* 137
Tanaga (L4)
Tanana (H1)* 228
Tanana (river) (K1)
Teller (E1)* 269
Tikchik (lakes) (G2)
Trinity (isls.) (H3)
Ugashik (G3)* 48
Umnak (isl.) (E4)
Umnak (passage) (D4)
Unalakleet (F2)* 469
Unalaska (E4)* 173
Unalaska (isl.) (E4)
Unga (F4)* 107
Unimak (E4)
Unimak (isl.) (E4)
Unimak (passage) (E4).
Valdez (K2)* 554
Wainwright (F1)* 227
Wales (E1)* 141
Walrus (isl.) (D3)
Wasilla (J2)* 97
White Mountain (E1)* 129
Whittier (J2)* 627
Wiseman (J1)*
Wrangell (O3)* 1,263
Wrangell (mts.) (L2)
Yakutat (L3)* 298
Yakutat (bay) (L3)
Yukon (river) (G2)

ARIZONA

Map on Page 50 — *Total Population 749,587*

14 COUNTIES

Apache (F3) 27,767
Cochise (F7) 31,488
Coconino (C3) 23,910
Gila (E5) 24,158
Graham (E6) 12,985
Greenlee (F5) 12,805
Maricopa (C5) 331,770
Mohave (A3) 8,510
Navajo (E3) 29,446
Pima (D6) 141,216
Pinal (D6) 43,191
Santa Cruz (E7) 9,344
Yavapai (C4) 24,991
Yuma (A5) 28,006

CITIES and TOWNS

Adamana (F4)* 60
Agua Caliente (B6)* 75
Aguila (B5)* 180
Ajo (C6)* 5,817
Alpine (F5)*
Amado (D7)*
Apache (F7) 36
Apache Junction (D5)* 50
Aripine (E4)* 45
Arivaca (D7)* 120
Arlington (C5)* 500
Ash Fork (C3)* 800
Ashurst (F5)* 135
Avondale (C5)* 2,505
Aztec (B6)* 49
Bagdad (B4)*
Bannon (F4) 14
Bapchule (D5)* 50
Bellemont (D3)* 100
Benson (E7)* 1,440
Betatakin (Shonto) (E2)
Bisbee (F7)* 3,801
Blue (F5)* 50
Blue Bell (C4)
Bonita (E6)* 100
Bouse (A5)* 150
Bowie (F6)* 300
Buckeye (C5)* 1,932
Bullhead City (A3)*
Bumble Bee (C4)* 36
Bylas (E5)* 750
Cactus (D5)* 125
Calva (E5) 25
Cameron (D3)* 25
Camp Verde (D4)* 550
Camp Wood (C4)* 35
Cane Beds (B2) 30
Casa Grande (D6)* 4,181
Cashion (C5)* 700
Castle Butte (E3)*
Castle Hot Springs (C5)* 30
Cavecreek (D5)* 250
Central (F6)* 300
Chambers (F3)* 106
Chandler (D5)* 3,799
Cherry (C4)
Chinle (F2)* 150
Chino Valley (C4)* 500
Chloride (A3)* 250
Christmas (E5) 60
Chrysotile (E5)
Cibecue (E4)* 35
Clarkdale (C4)* 1,609
Clay Springs (E4)* 199
Claypool (E5)* 1,200
Cleator (C4)* 60
Clemenceau (C4)* 300
Clifton (F5)* 3,466
Cochise (F6)* 90
Concho (F4)* 175
Congress (C4)* 30
Congress Jct. (B4) 95
Continental (D7) 12
Coolidge (D6)* 4,306
Coolidge Dam (E5)* 35
Cordes (C4)
Cornfields (F3) 204
Cornville (D4)* 21
Cortaro (D6)* 360
Cottonwood (D4)* 1,326
Courtland (F7) 25
Crown King (C4)* 100
Dateland (B6)*
Davis Dam (A3) 1,000
Dewey (C4)* 25
Dilkon (E3) 15
Dome (A6)* 35
Dos Cabezas (F6)* 80
Douglas (F7)* 9,442
Dragoon (F6)* 44
Drake (C4) 5
Duncan (F6)* 941
Eagar (F4)* 637
Eden (F6)* 200
Elfrida (F7)* 277
Elgin (E7)* 143
Eloy (D6)* 3,580
Emery Park (E6)* 600
Escuela (D6) 10
Estrella (C6) 21
Fairbank (E7)* 50
Flagstaff (D3)* 6,771
Florence (D5)* 1,776
Florence Jct. (D5)* 32
Fort Apache (F5)* 500
Fort Defiance (F3)* 500
Fort Grant (E6)*
Fort Huachuca (E7)* 100
Fort Thomas (E5)*
Franklin (F6)* 300
Fredonia (C2)* 350
Fry (E7)* 150
Gadsden (A6)* 250
Gando (F3)* 450
Geronimo (F5)* 23
Gila Bend (C6)* 873
Gilbert (D5)* 1,114
Gleeson (F7) 30
Glenbar (F6)* 170
Glendale (C5)* 8,179
Globe (E5)* 6,419
Goldroad (A3) 14
Goodwin (C4) 15
Goodyear (C5)* 1,254
Grand Canyon (C2)* 1,001
Greasewood Sprs. (F2).
Greaterville (E7)
Greer (F4)* 30
Hackberry (B3)* 250
Hassayampa (C5)
Hayden (E5)* 1,494
Hayden Junction (E6)*. 71
Heber (E4)* 250
Hereford (E7)* 90
Higley (D5)* 150
Hillside (B4)* 40
Hilltop (F6) 34
Holbrook (E4)* 2,336
Hotevilla (E3)* 572
Houck (F3)*
Humboldt (C4)* 350
Indian Wells (E3)* 2
Inspiration (D5)* 500
Iron Springs (C4)* 3
Jacob Lake (C2)* 10
Jeddito (E3) 6
Jerome (C4)* 1,233
Joseph City (E4)* 500
Kayenta (E2)* 100
Keams Canyon (E3)* 500
Kelvin (E5)* 35
Kingman (A3)* 3,342
Kirkland (C4)* 96
Klagetoh (F3)
Klondyke (E6)* 150
Komatke (C5) 200
Lakeside (E4)*
Laveen (C5)* 300
Leupp (E3)*
Liberty (C5)
Linden (E4)* 105
Litchfield (C5) 1,000
Litchfield Park (C5)* 450
Littlefield (B2)* 100
Lowell (F7)* 1,136
Lukachukai (F2)*
Lupton (F3)* 115
Madera Canyon (E7) 40
Mammoth (E6)* 275
Marana (D6)* 1,000
Marble Canyon (D2) 5
Maricopa (C5)* 150
Marinette (C5)* 500
Maverick (F5)* 450
Mayer (C4)* 500
Mc Nary (F4)* 1,902
McNeal (F7)* 101
Mesa (D5)* 16,790
Miami (E5)* 4,329
Miller Valley (C4) 2,953
Mobile (C5)* 120
Moccasin (C2)* 55
Mohawk (B6)* 18
Morenci (F5)* 6,541
Mormon Lake (D4)*
Morristown (C5)* 185
Mount Trumbull (B2)* 57
Naco (E7)* 400
Navajo (F3)* 50
Nelson (B3)* 155
Nogales (E7)* 6,153
North Rim (C2)* 2
Nutrioso (F5)* 100
Oatman (A3)* 600
Olberg (D5) 51
Oracle (E6)*
Oraibi (E3)*
Palo Verde (C5)*
Pantano (E7)* 40
Paradise (F7) 14
Parker (A4)* 1,201
Parks (C3)* 50
Patagonia (E7)* 700
Paul Spur (F7)* 300
Paulden (C4)* 25
Payson (D4)* 350
Peach Springs (B3)* 575
Pearce (F7)* 150
Peoria (C5)* 2,000
Perkinsville (C4) 15
PHOENIX (C5)* 106,818
Phoenix (urban area) 214,335
Picacho (D6)* 150
Pima (F6)* 824
Pine (D4)*
Pinedale (E4)* 87
Pinetop (F4)* 300
Pirtleville (F7)* 1,246
Polacca (E3)*
Pomerene (E6)* 100
Portal (F7)* 65
Poston (A3)*
Prescott (C4)* 6,764
Quartzsite (A5)* 153
Queen Creek (D5)* 1,200
Quijotoa (C6) 50
Randolph (D6)*
Ray (E5)* 2,000
Red Rock (D6)* 50
Redington (E6) 51
Rillito (D6)* 200
Rimrock (D4)* 20
Rock Springs (C3)*
Roll (A6)* 66
Roosevelt (D5)*
Rowood (C6)* 50
Ruby (D7)
Sacaton (D5)* 600
Safford (F6)* 3,756
Sahuarita (E7)* 500
Saint David (E7)* 750
St. Johns (F4)* 1,469
St. Michaels (F3)* 120
Salome (B5)* 300
San Carlos (E5)* 3,000
San Luis (A6)*
San Simon (F6)* 175
Sanders (F3)*
Sasabe (D7)* 75
Scottsdale (D5)* 2,032
Sedona (D4)* 350
Seligman (B3)* 1,000
Sells (D7)* 650
Sentinel (B6)* 60
Shonto (E2)
Short Creek (B2)* 200
Show Low (F4)* 1,000
Shumway (E4)* 88
Shungopavy (E3)
Skull Valley (C4)* 250
Snowflake (E4)* 929
Solomon (F6)* 700
Sombrero Butte (E6) 10
Somerton (A6)* 1,825
Sonoita (E7)* 150
Sonora (D5)* 1,821
South Tucson (D6) 2,364
Springerville (F4)* 689
Steamboat (F3)
Stoneman Lake (D4)
Supai (C2)* 16
Supai (C3)
Superior (D5)* 4,500
Tacna (B6)* 18
Taylor (E4)* 500
Tempe (D5)* 7,684
Thatcher (F6)* 1,284
Tiger (E6)* 1,800
Tolleson (C5)* 3,042
Toltec (D6) 30
Tombstone (F7)* 910
Tonalea (E2)*
Tonopah (B5)* 4
Tonto Basin (D5)* 111
Topawa (D7)* 342
Topock (A4)* 50
Toreva (E3)
Tortilla Flat (D5)* 65
Tuba City (D2)* 250
Tubac (E7) 25
Tucson (D6)* 45,454
Tuweep (B2) 10
Vail (E6)*
Valentine (B3)* 127
Valley Farms (D6)* 212
Vernon (F4)* 155
Vicksburg (B5)* 33
Waddell (C5)*
Wagoner (C4)* 55
Walker (C4) 20
Warren (F7)* 2,610
Wellton (A6)*
Wenden (B5)* 100
Whipple (C4)* 650
Whiteriver (E5)* 950
Wickenburg (C5)* 1,736
Wide Ruins (F3) 9
Wikieup (B4)* 6
Wilhoit (C4) 12
Willcox (F6)* 1,266
Williams (C3)* 2,152
Window Rock (F3)*
Winkelman (E6)* 548
Winona (D3) 30
Winslow (E3)* 6,518
Wintersburg (B5) 50
Wittmann (C5)* 170
Wolf Hole (B2) 12
Woodruff (E4)* 164
Yarnell (C4)* 450
Yava (C4)* 35
Young (D4)* 242
Yucca (A4)* 40
Yuma (A6)* 9,145

ARKANSAS

Map on Page 51 — *Total Population 1,909,511*

75 COUNTIES

Arkansas (H5) 23,665
Ashley (G7) 25,660
Baxter (F1) 11,683
Benton (B1) 38,076
Boone (D1) 16,260
Bradley (F7) 15,987
Calhoun (E6) 7,132
Carroll (C1) 13,244
Chicot (H7) 22,306
Clark (D5) 22,998
Clay (K1) 26,674
Cleburne (F2) 11,487
Cleveland (F6) 8,956
Columbia (D7) 28,770
Conway (E3) 18,137
Craighead (J2) 50,613
Crawford (B2) 22,727
Crittenden (K3) 47,184
Cross (J3) 24,757
Dallas (E6) 12,416
Desha (H6) 25,155
Drew (G6) 17,959
Faulkner (F3) 25,289
Franklin (C2) 12,358
Fulton (G1) 9,187
Garland (D4) 47,102
Grant (F5) 9,024
Greene (J1) 29,149
Hempstead (C6) 25,080
Hot Spring (E5) 22,181
Howard (C5) 13,342
Independence (G2) 23,488
Izard (G1) 9,953
Jackson (H2) 25,912
Jefferson (G5) 76,075
Johnson (C2) 16,138
Lafayette (C7) 13,203
Lawrence (H1) 21,303
Lee (J4) 24,322
Lincoln (G6) 17,079
Little River (B6) 11,690
Logan (C3) 20,260
Lonoke (G4) 27,278
Madison (C1) 11,734
Marion (E1) 8,609
Miller (C7) 32,614
Mississippi (K2) 82,375
Monroe (H4) 19,540
Montgomery (C4) 6,680
Nevada (D6) 14,781
Newton (D2) 8,685
Ouachita (E6) 33,051
Perry (E4) 5,978
Phillips (J5) 46,254
Pike (C5) 10,032
Poinsett (J2) 39,311
Polk (B5) 14,182
Pope (D3) 23,291
Prairie (G4) 13,768
Pulaski (F4) 196,685
Randolph (H1) 15,982
Saint Francis (J3) 36,841
Saline (E4) 23,816
Scott (B4) 10,057
Searcy (E2) 10,424
Sebastian (B3) 64,202
Sevier (B6) 12,293
Sharp (G1) 8,999
Stone (F2) 7,662
Union (E7) 49,686
Van Buren (E2) 9,687
Washington (B2) 49,979
White (G3) 38,040
Woodruff (H3) 18,957
Yell (D3) 14,057

CITIES and TOWNS

Abbott (B3)* 200
Adona (E3)* 194
Agnos (G1)* 80
Alabam (C1)* 37
Albert (C5) 5
Alco (F2)*
Alexander (F4)* 194
Algoa (H2)* 73
Alicia (H2)* 299
Alix (C3)*
Alleene (B6)*
Alma (B3)* 1,228
Almond (G2)* 150
Almyra (H5)* 235
Alpena (D1)* 304
Alpine (D5)* 100
Altheimer (G5)* 680
Altus (C3)* 431
Aly (D4)* 122
Amagon (H2)* 181
Amity (D5)* 591
Antoine (D5)* 209
Aplin (E4)* 125
Appleton (E3)* 265

Arden (B6)*...
Arkadelphia (D5)*...6,819
Arkansas City (H6)*...1,018
Arkansas Post (H5)... 30
Arkinda (B6)*... 92
Arlberg (F2)*... 20
Armorel (L2)*... 500
Arthur (J3)...
Ash Flat (G1)*... 265
Ashdown (B6)*...2,738
Athens (C5)*... 57
Atkins (E3)*...1,291
Atlanta (D7)*...
Aubrey (J4)*... 300
Augusta (H3)*...2,317
Aurora (C2)*... 26
Austin (G4)*... 154
Auvergne (H2)*...
Avoca (B1)*... 200
Bald Knob (G3)*...2,022
Banks (F6)*... 240
Barber (B3)*... 35
Barfield (L2)... 100
Barling (B3)*... 325
Barton (J4)*... 600
Bates (B4)*... 130
Batesville (G2)*...6,414
Bauxite (F4)*...2,459
Bauxite Junction (E4)..
Baxter (G6)*... 75
Bay (J2)*... 500
Bayou Meto (H5)*... 300
Bearden (E6)*...1,300
Beaton (D5)... 75
Beaver (C1)*... 50
Bee Branch (F3)*... 137
Beebe (G3)*...1,192
Beirne (D6)...
Bellefonte (D1)*... 250
Belleville (D3)*... 372
Belton (C6)... 50
Ben Lomond (B6)*... 284
Benton (E4)*...6,277
Bentonville (B1)*...2,942
Bergman (E1)*... 126
Berryville (C1)*...1,753
Bestwater (B1)... 50
Bethel (K2)... 50
Bethesda (G2)*... 300
Big Fork (B5)*... 60
Bigelow (E3)*... 292
Bigflat (F1)*... 197
Biggers (J1)*... 333
Bingen (C6)*... 50
Birdell (H1)... 36
Birdsong (K3)... 100
Birta (D3)*... 78
Biscoe (H4)*... 406
Bismarck (D5)*... 150
Black Oak (K2)*... 261
Black Rock (H1)*... 662
Black Springs (C5)*... 90
Blackton (H4)*... 300
Blackwell (E3)*... 240
Blevins (C6)*... 271
Bloomer (B3)... 250
Blue Ball (C4)*... 90
Blue Mountain
(C3)*... 122
Bluff City (D6)*... 200
Bluffton (C4)*... 400
Blytheville (L2)*...16,234
Board Camp (B4)*... 75
Bodcaw (D6)*... 200
Bolding (F7)*... 59
Boles (B4)*... 150
Bonanza (B3)*... 361
Bono (J2)*... 352
Bookman (F5)... 50
Booneville (C3)*...2,433
Boswell (F1)*...
Boughton (D6)*...
Boxley (D2)*...
Boydell (H7)*... 100
Boydsville (K1)*... 100
Boynton (K2)... 15
Bradford (G3)*... 720
Bradley (C7)*... 444
Branch (C3)*... 308
Brasfield (H4)*... 100
Brentwood (B2)*... 300
Brickeys (J4)*... 62
Briggsville (C4)*... 253
Bright Star (C7)...
Brinkley (H4)*...4,173
Brookland (J2)*... 334
Brownsville (G2)... 100
Bruins (K4)... 200
Brummitt (G4)... 70
Bruno (E1)*...
Bryant (F4)*... 387
Buckner (D7)*... 335
Buckville (D4)*... 225
Buena Vista (D7)*... 150
Buffalo (E1)*... 52
Burdette (L2)*... 122
Burg (B5)... 1
Butlerville (G4)... 75
Butterfield (E5)*... 150
Cabot (F4)*...1,147
Caddo Gap (C5)*... 150
Calamine (H1)*... 24
Caldwell (J3)*...
Cale (D6)*... 115
Calico Rock (F1)*... 963
Calion (E7)*... 536
Calmer (F6)... 25
Camden (E6)*...11,372
Cammack Village (E4). 987
Canehill (B2)*... 150
Canfield (C7)*... 125
Caraway (K2)*... 970
Carlisle (G4)*...1,396
Carryville (K1)*... 40
Carson (K2)... 150
Carthage (E5)*... 533
Casa (D3)*... 184
Cash (J2)*... 188
Cass (C2)*...
Casscoe (H4)*... 300
Cato (F4)*... 125
Cauthron (B4)*... 50
Cave City (G2)*... 372
Cave Springs (B1)*... 267
Cedar Glades (D4)*... 350
Cedarcreek (C4)... 50
Cedarville (B2)*... 43
Center (H1)*... 65
Center Hill (G3)... 100
Center Point (C5)*... 162
Center Ridge (E3)*... 100
Centerton (B1)*... 200
Centerville (D3)*... 160
Central City (B3)... 115
Cerrogordo (B6)... 77
Chapel Hill (B5)... 260
Charleston (B3)*... 968
Chatfield (K3)*... 200
Cherokee City (A1)*... 68
Cherry Hill (B4)*... 175
Cherry Valley (J3)*... 521
Chester (B2)*... 120
Chickalah (D3)*... 97
Chicot (H7)*... 100
Chidester (D6)*... 425
Chismville (C3)... 100
Choctaw (F2)*...
Chula (C4)*... 47
Cincinnati (B1)... 50
Clarendon (H4)*...2,547
Clarkedale (K3)*... 150
Clarksville (D3)*...4,343
Clay (G3)... 40
Cleveland (E3)*... 59
Clifty (C1)*... 50
Clinton (F2)*... 853
Clover Bend (H2)... 75
Clyde (B2)*... 78
Coal Hill (C3)*... 873
College (G6)...
Collins (G6)*... 183
Colt (J3)*... 267
Columbus (C6)*... 200
Combs (C2)*...
Conway (F3)*...8,610
Copeland (E2)*...
Cord (H2)*... 150
Corinth (C5)... 60
Corley (C3)*... 45
Cornerstone (G5)... 100
Cornerville (G6)*... 100
Corning (J1)*...2,045
Cotter (E1)*...1,089
Cotton Plant (H3)*...1,838
Cove (B5)*... 405
Coy (G4)*... 200
Crawfordsville (K3)*... 680
Creswell (F1)*...
Crocketts Bluff (H5)*.. 102
Crosses (C2)*... 75
Crossett (F7)*...4,619
Crumrod (H5)*... 300
Crystal Springs (D5)*... 118
Cullendale (E7)*...3,225
Cumi (F1)*... 3
Curtis (D6)*...
Cushman (G2)*... 314
Cypert (J5)... 53
Daisy (C5)*... 74
Dalark (E5)*... 142
Dalton (H1)*... 50
Damascus (F3)*... 80
Danville (D3)*... 829
Dardanelle (D3)*...1,772
Datto (J1)*... 176
De Queen (B5)*...3,015
De Roche (D5)... 200
De Valls Bluff (H4)*... 830
De Witt (H5)*...2,843
Decatur (A1)*... 350
Deckerville (K3)... 46
Deer (D2)*... 80
Delaney (C2)*...
Delaplaine (J1)*... 208
Delaware (D3)*... 500
Delight (C5)*... 574
Dell (K2)*... 384
Denning (C3)*... 268
Denver (D1)*... 50
Dermott (H7)*...3,601
Des Arc (G4)*...1,612
Diantha (G5)...
Diaz (H2)*... 150
Dierks (B5)*...1,253
Dillen (D2)*... 50
Dodd City (E1)...
Doddridge (C7)*... 128
Donaldson (E5)*... 500
Douglas ‡(H5)*... 1
Dover (D3)*... 510
Drakes Creek (C2)*...
Drasco (G2)*... 100
Driggs (C3)... 50
Dryden (J2)... 43
Dublin (D3)...
Dumas (H6)*...2,512
Durham (C2)*... 110
Dutch Mills (B2)*... 50
Dutton (C2)*... 50
Dyer (B3)*... 398
Eagle Mills (E6)*... 175
Eagleton (B4)*... 64
Earle (K3)*...2,375
Edgemont (F2)*... 89
Edmondson (K3)*... 283
El Dorado (E7)*...23,076
El Paso (F3)*... 200
Elaine (J5)*... 744
Elba (E2)*... 32
Elizabeth (F1)*... 100
Elkins (C1)*... 275
Elliott (E7)... 150
Ellisville (F6)...
Elm Springs (B1)*... 217
Elmore (E5)... 45
Emerson (D7)*... 523
Emmet (D6)*... 482
Enders (F3)... 25
England (G4)*...2,136
Enola (F3)*... 250
Ethel (H5)*...
Etowah (K2)*... 150
Eudora (H7)*...3,072
Eureka Springs (C1)*...1,958
Evadale (K2)... 100
Evansville (B2)*... 2
Evening Shade (G1)*... 360
Everton (E1)*... 198
Excelsior (B3)... 200
Faber (E5)*... 215

Fair Oaks (J3)*... 200
Faith (F5)... 100
Fallsville (D2)*...
Fargo (H4)*... 200
Farmington (B1)*... 300
Fayetteville (B1)*...17,071
Felsenthal (F7)*...
Felton (J4)... 100
Fenter (E5)*... 50
Ferda (G5)... 50
Fisher (J2)*... 289
Fitzhugh (H3)*... 165
Flippin (E1)*... 646
Floral (G2)*... 150
Florence (G6)*... 275
Floyd (G3)... 135
Fontain (J2)... 250
Fordyce (F6)*...3,754
Foreman (B6)*... 907
Forester (C4)*... 818
Formosa (E3)*... 195
Forrest City (J3)*...7,607
Fort Smith (B3)*...47,942
Fort Smith (urban
area)...55,947
Forum (C1)*... 45
Fouke (C7)*... 336
Fountain Hill (G7)*... 320
Fourche (E4)... 51
Fox (F2)*...
Franklin (G1)*... 100
Fredonia (Biscoe*)(H4) 406
Friendship (E5)*... 179
Frys Mill (K2)... 75
Fulton (C6)*... 385
Gaines Landing (H7)... 100
Gainesville (J1)... 200
Galloway (F4)... 350
Garfield (C1)*... 83
Garland (C7)*... 351
Garner (G3)*... 175
Gassville (F1)*... 273
Gateway (B1)*... 97
Genoa (C7)*... 100
Gentry (A1)*... 729
Georgetown (G3)*... 200
Gilbert (E2)*... 51
Gillett (H5)*... 774
Gillham (B5)*... 207
Gilmore (K3)*...
Glenville (D7)...
Glenwood* (C5)... 843
Goldman (G5)... 40
Goodwin (J4)*... 85
Goshen (C1)*... 65
Gould (G6)*...1,076
Grady (G5)*... 517
Grand Glaise (G2)*...
Grand Lake (H7)*...
Grandview (C1)*... 86
Grannis (B5)*... 193
Grapevine (F5)*... 200
Gravelly (C4)*... 150
Gravelridge (F7)... 250
Gravette (B1)*... 894
Grays (H3)*...
Graysonia (D5)...
Green Forest (D1)*... 738
Greenbrier (F3)*... 375
Greenland (B1)*... 164
Greenway (K1)*... 288
Greenwood (B3)*...1,634
Gregory (H3)*... 250
Griffithville (G3)*... 207
Grubbs (H2)*... 313
Guion (G2)*... 219
Gurdon (D6)*...2,390
Guy (F3)*... 100
Hackett (B3)*... 440
Hagarville (D2)*... 195
Halley (H6)*... 149
Hamburg (G7)*...2,655
Hampton (F6)*... 838
Hardy (H1)*... 599
Harmony (D2)*... 31
Harrell (F7)*... 342
Harris (B1)*... 2
Harrisburg (J2)*...1,498
Harrison (D1)*...5,542
Hartford (B3)*... 865
Hartman (C3)*... 418
Haskell (E4)*... 209
Harwood (H7)...
Hasty (D1)*... 25
Hatfield (B5)*... 364
Hattieville (E3)*... 150
Havana (D3)*... 348
Haynes (J4)*... 250
Hazen (G4)*...1,270
Heber Springs (G2)*...2,109
Hector (E3)*... 325
Helena (J4)*...11,236
Hensley (F4)*...1,200
Herbine (F6)*... 55
Hermitage (F7)*... 398
Heth (K3)*... 285
Hickman (L2)... 150
Hickory Plains (G3)*... 225
Hickory Ridge (J3)*... 345
Higden (F2)*... 115
Higginson (G3)*... 131
Highland (C5)*... 50
Hillemann (H3)*... 35
Hindsville (C1)*... 116
Hiram (G3)*... 100
Hiwasse (B1)*... 300
Holland (F3)... 100
Hollis (D4)*... 195
Holly Grove (H4)*... 761
Holly Springs (E6)*...
Hollywood (D5)*... 100
Homan (C6)... 75
Hon (B4)*... 200
Hope (C6)*...8,605
Hopper (C5)*... 200
Hopper (H4)... 60
Horatio (B6)*... 776
Hot Springs Nat'l
Park (D4)*...29,307
Houston (E3)*... 291
Howell (H3)*... 55
Hoxie (H1)*...1,855
Hudspeth (H7)... 40
Huffman (L2)*... 300
Hughes (J4)*...1,686
Hulbert (K3)*... 750
Humnoke (G4)*... 263
Humphrey (G5)*... 629
Hunter (H3)*... 286
Huntington (B3)*... 744
Huntsville (C1)*...1,010
Huttig (F7)*...1,038
Iceledo (D2)... 20
Imboden (H1)*... 447
Ingalls (F7)*... 300
Ione (B3)*... 80
Ivan (F6)*... 150
Ivy (E5)*... 80
Jacinto (E6)...
Jacksonport (H2)*...
Jacksonville (F4)*...2,474
Jamestown (G2)*... 84
Jasper (D1)*... 407
Jefferson (F5)*...
Jennie (H7)*...
Jenny Lind (B3)*... 513
Jericho (K3)... 250
Jerome (G7)*... 82
Jersey (F7)*...
Jerusalem (E3)*...
Jessieville (D4)*... 100
Johnson (B1)*... 350
Johnsville (F7)*...
Joiner (K2)*... 596
Jonesboro (J2)*...16,310
Judsonia (G3)*...1,122
Junction City (E7)*...1,013
Kedron (F5)*... 100
Keevil (H4)*... 350
Keiser (K2)*... 522
Kelso (H6)...
Kensett (G3)*... 829
Keo (G4)*... 200
Kerlin (D7)... 50
Kerrs (F4)... 100
Kiblah (C7)... 55
Kimberley ‡(C5)... 46
King (B5)*...
Kingsland (F6)*... 337
Kingston (C1)*... 208
Kinton (J3)*... 150
Kirby (C5)*...
Knobel (J1)*... 417
Knowlton (H5)...
Knoxville (D3)*... 367
Koch Ridge (E2)... 22
La Grange (J4)*... 250
Lacey (G7)...
Ladelle (G7)*... 38
Lafe (J1)*... 400
Lafferty (G2)*... 250
Lake City (K2)*... 783
Lake Frances (B1)... 15
Lake Village (H7)*...2,484
Lamar (D3)*... 555
Lambert (D5)*... 250
Laneburg (D6)*... 85
Langley (C5)*... 53
Lapile (F7)*... 55
Lavaca (B3)*... 373
Lawson (F7)*... 300
Leachville (K2)*...1,230
Lead Hill (E1)*... 110
Leecreek (B2)*... 25
Leola (E5)*... 313
Leonard (K1)... 10
Lepanto (K2)*...1,683
Leslie (E2)*... 610
Lester (E6)...
Letona (G3)*... 164
Levy (F4)*...
Lewisville (C7)*...1,237
Lexa (J4)*... 500
Lexington (F2)... 100
Limestone (D2)*...
Lincoln (B2)*... 771
Lisbon (E7)...
LITTLE ROCK (F4)*.102,213
Little Rock - North
Little Rock (urban
area)...150,758
Lockesburg (B6)*... 714
Locust Bayou (E6)... 75
Lodge Corner (H5)*... 43
London (D3)*... 353
Lonoke (G4)*...1,556
Lonsdale (E4)*... 91
Louann (E7)*... 291
Lowell (B1)*... 341
Lucas (B3)... 40
Luna Landing (H7)... 100
Lundell (H5)*... 350
Lunsford (K2)... 150
Lurton (D2)*...
Luxora (K2)*...1,302
Lynn (H2)*...
Mabelvale (F4)*... 200
Macedonia (D7)... 100
Macks (H2)*... 100
Madison (J4)*... 718
Magazine (C3)*... 503
Magness (H2)*... 229
Magnet (E5)*... 175
Magnolia (D7)*...6,918
Malvern (E5)*...8,072
Mammoth Spring(G1)*. 870
Mandalay (K2)... 15
Mandeville (C7)*... 150
Manila (K2)*...1,729
Manning (E5)*... 300
Mansfield (B3)*... 869
Marble (C1)*... 100
Marcella (G2)*... 75
Marche (F4)... 75
Marianna (J4)*...4,530
Marion (K3)*... 883
Marked Tree (K2)*...2,878
Marmaduke (K1)*... 643
Marshall (E2)*...1,189
Martinville (F3)*... 450
Marvell (J4)*...1,121
Mauldin (C4)...
Maumee (E1)*... 25
Mayflower (F4)*... 293
Maynard (J1)*... 216
Maysville (A1)*... 225
McCaskill (C6)*... 122
McClelland (H3)*... 150
McCrory (H3)*...1,115
McDougal (K1)*... 250
McFadden (H3)*...
McGehee (H6)*...3,854
McKamie (C7)*... 109
McNab (C6)*... 206
McNeil (D7)*... 597
McRae (G3)*... 414
Meg (C3)... 10
Melbourne (G1)*... 568
Mellwood (H5)*... 300
Mena (B4)*...4,445
Menifee (E3)*...
Meroney (G6)... 50
Mesa (G4)... 25
Meyers (D5)*... 100
Middlebrook (H1)*... 30
Midland (B3)*... 356
Midway (E6)*... 450
Millville (E6)... 100
Milner (D7)...
Milo (G7)... 12
Mineral (B5)*... 50
Mineral Springs (C6)*.. 751
Minturn (H2)*... 138
Mist (G7)... 15
Mitchell (G1)*... 44
Moark (J1)*... 125
Monette (K2)*...1,114
Monroe (H4)*... 75
Montana (C3)... 150
Monte Ne (B1)*... 100
Monticello (G6)*...4,501
Montrose (H7)*... 344
Moorefield (H2)*... 107
Moreland (E3)*... 50
Morganton (F3)*...
Moro (H4)*... 189
Morobay (F7)*... 77
Morrilton (E3)*...5,483
Morrison Bluff (D3)...
Morriston (G1)*... 50
Morrow (B2)*... 50
Moscow (G5)*...
Mount Holly (E7)*...
Mount Ida (C4)*... 566
Mount Judea (D2)*... 95
Mount Pleasant (G2)*.. 250
Mount Sherman (D1)... 130
Mount Vernon (F3)*... 200
Mountain Home (F1)*...2,217
Mountain Pine (D4)*...1,155
Mountain Valley (D4)*. 160
Mountain View (F2)*...1,043
Mountainburg (B2)*... 405
Mountaincrest (B2)...
Mulberry (B2)*... 952
Murfreesboro (C5)*...1,079
Nashville (C6)*...3,548
Nathan (C5)... 100
Natural Steps (E4)... 100
Nelsonville (H1)...
Nettleton (J2)*...1,382
Neuhardt (K3)... 190
New Blaine (D3)*...
New Edinburg (F6)*... 150
New London (F7)... 50
New Rocky Comfort
(Foreman*) (B6)... 907
Newark (H2)*... 913
Newburg (G1)*...
Newhope (C5)*... 162
Newport (H2)*...6,254
Nimmons (K1)*... 199
Nimrod (D4)*... 185
Noble Lake (G5)... 150
Nola (C4)*... 130
Norfork (F1)*... 431
Norman (C5)*... 401
Norphlet (E7)*... 653
No. Little Rock (F4)*..44,097
No. Little Rock-Little
Rock (urban area)..150,758
North Spadra (C3)... 75
Norvell (K3)... 372
Nunley (B4)... 50
Oakgrove (C1)*... 100
Oakhaven ‡(C6)... 81
Oden (C4)*... 133
Ogden (B6)*... 296
Ogemaw (E7)*... 75
Oil Trough (G2)*... 300
O'Kean (J1)*... 165
Okolona (D5)*... 458
Ola (D3)*... 880
Olena (H5)... 39
Olvey (E1)*...
Olyphant (H2)*...
Omaha (D1)*... 91
Oneida (J5)*...
Onyx (D4)*... 60
Oppelo (E3)... 100
Optimus (F1)*... 60
Osage (D1)*... 30
Osage Mills (B1)... 12
Osceola (K2)*...5,006
Otwell (J2)*...
Ouachita (E6)*... 75
Owensville (E4)... 100
Oxford (G1)*... 79
Ozan (C6)*... 124
Ozark (C3)*...1,757
Ozone (D2)*... 200
Palarm (F4)... 25
Palatka (J1)*... 40
Palestine (J4)*... 420
Pangburn (G3)*... 669
Paragould (J1)*...9,668
Paraloma (B6)*... 186
Paris (C3)*...3,731
Parkdale (G7)*... 385
Parkin (J3)*...1,414
Parks (B4)*... 200
Paron (E4)*... 75
Patmos (C7)*... 120
Patterson (H3)*... 357
Pea Ridge (B1)*... 268
Peach Orchard (J1)*... 327
Pearcy (D5)*... 200
Pearson (F3)*... 55
Pecan Point (L3)... 100
Penrose (H3)*... 50
Perla (E5)*... 400
Perry (E3)*... 284
Perryville (E3)*... 674
Pettigrew (C2)*...
Pfeiffer (G2)... 50
Pickens (H6)*... 86
Piggott (K1)*...2,558
Pike (C5)*... 123
Pinckney (K4)*... 175
Pindall (E1)*... 160
Pine Bluff (F5)*...37,162
Pine City (H4)... 75
Pine Grove (E6)... 300
Pine Ridge (C4)*...
Pinetree (J3)... 75
Piney (D3)... 50
Pitts (J2)... 40
Plainfield (D7)...
Plainview (D4)*... 637
Pleasant Plains (G2)*.. 153
Plumerville (E3)*... 550
Pocahontas (E1)*...3,840
Point Cedar (D5)*... 63
Pollard (K1)*... 165
Ponca (D1)*... 42
Poplar Grove (J4)*... 169
Portia (H1)*... 349
Portland (G7)*... 517
Postelle (J4)*... 42
Potter (B4)*... 175
Pottsville (D3)*... 224
Poughkeepsie (H1)*...
Powhatan (H1)*... 120
Poyen (E5)*...
Prague (F5)... 39
Prairie Grove (B2)*... 939
Prairie View (C3)*... 300
Prattsville (F5)*... 110
Prescott (D6)*...3,960
Princedale (J3)... 25
Princeton (E6)*... 112
Proctor (K3)*... 500
Provo (B5)*... 61
Pyatt (E1)*... 257
Quitman (F3)*... 345
Ratcliff (C3)*... 213
Ratio (J5)*... 375
Ravana (C7)*...
Ravenden (H1)*... 245
Ravenden Springs (H1)* 197
Reader (D6)*... 79
Readland (H7)*... 125
Rector (K1)*...1,855
Redfield (F5)*... 291
Redstar (C2)*...
Relfs Bluff (G6)*... 50
Rest (G6)... 10
Retta (E3)... 10
Rex (E2)... 40
Reydell (G5)*... 150
Reyno (J1)*... 292
Rich Mountain (B4)... 57
Richmond (B6)...
Rison (F6)*... 953
Rivervale (K2)*...
Rob Roy (G5)... 50
Robinson (B1)... 60
Roe (H4)*... 200
Rogers (B1)*...4,962
Rohwer (H6)*...
Roland (E4)*... 350
Rolla (E5)*... 150
Romance (F3)*... 100
Rondo (J4)*... 194
Rosboro (C5)*... 84
Rose Bud (F3)*... 181
Roseland (K2)*... 75
Rosetta (D2)... 50
Rosie (G2)*... 300
Rosston (D6)*... 200
Round Pond (J3)*... 250
Rover (D4)*... 182
Rowell (F6)*... 50
Rudy (B2)*... 97
Rush (E1)*... 250
Russell (G3)*... 241
Russellville (D3)*...8,166
Rye (F6)*... 40
Saddle (G1)*... 45
Sage (G1)*... 125
Saint Charles (H5)*... 313
St. Francis (K1)*... 292
St. James (F2)*...
St. Joe (E1)*... 187
St. Paul (C2)*... 136
St. Thomas (K3)... 100
Salado (G2)*... 200
Salem (G1)*... 687
Salus (D2)*... 100
Saratoga (C6)*... 110
Sayre (D6)...
Schaal (C6)*... 25
Scotland (E2)*... 200
Scott (F4)*... 350
Scottsville (D3)*... 150
Scranton (C3)*... 283
Searcy (G3)*...6,024
Sedgwick (J2)*... 196
Selma (G6)*... 275
Seyppel (K4)... 175
Shawmut (D5)... 26
Shelbyville (H2)*...
Sheridan (F5)*...1,893
Sherrill (G5)*... 263
Sherwood (F4)... 717
Shiloh (F2)*... 41
Shirley (F2)*... 259
Sidney (G1)*... 120
Sidon (G3)*... 75
Siloam Springs (B1)*...3,270

Map on Page 52   CALIFORNIA   Total Population 10,586,223

Lafayette (K2)*.........10,500
Laguna Beach (G10)*...6,661
Lagunitas (H1)*.......... 750
Lake Alpine (F5)*........ 3
Lake Arrowhead (H9)*.. 667
Lake City (E2)*.......... 94
Lake Hughes (G9)*....... 224
Lakeport (C4)*............1,983
Lakeside (J11)*...........1,500
Lakewood (C11)*.........31,000
Lamont (G8)*..............3,571
Lancaster (G9)*...........3,594
Larkspur (H1)*............2,905
Las Plumas (D4)*........ 55
Lathrop (D6)............... 600
Laton (F7)*................ 881
Laurel (K4)................. 64
Lawndale (C11)*.........31,000
Lawndale (Colma*)(H2) 297
Laws (G6)*................. 75
Laytonville (B4)*.........
Le Grand (E6)*............1,000
Lebec (G9)*................ 370
Leevining (F6)*........... 450
Lemoncove (G7)*..........1,100
Lemoore (F7)*.............2,153
Lennox (C11)*............25,000
Lenwood (H9).............. 250
Leucadia (H10)*.......... 500
Lewiston (C3)*............ 300
Likely (E2)*................ 200
Lincoln (B8)*...............2,410
Linden (D5)*............... 426
Lindsay (G7)*..............5,060
Little Lake (H8)*......... 50
Littleriver (B4)*.......... 300
Live Oak (D4)*.............1,770
Livermore (L2)*...........4,364
Livingston (E6)*..........1,502
Llano (H9)*................ 30
Locke (B9)*................ 295
Lockeford (C9)*...........1,000
Lodi (C9)*..................13,798
Loftus (C3)*............... 200
Loleta (A3)*............... 500
Loma Linda (E10)*......4,000
Loma Mar (J3)*.......... 125
Lomita (C11)*............10,000
Lomita Park (J2)*........1,800
Lompoc (E9)*...............5,520
Lone Pine (H7)*...........1,415
Long Beach (C11)*....250,767
Lonoak (E7)*............... 15
Lookout (D2)*............. 225
Loomis (C8)*............... 350
Los Alamitos (D11)*.....1,800
Los Alamos (E9)*......... 800
Los Altos (K3)*..........11,000
Los Angeles (C10)*.1,970,358
Los Angeles (urban area) 3,970,595
Los Banos (E6)*...........3,868
Los Gatos (K4)*............4,907
Los Molinos (D3)*........ 600
Los Olivos (E9)*.......... 500
Lost Hills (F8)*............ 300
Lotus (C8)*................. 150
Lower Lake (C5)*......... 275
Loyalton (E4)*............ 911
Lucerne (C4)*.............. 350
Lucerne Valley (J9)*.... 933
Ludlow (J9)*............... 250
Lynwood (C11)*...........25,823
Macdoel (D2)*............. 200
Madeline (E2)*............ 60
Madera (E7)*..............10,497
Madison (D5)*.............
Madrone (L4)*............. 720
Magalia (D4)*............. 200
Manchester (B5)*......... 500
Manhattan Beach (B11)* 17,330
Manteca (D6)*.............3,804
Manton (D3)*.............. 100
March Air Force Base (E11)* ....
Maricopa (F8)*............ 800
Mariposa (F6)*............ 700
Markleeville (F5)*........ 100
Martell (C9)*............... 200
Martinez (K1)*............8,268
Marysville (D4)*...........7,826
Maxwell (C4)*............. 750
Maywood (C10)*.........13,292
Mc Arthur (D2)*........... 398
Mc Cann (B3)............... 35
Mc Cloud (C2)*............1,394
Mc Farland (F8)*.........2,183
Mc Kittrick (F8)*......... 124
Meadow Valley (D4)*... 300
Mecca (K10)*.............. 837
Mendocino (B4)*..........1,250
Mendota (E7)*.............1,516
Menlo Park (J3)*........13,587
Mentone (H9)*.............3,525
Merced (E6)*.............15,278
Michigan Bar (C8)........ 132
Middletown (C5)*......... 400
Midland (L10)*............ 700
Midway City (D11)*......1,421
Milford (E3)*............... 55
Mill Valley (H2)*.........7,331
Millbrae (J2)*..............8,972
Mills (C8)..................... 300
Millville (C3)*.............. 246
Milpitas (L3)*.............
Milton (E5)..................
Mineral (D3)*.............. 125
Mira Loma (E10)*........1,555
Mission San Jose (L3)*1,080
Modesto (D6)*............17,389
Mojave (G8)*...............2,055
Mokelumne Hill (E5)*.. 495
Mono Lake (F5)*.......... 20
Monolith (G8)*............ 450
Monrovia (D10)*.........20,186
Montague (C2)*........... 579
Montalvo (F9)*.............1,200
Montara (H3)*............. 400
Monte Rio (B5)*.......... 750
Montebello (C10)*......21,735
Montecito (F9).............4,052
Monterey (D7)*..........16,205
Monterey Park (C10)*.20,395
Monticello (C5)*.........
Montrose (C10)*..........8,500
Moorpark (G9)*............1,146
Moraga (K2)*.............. 325
Moreno (H10)*............ 200
Morgan Hill (L4)*........1,627
Morro Bay (D8)*..........1,659
Moss Beach (H3)*......... 525
Moss Landing (C7)*..... 300
Mount Eden (K2)*........1,500
Mount Hamilton (L3)*..
Mount Hermon (K4)*.... 150
Mount Owen (H8).........
Mount Shasta (C2)*.....1,909
Mountain Center (J10)* 40
Mountain View (K3)*....6,563
Murphys (E5)*............. 650
Murray (E7)................ 150
Napa (C5)*.................13,579
Napa Junction (J1)...... 224
National City (J11)*..21,199
Natoma (C8)*.............. 65
Navarro (B4)*............. 117
Needles (L9)*..............4,051
Nevada City (D4)*........2,505
New Cuyuma (F9)* 1,079
Newark (K3)*...............1,532
Newberry (J9)*............ 520
Newcastle (C8)*.......... 800
Newhall (G9)*..............2,527
Newman (D6)*..............1,815
Newport Beach (D11)*12,120
Nicasio (H1)*.............. 133
Nicolaus (B8)*............ 400
Niland (K10)*.............. 700
Niles (K3)*..................1,519
Nipinnawasee (F6)*......
Nipomo (E8)*...............1,000
Nipton (K8)*................ 15
Norco (E11)*...............1,584
Norden (E4)*............... 220
N. Fork (F6)*...............1,453
N. Sacramento (B8)*....6,029
N. San Juan (E4)*........ 250
Norwalk (C11)*............6,300
Novato (H1)*................3,496
Nubieber (D2)*............ 400
Oakdale (E6)*...............4,064
Oakhurst (F6)*............ 325
Oakland (J2)*............384,575
Oakland-San Francisco (urban area)........1,997,303
Oakley (L1)*................2,892
Oasis (G6)..................... 25
Ocean Beach (H11)*....16,600
Oceano (E8)*...............1,446
Oceanside (H10)*........12,881
Oildale (F8)*.............,16,615
Ojai (F9)*....................2,519
Olancha (H7)*............. 200
Olema (H1)*.................
Oleum (J1)*..................1,200
Olinda (C3)*................ 411
Olinda (D11)............... 150
Olive (D11)*................ 700
Olympia (K4).............. 150
O'Neals (F6)*...............
Ono (C3)*.................... 38
Ontario (D10)*............22,872
Onyx (G8)*.................. 150
Orange (D11)*............10,027
Orange Cove (F7)*.......2,395
Orcutt (E9)*................1,001
Orick (A2)*.................. 600
Orinda (K2)*................5,000
Orland (C4)*................2,067
Orleans (B2)*.............. 263
Oro Grande (H9)*........ 556
Orosi (F7)*.................. 712
Oroville (D4)*...............5,387
Oxford (B9).................. 28
Oxnard (F9)*..............21,567
Pacheco (K1)............... 400
Pacific Beach (H11)*..23,600
Pacific Grove (C7)*......9,623
Paicines (D7)*............. 300
Palermo (D4)*..............1,200
Palm City (H11)*..........3,000
Palm Springs (J10)*....7,660
Palmdale (G9)*............3,300
Palo Alto (K3)*...........25,475
Palo Verde (L10)*........ 200
Palos Verdes Estates (B11)* 1,963
Paradise (D4)*.............4,426
Paramount (C11)*.......10,006
Parker Dam (L9)*........ 550
Parlier (F7)*.................1,419
Pasadena (C10)*.......104,577
Paskenta (C4)*............ 350
Paso Robles (E8)*........4,835
Patterson (D6)*............1,343
Paynes Creek (D3)*...... 35
Penryn (C8)*............... 500
Pepperwood (A3)*........ 300
Perkins (B8)*............... 600
Perris (F11)*.................1,807
Pescadero (J4)*............1,000
Petaluma (H1)*..........10,315
Philo (B4)*................... 700
Pico (C10)*...................9,000
Piedmont (J2)*............10,132
Pine Valley (J11)*........ 300
Pinecrest (F5)*............ 30
Pinedale (F7)*..............2,220
Pineridge (F6)............. 115
Pinole (J1)*..................1,147
Piru (G9)*.....................1,500
Pismo Beach (E8)*.......1,425
Pittsburg (K1)*...........12,763
Pittville (D2)*.............. 50
Pixley (F8)*..................2,000
Placentia (D11)*...........1,682
Placerville (C8)*...........3,749
Planada (E6)*...............1,200
Plaster City (K11)*...... 205
Pleasant Grove (B8)*... 30
Pleasanton (L2)*..........2,244
Plymouth (C8)*............ 382
Point Arena (B5)*........ 372
Point Reyes Sta. (H1)*. 500
Pollock Pines (E5)*...... 850
Pomona (D10)*...........35,405
Pondosa (D2)*............. 400
Port Chicago (K1)*.......3,000
Port Costa (J1)*........... 587
Port Hueneme (F9)*.....3,024
Porterville (F7)*...........6,904
Portola (E4)*................2,261
Potrero (J11)*............. 200
Potter Valley (B4)*......1,200
Pozo (E8)..................... 200
Princeton (C4)*........... 300
Project City (C3)*........1,200
Puente (D10)*..............3,000
Quincy (E4)*.................1,330
Raisin (E7)*................. 250
Ramona (J10)*..............1,158
Rancho Santa Fe (H10)* 750
Randsburg (H8)*.......... 300
Ravendale (E3)*........... 38
Raymond (F6)*............ 200
Red Bluff (C3)*............4,905
Red Mountain (H8)*..... 250
Redding (C3)*.............10,256
Redlands (H9)*...........18,429
Redondo Beach (B11)*25,226
Redwood City (J3)*.....25,544
Redwood Estates (K4)* 600
Reedley (F7)*...............4,135
Represa (C8)*...............3,000
Requa (A2)*.................
Rialto (E10)*.................3,156
Rice (L9)*.................... 109
Richmond (J1)*..........99,545
Richvale (D4)*............. 430
Ridgecrest (H8)*..........2,028
Rio Dell (A3)*...............1,862
Rio Linda (B8)*.............5,000
Rio Vista (L1)*..............1,831
Ripley (L10)*............... 300
Ripon (D6)*...................1,550
Riverbank (E6)*............2,662
Riverdale (E7)*............ 713
Riverside (E10)*.........46,764
Robbins (B8)*.............. 150
Rockaway Beach (H2)* 300
Rocklin (B8)*................1,155
Rockport (B4)*............ 750
Rodeo (J1)*...................6,500
Rohnerville (B3)*..........1,500
Rosamond (G9)*.......... 700
Rosemead (D10)*........15,230
Roseville (B8)*..............8,723
Ross (H1)*....................2,179
Round Mountain (D3)*. 450
Ryde (B9)*................... 397
SACRAMENTO (B8)* 137,572
Sacramento (urban area) 210,081
Sage (J10).................... 52
Saint Helena (C5)*.......2,297
Salinas (D7)*..............13,917
Salyer (B3)*................ 250
Samoa (A3)*................ 600
San Andreas (E5)*........1,263
San Anselmo (H1).........9,188
San Ardo (E7)*............ 500
San Benito (D7)*.......... 110
San Bernardino (E10)*63,058
San Bernardino (urban area) 135,394
San Bruno (J2)*.........12,478
San Carlos (J3)*.........14,371
San Clemente (H10)*....2,008
San Diego (J11)*.......334,387
San Diego (urban area) 413,274
San Dimas (D10)*.........1,840
San Fernando (C10)*..12,992
San Francisco (H2)*.775,357
San Francisco-Oakland (urban area).......1,997,303
San Gabriel (C10)*......20,343
San Geronimo (H1)*..... 300
San Gregorio (J3)*....... 250
San Jacinto (H10)*.......1,778
San Joaquin (E7)*........ 632
San Jose (L3)*............95,280
San Jose (urban area).....................175,983
San Juan Bautista (D7)* 1,031
San Juan Capistrano (H10)* 1,250
San Leandro (J2)*......27,542
San Lorenzo (K2)*......10,570
San Lucas (E7)*.......... 400
San Luis Obispo (E8)..14,180
San Marino (D10)*......11,230
San Martin (L4)*..........2,200
San Mateo (J3)*.........41,782
San Miguel (E8)*......... 800
San Pablo (J1)*..........14,476
San Pedro (C11)*........74,000
San Quentin (H1)*........
San Rafael (J1)*.........13,848
San Ramon (K2)*......... 250
San Simeon (D8)*......... 75
San Ysidro (J11)*.........2,381
Sanger (F7)*.................6,400
Sanitarium (C5)*......... 750
Santa Ana (D11)*.......45,533
Santa Barbara (F9)*...44,913
Santa Clara (K3)*.......11,702
Santa Cruz (K4)*........21,970
Santa Margarita (E8)*. 500
Santa Maria (E9)*......10,440
Santa Monica (B10)*..71,595
Santa Paula (F9)*......11,049
Santa Rosa (C5)*........17,902
Santa Susana (B10)*....1,000
Saratoga (K4)*............1,329
Saticoy (F9)*................2,216
Sausalito (H2)*.............4,828
Sawyers Bar (B2)*.......
Schellville (J1).............
Scotia (A3)*..................1,017
Seabright (K4)*............
Seal Beach (C11)*........3,553
Seaside (D7)...............10,226
Sebastopol (C5)*..........2,601
Seeley (K11)*.............. 500
Seiad Valley (B2)*........ 41
Selby (J1)*.................. 403
Selma (F7)*..................5,964
Seneca (D3).................
Sepulveda (B10)*..........4,500
Shafter (F8)*................2,207
Shandon (E8)*............. 510
Sharp Park (H2)*.........3,800
Shasta (C3)*................ 900
Shell Beach (E8)*.........1,000
Sheridan (D5)*............. 600
Shingle (C8)*............... 300
Shively (B3)*................ 196
Shoshome (J8)*............ 150
Sierra City (E4)*.......... 150
Sierra Madre (D10)*.....7,273
Sierraville (E4)*........... 400
Signal Hill (C11)*........4,040
Silverado (E11)*...........1,400
Simi (G9)*.................... 550
Sites (C4)*................... 200
Sloat (E4)*...................
Sloughhouse (C8)*........
Smartville (D4)*........... 350
Smith River (A2)*........ 700
Snelling (E6)*.............. 350
Soda Springs (E4)*...... 400
Solana Beach (H11)*...1,350
Soledad (D7)*...............2,441
Solvang (E9)*................1,025
Somesbar (B2)*............ 200
Sonoma (C5)*................2,015
Sonora (E6)*..................2,448
Soquel (K4)*..................2,400
Soulsbyville (E6)*......... 150
S. Bakersfield (F8).....12,120
S. Dos Palos (E7)*........ 503
S. Fork (A3)*................ 150
S. Gate (C11)*............51,116
S. Pasadena (C10)*.....16,935
S. San Francisco (J2)*19,351
Spadra (D10)*...............1,200
Spreckels (D7)*............
Spring Garden (D4)*.... 180
Springville (G7)*.......... 735
Stacy (E3)*................... 23
Standard (E6)*............. 300
Standish (E3)*............. 45
Stanford (J3)*............10,000
Stanton (D11)*..............1,762
Stauffer (F9)................ 100
Stege (J2)....................
Stewarts Point (B5)*... 200
Stinson Beach (H2)*.... 400
Stirling City (D4)*........ 750
Stockton (D6)*............70,853
Stockton(urban area)113,362
Stonyford (C4)*........... 125
Stratford (F7)*............ 400
Strathmore (F7)*.........2,500
Suisun City (K1)*......... 946
Summerland (F9)*........ 507
Summit City (C3)*........1,000
Sunland (C10)*.............5,000
Sunnymead (F11)*........ 885
Sunnyvale (K3)*...........9,829
Sunol (L2)*.................. 700
Sunset Beach (C11)*....1,500
Surf (E9)*..................... 50
Susanville (E3)*............5,338
Sutter (D4)*..................1,200
Sutter Creek (C9)*........1,151
Taft (F8)*.....................3,707
Tahoe City (E4)*.......... 250
Tahoe Valley (E5)*.......
Tarzana (B10)*...........10,000
Taylorsville (E3)*......... 250
Tecopa (J8)*................ 150
Tehachapi (G8)*...........1,685
Tehama (C3)*............... 314
Temecula (H10)*.......... 500
Temple City (C10)*.....25,000
Templeton (E8)*.......... 586
Tennant (C2)*.............. 450
Termo (E3)*................. 58
Terra Bella (G8)*......... 850
Thermal (J10)*............ 942
Thornton (B9)*.............1,800
Tiburon (J2)*................1,100
Tionesta (D2)*.............
Tipton (F7)*..................1,000
Tomales (C5)*..............
Topanga (B10)*.............3,728
Torrance (C11)*..........22,241
Tracy (D6)*...................8,410
Tranquillity (E7)*......... 500
Tres Pinos (D7)*.......... 180
Trigo (F7)....................
Trinidad (A2)*............. 188
Trinity Center (C2)*..... 100
Trona (H8)*...................2,450
Truckee (E4)*................1,025
Tujunga (C10)*...........14,000
Tulare (F7)*.................12,445
Tulelake (D2)*...............1,028
Tuolumne (E6)*.............1,284
Tupman (F8)*............... 187
Turlock (D6)*................6,235
Tustin (D11)*................1,143
Twain (D4)*................. 285
Twentynine Palms(K9)*10,22
Twin Lakes (K4)...........
Twin Peaks (H9)*........ 489
Ukiah (B4)*...................6,120
Upland (D10)*...............9,203
Upper Lake (C4)*......... 600
Vacaville (D5)*..............3,169
Vallejo (J1)*.................26,038
Valley Center (J10)*.... 50
Valley Springs (C9)*.... 500
Van Nuys (B10)*.........90,000
Venice (B11)*..............58,871
Ventucopa (F9)*.......... 40
Ventura (F9)*..............16,534
Verdugo City (C10)*.....2,100
Vernon (C10)*............. 432
Victor (C9)*.................
Victorville (H9)*...........3,241
Vidal (L9)*................... 50
Vina (D4)*................... 500
Visalia (F7)*................11,749
Vista (H10)*..................1,705
Volcano (E5)*.............. 150
Vorden (B9)................. 175
Wallace (C9)*.............. 55
Walnut Creek (K2)*......2,420
Walnut Grove (B9)*......1,250
Warm Springs (K3)*.... 600
Wasco (F8)*..................5,592
Waterford (E6)*............1,777
Watsonville (D7)*.......11,572
Weaverville (C3)*.........1,800
Weed (C2)*...................2,739
Weitchpec (B2)*.......... 300
Weldon (G8)*.............. 196
Wendel (E3)*............... 39
Weott (A3)*................. 450
W. Covina (D10)...........4,499
W. Point (E5)*..............1,500
W. Riverside (E10)........3,798
W. Sacramento (B8)*...8,200
Westend (H8)*............ 400
Westminster (D11)*.....3,131
Westmorland (K10)*....1,213
Westport (B4)*............ 157
Westwood (D3)*............3,618
Wheatland (D4)*.......... 581
Wheeler Ridge (G8)*.... 250
White Plains (E5)*....... 425
Whitmore (D3)............. 30
Whittier (D11)*...........23,820
Wildomar (H10)*......... 350
Williams (C4)*..............1,134
Willits (B4)*..................2,691
Willow Ranch (E2)*..... 275
Willows (C4)*................3,019
Wilmar (C10)*...............8,000
Wilmington (C11)*.....30,000
Wilton (C9)*................ 263
Windsor (C5)*............. 600
Winterhaven (L11)*..... 400
Winters (D5)*................1,265
Winton (E6)*................ 496
Woodbridge (B9)*........ 850
Woodlake (G7)*.............2,525
Woodland (B8)*.............9,386
Woodside (J3)*..............2,000
Woody (G8)*................ 150
Yermo (J9)*................. 775
Yettem (F7)*................ 150
Yolanda (H1)*..............
Yolo (B8)*................... 700
Yorba Linda (D11)*......2,000
Yosemite National Park (F6)*............... 900
Yountville (C5)*........... 690
Yreka (C2)*...................3,227
Yuba City (D4)*............7,861
Yucaipa (J9)*................1,515
Zamora (C5)*.............. 60
Zenia (B3)*.................. 100

Map on Page 53

COLORADO

Total Population 1,325,089

63 COUNTIES

Adams (L3)................40,234
Alamosa (H7)..............10,531
Arapahoe (L3).............52,125
Archuleta (E8)..............3,030
Baca (O8)....................7,964
Bent (N7).....................8,775
Boulder (J2)................48,296
Chaffee (G5)................7,168
Cheyenne (O5)..............3,453
Clear Creek (H3)...........3,289
Conejos (G8)...............10,171
Costilla (J8)..................6,067
Crowley (M6).................5,222
Custer (J6)....................1,573
Delta (D5)....................17,365
Denver (K3)................415,786
Dolores (C7)..................1,966
Douglas (K4)..................3,507
Eagle (F3).....................4,488
El Paso (K5)................74,523
Elbert (L4).....................4,477
Fremont (J5).................18,366
Garfield (C3).................11,625
Gilpin (H3)..................... 850
Grand (G2).....................3,963
Gunnison (E5).................5,716
Hinsdale (E7)................. 263
Huerfano (K7)................10,549
Jackson (G1)...................1,976
Jefferson (J3).................55,687
Kiowa (O6).......................3,003
Kit Carson (O4)................8,600
La Plata (D8)..................14,880
Lake (G4).........................6,150
Larimer (H1)...................43,554
Las Animas (L8)..............25,902
Lincoln (M5).....................5,909
Logan (N1).......................17,187
Mesa (B5).......................38,974
Mineral (F7)..................... 698
Moffat (C1).......................5,946
Montezuma (B8)................9,991
Montrose (C6).................15,220
Morgan (M2)....................18,074
Otero (M7).......................25,275
Ouray (D6)........................2,103
Park (H4)..........................1,870
Phillips (P1).......................4,924
Pitkin (F4)..........................1,646
Prowers (P7).....................14,836
Pueblo (K6).......................90,188
Rio Blanco (C3)..................4,719
Rio Grande (G7)................12,832
Routt (E1)..........................8,940
Saguache (G6)....................5,664
San Juan (D7).....................1,471
San Miguel (C6)..................2,693
Sedgwick (P1).....................5,095
Summit (G3).......................1,135
Teller (J5)..........................2,754
Washington (N3).................7,520
Weld (L1)..........................67,504
Yuma (P2).........................10,827

CITIES and TOWNS

Abarr (O3).................... 8
Ackmen (B7)..................
Adams City (K3).......... 800
Adena (M2)...................
Agate (M4)*................. 134
Aguilar (K8)* 1,038
Akron (N2)*...................1,605
Alamosa (H8)*...............5,354
Allenspark (J2)*........... 100
Allison (E8)*................ 105
Alma (G4)*................... 149
Almont (F5)*................
Amherst (P1)*.............. 101
Amity (P6)........ ....
Andrix (N8)*................ 10
Animas (D8).................2,500
Anthracite (E5)............
Antlers (D3)*............... 150
Anton (N3)*................. 50
Antonito (H8)*..............1,255
Arapahoe (P5)*............ 125
Arboles (E8)*............... 108
Arickaree (N3)*........... 13
Arlington (N6)*............ 25
Armel (P3)*................. 4
Aroya (N5)*.................
Arriba (N4)*................. 367
Arriola (B8)................. 350
Artesia (B2)*............... 281
Arvada (J3)*................2,359
Aspen (F4)*................. 916
Association Camp (J2)*
Atwood (N1)*.............. 200
Ault (K1)*.................... 866
Aurora (K3)*...............11,421
Avon (F3)*...................
Avondale (L6)*............ 152
Axial (D2)*..................
Ayer (M7)..................... 7
Bailey (H4)*................. 75
Barela (L8)................... 9
Barnesville (L2)........... 35
Barr Lake (K3)*........... 100
Bartlett (P8)................ 30
Basalt (E4)*................. 173
Battle Creek (E1)......... 18
Bayfield (D8)*.............. 335
Bedrock (B6)*.............. 15
Beecher Island (P3)*.... 10
Bellvue (J1)*................ 300
Bennett (L3)*............... 272
Berthoud (J2)*............. 867
Berthoud Pass (H3)......
Bethune (P4)*.............. 71
Beulah (K6)*...............
Big Bend (O6).............. 30
Black Forest (K4)......... 10
Black Hawk (J3)*......... 166
Blanca (H8)*................ 376
Blende (K6)................. 575
Blue Mountain (B2)*.... 6
Bonanza (G6).............. 51
Boncarbo (K8)*............ 97
Bond (F3)*.................. 125
Bondad (D8)................ 2
Boone (L6)*................. 468
Boulder (J2)*..............19,999
Bountiful (G8)............. 100
Bovina (N4)*................ 22
Bowie (D5)*................. 250
Boyero (N5)*................ 36

Bracewell (K2)............ 5	Critchell (J4).......... 75
Brandon (P6)*.......... 50	Crook (O1)*.......... 259
Branson (M8)*......... 157	Cross Mountain (B2).. 10
Breckenridge (G4)*.... 296	Crowley (M6)*....... 379
Breed (K5).............. 20	Cuchara Camps (J8)*.. 2
Breen (C8)*...........	Dacono (K2)*........ 258

Bracewell (K2)............ 5
Brandon (P6)*.......... 50
Branson (M8)*......... 157
Breckenridge (G4)*.... 296
Breed (K5).............. 20
Breen (C8)*...........
Bridges (C4)*.......... 60
Briggsdale (L1)*.......
Brighton (K3)*......4,336
Bristol (P6)*.......... 250
Brookside (J6)........ 175
Brookvale (H3)........ 15
Broomfield (J3)*...... 125
Brush (M2)*........2,431
Buckeye (J1).......... 37
Buckingham (L1)*..... 36
Buena Vista (G5)*..... 783
Buffalo Creek (J4)*... 50
Buford (D2)*.......... 30
Buick (M4)............ 31
Burlington (P4)*....2,247
Burns (F3)*........... 200
Byers (L3)*...........
Caddoa (O6)*......... 32
Cahone (B7)*......... 103
Calhan (L4)*......... 375
Cameo (C4)*.......... 100
Campion (J2)*........
Campo (O8)*......... 266
Canfield (J2)......... 65
Canon City (J6)*....6,345
Canyon (G8)*.........
Capulin (G8)*.........
Carbondale (E4)*..... 441
Carlton (P6)*......... 55
Carr (K1)*............ 98
Cascade (K5)*........ 75
Castle Rock (K4)*..... 741
Cedar (B7)...........
Cedaredge (D5)*..... 574
Cedarwood (K7)....... 85
Center (G7)*.......2,024
Central City (J3)*..... 371
Chama (J8)*.......... 760
Cheraw (N6)*......... 174
Cherry Hills Village ‡(K3)............... 750
Cheyenne Wells (P5)*.1,154
Chimney Rock (E8)*... 100
Chivington (O6)*......
Chromo (F8)*......... 200
Cimarron (D6)*....... 150
Clark (F1)*...........
Clarkville (P2)*....... 4
Clifton (C4)*......... 920
Climax (G4)*......... 750
Coalcreek (J6)*....... 195
Coaldale (H6)*....... 130
Coalmont (F1)*....... 26
Cokedale (K8)*....... 214
Collbran (C4)*....... 237
Colona (D6)*......... 125
Colorado Spgs. (K5)*..45,472
Columbine (E1)*......
Como (H4)*.......... 39
Conejos (G8)*........
Cope (O3)*........... 145
Copper Spur (F3)*.... 36
Cornish (L2)*........ 140
Cortez (B8)*.......2,680
Cory (C5)*...........
Cotopaxi (H6)*....... 210
Cowdrey (G1)*.......
Craig (D2)*........3,080
Crawford (D5)*....... 170
Creede (E7)*......... 503
Crested Butte (E5)*... 730
Crestone (H7)*....... 72
Cripple Creek (J5)*... 853

Critchell (J4).......... 75
Crook (O1)*.......... 259
Cross Mountain (B2).. 10
Crowley (M6)*....... 379
Cuchara Camps (J8)*.. 2
Dacono (K2)*........ 258
Dailey (O1)*......... 90
De Beque (C4)*...... 253
De Nova (O3)*....... 4
Deckers (J4)*........
Deer Trail (M3)*..... 421
Del Norte (G8)*....2,048
Delagua (K8)*........ 239
Delcarbon (K7)*...... 200
Delhi (M7)*.......... 36
Delta (D5)*........4,097
DENVER (K3)*....415,786
Denver (urban area).............495,513
Deora (O7)*.......... 41
Derby (K3)*........2,840
Devine (L6).......... 116
Dillon (H3)*......... 191
Divide (J5)*......... 50
Dolores (C8)*........ 729
Dotsero (E3)......... 58
Dove Creek (A7)*.... 702
Doyleville (F6)*...... 105
Drake (J2)*.......... 70
Dunton (C7)*........
Dupont (K3)*........ 400
Durango (D8)*......7,459
Eads (O6)*........1,015
Eagle (F3)*.......... 445
Earl (L8)............
East Canon (J6)...... 761
Eastlake (K2)........ 194
Eaton (K2)*........1,276
Eckert (C5)*.........
Eckley (P2)*......... 295
Edgewater (J3)*....2,580
Edison (L5)*......... 15
Edler (D3)*..........
Edwards (F3)*........
Egnar (B7)*.......... 35
Elba (N3)*........... 25
Elbert (L4)*.......... 200
Eldora (H3)*.........
Elizabeth (K4)*...... 253
Elk Springs (C2)*.... 35
Elkton (J3)*......... 10
Elwell (K2).......... 40
Empire (H3)*......... 228
Englewood (K3)*...16,869
Erie (K2)*........... 937
Escalante Forks (B5)*. 20
Estes Park (J2)*....1,617
Eureka (D7).......... 13
Evans (K2)*.......... 862
Evergreen (J3)*...... 800
Fairplay (H4)*....... 476
Falcon (K5)..........
Falfa (D8)*.......... 300
Fall Creek (C7)....... 25
Farisita (J7)*........ 125
Farmers Spur (K2).... 22
Farr (K7)............
Federal Heights...... 173
Firestone (K2)*...... 297
Firstview (O5)*...... 30
Fitzsimons (K3)*...5,000
Flagler (N4)*........ 793
Fleming (O1)*....... 377
Florence (J6)*......2,773
Florissant (J5)*..... 53
Fondis (L4)*......... 9
Forder (M5).......... 26
Fort Collins (J1)*..14,937
Fort Garland (J8)*...

Fort Lupton (K2)*...1,907
Fort Lyon (N6)*......
Fort Morgan (M2)*..5,315
Fosston (L1).........
Fountain (K5)*....... 713
Fowler (L6)*.......1,025
Foxton (J4)*.........
Franktown (K4)*..... 25
Fraser (H3)*.........
Frederick (K2)*...... 599
Freeman (G7)*....... 100
Freshwater (Guffey*) (H5)................ 20
Frisco (G3)*......... 87
Fruita (B4)*.......1,463
Fruitvale (B4)*.....2,275
Galatea (N6)......... 10
Galeton (K1)*........ 200
Garcia (J8)*......... 350
Garden City ‡(L1)... 104
Gardner (J7)*........ 200
Garfield (G5)*....... 100
Garo (H4)*.......... 50
Gary (M2)*.......... 6
Gateway (B5)*....... 250
Genoa (N4)*......... 257
Georgetown (H3)*.... 329
Gilcrest (K2)*....... 429
Gill (K2)*........... 375
Gilman (G3)*........ 300
Glade Park (B5)*.... 250
Glen Haven (H2)*.... 40
Glendevey (H1)*..... 15
Glentivar (H4)*...... 5
Glenwood Spgs. (E4)*.2,412
Golden (J3)*.......5,238
Goldfield (J5)....... 81
Good Pasture (K6)... 48
Goodrich (M2)*...... 30
Gordon (K7).........
Gould (G1)*......... 150
Gowanda (K2)....... 12
Granada (P6)*....... 551
Granby (H2)*........ 463
Grand Jct. (C4)*...14,504
Grand Lake (H2)*.... 309
Grand Mesa (D4)*....
Grand Valley (D4)*... 296
Granite (G4)*........ 75
Grant (H4)*......... 25
Greeley (K2)*......20,354
Green Mt. Falls (K5)*. 106
Greenhorn (K7)*..... 20
Greenland (K4)*..... 75
Greenwood (J6)......
Greystone (B1)*..... 2
Grover (L1)*......... 146
Guffey (Freshwater) (H5)................ 20
Gulnare (K8)*........ 200
Gunnison (E5)*.....2,770
Gypsum (F3)*........ 345
Hahns Peak (E1).....
Hale (P3)*........... 240
Hamilton (D2)*...... 25
Hardin (L2)*........
Harmony (J2)........ 18
Harrisburg (N3)*.... 6
Hartman (P6)*....... 181
Hartsel (H4)*........ 65
Hastings (K8).......
Hasty (O6)*.........
Haswell (N6)*....... 163
Haxtun (O1)*......1,006
Haybro (F2)*........ 150
Hayden (E2)*........ 767
Hebron (G1)*........ 4
Henderson (K3)*..... 50
Hereford (L1)*....... 100

Hesperus (C8)*......
Higbee (M7)......... 6
Hill Top (K4)........ 10
Hillrose (N2)*....... 190
Hillside (H6)*....... 10
Hoehne (L8)*........ 500
Holly (P6)*........1,236
Holyoke (P1)*......1,558
Homelake (G7)...... 250
Hooper (H7)*........ 103
Hot Sulphur Spgs.(H2)* 263
Hotchkiss (D5)*..... 715
Howard (H6)*....... 210
Howardsville (E7)... 20
Hoyt (L2)*.......... 250
Hudson (K2)*....... 365
Hughes (O3)*........ 6
Hugo (N4)*......... 943
Husted (K4)......... 30
Hyde (O2)...........
Hydrate (F2)........
Hygiene (J2)*....... 200
Idaho Springs (H3)*.1,769
Idalia (P3)*......... 74
Ignacio (D8)*....... 526
Iliff (N1)*.......... 235
Independence (K5)*.. 20
Indian Hills (J3)*... 300
Iola (E6)*.......... 50
Ione (K2)*.......... 100
Irondale (K5)....... 325
Ironton ‡(D7)....... 6
Ivywild (K5)........2,849
Jamestown (J2)*..... 118
Jansen (K8)*.......1,500
Jaroso (H8)*........ 250
Jefferson (H4)*..... 75
Joes (O3)*.......... 109
Johnstown (K2)*.... 897
Julesburg (P1)*....1,951
Juniper Springs (D2).. 6
Karval (N5)*........ 90
Kearns (E8).........
Keensburg (L2)*.... 432
Kelim (J2)*......... 50
Kendrick (M5)*...... 14
Keota (L1)*......... 21
Kersey (L2)*........ 304
Kim (M8)*.......... 475
King's Canyon (G1)*..
Kiowa (L4)*......... 173
Kirk (P3)*.......... 125
Kit Carson (O5)*.... 379
Kline (C8)*......... 110
Kokomo (G4)*....... 53
Kornman (O6)....... 75
Kremmling (G2)*.... 623
Kutch (M5)*........ 3
La Garita (G7)*.....
La Jara (H8)*....... 912
La Junta (M7)*.....7,712
La Salle (K2)*....... 797
La Sauces (H8).......
La Veta (J8)*....... 701
Lafayette (K3)*.....2,073
Laird (P2)*......... 155
Lake City (E6)*..... 141
Lake George (J5)*... 30
Lakeside ‡(J3)...... 46
Lamar (O6)*.......6,829
Lamport (O8)........
Laporte (J1)*....... 500
Larkspur (K4)*...... 200
Las Animas (N6)*...3,223
Lascar (K7).........
Last Chance (M3)*.. 25
Lavalley (J8)........
Lawson (H3)*.......
Lay (G1)*..........

Lazear (D5)*........ 100
Leader (L3)*........ 67
Leadville (G4)*....4,081
Lebanon (C8)*....... 150
Leonard (C6)*....... 10
Lester (K8)*........ 19
Lewis (B7)*......... 50
Lime (K6)*.......... 22
Limon (M4)*.......1,471
Lindon (N3)*........ 29
Littleton (K3)*.....3,378
Livermore (J1)*..... 150
Logan (N1)*.........
Logcabin (J1).......
Loma (B4)*.......... 400
Longmont (J2)*....8,099
Longs Peak (J2)*.... 7
Longview (J4).......
Louisville (J3)*....1,978
Louviers (K4)*...... 250
Loveland (J2)*.....6,773
Loyd (D2)*.......... 82
Lucerne (K2)*....... 100
Ludlow (L4)*........ 200
Lycan (P7)*......... 6
Lyons (J2)*......... 689
Mack (B4)*.......... 185
Maher (D5)*........
Maitland (K7).......
Malachite (J7)......
Malta (G4)*......... 25
Manassa (H8)*....... 832
Mancos (C8)*....... 785
Manitou Springs (J5)*.2,580
Manzanola (M6)*.... 543
Marble (E4).........
Marshall Pass (G6)*.. 8
Marvine (D2)........
Masonville (J2)*.....
Massadona (B2)..... 3
Masters (L2)*.......
Matheson (M4)*..... 100
May Valley (O6)*.... 20
Maybell (C2)*....... 106
McClave (O6)*...... 125
McClure Ranch (F4).. 25
McCoy (H3)*........
McElmo (B8)......... 50
McGregor (E2)*...... 25
McPhee (C7)......... 30
Mead (K2)*......... 186
Meeker (D2)*......1,658
Meredith (H6)*...... 25
Merino (N2)*........ 209
Mesa (C4)*......... 300
Mesa Verde National Park (C8)*......... 106
Mesita (H8)*........
Messex (N2)......... 25
Mildred (O3)*....... 3
Milliken (K2)*...... 510
Mineral Hot Spgs. (G6) 10
Minturn (G3)*....... 509
Model (L8)*......... 300
Moffat (H6)*........ 109
Mogote (G8)*....... 150
Molina (D4)*........
Monarch (G5)*...... 13
Monte Vista (G7)*..3,272
Montezuma (H3)*.... 48
Montrose (D6)*.....4,964
Monument (K4)*..... 126
Morley (L8)*........ 300
Morrison (J3)*...... 306
Mosca (H7)*........ 130
Mount Harris (E2)*.. 700
Mountain View ‡(J3). 878
Mustang (K7)........ 10
Nathrop (H5)*.......
Naturita (B6)*...... 500
Nederland (H3)*.... 266
Nevadaville ‡(H3)... 6
New Castle (E3)*.... 483
New Raymer (M1)*... 130
Ninaview (N7)*...... 2
Niwot (J2)*......... 160
North Avondale (L6)*. 22
North Creede (F7)....
Northdale (B7)......
Northglenn...........
Nortonville (G8).....
Norwood (C6)*...... 294
Nucla (B6)*......... 457
Nunn (K1)*......... 182
Oak Creek (F2)*....1,488
Oak Grove (C6)..... 35
Ohio (F5)*.......... 40
Olathe (D5)*........ 810
Olney Springs (M6)*. 279
Ophir (D7)*......... 2
Orchard (L2)*.......
Ordway (M6)*......1,290
Ortiz (H8)..........
Otis (O2)*.......... 532
Ouray (D6)*........1,089
Ovid (P1)*.......... 664
Oxford (D8)*........
Padroni (N1)*....... 153
Pagoda (E2).........
Pagosa Junction (E8)*.
Pagosa Springs (E8)*..†,379
Palisade (C4)*....... 861
Palmer Lake (J4)*... 263
Pando (G4).......... 17
Paoli (P1)*......... 91

Paonia (D5)*.......1,257
Paradox (B6)*....... 50
Parkdale (H6)*...... 20
Parker (K4)*........ 132
Parlin (F6)*......... 50
Parshall (G2)*...... 81
Pawnee (M2).........
Peagreen (C5)....... 10
Peckham (K2)........ 40
Peetz (N1)*......... 232
Penrose (K6)*....... 90
Peyton (K4)*........
Phippsburg (F2)*....
Piedra (E8)..........
Pierce (K1)*........ 372
Pikeview (K5)*...... 300
Pine (J4)*.......... 75
Pine River Dam (E8)..
Pinecliffe (J3)*..... 25
Pinon (K6).......... 65
Pitkin (F5)*......... 152
Placerville (D6)*.... 100
Plainview (J3)*...... 50
Plateau City (D4)*.. 20
Platner (N2)*....... 49
Platteville (K2)*.... 570
Poncha Springs (G6)*. 114
Portland (K6)*...... 205
Portland ‡(D6)...... 16
Powderhorn (E6)*... 90
Price Creek (C2).... 2
Pritchett (O8)*..... 286
Proctor (N1)*....... 40
Prospect (L2)....... 62
Prospect Heights ‡(J6). 50
Prowers (O6)........ 36
Pryor (K6).......... 25
Pueblo (K6)*......63,685
Pueblo (urban area)..73,102
Pumpkin Center (M5)..
Purcell (K1)*.......
Radium (E2)*....... 20
Ragged Mountain (E4)*.
Rago (N3)...........
Ramah (L4)*........ 142
Ramona (K5).........
Rand (G2)*..........
Rangely (B2)*....... 808
Rapson (K8).........
Ravenwood (K7).....
Raymer (New Raymer*) (M1)............... 130
Read (D5)...........
Recen (Kokomo*) (G4). 53
Red Feather Lakes(H1)* 93
Red Wing (J7)*..... 16
Redcliff (G4)*...... 556
Redmesa (C8)*......
Redstone (E4)....... 50
Redvale (B6)*....... 70
Rex (J1)............
Rico (C7)*.......... 212
Ridgway (D6)*...... 209
Rifle (D3)*........1,525
Riland (E3).........
Rio Blanco (C3)*.... 3
Roach (G1)..........
Rockport (K1)....... 2
Rockvale (J6)*...... 380
Rockwood (D8)...... 15
Rocky Ford (M6)*..4,087
Roggen (L2)*....... 150
Romeo (G8)*........ 404
Rosedale ‡(K2)...... 57
Rosita (J6)*........ 20
Roswell (K5)*.....1,029
Routt (E2)*......... 50
Rowena (J2)*....... 3
Ruedi (F4).......... 25
Rugby (K8)..........
Rush (L5)*.......... 18
Russell (J7)*........ 43
Rye (K7)*.......... 166
Saguache (G6)*....1,024
Saint Elmo (G5)*....
St. Peters (O2)......
Salida (H6)*.......4,553
Sams (D6)........... 15
San Acacio (H8)*.... 135
San Isabel (K7)..... 25
San Luis (J8)*.....1,239
San Pablo (J8)*.....
Sanford (H8)*....... 666
Sapinero (E6)*...... 30
Sargents (F6)*...... 135
Saw Pit (D7).......
Sedalia (K4)*.......
Sedgwick (O1)*..... 332
Segundo (K8)*...... 300
Seibert (O4)*....... 346
Severance (K1)...... 108
Shaffers Crossing (J4).. 6
Shaw (N3)*......... 4
Shawnee (H4)*......
Sheephorn (G3)......
Sheridan ‡(K3)*....1,715
Sheridan Lake (P6)*.. 100
Sidney (F2).........
Silica (J4)..........
Siloam (K6)......... 16
Silt (D4)*.......... 361
Silver Cliff (J6)*... 217
Silver Plume (H3)*.. 136
Silverton (D7)*....1,375
Simla (M4)*........ 424

Skyway (C4)........
Slater (E1)*........ 15
Sligo (L1)..........
Snowmass (E4)*.....
Snyder (M2)*....... 250
Somerset (E5)*......
Sopris (K8)*.......1,330
South Canon (J6)*..1,588
South Fork (F7)*....
Spicer (F2)*........
Spikebuck (H5).....
Springfield (O8)*...2,041
Starkville (L8)*....1,000
State Bridge (F3)... 2
Steamboat Spgs. (F2)*.1,913
Stellwagon (L5)..... 2
Sterling (N1)*.....7,534
Stone City (K6)*.... 75
Stoneham (M1)*..... 75
Stoner (C7)*........ 2
Stonington (P8)*.... 44
Strasburg (L3)*..... 520
Stratton (O4)*...... 720
Strong (K7)......... 20
Sugar City (M6)*.... 527
Sugar Loaf (J2)*.... 6
Summitville (G8)*... 4
Sunbeam (C1)*...... 29
Superior (J3)*...... 134
Swallows (K6)....... 50
Swing (M7)*........ 336
Tabernash (H3)*.... 260
Tacoma (D7)*....... 17
Telluride (D7)*....1,101
Tennessee Pass (G4)*. 25
Tercio (J8).......... 110
Texas Creek (H6)*... 25
Thatcher (L7)*......
Thurman (N3)*...... 10
Tiffany (D8)*.......
Tiger (G3).......... 8
Timnath (J1)*....... 177
Timpas (M7)*....... 50
Tioga (K7)*......... 250
Tobe (M8)*.........
Tolland (H3)........ 10
Toltec (K7)*........ 180
Toponas (F2)*....... 250
Towaoc (B8)*.......
Towner (P6)*....... 150
Trail Ridge (H2)*....
Trimble Springs (D8).. 30
Trinchera (M8)*..... 90
Trinidad (L8)*....12,204
Troutville (F4)*.... 16
Truckton (L5)....... 20
Trump (H5).......... 25
Tungsten (H3)....... 6
Twin Lakes (G4)*... 60
Two Buttes (P7)*.... 121
Tyrone (L8)*........ 50
Uravan (B6)*....... 700
Ute (C6)............ 9
Utleyville (O8)*.... 8
Valdez (K8)*....... 700
Vallorso (K8)*...... 90
Vanadium (C7)...... 2
Vernon (P3)*.......
Victor (J5)*......... 684
Vilas (P8)*......... 132
Villa Grove (G6)*... 200
Villegreen (M8)*.... 150
Vim (M1)........... 6
Vineland (K6)*...... 200
Virginia Dale (J1)*.. 100
Vona (O4)*......... 209
Vroman (M6)*.......
Wages (P2).........
Wagon Wheel Gap (F7)*.
Walden (G7)*....... 696
Walsenburg (K7)*..5,596
Walsh (P8)*........ 897
Ward (H2)*......... 10
Watkins (K3)*...... 85
Wattenberg (K2)....
Waunita Hot Spgs. (G6)
Waverly (J1)........ 20
Weldona (M2)*...... 300
Wellington (K1)*.... 541
Westcliffe (H6)*.... 390
Westcreek (J4)*.....
Westminster (J3)*..1,686
Weston (K8)*....... 500
Wetmore (J6)*...... 100
Wheat Ridge (J3)*..7,000
Whitewater (C5)*.... 150
Wiggins (L2)*....... 400
Wild Horse (N5)*... 60
Wilds (J2).......... 25
Wiley (O6)*........ 417
Willard (M1)*....... 29
Williamsburg (J6)*.. 65
Willow Creek (E2)...
Windsor (J2)*.....1,548
Winnview (M3)......
Winter Park (H3)*... 100
Wolcott (F3)*....... 50
Woodland Park (J4)*. 391
Woodrow (M3)*.....
Woody Creek (F4)*.. 7
Wray (P2)*........2,198
Yampa (F2)*........ 421
Yellow Jacket (B8)*..
Yoder (L5)*......... 30
Yuma (O2)*.......1,908

Map on Page 54   **CONNECTICUT**   **Total Population 2,007,280**

8 COUNTIES
Fairfield (B3).......504,342
Hartford (E1).......539,661
Litchfield (C1).......98,872
Middlesex (E3)......67,332
New Haven (D3)....545,784
New London (G2)...144,821
Tolland (F1).........44,709
Windham (H1)......61,759

CITIES and TOWNS
Abington (G1)*...... 450
Addison (E2)........ 900
Allingtown (D3)....4,800
Amston (E3).........
Andover (F2)*.....△1,034
Ansonia (C3)*.....18,706
Arnolds (E3).........
Ashford (G1)........△ 845

Aspetuck (B4)*....
Atwoodville (G1)..... 35
Avon (D1)*........△3,171
Bakersville (C1)......
Ballouville (H1)*....
Baltic (G2)*........1,345
Bantam (B2)*....... 940
Barkhamsted (D1)...△ 946
Beach Park (E3)..... 500
Beacon Falls (C3)*.△2,067

Beckleys (E2)....... 100
Berkshire Junction (B3)
Berlin (E2)*.......△7,470
Bethany (C3)*.....△1,318
Bethel (B3)*.......△5,104
Bethlehem (C2)*...△1,015
Black Hall (F3)......
Black Point Beach Club (G3)*......... 100
Bloomfield (E1)*...△5,746

Boardmans Bridge (B2) 75
Bolton (F1)*........△1,279
Botsford (C3)*......
Branchville (B3)..... 300
Branford (D3)*.....2,552
Bridgeport (C4)*..158,709
Bridgeport (urban area)............237,954
Bridgewater (B2)*..△ 639
Bristol (D2)*......35,961

Bristol-New Britain (urban area)......122,618
Broad Brook (E1)*.. 2,140
Brookfield (B3)*....△1,688
Brookfield Center (B3)*
Brookfield Junction (B3)
Brooklyn (H1)*....△2,652
Brooksvale (D3)..... 500
Buckingham (E2).... 350
Buckland (E1)*...... 750

Burlington (D1)....△1,846
Burnside (E1)*......
Burrville (C1)....... 250
Byram (A4)*.......8,000
Campbell (F1).......
Campville (C2)......
Canaan (B1)*......1,189
Cannondale (B4)*... 300
Canterbury (H2)*..△1,321
Canton (D1)*......△3,613

Canton Center (D1)*... 300	E. Canaan (B1)*...... 800	Franklin (G2)......△ 727	Hawleyville (B3)*......	New London (G3)*...30,551	Ridgefield (A3)*...△4,356	Torrington (C1)*....27,820
Centerbrook (F3)*..... 487	E. Glastonbury	Gales Ferry (G3)*..... 300	Hazardville (E1)*.. 1,272	New Milford (B2)*...△5,799	Riverside (A4)*..... 2,000	Tracy (D2)
Central Village (H2)*.. 800	(E2)*.......... 450	Gardner Lake (G2).....	Hebron (F2)*.......△1,320	New Preston (B2)*..... 500	Riverton (D1)*....... 220	Trumbull (C4).....△8,641
Chaplin (G1)*........△ 712	E. Granby (E1)*....△1,327	Gaylordsville (B2)*.... 200	Higganum (E2)*......	Newington (E2)*...△9,110	Robertsville (C1)..... 130	Twin Lakes (B1)
Cheshire (D2)*......△6,295	E. Haddam (F3)*....△2,554	Georgetown (B4)*.....	High Ridge (A4)...... 1,015	Newtown (B3)*....... 782	Rockfall (E2)*...... 2,000	Tyler City (D3)
Chester (F3)*.......△1,920	E. Hampton (E2)*...△4,000	Gildersleeve (E2)*....	Highland Park (F1)...	Niantic (G3)*...... 1,746	Rockville (F1)*..... 8,016	Tylerville (F3)
Chesterfield (G3)..... 120	E. Hartford (E1)*..△29,933	Gilead (F2)........... 70	Highwood (D3).......	Nichols (C4)....... 1,171	Rocky Hill (E2)*...△5,108	Uncasville (G3)*
Chestnut Hill (G2)*...	E. Hartland (D1)*.... 400	Gilman (G2)......... 400	Hockanum (E2)......	Noank (G3)*....... 1,149	Romford (B2)........ 30	Union (G1).........△ 261
Clarks Corner (G1)... 78	E. Haven (D3)*....△12,212	Glasgo (H2)*........	Hop River (F2)......	Norfolk (E1)*......△1,572	Round Hill (A4)..... 600	Union City (C2)*.... 5,000
Clarks Falls (H3)..... 200	E. Kent (B2)........	Glastonbury (E2)*..△8,818	Hotchkissville (C2)... 300	Noroton (B4)*..... 3,000	Rowayton (B4)*.... 3,200	Unionville (D1)*.... 2,197
Clinton (E3)*......△2,466	E. Killingly (H1)*.... 800	Glenbrook (A4)*.....	Huntington (C3).....	Noroton Heights (B4)* 3,918	Roxbury (B2)*......△ 740	Vernon (F1)*.......△10,115
Clintonville (D3)..... 850	E. Litchfield (C1)..... 60	Glenville (A4)....... 976	Hurlbutt (B4).......	North Ashford (G1)...	Roxbury Falls (B2)..	Versailles (G2)*
Cobalt (E2)*........ 500	E. Lyme (G3)*.....△3,870	Goodyear (H1)*..... 1,000	Ivoryton (F3)*...... 885	N. Branford (E3)....△2,017	Roxbury Station (B2)..	Voluntown (H2)*....△ 825
Colchester (F2)*..... 1,522	E. Morris (C2).......	Goshen (C1)*......△ 940	Jewett City (H2)*... 3,702	N. Canton (D1)*..... 250	Sachem Head (E3)*...	Wallingford (D3)*...11,994
Colebrook (C1)*.....△ 592	E. Norwalk (B4)..... 5,000	Granby (D1)*.......△2,693	Jordan Village	N. Franklin (G2)..... 735	Salem (F3)..........△ 618	Wapping (E1)*...... 1,000
Collinsville (D1)..... 2,078	E. River (E3)*....... 450	Greenfield Hill (B4)...	(Waterford*) (G3)..△9,100	N. Granby (D1)*..... 650	Salisbury (B1)*....△3,132	Warehouse Point (E1)*1,283
Columbia (F2)*......△1,327	E. Thompson (H1)..... 200	Greens Farms (B4)*... 500	Judds Bridge (B2)... 30	N. Grosvenor Dale	Sandy Hook (B3)*... 1,600	Warren (B2).........△ 437
Cooper (B3).........	E. Wallingford (D3)...	Greenville (G2)*.....	Kensington (D2)*.... 4,700	(H1)*............ 2,232	Saugatuck (B4)*.... 1,500	Warrenville (G1)*
Cornwall (B1)*......△ 896	E. Willington (F1)..... 50	Greenwich (A4)*...△40,835	Kent (B2)*........△1,392	N. Guilford (E3)..... 1,000	Saybrook Point (F3)*. 250	Washington (B2)*...△2,227
Cornwall Bridge (B1)*	E. Windsor (E1)*...△4,859	Greystone (C2)...... 150	Kent Furnace (B2)...	N. Haven (D3)*....△9,444	Scitico (E1)......... 125	Washington Depot
Cos Cob (A4)*...... 6,800	E. Windsor Hill (E1)* 671	Griffins (E1)........	Killingly (H1)...... 1,105	N. Kent (B1).......	Scotland (G2)*.....△ 513	(B2)*............ 700
Coventry (F1)*......△4,043	E. Woodstock (H1)*... 275	Grosvenor Dale (H1)*. 800	Killingworth (E3)....△ 677	N. Madison (E3).....	Seymour (C3)*.....△7,832	Waterbury (C2)*...104,477
Cranbury (B4)...... 3,000	Eastford (G1)*......△ 598	Groton (G3)*....... 7,036	Lakeside (B2)*......	N. Newington (D2)...	Sharon (C3)*......△1,889	Waterbury (urban
Crescent Beach (G3)*.	Easton (B4)*.......△2,165	Groton Long Point (G3)*	Lakeville (B1)*......	N. Plain (F3).......	Sharon Valley (B1).. 174	area)...........131,442
Cromwell (E2)*.....△4,286	Ellington (F1)*.....△3,099	Grove Beach (E3)....	Lebanon (G2)*.....△1,654	N. Stamford (A4)....	Shelton (C3)*......12,694	Waterford (Jordan
Crystal Lake (F1).... 350	Elliott (G1).........	Guilford (E3)*......△5,092	Lebanon Station (G2)..	N. Sterling (H1).....	Sherman (B2)*......△ 549	Village) (G3)*....△9,100
Danbury (B3)*.....22,067	Elmwood (D2)*..... 6,000	Gurleyville (G1)..... 120	Ledyard (G3).......△1,749	N. Stonington (H3)*.△1,367	Short Beach (D3)*...	Watertown (C2)*...△10,699
Danielson (H1)*..... 4,554	Enfield (E1)*......△15,464	Haddam (E3)*......△2,636	Leetes Island (E3)...	N. Westchester (F2)*. 100	Silver Lane (E1)....	Waterville (C2)*
Darien (B4)*.......11,767	Essex (E3)*........△3,491	Haddam Neck (E2)... 50	Lime Rock (B1)*.... 186	N. Wilton (B4)......	Simsbury (D1)*....△4,822	Wauregan (H2)*.... 1,002
Dayville (Killingly)	Fabyan (H1)*....... 425	Hadlyme (E3)*...... 300	Litchfield (C2)*.... 1,174	N. Windham (G1)*... 300	Somers (F1)*......△2,631	Weatogue (D1)*.... 800
(H1)*............ 1,105	Fairfield (B4)*.....△30,489	Hallville (G2).......	Long Hill (C3)......	N. Woodbury (C2)...	Somersville (F1)*.... 750	West Ashford (G1)...
Deep River (F3)*....△2,570	Falls Village (B1)*... 640	Hamburg (F3)*......	Long Ridge (A4)....	N. Woodstock (G1)*..	Sound View (F3).... 100	W. Avon (D1)...
Derby (C3)*.......10,259	Farmington (D2)*...△7,026	Hamden (D3)*.....△29,715	Lords Point (H3).... 400	Northfield (C2)*.....	South Britain (B3)*.. 400	W. Cheshire (D2)*... 1,000
Devon (C4)*........	Farmington Station (D2)	Hampton (G1)*.....△ 672	Lyme (F3)*......... 857	Northford (D3)*..... 800	S. Coventry (F1)*... 1,617	W. Cornwall (B1)*
Durham (E3)*...... 1,804	Fenwick (F3)....... 16	Hancock (C2).......	Madison (E3)*.....△3,078	Northville (B2)...... 150	S. Glastonbury (E2)*.	W. Goshen (B1)*
Durham Center (E3)*.	Fitchville (G2)*...... 300	Hanover (G2)....... 300	Manchester (D3)*..△34,116	Norwalk (B4)*.....49,460	S. Kent (B2)*...... 108	W. Granby (D1)*
Eagleville (F1)*..... 265	Flanders (B1).......	HARTFORD (E1)*..177,397	Manchester Green (E1)	Norwalk-Stamford	S. Killingly (H1)..... 250	W. Hartford (D1)*..△44,402
East Berlin (E2)*.... 1,000	Florida (B3)........	Hartford (urban area) 299,676	Mansfield (F1)*....△10,008	(urban area).....172,197	S. Lyme (F3)*...... 150	W. Hartland (D1)*.. 196
E. Brooklyn (H1).... 1,062	Forestville (D2)*.... 6,000	Harwinton (C1).....△1,858	Mansfield Center (G1)* 600	Norwich (D2)*.....23,429	S. Manchester (E1)...	W. Haven (D3)*....△32,010
			Mansfield Depot (F1)*	Norwichtown (G2)*. 2,916	S. Meriden (D2)*... 1,600	W. Mystic (H3)*.... 2,362
			Marble Dale (B2)*... 150	Oakdale (G3)*......	S. Norwalk (B4)*...18,000	W. Norwalk (B4)... 724
			Marion (D2)*....... 366	Oakville (C2)*...... 5,100	S. Wethersfield (E2)... 200	W. Redding (B3)*... 1,000
			Marlborough (F2)....△ 901	Occum (G2)........	S. Willington (F1)*...	W. Simsbury (D1)*.. 300
			Massapeag (G3).....	Old Greenwich (A4)*.5,348	S. Wilton (B4)......	W. Stafford (F1)... 312
			Mechanicsville (H1)*..	Old Lyme (F3)*....△2,141	S. Windham (G2)*... 450	W. Suffield (E1)*... 1,800
			Melrose (E1)*.......	Old Mystic (H3)*.... 600	S. Windsor (E1)*...△4,066	W. Thompson (H1)...
			Meriden (D2)*.....44,088	Old Saybrook (F3)*..△2,499	S. Woodstock (G1)*..	W. Torrington (C1)... 240
			Merrow (F1)*....... 125	Oneco (H2)*........ 450	Southbury (C3)*....△3,828	W. Willington (F1)*.. 100
			Mianus (A4)........	Orange (C3)*......△3,032	Southford (C3)......	W. Woodstock (G1)... 100
			Middle Haddam (E2)*	Orcutts (C1)........ 150	Southington (D2)*..△13,061	Westbrook (F3)*....△1,549
			Middlebury (D2)*...△3,318	Oronoque (C4)*..... 650	Southport (B4)*.... 3,000	Westfield (C2)..... 1,250
			Middlefield (E2)*...△1,983	Oxford (C3)*......△2,037	Springdale (A4)*.... 5,280	Westford (G1)...
			Middletown (E2)*...29,711	Pachaug (H2)*...... 75	Stafford (F1)*.....△6,471	Weston (B4)........△1,988
			Milford (C4)*......△26,870	Packer (H2)*....... 65	Stafford Sprs. (F1)*.. 3,396	Westport (B4)*....△11,667
			Mill Plain (A3)..... 125	Pawcatuck (H3)..... 5,269	Staffordville (G1)*... 1,000	Westway (F1)...
			Milldale (D2)*...... 1,200	Pequabuck (C2)*.... 600	Stamford (A4)*.....74,293	Wethersfield (E2)*..△12,533
			Millstone (G3)......	Phoenixville (G1)....	Stamford-Norwalk	Whitneyville (D3)*
			Milton (C1)........ 200	Pine Meadow (D1)*.. 425	(urban area).....172,197	Wildermere Beach (C4)
			Minortown (C2)..... 100	Pine Orchard (D3)*.. 5,100	Stepney (B3).......	Willimantic (G2)*...13,586
			Mohegan (G3)......	Plainfield (H2)*....△8,071	Stepney Depot (B3)*. 3,000	Wilson (E1)*...... 3,500
			Monroe (C3)........△2,892	Plainville (D2)*....△9,994	Sterling (H1)*......△1,298	Wilson Point (B4)... 200
			Montowese (D3).....	Plantsville (D2)*.... 1,536	Stevenson (C3)*..... 200	Wilsonville (H1)*... 385
			Montville (G3)*.....△4,766	Pleasant Valley (C1)*. 325	Still River (B2)..... 200	Wilton (B4)*.......△4,558
			Moodus (F2)*...... 1,400	Plymouth (C2)*.....△6,771	Stonington (H3)*.... 1,739	Winchester Center (C1)*
			Moosup (H2)*...... 2,909	Pomfret (H1)*......△2,018	Stony Creek (E3)*... 1,800	Windermere (F1)..... 95
			Morris (C2)*........ 799	Pomfret Center (H1)*. 675	Storrs (F1)*.......	Windham (G2)*....△15,884
			Mount Carmel (D3)*..	Poquetanuck (G3)....	Stratford (C4)*.....△33,428	Windsor (E1)*.....△11,833
			Mount Hope (G1).... 50	Poquonock (E1)*.... 1,200	Suffield (E1)*......△4,895	Windsor Locks (E1)*.△5,221
			Mystic (H3)*....... 2,266	Poquonock Bridge	Taconic (B1)*...... 150	Windsorville (F1)*
			Naugatuck (C3)*...17,455	(G3)............. 4,050	Taftville (F1)*...... 3,598	Winnipauk (B4)..... 3,600
			New Britain (E2)*..73,726	Portland (E2)*.....△5,186	Talcottville (F1)*.... 568	Winsted (C1)*...... 8,781
			New Britain-Bristol	Preston (H2)*......△1,775	Talmadge Hill (A4)...	Wolcott (D2).......△3,553
			(urban area).....122,618	Prospect (D2)......△1,896	Tariffville (D1)*.... 800	Woodbridge (D3)*..△2,822
			New Canaan (B4)*...△8,001	Putnam (H1)*...... 8,181	Terryville (C2)*..... 6,500	Woodbury (C2)*....△2,564
			New Fairfield (B3)...△1,236	Quaker Hill (G3)*... 1,260	Thamesville (G2)... 5,518	Woodmont (C4)*.... 5,000
			New Hartford (C1)*.△2,395	Quinebaug (H1)*.... 400	Thomaston (C2)*...△4,896	Woodstock (G1)*...△2,271
			New Haven (D3)*..164,443	Rainbow (E1).......	Thompson (H1)*....△5,585	Woodstock Valley (G1)*
			New Haven (urban	Redding (B3)*......△2,037	Thompsonville (E1)*.. 9,633	Woodville (B2)
			area)...........242,589	Redding Ridge (B3)*..	Tolland (F1)*......△1,659	Yalesville (D3)*..... 1,122
				Reynolds Bridge (C2). 600	Topstone (B3)......	Yantic (G2)*...... 800

DELAWARE Total Population 318,085

Map on Page 65

3 COUNTIES

Kent (M4)........37,870	Bethel (M6)*....... 271	Cool Spring (06)..... 25	Greenville (M1)*....	Lewes (05)*....... 2,904	New Castle (M2)*...5,396	Selbyville (N7)*.... 1,086
New Castle (M2)...218,879	Blackbird (M3)...... 50	Dagsboro (N6)*..... 474	Greenwood (M5)*... 746	Lincoln (N5)*...... 400	Newark (M2)*..... 6,731	Slaughter Beach (N5).. 85
Sussex (N6)......61,336	Blades (M6)........ 789	Delaware City (M2)*.1,363	Harbeson (N6)*.... 142	Little Creek (N4)*... 266	Newport (M2)*.... 1,171	Smyrna (M3)*..... 2,346
	Bowers (N4)*....... 284	Delmar (M7)*...... 1,015	Harrington (M5)*... 2,241	Magnolia (M4)*.... 207	Oak Grove (M6)..... 50	Stanton (M2)*......
CITIES and TOWNS	Bridgeville (M6)*....1,468	DOVER (M4)*......6,223	Hartly (M4)........ 139	Marshallton (M2)*... 1,600	Oak Orchards (06)...	Stockley (N6)*......
	Camden (M4)*...... 606	Edge Moor (N1)..... 25	Hazlettville (M4)..... 20	Masten's Corner (M5).. 30	Oakley (M5)........	Summit Bridge (M2)..
Angola (06)*....... 22	Cannon (M6)....... 150	Ellendale (N5)*..... 321	Hickman (M5)...... 200	McDonough (M3)...	Ocean View (06)*... 450	Townsend (M3)*.... 441
Arden (M1)*....... 842	Canterbury (M4).... 50	Elsmere (M2)....... 5,314	Hockessin (M1)*.... 1,200	Middletown (M3)*... 1,755	Odessa (M3)*...... 467	Viola (M4)........ 134
Bacons (M6)....... 28	Centerville (M1).... 225	Farmington (M5)*... 113	Hollyoak (N1)...... 1,450	Midway (06)....... 45	Port Penn (M2)*....	Williamsville (07)...
Bayard (06)........	Cheswold (M4)..... 292	Farnhurst (M2)*.... 150	Hollyville (06)...... 20	Milford (N5)*...... 5,179	Red Lion (M2)..... 50	Willowgrove (M4)... 65
Bear (M2)*........ 150	Christiana (M2)..... 500	Felton (M4)*....... 455	Houston (N5)*..... 332	Millsboro (N6)*.... 470	Redden (N5).......	Wilmington (M2)*..110,356
Bellefonte (N1)..... 1,472	Clarksville (06)*.... 150	Frankford (N6)*.... 615	Kenton (M4)*...... 211	Millville (06)*..... 270	Rehoboth Beach (06)*1,794	Wilmington (urban
Bethany Beach (06)*.. 190	Claymont (N1)*.... 5,370	Frederica (N4)*.... 675	Kirkwood (M2)*....	Milton (N5)*...... 1,321	Rockland (M1)*.... 350	area)...........186,265
	Clayton (M3)*...... 825	Georgetown (N6)*... 1,923	Laurel (M6)*...... 2,700	Mount Cuba (M1)... 300	Roxana (06)....... 100	Woodside (M4)*.... 157
	Concord (M6)...... 100	Glasgow (M2)......	Lebanon (N4)...... 150	Mount Pleasant (M2)*. 87	Saint Georges (M2)*..	Wyoming (M4)*.... 911
	Cooch (M2)........ 12	Glasgow Station (M2)...	Leipsic (N4)....... 253	Nassau (06)*...... 120	Seaford (M6)*..... 3,087	Yorklyn (M1)*..... 500

FLORIDA Total Population 2,771,305

Map on Page 55

67 COUNTIES

Alachua (D2)......57,026	Hamilton (D1)...... 8,981	Osceola (E3)......11,406	Allenhurst (F3)..... 60	Aucilla (C1)*......	Belleville (C1)..... 20	Brighton (E4)*..... 175
Baker (D1)........ 6,313	Hardee (E4)....... 10,073	Palm Beach (F5)...114,688	Alliance (D2)....... 250	Avon Park (E4)*... 4,612	Benhaden (B1)..... 25	Bristol (B1)*...... 1,800
Bay (C6)........ 42,689	Hendry (E5)....... 6,051	Pasco (D3)....... 20,529	Altamonte Spgs. (E3)*. 858	Babson Park (E4)*... 1,000	Bennett (D6)....... 200	Bronson (D2)*..... 624
Bradford (D2)..... 11,457	Hernando (D3)..... 6,693	Pinellas (D4).....159,249	Altha (A1)*....... 434	Bagdad (B6)*..... 1,500	Beresford (E2)*.... 100	Brooker ‡(D2)*.... 277
Brevard (F3)..... 23,653	Highlands (E4)....13,636	Polk (E4).......123,997	Altoona (E3)*..... 500	Baker (C5)*.......	Biscayne Park ‡(F6).. 200	Brooksville (D3)*... 1,818
Broward (F5)..... 83,933	Hillsborough (D4).249,894	Putnam (E2)...... 23,615	Alturas (E4)*..... 350	Bal Harbour ‡(F6).. 224	Bithlo (E3)*...... 50	Broscan (C2)...... 10
Calhoun (D6)...... 7,922	Holmes (C5)....... 13,988	St. Johns (E2)..... 24,998	Alva (E5)*........ 300	Baldwin (E1)*..... 1,048	Blanton (D3)*..... 75	Brownville (E4)*.... 200
Charlotte (E5)..... 4,286	Indian River (F4)...11,872	St. Lucie (F4)..... 20,180	Amelia City (E1)*... 150	Barberville (E2)*... 350	Blountstown (A1)*.. 2,118	Bruce (C6)*...... 200
Citrus (D3)....... 6,111	Jackson (D5).....34,645	Santa Rosa (B6)...18,554	Anastasia (E2)*.... 500	Barrineau Park (B6)*. 200	Bluffsprings (B5)*... 100	Bryant (F5)*...... 400
Clay (E2)........ 14,323	Jefferson (C1).....10,413	Sarasota (D4).....28,827	Ankona (F4)*...... 75	Barth (B6)*....... 300	Boca Ciega ‡(D4)... 159	Bryceville (D1)*.... 150
Collier (E5)....... 6,488	Lafayette (C2)...... 3,440	Seminole (E3).....26,883	Anna Maria (D4)*... 345	Bartow (E4)*...... 8,694	Boca Grande (D5)*.. 400	Bulow (E2)........ 25
Columbia (D1).....18,216	Lake (E3)....... 36,340	Sumter (D3)...... 11,330	Anthony (D2)*..... 400	Bascom (A1)*...... 150	Boca Raton (F5)*... 992	Bunnell (E2)*..... 1,341
Dade (F6)......495,084	Lee (E5)......... 23,404	Suwannee (C1)....16,986	Apalachicola (A2)*.. 3,222	Basinger (E4)*.... 150	Bokeelia (D5)*.... 100	Burbank (E2)*..... 80
De Soto (E4)...... 9,242	Leon (B1)........51,590	Taylor (C1)...... 10,416	Apopka (E3)*..... 2,254	Bay Harbor (D6)*.. 1,676	Bonifay (C5)*..... 2,252	Bushnell (D3)*.... 536
Dixie (C2)........ 3,928	Levy (D2)........ 10,637	Union (D1)....... 8,906	Arcadia (E4)*..... 4,764	Bay Harbor Isls. ‡(F6). 296	Bonita Springs (E5)*.	Callahan (E1)*.... 722
Duval (E1)......304,029	Liberty (B1)....... 3,182	Volusia (E2)...... 74,229	Archer (D2)*...... 586	Bay Springs (B6)*...	Bostwick (E2)*.... 500	Campbellton (D5)*.. 307
Escambia (B6)....112,706	Madison (C1)......14,197	Wakulla (B1)....... 5,258	Argyle (C6)*......	Bayard (E1)*..... 300	Bowling Green (E4)*. 884	Campville (D2)*.... 250
Flagler (E2)....... 3,367	Manatee (D4)......34,704	Walton (C6)...... 14,725	Aripeka (D3)*..... 75	Bayport (D3)*..... 45	Boyd (C1)*....... 200	Canal Point (F5)*.. 1,022
Franklin (B2)...... 5,814	Marion (D2)...... 38,187	Washington (C6)... 11,888	Arlington · (E1)*.. 3,200	Bayshore (E5)..... 15	Boynton Beach (F5)*. 2,542	Canaveral (F3)...
Gadsden (B1)..... 36,457	Martin (F4)....... 7,807		Arran (B1)*.......	Bean City (F5)*.... 268	Bradenton (D4)*...13,604	Candler (E2)*..... 150
Gilchrist (D2)...... 3,499	Monroe (E7)...... 29,957	**CITIES and TOWNS**	Artesia (F3)*......	Bee Ridge (D4)*.... 500	Bradenton Beach(D4)*. 500	Cantonment (B6)*..
Glades (E5)....... 2,199	Nassau (E1)....... 12,811		Astatula (E3)*..... 255	Bell (C2)*........ 108	Bradley (D4)*..... 422	Captiva (D5)*..... 50
Gulf (D7)........ 7,460	Okaloosa (C6)..... 27,533	Alachua (D2)*.... 1,116	Astor (E2)*.......	Belle Glade (F5)*... 7,219	Brandon (D4)*.... 1,250	Carrabelle (B2)*... 970
	Okeechobee (F4).... 3,454	Alford (D6)....... 375	Atlantic Beach (E1)*. 1,604	Belleair (D4)...... 961	Branford (D2)*.... 753	Caryville (C6)*.... 525
	Orange (E3)......114,950		Auburndale (E3)*... 3,763	Belleview (D2)*.... 595	Brewster (E4)*.... 800	

Cassadaga (E3)*...... 200
Casselberry ‡(E3)...... 407
Cedar Key (C2)*...... 900
Center Hill (D3)*...... 522
Century (B5)*......1,350
Chaires (B1)*......
Charlotte Harbor (E5)*. 330
Chattahoochee (B1)*......8,473
Cherry Lake Farms (C1)...... 600
Chiefland (D2)*...... 843
Chipley (D6)*......2,959
Chokoloskee (E6)*...... 148
Chosen (F5)*......1,873
Christmas (E3)*...... 250
Citra (D2)*...... 500
Citrus Center (E5)...... 15
City Point (F3)*...... 250
Clarksville (D6)*......
Clearwater (D4)*......15,581
Clermont (E3)*......2,168
Cleveland (E5)*...... 104
Clewiston (E5)*......2,499
Cloud Lake ‡(F5)...... 132
Cocoa (F3)*......4,245
Cocoa Beach (F3)*...... 246
Coleman (D3)*...... 849
Collier City (Goodland*) (E6)...... 337
Columbia (D1)...... 75
Compass Lake (D6)*......
Concord (B1)*......
Conner (E2)...... 100
Coral Gables (F6)*......19,837
Coreytown ‡(D4)...... 23
Cornwell (E4)*...... 10
Coronado (F2)......
Cortez (D4)*...... 600
Cottagehill (B6)*...... 500
Cottondale (D6)*...... 737
Craig (F7)*...... 10
Crawfordville (B1)*...... 525
Crescent City (E2)*......1,393
Crestview (C6)*......5,003
Cross City (C2)*......1,522
Crystal Lake (D6)*...... 250
Crystal River (D3)*......1,026
Crystal Springs (D3)*... 250
Curtis (D2)...... 50
Cypress (A1)*...... 262
Dade City (D3)*......3,806
Dania (F5)*......4,540
Darlington (C5)*......
Davenport (E3)*...... 760
Davie (F5)...... 728
Day (C1)*...... 300
Daytona Beach (F2)*..30,187
De Funiak Springs (C6)*......3,077
De Land (E2)*......8,652
De Leon Springs (E2)*.. 900
De Soto City (E4)*...... 220
Deer Park (F3)*......
Deerfield Beach (F5)*..2,088
Delray Beach (F5)*......6,312
Denaud (E5)...... 100
Destin (C6)*......
Dinsmore (E1)*......1,010
Doctors Inlet (E1)*...... 490
Dover (D4)*......1,000
Dowling Park (C1)...... 35
Drifton (C1)*...... 200
Dundee (E3)*......1,152
Dunedin (D3)*......3,202
Dunnellon (D2)*......1,110
Eagle Lake (E4)*......1,060
Earleton (D2)*...... 100
East Palatka (E2)*......1,367
Eastpoint (B2)*...... 600
Eastport (E1)......
Eau Gallie (F3)*......1,554
Ebb (C1)*...... 100
Ebro (C6)*...... 200
Edgewater (F3)*...... 837
Edgewood ‡(E3)...... 217
El Jobean (D5)*...... 60
El Portal ‡(F6)......1,371
Elfers (D3)*...... 560
Elkton (E2)*......
Ellaville (C1)...... 5
Ellenton (D4)*...... 700
Ellzey (D2)...... 150
Emporia (E2)*...... 420
Englewood (D5)*......1,206
Enterprise (E3)*...... 300
Espanola (E2)*...... 125
Estero (E5)*...... 250
Esto (C5)*...... 217
Eureka (E2)*...... 300
Eustis (E3)*......4,005
Everglades (E6)*...... 625
Fairbanks (D2)...... 35
Fairfield (D2)*...... 135
Fairvilla (E3)......1,000
Falmouth (C1)*......
Felda (E5)*...... 300
Fellsmere (F4)*...... 649
Fernandina (E1)*......4,420
Fernandina Beach ‡(E1)...... 554
Flagler Beach (E2)*...... 374
Fletcher (C2)...... 100
Florahome (E2)*...... 400
Floral City (D3)*...... 700
Florence Villa (E3)*......2,500
Florida City (F6)*......1,547
Floridatown (B6)......1,200
Florosa (B6)......
Foley (C1)*......1,014
Ft. Barrancas (B6)...... 300
Ft. Drum (F4)...... 50
Ft. George (E1)*...... 150
Ft. Green (E4)*......
Ft. Lauderdale (F5)*..36,328
Ft. Mc Coy (E2)*...... 500
Ft. Meade (E4)*......2,803
Ft. Myers (E5)*......13,195
Ft. Ogden (E4)*...... 750
Ft. Pierce (F4)*......13,502
Ft. Walton (C6)*......2,463
Ft. White (D2)*...... 329
Fountain (D6)*...... 150
Freeport (C6)*......
Frink (D6)*...... 300
Frostproof (E4)*......2,329
Fruitland Park (D3)*.... 551
Fruitville (D4)...... 900
Gainer (D6)...... 25
Gainesville (D2)*......26,861
Garden City (E1)*...... 500
Gardner (E4)*...... 110
Gasparilla (D5)*...... 250
Geneva (E3)*...... 600
Genoa (D1)...... 100
Georgetown (E2)*...... 300
Gibsonton (D4)*......
Gifford (F4)*......1,459
Glen Ridge ‡(F5)...... 126
Glen Saint Mary (D1)*.
Glendale (C5)...... 250
Glenwood (E2)*...... 155
Golden Beach ‡(F6)*.... 156
Golfview ‡(F5)...... 84
Gomez (F4)...... 65
Gonzalez (B6)*...... 700
Goodland (E6)*...... 337
Gotha (E3)*...... 275
Goulding (B6)...... 300
Goulds (F6)*......1,000
Graceville (D5)*......1,638
Graham (D2)*...... 50
Grand Ridge (A1)*...... 300
Grandin (E2)*...... 200
Grant (F4)*......
Green Cove Spgs. (E2)*.3,291
Greenacres City (F5)*... 531
Greensboro (B1)*...... 565
Greenville (C1)*......1,163
Greenwood (A1)*......
Gretna (B1)*...... 385
Groveland (E3)*......1,028
Gulf Breeze (B6)*...... 287
Gulf Hammock (D2)*.... 250
Gulf Stream ‡(F5)...... 163
Gulfport (D4)*......3,702
Gull Point (B6)*...... 65
Hague (D2)...... 150
Haines City (E3)*......5,630
Hallandale (F6)*......3,886
Hampton (D2)*...... 386
Hampton Spgs. (C1)...... 15
Hardee Town (D2)......
Harold (B6)*...... 75
Hastings (E2)*...... 577
Havana (B1)*......1,634
Hawthorne (D2)*......1,058
Hernando (D3)*...... 304
Hesperides (E4)...... 70
Hialeah (F6)*......19,676
Hicora (E4)......
High Springs (D2)*......2,088
Highland (E1)*...... 350
Highland Beach ‡(F5)... 52
Highland City (E4)*......1,600
Highland Park ‡(E4)...... 52
Hildreth (D2)*...... 22
Hillcrest Hts. ‡(E4)...... 91
Hilliard (E1)*...... 607
Hillsboro Beach ‡(F5).. 84
Hines (C2)...... 400
Hinson (B1)*...... 500
Hobe Sound (F5)*...... 950
Holder (D3)*...... 75
Hollister (E2)*......
Holly Hill (E2)......3,232
Hollywood (F5)*......14,351
Holmes Beach ‡(D4).... 137
Holopaw (E3)*......
Holt (C6)*......
Homestead (F6)*......4,573
Homosassa (D3)*...... 500
Homosassa Spgs. (D3)*. 100
Horseshoe Beach (C2)*. 150
Hosford (B1)*......
Houston (D1)*...... 140
Howey in the Hills, (E3)*...... 188
Hudson (D3)*...... 350
Hull (E4)*......
Immokalee (E5)*......1,200
Indian Creek ‡(F6)...... 44
Indian Pass (D7)...... 60
Indian River City (F3)*. 450
Indian Rocks Beach (D4)*...... 198
Indian Town (F4)*......
Inglis (D2)*...... 200
Intercession City (E3)*.
Interlachen (E2)*...... 297
Inverness (D3)*......1,471
Inwood (A1)...... 100
Islamorada (F7)*...... 600
Island Grove (D2)*...... 400
Jacksonville (E1)*......204,517
Jacksonville (urban area)......241,579
Jacksonville Beach(E1)*6,430
Jamieson 'B1)*...... 120
Jasper (D1)*......2,327
Jay (B5)*...... 547
Jennings (C1)*...... 549
Jensen Beach (F4)*......
Johnson (E2)*......
Jupiter (F5)*...... 313
Kathleen (D3)*...... 750
Kenansville (F4)*...... 250
Kendall (F6)*......2,100
Kendrick (D2)*...... 600
Key Largo (F6)...... 60
Key West (E7)*......26,433
Keystone Heights (E2)* 307
Keysville (D4)*...... 500
Kinard (D6)*...... 300
Kissimmee (E3)*......4,310
Korona (E2)*......
Kynesville (D6)...... 400
La Belle (E5)*...... 945
La Crosse (D2)*...... 146
Lacoochee (D3)*......1,792
Lady Lake (E3)*...... 331
Lake Alfred (E3)*......1,270
Lake Butler (D1)*......1,040
Lake City (D1)*......7,571
Lake City Jct. (D2)...... 11
Lake Como (E2)*...... 200
Lake Hamilton (E3)*.... 604
Lake Harbor (F5)*...... 800
Lake Helen (E3)*...... 926
Lake Jem (E3)*...... 300
Lake Maitland ‡(E3).... 889
Lake Mary (E3)*...... 500
Lake Monroe (E3)*...... 300
Lake Park (F5)*...... 489
Lake Placid (E4)*...... 417
Lake Wales (E4)*......6,821
Lake Worth (G5)*......11,777
Lakeland (D3)*......30,851
Lakeport (E5)...... 70
Lakewood (C5)*......
Lamont (C1)*......
Land O'Lakes (D3)*...... 75
Lantana (F5)*...... 773
Largo (D4)*......1,547
Laurel (D4)*...... 500
Lauderdale-by-the-Sea ‡(F5)...... 234
Laurel Hill (C5)*...... 327
Lawtey (D1)*...... 576
Lebanon (D2)...... 75
Lecanto (D3)*...... 182
Lee (C1)*...... 228
Leesburg (E3)*......7,395
Leonia (C5)*...... 105
Limestone (E4)*...... 150
Linden (D3)*...... 250
Live Oak (D1)*......4,064
Lloyd (C1)*...... 325
Lochloosa (E2)*...... 200
Lockhart (E3)*......1,200
Longwood (E3)*...... 717
Lorida (E4)*...... 225
Loughman (E3)*...... 350
Lovett (C1)*...... 18
Lowell (D2)*...... 150
Loxahatchee (F5)*...... 200
Lulu (D1)*...... 100
Lumberton (D3)...... 25
Luraville (C1)...... 20
Lutz (D3)*......1,800
Lynn Haven (C6)*......1,787
Lynne (E2)*...... 125
Macclenny (D1)*......1,177
Madeira Beach ‡(D4)*.. 916
Madison (C1)*......3,150
Maitland (E3)*......
Malabar (F3)*...... 375
Malone (A1)*...... 521
Manalapan ‡(F5)...... 54
Manatee (D4)......
Mandarin (E1)*...... 800
Mango (D4)*...... 350
Mangonia Park ‡(F5)... 348
Mannville (E2)*...... 70
Marathon (E2)*......1,200
Marco (E6)*...... 250
Marianna (A1)*......5,845
Marineland (E2)...... 40
Martin (D2)*...... 100
Mary Esther (B6)*...... 332
Masaryktown (D3)...... 190
Mascotte (E3)*...... 440
Mason (D1)...... 20
Maxville (E1)*......
Mayo (C1)*...... 679
Mayport (E1)*......1,300
Maytown (F3)...... 25
Mc Alpin (D1)*...... 100
Mc David (B5)*...... 700
Mc Intosh (D2)*...... 247
Mc Neal (A1)...... 500
Medley ‡(F6)...... 106
Melbourne (F3)*......4,223
Melbourne Beach (F3)*. 230
Melrose (D2)*...... 750
Merritt Island (F3)*......
Miami (F6)*......249,276
Miami (urban area) ..453,004
Miami Beach (F6)*......46,282
Miami Shores (F6)*......5,086
Miami Springs (F6)*......5,108
Micanopy (D2)*...... 612
Micco (F4)*...... 250
Miccosukee (B1)*...... 160
Middleburg (E1)*...... 500
Midway (B1)*...... 500
Millers Ferry (C6)*...... 40
Milligan (C6)*...... 600
Millview (B6)...... 150
Milton (B6)*......2,040
Mims (F3)*......1,500
Minneola (E3)*...... 399
Molino (B6)*...... 600
Montbrook (D2)*...... 200
Monticello (C1)*......2,264
Montverde (E3)*...... 293
Moore Haven (E5)*...... 636
Morriston (D2)*...... 150
Mossy Head (C6)*...... 125
Moultrie (E2)...... 50
Mt. Dora (E3)*......3,028
Mt. Pleasant (B1)*...... 300
Mulat (B6)*...... 80
Mulberry (E4)*......2,024
Munson (B5)*...... 300
Murdock (D4)*...... 100
Muscogee (B6)*...... 165
Myakka City (D4)*...... 450
Myrtle Grove (B6)*......
Naples (E5)*......1,465
Naranja (F6)*...... 500
Narcoossee (E3)*...... 120
National Gardens(E2)*. 125
Neptune Beach (E1)*...1,767
New Berlin (E1)...... 100
New Port Richey (D3)*.1,512
New River (D2)*...... 150
New Smyrna Beach (F2)*......5,775
Newberry (D2)*...... 873
Newburn (C1)...... 10
Niceville (C6)*......2,497
Nichols (E4)*...... 550
Nobleton (D3)*...... 72
Nocatee (E4)*......1,200
Nokomis (D4)*...... 800
Noma (C5)*......
North Bay ‡(F6)...... 198
North Miami (F6)*......10,734
N. Miami Beach (F6)*..2,129
O'Brien (D1)*...... 300
Oak Hill (F3)*...... 683
Oakland (E3)*...... 548
Oakland Park (F5)*......1,295
Ocala (D2)*......11,741
Ocean Ridge ‡(F5)...... 67
Ochopee (E6)*...... 300
Ocoee (E3)*......1,370
Odessa (D3)*......
Ojus (F6)*......3,791
Okahumpka (D3)*...... 450
Okeechobee (F4)*......1,849
Oklawaha (E2)*...... 500
Old Town (C2)*...... 300
Oldsmar (D3)*...... 345
Olive (B6)...... 200
Olustee (D1)*......
Ona (E4)*...... 89
Oneco (D4)*...... 650
Opa-Locka (F6)*......5,271
Orange (B1)*......
Orange City (E3)*...... 797
Orange Lake (D2)*...... 500
Orange Park (E1)*......1,502
Orange Springs (E2)*.... 275
Orlando (E3)*......52,367
Orlando (urban area)..72,572
Ormond (E2)*......3,418
Ormond Beach (F2)*.... 900
Orsino (F3)*...... 55
Osceola (E3)......
Osprey (D4)*...... 350
Osteen (E3)*...... 300
Otter Creek (D2)*......1,050
Overstreet (D6)*...... 100
Oviedo (E3)*......1,601
Oxford (D3)*...... 304
Ozona (D3)*...... 600
Pahokee (F5)*......4,472
Palatka (E2)*......9,176
Palm Bay (F3)*...... 300
Palm Beach (G5)*......3,886
Palm City (F4)*......
Palm Harbor (D3)*...... 750
Palma Sola (D4)*...... 300
Palmdale (E5)*...... 82
Palmetto (D4)*......4,103
Panacea (B1)*......
Panama City (C6)*......25,814
Panama City Beach(C6)*
Paola (E3)*...... 400
Parrish (D4)*......1,200
Parker (D6)*......
Pass-a-Grille Beach (D4)*......1,000
Paxton (C5)...... 300
Pelican Lake (F5)*......
Pembroke (E4)*...... 50
Penney Farms (E2)*...... 445
Pennsuco ‡(F6)...... 133
Pensacola (B6)*......43,479
Perrine (F6)*......2,859
Perry (C1)*......2,797
Pierce (E4)*...... 975
Pierson (E2)*...... 657
Pine Castle (E3)*......2,000
Pineland (D5)*...... 50
Pinellas Park (D4)*......2,924
Pinetta (C1)*...... 250
Pirates Cove (E7)......
Plant City (D3)*......9,230
Plymouth (E3)*...... 300
Point Washington (C6)*
Polk City (E3)*...... 171
Pomona Park (E2)*...... 443
Pompano Beach (F5)*...5,682
Ponce de Leon (C6)*.... 600
Ponce Park (F2)...... 39
Ponte Vedra Beach (E1)*......1,000
Port Boca Grande (D5). 75
Port Everglades (F5)*... 100
Port Mayaca (F5)*...... 155
Port Orange (F2)*......1,201
Port Richey (D3)*...... 376
Port Saint Joe (D6)*......2,752
Port Sewall (F4)...... 210
Port Tampa (D4)*......1,497
Portland (C6)*...... 350
Princeton (F6)*......1,300
Providence (D2)...... 16
Punta Gorda (E5)*......1,915
Punta Rassa (E5)...... 25
Quincy (B1)*......6,505
Raiford (D1)*...... 40
Raleigh (D2)*...... 156
Ramrod Key (E7)*...... 3
Redbay (C6)*...... 250
Reddick (D2)*...... 433
Redington Beach ‡(D4). 384
Richland (D3)...... 100
Richloam (D3)...... 10
River Junction (B1)*......
Riverdale (E2)...... 100
Riverview (D4)*......
Riviera Beach (F5)*......4,065
Rock Bluff (B1)*...... 250
Rock Harbor (F6)*...... 185
Rockledge (F3)*......1,347
Romeo (D2)*...... 300
Roseland (F4)*...... 100
Round Lake (D6)*...... 250
Ruskin (D4)*......
Safety Harbor (D4)*...... 894
St. Augustine (E2)*....13,555
St. Catherine (D3)*...... 250
St. Cloud (E3)*......3,001
St. James City (E5)*.... 35
St. Leo (D3)*...... 261
St. Lucie (F4)*...... 300
St. Marks (B1)*...... 391
St. Petersburg (D4)*...96,738
St. Petersburg (urban area)......113,378
St. Petersburg Beach ‡(D4)...... 722
Salem (C2)*...... 200
Salerno (F4)*...... 789
Samoset (D4)*......1,617
Sampson (D2)*...... 125
Samsula (E2)...... 500
San Antonio (D3)*...... 286
San Carlos (E5)......
San Mateo (E2)*...... 750
Sanderson (D1)*...... 100
Sanford (E3)*......11,935
Sanibel (D5)*...... 125
Santa Fe (D2)*...... 100
Santa Rosa (C6)*...... 300
Santos (D2)...... 100
Sarasota (D4)*......18,896
Satsuma (E2)*...... 250
Scottsmoore (F3)*...... 150
Sears (E5)......
Sebastian (F4)*...... 376
Sebring (E4)*......5,006
Seffner (D4)*...... 850
Seville (E2)*...... 427
Shady Grove (C1)*...... 50
Shalimar ‡(C6)*...... 694
Shamrock (C2)*...... 700
Sharpes (F3)*...... 300
Shiloh (F3)*...... 150
Silver Springs (D2)*..... 350
Slater (E5)...... 25
Sneads (B1)*......1,074
Sopchoppy (B1)*......
Sorrento (E3)*...... 300
South Bay (F5)*......1,050
South Daytona (E2)...... 692
South Flomatin ‡(B5)... 395
South Miami (F6)*......4,809
Southport (C6)*...... 825
Sparr (D2)*...... 450
Springfield (D6)......1,084
Starke (D2)*......2,944
Steinhatchee (C2)*...... 900
Stuart (F4)*......2,912
Sumatra (B1)*......
Summerfield (D2)*...... 400
Sumner (D2)...... 25
Sun City (D4)*...... 325
Sunnyside (C6)*...... 85
Sunshine Beach ‡(D4).. 469
Surfside ‡(F6)......1,852
Suwannee (C2)*...... 125
Sweetwater ‡(F6)...... 230
Switzerland (E1)*...... 350
Taft (E3)*...... 800
TALLAHASSEE (B1)*.27,237
Tampa (D4)*......124,681
Tampa (urban area)..178,398
Tarpon Springs (D3)*..4,323
Tavares (E3)*......1,763
Tavernier (F6)*...... 480
Telogia (B1)*......
Temple Terrace (D3)*... 433
Terra Ceia (D4)*......1,500
Thonotosassa (D3)*......
Tice (E5)*......1,133
Titusville (F3)*......2,604
Treasure Island ‡(D4)... 75
Trenton (D2)*...... 904
Trilby (D3)*...... 500
Uleta (F6)*......
Umatilla (E3)*......1,312
Useppa Island (D5)...... 25
Valparaiso (C6)*......1,047
Venice (D4)*...... 727
Venus (E4)*...... 35
Vernon (C6)*...... 610
Vero Beach (F4)*......4,746
Virginia Gardens ‡(F6) 235
Villa Tasso (C6)...... 75
Wabasso (F4)*...... 300
Wacissa (B1)*...... 450
Wakulla (B1)*......
Waldo (D2)*...... 647
Walnut Hill (B5)*......
Walton (F4)...... 175
Ward (B1)...... 30
Warrington (B6)*......13,570
Watertown (D1)*......1,473
Wauchula (E4)*......2,872
Waukeenah (C1)*...... 200
Wausau (D6)*...... 350
Waverly (E4)*......1,000
Webster (D3)*...... 569
Weirsdale (D3)*...... 800
Welaka (E2)*...... 459
Wellborn (D1)*...... 450
West Miami (F6)......4,043
W. Palm Beach (F5)*..43,162
Westbay (C6)*...... 400
Westgate (F6)......3,303
Westville (C6)*...... 428
Wewahitchka (D6)*......1,289
White City (F4)...... 750
White Springs (D1)*..... 700
Whitehouse (E1)*...... 175
Wilcox (D2)*...... 125
Wildwood (D3)*......2,019
Williston (D2)*......1,323
Wilma (B1)*...... 50
Wilton Manor ‡(F5)...... 883
Wimauma (D4)*...... 440
Windermere (E3)*...... 317
Winfield (D1)...... 100
Winter Beach (F4)*...... 350
Winter Garden (E3)*....3,503
Winter Haven (E3)*......8,605
Winter Park (E3)*......8,250
Woodville (B1)*......
Worthington (D2)*...... 30
Yalaha (E3)*...... 600
Yankeetown (D2)*...... 322
Youngstown (D6)*...... 500
Yukon (E1)*......2,000
Yulee (E1)*...... 500
Zellwood (E3)*......1,500
Zephyrhills (D3)*......1,826
Zolfo Springs (E4)*...... 334

Map on Page 56

GEORGIA

Total Population 3,444,578

159 COUNTIES

Appling (H7)......14,003
Atkinson (G8)......7,362
Bacon (G7)......8,940
Baker (D8)......5,952
Baldwin (F4)......29,706
Banks (E2)......6,935
Barrow (E2)......13,115
Bartow (C2)......27,370
Ben Hill (F7)......14,879
Berrien (F8)......13,966
Bibb (E5)......114,079
Bleckley (F6)......9,218
Brantley (J8)......6,387
Brooks (E9)......18,169
Bryan (K6)......5,965
Bulloch (J6)......24,740
Burke (J4)......23,458
Butts (E4)......9,079
Calhoun (C7)......8,578
Camden (J9)......7,322
Candler (H6)......8,063
Carroll (B3)......34,112
Catoosa (B1)......15,146
Charlton (H9)......4,821
Chatham (K6)......151,481
Chattahoochee (C6)....12,149
Chattooga (B1)......21,197
Cherokee (D2)......20,750
Clarke (F3)......36,550
Clay (B7)......5,844
Clayton (D3)......22,872
Clinch (G9)......6,007
Cobb (C3)......61,830
Coffee (G8)......23,961
Colquitt (E8)......33,999
Columbia (H3)......9,525
Cook (F8)......12,201
Coweta (C4)......27,796
Crawford (E5)......6,080
Crisp (E7)......17,663
Dade (A1)......7,364
Dawson (D2)......3,712
De Kalb (D3)......136,395
Decatur (C9)......23,620
Dodge (F6)......17,865
Dooly (E6)......14,159
Dougherty (D7)......43,617
Douglas (C3)......12,173
Early (C8)......17,413
Echols (G9)......2,494
Effingham (K6)......9,133
Elbert (G2)......18,585
Emanuel (H5)......19,789
Evans (J6)......6,653
Fannin (D1)......15,192
Fayette (C4)......7,978
Floyd (B2)......62,899
Forsyth (D2)......11,005
Franklin (F2)......14,446
Fulton (D3)......473,572
Gilmer (D1)......9,963
Glascock (G4)......3,579
Glynn (J8)......29,046
Gordon (C2)......18,922
Grady (D9)......18,928
Greene (F3)......12,843
Gwinnett (D2)......32,320
Habersham (E1)......16,553
Hall (E2)......40,113
Hancock (G4)......11,052
Haralson (B3)......14,663
Harris (C5)......11,265
Hart (G2)......14,495
Heard (B4)......6,975
Henry (D4)......15,857
Houston (E6)......20,964
Irwin (F7)......11,973
Jackson (E2)......18,997
Jasper (E4)......7,473
Jeff Davis (G7)......9,299
Jefferson (H4)......18,855
Jenkins (J5)......10,264
Johnson (G5)......9,893
Jones (E5)......7,538
Lamar (D4)......10,242
Lanier (F8)......5,151
Laurens (G6)......33,123
Lee (D7)......6,674
Liberty (J7)......8,444
Lincoln (H3)......6,462
Long (J7)......3,598
Lowndes (F9)......35,211
Lumpkin (D1)......6,574
Macon (D6)......14,213
Madison (F2)......12,238
Marion (C6)......6,521
Mc Duffie (H4)......11,443
Mc Intosh (K7)......6,008
Meriwether (C4)......21,055
Miller (C8)......9,023
Mitchell (D8)......22,528
Monroe (E4)......10,523
Montgomery (G6)......7,901

Morgan (F3)......11,899
Murray (C1)......10,676
Muscogee (C6)......118,028
Newton (E3)......20,185
Oconee (F3)......7,009
Oglethorpe (F3)......9,958
Paulding (C3)......11,752
Peach (E5)......11,705
Pickens (D2)......8,855
Pierce (H8)......11,112
Pike (D4)......8,459
Polk (B3)......30,976
Pulaski (E6)......8,808
Putnam (F4)......7,731
Quitman (B7)......3,015
Rabun (F1)......7,424
Randolph (C7)......13,804
Richmond (H4)......108,876
Rockdale (D3)......8,464
Schley (D6)......4,036
Screven (J5)......18,000
Seminole (C9)......7,904
Spalding (D4)......31,045
Stephens (F1)......16,647
Stewart (C6)......9,194
Sumter (D6)......24,208
Talbot (C5)......7,687
Taliaferro (G3)......4,515
Tattnall (J6)......15,939
Taylor (D5)......9,113
Telfair (G7)......13,221
Terrell (D7)......14,314
Thomas (E9)......33,932
Tift (E8)......22,645
Toombs (H6)......17,382
Towns (E1)......4,803
Treutlen (G6)......6,522
Troup (B4)......49,841
Turner (E7)......10,479
Twiggs (F5)......8,308
Union (E1)......7,318
Upson (D5)......25,078
Walker (B1)......38,198
Walton (E3)......20,230
Ware (H8)......30,289
Warren (G4)......8,779
Washington (G4)......21,012
Wayne (J7)......14,248
Webster (C6)......4,081
Wheeler (G6)......6,712
White (E1)......5,751
Whitfield (B1)......34,432
Wilcox (F7)......10,167
Wilkes (G3)......12,388
Wilkinson (F5)......9,781
Worth (E8)......19,357

CITIES and TOWNS

Aaron (J5)......50
Abac (E8)......
Abba (F7)*......
Abbeville (F7)*......890
Abbottsford (B4)......40
Acree (D7)*......225
Acworth (C2)*......1,466
Adairsville (C2)*......916
Adel (F8)*......2,776
Adgateville (E4)......75
Adrian (G5)*......503
Afton (D2)......7
Agnes (H3)*......30
Agricola (G4)......45
Aikenton (E4)......
Ailey (G6)*......508
Akes (B3)......400
Alamo (G6)*......800
Alapaha (F8)*......505
Albany (D7)*......31,155
Aldora (D4)......591
Alexander (J4)*......90
Aline (H6)......100
Allenhurst (J7)*......150
Allentown (F5)*......450
Allenville (F8)......15
Alma (G7)*......2,588
Almon (E3)......135
Alpharetta (D2)*......917
Alston (H6)*......147
Altamaha (H7)......
Alto (E2)*......302
Alvaton (C4)*......95
Amboy (E7)......50
Ambrose (G7)*......470
Americus (D6)*......11,389
Amity (H3)*......
Amsterdam (D9)*......700
Andersonville (D6)*......281
Apalachee (E3)*......178
Apollo (F4)*......25
Appling (H3)*......250
Arabi (E7)*......376
Aragon (B2)*......1,272
Arcade (E2)......114
Arcola (J6)......86
Argyle (G8)*......244
Arlington (C8)*......1,382
Armuchee (B2)*......
Arnoldsville (F3)*......150
Arp (F7)......
Ashburn (E7)*......2,918
Ashland (F2)*......250
Aska (D1)*......35
Atco (C2)*......1,443
Athens (F3)*......28,180
Atkinson (J8)*......500
ATLANTA (D3)*......331,314
Atlanta (urban area)......502,204
Attapulgus (D9)*......457
Auburn (E2)*......301
Augusta (J4)*......71,508
Augusta (urban area)......87,823
Auraria (E1)......200
Austell (C3)*......1,413
Autreyville (E8)......100
Avalon (F1)*......151
Avans (A1)*......
Avera (H4)*......230
Avondale Estates (D3)*......1,070
Axson (G8)*......200
Babcock (C8)......
Baconton (D8)*......500
Bainbridge (C9)*......7,562
Bairdstown (F3)*......75
Baldwin (E2)*......490
Ball Ground (D2)*......700
Banning (C3)......225
Bannockburn (F8)......15
Barnesville (D4)*......4,185
Barnett (G3)*......60
Barnett Shoals (F3)......
Barney (E8)*......157
Barretts (F8)*......150
Bartow (G5)*......347
Barwick (E9)*......436
Bascom (J5)......30
Baxley (H7)*......3,409
Baxter (D1)*......
Beach (G8)......62
Beachton (D9)......50
Belair (H4)......
Bellton (E2)*......266
Bellville (H6)*......300
Belmont (E2)......100
Bemiss (F9)......50
Benevolence (C7)*......157
Berlin (E8)*......309
Berner (E4)*......175
Berryton (B2)*......520
Bethlehem (E3)*......240
Between (E3)......120
Beverly (G2)......
Bibb City (B5)*......1,452
Big Springs (C5)......25
Bingen (C9)......4
Bishop (F3)*......253
Blackshear (H8)*......2,271
Bladen (J8)......8
Blaine (C1)......95
Blairsville (E1)*......430
Blakely (C8)*......3,234
Blalock (E1)......50
Blitchton (J6)*......50
Bloomingdale (K6)*......350
Blue Ridge (D1)*......1,718
Bluffton (C7)*......244
Blun (H5)......150
Blundale (H5)*......116
Blythe (H4)*......268
Bogart (E3)*......459
Bolen (G8)......90
Bolingbroke (E5)*......87
Bolton (D3)*......
Boneville (G4)*......100
Boston (E9)*......1,035
Bostwick (E3)*......287
Bowdon (B3)*......1,155
Bowdon Junction (B3)*......450
Bowens Mill (F7)......
Bowersville (G2)*......303
Bowman (G2)*......714
Box Springs (C5)*......100
Boykin (C8)......120
Bradley (E4)*......100
Braselton (E2)*......165
Braswell (C3)......25
Bremen (B3)*......2,299
Brentwood (H7)......50
Brest (D8)......
Brewton (G5)*......
Bridgeboro (E8)......
Briggston (F9)......35
Bright (D2)......150
Brighton (E7)......35
Brinson (C9)*......248
Bristol (H8)*......137
Broadhurst (J8)......225
Brobston (K8)......8
Bronwood (D7)*......337
Brooker (G7)......50
Brookfield (F8)*......350
Brooklet (J6)*......536
Brooklyn (C6)*......300
Brooks (D4)*......136
Brookton (E2)......200
Browns Crossing (F4)......50
Broxton (G7)*......890
Brunswick (K8)*......17,954
Buchanan (B3)*......651
Buckhead (F3)*......220
Buena Vista (C6)*......1,428
Buford (D2)*......3,812
Bullard (F5)......
Burnt Fort (J9)......75
Burtsboro (D1)......25
Burwell (B3)*......60
Bushnell (G7)......27
Butler (D5)*......1,182
Butts (J5)......10
Byromville (E6)*......288
Byron (E5)*......379
Cadwell (G6)*......310
Cairo (D9)*......5,577
Calhoun (B1)*......3,231
Calvary (D9)*......600
Calvin (F6)......50
Camak (G4)*......379
Camilla (D8)*......3,745
Camp Creek (D1)......
Campania (H4)......350
Campton (E3)*......163
Canon (F2)*......596
Canoochee (H5)*......62
Canton (C2)*......2,716
Carbondale (B1)......75
Carl (E3)*......214
Carlton (F2)*......249
Carnegie (C7)*......197
Carnesville (F2)*......349
Carrollton (C3)*......7,753
Carrs Station (F4)......50
Cartecay (D1)*......
Carters (C1)*......35
Cartersville (C2)*......7,270
Cass (C2)*......
Cassandra (B1)......125
Cassville (C2)*......
Cataula (C5)*......500
Cave (C2)......8
Cave Spring (B2)*......959
Cecil (F8)*......254
Cedar Grove (A1)*......75
Cedar Springs (C8)*......
Cedartown (B2)*......9,470
Center (F2)*......112
Centralhatchee (B4)......239
Chalybeate Spgs. (C5)......255
Chamblee (D3)*......3,445
Charing (D6)*......
Charles ‡(H6)......20
Chatsworth (C1)*......1,214
Chattahoochee (C3)*......
Chauncey (F6)*......348
Cherrylog (D1)*......
Chester (F6)*......315
Chickamauga (B1)*......1,747
Chipley (C5)*......817
Choestoe (E1)......
Chula (E7)*......210
Cisco (C1)*......100
Clarkdale (C3)*......750
Clarkesville (F1)*......1,106
Clarkston (D3)*......1,165
Claxton (J6)*......1,923
Clay Hill (H3)*......17
Clayton (F1)*......1,302
Clem (B3)*......400
Clermont (E2)*......323
Cleveland (E1)*......589
Climax (D9)*......373
Clinchfield (E6)*......200
Clito (J5)......25
Cloudland (A1)*......100
Clyattville (F9)*......75
Clyo (K6)*......600
Cobb (E7)*......150
Cobbtown (H6)*......288
Cobbville (G7)......126
Cobert (F2)......
Cochran (F6)*......3,357
Coffee (H7)*......200
Coffinton (C6)......
Cogdell (G8)*......
Cohutta (C1)*......450
Colbert (F2)*......407
Coleman (C7)*......295
Coleman (G4)......35
Colesburg (J9)......100
College Park (C3)*......14,535
Collegeboro (J6)*......1,000
Collins (H6)*......638
Colon (G9)......25
Colquitt (C8)*......1,664
Columbus (C6)*......79,611
Columbus (urban area)......118,122
Comer (F2)*......882
Commerce (E2)*......3,351
Concord (D4)*......360
Conyers (D3)*......2,003
Coolidge (E8)*......764
Coosa (B2)*......125
Cordele (E7)*......9,462
Corinth (B4)......135
Cork (E4)......50
Cornelia (E1)*......2,424
Cotton (D8)*......146
Council (G9)*......125
Covena (H6)*......
Coverdale (E7)......50
Covington (E3)*......5,192
Covington Mills (E3)......
Crandall (C1)*......202
Crawford (F3)*......555
Crawfordville (G3)*......966
Crest (D5)......96
Crosland (E8)*......127
Crystal Springs (B2)......
Culloden (D5)*......261
Culverton (G4)*......250
Cumming (D2)*......1,264
Curryville (B2)*......54
Cusseta (C6)*......571
Cuthbert (C7)*......4,025
Cutting (G8)......100
Cyrene (C9)......35
Dacula (E3)*......369
Dahlonega (D1)*......2,152
Daisy (J6)*......195
Dakota (E7)......40
Dallas (C3)*......1,817
Dalton (B1)*......15,968
Damascus (C8)*......402
Dames Ferry (E4)*......225
Danburg (G3)*......181
Danielsville (F2)*......298
Danville (F5)*......461
Darien (K8)*......1,380
Dasher (F9)*......100
Davisboro (G5)*......469
Dawson (D7)*......4,411
Dawsonville (D2)*......318
De Soto (D7)*......309
Dearing (H4)*......325
Decatur (D3)*......21,635
Deepstep (G4)*......159
Demorest (F1)*......1,166
Dennis (F4)......50
Denton (G7)*......273
Devereux (F4)*......170
Dewey Rose (G2)*......375
Dewitt (D8)......
Dexter (G6)*......264
Dial (D1)*......89
Dickey (C7)......135
Dillard (F1)*......186
Dixie (E9)*......261
Doctortown (J7)*......350
Doerun (E8)*......902
Doles (E7)*......125
Donalsonville (C8)*......2,569
Donovan (G5)*......225
Doogan (C1)......30
Dooling (E6)*......300
Doraville (D3)*......472
Dorchester (K7)*......150
Double Branches (H3)......100
Doublerun (E7)......
Douglas (G7)*......7,428
Douglasville (C3)*......3,400
Dover (J5)*......150
Doverel (D7)......25
Doyle (D6)*......
Draketown (B3)......200
Dry Branch (F5)*......250
Du Pont (G9)*......285
Dublin (G5)*......10,232
Ducktown (D2)......58
Dudley (F5)*......272
Due (D1)......50
Duluth (D2)*......842
Dunwoody (D3)*......240
Durand (C5)*......186
Dyas (E5)......12
Early (B2)......100
East Ellijay (C1)*......549
East Juliette (E4)......303
East Point (C3)*......21,080
East Thomaston (D5)......3,082
Eastanollee (F1)*......225
Eastman (F6)*......3,597
Eastville (F3)......96
Eatonton (F4)*......2,749
Echeconnee (E5)......56
Eden (K6)*......300
Edison (C7)*......1,247
Edith (G9)......150
Egypt (K6)*......
Elberton (G2)*......6,772
Eldora (J6)......50
Eldorendo (C8)*......250
Elko (E6)*......188
Ella Gap (C1)......
Ellabell (K6)*......100
Ellaville (D6)*......886
Ellenton (E8)*......429
Ellenwood (D3)*......250
Ellerslie (C5)*......650
Ellijay (C1)*......1,527
Elmodel (D8)*......125
Emerson (C2)*......508
Emma (D1)*......135
Emmalane (H5)......10
Empire (F6)*......157
Enigma (F8)*......499
Epworth (D1)*......100
Erick (G6)......20
Esom Hill (B3)*......175
Eton (C1)*......297
Eulonia (K7)*......
Evans (H3)*......
Everett (J8)*......200
Experiment (D4)*......4,265
Faceville (C9)*......700
Fairburn (C3)*......1,889
Fairfax (G8)......
Fairmount (C2)*......573
Fargo (G9)*......
Farmdale (J5)......
Farmington (F3)*......121
Farrar (E4)*......30
Fayetteville (C4)*......1,032
Felton (B3)*......250
Fender (E8)*......150
Ficklin (G3)*......100
Findlay (E6)......50
Finleyson (F6)*......79
Fish (B2)......200
Fitzgerald (F7)*......8,130
Fitzpatrick (F5)......150
Fleming (K7)*......200
Flemington (J7)*......90
Flint (D8)......
Flintstone (B1)*......200
Flippen (D3)*......500
Florence (C6)......
Flovilla (E4)*......315
Flowery Branch (E2)*......610
Folkston (H9)*......1,515
Forest Glen (F7)......
Forest Park (D3)*......2,653
Forsyth (E4)*......3,125
Fort Gaines (C7)*......1,339
Fort Lamar (F2)......15
Fort Mudge (H8)......25
Fort Oglethorpe ‡(B1)*......692
Fort Screven (L6)*......300
Fort Valley (E5)*......6,820
Fortson (C5)*......300
Fowlstown (D9)*......300
Franklin (B4)*......425
Franklin Spgs. (F2)*......182
Frolona (B4)*......123
Fry (D1)*......250
Fullerville (C3)......529
Funston (E8)*......233
Gabbettville (B5)*......275
Gaddistown (D1)*......175
Gaillard (D5)*......80
Gainesville (E2)*......11,936
Garden City (K6)*......1,557
Gardi (J7)*......225
Gardners (G5)*......150
Garfield (H5)*......213
Gay (C4)*......241
Geneva (C5)*......209
Georgetown (B7)*......550
Gibson (G4)*......460
Gillsville (E2)*......152
Girard (J4)*......244
Glenmore (H8)......30
Glenn (B4)*......
Glennville (J7)*......2,327
Glenwood (G6)*......684
Gloster (D3)......100
Godfrey (F4)*......168
Godwinsville (F6)......100
Goggins (D4)*......130
Good Hope (E3)*......189
Gordon (F5)*......1,761
Gore (B2)*......65
Gough (H4)*......450
Gracewood (H4)*......
Graham (H7)*......160
Grangerville (J8)......25
Grantville (C4)*......1,359
Gratis (E3)......70
Graves (C7)*......200
Gray (F4)*......866
Graymont (Twin City) (H5)*......1,018
Grayson (E3)*......227
Graysville (B1)*......120
Greenbush (B1)......150
Greenough (D8)......
Greensboro (F3)*......2,688
Greenville (C4)*......733
Greggs (F8)......4
Greshamville (F3)*......100
Gresston (F6)*......200
Griffin (D4)*......13,982
Griswoldville (F5)......
Grovania (E6)*......225
Groveland (J6)*......140
Grovetown (H4)*......500
Guyton (K6)*......633
Habersham (F1)*......750
Haddock (F4)*......475
Hagan (J6)*......525
Hahira (F9)*......1,010
Halcyon Dale (J5)*......330
Hamilton (C5)*......449
Hammett (D5)......15
Hampton (D4)*......864
Hanlin (C3)......50
Hapeville (D3)*......8,560
Haralson (C4)*......142
Hardwick (F4)*......3,000
Harlem (H4)*......1,033
Harris (C5)......250
Harrison (G5)*......261
Hartsfield (E8)*......113
Hartwell (G2)*......2,964
Hatcher (B7)*......90
Hatley (E7)......100
Hawkinsville (E6)*......3,342
Haylow (G9)*......
Hayner (J8)......20
Haywood (H8)......20
Hazlehurst (G7)*......2,687
Headlight (G9)......4
Heardmont (G2)*......65
Hebardville (H8)......1,113
Helen (E1)*......191
Helena (G6)*......1,027
Hephzibah (H4)*......525
Hermitage (B2)......25
Herndon (H5)*......300
Herod (D7)......126
Hiawassee (E1)*......375
Hickox (H8)*......139
Higgston (G6)*......155
High Shoals (F3)*......
High Tower (D2)......75
Hill City (C1)*......100
Hillsboro (E4)*......300
Hilltonia (J5)*......318
Hilton (C8)*......
Hinesville (J7)*......1,217
Hinsonton (D8)*......
Hiram (C3)*......299
Hoboken (H8)*......492
Hogansville (C4)*......3,769
Holland (B2)*......300
Holly Springs (D2)*......386
Hollywood (E1)*......100
Homeland (H9)......276
Homer (F2)*......340
Homerville (G8)*......1,787
Homestead (H8)......13
Hortense (J8)*......175
Hoschton (E2)*......378
Howard (D5)*......
Howell (F9)*......169
Huching (F3)......145
Hull (F2)*......153
Hunters (K5)......60
Huntington (D6)......100
Hurst (D1)*......195
Ideal (D6)*......318
Ila ((F2)*......225
Inaha (E7)......100
Indian Springs (E4)*......200
Inman (D4)*......300
Iron City (C8)*......293
Irwinton (F5)*......750
Irwinville (F7)*......275
Isle of Hope (K7)......800
Ivey (F5)......46
Jackson (E4)*......2,053
Jacksonville (G7)*......300
Jakin (B8)*......264
James (E5)*......150
Jasper (D2)*......1,380
Jefferson (F2)*......2,040
Jeffersonville (F5)*......787
Jenkinsburg (E4)*......166
Jersey (E3)*......182
Jesup (J7)*......4,605
Jewell (G4)*......200
Jimps (J6)......25
Johntown (D1)......8
Jonesboro (D4)*......1,741
Julia (C6)......
Juliette (E4)*......283
Junction City (C5)*......259
Juniper (C6)*......150
Juno (D2)*......30
Kathleen (E6)*......100
Keithsburg (C2)......150
Kelly (E4)*......100
Kennesaw (C2)*......564
Kenwood (D3)*......300
Keysville (H4)*......304
Kibbee (H6)*......100
Kildare (K5)......75
Killen (C7)......40
Kimbrough (C7)......100
Kingsland (J9)*......1,169
Kingston (C2)*......675
Kinlaw (J9)......35
Kirkland (G8)*......100
Kite (G5)*......447
Knoxville (E5)*......400
La Cross (D6)......
La Grange (B4)*......25,025
Ladds (C2)......75
LaFayette (B1)*......4,884
Lake Park (F9)*......334
Lake Tara ‡(D3)......224
Lakeland (F8)*......1,551
Lakemont (F1)*......500
Lanier (J6)*......100
Lavonia (F2)*......1,766
Lawrenceville (D3)*......2,932
Lax (F8)......100
Leaf (E1)*......251
Leah (H3)......200
Leary (C8)*......721
Leathersville (H3)*......
Lebanon (D2)*......200
Lee Pope (E5)*......75
Leesburg (D7)*......659
Lenox (F8)*......789
Leslie (D7)*......417
Lewiston (F5)......
Lexington (F3)*......514
Lexsy (H6)*......75
Lilburn (D3)*......567
Lilly (E6)*......177
Lincolnton (H3)*......1,315
Lindale (B2)*......2,834
Linton (F4)*......150
Linwood (B1)......858
Linwood (B2)......100
Lisbon (G3)*......95
Lithia Springs (C3)*......
Lithonia (D3)*......1,538
Little River (G3)......80
Lizella (E5)*......350
Loco (G3)......
Locust Grove (D4)*......405
Loganville (E3)*......699
Lollie (Minter) (G6)*......143
Lone Oak (C4)......120
Lookout (B1)......
Lorane (E5)......
Louisville (H4)*......2,231
Louvale (C6)*......
Lovejoy (D4)*......204
Lovett (G5)*......80
Lucile (C8)......50
Lucius (D1)......
Ludowici (J7)*......1,332
Ludville (C2)......
Luella (D4)*......200
Lula (E2)*......378
Lumber City (G7)*......1,232
Lumpkin (C6)*......1,209
Luthersville (C4)*......312
Lyerly (B2)*......524
Lynn (J7)......
Lynn Station (C8)......25
Lyons (H6)*......2,799
Machen (E4)*......40
Macon (E5)*......70,252
Macon (urban area)......93,305
Madison (F3)*......2,489
Madras (C4)*......185
Manassas (H6)*......128
Manchester (C5)*......4,036
Manor (G8)*......
Mansfield (E4)*......446
Marblehill (D2)*......
Margret (D1)*......145
Marietta (D3)*......20,687
Marion (D1)*......
Marlow (K6)*......250
Marshallville (D6)*......1,121
Martin (F2)*......207
Martinez (H3)*......2,500
Matthews (H4)*......100
Mauk (D6)*......100
Maxeys (F3)*......204
Maxim (H3)......25
Mayfield (G4)*......250
Maysville (E2)*......533
Mc Bean (J4)*......200
Mc Caysville (D1)*......2,067
Mc Collum (C4)......100
Mc Donough (D4)*......1,635
Mc Intosh (K7)*......
Mc Intyre (F5)*......194
Mc Kinnon (J8)*......65
Mc Rae (G6)*......1,904
Mc Whorter (C3)......45
Meansville (D4)*......224
Meda (F4)......20
Meeks (G5)*......100
Meigs (D8)*......1,125
Meinhard (K6)......160
Meldrim (K6)*......250
Mendes (H7)*......300
Menlo (B2)*......453
Meridian (K8)*......
Merrillville (E9)......109
Mershon (H8)*......
Mesena (G4)*......150
Metasville (G3)......82
Metcalf (E9)*......206
Metter (H6)*......2,091
Middleton (G2)*......144
Midland (C5)*......200
Midville (H5)*......682
Midway (K7)*......228
Milan (G6)*......750
Milford (C8)*......
Milledgeville (F4)*......8,835
Millen (J5)*......3,449
Millhaven (J5)*......50
Millwood (G8)*......
Milner (D4)*......345
Milstead (D3)*......1,075
Mineral Bluff (D1)*......209
Minter (Lollie*) (G6)......143
Minter (G6)*......143
Mitchell (G4)*......240
Mize (F2)......75
Molena (D4)*......307
Moniac (H9)*......200
Monroe (E3)*......4,542
Modoc ‡(A5)......32
Montezuma (E6)*......2,921
Monticello (E4)*......1,918
Montrose (F5)*......242
Moran (E5)*......250
Moreland (C4)*......306
Morgan (C7)*......304
Morganton (D1)*......244
Morris (C7)*......
Morrow ‡(D3)*......326
Morven (E9)*......474
Moultrie (E8)*......11,639
Mount Airy (F1)*......416
Mount Berry (B2)*......1,500
Mount Pleasant (J8)......50
Mount Vernon (H6)*......990
Mount Zion (B3)*......141
Mountain City (F1)*......524
Mountain Park ‡(D3)......15
Mountville (C4)*......142

Moxley (H5) 50
Munnerlyn (H5)* 75
Murrayville (E2)* 1,000
Musella (E5)* 68
Mystic (F7)* 281
Nacoochee (E1)* 250
Nahunta (H8)* 738
Nankipooh (C5) 100
Nashville (F8)* 3,414
Natal (E1)
Naylor (F9)* 290
Neal (D4) 50
Nelson (D2)* 645
Nevils (J6) 160
New Holland (E2)* 1,618
New Lacy (H7) 25
Newborn (E3)* 298
Newington (J5)* 429
Newnan (C4)* 8,218
Newton (D8)* 503
Nicholls (G7)* 806
Nicholson (F2)* 252
Noble (B1) 200
Norcross (D3)* 1,340
Norman Park (E8)* 832
Normantown (H6) 78
Norristown (H5)* 150
North Atlanta ‡(D3) 5,930
North High Shoals ‡(F3) 124
Norwood (G4)* 268
Nuberg (G2) 273
Nunez (H5)* 82
Oak Hill (D1) 50
Oak Park (H6)* 308
Oakfield (E7)* 108
Oaklawn (E9) 75
Oakman (C1)* 127
Oakwood (E2)* 225
Oasis (C1) 15
Ochlochnee (E9)* 503
Ocilla (F7)* 2,697
Oconee (G5)* 1,500
Odessa (J7) 5
Odessadale (C5)* 55
Odum (H7)* 389
Offerman (H8)* 500
Ogeechee (J5)* 40
Oglesby (G2) 15
Oglethorpe (D6)* 1,204
Ohoopee (H6)* 53
Ola (4) 100
Oliver (J5)* 223
Omaha (C6)* 217
Omega (E8)* 966
Oostanaula (B1) 50
Ophir (D2) 40
Orange (D2) 50
Orchard Hill (D4)* 82
Orland (G6) 40
Oscarville (E2) 25
Osierfield (F7)* 147
Ousley (F9)* 35
Owen (H5)* 50
Oxford (E3)* 817
Padena (D1) 105
Palmetto (C3)* 1,257
Parish (J6) 15
Parrott (D7)* 291
Patterson (H8)* 656
Pavo (E9)* 806
Payne (E5) 520
Pearson (G8)* 1,402
Pelham (D8)* 4,365
Pembroke (J6)* 1,171
Pendergrass (E2)* 189
Penfield (F3)* 74
Penia (E7) 50
Pennick (J8) 300
Pepperton (E4) 572
Perkins (J5)* 210
Perry (E6)* 3,849
Persimmon (E1)
Philomath (G3)* 200
Pickard (D5)* 150
Pidcock (E9)* 100
Piedmont (D4) 34
Pike (D1)* 44
Pine Grove (H7) 135
Pine Lake ‡(D3)* 566
Pine Log (C2)*
Pine Park (D9)* 126
Pinehurst (E6)* 430
Pineora (K6)* 450
Pineview (F6)* 310
Pisgah (D1)*
Pitts (E7)* 397
Pittsburg (B1) 40
Plainfield (F6)* 117
Plains (D6)* 546
Plainville (C2)* 142
Pocotalago (F2) 68
Point Peter (F3)* 100
Pooler (K6)* 818
Pope City (F6)
Port Wentworth (K6)* 1,500
Portal (J5)* 532
Porter Springs (E1) 125
Porterdale (E3)* 3,207
Portland (C2) 300
Poulan (E8)* 750
Powder Springs (C3)* 619
Powelton (G4) 50
Powersville (E5)* 100
Prattsburg (D5) 50
Preston (C6)* 260
Pridgen (G7) 200
Primrose (C4) 24
Princeton (F3) 100
Priors (B2) 50
Pulaski (J6)* 234
Putnam (D6)* 60
Putney (D8)* 200
Quill (D1)*
Quitman (E9)* 4,769
Rabun Gap (F1)* 250
Racepond (H8)* 158
Rahns (K6)
Raleigh (C5)* 48
Ramhurst (C1)* 100
Randolph (C7)
Ranger (C2)* 183
Ray City (F8)* 576
Raybon (H8)
Rayle (G3) 300
Raymond (C4)* 200
Rebecca (E7)* 295
Recovery (C9) 100
Red Oak (C3)* 675
Register (J6)* 300
Reidsville (H6)* 1,266
Relay (B2) 100
Relee (G7)
Remerton (F9)* 500
Renfroe (C6) 56
Reno (D9) 108
Rentz (G6)* 302
Resaca (C1)* 300
Rest Haven ‡(D3) 147
Reynolds (D5)* 906
Rhine (F7)* 514
Riceboro (K7)* 267
Richland (C6)* 1,571
Richmond Hill (K7)* 500
Richwood (E6) 75
Riddleville (G5) 106
Ridgeville (K8)*
Rincon (K6)* 424
Ringgold (B1)* 1,192
Rising Fawn (A1)* 300
Riverdale (D3)* 263
Riverside (E8) 395
Roberta (D5)* 673
Robertstown (E1)* 150
Robinson (B2)* 75
Rochelle (F7)* 1,097
Rockingham (H7) 60
Rockledge (G6)* 100
Rockmart (C2)* 3,821
Rockville (F4) 30
Rocky Face (C1)* 300
Rocky Ford (J5)* 278
Rocky Mount ‡(C4) 27
Rome (B2)* 29,615
Roopville (B4)* 202
Rosebud (D3) 100
Rosier (H5)* 125
Rossville (B1)* 3,892
Roswell (D2)* 2,123
Round Oak (E4)* 165
Rowell (B2) 45
Rowena (C8) 200
Roy (D1)* 15
Royston (F2)* 2,039
Ruckersville (G2) 74
Rupert (D6)*
Russell (E3) 129
Ruth (F4) 200
Rutland (E5)
Rutledge (E3)* 482
Rydal (C2)* 100
St. Charles (C4)
St. Clair (H4) 150
St. George (H9)* 582
St. Marks (C4) 43
St. Marys (J9)* 1,348
St. Simons Isl. (K8)* 1,706
Sale City (D8)* 289
Sandersville (G5)* 4,480
Sapelo Island (K8)* 307
Sarah (D1)* 75
Sardis (J5)* 695
Sargent (C4)* 1,250
Sasser (D7)* 371
Satolah (F1)* 165
Sautee (E1)* 314
Savannah (L6)* 119,638
Savannah (urban area) 128,190
Savannah Beach (L7)* 1,036
Scarboro (J5) 150
Scotland (G6)* 218
Scott (G5)* 194
Screven (H7)* 752
Sea Island (K8)* 500
Sells (E2) 30
Seney (B2) 50
Senoia (C4)* 770
Sessoms (G8) 100
Seville (E7)* 187
Shady Dale (E4)* 253
Shannon (B2)* 1,676
Sharon (G3)* 224
Sharpsburg (C4)* 133
Shell Bluff (J4) 20
Shellman (C7)* 1,090
Shiloh (C5)* 250
Shingler (E7)
Siloam (F3)* 324
Silver City (D2) 150
Silver Creek (B2)* 400
Silvertown (D5)* 3,387
Smarr (E5)* 100
Smithonia (F2) 80
Smithville (D7)* 676
Smyrna (D3)* 2,005
Snellville (D3)* 309
Social Circle (E3)* 1,685
Sofkee (E5)
Soperton (G6)* 1,667
South Georgia (G8) 650
South Newport (K7) 50
Sparks (F8)* 887
Sparta (F4)* 1,954
Spring Place (C1)* 214
Springfield (K6)* 627
Springvale (C7)* 127
Sprite (B2) 25
Stapleton (H4)* 355
Statenville (G9)* 1,000
Statesboro (J6)* 6,097
Statham (E3)* 626
Stellaville (H4)* 69
Stephens (F3)* 100
Sterling (K8) 30
Stevens Crossing (H5)
Stevens Pottery (F5)*
Stilesboro (B2)*
Stillmore (H6)* 420
Stilson (J6)* 165
Stockbridge (D3)* 717
Stockton (G9)* 300
Stone Mountain (D3)* 1,899
Stonewall (C3)* 510
Stovall (C5)* 150
Stuckey (G6)* 150
Subligna (B1)* 152
Suches (E1)*
Sugar Hill ‡(D3) 783
Sugar Valley (C1)* 214
Sulphur Springs (A1)* 175
Summertown (H5)* 137
Summerville (B2)* 3,973
Summit (Twin City) (H5)* 1,018
Sumner (E7)* 226
Sumter (D7)* 40
Sunny Side (D4)* 169
Suomi (G6) 40
Surrency (H7)* 295
Suwanee (E2)* 357
Swainsboro (H5)* 4,300
Swords (F3)* 35
Sycamore (E7)* 624
Sylvania (J5)* 2,939
Sylvester (E7)* 2,623
Talbotton (C5)* 1,175
Talking Rock (D1)* 94
Tallapoosa (B3)* 2,826
Tallulah Falls (F1)* 239
Tallulah Park (F1)
Talmo (E2)* 152
Talona (C1)* 41
Tarboro (J8) 180
Tarrytown (H6)* 250
Tarver (G9)
Tate (D2)* 100
Taylorsville (C2)* 260
Tazewell (D6)* 105
Temple (B3)* 676
Tennga (C1)* 200
Tennille (G5)* 1,713
Texas (B4) 40
Thalmann (J8)* 150
The Rock (D5)* 147
Thomasboro (J5)* 30
Thomaston (D5)* 6,580
Thomasville (E9)* 14,424
Thomson (H4)* 3,489
Thunderbolt (K6)* 1,238
Tifton (F8)* 6,831
Tiger (F1)* 269
Tignall (G3)* 502
Tilton (B1)* 100
Tippettville (E6) 50
Titus (E1)* 200
Toccoa (F1)* 6,781
Toledo (H9) 134
Toomsboro (F5)* 711
Towns (G7)* 96
Townsend (J7)*
Trenton (A1)* 755
Trimble (C4) 150
Trion (B1)* 3,028
Troutman (C7) 25
Tugalo (F1)* 25
Tunnell Hill (C1)*
Turin (C4)* 185
Tusculum (K6)* 100
Twin City (H5) 1,018
Ty Ty (E8)* 478
Tyrone (C4)* 156
Unadilla (E6)* 1,098
Union City (D3)* 1,490
Union Point (F3)* 1,724
Upatoi (C5)* 300
Uvalda (H6)* 987
Valdosta (K9)* 20,046
Valona (K8)* 50
Van Wert (B3)
Vanna (F2)* 145
Varnell (C1)* 500
Vaughn (D4)* 100
Veazey (F3) 40
Vidalia (H6)* 5,819
Vidette (H4)* 159
Vienna (E6)* 2,202
Villa Rica (C3)* 1,703
Villanow (B1) 150
Waco (B3)* 328
Wade (H5)
Wadley (H5)* 1,624
Walburg (J8) 4
Walden (E5)* 100
Waleska (D2)* 385
Walker Park (E3)* 150
Walnutgrove (E3) 121
Waltertown (H8) 2
Walthourville (J7)* 300
Waresboro (H8)*
Warm Springs (C5)* 557
Warner Robins (E5)* 7,986
Warrenton (G4)* 1,442
Warsaw (K7)
Warthen (G4)* 240
Warwick (E7)* 449
Washington (G3)* 3,802
Watkinsville (E3)* 662
Waverly (J8)* 100
Waverly Hall (C5)* 690
Waycross (H8)* 18,899
Waynesboro (J4)* 4,461
Waynesville (J8)*
Wayside (E4)* 150
Wenona (E7) 75
Wesley (H6)* 66
West Bainbridge (C9)* 3,000
West Georgia College (B3) 700
West Green (G7)*
West Point (B5)* 4,076
Westlake (F5)
Weston (C7)* 162
Westwood (F7) 75
Whigham (D9)* 471
White (C2)* 454
White Hall (F3)* 493
White Oak (J8)* 150
White Plains (F4)* 359
White Sulphur Springs ‡(C5) 32
Whitepath (D1) 100
Whites Mill (C9) 5
Whitesburg (B4)* 400
Whitestone (D1)*
Whitesville (C5) 100
Wiley (F1)* 125
Willacoochee (G8)* 987
Willard (F4) 25
Williamson (D4)* 211
Winchester (E6) 25
Winder (E3)* 4,604
Winfield (H3) 25
Winokur (H8)* 100
Winston (C3)* 154
Winterville (F3)* 453
Woodbine (J9)* 750
Woodbury (C5)* 985
Woodcliff (J5)* 175
Woodland (D5)* 621
Woodstock (D2)* 545
Woodville (F3)* 484
Woolsey (D4)* 90
Worth (E7)
Wray (F7)* 45
Wrayswood (F3) 30
Wrens (H4)* 1,380
Wrightsville (G5)* 1,750
Yahoolah (D1) 125
Yatesville (D5)* 290
Yonkers (F6) 33
Young Harris (E1)* 450
Youngcane (E1)* 500
Youngs (B3)
Ypsilanti (D5) 35
Zebulon (D4)* 539
Zeigler (J5) 100
Zenith (E5) 10

HAWAII

Map on Page 95

Total Population 499,794

Ahua (point) (B4)
Aiea (B3)* 3,714
Ainahou Ranch (J6)
Alalakeiki (channel) (J3)
Alenuihaha (channel) (E7)
Alili Camp (H6)
Anahola (C1)* 326
Apua (point) (J6)
Auau (channel) (H2)
Barbers (point) (E2)
Bishop (point) (A4)
Brodie Camp (E1)
Bryant Camp (G3)
Camp Eight (J5) 75
Camp Two (C2)
Camp Two (J5) 200
Captain Cook (G5)* 316
Dairy Camp (G7)
Diamond Head (crater) (C5)
Diamond Head (promontory) (C5)
East Loch (inlet) (B3)
Eastern (isl.) (E4)
Eleele (C2)* 993
Elevenmile Homestead (J5)
Eo (lake) (A3)
Ewa (A4)* 3,429
Ewa (beach) (A4)
Ewa Field (A4)
Ford (isl.) (B3)
Gardner Pinnacles (isls.) (C6)
Gilbert (E2)
Glenwood (J5)
Haena (C1) 90
Haiku (J2)* 729
Haina (H3)* 695
Hakalau (J4)* 688
Halalii (lake) (A2)
Halama (K6)
Halaula-Kapaau (G3)* 1,309
Halawa (G3) 900
Halawa (H1)
Halawa (bay) (H1)
Halawa (cape) (H1)
Halawa (stream) (B3)
Haleakala (crater) (K2)
Haleiwa (E1)* 2,142
Halfway House (H6)
Hamakuapoko (J1)* 300
Hamoa (K2)
Hana (K2)* 547
Hanalei (C1)* 364
Hanalei (bay) (C1)
Hanalei (river) (C1)
Hanaloa (lake) (A3)
Hanamalo (point) (F7)
Hanamanioa (cape) (J3)
Hanamaulu (C2)* 1,031
Hanapepe (C2)* 1,259
Haou (K2)
Hauula (E1)* 631
Hawaii (county) (K7) 68,350
Hawaii (isl.) (H5) 68,350
Hawaii National Park (J6)*
Hawaii National (park) (K2)
Hawaii National (park) (H6)
Hawea (point) (H1)
Hawi (G3)* 951
Hickam Field (B4)
Hilea (H7) 8
Hilo (J5)* 27,198
Hilo (bay) (J5)
Hoaeae (A3) 50
Hoea Mill (G3) 125
Holualoa (G5)* 475
Honaunau (G6)*
Honohina (J4) 200
Honoipu (G3)
Honokaa (H4)* 1,021
Honokahau (F5)* 650
Honokohau (J1)
Honokohau (G5)
Honokahua (H1) 475
Honokowai Camp (H1)
HONOLULU (C4)* 248,034
Honolulu (county) (D3) 353,020
Honolulu (harbor) (C4)
Honomaele (K2)
Honomalino Camp (G6)
Honomu (J4)* 600
Honouliuli (A3)
Honuapo (H7) 25
Hookena (G6) 20
Hoolehua (G1)* 709
Hoopuloa (G6)
Hualalai (mt.) (G5)
Huehue (G5)
Huumula Sheep Station (H5) 6
Ilio (point) (G1)
Iseri Camp (H6)
Iwilei (C4)
John Rogers Field (B4)
Johnston (isl.) (C7)
Kaala (mt.) (E1)
Kaalaika Camp (G7) 6
Kaalualu (G7) 48
Keenapali (H2)
Kaeleku (K2)
Kaena (point) (D1)
Kahakuloa (J1) 20
Kahala (D5)
Kahala (point) (D1)
Kahana (F1)
Kahana (bay) (F1)
Kahoolawe (isl.) (H3)
Kahua (G3)
Kahuku (E1)* 1,602
Kahuku (point) (E1)
Kahuku Ranch (G7) 36
Kahului (J2)* 6,306
Kahului (harbor) (J1)
Kailio (point) (C1)
Kailua (F2) 326
Kailua (K2)
Kailua-Lanikai (F5)* 7,740
Kailua (bay) (F5)
Kailua (bay) (F2)
Kaimu (K6)
Kaimuli (D4)
Kainaliu (G5) 510
Kaiwi (channel) (E6)
Kakaako (C4)
Kalae (G1)
Kalae (South) (cape) (G7)
Kalaheo (C2)* 972
Kalaoa (G5) 40
Kalapana (K6) 60
Kalaua (B3)
Kalaupapa (G1)*
Kalawa (G1)
Kalawao (H1)
Kalawao (county) (G1). 340
Kalihi (stream) (C3)
Kalihi Entrance (strait) (B4)
Kalihiwai (C1) 44
Kalohi (channel) (G1)
Kaloli (point) (K5)
Kaluaaha (H1) 300
Kamaiki (point) (H2)
Kamakou (mt.) (H1)
Kamalino (A2) 15
Kamalo (H1) 300
Kamilo (point) (H7)
Kamuela-Waimea (G4)* 560
Kanaio (J3) 24
Kanapou (bay) (J3)
Kaneohe (F2)* 3,208
Kaneohe (bay) (F2)
Kapaa (D1)* 3,177
Kapaau-Halaula (G3) 1,309
Kapalaoa (G4)
Kapapala (H6) 251
Kapoho (K5)* 335
Kapulena (H4)
Kau (desert) (J6)
Kauai (channel) (E6)
Kauai (county) (A1) 29,905
Kauai (isl.) (C1) 29,683
Kaueleau (K6)
Kauhola (point) (G3)
Kauiki Head (promontory) (K2)
Kaula (isl.) (D6)
Kaulakahi (channel (B2)
Kaumalapau (harbor) (G2)
Kaumana (J5)
Kauna (point) (G7)
Kaunakakai (G1)* 973
Kaunakakai (harbor) (G1)
Kaunalewa (B2)
Kauno-o-Kaleioohie (mt.) (G3)
Kaunuopou (point) (B2)
Kaupakulua (K2)
Kaupo (K2)
Kawaihae (G4)* 152
Kawaihae (bay) (G4)
Kawaihapai (D1)
Kawaihau (C1) 6,290
Kawaihoa (cape) (A2)
Kawaikini (mt.) (C1)
Kawailoa (E1)*
Kawainui (J4) 193
Kawela Camp (H3)
Keaau (K5)
Keaau-Olaa (J5) 1,620
Keahiakahoe (mt.) (D3)
Keahole (point) (F5)
Keahua (J2)* 200
Keaiwa Camp (H6) 110
Kealaikahiki (channel) (H3)
Kealaikahiki (point) (H3)
Kealakekua (G5)* 325
Kealakekua (bay) (F6)
Kealapuali (G5)
Kealia (D1)* 655
Kealia (G5) 184
Keamuku (G4) 11
Keanae (K2)* 54
Keanapapa (point) (G2)
Keauhou (F5)* 196
Keaukaha (J5) 2,500
Keawekaheka (point) (F5)
Keehi (lagoon) (B4)
Kekaa (point) (H2)
Kekaha (C2)* 1,989
Kemoo Camp (E2)
Keokea (G6) 150
Keokea (J2) 698
Keomuku (H2) 8
Keoneoio (J3)
Kepuhi (G1) 1
Kiekie (A2)
Kihei (J2)* 1,500
Kiholo (G4) 1
Kiholo (bay) (F4)
Kikoa (point) (H2)
Kilauea (C1)* 757
Kilauea (crater) (H6)
Kilauea (point) (C1)
Kilauea Ranger Station (J6) 135
Kingman (reef) (C7)
Kipahulu (K2)
Kipapa Camp 5 (E2)
Koa Mill (G6)
Koae (K5) 65
Koali (K2)
Koele (H2) 45
Kohala (mts.) (G4)
Koko Head (promontory) (F2)
Kokole (point) (B2)
Kokomo (K2) 181
Kolekole (creek) (J4)
Koloa (C2)* 1,470
Kolukahi (H7)
Kona Mill (G5)
Konahuanui (mt.) (D3)
Koolau (mt. range) (E2)
Kualapuu (G1) 607
Kukalau (H4)
Kukui (J5)
Kukui (mt.) (J2)
Kukuihaele (H3)* 590
Kula (J2)
Kumukahi (cape) (K5)
Kunia Camp (E2)*
Kupaahu (J6)
Kure (isl.) (A5)
Kurtistown (J5)* 1,500
La Perouse Pinnacle (isl.) (C6)
Laau (point) (G1)
Lahaina (H2)* 4,025
Laie (E1)* 841
Lanai (isl.) (H2) 3,136
Lanai City (H2)* 2,746
Lanaihale (mt.) (H2)
Lanihuli (mt.) (D3)
Lanikai-Kailua (F2)* 7,740
Laupahoehoe (J4)* 401
Lawai (C2)*
Laysan (isl.) (B5)
Lehua (isl.) (A2)
Leleiwi (point) (K5)
Libbyville (E2) 85
Lihue (C2)* 3,870
Lisianski (isl.) (B5)
Lower Paia (J1) 1,137
Lua Makika (mt.) (J3)
Lualualei (D2) 1,528
Luke Field (B3)
Maalaea (J2) 500
Maalaea (bay) (J2)
Mahinahina Camp (J1) 50
Mahukona (G3) 132
Makaha (D2) 1,500
Makaha (point) (B1)
Makahuena (point) (C2)
Makalawena (F4) 2
Makanalua (peninsula) (H1)
Makapala (G3) 381
Makapuu Head (promontory) (F2)
Makawao (K2)* 1,098
Makaweli (C2)* 1,283
Makeweli Landing (B2)
Makena (J2)* 6
Makua (D1) 1,500
Mala (H2) 100
Mamalu (bay) (A4)
Mamalu (bay) (K3)
Mana (B2) 276
Manana (isl.) (F2)
Maro (reef) (C6)
Maui (county) (J1) 48,519
Maui (isl.) (J2) 46,919
Mauna Kea (mt.) (H4)
Mauna Loa (mt.) (G5)
Maunalua (bay) (F2)
McBryde Plantation Mill (C2) 1,500
Middle Loch (inlet)(A3)
Middle Moaula Camp (H6)
Midway (isls.) (D5)
Milolii (G6) 95

Moanalua (stream) (C3)
Mokapu (peninsula) (F2)
Mokolii (isl.) (F1)
Moku (G1)
Mokuaweoweo (crater) (H6)
Mokuhooniki (isl.) (J1)
Mokulau (K3)
Mokuleia (D1) 150
Moloaa (D1)
Molokai (isl.) (G1) 5,280
Molokini (isl.) (J2)
Monohaa (G5) 2
Mopua (J2) 600
Mountainview (J5)* 747
Muolea (K2)
Naalehu (H7)* 1,004
Nahiku (K2)
Nakalele (point) (J1)
Nanakuli (D2)* 2,002
Napoopoo (G6)* 103
Nawiliwili (D2)
Nawiliwili (bay) (D2)
Necker (isl.) (D6)
Nihoa (isl.) (D6)
Niihau (isl.) (A2) 222
Ninini (point) (D2)
Ninole (J4)* 112
Niulii (G3)
Nohili (point) (B1)
Nonopapa (A2)
Nuuanu (stream) (C4)
Oahu (isl.) (E2) 353,020
Olaa-Keaau (J5)* 1,620
Olowalu (H2) 100
Onomea (J4) 300
Ookala (J4)* 662
Opihikao (K6)
Paauhau (H4)* 400
Paauilo (H4)*
Pacific Heights (C4)
Pacific Ocean (B6)
Pacific Sugar Mill (H3)
Pahala (H6)* 1,602
Pahoa (J5)* 990
Paholoi (J2) 50
Paia (J2)* 3,195
Paihaaloa (J4) 98
Pailolo (channel) (H1)
Palama (C4)
Palaoa (point) (G2)
Palmyra (isl.) (C7)
Palolo (stream) (D4)
Paniau (mt.) (A2)
Papa (G6)
Papaaloa (G5)
Papaaloa (J4)* 597
Papaikou (J5)* 1,427
Paukaa (J5) 200
Pauwalu (point) (K2)
Pauwela (K1)* 618
Pauwela (point) (K1)
Peahi (K2)
Pearl (harbor) (A3)
Pearl and Hermes (reef) (B5)
Pearl City (B3)* 2,663
Pelekunu (H1)
Pepeekeo (J4)* 1,002
Pepeekeo (point) (J4)
Piihonua (J5) 600
Pohakuloa (point) (H2)
Pohoiki (K6) 3
Port Allen (C2) 450
Pua Akala (H5)
Puako (G4)
Pueo (point) (A2)
Puhi (C2)* 765
Pukoo (H1)* 42
Pulehu (J2) 200
Pulehu Camp (J2)
Punahou (C4)
Punaluu (E1)
Punaluu (H7) 30
Punaluu (harbor) (H7)
Punchbowl (hill) (C4)
Puolo (point) (C2)
Puu Hue (G3)
Puu Lehua Ranch (G5)
Puu Makani Camp (H7)
Puuanahulu (G4) 62
Puuiki (E1) 170
Puuiki (K2)
Puukolii (J2) 689
Puuloa Station (B4)
Puunene (J2)* 5,000
Puunui (C4)
Puuwai (A2) 185
Red Hill (mt.) (K2)
Roundtop (hill) (C4)
Salt (lake) (B3)
Sand (isl.) (E4)
Sand (isl.) (C4)
Sand (isl.) (E4)
Schofield Barracks (E2)
Seward Roads (channel) (D4)
South (Kalae) (cape) (G7)
Southeast Loch (inlet) (B3)
Spreckelsville (J1)*
Sugarloaf (hill) (C4)
Summer Camp (J6) 400
Tantalus (mt.) (D4)
Ulumahi (K2)
Ulupalakua (J2)
Umikoa (J4)
Upolu (point) (G3)
Wahiawa (E2)* 8,369
Waiahukini (G7) 175
Waiakea (J5) 5,000
Waiakoa (J2)* 517
Waialee (E1) 72
Waialua (E1)* 2,602
Waialua (H1)
Waialua Camp (E1)
Waianae (D2)* 1,000
Waianuenue (C1)
Waihee (J2) 600
Waikane (F2) 85
Waikapu (J2) 549
Waikii (H4)
Waikiki (C4)* 50
Waikiki (beach) (C4)
Wailau (H1) 300
Wailea (J4) 341
Wailua (D2)
Wailua (K2)
Wailuku (J2)* 7,424
Wailuku (river) (J5)
Wailupe (F2)
Waimanalo (F2)* 868
Waimanalo (bay) (F2)
Waimea (B2)* 1,648
Waimea (E1)
Waimea-Kamuela (H4)
Waimea (bay) (B2)
Waimea (river) (C2)
Waimea Camp (E1)
Wainiha (C1) 60
Wainiha (river) (C1)
Waiohinu (G7) 163
Waipahu (A3)* 7,169
Waipio (K2)
Waipio (H3) 95
Waipio (peninsula) (A3)
Waipio (point) (A4)
Welles (harbor) (D4)
West Loch (inlet) (A3)
Wood Valley Camp (H6)
Woodlawn (D4)

IDAHO

Map on Page 57

Total Population 588,637

45 COUNTIES

Ada (B6) 70,649
Adams (B5) 3,347
Bannock (F7) 41,745
Bear Lake (G7) 6,834
Benewah (B2) 6,173
Bingham (F6) 23,271
Blaine (D6) 5,384
Boise (C6) 1,776
Bonner (B1) 14,853
Bonneville (G6) 30,210
Boundary (B1) 5,908
Butte (E6) 2,722
Camas (D6) 1,079
Canyon (B6) 53,597
Caribou (G7) 5,576
Cassia (E7) 14,629
Clark (F5) 918
Clearwater (C3) 8,217
Custer (D5) 3,318
Elmore (C6) 6,687
Franklin (G7) 9,867
Fremont (G5) 9,351
Gem (B6) 8,730
Gooding (D6) 11,101
Idaho (C4) 11,423
Jefferson (F6) 10,495
Jerome (D7) 12,080
Kootenai (B2) 24,947
Latah (B3) 20,971
Lemhi (D4) 6,278
Lewis (B3) 4,208
Lincoln (D6) 4,256
Madison (G6) 9,156
Minidoka (E7) 9,785
Nez Perce (B3) 22,658
Oneida (F7) 4,387
Owyhee (B7) 6,307
Payette (B5) 11,921
Power (F7) 3,988
Shoshone (B2) 22,806
Teton (G6) 3,204
Twin Falls (D7) 40,979
Valley (C5) 4,270
Washington (B5) 8,576
Yellowstone Nat'l. Park† (G5)

† Part. See also Wyoming and Montana.

CITIES and TOWNS

Aberdeen (F7)* 1,486
Acequia (E7)* 125
Addie (B1)* 15
Ahsahka (B3)*
Alameda (F7)* 4,694
Albion (E7)* 610
Alexander (G7)*
Almo (E7)*
Alpha (C5)*
Alpine (G6)* 172
Alridge (G6)
American Falls (E7)* 1,874
Ammon (G6) 447
Amsterdam (D7)* 100
Arbon (F7)
Archer (G6) 400
Arco (E6)* 961
Arimo (F7)* 337
Ashton (G5)* 1,256
Athol (B2)* 226
Atlanta (C6)* 300
Atomic City (F6)* 500
Avery (C2)* 350
Avon (B3)* 6
Baker (E4)* 150
Bancroft (G7)* 495
Banida (G7)* 140
Banks (B5)*
Basalt (F6)* 227
Bayview (B2)* 150
Bear (B4)*
Bellevue (D6)* 528
Benewah (B2) 50
Bennett (C6) 10
Bennington (G7)* 200
Berger (D7)
Bern (G7)* 140
Big Creek (C4)* 24
Big Springs (G5)* 5
Blackfoot (F6)* 5,180
Blanchard (A1)* 200
Bliss (D7)* 126
Bloomington (G7)* 302
BOISE (B6)* 34,393
Boles (B4) 25
Bone (G6) 50
Bonners Ferry (B1)* 1,776
Bovill (B3)* 437
Bowmont (B6)*
Bridge (E7)*
Broten (B1)* 30
Bruneau (C7)* 100
Buhl (D7)* 2,870
Burgdorf (B4)
Burke (C2)* 800
Burley (E7)* 5,924
Burmah (D6)
Cabinet (B1)* 60
Calder (B2)* 65
Caldwell (B6)* 10,487
Camas (F5)* 40
Cambridge (B5)* 354
Cameron (B3)* 83
Canfield (B4)* 50
Carey (E6)* 1,100
Careywood (B1)* 50
Carmen (E4)*
Cascade (C5)* 943
Castleford (C7)* 500
Cavendish (B3)
Centerville (C6)* 25
Central (G7)* 120
Challis (D5)* 728
Chatcolet (B2) 92
Chester (G5)* 247
Chesterfield (F7)*
Chilco (B2)* 45
Chilly (E5)* 84
Chubbuck ‡(F7)* 120
Churchill (D7)
Clagstone (B1) 15
Clark Fork (B1)* 387
Clarkia (B2)* 150
Clarkville ‡(B2) 19
Clawson (G6) 34
Clayton (D5)* 75
Clearwater (C3)* 38
Clementsville (G6) 38
Cleveland (G7)* 135
Cliffs (B7) 32
Clifton (F7)* 201
Coeur D'Alene (B2)* 12,198
Colburn (B1)*
Conda (G7)* 330
Coolin (B1)*
Copeland (B1)* 11
Corral (D6)* 157
Cottonwood (B3)* 689
Council (B5)* 748
Craigmont (B3)* 594
Crouch (B5)* 60
Crystal (F7)
Culdesac (B3)* 175
Cuprum (B4)* 20
Dalby ‡(G6) 13
Darlington (E6)* 200
Dayton (F7)* 287
De Lamar (B6)
Deary (B3)* 320
Declo (E7)* 219
Dent (B3)*
Denver (B4) 29
Desmet (B2)* 5
Dietrich (D7)* 160
Dingle (G7)*
Dixie (C4)* 56
Donnelly (C5)* 595
Dover (B1)* 385
Downey (F7)* 748
Driggs (G6)* 941
Drummond (G5)* 59
Dubois (F5)* 430
Dudley (B2)*
Eagle (B6)* 500
East Hope (B1) 149
Eastport (B1)* 108
Eddiville‡ (B2) 10
Eden (D7)* 456
Edgemere (B1)* 96
Elba (E7)* 180
Elk City (C4)* 300
Elk River (B3)* 312
Ellis (D5)*
Elmira (B1)* 128
Emida (B2)* 125
Emmett (B6)* 3,067
Enaville (B2)* 60
Fairfield (D6)* 502
Fairview (G7) 398
Felt (G6)* 120
Fenn (B4)* 57
Ferdinand (B3)* 206
Fernwood (B2)* 200
Filer (D7)* 1,425
Firth (F6)* 293
Fish Haven (G7)*
Forest (B3)
Forney (D4)*
Fort Hall (F6)*
Franklin (G7)* 467
French Creek (B4) 65
Fruitland (B6)* 573
Fruitvale (B5)* 125
Gannett (D6)* 43
Garden City (B6) 764
Garden Valley (C5)* 210
Gardena (B5)*
Gardner (F6)
Gem (C2)* 500
Genesee (B3)* 552
Geneva (G7)*
Georgetown (G7)* 404
Gibbonsville (E4)* 200
Gibbs (B2)* 35
Gifford (B3)* 51
Gilmore (E5)* 50
Glengary (B1)
Glenns Ferry (C7)* 1,515
Goldburg (E5)
Golden (C4)* 100
Gooding (D7)* 3,099
Goodrich (B5)* 16
Grace (G7)* 761
Grainville (G5) 30
Grand View (B7)*
Grangemont (C3)* 130
Grangeville (B4)* 2,544
Granite (B1)* 150
Gray (G6)*
Greencreek (B3)* 51
Greenleaf (B6)*
Greer (B3)* 127
Grimes Pass (C5)
Grouse (E6)* 43
Hagerman (D7)* 520
Hailey (D6)* 1,464
Hamer (F6)*
Hammett (C7)* 350
Hansen (D7)* 463
Harpster (C4)*
Harrison (B2)* 322
Harvard (B3)* 102
Hauser (B2) 70
Hayden Lake (B2)* 39
Hazelton (E7)* 429
Headquarters (C3)* 300
Heath (B5) 15
Heglar (E7) 10
Heise (G6) 87
Henry (G7)*
Heyburn (E7)* 539
Hibbard (G6) 400
Hill City (D6)* 15
Holbrook (F7)*
Hollister (D7)* 80
Homedale (A6)* 1,411
Hope (B1)* 111
Horse Shoe Bend (B6)* 401
Howe (F6)* 200
Huetter (B2)* 84
Humphrey (F5)* 35
Idaho City (C6)* 246
Idaho Falls (F6)* 19,218
Indian Valley (B5)* 50
Inkom (F7)* 434
Iona (G6)* 502
Irwin (G6)* 147
Island Park (G5)*
Jerome (D7)* 4,523
Joseph (B4)* 23
Juliaetta (B3)* 365
Juniper (F7)
Kamiah (B3)* 812
Kellogg (B2)* 4,913
Kendrick (B3)* 409
Ketchum (D6)* 757
Keuterville (B3)* 25
Kilgore (G5)* 160
Kimberly (D7)* 1,347
King Hill (C6)*
Kingston (B2)*
Kooskia (C3)* 629
Kootenai (B1)* 199
Kuna (B6)* 534
Laclede (B1)* 200
Lago (G7)* 250
Lake (G5) 8
Lake Fork (B5)* 11
Lakeview (B2)
Lamont (G6)* 50
Lane (B2)*
Lapwai (B3)* 480
Lava Hot Springs (F7)* 591
Leadore (E5)* 159
Leesburg (D4)
Lemhi (E5)* 150
Leonia (B1)*
Leslie (E6)* 40
Letha (B6)* 376
Lewiston (A3)* 12,985
Lewisville (F6)*
Liberty (G7)
Lincoln (F6)
Lorenzo (G6)* 250
Lost River (E6) 37
Lowell (C3)
Lowman (C5)* 30
Lucile (B4)* 13
Lund (G7)* 103
Mackay (E6)* 760
Macks Inn (G5)* 100
Maland City (F7)* 2,715
Malta (E7)* 518
Marble Creek (C2) 6
Marsing (B6)* 643
Marysville (G5) 190
May (E5)* 75
Mayfield (B6)
Mc Call (C5)* 1,173
Mc Cammon (F7)* 578
Meadow Creek (B1) 15
Meadows (B5)* 190
Melba (B6)* 203
Melrose (B3) 5
Menan (F6)* 430
Meridian (B6)* 1,810
Mesa (B5)* 179
Middleton (B6)* 496
Midvale (B5)* 231
Milner (D7)
Minidoka (E7)* 113
Minkcreek (G7)* 124
Monteview (F6)*
Montour (B6)* 155
Montpelier (G7)* 2,682
Moore (E6)* 256
Moravia (B1)
Moreland (F6)* 250
Moscow (B3)* 10,593
Mountain Home (C6)* 1,887
Moyie Springs (B1)* 109
Muldoon (E6)*
Mullan (C2)* 2,036
Murphy (B6)* 37
Murray (C2)* 158
Murtaugh (D7)* 239
Myrtle (B3)* 20
Naf (E7)*
Nampa (B6)* 16,185
Naples (B1) 300
New Meadows (B4)* 621
New Plymouth (B6)* 942
Newdale (G6)* 312
Nezperce (B3)* 543
Nordman (B1)* 18
North Fork (D4)* 100
N. Pocatello (F7) 575
Norwood (C5)
Notus (B6)* 313
Nounan (G7)*
Oakley (D7)* 684
Obsidian (D6)* 11
Ola (B5)* 300
Oldtown (A1) 358
Onaway (B3) 81
Orchard (B6)*
Orchards (A3) 4,494
Oreana (B6)* 100
Orofino (B3)* 1,656
Orogrande (C4)* 12
Ovid (G7)* 200
Oxford (F7)* 110
Pardee (B3)
Paris (G7)* 774
Parker (G6)* 306
Parma (B6)* 1,369
Patterson (E5)* 112
Paul (E7)* 560
Payette (B5)* 4,032
Pearl (B6) 38
Peck (B3)* 170
Pegram (G7)* 75
Picabo (D6)* 100
Pierce (C3)* 544
Pine (C6)*
Pingree (F6)* 102
Pioneerville (C6) 8
Placerville (C6)* 17
Plano (G6) 403
Plummer (B2)* 395
Pocatello (F7)* 26,131
Polaris (B2)* 214
Pollock (B4)*
Ponderay (B1)* 248
Porthill (B1)* 68
Portneuf (F7) 65
Post Falls (A2)* 1,069
Potlatch (A3)* 1,024
Prairie (C6)* 150
Preston (G7)* 4,045
Prichard (B2) 40
Priest River (A1)* 1,592
Princeton (B3)* 84
Rathdrum (A2)* 610
Raymond (G7)* 88
Red River Hot Springs (C4) 12
Regena (C6)
Reno (F5)
Reubens (B3)* 116
Rexburg (G6)* 4,253
Richfield (D6)* 429
Riddle (B7)* 35
Rigby (G6)* 1,826
Riggins (B4)* 287
Ririe (G6)* 527
Riverside (F6)
Roberts (F6)* 341
Robin (F7)* 165
Rockford (F6)
Rockford Bay (B2)* 27
Rockland (F7)* 277
Rocky Bar (C6)
Rogerson (D7)* 75
Roseberry (C5)
Roselake (B2)* 212
Roswell (A6)* 92
Roy (F7)* 25
Rupert (E7)* 3,098
Sagle (B1)* 75
Saint Anthony (G6)* 2,695
St. Charles (G7)* 363
St. Joe (B2) 75
St. Maries (B2)* 2,220
Salmon (D4)* 2,648
Samaria (F7)*
Samuels (B1)*
Sanders (B2)* 25
Sandpoint (B1)* 4,265
Santa (B2)*
Shelley (F6)* 1,856
Shoshone (D7)* 1,420
Shoup (D4)*
Silver City (B6)
Small (F5)*
Smelterville (B2)* 76
Smiths Ferry (C5)*
Soda Springs (G7)* 1,329
Southwick (B3)* 200
Spencer (F5)* 70
Spirit Lake (A2)* 823
Springfield (F6)* 435
Springston (B2)* 57
Squirrel (G5)*
Stanley (D5)* 33
Star (B6)* 525
Starkey (B5) 3
State Line ‡(B2) 52
Sterling (F6)*
Stibnite (C5)* 717
Stites (C3)* 227
Stone (F7)* 170
Strevell (E7) 25
Sugar City (G6)* 684
Sun Valley (D6)* 428
Sunbeam (D5)* 6
Swan Valley (G6)* 203
Swanlake (F7)* 250
Sweet (B6)* 200
Sweetwater (B3)* 80
Taber (F6)
Tamarack (B5)*
Tendoy (E5)*
Tensed (B2)* 189
Terreton (F6)* 35
Teton (G6)* 463
Tetonia (G6)* 232
Thatcher (G7)* 50
Thornton (G6)* 300
Three Creek (C7) 65
Tindall (C7) 5
Treasureton (G7)
Triangle (B7)* 35
Triumph (D6)* 97
Troy (B3)* 531
Tuttle (D7)* 15
Twin Falls (D7)* 17,600
Twin Lakes (B2) 225
Twin Springs (C6)*
Tyhee (F7) 350
Ucon (F6)* 356
Ustick (B6)* 200
Vay (B1)* 80
Victor (G6)* 431
Viola (B3)* 150
Virginia (F7)* 245
Wallace (C2)* 3,140
Wapello (F6)
Wardner (B2)* 772
Warm Lake (C5)* 500
Warren (C4)* 30
Wayan (G7)*
Weippe (C3)* 1,000
Weiser (B5)* 3,961
Wendell (D7)* 1,483
Westlake (B3)* 35
Weston (F7)* 382
White Bird (B4)*
Wilder (A6)* 555
Wildhorse (B5)* 18
Winchester (B3)* 488
Winona (B3)
Winsper (F5) 62
Woodland (C3)*
Worley (B2)* 233
Yellow Pine (C4)* 35

ILLINOIS

Map on Page 58

Total Population 8,712,176

102 COUNTIES

Adams (B4) 64,690
Alexander (D6) 20,316
Bond (D5) 14,157
Boone (E1) 17,070
Brown (C4) 7,132
Bureau (D2) 37,711
Calhoun (C4) 6,898
Carroll (D1) 18,976
Cass (C4) 15,097
Champaign (E3) 106,100
Christian (D4) 38,816
Clark (F4) 17,362
Clay (E5) 17,445
Clinton (D5) 22,594
Coles (E4) 40,328
Cook (F2) 4,508,792
Crawford (F4) 21,137
Cumberland (E4) 10,496
De Kalb (E2) 40,781
De Witt (E3) 16,894
Douglas (E4) 16,706
Du Page (E2) 154,599
Edgar (F4) 23,407
Edwards (E5) 9,056
Effingham (E4) 21,675
Fayette (D4) 24,582
Ford (E3) 15,901
Franklin (E5) 48,685
Fulton (C3) 43,716
Gallatin (E6) 9,818
Greene (C4) 18,852
Grundy (E2) 19,217
Hamilton (E5) 12,256
Hancock (B3) 25,790
Hardin (E6) 7,530
Henderson (C3) 8,416
Henry (C2) 46,492
Iroquois (F3) 32,348
Jackson (D6) 38,124
Jasper (E4) 12,266
Jefferson (E5) 35,892
Jersey (C4) 15,264
Jo Daviess (C1) 21,459
Johnson (E6) 8,729
Kane (E2) 150,388
Kankakee (F2) 73,524
Kendall (E2) 12,115
Knox (C3) 54,366
La Salle (E2) 100,610
Lake (E1) 179,097
Lawrence (F5) 20,539
Lee (D2) 36,451
Livingston (E3) 37,809
Logan (D3) 30,671
Macon (E4) 98,853
Macoupin (D4) 44,210
Madison (D5) 182,307
Marion (E5) 41,700
Marshall (D2) 13,025
Mason (D3) 15,326
Massac (E6) 13,594
Mc Donough (C3) 28,199
Mc Henry (E1) 50,656
Mc Lean (E3) 76,577
Menard (D3) 9,639
Mercer (C2) 17,374
Monroe (C5) 13,282
Montgomery (D4) 32,460
Morgan (C4) 35,568
Moultrie (E4) 13,171
Ogle (D1) 33,429
Peoria (D3) 174,347
Perry (D5) 21,684
Piatt (E4) 13,970
Pike (C4) 22,155
Pope (E6) 5,779
Pulaski (D6) 13,639
Putnam (D2) 4,746
Randolph (D5) 31,673
Richland (E5) 16,889
Rock Island (C2) 133,558
Saint Clair (D5) 205,995
Saline (E6) 33,420
Sangamon (D4) 131,484
Schuyler (C3) 9,613
Scott (C4) 7,245
Shelby (E4) 24,434
Stark (D2) 8,721
Stephenson (D1) 41,595
Tazewell (D3) 76,165
Union (D6) 20,500
Vermilion (F3) 87,079
Wabash (F5) 14,651
Warren (C3) 21,981
Washington (D5) 14,460
Wayne (E5) 20,933
White (E5) 20,935
Whiteside (D2) 49,336
Will (F2) 134,336
Williamson (E6) 48,621
Winnebago (D1) 152,385
Woodford (D3) 21,335

CITIES and TOWNS

Abingdon (C3)* 3,300
Adair (C3)* 400
Addieville (D5)* 271
Addison (A2)* 813
Adeline (D1) 1,135
Adrian (B3)* 63
Akin (E6)*
Albany (C2)* 544
Albers (D5)* 365
Albion (E5)* 2,287
Alden (E1)* 200
Aledo (C2)* 2,919
Alexander (D4)* 350
Alexis (C2)* 821
Algonquin (E1)* 1,223
Alhambra (D5)* 476
Allendale (F5)* 442
Allenville (E4)* 253
Allerton (F4)* 244
Alma (E5)* 404
Alorton (B6) 2,547
Alpha (C2)* 630
Alsey (C4)* 294
Alsip (B2) 1,228
Altamont (E4)* 1,580
Alto Pass (D6)* 462
Alton (A6)* 32,550
Altona (C2)* 462
Alvin (F3)* 287
Amboy (D2)* 2,128
America (D6)
Anchor (E3)* 175
Ancona (E2)*
Andalusia (C2)* 510
Andover (C2)* 256
Anna (D6)* 4,380
Annapolis (F4)* 147
Annawan (D2)* 592
Antioch (E1)* 1,307
Apple River (C1)* 431
Arcola (E4)* 1,700
Arenzville (C4)* 513
Argenta (E4)* 575
Argo (B2)* 9,000
Arlington (D2)* 247
Arlington Hts. (A1)* 8,768
Armington (D3)* 314
Armstrong (F3)* 325
Aroma Park (F2)* 544
Arrowsmith (E3)* 316
Arthur (E4)* 1,573
Ashkum (E3)* 420
Ashland (C4)* 1,039

Matteson (B3)*....1,211
Mattoon (E4)*....17,547
Maunie (E5)*.... 412
Maywood (A2)*....27,473
Mazon (E2)*.... 586
Mc Clure (D6)*.... 350
Mc Connell (D1)*.... 200
Mc Cook (A2)*.... 361
Mc Dowell (E3).... 50
Mc Henry (E1)*....2,080
Mc Lean (D3)*.... 667
Mc Leansboro (E5)*....3,008
Mc Nabb (D2)*.... 190
Meadows (E3)*.... 150
Mechanicsburg (D4)*.... 464
Media (C3)*.... 148
Medora (C4)*.... 432
Melrose Park (A2)*....13,366
Melvin (E3)*.... 535
Mendon (B3)*.... 625
Mendota (D2)*....5,129
Menominee (C1).... 132
Meredosia (C4)*.... 940
Merrionette Park (B2)..1,101
Merritt (C4).... 80
Metamora (D3)*....1,368
Metcalf (F4)*.... 312
Metropolis (E6)*....6,093
Middlegrove (C3)*.... 200
Middletown (D3)*.... 480
Midlothian (B2)*....3,216
Milan (C2)*....1,737
Milford (F3)*....1,648
Mill Shoals (E5).... 417
Millbrook (E2)*.... 100
Millcreek (D6)*.... 127
Milledgeville (D1)*....1,044
Millington (E2)*.... 270
Millstadt (B6)*....1,566
Milmine (E4)*.... 95
Milton (C4)*.... 337
Milton (B6)....8,232
Mineral (D2)*.... 274
Minier (D3)*.... 780
Minonk (D3)*....1,955
Minooka (E2)*.... 369
Mitchellsville (E6).... 20
Mode (E4)*.... 133
Modesto (D4)*.... 232
Modoc (C5)*.... 108
Mokena (F2)*.... 903
Moline (C2)*....37,397
Moline-Rock Island, Ill.-
Davenport, Iowa
(urban area)....193,733
Momence (F2)*....2,644
Monee (F2)*.... 554
Monica (D3)*.... 185
Monmouth (C3)*....10,193
Monroe Center (E1)*... 215
Monsanto (B6)*.... 357
Montgomery (E2)*.... 773
Monticello (E3)*....2,612
Montrose (E4)*.... 309
Moon (E5).... 50
Mooseheart (E2)*....
Moro (B6)*.... 275
Morris (E2)*....6,926
Morrison (C2)*....3,531
Morrisonville (D4)*....1,182
Morton (D3)*....3,693
Morton Grove (B1)*....3,926
Mossville (D3)*.... 350

Mound City (D6)*....2,167
Mound Station
(Timewell*) (C3).... 184
Mounds (D6)*....2,001
Mt. Auburn (D4)*.... 414
Mt. Carmel (F5)*....8,732
Mt. Carroll (D1)*....1,950
Mt. Clare ‡(D4)*.... 260
Mt. Erie (E5)*.... 149
Mt. Morris (D1)*....2,709
Mt. Olive (D4)*....2,401
Mt. Prospect (A1)*....4,009
Mt. Pulaski (D3)*....1,526
Mt. Sterling (C4)*....2,246
Mt. Vernon (E5)*....15,600
Mt. Zion (E4)*.... 438
Moweaqua (E4)*....1,475
Mozier (C4)*.... 125
Muddy (E6)*.... 500
Mulberry Grove (D5)*.. 712
Muncie (F3)*.... 197
Mundelein (E1)*....3,189
Murdock (E4)*.... 300
Murphysboro (D6)*....9,241
Murrayville (C4)*.... 405
Nachusa (D2)*.... 150
Nameoki (B6)*....
Naperville (E2)*....7,013
Naplate (E2).... 783
Naples (C4)*.... 141
Nashville (D5)*....2,432
Nason (D5)*.... 199
National Stock Yards
(National City)(B6)* 207
Nauvoo (B3)*....1,242
Nebo (C4)*.... 413
Nelson (D2)*.... 289
Neoga (E4)*....1,125
Neponset (D2)*.... 501
New Athens (D5)*....1,518
New Baden (D5)*....1,428
New Bedford (D2)*.... 225
New Berlin (D4)*.... 622
New Boston (B2)*.... 767
New Burnside (E6)*.... 244
New Canton (B4)*.... 449
New Douglas (D5)*.... 359
New Grand Chain
(Grand Chain*) (D6). 330
New Haven (E6)*.... 819
New Holland (D3)*.... 343
New Lenox (F2)*....1,235
New Memphis (D5)*.... 350
New Milford (D1).... 340
New Minden (D5)*.... 160
New Philadelphia (C3)*
New Salem (C4)*.... 184
New Windsor (C2)*.... 569
Newark (E2)*.... 457
Newman (F4)*....1,140
Newton (E5)*....2,780
Niantic (D4)*.... 625
Niles (A1)....3,587
Nilwood (D4)*.... 321
Niota (B3)*.... 250
Noble (E5)*.... 776
Nokomis (D4)*....2,544
Nora (D1)*.... 208
Normal (E3)*....9,772
Norridge (B1)....3,428
Norris (C3)*.... 319
Norris City (E6)*....1,370
North Aurora (E2)*.... 921

N. Chicago (F1)*....8,628
N. Chillicothe (D3)....1,741
N. City (Coello*) (E5). 513
N. Henderson (C2)*....
N. Lake (A2)*....4,361
N. Pekin ‡(D3)....1,758
N. Quincy (B4)....2,985
N. Riverside (B2)....3,230
N. Utica (Utica*) (E2). 985
Northbrook (A1)*....3,348
Northfield (B1)*....1,426
Oak (E6)....
Oak Forest (B2)*....1,856
Oak Hill (D3)*....
Oak Park (B2)*....63,529
Oakdale (D5)*.... 570
Oakford (D3)*.... 281
Oakglen (B3)*....
Oakland (F4)*.... 980
Oaklawn (B2)*....8,751
Oakley (E4)*.... 150
Oakwood (F3)*.... 641
Oblong (F5)*....1,639
Oconee (D4)*.... 256
Odell (E2)*.... 908
Odin (D5)*....1,341
O'Fallon (B6)*....3,022
Ogden (F3)*.... 436
Oglesby (D2)*....3,922
Ohio (D2)*.... 561
Ohlman (D4)*....
Okawville (D5)*.... 855
Old Marissa (D5).... 200
Old Ripley (D5).... 135
Olive Branch (D6)*....
Olivet (F4)*.... 325
Olmsted (D6)*.... 525
Olney (E5)*....8,612
Olympia Fields (B3)*.... 160
Omaha (E6)*.... 394
Onarga (F3)*....1,455
Oneida (C2)*.... 554
Opdyke (E5)*.... 200
Ophiem (C2)*.... 150
Oquawka (C3)*.... 929
Orangeville (D1)*.... 460
Oraville (D6)*.... 200
Orchard Place (A1).... 500
Oreana (E4)*.... 148
Oregon (D1)*....3,205
Orient (E6)*.... 801
Orion (C2)*.... 829
Orlando Park (A2)*.... 788
Oswego (E2)*....1,220
Ottawa (E2)*....16,957
Otterville (C4).... 118
Owaneco (D4)*.... 343
Ozark (E6)*....
Palatine (E1)*....4,079
Palestine (F4)*....1,589
Palmer (D4)*.... 335
Palmyra (C4)*.... 746
Paloma (B3)*.... 150
Palos Heights (A2)*....1,600
Palos Park (A2)*.... 854
Pana (D4)*....6,178
Panama (D4)*.... 520
Panola (E3)*.... 52
Papineau (F3)*.... 157
Paris (F4)*....9,460
Park Forest (B3)*....8,138
Park Ridge (A1)*....16,602
Parkersburg (F5)*.... 288

Patoka (D5)*.... 602
Patterson (C4)*.... 147
Pawnee (D4)*.... 974
Pawpaw (E2)*.... 594
Paxton (E3)*....3,795
Payson (B4)*.... 490
Pearl (C4)*.... 472
Pearl City (D1)*.... 491
Pecatonica (D1)*....1,438
Pekin (D3)*....21,858
Penfield (F3)*.... 300
Peoria (D3)*....111,856
Peoria (urban area)..154,084
Peoria Heights (D3)*....5,425
Peotone (F2)*....1,395
Percy (D5)*.... 933
Perks (D6)*.... 295
Perry (C4)*.... 444
Peru (D2)*....8,653
Pesotum (E4)*.... 415
Petersburg (D4)*....2,325
Petrolia (F5).... 200
Philadelphia (C4)*.... 110
Phillipstown (F5).... 102
Philo (E3)*.... 525
Phoenix (B2)....3,606
Pierron (D5)*.... 371
Pierson Station (E4)*.. 130
Pinckneyville (D5)*....3,299
Pingree Grove (E1).... 162
Pinkstaff (F5)*.... 235
Piper City (E3)*.... 735
Pittsburg (E6)*.... 612
Pittsfield (C4)*....3,564
Pittwood (F3)*....
Plainfield (E2)*....1,764
Plainview (C4)*.... 210
Plainville (B4)*.... 242
Plano (E2)*....2,154
Plattville (E2)....
Pleasant Hill (C4)*.... 856
Pleasant Mound (D5)*.. 110
Pleasant Plains (D4)*... 500
Pleasant View (C3).... 150
Plymouth (C3)*.... 854
Pocahontas (D5)*.... 667
Polo (D1)*....2,242
Pontiac (E3)*....8,990
Pontoosuc (B3)*.... 214
Poplar Grove (E1)*.... 417
Port Byron (C2)*....1,050
Posen (B2)*....1,795
Potomac (F3)*.... 602
Prairie City (C3)*.... 500
Prairie du Rocher (C5)* 662
Prairietown (B5).... 150
Preemption (C2)*.... 150
Prentice (C4)*.... 60
Preston (D5)*.... 103
Princeton (D2)*....5,765
Princeville (D3)*....1,113
Prophetstown (D2)*....1,691
Prospect Hts. (A1)*....1,800
Pulaski (D6)*.... 478
Putnam (D2)*.... 90
Quincy (B4)*....41,450
Radom (D5)*.... 134
Raleigh (E6)*.... 262
Ramsey (D4)*.... 808
Rankin (F3)*.... 737
Ransom (E2)*.... 411
Rantoul (E3)*....6,387
Rapids City (C2)*.... 487
Rardin (E4)*.... 230
Raritan (C3)*.... 228
Ray (C3)*.... 85
Raymond (D4)*.... 779
Red Bud (D5)*....1,519
Reddick (E2)*.... 208
Redmon (F4)*.... 226
Reevesville (E6)*.... 110
Renault (C5)*....
Reno (D5)*.... 224
Rentchler (B6)....
Reynolds (C2)*.... 409
Richmond (E1)*.... 623
Richton Park (B3)*.... 232
Richview (D5)*.... 352
Ridge Farm (F4)*.... 905
Ridgway (E6)*....1,148
Ridott (D1)*.... 187
Rinard (E5)*.... 100
Ringwood (E1)*.... 175
Rio (C2)*.... 200
Ripley (C3)*.... 177
River Forest (B2)*....10,823
River Grove (A2)*....4,839
Riverdale (B2)*....5,840
Riverside (B2)*....9,153
Riverton (D4)*....1,450
Roanoke (D3)*....1,368
Robbins (B2)*....4,766
Roberts (E3)*.... 416
Robinson (F5)*....6,407
Rochelle (D2)*....5,449
Rochester (D4)*.... 506
Rock City (D1)*.... 157
Rock Falls (D2)*....7,983
Rock Grove (D1).... 150
Rock Island (C2)*....48,710
Rock Island-Moline, Ill.-
Davenport, Iowa
(urban area)....193,733
Rockbridge (C4)*.... 243

Rockdale (E2)....1,393
Rockford (D1)*....92,927
Rockford (urban
area)....121,723
Rockport (B4)*.... 232
Rockton (E1)*....1,432
Rockwood (D6)*.... 175
Rollo (E2).... 24
Rome (D3)*.... 600
Rome (Dix*) (E5).... 190
Romeoville (E2).... 147
Roodhouse (C4)*....2,368
Rosamond (D4)*.... 300
Roscoe (D1)*.... 700
Rose Hill (E4)*.... 128
Roselle (E1)*....1,038
Roseville (C3)*....1,080
Rosiclare (E6)*....2,086
Rossville (F3)*....1,382
Round Grove (D2)*....
Round Lake ‡(E1)*.... 573
Round Lake Beach
‡(E1)....1,892
Round Lake Park ‡(E1)1,836
Roxana (B6)*....1,911
Royal (E3)*.... 156
Royalton (D6)*....1,506
Ruma (C5).... 107
Rushville (C3)*....2,682
Russellville (F5).... 207
Rutland (D3)*.... 486
Sadorus (E4)*.... 388
Sailor Springs (E5)*.... 259
St. Anne (F2)*....1,403
St. Augustine (C3)*.... 198
St. Charles (E2)*....6,709
St. David (C3)*.... 812
St. Elmo (E4)*....1,716
St. Francisville (F5)*....1,117
St. Jacob (D5)*.... 478
St. James (E5)*.... 60
St. Johns (D5).... 275
St. Joseph (E3)*.... 941
St. Libory (D5)*.... 324
St. Peter (E5)*.... 354
St. Rose (D5).... 125
Ste. Marie (E5)*.... 352
Salem (E5)*....6,159
San Jose (D3)*.... 562
Sandoval (D5)*....1,531
Sandusky (D6).... 350
Sandwich (E2)*....3,027
Saunemin (E3)*.... 338
Savanna (C1)*....5,058
Savoy (E3)*.... 145
Sawyerville (D4)*.... 390
Saybrook (E3)*.... 758
Scales Mound (C1)*.... 385
Schiller Park (A1)*....1,384
Schram City (D4).... 793
Sciota (C3)*.... 128
Scottland (F4)*.... 100
Scottville (C4)*.... 200
Seaton (C2)*.... 285
Seatonville (D2)*.... 405
Secor (D3)*.... 375
Seneca (E2)*....1,435
Serena (E2)*.... 165
Sesser (D5)*....2,086
Seymour (E3)*.... 275
Shabbona (E2)*.... 667
Shannon (D1)*.... 668
Shattuc (D5)*.... 200
Shawneetown (E6)*....1,917
Sheffield (D2)*.... 995
Shelbyville (E4)*....4,462
Sheldon (F3)*....1,114
Sheridan (E2)*.... 476
Sherman (D4)*....
Sherrard (C2)*.... 484
Shiloh (B6).... 453
Shipman (C4)*.... 376
Shirland (D1)*....
Shirley (E3)*.... 140
Shobonier (D5)*.... 315
Shumway (E4)*.... 248
Sibley (E3)*.... 345
Sidell (F4)*.... 554
Sidney (E3)*.... 653
Sigel (E4)*.... 296
Silvis (C2)*....3,055
Simpson (E6)*.... 119
Sims (E5)*.... 408
Skokie (B1)*....14,832
Smithboro (D5)*.... 253
Smithfield (C3)*.... 355
Smithshire (C3)*.... 150
Smithton (C5)*.... 515
Somonauk (E2)*.... 721
Sorento (D5)*.... 692
S. Beloit (E1)*....3,221
S. Chicago Hts. (B3)....2,129
S. Elgin (E2)*....1,220
S. Holland (B2)*....3,247
S. Jacksonville (C4)....1,165
S. Pekin (D3)*....1,043
S. Standard (D4)*.... 192
S. Wilmington (E2)*.... 662
Southern View ‡(D4).... 898
Sparland (D2)*.... 509
Sparta (D5)*....3,576
Spaulding (D4).... 211
Spillertown ‡(E6).... 196
Spring Bay (D3).... 203

Spring Garden (E5)....
Spring Grove (E1)*.... 269
Spring Valley (D2)*....4,916
Springerton (E5)*.... 279
SPRINGFIELD (D4)*..81,628
Springfield (urban
area)....96,649
Standard (D2)*.... 290
Standard City (South
Standard*) (D4).... 192
Stanford (D3)*.... 457
Staunton (D5)*....4,047
Steeleville (D6)*....1,353
Steger (F2)*....4,358
Sterling (D2)*....12,817
Steward (D2)*.... 270
Stewardson (E4)*.... 666
Stickney (B2)....3,317
Stillman Valley (D1)*... 362
Stillwell (B3)*.... 100
Stockland (F3)*.... 149
Stockton (C1)*....1,445
Stone Park ‡(A2)....1,414
Stonefort (E6)*.... 490
Stonington (D4)*....1,120
Stoy (F5)*.... 161
Strasburg (E4)*.... 436
Strawn (E3)*.... 173
Streator (E2)*....16,469
Stronghurst (C3)*.... 741
Sublette (D2)*.... 290
Sullivan (E4)*....3,470
Summer Hill (C4)*.... 145
Summerfield (D5)*.... 378
Summit (B2)*....8,957
Summum (C3)*.... 225
Sumner (F5)*....1,170
Sunfield (D5)....
Swan Creek (C3)*.... 160
Swansea (B6)....1,816
Swanwick (D5)*.... 154
Sycamore (E2)*....5,912
Symerton (F2)*.... 119
Table Grove (C3)*.... 481
Tallula (D4)*.... 527
Tamalco (D5)*.... 50
Tamaroa (D5)*.... 849
Tamms (D6)*.... 665
Tampico (D2)*.... 760
Taylor Spgs. (D4)*.... 627
Taylorville (D4)*....9,188
Tennessee (C3)*.... 249
Terre Haute (C3)....
Teutopolis (E4)*.... 919
Thackeray (E5)*.... 100
Thawville (E3)*.... 267
Thayer (D4)*.... 695
Thebes (D6)*.... 541
Thomasboro (E3)*.... 330
Thompsonville (E6)*.... 530
Thomson (C2)*.... 559
Thornton (B3)*....1,217
Tiedtville (A2)....
Tilden (D5)*.... 906
Tilton (F3)*....1,638
Time (C4).... 57
Timewell (C3)*.... 184
Tinley Park (B2)*....2,326
Tioga (B3)*.... 90
Tiskilwa (D2)*.... 962
Toledo (E4)*.... 905
Tolono (E3)*....1,065
Toluca (D2)*....1,419
Tonica (E2)*.... 585
Tonti (E5).... 100
Topeka (D3)*.... 72
Torino ‡(E2).... 9
Toulon (D2)*....1,173
Tovey (D4)*.... 593
Towanda (E3)*.... 400
Tower Hill (E4)*.... 784
Tremont (D3)*....1,138
Trenton (D5)*....1,432
Trilla (E4)*.... 250
Trimble (F4)*.... 165
Triumph (E2)*....
Trivoli (D3)*.... 395
Troy (B6)*....1,260
Troy Grove (E2)*.... 258
Tuscola (E4)*....2,950
Ullin (D6)*.... 772
Union (E1)*.... 435
Union Hill ‡(E2)*.... 138
Unionville (E6).... 140
Urbain ‡(E6).... 57
Urbana (E3)*....22,835
Ursa (B3)*.... 400
Utica (E2)*.... 985
Valier (D5)*.... 808
Valley City (C4)*.... 200
Valmeyer (C5)*.... 656
Van Orin (D2)*.... 105
Vandalia (D5)*....5,471
Varna (D2)*.... 400
Venedy (D5)*.... 149
Venice (A6)*....6,226
Vera (D4).... 125
Vergennes (D6)*.... 312
Vermilion (F4)*.... 316
Vermilion Grove (F4)*.. 200
Vermont (C3)*.... 940
Vernon (D5)*.... 243
Verona (E2)*.... 205
Versailles (C4)*.... 472

Victoria (C2)*.... 472
Vienna (E6)*....1,085
Villa Grove (E4)*....2,026
Villa Park (A2)*....8,821
Villa Ridge (D6)*.... 550
Viola (C2)*.... 826
Virden (D4)*....3,206
Virginia (C4)*....1,572
Wadsworth (F1)*.... 500
Waggoner (D4)*.... 239
Walnut (D2)*....1,093
Walnut Grove (C3)*.... 77
Walnut Hill (E5)*.... 156
Walshville (D4)*.... 113
Waltonville (D5)*.... 459
Wamac (D5)....1,429
Wapella (E3)*.... 504
Warren (C1)*....1,378
Warrensburg (D4)*.... 549
Warsaw (B3)*....2,002
Washburn (D3)*.... 999
Washington (D3)*....4,285
Washington Park (B6)*5,840
Wasson (E6).... 300
Wataga (C2)*.... 550
Waterloo (C5)*....2,821
Waterman (E2)*.... 750
Watseka (F3)*....4,235
Watson (E4)*.... 288
Wauconda (E1)*....1,173
Waukegan (F1)*....38,946
Waverly (D4)*....1,330
Wayne City (E5)*.... 726
Waynesville (D3)*.... 516
Weldon (E3)*.... 492
Welland (D2).... 60
Wellington (F3)*.... 300
Wenona (E2)*....1,005
Wenonah (D4).... 125
West Brooklyn (D2)*.... 194
W. Chicago (E2)*....3,973
W. City (E5)....1,081
W. Dundee (Dundee*)
(E1)....1,948
W. Frankfort (E6)*....11,384
W. Jersey (D2).... 75
W. Liberty (E5)*.... 150
W. Point (B3)*.... 275
W. Salem (F5)*.... 902
W. Union (F4)*.... 375
W. York (F4).... 250
Westchester (A2)....4,308
Western Springs (A2)*.6,364
Westervelt (E4)*.... 200
Westfield (F4)*.... 661
Westmont (A2)*....3,402
Weston (E3)*.... 150
Westville (F3)*....3,196
Wheaton (E2)*....11,638
Wheeler (E4)*.... 178
Wheeling (F1)*.... 916
White City (D4).... 275
White Hall (C4)*....3,082
White Heath (E3)*.... 250
Whiteash ‡(E6).... 204
Whittington (E5)*.... 200
Wichert (F2)*.... 250
Williamsfield (C3)*.... 542
Williamson (D5).... 319
Williamsville (D4)*.... 656
Willisville (D6)*.... 635
Willow Hill (E5)*.... 333
Willow Springs (A2)*...1,314
Wilmette (B1)*....18,162
Wilmington (Patterson*)
(C4).... 147
Wilmington (E2)*....3,354
Wilsonville (D4)*.... 822
Winchester (C4)*....1,591
Windsor (E4)*....1,008
Windsor (New Windsor*)
(C2).... 569
Winfield (E2)*.... 714
Wing (E3).... 50
Winkle (D5).... 114
Winnebago (D1)*.... 752
Winnetka (B1)*....12,105
Winslow (D1)*.... 355
Winthrop Harbor (F1)*1,765
Witt (D4)*....1,156
Woburn (D5).... 110
Wolf Lake (D6)*.... 135
Wood Dale (A1)*....1,857
Wood River (B6)*....10,190
Woodbine (C1)*....
Woodhull (C2)*.... 718
Woodland (F3)*.... 334
Woodlawn (D5)*.... 320
Woodson (C4)*.... 211
Woodstock (E1)*....7,192
Woodworth (F3).... 89
Woosung (D2)*.... 167
Worden (B6)*.... 968
Worth (A2)*....1,472
Wrights (C4)*.... 150
Wyanet (D2)*.... 950
Wyoming (D2)*....1,496
Xenia (E5)*.... 643
Yale (E4)*.... 153
Yates City (C3)*.... 623
Yorkville (E2)*.... 632
Zeigler (D6)*....2,516
Zenith (E5).... 59
Zion (F1)*....8,950

INDIANA

Map on Page 59

Total Population 3,934,224

92 COUNTIES

Adams (H3)....22,393
Allen (G2)....183,722
Bartholomew (F6)....36,108
Benton (C3)....11,462
Blackford (G4)....14,026
Boone (E4)....23,993
Brown (E6)....6,209
Carroll (D3)....16,010
Cass (E3)....38,793
Clark (F8)....48,330
Clay (C6)....23,918
Clinton (E4)....29,734
Crawford (E8)....9,289
Daviess (C7)....26,762
De Kalb (H2)....26,023
Dearborn (H6)....25,141
Decatur (G6)....18,218
Delaware (G4)....90,252
Dubois (D8)....23,785
Elkhart (F1)....84,512
Fayette (G5)....23,391
Floyd (F8)....43,955
Fountain (C4)....17,836
Franklin (G6)....16,034
Fulton (E2)....16,565
Gibson (B8)....30,720
Grant (F3)....62,156
Greene (D6)....27,886
Hamilton (E4)....28,491
Hancock (F5)....20,332
Harrison (E8)....17,858
Hendricks (D5)....24,594
Henry (G5)....45,505
Howard (E4)....54,498
Huntington (G3)....31,400
Jackson (E7)....28,237
Jasper (C2)....17,031
Jay (G4)....23,157
Jefferson (G7)....21,613
Jennings (F7)....15,250
Johnson (E6)....26,183
Knox (C7)....43,415
Kosciusko (F2)....33,002
La Porte (D1)....76,808
La Grange (G1)....15,347
Lake (C2)....368,152
Lawrence (E7)....34,346
Madison (F4)....103,911
Marion (E5)....551,777
Marshall (E2)....29,468
Martin (D7)....10,678
Miami (E3)....28,201
Monroe (D6)....50,080
Montgomery (D4)....29,122
Morgan (E6)....23,726
Newton (C3)....11,006
Noble (G2)....25,075
Ohio (H7)....4,223
Orange (E7)....16,879
Owen (D6)....11,763
Parke (C5)....15,674
Perry (D8)....17,367
Pike (C8)....14,995
Porter (C2)....40,076
Posey (B8)....19,818
Pulaski (D2)....12,493
Putnam (D5)....22,950
Randolph (G4)....27,141
Ripley (G6)....18,763
Rush (G5)....19,799
Saint Joseph (E1)....205,058
Scott (F7)....11,519
Shelby (F5)....28,026
Spencer (C9)....16,174
Starke (D2)....15,282
Steuben (G1)....17,087
Sullivan (C6)....23,667
Switzerland (G7)....7,599
Tippecanoe (D4)....74,473
Tipton (E4)....15,566
Union (H5)....6,412
Vanderburgh (B8)....160,422

Manhattan (D5)
Manilla (F5)* 400
Mansfield (C5) 35
Manson (D4) 65
Maples (H2) 110
Marco (C7)* 195
Marengo (E8)* 801
Mariah Hill (D8)*
Marietta (F6) 150
Marion (F3)* 30,081
Markland (G7) 200
Markle (G3)* 733
Markleville (F5)* 314
Marshall (C5)* 326
Marshfield (C4)* 100
Martinsburg (E8) 125
Martinsville (D6)* 5,991
Marysville (F7)* 98
Matthews (F4)* 501
Mauckport (E8)* 154
Maumee (E6) 25
Maxinkuckee (E2) 75
Maxwell (F5)* 285
Mays (G5)* 200
Maywood (E5)* 525
Mc Cool (C1)* 250
Mc Cordsville (F5)* 735
Mc Coysburg (C3)
Mc Grawsville (E3) 50
Mc Natts (G3) 25
Mecca (C5)*
Mechanicsburg (G5) 250
Medaryville (D2)* 833
Medora (E7)* 627
Mellott (C4)* 266
Memphis (F8)* 380
Mentone (E2)* 798
Merom (B6)* 374
Merriam (G2) 110
Merrillville (C2) 1,400
Metamora (G6)* 400
Metea (E3) 45
Metz (H1)* 175
Mexico (E3)* 521
Miami (E3)*
Michigan
City (C1)* 28,395
Michigantown (E4)* 443
Middlebury (F1)* 839
Middlefork (E4) 62
Middletown (F4)* 1,731
Midland (C6)*
Midway (C8) 20
Mier (F3) 63
Milan (G6)* 1,014
Milford (F2)* 952
Milford (Clifty*) (F6) 175
Mill Creek (D1)* 162
Millersburg (C8)
Millersburg (F1)* 437
Millgrove (G4)* 160
Millhousen (G6)* 184
Milligan (C5)* 100
Milltown (E8)* 760
Millville (G5) 120
Milo (G3)
Milroy (G6)* 800
Milton (G5)* 752
Mineral (D7) 55
Mishawaka (E1)* 32,913
Mitchell (E7)* 3,245
Modoc (G4)* 275
Mohawk (F5)* 150
Mongo (G1)* 225
Monitor (D4) 50
Monmouth (H3) 100
Monon (D3)* 1,439
Monroe (H3)* 428
Monroe City (C7)* 453
Monroeville (H3)* 1,150
Monrovia (E5)* 375
Monterey (D2)* 250
Montezuma (C5)* 1,220
Montgomery (C7)* 538
Monticello (D3)* 3,467
Montmorenci (D4)* 235
Montpelier (G3)* 1,826
Moody (C3)
Moore (H2) 30
Moorefield (G7)
Mooreland (G5)* 497
Moores Hill (G6)* 445
Mooresville (E5)* 2,264
Moran (D4)* 140
Morgantown (E6)* 838
Morocco (C3)* 1,141
Morris (G6)* 500
Morristown (F5)* 679
Morton (D5)
Moscow (F6)
Mount Auburn ‡(G5) 164
Mt. Ayr (C3)* 222
Mt. Carmel (H6) 134
Mt. Comfort (F5)* 115
Mt. Etna (F3) 171
Mt. Meridian (D5)
Mt. Pisgah (G1) 54
Mt. Pleasant (D8)* 24
Mt. Sterling (G7) 40
Mt. Summit (G4)* 295
Mt. Vernon (B9)* 6,150
Mt. Zion (G3) 30
Mulberry (D4)* 950
Muncie (G4)* 58,479
Munster (B1)* 4,753
Murray (G3) 94
Nabb (F7)* 110
Napoleon (G6)* 350
Nappanee (F2)* 3,393
Nashville (E6)* 526
Nead (E3) 48
Nebraska (F6)* 104
Needham (E5)* 110
Needmore (E7) 150
Nevada (F4) 45
Nevada Mills (G1) 75
New Albany (F8)* 29,436
New Amsterdam (E8) 76
New Augusta (E5)* 225
New Bellsville (E6) 20
New Burlington (G4) 100
New Carlisle (E1)* 983
New Castle (G5)* 18,271
New Chicago (C1) 921
New Corydon (H3)* 105
New Goshen (B5)* 600
New Harmony (B8)* 1,360
New Haven (H2)* 2,336
New Holland (F3) 20
New Hope (D6) 11
New Lebanon (C6)* 125
New Lisbon (G5)* 290
New London (E4) 210
New Marion (G6) 150
New Market (D5)* 370
New Middletown (E8)* 153
New Mt. Pleasant (G4) 100
New Palestine (F5)* 504
New Paris (F2)* 985
New Pekin (F7) 543
New Philadelphia (F7)*
New Point (G6)* 322
New Providence
(Borden*) (F8) 426
New Richmond (D4)* 391
New Ross (D5)* 336
New Salem (G5) 206
New Salisbury (E8)* 215
New Trenton (H6)* 150
New Washington (F7)* 750
New Waverly (E3)* 190
New Winchester (D5) 75
Newbern (F6)
Newberry (C7)* 340
Newburgh (C9)* 1,324
Newland (C2)
Newport (C5)* 660
Newton Stewart (D8)* 40
Newtonville (D8)* 123
Newtown (C4)* 287
Newville (H2) 75
Nineveh (E6)* 300
Noblesville (F4)* 6,567
Norman (E7)* 110
Norristown (F6) 75
North Grove (F3) 126
N. Hayden (B2) 150
N. Judson (D2)* 1,705
N. Liberty (E1)* 1,165
N. Madison (G7)* 715
N. Manchester (F3)* 3,977
N. Salem (D5)* 544
N. Terre Haute (C5)*
N. Vernon (F6)* 3,488
N. Webster (F2)* 487
Norway (D3)
Notre Dame (E1)* 5,000
Nulltown (G5)
Oak (D3)* 150
Oak Forest (G6) 120
Oakford (E4)* 230
Oakland City (C8)* 3,539
Oaklandon (E5)* 346
Oaktown (C7)* 763
Oakville (G4)* 224
Oatsville (C8) 100
Obed (D2)* 100
Ockley (D4)* 140
Odell (C4) 210
Odon (C7)* 1,177
Ogden Dunes (C1) 429
Oldenburg (G6)* 591
Olean (G7) 225
Oliver (B8)
Omega (F4) 50
Ontario (G1) 150
Onward (E3)* 140
Oolitic (E7)* 1,125
Ora (D2)* 140
Orange (G5) 200
Orangeville (D7) 85
Orestes (F4)* 482
Orland (G1)* 386
Orleans (D7)* 1,531
Osceola (E1)* 1,091
Osgood (G6)* 1,228
Ossian (G3)* 761
Oswego (F2)
Otis (D1)*
Otisco (F7)* 250
Otterbein (C4)* 641
Otto (G7)
Otwell (C8)* 400
Owensburg (D7)* 400
Owensville (B8)* 1,110
Oxford (C3)* 888
Packertown (F2) 72
Palestine (F2) 90
Palmer (C2) 200
Palmyra (E8)* 327
Paoli (E7)* 2,575
Paragon (D6)* 463
Paris Crossing (F7)* 132
Parker (G4)* 915
Parkersburg (D5) 100
Parr (C2)* 132
Patoka (B8)* 626
Patricksburg (D6)* 450
Patriot (H7)* 315
Patronville (C9) 30
Paxton (C6)* 275
Paynesville (F7) 50
Peabody (G2)
Pekin (E7)* 553
Pelzer (C8) 49
Pence (C4)* 122
Pendleton (F5)* 2,082
Pennville (G4)* 626
Peoga (E6) 48
Percy Junction (C3) 4
Perkinsville (F4) 250
Perrysburg (E3) 50
Perrysville (C4)* 462
Pershing (G5)* 389
Pershing (E2) 50
Peru (E3)* 13,308
Petersburg (C7)* 3,035
Peterson (G3) 50
Petersville (F6)
Petroleum (G3)*
Phenix (G3)
Pickard (E4)
Pierceton (F2)* 973
Pierceville (G6)*
Pikes Peak (E6)
Pikeville (C8) 50
Pilot Knob (E8)* 200
Pimento (C6)* 125
Pine Village (C4)* 311
Pinelake (D1)* 250
Pinola (D1) 50
Pittsboro (D5)* 599
Pittsburg (D3) 350
Plainfield (E5)* 2,585
Plainville (C7)* 568
Plato (G1) 40
Pleasant (G7) 15
Pleasant Lake (H1)* 500
Pleasant Mills (H3)* 175
Pleasant Ridge (C3)
Pleasant View (F5) 11
Pleasantville (C7)* 200
Plevna (E3) 72
Plum Tree (G3) 40
Plummer (C7) 10
Plymouth (E2)* 6,704
Poe (G3) 80
Point Isabel (F4) 75
Poland (C6)* 150
Poneto (G3)* 244
Porter (C1)* 1,458
Portersville (C8) 75
Portland (H4)* 7,064
Poseyville (B8)* 1,005
Pottawattomie Park (D1) 35
Powers (G4) 50
Prairie Creek (C6)* 225
Prairieton (B6)*
Preble (H3)* 150
Prescott (F6) 30
Priam (G4)
Princeton (B8)* 7,673
Providence (E6) 100
Pulaski (D3) 100
Putnamville (D5)* 165
Pyrmont (D4) 100
Queensville (F6) 70
Quincy (D6)* 320
Raber (G2)
Raccoon (D5) 100
Radley (F4) 150
Radnor (D3)* 110
Ragsdale (C7)* 230
Rainsville (C4) 130
Raleigh (G5) 150
Ramsey (E8)* 106
Ranger (D8)*
Raub (C3)* 110
Ravenswood (E5)* 498
Ray (H1)* 175
Raymond (H6) 62
Rays Crossing (F5) 75
Reagan (D4) 2
Red Key (G4)* 1,639
Redbridge (F3) 75
Reddington (F6) 220
Reelsville (D5)* 90
Reese Mill (D4) 130
Reiffsburg (G3) 43
Remington (C3)* 1,053
Rensselaer (C3)* 4,072
Rexville (G7) 60
Reynolds (D3)* 499
Riceville (D8) 4
Richland (C9)* 530
Richland Center (E2) 10
Richmond (H5)* 39,539
Richvalley (F3)* 111
Ridgeview (E3)
Ridgeville (G4)* 950
Rigdon (F4) 80
Riley (C6)* 251
Rileysburg (B4) 40
Rising Sun (H7)* 1,930
River (G3) 75
Riverside (C4) 120
Riverton (B6) 54
Roachdale (D5)* 918
Roann (F3)* 492
Roanoke (G3)* 905
Rob Roy (C4) 54
Rochester (E2)* 4,673
Rock Creek (G3)
Rockfield (D3)* 325
Rocklane (E5)
Rockport (C9)* 2,493
Rockville (C5)* 2,467
Rocky Ripple (E5) 528
Roll (G3)* 150
Rolling Prairie (D1)* 625
Rome (D9)*
Rome City (G1)* 1,303
Romney (D4)* 500
Rosedale (C5)* 673
Roseland (E1) 984
Roselawn (C2)*
Rosston (E4) 35
Rossville (D4)* 739
Royal Center (E3)* 876
Royalton (E5) 50
Royerton (G4) 400
Rumble (C8) 21
Rushville (G5)* 6,761
Rusk (D7)*
Russellville (D5)* 361
Russiaville (E4)* 1,025
Saint Anthony (D8)* 152
St. Bernice (C5)* 1,200
St. Croix (D8)* 100
St. Henry (D8) 183
St. Joe (H2)* 479
St. John (C2)* 684
St. Joseph Hill (F8) 200
St. Leon (H6)* 288
St. Louis Crossing (F6)* 150
St. Mary of the Woods
(B6)* 1,300
St. Mary's (E1)*
St. Maurice (G6) 60
St. Meinrad (D8)* 720
St. Omer (F6) 75
St. Paul (F6)* 669
St. Peters (H6) 130
St. Philip (B9) 200
St. Wendells (B8)
Salamonia (H4)* 181
Salem (E7)* 3,271
Salem Center (G1) 50
Saline City (C6)* 115
Saltillo (E7)* 122
Samaria (E6) 88
San Pierre (D2)* 350
Sandborn (C7)* 572
Sanders (E6) 200
Sandford (B5)* 195
Sandusky (G6) 200
Santa Claus (D8)* 45
Santa Fe (E3) 92
Saratoga (H4)* 333
Sardinia (F6)* 150
Savah (B8) 100
Schererville (C2)* 1,457
Schneider (C2)* 356
Schnellville (D8)* 300
Scipio (H6) 75
Scipio (F6)* 200
Scircleville (E4)* 181
Scotland (D7)* 100
Scott (F1) 100
Scottsburg (F7)* 2,953
Sedalia (E4)* 180
Sedan (G2) 30
Seelyville (C6)* 898
Sellersburg (F8)* 1,664
Selma (G4)* 499
Selvin (C8)*
Servia (F3)* 143
Sevastopol (F2) 50
Sexton (G5) 80
Seybert (F1) 30
Seymour (F7)* 9,629
Shadeland (C4) 78
Shannondale (D4) 20
Sharpsville (E4)* 508
Shelburn (C6)* 1,412
Shelby (C2)* 519
Shelbyville (F6)* 11,734
Shepardsville (B5)* 300
Sheridan (E4)* 1,965
Shideler (G4)
Shipshewana (F1)* 277
Shirley (F5)* 1,087
Shirley City
(Woodburn*) (H2) 540
Shoals (D7)* 1,039
Shooters Hill ‡(E5) 13
Shrock (F1)
Siberia (D8)* 50
Sidney (F2)* 168
Silver Lake (F2)* 472
Silverville (D7) 60
Silverwood (C5) 75
Simpson (G3) 9
Sims (F3)* 231
Skelton (B8) 50
Smartsburg (D4) 55
Smith Valley (E5) 150
Smithville (D6)* 425
Snow Hill (H4) 15
Solon (F7) 137
Solsberry (D6)* 500
Somerset (F3)* 255
Somerville (C8)* 353
South Bend (E1)* 115,911
South Bend (urban
area) 167,879
S. Boston (F7) 125
S. Milford (G1)* 350
S. Raub (D4) 30
S. Wanatah (D2) 95
S. Whitley (F2)* 1,299
Southport (E5)* 730
Spades (G6)
Sparksville (E7)* 136
Spartanburg (H4) 200
Spearsville (E6) 38
Speed (F8)* 1,000
Speedway (E5)* 5,498
Speicher (F3) 60
Spelterville (C5) 150
Spencer (D6)* 2,394
Spencerville (G2)* 450
Spiceland (F5)* 739
Spraytown (E6) 63
Spring Grove (H5) 333
Spring Hills ‡(E5) 27
Spring Lake Park (F5) 156
Springfield (B8)
Springport (G4)* 217
Springville (D7)* 500
Spurgeon (C8)* 327
Stacer (B8)
Stanford (D6)* 100
Star City (D3)* 600
Starlight (F8) 50
State Line (C4)* 152
Staunton (C6)* 487
Steele (H3) 26
Stendal (C8)* 175
Stewartsville (B8)* 240
Stilesville (D5)* 330
Stillwell (D1)*
Stinesville (D6)* 355
Stockwell (D4)* 632
Stone (G4) 10
Stonebluff (C4)* 172
Stones Crossing (E5) 75
Story (E6)
Straughn (G5)* 345
Stroh (G1)* 475
Strouse (G2)
Sullivan (C6)* 5,423
Sulphur (E8)* 43
Sulphur Springs (G4)* 351
Sumava Resorts (C2)* 125
Summit (G1) 2
Summitville (F4)* 1,061
Sunman (G6)* 358
Surprise (E7) 55
Swanington (C3) 125
Swayzee (F4)* 690
Sweetsers (F3)* 535
Switz City (C6)* 328
Sycamore (F4) 76
Sylvania (C5) 35
Syracuse (F2)* 1,453
Tab (C4)*
Talbot (C3)*
Talma (E2) 150
Tampico (F7) 150
Tangier (C5)* 100
Taswell (D8)* 110
Taylorsville (F6)* 290
Tecumseh (C8)
Teegarden (E2)*
Tefft (D2)* 140
Tell City (D9)* 5,735
Templeton (C3)* 143
Tennyson (C8)* 409
Terhune (E4) 100
Terre Haute (C6)* 64,214
Terre Haute (urban
area) 77,845
Thayer (C2)* 250
Thorntown (D4)* 1,380
Tiosa (E2) 125
Tippecanoe (E2)* 400
Tipton (E4)* 5,633
Tobinsport (D9)* 205
Tocsin (G3)* 175
Topeka (F1)* 557
Toto (D2) 275
Tower (E8)
Trafalgar (E6)* 439
Trail Creek (D1) 817
Treaty (F3) 90
Trevlac (E6)* 48
Trinity Springs (D7) 150
Troy (D9)* 537
Tulip (D6) 20
Tunker (F2) 40
Tunnelton (E7)* 300
Twelve Mile (E3)* 247
Tyner (E2)* 250
Ulen (E4) 83
Underwood (F7)* 328
Union (C8)* 209
Union City (H4)* 3,572
Union Mills (D2)* 450
Uniondale (G3)* 293
Unionport (G4) 50
Uniontown (D8)*
Unionville (E6)* 475
Universal (C5)* 479
Upland (F4)* 1,565
Urbana (F3)* 400
Utica (F8) 250
Valeene (E8)* 94
Valentine (G1) 110
Vallonia (E7)* 510
Valparaiso (C2)* 12,028
Van Buren (F3)* 815
Veedersburg (C4)* 1,719
Velpen (C8)* 197
Vera Cruz (G3) 143
Verne (C7) 50
Vernon (F7)* 480
Versailles (G6)* 886
Veterans Adm. Hospital
(F3)* 3,950
Vevay (G7)* 1,309
Vicksburg (C6) 390
Vienna (F7) 80
Vincennes (C7)* 18,831
Vine (C4) 15
Virgie (C2)
Vistula (F1) 100
Wabash (F3)* 10,621
Wadena (C3) 65
Wadesville (B8)*
Wakarusa (F1)* 1,143
Wakefield (F7) 45
Waldron (F6)* 700
Walesboro (F6)
Walkerton (E2)* 2,102
Wallace (C5)* 123
Wallace Junction (D6)
Wallen (G2) 120
Walton (E3)* 837
Wanamaker (E5)* 325
Wanatah (D2)* 750
Warren (G3)* 1,247
Warren Park (F5) 336
Warrenton (B8) 100
Warrington (F5) 95
Warsaw (F2)* 6,625
Washington (C7)* 10,987
Waterloo (G2)* 1,414
Waterman (C5) 100
Watson (F8) 200
Waveland (D5)* 553
Waverly (E5) 150
Wawaka (F2)* 300
Wawasee (F2)* 400
Wawpecong (F3) 84
Waymansville (E6) 250
Waynedale (G3)
Waynesville (F6)
Waynetown (C4)* 658
Webster (H5)* 175
Weisburg (H6)* 148
Wellsboro (D1)* 170
West Baden Springs
(D7)* 1,047
W. College Corner (H5) 513
W. Fork (D8)* 58
W. Franklin (B9) 100
W. Harrison (H6) 308
W. Lafayette (D4)* 11,873
W. Lebanon (C4)* 642
W. Middleton (E4)* 250
W. Newton (E5)*
W. Terre Haute (B6)* 3,357
Westchester (H4) 8
Westfield (E4)* 849
Westphalia (C7)* 250
Westpoint (C4)* 315
Westport (F6)* 658
Westville (D1)* 624
Wheatfield (C2)* 496
Wheatland (C7)* 735
Wheeler (C1)* 400
Wheeling (G4)
Wheeling (C8) 50
Whitaker (D6) 25
Whitcomb (H6) 150
White Cloud (E8) 50
White Lick (E5)
Whitehall (D6) 80
Whiteland (E5)* 465
Whitestown (E5)* 550
Whitesville (D5) 75
Whitewater (H5) 104
Whiting (C1)* 9,669
Wickliffe (D8)* 9
Wilbur (D5) 75
Wilfred (C6) 50
Wilkinson (F5)* 365
Williams (D7)* 400
Williams (H3) 75
Williams Creek (E5) 288
Williamsport (C4)* 1,241
Willow Branch (F5)*
Wilmington (H6) 200
Wilmot (F2) 100
Wilson (F6) 25
Winamac (D2)* 2,166
Winchester (G4)* 5,467
Windfall (F4)* 963
Windom (D7) 8
Windsor (G4)
Wingate (C4)* 400
Winona Lake (F2)* 1,366
Winslow (C8)* 1,322
Wirt (G7)
Wolcott (C3)* 778
Wolcottville (G1)* 672
Wolflake (F2)* 250
Woodburn (H2)* 540
Woodland (E1) 115
Woodlawn Heights (F4)
Woodruff Place (E5) 1,557
Woodstock ‡(E5) 29
Worthington (C6)* 1,627
Wyandotte (E8)* 50
Wyatt (E1)* 250
Wynedale ‡(E5) 75
Yankeetown (C9) 323
Yeddo (C4)* 115
Yeoman (D3)* 180
Yoder (G3)* 200
Yorktown (G4)* 1,109
Yorkville (H6)* 87
Young America (E3)* 250
Youngs Creek (D8)* 79
Youngstown (C6) 72
Zanesville (G3)* 300
Zenas (G6) 44
Zionsville (E5)* 1,536
Zipp (B8)
Zoar (C8) 5
Zulu (H2) 175

Map on Page 60

IOWA

Total Population 2,621,073

99 COUNTIES

Adair (E6) 12,292
Adams (D6) 8,753
Allamakee (L2) 16,351
Appanoose (H7) 19,683
Audubon (D5) 11,570
Benton (J4) 22,656
Black Hawk (J4) 100,448
Boone (F5) 28,139
Bremer (J3) 18,884
Buchanan (K4) 21,927
Buena Vista (C3) 21,113
Butler (H3) 17,394
Calhoun (D4) 16,925
Carroll (D4) 23,065
Cass (D6) 18,532
Cedar (L5) 16,910
Cerro Gordo (G2) 46,053
Cherokee (B3) 19,052
Chickasaw (J2) 15,228
Clarke (F6) 9,369
Clay (C2) 18,103
Clayton (L3) 22,522
Clinton (M5) 49,664
Crawford (C4) 19,741
Dallas (E5) 23,661
Davis (J7) 9,995
Decatur (F7) 12,601
Delaware (L4) 17,734
Des Moines (L7) 42,056
Dickinson (C2) 12,756
Dubuque (M4) 71,337
Emmet (D2) 14,102
Fayette (K3) 28,294
Floyd (H2) 21,505
Franklin (G3) 16,268
Fremont (B7) 12,323
Greene (E5) 15,544
Grundy (H4) 13,722
Guthrie (D5) 15,197
Hamilton (F4) 19,660
Hancock (F2) 15,077
Hardin (G4) 22,218
Harrison (B5) 19,560
Henry (K6) 18,708
Howard (J2) 13,105
Humboldt (E3) 13,117
Ida (C4) 10,697
Iowa (J5) 15,835
Jackson (M4) 18,622
Jasper (G5) 32,305
Jefferson (K6) 15,696
Johnson (K5) 45,756
Jones (L4) 19,401
Keokuk (J6) 16,797
Kossuth (E2) 26,241
Lee (L7) 43,102
Linn (K4) 104,274
Louisa (L6) 11,101
Lucas (G6) 12,069
Lyon (A2) 14,697
Madison (E6) 13,131
Mahaska (H6) 24,672
Marion (G6) 25,930
Marshall (G4) 35,611
Mills (B6) 14,064
Mitchell (H2) 13,945
Monona (B4) 16,303
Monroe (H7) 11,814

Montgomery (C6)........15,685
Muscatine (L5)........32,148
O'Brien (B2)........18,970
Osceola (B2)........10,181
Page (C7)........23,921
Palo Alto (D2)........15,891
Plymouth (A3)........23,252
Pocahontas (D3)........15,496
Polk (F5)........226,010
Pottawattamie (B6)....69,682
Poweshiek (H5)........19,344
Ringgold (E7)........9,528
Sac (C4)........17,518
Scott (M5)........100,698
Shelby (C5)........15,942
Sioux (A2)........26,381
Story (G4)........44,294
Tama (H4)........21,688
Taylor (D7)........12,420
Union (E7)........15,651
Van Buren (K7)........11,007
Wapello (J6)........47,397
Warren (F6)........17,758
Washington (K6)........19,557
Wayne (G7)........11,737
Webster (E4)........44,241
Winnebago (F2)........13,450
Winneshiek (K2)........21,639
Woodbury (B4)........103,917
Worth (G2)........11,068
Wright (F3)........19,652

CITIES and TOWNS

Abingdon (J6)........ 70
Ackley (G3)*........1,608
Ackworth (G6)*........ 95
Adair (D6)*........ 827
Adaza (E4)*........ 51
Adel (E5)*........1,799
Afton (E6)*........ 936
Agency (J7)*........ 524
Ainsworth (K6)*........ 396
Akron (A3)*........1,251
Albert City (C3)*........ 736
Albia (H6)*........4,838
Albion (H4)*........ 492
Alburnett (K4)*........ 254
Alden (G4)*........ 829
Alexander (G3)*........ 278
Algona (E2)*........5,415
Alleman (F5)*........ 108
Allendorf (B2)*........ 55
Allerton (G7)*........ 761
Allison (H3)*........ 771
Alpha (K3)*........ 122
Alta (C3)*........1,348
Alta Vista (J2)*........ 312
Alton (A3)*........1,038
Altoona (G5)*........ 736
Alvord (A2)*........ 263
Amana (K5)*
Amber (L4)*........ 115
Ames (F4)*........22,898
Anamosa (L4)*........3,910
Anderson (B7)*........ 120
Andover (N5)*........ 80
Andrew (M4)*........ 280
Angus (E5)*........ 150
Anita (D6)*........1,112
Ankeny (F5)*........1,229
Anthon (B4)*........ 770
Aplington (H3)*........ 702
Arcadia (C4)*........ 425
Archer (B2)*........ 167
Ardon (L6)*........ 20
Aredale (H3)*........ 204
Argyle (K7)*........ 85
Arion (B5)*........ 220
Arispe (E7)*........ 110
Arlington (K3)*........ 661
Armstrong (D2)*........ 943
Arnolds Park (C2)*........1,078
Arthur (C4)*........ 243
Asbury (M4)........ 52
Ashton (B2)*........ 588
Aspinwall (C5)*........ 107
Astor (C5)
Atalissa (L5)*........ 204
Athelstan (D7)*........ 115
Atkins (K4)*........ 387
Atlantic (D6)*........6,480
Attica (G6)*
Auburn (D4)*........ 350
Audubon (D5)*........2,808
Augusta (L7)........ 50
Aurelia (C3)*........ 807
Aurora (K3)*........ 225
Austinville (H3)*........ 130
Avery (H6)*........ 175
Avoca (C6)*........1,955
Ayrshire (D2)*........ 334
Badger (E3)*........ 301
Bagley (E5)*........ 392
Bailey (H2)........ 25
Baldwin (M4)*........ 208
Balltown (M3)........ 49
Bancroft (E2)*........ 901
Bankston (L3)........ 40
Barnes City (H6)*........ 326
Barnum (E3)*........ 193
Bartlett (B7)*........ 88
Bassett (J2)*........ 125
Batavia (J7)*........ 524
Battle Creek (B4)*........ 873
Baxter (G5)*........ 618
Bayard (D5)*........ 634
Beacon (H6)*........ 371
Beaconsfield (E7)*........ 104
Beaman (H4)*........ 191
Beaver (E4)*........ 114
Bedford (D7)*........2,000
Beech (G6)*........ 106
Belknap (J7)*........ 80
Belle Plaine (J5)*........3,056
Bellevue (M4)*........1,932
Belmond (F3)*........2,169
Beloit (A2)*........ 90
Bennett (L5)*........ 357
Bentley (B6)*........ 50
Benton (E7)*........ 128
Bentonsport (K7)........ 60
Berkley (E5)........ 71
Bernard (M4)*........ 149
Bertram (K5)........ 128
Berwick (G5)*........ 113
Bethlehem (G7)........ 52
Bettendorf (N5)*........5,132
Bevington (F6)*........ 48
Big Rock (M5)*........ 106
Birmingham (K7)*........ 643
Blairsburg (F4)*........ 257
Blairstown (J5)*........ 523
Blakesburg (H7)*........ 401
Blanchard (C7)*........ 214
Blencoe (A5)*........ 328
Blockton (D7)*........ 407
Bloomfield (J7)*........2,688
Blue Grass (M5)*........ 337
Bode (E3)*........ 492
Bonair (J2)........ 80
Bonaparte (K7)*........ 642
Bondurant (G5)*........ 328
Boone (F4)*........12,164
Botna (C5)*........ 54
Bouton (E5)*........ 159
Boxholm (E4)*........ 304
Boyden (B2)*........ 541
Boyer (C4)*........ 70
Braddyville (D7)*........ 249
Bradford (G3)*
Bradgate (E3)*........ 188
Brandon (K4)*........ 319
Brayton (D5)*........ 239
Brazil (H7)*
Breda (C4)*........ 506
Bremer (J3)*........ 80
Bridgewater (D6)*........ 296
Brighton (K6)*........ 705
Bristow (H3)*........ 313
Britt (F2)*........1,908
Bronson (A4)*........ 295
Brooklyn (J5)*........1,323
Brooks (D7)*........ 180
Brunsville (A3)*........ 112
Bryant (N5)*........ 45
Buchanan (L5)........ 36
Buck Grove (C5)*........ 67
Buckeye (G4)*........ 192
Buckingham (J4)*........ 68
Buffalo (M6)*........ 695
Buffalo Center (F2)*....1,087
Bunch (H7)*........ 103
Burchinal (G2)*........ 75
Burdette (G3)........ 18
Burlington (L7)*........30,613
Burnside (E4)*........ 105
Burroak (K2)*........ 250
Burt (E2)*........ 572
Bussey (H6)*........ 633
Calamus (M5)*........ 381
California (B5)*........ 125
Callender (E4)*........ 387
Calmar (K2)*........ 937
Calumet (B3)*........ 250
Camanche (N5)*........1,212
Cambria (G7)*........ 125
Cambridge (G5)*........ 573
Cantril (J7)*........ 353
Carbon (D6)*........ 282
Carl (D6)........ 40
Carlisle (G6)*........ 903
Carnarvon (C4)*........ 115
Carney (F5)
Carpenter (H2)*........ 165
Carroll (D4)*........6,231
Carrollton (D5)........ 17
Carson (C6)*........ 596
Carter Lake (B6)........1,183
Cartersville (G2)........ 25
Cascade (L4)*........1,299
Casey (D5)*........ 703
Castalia (K2)*........ 221
Castana (B4)*........ 265
Castle Hill (J3)........ 425
Cedar (H6)*........ 110
Cedar Bluff (L5)*........ 75
Cedar Falls (H3)*........14,344
Cedar Heights (H3)
Cedar Rapids (K5)*....72,296
Cedar Rapids (urban area)........77,990
Center Junction (L4)*... 153
Center Point (K4)*........ 987
Centerdale (L5)........ 34
Centerville (H7)*........7,625
Central City (K4)*........ 965
Central Heights ‡(G2)*. 766
Centralia (M4)........ 78
Chapin (G3)*........ 200
Chariton (G6)*........5,320
Charles City (H2)*........10,309
Charleston (K7)........ 30
Charlotte (M5)*........ 427
Charter Oak (C4)*........ 710
Chatsworth (A3)*........ 102
Chelsea (J5)*........ 482
Cherokee (B3)*........7,705
Chester (J2)*........ 226
Chester Center (H5)
Chillicothe (J6)*........ 196
Church (L2)........ 40
Churchville (F6)........ 25
Churdan (D4)*........ 593
Cincinnati (G7)*........ 703
Clare (E3)*........ 179
Clarence (M5)*........ 791
Clarinda (C7)*........5,086
Clarion (F3)*........3,150
Clarksville (H3)*........1,210
Clay Works (E4)........ 175
Clayton (L3)*........ 136
Clear Lake (G2)*........4,977
Clearfield (D7)*........ 547
Cleghorn (B3)*........ 246
Clemons (G4)*........ 202
Clermont (K3)*........ 625
Cleves (G4)*........ 50
Climbing Hill (B4)*........ 140
Clinton (N5)*........30,379
Clio (G7)*........ 162
Clive (F5)*........ 250
Clover Hills (F5)........ 408
Clutier (J4)*........ 302
Coal City (H7)
Coalville (E4)........ 350
Coburg (C7)*........ 83
Coggon (L4)*........ 604
Coin (C7)*........ 407
Colesburg (L3)*........ 326
Colfax (G5)*........2,279
College Springs (C7)*... 368
Collins (G5)*........ 432
Colo (G4)*........ 538
Columbia (G6)*........ 110
Columbus City (L6)*........ 319
Columbus Junction(L6)*1,123
Colwell (H2)*........ 122
Commerce (F5)........ 152
Conesville (L6)*........ 252
Confidence (G7)........ 65
Conover (K2)
Conrad (H4)*........ 649
Conroy (J5)*........ 200
Conway (D7)*........ 168
Coon Rapids (D5)*........1,676
Cooper (E5)*........ 99
Coppock (K6)*........ 81
Coralville (K5)........ 977
Cordova (G6)........ 15
Corley (C5)*........ 60
Cornell (C3)*
Corning (D7)*........2,104
Correctionville (B4)*........ 992
Corwith (F3)*........ 480
Corydon (G7)*........1,870
Cotter (L6)*........ 49
Coulter (G3)*........ 271
Council Bluffs (B6)*....45,429
Covington (K5)........ 82
Craig (A3)*........ 142
Cranston (L6)*
Crawfordsville (K6)*........ 286
Crescent (B6)*
Cresco (J2)*........3,638
Creston (E6)*........8,317
Cricket (H6)
Cromwell (E6)*........ 147
Croton (K7)........ 55
Crystal Lake (F2)*........ 286
Cumberland (D6)*........ 493
Cumming (F6)*........ 131
Curlew (D3)*........ 151
Cushing (B4)*........ 248
Cylinder (D2)*........ 143
Dakota City (E3)*........ 637
Dale (E5)........ 30
Dallas (G6)*........ 421
Dallas Center (E5)*........ 944
Dana (E4)*........ 184
Danbury (B4)*........ 601
Danville (L7)*........ 450
Davenport (M5)*........74,549
Davenport, Iowa — Rock Island, Ill.—Moline, Ill. (urban area)........193,733
Davis City (F7)*........ 432
Dawson (E5)*........ 286
Dayton (E4)*........ 793
De Soto (E5)*........ 274
De Witt (N5)*........2,644
Dean (H7)*........ 45
Decatur (F7)*........ 196
Decorah (K2)*........6,060
Dedham (D5)*........ 360
Deep River (J5)*........ 379
Defiance (C5)*........ 368
Delaware (L4)*........ 192
Delhi (L4)*........ 383
Delmar (M4)*........ 415
Deloit (C4)*........ 235
Delphos (E7)*........ 74
Delta (J6)*........ 562
Denison (C4)*........4,554
Denmark (L7)*........ 300
Denver (J3)*........ 635
Derby (G7)*........ 194
DES MOINES (F5)*....177,965
Des Moines (urban area)........198,892
Dewar (J3)*........ 150
Dexter (E5)*........ 643
Diagonal (E7)*........ 472
Dickens (C2)*........ 311
Dike (H4)*........ 517
Dinsdale (H4)*........ 80
Dixon (M5)*........ 208
Dolliver (D2)*........ 130
Donahue (M5)*........ 105
Donnan (K3)*........ 36
Donnellson (K7)*........ 589
Doon (A2)*........ 517
Dorchester (L2)*........ 120
Douds (K7)*........ 425
Dougherty (G3)*........ 212
Dow City (B5)*........ 524
Downey (L5)*........ 126
Dows (F3)*........ 948
Drakesville (J7)*........ 222
Dubuque (M3)*........49,671
Dudley (H6)........ 54
Dumont (H3)*........ 718
Dunbar (H5)*........ 80
Duncombe (E4)*........ 378
Dundee (L3)*........ 176
Dunkerton (J3)*........ 409
Dunlap (B5)*........1,409
Durango (M3)*........ 71
Durant (M5)*........1,075
Dyersville (L3)*........2,416
Dysart (J4)*........1,089
Eagle Grove (F3)*........4,176
Earlham (E6)*........ 771
Earling (C5)*........ 341
Earlville (L4)*........ 661
Early (C4)*........ 742
East Peru (F6)........ 204
East Pleasant Plain (K6)*
Eddyville (H6)*........ 941
Edgewood (L3)*........ 696
Edna (A2)*........ 80
Elberon (J4)*........ 225
Eldon (J7)*........1,457
Eldora (G4)*........3,107
Eldorado (K2)*........ 100
Eldridge (M5)*........ 376
Elgin (K3)*........ 642
Elk Horn (C5)*........ 566
Elkader (L3)*........1,584
Elkhart (F5)*........ 222
Elkport (L3)*........ 99
Elliott (C6)*........ 482
Ellston (E7)*........ 158
Ellsworth (F4)*........ 439
Elma (J2)*........ 731
Elvira (N5)........ 210
Elwood (M4)*........ 125
Ely (K5)*........ 155
Emerson (C6)*........ 556
Emmetsburg (D2)*........3,760
Epworth (M4)*........ 536
Essex (C7)*........ 763
Estherville (D2)*........6,719
Evansdale (J4)*........3,571
Everly (C2)*........ 547
Ewart (H5)........ 34
Exira (D5)*........1,129
Exline (H7)*........ 342
Fairbank (K3)*........ 653
Fairfax (K5)*........ 335
Fairfield (J6)*........7,299
Fairport (M6)........ 150
Farley (L4)*........ 745
Farlin (E4)*........ 85
Farmersburg (L3)*........ 263
Farmington (K7)*........ 899
Farnhamville (D4)*........ 399
Farragut (C7)*........ 495
Farrar (G5)*........ 64
Farson (J6)*........ 100
Faulkner (G3)*........ 50
Fayette (K3)*........1,469
Fenton (E2)*........ 446
Ferguson (H5)*........ 178
Fernald (G4)*........ 100
Fertile (G2)*........ 397
Festina (K2)*........ 160
Flagler (G6)........ 55
Floris (J7)*........ 215
Floyd (H2)*........ 440
Fonda (D3)*........1,120
Fontanelle (E6)*........ 812
Forest City (F2)*........2,766
Fort Atkinson (J2)*........ 273
Ft. Des Moines (F5)*
Ft. Dodge (E3)*........25,115
Ft. Madison (L7)*........14,954
Fostoria (C2)*........ 147
Franklin (L7)........ 146
Frankville (K2)........ 169
Fraser (E4)*........ 219
Fredericksburg (J3)*........ 701
Frederika (J3)*........ 210
Fredonia (L6)........ 133
Fredric (H6)........ 28
Fremont (H6)*........ 471
Froelich (L2)*........ 65
Fruitland (L6)*........ 150
Fulton (M4)
Galt (F3)*........ 117
Galva (C3)*........ 492
Garber (L3)*........ 153
Garden City (G4)*........ 150
Garden Grove (F7)*........ 417
Garnavillo (L3)*........ 581
Garner (F2)*........1,696
Garrison (J4)*........ 457
Garwin (H4)*........ 518
Gaza (B2)*........ 85
Geneva (G3)*........ 242
George (B2)*........1,210
Gerled (E2)*........ 41
Gibson (J6)*........ 101
Gifford (G4)*........ 118
Gilbert (F4)*........ 297
Gilbertville (J4)*........ 399
Gillett Grove (C2)*........ 150
Gilman (H5)*........ 508
Gilmore City (D3)*........ 746
Givin (H6)*........ 75
Gladbrook (H4)*........ 862
Gladwin (L6)........ 50
Glasgow (K7)........ 85
Glendon (E5)........ 44
Glenwood (B6)*........4,664
Glidden (D4)*........ 996
Goldfield (F3)*........ 665
Goodell (F3)*........ 242
Gooselake (N5)*........ 148
Gowrie (E4)*........1,052
Graettinger (D2)*........1,016
Graf (M3)*........ 44
Grafton (G2)*........ 278
Graham (L3)
Grand Junction (E4)*...1,036
Grand Mound (M5)*........ 526
Grand River (F7)*........ 350
Grandview (L6)*........ 311
Granger (F5)*........ 300
Granite (A2)........ 15
Grant (C6)*........ 237
Grant Center (A4)*
Granville (B3)*........ 350
Gravity (D7)*........ 369
Gray (D5)*........ 183
Greeley (L3)*........ 360
Green Island (N4)*........ 120
Green Mountain (H4)*........ 199
Greene (H3)*........1,347
Greenfield (D6)*........2,102
Greenville (C3)*........ 173
Grimes (F5)*........ 582
Grinnell (H5)*........6,828
Griswold (C6)*........1,149
Grundy Center (H4)*........2,135
Gruver (D2)*........ 135
Guernsey (J5)*........ 113
Guthrie Center (D5)*...2,042
Guttenberg (L3)*........1,912
Halbur (D4)*........ 235
Hale (L4)*........ 75
Hamburg (B7)*........2,086
Hamilton (H6)*........ 245
Hamlin (D5)*........ 200
Hampton (G3)*........4,432
Hancock (C6)*........ 264
Hanlontown (G2)*........ 257
Hansell (G3)*........ 190
Harcourt (E4)*........ 303
Hardy (E3)*........ 139
Harlan (C5)*........3,915
Harper (J6)*........ 182
Harpers Ferry (L2)*........ 252
Harris (C2)*........ 319
Hartford (G6)*........ 221
Hartley (C2)*........1,611
Hartwick (J5)*........ 107
Harvard (G7)*
Harvey (H6)*........ 346
Haskins (K6)*........ 65
Hastings (C6)*........ 308
Havelock (D3)*........ 307
Haven (H5)........ 50
Haverhill (H5)*
Hawarden (A2)*........2,625
Hawkeye (J3)*........ 511
Hayesville (J6)*........ 137
Hayfield (F2)*........ 200
Hazleton (K3)*........ 550
Hedrick (J6)*........ 733
Henderson (B6)*........ 208
Hepburn (C7)*........ 64
Herndon (E5)*........ 100
Herring (C4)*........ 15
Herrold (F5)........ 45
Hesper (K2)*
High (K5)*........ 130
Highland Center (J6)*.. 85
Highlandville (K2)*........ 57
Hills (K5)*........ 248
Hillsboro (K7)*........ 253
Hinton (A3)*........ 345
Hiteman (H6)*........ 250
Holbrook (K5)*........ 29
Holland (H4)*........ 221
Holmes (F3)*........ 65
Holstein (B4)*........1,336
Holy Cross (L3)........ 139
Homestead (K5)*........ 150
Honey Creek (B6)*........ 62
Hopeville (F7)
Hopkinton (L4)*........ 731
Hornick (A4)*........ 310
Horton (J3)........ 66
Hospers (B2)*........ 604
Houghton (K7)*
Hubbard (G4)*........ 836
Hudson (H4)*........ 613
Hull (A2)*........1,127
Humboldt (E3)*........3,219
Humeston (G7)*........ 750
Huntington (D2)*........ 39
Hurstville (M4)........ 83
Huxley (F5)*........ 422
Iconium (H7)........ 75
Ida Grove (B4)*........2,202
Imogene (C7)*........ 274
Independence (K4)*........4,865
Indianola (F6)*........5,145
Inwood (A2)*........ 644
Ionia (J2)*........ 301
Iowa City (L5)*........27,212
Iowa Falls (G3)*........4,900
Ira (G5)*........ 103
Ireton (A3)*........ 573
Irving (J5)........ 78
Irvington (E3)*........ 110
Irwin (C5)*........ 381
Jackson Junction (K2)* 107
Jamaica (E5)*........ 303
James (A3)........ 36
Jamison (F6)........ 40
Janesville (J3)*........ 445
Jefferson (E4)*........4,326
Jerome (G7)*........ 130
Jesup (J4)*........1,158
Jewell (F4)*........ 973
Johnston (F5)*........ 750
Joice (G2)*........ 244
Jolley (D4)*........ 195
Jordan (F4)*........ 50
Kalo (E4)........ 150
Kalona (K6)*........ 947
Kamrar (F4)*........ 261
Kanawha (F3)*........ 747
Kellerton (E7)*........ 483
Kelley (F5)*........ 244
Kellogg (H5)*........ 670
Kendallville (K2)
Kensett (G2)*........ 424
Kent (E7)*........ 169
Keokuk (L8)*........16,144
Keosauqua (J7)*........1,101
Keota (K6)*........1,145
Kesley (H3)*........ 125
Keswick (J6)*........ 276
Keystone (J5)*........ 438
Kiene (K4)........ 11
Kilbourn (K7)*........ 73
Killduff (H5)*........ 145
Kimballton (D5)*........ 428
Kingsley (A3)*........1,098
Kingston (L7)........ 150
Kinross (J6)*........ 105
Kirkman (C5)*........ 131
Kirkville (H6)*........ 213
Kiron (C4)*........ 255
Klemme (F3)*........ 555
Knierim (D4)*........ 133
Knoke (D3)*........ 49
Knowlton (E7)........ 60
Knoxville (G6)*........7,625
Koszta (J5)........ 45
La Moille (G4)*........ 151
La Motte (M4)*........ 280
La Porte City (J4)*......1,770
Lacona (G6)*........ 430
Ladora (J5)*........ 273
Lake City (D4)*........2,308
Lake Mills (F2)*........1,560
Lake Park (C2)*........ 924
Lake View (C4)*........1,158
Lakeside (C3)........ 219
Lakota (E2)*........ 443
Lamoni (F7)*........2,196
Lamont (K3)*........ 574
Lancaster (J6)........ 25
Lanesboro (D4)*........ 280
Langdon (C2)*........ 60
Langworthy (L4)*........ 64
Lansing (L2)*........1,536
Lanyon (E4)*........ 120
Larchwood (A2)*........ 415
Larrabee (B3)*........ 158
Latimer (G3)*........ 434
Laurel (H5)*........ 257
Laurens (D3)*........1,556
Lavinia (D4)*........ 65
Lawler (J2)*........ 539
Lawn Hill (G4)........ 40
Lawton (A4)*........ 254
Le Claire (N5)*........1,124
Le Grand (H5)*........ 393
Le Mars (A3)*........5,844
Le Roy (F7)*........ 91
Leando (J7)
Ledyard (E2)*........ 327
Lehigh (E4)*........ 881
Leighton (H6)*........ 118
Leland (F2)*........ 209
Lenox (D7)*........1,171
Leon (F7)*........2,139
Leslie (F7)........ 25
Lester (A2)*........ 217
Letts (L6)*........ 404
Lewis (C6)*........ 511
Liberty (F6)........ 56
Liberty Center (F6)*........ 110
Libertyville (K7)*........ 311
Lidderdale (D4)*........ 180
Lime Springs (J2)*........ 551
Linby (J6)........ 50
Lincoln (H4)*........ 194
Linden (E5)*........ 290
Lineville (G7)*........ 482
Linn Grove (C3)*........ 320
Linwood (M6)........ 100
Lisbon (L5)*........ 952
Liscomb (H4)*........ 278
Little Cedar (H2)*........ 80
Little Rock (B2)*........ 533
Little Sioux (B5)*........ 349
Littleport (L3)*........ 139
Littleton (K3)........ 75
Livermore (E3)*........ 615
Lockridge (K7)*........ 233
Logan (B5)*........1,550
Lohrville (D4)*........ 698
Lone Rock (E2)*........ 188
Lone Tree (L6)*........ 639
Long Grove (M5)*........ 156
Lorimor (E6)*........ 505
Lost Nation (M5)*........ 557
Loveland (B6)*........ 55
Lovilia (H6)*........ 619
Low Moor (N5)*........ 279
Lowden (M5)*........ 642
Lowell (L7)*........ 85
Luana (K2)*........ 220
Lucas (G6)*........ 420
Luther (F5)*........ 131
Luton (A4)*........ 154
Luverne (E3)*........ 553
Luxemburg (L3)*........ 120
Luzerne (J5)*........ 186
Lynnville (H5)*........ 406
Lytton (D4)*........ 373
Macedonia (C6)*........ 298
Macksburg (E6)*........ 220
Madrid (F5)*........1,829
Magnolia (B5)*........ 207
Malcom (H5)*........ 406
Mallard (D3)*........ 399
Maloy (E7)*........ 90
Malvern (B7)*........1,263
Manchester (L3)*........3,987
Manilla (C5)*........1,035
Manly (G2)*........1,473
Manning (C5)*........1,801
Manson (D3)*........1,622
Maple Hill (D2)*........ 60
Maple River (D4)*........ 120
Mapleton (B4)*........1,857
Maquoketa (M4)*........4,307
Marathon (C3)*........ 565
Marble Rock (H3)*........ 470
Marcus (B3)*........1,263
Marengo (J5)*........2,151
Marion (K4)*........5,916
Marne (C6)*........ 214
Marquette (L2)*........ 641
Marshalltown (G4)*....19,821
Martelle (L4)*........ 228
Martensdale (F6)*........ 161
Martinsburg (J6)*........ 219
Marysville (G6)........ 165
Mason City (G2)*........27,980
Masonville (K4)*........ 133
Massena (D6)*........ 459
Massillon (L5)*........ 90
Matlock (A2)*........ 104
Maurice (A3)*........ 256
Maxwell (G5)*........ 802
Maynard (K3)*........ 455
Maysville (M5)........ 70
Mc Callsburg (G4)*........ 290
Mc Causland (M5)*........ 150
Mc Clelland (B6)*........ 159
Mc Gregor (L2)*........1,138
Mc Intire (H2)*........ 300
Mc Paul (B7)*........ 35
Mechanicsville (L5)*........ 850
Mederville (K3)
Mediapolis (L6)*........ 834
Melbourne (G5)*........ 510
Melcher (G6)*........ 898
Melrose (G7)*........ 310
Meltonville (G2)*
Melvin (B2)*........ 325
Menlo (E5)*........ 421
Meriden (B3)*........ 164
Merrill (A3)*........ 605
Meservey (G3)*........ 297
Meyer (H2)
Middle (K5)*
Middletown (L7)*........ 229
Miles (N4)*........ 344
Milford (C2)*........1,375
Miller (F2)*........ 75
Millersburg (J5)*........ 200
Millerton (G7)*........ 140
Milo (G6)*........ 525
Milton (J7)*........ 719
Minburn (E5)*........ 353
Minden (C6)*........ 328
Mineola (B6)*........ 145
Mingo (G5)*........ 227
Missouri Valley (B5)*...3,546
Mitchell (H2)*........ 168
Mitchellville (G5)*........ 906
Modale (B5)*........ 283
Moingona (F4)........ 150
Mondamin (B5)*........ 489
Moneta (C2)*........ 89
Monmouth (M4)*........ 198
Monona (L2)*........1,346
Monroe (G5)*........1,108
Monteith (E5)*
Monterey (H7)........ 35
Montezuma (H5)*........1,460
Montgomery (C2)*........ 150
Monticello (L4)*........2,888
Montour (H5)*........ 380
Montpelier (M6)*........ 200
Montrose (L7)*........ 643
Mooar (L8)........ 235
Moorhead (B5)*........ 392
Moorland (E4)*........ 248
Moran (F5)........ 150
Moravia (H7)*........ 652
Morley (L4)*........ 157
Morning Sun (L6)*........ 939
Morrison (H4)*........ 169
Morse (L5)
Morton Mills (C6)........ 70
Moscow (L5)*........ 195
Moulton (H7)*........ 985
Mount Auburn (J4)*........ 216
Mt. Ayr (E7)*........1,793
Mt. Etna (D6)*........ 90
Mt. Hamill (K7)*........ 44
Mt. Pleasant (L7)*........5,843
Mt. Sterling (J7)*........ 144
Mt. Union (L6)*........ 167
Mt. Vernon (K5)*........2,320
Mt. Zion (K7)*........ 50
Moville (A4)*........ 964
Murray (F6)*........ 767
Muscatine (L6)*........19,041
Mystic (H7)*........1,233
Nashua (J3)*........1,609
Nemaha (C3)*........ 184
Neola (B6)*........ 839
Nevada (G5)*........3,763
Nevinville (D6)*........ 75
New Albin (L2)*........ 568
New Boston (L7)*........ 116
New Hampton (J2)*........3,323
New Hartford (H3)*........ 584
New Liberty (M5)*........ 126
New London (L7)*........1,510
New Market (D7)*........ 573
New Providence (G4)*.. 212
New Sharon (H6)*........1,089
New Vienna (L3)*........ 204
New Virginia (F6)*........ 342
Newbern (G6)........ 24
Newburg (H5)*........ 105
Newell (D3)*........ 884
Newhall (K5)*........ 366
Newton (H5)*........11,723
Nichols (L6)*........ 348
Noble (K6)........ 34
Nodaway (D7)*........ 233
Nora Springs (H2)*........1,257
North Buena Vista (L3)* 148
N. English (J5)*........ 853
N. Liberty (K5)*........ 309
N. Washington (J2)*........ 159
Northboro (C7)*........ 167
Northwood (G2)*........1,767
Norwalk (F6)*........ 435
Norway (K5)*........ 441
Numa (G7)*........ 248
Oakdale (K5)*........ 650
Oakland (C6)*........1,296
Oakland Mills (K7)........ 37
Oakley (G6)........ 25
Oakville (L6)*........ 360
Oasis (L5)........ 27
Ocheyedan (B2)*........ 700
Odebolt (C4)*........1,279
Oelwein (K3)*........7,859
Ogden (E4)*........1,486
Okoboji (C2)*........ 336
Old Town ‡(C2)........ 40
Olds (K6)*........ 187
Olin (L5)*........ 626
Ollie (J6)*........ 298
Onawa (A4)*........3,498
Oneida (L3)*........ 75
Onslow (M4)*........ 244
Ontario (F4)*........ 140
Oran (J3)*........ 110
Orange City (A2)*........2,166
Orchard (H2)*........ 114
Orient (E6)*........ 427
Orillia (F6)........ 25
Orleans (C2)*........ 317
Orson (B5)*........ 21
Osage (H2)*........3,436
Osceola (F6)*........3,422
Osgood (D2)*........ 50
Oskaloosa (H6)*........11,124

Ossian (K2)* 804
Osterdock (L3)* 51
Otho (E4)* 403
Otley (G6)* 177
Oto (B4)* 302
Otranto (H2)* 75
Otterville (K3)
Ottosen (E3)* 127
Ottumwa (J6)* 33,631
Owasa (G4)* 100
Oxford (K5)* 543
Oxford Junction (M4)* 663
Oxford Mills (L5) 103
Oyens (A3)* 95
Pacific Junction (B6)* 550
Packwood (J6)* 211
Page (C7) 9
Palmer (D3)* 296
Palo (K4)* 285
Panama (B5)* 230
Panora (E5)* 1,062
Paris (K4) 75
Parkersburg (H3)* 1,300
Parnell (J5)* 206
Paton (E4)* 404
Patterson (F6)* 133
Paullina (B3)* 1,289
Payne (B7)* 14
Pekin (J6) 75
Pella (H6)* 4,427
Peoria (H6) 150
Peosta (M4)* 60
Percival (B7)* 250
Percy (G6)*
Perkins (A2) 50
Perlee (K6) 22
Perry (E5)* 6,174
Pershing (G6)* 300
Persia (B5)* 373
Peru (F6)* 250
Peterson (C3)* 589
Pierson (B3)* 453
Pilot Grove (L7)* 50
Pilot Mound (F4)* 246
Pioneer (E3)* 83
Pisgah (B5)* 327
Plain View (M5) 42
Plainfield (J3)* 387
Plano (G7)* 106
Pleasant Plain (K6)* 148
Pleasant Valley (N5)* 500
Pleasanton (F7)* 130
Pleasantville (G6)* 893
Plover (D3)* 243
Plymouth (G2)* 395
Pocahontas (D3)* 1,949
Polk City (F5)* 336
Pomeroy (D3)* 868
Popejoy (G3)* 201
Portsmouth (C5)* 299
Postville (K2)* 1,343
Powersville (H3) 25
Prairie City (G5)* 834
Prairieburg (L4)* 210
Prescott (D6)* 372
Preston (N4)* 684
Primghar (B2)* 1,152
Primrose (K7)* 65
Princeton (N5)* 495
Prole (F6)*
Promise City (G7)* 218
Protivin (J2)* 283
Pulaski (J7)* 381
Purdy (G6)
Quarry (H4) 204
Quasqueton (K4)* 374
Quimby (B3)* 398
Quincy (D6)
Radcliffe (G4)* 638
Rake (F2)* 351
Ralston (D4)* 166
Randalia (K3)* 132
Randall (F4)* 202
Randolph (B7)* 295
Rathbun (H7)* 229
Raymond (J4)* 260
Read (L3)
Readlyn (J3)* 468
Reasnor (G5)* 227
Red Oak (C6)* 6,526
Redding (E7)* 200
Redfield (E5)* 892
Reinbeck (H4)* 1,460
Rembrandt (C3)* 296
Remsen (B3)* 1,280
Renwick (E3)* 474
Rhodes (G5)* 369
Riceville (H2)* 962
Richards (D4)* 48
Richland (K6)* 591
Richmond (K6)* 140
Rickardsville (M3) 75
Ricketts (B4)* 166
Ridgeway (K2)* 307
Rinard (D4)* 115
Ringsted (D2)* 578
Rippey (E5)* 354
River Junction (L5) 36
River Sioux (B5)* 135
Riverside (K6)* 631
Riverton (B7)* 472
Robertson (G3) 30
Robins (K4)* 272
Robinson (K4) 50
Rochester (L5) 67
Rock Falls (G2)* 139
Rock Rapids (A2)* 2,640
Rock Valley (A2)* 1,581
Rockdale (M4) 132
Rockford (H2)* 979
Rockwell (G3)* 753
Rockwell City (D4)* 2,333
Rodman (D2)* 123
Rodney (A4)* 127
Roland (F4)* 687
Rolfe (D3)* 997
Rome (K7)* 134
Roscoe (L6) 2
Rose Hill (J6)* 243
Roselle (D5) 82
Ross (D5) 50
Rossie (C2)* 112
Rossville (L2)
Rowan (F3)* 304
Rowley (K4)* 249
Royal (C2)* 495
Rubio (K6)* 70
Rudd (H2)* 398
Runnells (G5)* 307
Russell (G7)* 566
Ruthven (D2)* 868
Rutland (E3)* 225
Ryan (K4)* 362
Sabula (N4)* 888
Sac City (C4)* 3,170
Sageville (M3) 118
Saint Ansgar (H2)* 981
St. Anthony (G4)* 175
St. Benedict (E2)* 135
St. Charles (F6)* 319
St. Donatus (M4)* 100
St. Lucas (K2)* 158
St. Marys (F6)* 89
St. Olaf (L3)* 158
St. Paul (L7) 113
Salem (K7)* 473
Salina (K6) 50
Salix (A4)* 337
Sanborn (B2)* 1,337
Sand Springs (L4) 50
Sandyville (G6) 92
Saratoga (J2)* 85
Saylor (F5) 100
Scarville (F2)* 105
Schaller (C4)* 841
Schleswig (B4)* 751
Scotch Grove (L4)* 55
Scranton (D4)* 891
Searsboro (H5)* 183
Sedan (H7) 80
Selma (J7)* 175
Seney (A3) 82
Sergeant Bluff (A4)* 569
Sewal (G7)* 100
Sexton (E2)*
Seymour (G7)* 1,223
Shambaugh (D7)* 251
Shannon City (E7)* 171
Sharpsburg (D7)* 147
Sheffield (G3)* 1,163
Shelby (C5)* 592
Sheldahl (F5)* 211
Sheldon (B2)* 4,001
Shell Rock (H3)* 1,013
Shellsburg (K4)* 632
Shenandoah (C7)* 6,938
Sherrill (M3) 162
Sherwood (D4) 21
Shueyville (K5) 75
Sibley (B2)* 2,559
Sidney (B7)* 1,132
Sigourney (J6)* 2,343
Silver City (B6)* 311
Sioux Center (A2)* 1,860
Sioux City (A3)* 83,991
Sioux City (urban area) 90,144
Sioux Rapids (C3)* 1,010
Slater (F5)* 583
Sloan (A4)* 654
Smithland (B4)* 373
Soldier (B5)* 323
Solon (L5)* 527
Somers (E4)* 217
South Amana (J5)* 185
S. English (J6)* 248
Spechts Ferry (M3) 10
Spencer (C2)* 7,446
Sperry (L7)* 65
Spillville (J2)* 363
Spirit Lake (D2)* 2,467
Spragueville (N4)* 115
Spring Hill (F6)* 86
Springbrook (N4)* 109
Springdale (L5) 72
Springville (L4)* 680
Stacyville (H2)* 544
Stanhope (F4)* 420
Stanley (K3)* 158
Stanton (C7)* 570
Stanwood (L5)* 547
Stanzel (E6)* 25
State Center (G5)* 1,040
Steamboat Rock (G4)* 395
Stennett (C6) 28
Stiles (J7) 50
Stockport (K7)* 346
Stockton (M5)* 165
Stone City (L4)* 200
Storm Lake (C3)* 6,954
Story City (F4)* 1,545
Stout (H3)* 135
Strahan (B7)* 100
Stratford (F4)* 673
Strawberry Point (K3)* 1,247
Struble (A3)* 91
Stuart (E6)* 1,500
Sully (H5)* 452
Sulphur Springs (C3)* 90
Summerset (F6)
Summitville (K8) 86
Sumner (J3)* 1,911
Sunbury (M5)* 100
Superior (D2)* 240
Sutherland (B3)* 835
Swaledale (G3)* 205
Swan (G6)* 194
Swea City (E2)* 869
Swedesburg (L6)* 104
Swisher (K5)* 205
Tabor (B7)* 869
Taintor (H6)* 78
Talleyrand (J6) 24
Talmage (E6) 44
Tama (H5)* 2,930
Tara (E4) 70
Teeds Grove (N4)*
Templeton (D5)* 385
Tennant (C5)* 95
Terril (C2)* 425
Thayer (E6)* 152
The Inn (C2)
Thompson (F2)* 698
Thor (E3)* 271
Thornburg (J6)* 138
Thornton (G3)* 441
Thurman (B7)* 284
Ticonic (B4) 35
Tiffin (K5)* 256
Tingley (E7)* 333
Tipton (L5)* 2,633
Titonka (E2)* 589
Toddville (K4)* 200
Toeterville (H2)* 75
Toledo (H4)* 2,106
Toronto (M5)* 165
Tracy (H6)*
Traer (J4)* 1,627
Trenton (K6) 104
Treynor (B6)* 247
Tripoli (J3)* 1,124
Troy (J7)* 103
Troy Mills (K4)*
Truax (H6) 60
Truesdale (C3)* 158
Truro (F6)* 354
Turin (B4)* 160
Turkey River (L3) 9
Udell (H7)* 96
Ulmer (D4)*
Underwood (B6)* 278
Union (G4)* 490
Unionville (H7)* 204
University Heights (K5) 446
University Park (H6)* 457
Urbana (K4)* 414
Urbandale (F5)* 1,777
Ute (B4)* 563
Vail (C4)* 532
Valeria (G5)* 57
Van Cleve (G5) 25
Van Horne (J4)* 511
Van Meter (E5)* 364
Van Wert (F7)* 318
Vandalia (G5) 55
Varina (D3)* 144
Ventura (F2)* 300
Victor (J5)* 741
Villisca (C7)* 1,838
Vincennes (K7)* 72
Vincent (E3)* 193
Vining (J5)* 112
Vinton (J4)* 4,307
Viola (L4)*
Volga (L3)* 423
Voorhies (J4)* 56
Wadena (K3)* 316
Wahpeton ‡(C2) 127
Walcott (M5)* 480
Walford (K5)* 165
Walker (K4)* 549
Wall Lake (C4)* 753
Wallingford (D2)* 229
Walnut (C6)* 888
Wapello (L6)* 1,755
Ware (D3)*
Washburn (J4)* 132
Washington (K6)* 5,902
Washta (B3)* 403
Waterloo (J4)* 65,198
Waterloo (urban area) 83,551
Waterville (L2)* 199
Watkins (J5)* 130
Waubeek (K4)* 120
Waucoma (J2)* 385
Waukee (F5)* 501
Waukon (L2)* 3,158
Waukon Junction (L2)* 40
Waupeton (M3)* 11
Waverly (J3)* 5,124
Wayland (K6)* 600
Webb (D3)* 235
Webster (J6)* 136
Webster City (F4)* 7,611
Weldon (F7)* 229
Wellman (K6)* 1,071
Wellsburg (H4)* 744
Welton (M5)* 93
Wesley (E2)* 509
West (J5)*
West Bend (D3)* 772
W. Branch (L5)* 769
W. Burlington (L7)* 1,614
W. Chester (K6)* 218
W. Des Moines (F5)* 5,615
W. Grove (J7)* 90
W. Liberty (L5)* 1,866
W. Mitchell (H2) 112
W. Okoboji (C2) 158
W. Point (K7)* 662
W. Union (K3)* 2,141
Western College (K5)
Westfield (A3)* 172
Westgate (K3)* 226
Weston (B6) 75
Westphalia (C5)* 160
Westside (C4)* 393
Wever (L7)* 100
What Cheer (J6)* 1,119
Wheatland (M5)* 568
Whiting (A4)* 663
Whittemore (E2)* 678
Whitten (H4)* 174
Whittier (K4)* 134
Wick (F6)* 58
Willey (D5) 94
Williams (F3)* 519
Williamsburg (J5)* 1,183
Williamson (G6)* 294
Wilton Junction (M5)* 1,446
Winfield (L6)* 888
Windsor Heights (F5) 1,414
Winterset (E6)* 3,570
Winthrop (K4)* 604
Wiota (D6)* 227
Woden (F2)* 272
Woodbine (B5)* 1,304
Woodburn (F7)* 255
Woodland (F7)
Woodward (F5)* 908
Woolstock (F3)* 255
Worthington (L4)* 337
Wright (J6)* 125
Wyman (L6)* 100
Wyoming (L4)* 724
Yale (E5)* 293
Yarmouth (L6)* 160
Yetter (D4)* 121
Yorkshire (B5)
Yorktown (C7)* 146
Zearing (G4)* 514
Zook Spur (F5) 20
Zwingle (M4)* 132

Map on Page 61

KANSAS

Total Population 1,905,299

105 COUNTIES

Allen (G4) 18,187
Anderson (G3) 10,267
Atchison (G2) 21,496
Barber (D4) 8,521
Barton (D3) 29,909
Bourbon (H4) 19,153
Brown (G2) 14,651
Butler (F4) 31,001
Chase (F3) 4,831
Chautauqua (F4) 7,376
Cherokee (H4) 25,144
Cheyenne (A2) 5,668
Clark (C4) 3,946
Clay (E2) 11,697
Cloud (E2) 16,104
Coffey (G3) 10,408
Comanche (C4) 3,888
Cowley (F4) 36,905
Crawford (H4) 40,231
Decatur (B2) 6,185
Dickinson (E3) 21,190
Doniphan (G2) 10,499
Douglas (G3) 34,086
Edwards (C4) 5,936
Elk (F4) 6,679
Ellis (C3) 19,043
Ellsworth (D3) 8,465
Finney (B3) 15,092
Ford (C4) 19,670
Franklin (G3) 19,928
Geary (F3) 21,671
Gove (B3) 4,447
Graham (C2) 5,020
Grant (A4) 4,638
Gray (B4) 4,894
Greeley (A3) 2,010
Greenwood (F4) 13,574
Hamilton (A3) 3,696
Harper (D4) 10,263
Harvey (E3) 21,698
Haskell (B4) 2,606
Hodgeman (C3) 3,310
Jackson (G2) 11,098
Jefferson (G2) 11,084
Jewell (D2) 9,698
Johnson (H3) 62,783
Kearny (A3) 3,492
Kingman (D4) 10,324
Kiowa (C4) 4,743
Labette (G4) 29,285
Lane (B3) 2,808
Leavenworth (G2) 42,361
Lincoln (D2) 6,643
Linn (H3) 10,053
Logan (A3) 4,206
Lyon (F3) 26,576
Marion (E3) 16,307
Marshall (F2) 17,927
Mc Pherson (E3) 23,670
Meade (B4) 5,710
Miami (H3) 19,698
Mitchell (D2) 10,320
Montgomery (G4) 46,487
Morris (F3) 8,485
Morton (A4) 2,610
Nemaha (F2) 14,341
Neosho (G4) 20,348
Ness (C3) 6,322
Norton (C2) 8,808
Osage (G3) 12,811
Osborne (D2) 8,558
Ottawa (E2) 7,265
Pawnee (C3) 11,041
Phillips (C2) 9,273
Pottawatomie (F2) 12,344
Pratt (D4) 12,156
Rawlins (A2) 5,728
Reno (D4) 54,058
Republic (E2) 11,478
Rice (D3) 15,635
Riley (F2) 33,405
Rooks (C2) 9,043
Rush (C3) 7,231
Russell (D3) 13,406
Saline (E3) 33,409
Scott (B3) 4,921
Sedgwick (E4) 222,290
Seward (B4) 9,972
Shawnee (G2) 105,418
Sheridan (B2) 4,607
Sherman (A2) 7,373
Smith (D2) 8,846
Stafford (D3) 8,816
Stanton (A4) 2,263
Stevens (A4) 4,516
Sumner (E4) 23,646
Thomas (A2) 7,572
Trego (C3) 5,868
Wabaunsee (F3) 7,212
Wallace (A3) 2,508
Washington (E2) 12,977
Wichita (A3) 2,640
Wilson (G4) 14,815
Woodson (G4) 6,711
Wyandotte (H2) 165,318

CITIES and TOWNS

Abbyville (D4)* 99
Abilene (E3)* 5,775
Achilles (B2)* 18
Acres (C4)* 2
Ada (E2)* 175
Adams (E4)* 45
Admire (F3)* 184
Aetna (D4) 40
Agenda (E2)* 159
Agra (C2)* 354
Agricola (G3)* 30
Alamota (B3)* 39
Albert (C3)* 218
Alden (D3)* 286
Alexander (C3)* 188
Aliceville (G3)* 100
Alida (F2) 81
Alki (F3) 10
Allen (F3)* 241
Alma (F2)* 716
Almena (C2)* 616
Alta Vista (F3)* 420
Altamont (G4)* 652
Alton (D2)* 317
Altoona (G4)* 582
America City (F2) 10
Americus (F3)* 339
Ames (E2)* 67
Amiot (G3)*
Amy (B3)* 35
Andale (E4)* 316
Andover (E4)* 250
Angola (G4)* 50
Anness (E4)* 11
Anson (E4)* 50
Antelope (F3)* 45
Anthony (D4)* 2,792
Antonino (C3)* 75
Arcadia (H4)* 572
Argonia (E4)* 562
Arkansas City (E4)* 12,903
Arlington (D4)* 405
Arma (H4)* 1,334
Arnold (B3)* 108
Arrington (G2)* 50
Ash Grove (D2) 55
Ash Valley (C3)
Asherville (D2)* 105
Ashland (C4)* 1,493
Ashton (E4)* 45
Assaria (E3)* 221
Atchison (G2)* 12,792
Athol (D2)* 203
Atlanta (F4)* 309
Attica (D4)* 622
Atwood (B2)* 1,613
Auburn (G3)* 110
Augusta (F4)* 4,483
Aulne (E3)* 182
Aurora (E2)* 221
Axtell (F2)* 510
Baileyville (F2)* 150
Bala (F2)* 50
Baldwin City (G3)* 1,741
Bancroft (G2) 26
Barclay (G3)* 47
Barker (H2) 735
Barnard (D2)* 250
Barnes (F2)* 308
Bartlett (G4)* 143
Basehor (G2)* 275
Bassett (G4) 117
Bavaria (E3)* 50
Baxter Springs (H4)* 4,647
Bazaar (F3) 64
Bazine (C3)* 456
Beagle (G3)* 156
Beardsley (A2)* 35
Beattie (F2)* 321
Beaumont (F4)* 150
Beaver (D3)* 118
Beeler (B3)* 100
Bellaire (D2)* 55
Belle Plaine (E4)* 971
Bellefont (C4)* 35
Belleville (E2)* 2,858
Belmont (D4)* 48
Beloit (D2)* 4,035
Belpre (C4)* 231
Belvidere (C4)* 52
Belvue (F2)* 193
Bendena (G2)* 94
Benedict (G4)* 176
Bennington (E2)* 325
Bentley (E4)* 200
Benton (E4)* 269
Bern (F2)* 216
Berryton (G3)* 213
Berwick (G2) 14
Beverly (E2)* 255
Big Bow (A4)* 100
Bigelow (F2)* 170
Bird City (A2)* 784
Bison (C3)* 326
Black Wolf (D3)* 23
Blaine (F2)* 45
Blair (H2)* 100
Blakeman (A2)* 10
Block (H3) 21
Bloom (C4)* 125
Bloomington (D2)* 50
Blue Mound (H3)* 424
Blue Rapids (F2)* 1,430
Bluff City (E4)* 172
Bogue (C2)* 211
Boicourt (H3)* 30
Bonner Springs (H2)* 2,277
Bradford (F3) 25
Brantford (E2) 23
Brazilton (H4)* 75
Bremen (F2)* 80
Brenham (C4) 21
Brewster (A2)* 467
Bridgeport (E3)* 53
Bronson (H4)* 415
Brookville (E3)* 213
Broughton (E2)* 96
Brownell (C3)* 211
Buckeye (E2) 15
Bucklin (C4)* 824
Bucyrus (H3) 131
Buffalo (G4)* 437
Buffville (G4) 50
Buhler (E3)* 750
Bunker Hill (D3)* 271
Burden (F4)* 541
Burdett (C3)* 355
Burdick (F3)* 110
Burlingame (G3)* 1,065
Burlington (G3)* 2,304
Burns (F3)* 294
Burr Oak (D2)* 505
Burrton (E3)* 749
Burt (G4) 35
Busby (F4) 42
Bush City (G3)* 65
Bushong (F3)* 93
Bushton (D3)* 532
Byers (D4)* 83
Cairo (D4) 40
Caldwell (E4)* 2,000
Calista (D4)* 12
Calvert (C2)* 22
Cambridge (F4)* 221
Canada (E3)* 38
Caney (G4)* 2,876
Canton (E3)* 771
Carbondale (G3)* 453
Carlton (E3)* 76
Carlyle (G4)* 45
Carneiro (D3)* 55
Carona (H4)* 175
Cassoday (F3)* 150
Castleton (E4)* 64
Catharine (C3)* 218
Cawker City (D2)* 691
Cedar (D2)* 86
Cedar Bluffs (B2)* 45
Cedar Point (F3)* 107
Cedar Vale (F4)* 1,010
Centerview (C4)* 30
Centerville (H3)* 155
Centralia (F2)* 574
Chanute (G4)* 10,109
Chapman (E3)* 990
Chardon (A2)
Charleston (B4) 12
Chase (D3)* 961
Chautauqua (F4)* 215
Cheney (E4)* 777
Cherokee (H4)* 849
Cherryvale (G4)* 2,952
Chetopa (G4)* 1,671
Chicopee (H4) 250
Chiles (H3) 20
Cimarron (B4)* 1,189
Circleville (G2)* 169
Claflin (D3)* 921
Claudell (C2)* 25
Clay Center (E2)* 4,528
Clayton (B2)* 157
Clearwater (E4)* 647
Cleburne (F2)* 150
Clements (F3)* 75
Clifton (E2)* 743
Climax (F4)* 91
Clonmel (E4) 25
Cloverdale (F4)
Clyde (E2)* 1,067
Coats (D4)* 255
Codell (C2)* 100
Coffeyville (G4)* 17,113
Colby (A2)* 3,859
Coldwater (C4)* 1,208
Collano (B4) 25
Collyer (B2)* 282
Colony (G3)* 387
Columbus (H4)* 3,490
Colwich (E4)* 339
Como (E2) 17
Concordia (E2)* 7,175
Conway (E3)* 101
Conway Springs (E4)* 816
Coolidge (A3)* 168
Copeland (B4)* 242
Corbin (E4)* 100
Corinth (D2) 3
Corning (F2)* 254
Corwin (D4)* 60
Cottonwood Falls (F3)* 957
Council Grove (F3)* 2,722
Courtland (E2)* 367
Covert (D2)* 75
Coyville (G4)* 106
Crawford (E3)* 50
Crestline (H4)* 150
Crisfield (D4)* 11
Croft (D4)* 6
Crystalsprings (D4)* 73
Cuba (E2)* 345
Cullison (D4)* 174
Culver (E3)* 153
Cummings (G2)* 52
Cunningham (D4)* 510
Damar (C2)* 305
Danville (E4)* 122
Day (E2) 6
De Graff (F4) 30
De Soto (H3)* 518
Dearing (G4)* 261
Deerfield (A4)* 440
Delavan (F3)* 75
Delia (G2)* 164
Dellvale (B2)* 12
Delphos (E2)* 676
Denison (G2)* 166
Denmark (D2)* 50
Dennis (G4)* 200
Densmore (C2)* 61
Denton (G2)* 157
Derby (E4)* 432
Detroit (E3)* 124
Devon (H4)* 124
Dexter (F4)* 354
Dighton (B3)* 1,246
Dillon (E3) 35
Dillwyn (D4) 10
Dispatch (D2) 17
Dodge City (B4)* 11,262
Doniphan (G2) 50
Dorrance (D3)* 365
Douglass (F4)* 729
Dover (G3)* 50
Downs (D2)* 1,221
Dresden (B2)* 162
Dubuque (D3) 12
Duluth (F2)* 70
Dundee (D3)
Dunlap (F3)* 134
Duquoin (D4)* 15
Durham (E3)* 229
Dwight (F3)* 281
Earlton (G4)* 141
Eastborough (E4) 708
Easton (G2)* 255
Edgerton (H3)* 266
Edmond (C2)* 110
Edna (G4)* 422
Edson (A2)* 70
Edwardsville ‡(H2)* 274
Effingham (G2)* 525
El Dorado (F4)* 11,037
Elbing (E3)* 98
Elgin (F4)* 212
Elk City (G4)* 524
Elk Falls (F4)* 276
Elkader (B3) 5
Elkhart (A4)* 1,132
Ellinwood (D3)* 2,569
Ellis (C3)* 2,649
Ellsworth (D3)* 2,193
Elmdale (F3)* 180
Elmo (E3)* 50
Elmont (G2)* 65
Elsmore (G4)* 152
Elwood (H2)* 1,020
Elyria (E3)* 65
Emmett (F2)* 143
Emporia (F3)* 15,669
Englevale (H4)* 150
Englewood (C4)* 341
Enosdale (E2) 11
Ensign (B4)* 227
Enterprise (E3)* 795
Erie (G4)* 1,296
Esbon (D2)* 278
Eskridge (F3)* 601
Eudora (G3)* 929
Eureka (F4)* 3,958
Everest (G2)* 368
Fact (E2) 15
Fairport (C2)* 35
Fairview (G2)* 336
Fairway ‡(H2) 1,816
Fall River (G4)* 261
Falun (E3)* 92
Farlington (H4)* 96
Farlinville (H3) 15
Faulkner (H4) 36
Fellsburg (C4)* 43
Feterita (A4) 10
Florence (E3)* 1,009
Flush (F2) 304
Fontana (H3)* 168
Ford (C4)* 244
Formoso (D2)* 271
Fort Dodge (C4)* 500
Ft. Leavenworth (H2)*
Ft. Riley (F2)* 2,531
Ft. Scott (H4)* 10,335
Fostoria (F2)* 100
Fowler (B4)* 778
Frankfort (F2)* 1,237
Franklin (H4)* 600
Frederick (D3)* 53
Fredonia (G4)* 3,257
Freeport (E4)* 30
Friend (B3)* 44
Frontenac (H4)* 1,569
Fulton (H4)* 243
Furley (E4)* 75
Galatia (D3)* 89
Galena (H4)* 4,029
Galesburg (G4)* 189
Galva (E3)* 426
Garden City (B4)* 10,905
Garden Plain (E4)* 323
Gardner (H3)* 676
Garfield (C3)* 297
Garfield Center (E2)
Garland (H4)* 280

KENTUCKY

Map on Page 62

Total Population 2,944,806

120 COUNTIES

Lincoln (H6)...........18,668
Livingston (D2)...........7,184
Logan (D7)...........22,335
Lyon (E5)...........6,853
Madison (J5)...........31,179
Magoffin (L5)...........13,839
Marion (G5)...........17,212
Marshall (D3)...........13,387
Martin (M5)...........11,677
Mason (K3)...........18,486
McCracken (D3)...........49,137
McCreary (J7)...........16,660
McLean (C5)...........10,021
Meade (E5)...........9,422
Menifee (K5)...........4,798
Mercer (H5)...........14,643
Metcalfe (F7)...........9,851
Monroe (F7)...........13,770
Montgomery (K4)...........13,025
Morgan (L5)...........13,624
Muhlenberg (C6)...........32,501
Nelson (F5)...........19,521
Nicholas (J4)...........7,532
Ohio (D6)...........20,840
Oldham (G4)...........11,018
Owen (H3)...........9,755
Owsley (K6)...........7,324
Pendleton (J3)...........9,610
Perry (L6)...........46,566
Pike (N6)...........81,154
Powell (K5)...........6,812
Pulaski (H6)...........38,452
Robertson (J3)...........2,881
Rockcastle (J6)...........13,925
Rowan (L4)...........12,708
Russell (G7)...........13,717
Scott (H4)...........15,141
Shelby (G4)...........17,912
Simpson (D7)...........11,678
Spencer (G4)...........6,157
Taylor (G6)...........14,403
Todd (C7)...........12,890
Trigg (E3)...........9,683
Trimble (G3)...........5,148
Union (E2)...........14,893
Warren (E6)...........42,758
Washington (G5)...........12,777
Wayne (H7)...........16,475
Webster (E2)...........15,555
Whitley (J7)...........31,940
Wolfe (K5)...........7,615
Woodford (H4)...........11,212

CITIES and TOWNS

Aberdeen (D6)*........... 50
Adair (D5)*........... 100
Adairville (D7)*........... 800
Adams (M4)*........... 300
Adolphus (E7)*........... 500
Aflex (N5)*........... 250
Akersville (F7)*........... 152
Albany (G7)*...........1,920
Alcalde (J6)*...........
Alcorn (K5)*........... 100
Alexandria (J3)*........... 536
Allais (L6)*........... 600
Allegre (C7)*........... 125
Allen (M5)*........... 421
Allen Springs (E7)*...........
Allensville (C7)*........... 337
Allock (L6)*........... 608
Almo (D3)*........... 150
Alpha (G7)*........... 75
Alpine (H7)*........... 150
Alton Station (H4)*........... 75
Altro (L6)*........... 75
Alva (L7)*...........1,341
Alvaton (E7)*........... 250
Amburgey (M6)*...........
Ammie (K6)*...........
Anchorage (F4)*........... 883
Anco (L6)*........... 400
Anna (E6)*...........
Anneta (E6)*........... 100
Annville (K6)*........... 350
Ansel (H6)*........... 195
Arabia (H6)*........... 229
Arjay (K7)*...........1,000
Arlington (C3)*........... 584
Artemus (K7)*...........1,000
Arvel (K5)*...........
Ashbyburg (C5)*...........
Ashcamp (N6)*...........
Ashland (M4)*...........31,131
Ashland, Ky.—Huntington, W. Va. (urban area) 156,136
Athertonville (F5)*........... 166
Auburn (D7)*........... 994
Audubon Park (F4)...........1,790
Augusta (J3)*...........1,599
Austin (F7)*........... 150
Auxier (M5)*...........1,000
Avenstoke (H4)........... 125
Bagdad (G4)*........... 400
Baizetown (D6)*........... 127
Bakerton (G7)*...........
Balkan (K7)*...........
Bandana (C2)*........... 300
Bangor (L4)*........... 155
Banner (M5)*...........
Barbourville (K7)*...........2,926
Bardstown (G5)*...........4,154
Bardstown Jct. (F5)*. 75
Bardwell (C3)*...........1,033
Barlow (C3)*........... 657
Barnrock (M5)*...........
Barretts Ferry (D5)*.... 10
Barterville (J4)*........... 100
Baskett (B5)*........... 275
Battletown (E4)*........... 125
Bayou (D2)........... 125
Bays (L5)*...........
Beals (C5)*........... 150
Beattyville (K5)*...........1,042
Beauty (N5)*........... 577
Beaver Dam (D6)*...........1,349
Bedford (G3)*........... 533
Bee Spring (E6)*...........
Beech Creek (C6)*...........
Beech Grove (C5)*........... 162
Belcher (N6)*...........
Belfry (N5)*...........1,315
Bell Farm (H7)*...........
Bellevue (L1)*...........9,040
Belmont (F5)*........... 75
Belton (D6)*...........
Benham (M7)*...........3,982
Benton (D3)*...........1,980
Berea (J5)*...........3,372
Bernstadt (J6)*........... 300
Berry (J3)*........... 312
Berrys Lick (D6)*........... 50
Bertis (K4)*........... 97
Bethel (K4)*........... 225
Bethelridge (H6)*........... 190
Bethlehem (G4)*........... 188
Betsy Layne (M5)*...........1,500
Beverly (L7)*........... 500
Bevier (C6)*........... 175
Big Branch (M6)*...........
Big Clifty (E5)*........... 500
Big Creek (K6)*........... 560
Big Rock (L6)*........... 430
Big Spring (E5)*........... 250
Billows (J6)........... 50
Birdsville (D2)*........... 113
Black Rock (E6)*........... 25
Blackey (M6)*........... 393
Blackford (B6)*........... 165
Blacks Ferry (G7)*...........
Blaine (M4)*...........
Blairs Mills (L4)*...........
Blanche (K7)*........... 455
Blandville (C3)*........... 124
Bloomfield (G5)*........... 666
Blue Diamond (L6)*...........1,968
Bluestone (L4)*........... 60
Boaz (D3)*........... 100
Boldman (M5)*........... 300
Bolyn (M6)*........... 150
Bond (J6)*...........
Bondville (H5)*........... 91
Bonnieville (F6)*........... 300
Bonnyman (L6)*........... 900
Boone (J5)*........... 137
Booneville (K6)*........... 165
Boreing (J6)*........... 250
Boston (F5)*........... 300
Botto (K6)*........... 60
Bowen (K5)*........... 150
Bowling Green (D7)*...18,347
Boyd (J3)*........... 55
Bradford (J3)*........... 45
Bradfordsville (G6)*........... 450
Brandenburg (E4)*........... 755
Brazil (J5)*...........
Breeding (G7)*........... 100
Bremen (C6)*........... 410
Brent (L2)...........
Brewers (D3)*........... 57
Brightshade (K7)*........... 200
Bristow (E6)* 73
Brodhead (J6)*........... 808
Bromley (K1)*........... 980
Bronston (H7)*........... 300
Brooklyn (D6)*........... 50
Brooks (F4)*........... 150
Brookside (L7)*........... 600
Brooksville (J3)*........... 622
Browder (D6)*........... 350
Brownsville (E6)*........... 447
Bruin (L4)*........... 125
Brushart (L3)*........... 50
Bryan (G7)*........... 137
Bryantsville (H5)*........... 126
Buchanan (M4)*........... 160
Buckner (G4)*........... 250
Buechel (F4)*...........1,500
Buffalo (F6)*........... 495
Buford (D5)........... 100
Bulan (L6)*...........1,446
Bunch (J6)*...........
Burgin (H5)*........... 777
Burkesville (G7)*...........1,278
Burkley (C3)*........... 340
Burlington (J2)*........... 400
Burna (D2)*........... 300
Burning Springs (K6)*.. 350
Burnside (H6)*........... 615
Burton (Bypro*) ‡(M6) 257
Burtonville (L4)*........... 200
Bush (K6)*........... 200
Buskirk (L5)*...........
Busseyville (M4)*........... 100
Butler (J3)*........... 404
Cadiz (B7)*...........1,280
Cains Store (H6)*...........
Calhoun (C5)*........... 746
California (J3)*........... 117
Calvary (G6)........... 250
Calvert City (D3)*........... 900
Calvin (K7)*...........
Camp Dix (L3)*........... 75
Camp Taylor (F4)*...........
Campbellsburg (G3)*.... 361
Campbellsville (G6)*.....3,477
Campton (K5)*........... 431
Canada (N5)*...........1,500
Cane Valley (G6)*........... 150
Caney (L5)*........... 400
Caneyville (E6)*........... 377
Canmer (F6)*...........
Cannel City (L5)*........... 400
Canton (B7)*........... 250
Carbon Glow (M6)*........... 300
Carlisle (J4)*...........1,524
Carntown (J3)........... 100
Carpenter (K7)*...........
Carrollton (G3)*........... 226
Carrsville (D2)*........... 205
Carter (L4)*........... 84
Cartwright (G7)*........... 110
Casey Creek (G6)*........... 117
Caseyville (B5)*........... 73
Cash (F6)*........... 75
Catlettsburg (M4)*...........4,750
Cave City (F6)*...........1,119
Cawood (L7)*...........1,232
Cayce (C4)*........... 200
Cecilia (F5)*........... 400
Center (F6)*........... 175
Centertown (C6)*........... 370
Central City (C6)*...........4,110
Cerulean (B7)*........... 218
Chance (G7)*........... 350
Chaplin (G5)*........... 200
Chappell (L7)*...........

Charley (M5)*...........
Charters (L3)*........... 20
Chavies (L6)*........... 300
Chenoa (K7)*...........
Cherokee (M4)*...........
Chevrolet (L7)*........... 500
Chilesburg (J4)*........... 50
Christianburg (G4)*........... 100
Clark Hill (L4)*........... 400
Clarkson (E6)*........... 489
Claxton (B6)*........... 72
Clay (B6)*...........1,291
Clay City (K5)*........... 636
Claymour (C7)........... 150
Claypool (E7)*........... 50
Clearfield (L4)*...........
Cleaton (C6)*........... 450
Clermont (F5)*........... 40
Cliff (M5)*........... 500
Clifford (N4)*........... 50
Clifty (C7)*........... 200
Climax (J6)*........... 75
Clinton (C3)*...........1,593
Clintonville (J4)*........... 100
Closplint (L7)*........... 600
Clover Bottom (J5)*........... 600
Cloverport (D5)*...........1,357
Co-Operative (H7)*........... 400
Coakley (F6)*........... 150
Cobb (B6)*........... 200
Cold Spring (L2)*........... 518
Coleman (N6)*........... 200
Colesburg (F5)*........... 73
College Hill (J5)*........... 400
Collista (M5)*........... 175
Colmar (K7)*........... 500
Colson (M6)*........... 200
Columbia (G6)*...........2,167
Columbus (C3)*........... 482
Combs (L6)*........... 800
Concord (L3)*........... 142
Concordia (D4)*........... 75
Confluence (L6)*........... 285
Constance (J1)*........... 150
Conway (J6)*........... 75
Cooper (H7)*........... 275
Coopersville (H7)*........... 250
Coral Ridge (F4)*...........3,010
Corbin (J7)*...........7,744
Corinth (H3)*........... 283
Cork (F6)*........... 83
Cornishville (H5)*........... 230
Corydon (B5)*........... 742
Cottle (L5)*...........
Cottonburg (J5)*........... 122
Covington (K1)*...........64,452
Cowan (K4)*........... 200
Cowcreek (K6)*........... 250
Coxton (L7)*........... 700
Crab Orchard (H6)*........... 757
Crailhope (F6)*........... 50
Crane Nest (K7)*........... 200
Crayne (A6)*........... 300
Creal (F6)*........... 30
Creekville (L6)*........... 67
Creelsboro (G7)*........... 50
Crescent Springs (K1)...
Creston (G6)*........... 25
Crestwood (G4)*........... 450
Crider (B6)*........... 125
Crittenden (H3)*........... 287
Crofton (C6)*........... 500
Cromwell (D6)*........... 200
Cropper (G4)*........... 175
Crummies (L7)*........... 400
Crutchfield (C4)*........... 170
Cub Run (E6)*........... 250
Cubage (K7)*........... 325
Cumberland (M6)*...........4,249
Cundiff (G7)*........... 125
Cunningham (C3)*........... 275
Curdsville (C5)*........... 169
Custer (E5)*........... 200
Cutshin (L6)*...........
Cynthiana (J4)*...........4,847
Dabney (H6)*...........
Daisy (L6)*........... 300
Dalton (B6)*........... 75
Daniel Boone (C6)...........
Danville (H5)*...........8,686
David (M5)*........... 800
Dawson Springs (B6)*..2,374
Daysville (C7)........... 50
Dayton (L1)*...........8,977
De Coursey (L2)...........
De Mossville (J3)*........... 104
Decoy (L5)*........... 250
Defoe (G4)*........... 142
Dekoven (B5)*...........
Delaware (C5)*........... 28
Delphia (L6)*........... 395
Denton (M4)*........... 200
Depoy (C6)*...........
Dewitt (K7)*........... 250
Dexter (D3)*........... 277
Dixon (B5)*........... 624
Donansburg (F6)*........... 200
Donerail (J4)*........... 91
Dorton (M6)*........... 500
Dover (K3)*........... 334
Drakesboro (D6)*...........1,102
Dreyfus (J5)*........... 150
Dry Ridge (H3)*........... 640
Dublin (C3)........... 100
Duckers (H4)*........... 50
Duncan (H5)........... 125
Dundee (D5)*........... 150
Dunham (M6)*...........1,200
Dunmor (C6)*........... 156
Dunnville (H6)*........... 140
Dwale (M5)*........... 495
Dycusburg (E3)*........... 147
Dyer (E5)*........... 39
Eadsville (H7)........... 300
Eagle Station (G3)*........... 35
Earlington (B6)*...........2,753
East Bernstadt (J6)*.... 900
East Point (M5)*........... 200
Eby (L4)*........... 50
Echols (D6)*........... 50
Eddyville (B6)*...........1,840
Edmonton (F7)*........... 519
Edo (N6)*........... 200
Edsel (M4)*........... 50
Eighty Eight (F7)*........... 75
Ekron (E5)*........... 188
Elamton (L5)*...........
Eli (H6)*........... 250
Elias (K6)*...........
Elihu (H6)*...........
Elizabethtown (F5)*.....5,807
Elizaville (K4)*........... 150
Elk Creek (G4)........... 90
Elk Horn (G6)*...........
Elkatawa (K5)*........... 250
Elkfork (L5)*...........
Elkhorn City (Praise*) (N6) 1,349
Elkton (C7)*...........1,312
Elliottville (L4)*........... 100
Elmrock (L6)*........... 276
Elrod (J6)*........... 75
Elsmere (K2)...........3,483
Elva (D3)*........... 95
Eminence (G4)*...........1,462
Emlyn (J7)*........... 700
Emma (M5)*........... 600
English (G3)*........... 150
Ennis (D6)*........... 612
Eolia (M6)*........... 100
Erlanger (K2)*...........3,694
Essie (L6)*...........
Estill (M6)*...........
Etoile (F7)*........... 40
Etty (M6)*........... 200
Eubank (H6)*........... 322
Evarts (L7)*...........1,937
Evelyn (K5)*...........
Ewing (K4)*........... 400
Ezel (L5)*...........
Fagan (K5)*........... 50
Fairfield ‡(G5)*........... 202
Fairplay (G7)*........... 78
Fairview (C7)*...........
Falcon (L5)*........... 300
Falls of Rough (D5)*.... 195
Fallsburg (M4)*........... 200
Falmouth (J3)*...........2,186
Fancy Farm (C3)*........... 419
Fariston (J6)*........... 290
Farler (L6)*........... 200
Farmers (L4)*...........
Farmington (D4)*........... 221
Faubush (H6)*........... 300
Fedscreek (N6)*...........
Felty (K6)*........... 200
Ferguson (D7)........... 50
Ferguson (H6)*........... 550
Field (K7)*........... 300
Finchville (G4)*........... 75
Finley (G6)*........... 105
Finney (E7)*........... 75
Firebrick (L3)*........... 150
Fishtrap (N6)*...........1,000
Fitchburg (K5)*........... 200
Flat (K5)*........... 200
Flat Fork (L5)*...........
Flat Lick (K7)*...........1,000
Flat Rock (H7)*...........
Flatgap (M5)*........... 130
Fleming (M6)*........... 943
Flemingsburg (K4)*...........1,502
Flint (M6)*........... 100
Flippin (F7)*........... 150
Florence (J2)*...........1,325
Fonde (K7)*...........1,300
Fonthill (H6)*........... 50
Ford (J5)*........... 250
Fordsville (D5)*........... 533
Forks of Elkhorn (H4)* 400
Fort Knox (F5)*...........10,000
Fort Mitchell (K1)........... 312
Fort Thomas (L1)*...........10,870
Fort Wright ‡(K2)........... 594
Foster (J3)*........... 108
Fountain Run (F7)*........... 218
Francisville (J1)........... 25
FRANKFORT (H4)*....11,916
Franklin (D7)*...........4,343
Fredonia (B6)*........... 395
Freeburn (N5)*...........2,200
Freedom (F7)*........... 75
Frenchburk (K5)*........... 268
Frew (L6)*........... 162
Frogue (G7)*........... 300
Fry (G6)*........... 50
Frymire (E5)*........... 25
Fullerton (L3)*...........1,501
Fulton (C4)*...........3,224
Furnace (K5)*........... 75
Gabbard (K6)...........
Gallup (M4)*...........
Gamaliel (F7)*........... 500
Gapcreek (H7)*........... 300
Garfield (E5)*........... 150
Garlin (G6)*........... 75
Garrett (M6)*...........
Garrison (L3)*........... 300
Gatliff (K7)*........... 500
Gatton (F6)*........... 101
Gausdale (J7)*...........
Geneva (B5)*........... 195
Georges Creek (M5)*.... 300
Georgetown (H4)*...........5,516
Germantown (K3)*........... 260
Gesling (L4)*........... 100
Gest (H4)*........... 47
Ghent (G3)*........... 368
Gilbertsville (D3)*........... 700
Gimlet (L4)*........... 100
Girdler (K7)*........... 500
Glasgow (E6)*...........7,025
Glen Dean (E5)*........... 100
Glen Springs (K3)*........... 50
Glencoe (H3)*........... 500
Glendale (F5)*........... 300
Glens Fork (G6)*........... 213
Glenwood (M4)...........
Glo (M6)*........... 500
Glomawr (L6)*........... 800
Golden Pond (B7)*........... 125
Goodloe (M5)*...........
Gooserock (K6)*...........
Goshen (F4)*........... 100
Gracey (B7)*...........
Gradyville (G6)*........... 200
Graham (C6)*...........1,100
Grahn (L4)*........... 600
Grand Rivers (E3)*........... 234
Grange City (K4)*........... 225
Grant (H3)*........... 100
Grassland (E6)*........... 79
Gratz (H4)*........... 150
Gravel Switch (G5)*........... 200
Gray (K7)*........... 300
Gray Hawk (J6)*........... 300
Graysbranch (M3)*........... 156
Grayson (M4)*...........1,383
Green Hall (K6)*........... 120
Greenmount (J6)*........... 119
Greensburg (F6)*...........1,032
Greenup (M3)*...........1,276
Greenville (C6)*...........2,661
Greenwood (J7)*........... 100
Grove Center (B5)*........... 200
Guage (L5)*........... 50
Gulnare (M5)*........... 150
Gus (D6)*...........
Guston (E5)*........... 108
Guthrie (C7)*...........1,253
Guy (D6)*...........
Haddix (L6)*........... 500
Hadensville (C7)........... 85
Hadley (D6)*........... 675
Haldeman (L4)*...........
Haleys Mill (C6)*...........
Halfway (E7)*........... 200
Hall (M6)*...........
Hamilton (H3)........... 25
Hamlin (E4)*........... 20
Hammond (K7)*........... 400
Hampton (D2)*........... 120
Hanson (C6)*........... 393
Happy (L6)*........... 800
Hardburly (L6)*........... 800
Hardin (D3)*........... 324
Hardin Springs (E5)*.... 112
Hardinsburg (D5)*........... 902
Hardshell (L6)*........... 50
Hardy (N5)*...........
Hardyville (F6)*........... 300
Harlan (L7)*...........4,786
Harned (E5)*........... 140
Harold (M5)*........... 500
Harrods Creek (F4)*...........
Harrodsburg (H5)*...........5,262
Hartford (D6)*...........1,564
Harveyton (L6)*........... 368
Hatcher (G6)*...........
Hatfield (N5)*........... 250
Hawesville (D5)*...........925
Hazard (L6)*...........6,985
Hazel (D4)*........... 444
Hazel Green (K5)*........... 264
Hazle Patch (J6)*...........
Head of Grassy (L4)*.... 50
Hebbardsville (C5)*........... 238
Hebron (J1)*........... 250
Heidelberg (K5)*...........
Heidrick (K7)*........... 600
Heisey (N5)........... 150
Helechawa (L5)*........... 120
Hellier (N6)*........... 346
Helton (L7)*...........
Henderson (B5)*...........16,837
Hendricks (L5)*...........
Henshaw (B5)*........... 210
Herndon (C7)*........... 250
Hesler (H4)...........
Hi Hat (M6)*........... 650
Hibernia (G6)*........... 100
Hickman (C4)*...........2,037
Hickory (D3)*........... 185
High Bridge (H5)*........... 350
Highland Heights (L1)..1,569
Highsplint (L7)*...........1,500
Highway (G7)*........... 100
Hillsboro (K4)*........... 141
Hima (K6)*........... 200
Himlerville (Beauty*) (N5) 577
Himyar (K7)*........... 400
Hindman (M6)*........... 521
Hinton (J4)*........... 125
Hiram (L7)*........... 300
Hiseville (F6)*...........
Hitchins (M4)*...........1,000
Hodgenville (F5)*...........1,695
Holland (E7)*........... 120
Homer (D7)*........... 58
Hope (K4)*...........
Hopewell (M4)*........... 158
Hopkinsville (B7)*...........12,526
Horse Branch (D6)*........... 225
Horse Cave (F6)*...........1,545
Horton (D6)*........... 30
Howardstown (F5)*........... 100
Howel (B7)*........... 50
Huddy (N5)*...........
Hudson (E5)*........... 133
Huntersville (G7)*........... 193
Huntsville (D6)*........... 140
Hustonville (H6)*........... 435
Hyden (L6)*........... 647
Ilsley (B6)*........... 400
Independence (H3)*........... 285
Indian Hills ‡(F4)........... 291
Inez (N5)*........... 622
Irad (M4)*...........
Irvine (K5)*...........3,259
Irvington (E5)*........... 831
Island (C6)*........... 566
Isonville (L4)*........... 150
Iuka (D3)*........... 21
Ivel (M5)*...........1,200
Ivis (M6)*...........
Ivyton (L5)*........... 300
Jackson (L5)*...........1,978
Jamestown (G7)*...........1,064
Jason (K6)*........... 250
Jeff (L6)*...........1,500
Jeffersontown (G4)*.....1,246
Jeffersonville (K5)*........... 479
Jellicocreek (J7)*...........
Jenkins (M6)*...........6,921
Jericho (G4)*........... 110
Jeriel (M4)*........... 175
Jett (H4)*........... 240
Jetts Creek (K6)*........... 75
Johnetta (J6)*........... 100
Jonesville (H3)*........... 158
Joy (D2)*........... 70
Junction City (H5)*........... 988
Kayjay (K7)*........... 350
Keaton (L5)*...........
Keavy (J6)*...........
Keene (H5)*........... 500
Kehoe (L4)*........... 175
Kelly (C7)........... 90
Keltner (F6)*...........
Kemp (F6)*...........
Kenton (J3)*........... 165
Kenvir (L7)*...........3,250
Kevil (C3)*........... 202
King (K7)........... 50
Kings Mountain (H6)*.. 350
Kingsley ‡(F4)........... 488
Kingswood (E5)*........... 225
Kirk (D5)*........... 75
Kirkmansville (C6)*........... 138
Kirksey (D3)*........... 182
Kirksville (J5)*...........1,500
Kite (M6)*...........
Kitts (L7)*...........1,431
Knifley (G6)*........... 225
Knob Lick (F6)*...........
Knottsville (D5)........... 250
Kona (M6)*........... 400
Kosmosdale (E4)*........... 375
Krypton (L6)*........... 88
Kuttawa (E3)*........... 794
Kyrock (E6)*...........
La Center (C3)*........... 593
La Fayette (B7)*........... 246
La Grange (G4)*...........1,558
Lackey ‡(M6)*........... 452
Lair (J4)........... 65
Lake (K6)*........... 250
Lakeside (K2)........... 988
Lamasco (B7)*........... 100
Lambric (L5)*........... 75
Lancaster (H5)*...........2,402
Latonia (K2)...........
Laurel Creek (K6)*........... 300
Lawrenceburg (H4)*...........2,369
Lawton (L4)*........... 375
Lebanon (G5)*...........4,640
Lebanon Junction(F5)*.1,243
Lecta (F6)*........... 50
Lee (E6)*........... 25
Lee City (L5)*........... 120
Leeco (K5)*........... 200
Leighton (K5)*........... 500
Leitchfield (E6)*...........1,312
Lejunior (L7)*...........
Leon (M4)*........... 125
Levee (K5)*...........
Level Green (J6)*........... 75
Lewisburg (C6)*........... 496
Lewisport (D5)*........... 656
Lexington (J4)*...........55,534
Liberty (H6)*...........1,291
Lida (K6)*........... 200
Liggett (L7)*........... 450
Ligon (M6)*........... 396
Lily (J6)*...........
Limaburg (J2)........... 45
Linton (E3)........... 200
Linwood (F6)*...........
Lisman (B6)*........... 175
Littcarr (M6)*...........
Livermore (C5)*...........1,441
Livia (C5)*........... 75
Livingston (J6)*........... 378
Lockport (H4)*...........
Locust Branch (J5)*........... 300
Locust Hill (E5)*........... 50
Logansport (D6)*........... 125
Lola (D2)*........... 150
London (J6)*...........3,426
Loneoak (D3)...........1,250
Lookout (N6)*...........1,300
Lookout Heights (K1)... 603
Loretto (G5)*........... 600
Lost Creek (L6)*........... 250
Lothair (L6)*...........1,313
Louellen (L7)*...........1,600
Louisa (M4)*...........2,015
Louisville (F4)*...........369,129
Louisville (urban area) 470,394
Lovelaceville (C3)*........... 275
Lovely (N5)*........... 500
Lowes (C3)*........... 150
Lomansville (M5)*........... 500
Loyall (L7)*...........1,548
Lucas (F7)*........... 150
Lucile (L4)........... 75
Ludlow (K1)*...........6,374
Lynch (M7)*...........3,970
Lynn Grove (D4)*........... 75
Lynnville (D4)*........... 100
Lyons (F5)*...........
Mac (G6)*...........
Maceo (D5)*........... 350
Mackville (G5)*........... 250
Macon (E6)*...........
Madisonville (B6)*...........11,132
Majestic (N5)*...........1,140
Malone (L5)*........... 260
Maloneton (M3)*........... 100
Manchester (K6)*...........1,706
Manitou (B6)*........... 100
Mannington (C6)*........... 300
Mannsville (G6)*........... 200
Mariba (K5)*........... 75
Marion (A6)*...........2,375
Marrowbone (F7)*........... 250
Marshes Siding (H7)*... 500

LOUISIANA

Map on Page 63

Total Population 2,683,516

Warnerton (K5)*
Washington (G5)* 1,291
Water Proof (H3)* 1,180
Watson (L1)* 400
Waverly (H2)*
Waxia (G5)* 567
Weeks (G7)* 1,499
Weiss (L1)
Welcome (L3)* 300
Weldon (E1) 35
Welsh (E6)* 2,416
West Monroe (F1)* 10,302
Westlake (D6)* 1,871
Westwego (O4)* 8,281
Weyanoke (H5)*
White Castle (J3)* 1,839
White Sulphur Springs (F3) 50
Whitehall (M2)* 450
Whiteville (F5)*
Wilda (E4)*
Wildsville (G3)*
Willetts (G3)* 12
Wills Point (L7)
Wilmer (K5)* 75
Wilson (H5)* 375
Winnfield (E3)* 5,629
Winnsboro (G2)* 3,655
Wisner (G3)* 738
Woodland (J5)*
Woodlawn (E6) 210
Woodside (G5)*
Woodworth (E4)* 392
Wright (F6)* 36
Wyatt (E2)* 40
Yellow Pine (D2) 90
Youngsville (G6)* 769
Zachary (K1)* 1,542
Zenoria (F3)* 100
Zimmerman (E4)* 500
Zwolle (C3)* 1,555

Map on Page 64

MAINE

Total Population 913,774

16 COUNTIES

Androscoggin (C7) 83,594
Aroostook (F2) 96,039
Cumberland (C8) 169,201
Franklin (B5) 20,682
Hancock (G6) 32,105
Kennebec (D7) 83,881
Knox (E7) 28,121
Lincoln (D7) 18,004
Oxford (B6) 44,221
Penobscot (F5) 108,198
Piscataquis (E4) 18,617
Sagadahoc (D7) 20,911
Somerset (C4) 39,785
Waldo (E6) 21,687
Washington (H6) 35,187
York (B9) 93,541

CITIES and TOWNS

Abbot Village (E5)* ▲462
Acton (B8)* ▲473
Addison (H6)* ▲846
Albion (E6)* ▲992
Alexander (H5) ▲282
Alfred (B9)* ▲1,112
Allagash (F1) ▲680
Allens Mills (C6) 175
Alna (D7)* ▲350
Alton (F5) ▲314
Amherst (G6)* ▲151
Andover (B6)* ▲756
Anson (D6)* ▲2,199
Appleton (E7)* ▲671
Argyle (F5) ▲133
Ashdale (D8) 60
Ashland (G2)* ▲2,370
Ashville (G7)* 100
Athens (D6)* ▲725
Atkinson (E5) ▲400
Atlantic (G7)*
Auburn (C7)* 23,134
AUGUSTA (D7)* 20,913
Aurora (G6)* ▲91
Ayers (J6)*
Bailey Island (D8)* 175
Bancroft (H4)* ▲165
Bangor (F6)* 31,558
Bar Harbor (G7)* ▲3,864
Bar Mills (C8)* 800
Baring (J5)* ▲157
Bath (D8)* 10,644
Bay Point (D8)
Bayside (F7)*
Beals (H7)* ▲590
Beddington (H6) ▲26
Belfast (F7)* 5,960
Belgrade (D7)* ▲1,099
Belgrade Lakes (D6)* 450
Belmont (E7) ▲258
Bemis (B6)
Benedicta (G4)* ▲225
Benton (D6)* ▲1,421
Berry Mills (C6) 100
Berwick (B9)* ▲2,166
Bethel (B7)* ▲2,367
Biddeford (C9)* 20,836
Biddeford Pool (C9)*
Bingham (D5)* ▲1,354
Birch Harbor (H7)*
Birches (B6)
Blaine (H2)* ▲1,118
Blanchard (D5)* ▲75
Blue Hill (F7)* ▲1,308
Bolsters Mills (B7)* 115
Boothbay (D8)* ▲1,559
Boothbay Harbor (D8)* ▲2,290
Boundary (H3) 100
Bowdoinham (D7)* ▲1,039
Bowerbank (E5)* ▲20
Boyd Lake (F5)
Bradford (F5)* ▲793
Bradford Center (F5)* 150
Bradley (F6)* ▲786
Bremen (E8) ▲409
Brewer (F6)* 6,862
Bridgewater (H3)* ▲1,279
Bridgton (B7)* ▲2,950
Brighton (D5)* ▲106
Bristol (E8)* ▲1,476
Brooklin (F7)* ▲546
Brooks (E6)* ▲747
Brooksville (F7)* ▲751
Brookton (H4)* ▲206
Brownfield (B8)* ▲612
Brownville (E5)* ▲1,964
Brownville Jct. (E5)* 1,086
Brunswick (C8)* ▲10,996
Bryant Pond (B7)* 500
Buckfield (C7)* ▲899
Bucks Harbor (J6)* 160
Bucksport (F6)* ▲3,120
Burkettville (E7)* 100
Burlington (G5)* ▲425
Burnham (E6)* ▲706
Buxton (C8) ▲2,009
Buxton Center (B8)
Byron (B6) ▲96
Calais (J5)* 4,589
Cambridge (E5)* ▲326
Camden (F7)* ▲3,670
Canaan (D6)* ▲785
Canton (C7)* ▲746
Cape Neddick (B9)*
Cape Porpoise (C9)* 400
Capens (D4) 1
Caratunk (C5)* ▲96
Cardville (F5)* 200
Caribou (G2)* ▲9,923
Carmel (E6)* ▲996
Carrabassett (C5) 10
Carroll (G5)* ▲288
Carry Pond (C5)
Carthage (C6) ▲339
Cary (H4) ▲278
Casco (B7)* ▲881
Castine (F7)* ▲793
Cedar (J5)
Center Belmont (E7)
Center Lovell (B7)*
Center Montville (E7) 175
Centerville (H6)* ▲63
Chapman (G2) ▲381
Charleston (F5)* ▲771
Charlotte (J5) ▲252
Chebeague Island (C8)* 300
Chelsea (D7) ▲2,169
Cherryfield (H6)* ▲904
Chester (F5) ▲256
Chesterville (C6) ▲588
Chesuncook (D3)* 18
China (E7)* ▲1,375
Chisholm (C7)* 1,135
Citypoint (E7)
Clark Island (E8)* 175
Clarks Mill (B8)
Clayton Lake (E2)* 6
Cleveland (G1) 200
Cliff Island (C8)*
Clifton (G6) ▲193
Clinton (D6)* ▲1,623
Columbia (H6) ▲352
Columbia Falls (H6)* ▲550
Cooper (H6) ▲128
Coopers Mills (E7)* 239
Corea (H7)* 156
Corinna (E6)* ▲1,752
Cornish (B8)* ▲795
Cornville (D6) ▲563
Costigan (F5)* 158
Cranberry Isles (G7)* ▲228
Crawford (H5)* ▲83
Crescent Lake (C7)*
Criehaven (F8)* 60
Crouseville (G2)* 400
Crystal (G4) ▲373
Cumberland Ctr. (C8)* ▲2,030
Cumberland Mills (C8)*
Cundys Harbor (D8)* 80
Curtis Corner (C7)*
Cushing (E7) ▲376
Cutler (J6)* ▲483
Daigle (G1)
Damariscotta (E7)* ▲1,113
Danforth (H4)* ▲1,174
Danville (C7)*
Darkharbor (F7)*
Davidson (F4) 45
Dayton (B8) ▲502
Deblois (H6)* ▲59
Dedham (F6) ▲374
Deer Isle (F7)* ▲1,234
Denmark (B8)* ▲447
Dennistown (C4) ▲24
Dennysville (J6)* ▲345
Derby (E5)* 500
Detroit (E6)* ▲492
Dexter (E5)* ▲4,126
Dixfield (C6)* ▲2,022
Dixmont (E6)* ▲631
Dorman (H6)
Dover-Foxcroft (E5)* ▲4,218
Dover South Mills (E5)
Dresden Mills (D7)* 100
Dry Mills (C8)* 220
Dryden (C6)* 800
Dyer Brook (G3) ▲219
Eagle Lake (F1)* ▲1,516
East Andover (B6)* 150
E. Baldwin (B8)*
E. Blue Hill (G7)* 200
E. Boothbay (D8)* 500
E. Brownfield (B8)* 130
E. Corinth (F5)* 450
E. Dixfield (C6)* 242
E. Dixmont (E6)
E. Dover (E5)* 67
E. Eddington (F6)* 300
E. Franklin (G6)* 78
E. Hampden (F6)
E. Hiram (B8)* 350
E. Holden (F6)*
E. Jackson (E6)
E. Knox (E7)
E. Lebanon (B9)*
E. Limington (B8) 150
E. Livermore (C7)* 500
E. Lowell (G5)
E. Machias (J6)* ▲1,101
E. Madison (D6) 692
E. Millinocket (F4)* ▲1,358
E. New Portland (D6)* 43
E. Orland (F6)*
E. Otisfield (B7) 50
E. Parsonfield (B8)* 175
E. Peru (C7)
E. Pittston (D7) 1,050
E. Poland (C7)* 490
E. Sebago (B8)*
E. Stoneham (B7)* 300
E. Sullivan (G6)* 250
E. Sumner (C7)* 114
E. Union (E7)* 190
E. Vassalboro (D7)* 200
E. Waterboro (B8)* 175
E. Waterford (B7)* 175
E. Wilton (C6)* 450
E. Winn (G5) 75
Easton (H2)* ▲1,664
Eastport (K6)* 3,123
Eaton (H4)* 120
Eddington (F6) ▲664
Edgecomb (D8)* ▲447
Edmunds (J6) ▲288
Eliot (B9)* ▲2,509
Ellsworth (F6)* 3,936
Ellsworth Falls (G6)* 500
Elms (B9)
Emery Mills (B9)* 150
Enfield (F5)* ▲1,196
Etna (E6)* ▲458
Eustis (B5)* ▲763
Exeter (E6)* ▲734
Fairbanks (C6) 200
Fairfield (D6)* ▲5,811
Fairfield Center (D6) 150
Falmouth (C8) ▲4,342
Farmington (C6)* ▲4,677
Farmington Falls (D6)*
Fayette (C7)* ▲397
Five Islands (D8)* 200
Forest City (H4)* 27
Forest Station (H4)* 30
Fort Fairfield (H2)* ▲5,791
Fort Kent (F1)* ▲5,343
Fort Kent Mills (F1)* 175
Fortunes Rocks (C9) 82
Frankfort (F6)* ▲578
Franklin (G6)* ▲709
Freedom (E7)* ▲466
Freeport (C8)* ▲3,280
Frenchboro (G7)* 104
Frenchville (G1)* ▲1,528
Friendship (E7)* ▲772
Frye (B6)* 150
Fryeburg (A7)* ▲1,926
Gardiner (D7)* 6,649
Garland (E5)* ▲581
Georgetown (D8)* ▲510
Gerard (C5) 20
Gilbertville (C7) 100
Gilead (B7)* ▲140
Glen Cove (E7)* 200
Glenburn (F6) ▲694
Goodrich (H2)
Goodwins Mills (B8) 200
Goose Rocks Beach (C9) 135
Gorham (C8)* ▲4,742
Gouldsboro (H7)* 1,168
Grand Isle (G1)* ▲1,230
Grand Lake Stream (H5)* ▲294
Grants (B5)* 9
Gray (C8)* ▲1,631
Great Pond (G6) 40
Great Works (F6)*
Green Lake (F6)* 40
Greene (C7)* ▲974
Greenville (D5)* ▲1,889
Greenville Jct. (D5)* 780
Grindstone (F4)* 60
Grove (J5)* 125
Guerette (G1)
Guilford (E5)* ▲1,842
Haines Landing (B6)
Hale (B6) 60
Hallowell (D7)* 3,404
Hamlin (H1) ▲430
Hampden (F6)* ▲3,608
Hampden Highlands (F6)*
Hancock (G6)* ▲755
Hanover (B7)* ▲211
Harmony (D6)* ▲709
Harpswell Center (D8) 100
Harrington (H6)* ▲853
Harrison (B7)* ▲1,026
Hartford (C7) ▲381
Hartland (D6)* ▲1,310
Haynesville (G4)* ▲185
Hebron (C7)* ▲829
Hermon (F6) 1,728
Highland Lake (C8)
Highpine (B9)* 125
Hinckley (D6)* 250
Hiram (B8)* ▲804
Hodgdon (H3)* ▲1,162
Holeb (C4)* 54
Hollis Center (B8)* 230
Hope (E7)* ▲504
Houghton (B6)
Houlton (H3)* ▲8,377
Howland (F5)* ▲1,441
Hudson (F5)* ▲455
Hulls Cove (G7)* 450
Indian River (H6)
Intervale (C8)* 45
Island Falls (G3)* ▲1,237
Isle au Haut (F7)* ▲82
Islesboro (F7)* ▲529
Islesford (G7)* 150
Jackman (C4)* ▲964
Jackman Station (C4)* 980
Jacksonville (J6)* 300
Jay (C7)* ▲3,102
Jefferson (D7)* ▲1,215
Jemtland (G1) 100
Jimpond (B5) 8
Jonesboro (J6)* ▲459
Jonesport (H6)* ▲1,727
Katahdin Iron Works (E5) 15
Keegan (G1)* 1,100
Kellyland (H5) 23
Kenduskeag (E6)* ▲387
Kennebago Lake (B5)*
Kennebunk (B9)* ▲4,273
Kennebunk Beach (C9)* 125
Kennebunk Port (C9)* ▲1,522
Kents Hill (D7)* 170
Kezar Falls (B8)* 1,400
Kineo (D4) ▲40
Kingfield (C6)* ▲963
Kingman (G4)* ▲358
Kingsbury (D5)* ▲35
Kittery (B9)* ▲8,380
Kittery Depot (B9) 1,220
Kittery Point (B9)* 1,137
Knox (E6) ▲445
Kokadjo (E4)*
La Grange (F5)* ▲511
Lake Moxie (D5)
Lake View (F5) ▲23
Lambert Lake (H4)*
Lamoine (G7) ▲443
Lebanon (B9) ▲1,499
Lee (G5)* ▲610
Leeds (C7) ▲797
Leeds Junction (C7)* 54
Levant (F6)* ▲706
Lewiston (C7)* 40,974
Liberty (E7)* ▲497
Lille (G1)*
Limerick (B8)* ▲961
Limestone (H2)* ▲2,427
Limington (B8)* ▲851
Lincoln (G5)* ▲4,030
Lincoln Center (G5)*
Lincolnville (E7)* 881
Lincolnville Ctr. (E7)*
Linneus (H3)* ▲777
Lisbon (C7)* ▲4,318
Lisbon Center (C7)* 300
Lisbon Falls (D7)* 2,155
Litchfield (D7)* ▲953
Little Deer Isle (F7)* 350
Littleton (H3) ▲1,001
Livermore (C7)* ▲1,313
Livermore Falls (C7)* ▲3,359
Locke Mills (B7)* 380
Long Island (C8)* 350
Long Pond (C4)* 84
Longcove (E8)
Loon Lake (B5) 10
Lovell (B7)* ▲640
Lowell (F5)* ▲192
Lubec (K6) ▲2,973
Ludlow (G3) ▲361
Machias (J6)* ▲2,063
Machiasport (H6)* ▲781
Macwahoc (G4) ▲131
Madawaska (G1)* ▲4,900
Madison (D6)* ▲3,639
Madrid (B6) ▲162
Mainstream (D6)
Manchester (D7)* ▲664
Mapleton (G2)* ▲1,367
Mariner (C8)
Mars Hill (H2)* ▲2,060
Masardis (G3)* ▲523
Matagamon (F3) 3
Matinicus (F8)* ▲188
Mattawamkeag (G4)* ▲803
Maysville (G2) 150
McKinley (G7)*
Mechanic Falls (C7)* ▲2,061
Meddybemps (J5)* ▲109
Medford (F5) ▲191
Medford Center (F5) 25
Medway (G4)* ▲725
Mercer (D6)* ▲348
Mexico (B6)* ▲4,762
Michaud (F1)
Middledam (B6) 25
Milbridge (H6)* ▲1,199
Milford (F6)* ▲1,435
Millinocket (F4)* ▲5,890
Milltown (J5)*
Milo (F5)* ▲2,898
Minot (C7)* ▲750
Minturn (G7)* 134
Monarda (G4)* 250
Monhegan (E8)* ▲75
Monmouth (D7)* ▲1,683
Monroe (E6)* ▲593
Monson (E5)* ▲855
Monticello (H3)* ▲1,284
Montville (E7) ▲466
Moody (B9)*
Moose River (C4)* ▲203
Moosehead (D4) 17
Morrill (E7)* ▲306
Mount Desert (G7)* ▲1,776
Mount Vernon (D7)* ▲653
Naples (B8)* ▲747
New Gloucester (C8)* ▲2,628
New Harbor (E8)* 500
New Limerick (G3)* ▲543
New Portland (C6)* ▲733
New Sharon (C6)* ▲755
New Sweden (G2)* ▲827
New Vineyard (C6)* ▲447
Newagen (D8)*
Newburgh (F6) ▲599
Newcastle (D7)* ▲1,021
Newfield (B8)* ▲355
Newport (E6)* ▲2,190
Nobleboro (D7)* ▲654
Norcross (F4) 46
Norridgewock (D6)* ▲1,784
North Amity (H4)* 250
N. Anson (D6)* 1,000
N. Bancroft (G4)* 71
N. Belgrade (D7)* 200
N. Berwick (B9)* ▲1,655
N. Bradford (F5) 25
N. Bridgton (B7)*
N. Brooksville (F7)* 190
N. Buckfield (C7)
N. Cutler (J6)
N. Dexter (E5) 60
N. Dixmont (E6)
N. East Carry (D4)* 13
N. Ellsworth (G6)
N. Fryeburg (B7)* 200
N. Gorham (C8) 500
N. Haven (F7)* ▲410
N. Islesboro (F7)
N. Jay (C6)* 550
N. Lebanon (B9)
N. Leeds (C7)* 47
N. Limington (B8) 150
N. Livermore (C7)* 145
N. Lovell (B7)* 85
N. Lubec (J6)* 150
N. Lyndon (G2) 200
N. New Portland (C6)* 350
N. Newry (B6)* 100
N. Parsonfield (A8) 67
N. Penobscot (F7)* 150
N. Perry (J5)
N. Raymond (C8) 50
N. Searsmont (E7) 150
N. Shapleigh (B8)* 90
N. Sullivan (G6)* 850
N. Turner (C7)* 232
N. Vassalboro (D7)* 1,000
N. Waldoboro (E7)*
N. Waterboro (B8)* 500
N. Waterford (B7)* 450
N. Wayne (C7)*
N. Whitefield (D7)* 200
N. Windham (C8)* 500
N. Yarmouth (C8) ▲942
Northeast Harbor (G7)* 700
Northfield (H6) ▲75
Northport (E7)* ▲574
Norway (B7)* ▲3,811
Norway Lake (B7) 150
Oakfield (G3)* ▲1,009
Oakland (D6)* ▲2,679
Ocean Park (C9)*
Ogunquit (B9)* 800
Olamon (F5)* 600
Old Orchard Beach (C9)* ▲4,707
Old Town (F6)* 8,261
Onawa (E5)* 25
Oquossoc (B6)*
Orient (H4)* ▲176
Orland (F6)* ▲1,155
Orono (F6)* ▲7,504
Orrington (F6)* ▲1,895
Orrs Island (D8)* 450
Otisfield (B7) ▲599
Otter Creek (G7)* 1,000
Ouellette (G1)
Owls Head (F7)* ▲784
Oxbow (G3)* ▲189
Oxford (C7)* ▲1,569
Palermo, (E7)* ▲511
Palmyra (E6)* ▲965
Paris (B7)* ▲4,358
Parkman (D5)* ▲590
Passadumkeag (F5)* ▲331
Patten (F4)* ▲1,536
Pejepscot (D8)*
Pemaquid (E8)*
Pemaquid Beach (E8)*
Pembroke (J6)* ▲998
Penobscot (F7)* ▲699
Perham (G2)* ▲572
Perkins (F4) ▲5
Perry (J6)* ▲613
Peru (C6)* ▲1,080
Phair (G2) 150
Phillips (C6)* ▲1,088
Phippsburg (D8)* ▲1,134
Pine Point (C8) 650
Pittsfield (E6)* ▲3,909
Pittston (D7) ▲1,258
Plaisted (F1)* 300
Pleasant Island (B5)*
Pleasant Pond (D5) 11
Plymouth (E6)* ▲496
Poland (C7)* ▲1,503
Poland Spring (C7)* 500
Popham Beach (D8)*
Port Clyde (E8)* 350
Portage (G2)* ▲542
Porter (B8)* ▲1,052
Portland (C8)* 77,634
Portland (urban area) 112,659
Pownal (C8)* ▲752
Prentiss (G5)* ▲315
Presque Isle (H2)* ▲9,954
Princeton (H5)* ▲865
Prospect (F6) ▲392
Prospect Harbor (H7)* 270
Prouts Neck (C9)* 2,000
Pulpit Harbor (F7) 25
Quimby (F2)*
Randolph (D7) ▲1,733
Rangeley (B6)* ▲1,228
Raymond (B8)* ▲620
Readfield (D7)* ▲1,022
Red Beach (J5)*
Redding (B7) 11
Richmond (D7)* ▲2,217
Richmond Corner (D7)* 43
Ridlonville (C6)* 2,000
Riley (C6)* 175
Ripley (E5)* ▲389
Robbinston (J5)* ▲554
Robinsons (H3)* 350
Rockland (E7)* 9,234
Rockport (F7)* ▲1,656
Rockville (E7) 265
Rockwood (D4)* 300
Rome (D6) ▲420
Roque Bluffs (H6)* ▲80
Round Mountain (B5) 3
Round Pond (E8)* 500
Roxbury (B6)* ▲348
Rumford (B6)* ▲9,954
Rumford Center (B7)* 300
Rumford Point (B6)* 200
Sabattus (C7)* 1,216
Saco (C9)* 10,324
Saint Agatha (G1)* ▲1,512
St. Albans (E6)* ▲1,035
St. David (G1)* 1,000
St. Francis (E1)* ▲1384
St. George (E7)* ▲1,482
St. John (F1) ▲569
Salem (C6) ▲67
Sandy Creek (B7)
Sandy Point (F7)* 250
Sanford (B9)* ▲15.177
Sangerville (E5)* ▲1,161
Saponac (G5)* 25
Scarboro (C8)* ▲4,600
Seal Cove (G7)*
Seal Harbor (G7)* 400
Searsmont (E7)* ▲558
Searsport (F7)* ▲1,457
Sebago (B8) ▲577
Sebago Lake (B8)* 346
Sebec (E5)* ▲442
Sebec Lake (E5)* 7
Sebec Station (E5)* 23
Seboeis (F5)* ▲70
Sebomook (D4) ▲18
Sedgwick (F7)* ▲614
Selden (H4)* 25
Shapleigh (B8)* ▲531
Shawmut (D6)* 1,200
Sheepscott (D7)* 100
Sheridan (F2)* 310
Sherman (G4)* ▲1,029
Sherman Mills (G4)* 1,030
Sherman Station (F4)* 400
Shin Pond (F3)* 17
Shirley Mills (D5)* 250
Sidney (D7) ▲918
Silvers Mills (E5)* 55
Sinclair (G1)* 800
Skinner (B4)
Skowhegan (D6)* ▲7,422
Small Point Beach (D8)*
Smithfield (D6)* ▲354
Smyrna Mills (G3)* 650
Soldier Pond (F1)*
Solon (D6)* ▲746
Somerville (D7) ▲227
Sorrento, (G7)* ▲201
South Acton (B9) 200
S. Addison (H6) 170
S. Bancroft (G4)
S. Berwick (B9)* ▲2,646
S. Blue Hill (F7) 141
S. Brewer (F6)*
S. Bridgton (B8)* 125
S. Bristol (D8)* ▲631
S. Brooksville (F7)* 140
S. Casco (B8)* 150
S. China (D7)* 310
S. Deer Isle (F7) 85
S. Eliot (B4) 1,331
S. Exeter (E6) 25
S. Harpswell (C8)* 300
S. Hiram (B8)* 250
S. Hollis (B8) 30
S. Hope (E7)* 125
S. Jefferson (D7)
S. La Grange (F5) 150
S. Lebanon (A9)
S. Levant (E6) 110
S. Liberty (E7) 47
S. Lincoln (G5) 164
S. Monmouth (D7)
S. Orrington (F6)* 300
S. Paris (C7)* 2,067
S. Penobscot (F7)*
S. Portland (C8)* 21,866
S. Robbinston (J5)
S. Sanford (B9) 600
S. Thomaston (E7)* ▲654
S. Union (E7)*
S. Waldoboro (E7)
S. Warren (E7)
S. Waterford (B7)*
S. Windham (C8)* 1,569
Southport (D8)* ▲435
Southwest Harbor (G7)* ▲1,534
Spencer (C5)
Springfield (G5)* ▲414
Springvale (B9)* 2,745
Squa Pan (G2) 75
Stacyville (F4)* ▲679
Standish (B8)* ▲1,786
Starks (D6)* ▲421
Steep Falls (B8)* 480
Stetson (E6)* ▲434
Steuben (H6)* ▲784
Stillwater (F6)* 800
Stockholm (G1)* ▲641
Stockton Springs (F7)* ▲949
Stonington (F7)* ▲1,660
Stow, (A7)* ▲147
Stratton (B5)* 560
Strong (C6)* ▲1,036
Sugar Island (D4) 4
Sullivan (G6)* ▲762
Sumner (C7) ▲526
Sunset (F7)*
Sunshine (G7) 120
Surry (F7)* ▲448
Swans Island (G7)* ▲468
Swanville (E6) ▲437
Sweden (B7) ▲212
Sweden (G2)
Tarratine (D4) 8
Temple (C6)* ▲284
Tenants Harbor (E8)* 400
The Forks (D5)* ▲45
Thomaston (E7)* ▲2,810
Thorndike (E6)* ▲534
Topsfield (H5)* ▲231
Topsham (D8)* ▲2,626
Tremont (G7) ▲1,115
Trenton (G7) ▲358
Trescott (J6) ▲362
Trevett (D8)* 350
Troutdale (D5) 25
Troy (E6)* ▲553
Turner (C7)* ▲1,712
Turner Center (C7)*
Union (E7)* ▲1,085
Unionville (H6) 150
Unity (E6)* ▲1,014
Upper Dam (B6)
Upper Frenchville (G1)* 500
Upper Gloucester (C8)* 150
Upton (B6)* ▲105
Van Buren (G1)* ▲5,094
Vanceboro (H4)* ▲497
Vassalboro (D7)* ▲2,261
Veazie (F6) ▲776
Vienna (D6)* ▲231
Vinalhaven (F7)* ▲1,427
Waite (H5)* ▲117
Waldo (E7) ▲324
Waldoboro (E7)* ▲2,536
Walnut Hill (C8) 250
Waltham (G6) ▲154
Warren (E7)* ▲1,576
Washburn (G2)* ▲1,913
Washington (E7)* ▲722
Waterboro (B8)* ▲1,071
Waterford (B7)* ▲828
Waterville (E6)* 18,287
Wayne (D7)* ▲459
Webhannet (C9)*
Weeks Mills (E7)* 100
Welchville (C7)*
Weld (C6)* ▲361
Wellington (D5)* ▲252
Wells (B9)* ▲2,321
Wells Beach (C9)
Wesley (H6)* ▲149
West Athens (D6) 175
W. Baldwin (B8)*
W. Bath (D8) ▲578
W. Bethel (B7)* 250
W. Boothbay Harbor (D8)*
W. Brooksville (F7)* 140
W. Buxton (B8)* 350
W. Enfield (F5)*
W. Falmouth (C8) 1,500
W. Farmington (C6)* 500
W. Franklin (G6)* 115
W. Gardiner (D7) ▲946
W. Garland (E5) 50
W. Gorham (C8)
W. Gouldsboro (G7)* 105
W. Hampden (E6)
W. Harpswell (C8) 100
W. Jonesport (H6) 850
W. Kennebunk (B9)*
W. Lebanon (B9)* 150
W. Lubec (J6)*
W. Mills (C6) 50
W. Minot (C7)* 300
W. Newfield (B8)* 175
W. Old Town (F6) 35
W. Paris (B7)* 800
W. Pembroke (J6)* 500
W. Penobscot (F7)
W. Peru (C7)* 300
W. Poland (C7)*
W. Ripley (E6)
W. Rockport (E7)* 200
W. Scarboro (C8)* 1,500
W. Seboois (F4)*
W. Sumner (C7)* 101
W. Tremont (G7)* 250
W. Winterport (E6) 30
Westbrook (C8)* 12,284
Westfield (G2)* ▲557
Weston (H4)* ▲248
Wheelock (F1)
Whitefield (D7)* ▲1,030
Whiting (J6)* ▲354
Whitneyville (H6)* ▲227
Willimantic (E5) ▲189
Wilsons Mills (B6)* ▲80
Wilton (C6)* ▲3,455
Windsor (D7)* ▲740
Winn (G5)* ▲497
Winnecook (E6) 35
Winslow (D6) ▲4,413
Winslows Mills (E7)* 200
Winter Harbor (G7)* ▲568
Winterport (F6)* ▲1,694
Winterville (F2)* ▲373
Winthrop (C7)* ▲3,026
Wiscasset (D7)* ▲1,584
Woodland (H5)* ▲1,292
Wollwich (D8)* ▲1,344
Wyman Dam (D5)* 451
Wytopitlock (G4)* 352
Yarmouth (C8)* ▲2,669
York (B9) 2,000
York Beach (B9)* 500
York Corners (B9) 100
York Harbor (B9)* 750

Map on Page 65

MARYLAND

Total Population 2,343,001

24 COUNTIES

Allegany (A2).....89,556
Anne Arundel (H4)....117,392
Baltimore (H3).....270,273
Baltimore City (H3).949,708
Calvert (H6).....12,100
Caroline (L5).....18,234
Carroll (F2).....44,907
Cecil (L2).....33,356
Charles (F6).....23,415
Dorchester (K7).....27,815
Frederick (E3).....62,287
Garrett (A7).....21,259
Harford (J2).....51,782
Howard (G4).....23,119
Kent (K3).....13,667
Montgomery (E4).....164,401
Prince Georges (G5)..194,182
Queen Annes (L4).....14,579
Saint Marys (H7).....29,111
Somerset (M8).....20,745
Talbot (K5).....19,428
Washington (C2).....78,886
Wicomico (M7).....39,641
Worcester (N8).....23,148

CITIES and TOWNS

Abell (H8)*..... 400
Aberdeen (K2)*.....2,944
Abingdon (J3)*..... 650
Accident (A7)*..... 242
Accokeek (G6)*.....
Adamstown (D3)*..... 265
Aikin (K2).....
Aireys (K6)*..... 110
Allen (M7)*..... 350
Alta Vista (A4).....3,000
American Corner (L5).. 15
Andrews (K7)*.....
ANNAPOLIS (H5)*.....10,047
Annapolis Jct. (H4)*..... 322
Antietam (D3)..... 250
Antietam Station (D3). 50
Aquasco (G6).....
Arbutus (H3).....4,000
Ardmore (C4)..... 500
Arlington (H3)*.....71,750
Baden (H6)..... 150
Baldwin (J3)*..... 350
Balnew (H4).....1,500
Baltimore (H3)*.....949,708
Baltimore (urban area).....1,151,050
Barclay (L4)*..... 108
Barnesville (E4)*..... 130
Barstow (H6)*..... 151
Bartholows (F3)..... 100
Barton (C7)*..... 695
Bayview (L2).....
Beane (A4)..... 50
Beaver Creek (D2)..... 50
Bel Air (J2)*.....2,578
Bel Alton (G7)*..... 250
Bellevue (K6)*..... 300
Beltsville (C3)*..... 800
Benedict (H6)*..... 250
Bengies (J3)..... 500
Bentley Springs (H2)*.. 130
Berlin (O7)*.....2,001
Berwyn (B4)*.....
Berwyn Heights (C4)..... 674
Bethesda (A4)*..... 36,000
Bethlehem (L6)*.....
Betterton (K3)*..... 314
Big Spring (C2)*..... 125
Bigpool (C2)*..... 175
Bishop (N7)*..... 25
Bishops Head (K7)*..... 300
Bishopville (O7)*..... 375
Bivalve (L7)*..... 270
Bladensburg (C4)*.....2,899
Bloomington (B8)*..... 400
Blythedale (K2)..... 100
Boonsboro (D2)*.....1,071
Borden Shaft (C7)..... 419
Boring (G2)*..... 130
Boulevard Heights (B5)
Bowens (H6)*..... 220
Bowie (G4)*..... 860
Boyds (E4)*..... 250
Bozman (J5)*.....
Bradbury Heights (C5).1,800
Bradbury Park (C5)..... 500
Bradshaw (J3)*..... 500
Branchville (B4)*..... 500
Brandywine (G6)*.....1,000
Breathedsville (C2)*..... 150
Brentwood (B4)*.....3,523
Bridgetown (L4)..... 16
Bristol (H5)*..... 300
Broad Creek (B6)..... 50
Brookeville (F4)*..... 117
Brookview (L6)..... 150
Brown (C5)..... 200
Brownsville (D3)*..... 202
Brunswick (D3)*.....3,752
Buck Lodge (E4)..... 100
Buckeystown (E3)*.....
Burkittsville (D3)*..... 190
Burnt Mills (B3)..... 100
Burrsville (L5)..... 200
Burtonsville (G4)*.....
Bushwood (G7)*..... 300
Butler (H2)*..... 57
Cabin Creek (L6).....
Cabin John (A4)*.....2,000
California (H7)*..... 250
Calvert (K2)..... 150
Cambridge (K6)*.....10,351
Camp Springs (C6)..... 315
Capitol Heights (C5)*..2,729
Cardiff (J2)*..... 325
Carney (H3).....1,523
Carrollton (G2)*..... 180
Castleton (J2)*..... 343
Catoctin (E2)..... 300
Catonsville (H3)*.....29,638
Cavetown (D2)*..... 300
Cecilton (L3)*..... 510
Cedar Grove (F4)..... 200
Cedar Heights (C5)..... 788
Cedartown (N8)..... 50
Cedarville (G6)..... 200
Centreville (K4)*.....1,804
Chance (L8)*..... 400
Chaptico (H7)*..... 350
Charlestown (L2)*..... 551
Charlotte Hall (H7)*..... 150
Chase (J3)*..... 900
Cheltenham (G6)*..... 500
Cherry Hill (L2)..... 300
Chesapeake Beach (J6)* 504
Chesapeake City (L2)*.1,154
Chester (J5)*.....1,100
Chestertown (K4)*.....3,143
Chesterville (L3)..... 36
Cheverly (C4)*.....3,318
Chevy Chase (A4)*.....1,971
Chewsville (D2)*..... 180
Childs (L2)*..... 90
Chillum (B4)*.....15,000
Choptank (L6)*.....
Church Creek (K6)*..... 187
Church Hill (K4)*..... 271
Churchton (J5)*.....
Churchville (J2)*.....
Claiborne (J5)*..... 150
Clara (L7)..... 200
Clarksburg (E4)*..... 367
Clarksville (G4)*..... 200
Clear Spring (C2)*..... 558
Clements (G7)*..... 300
Clinton (C6)*..... 500
Cockeysville (H3)*.....3,000
College Park (C4)*.....11,170
Collington (G5).....
Colmar Manor (B4).....1,732
Colora (K2)*..... 190
Compton (H7)*..... 500
Conowingo (K2)*..... 500
Cooksville (F3)*..... 150
Cordova (K5)*..... 500
Cornersville (K6)..... 100
Corriganville (D7)*.....
Cottage City (B4).....1,249
Crapo (K7)*.....
Creagerstown (E2)..... 325
Crellin (A8)*..... 500
Cresaptown (C7)*.....2,000
Crisfield (L9)*.....3,688
Crocheron (K8)*.....
Crownsville (H4)*..... 350
Crumpton (L4)*.....
Cumberland (D7)*.....37,679
Damascus (F3)*.....1,000
Dameron (J8)*..... 250
Dames Quarter (L8)*..... 450
Daniels (G3)*..... 800
Daniels Park (C4)..... 750
Dargan (D3)..... 300
Darlington (J2)*..... 500
Darnestown (E4)..... 200
Davidsonville (H5)*..... 900
Day (F3).....
Deal Island (L8)*.....1,200
Deer Park (A8)*..... 320
Delmar (M7).....1,328
Denton (L5)*.....1,806
Derwood (F4)*..... 300
Dickerson (E4)*..... 300
District Heights (C5)....1,735
Doncaster (F7)*.....
Doubs (E3)*..... 250
Downsville (C2)..... 210
Drayden (J8)*..... 300
Dublin (J2)..... 250
Dundalk (J3)*.....40,182
Eagle Harbor ‡(F6)..... 7
Earleigh Heights (H4).. 400
Earleville (L3)*..... 42
East New Market (L6)* 264
East Riverdale (C4).....1,200
Easton (K5)*.....4,836
Eastport (J5)*.....
Eckhart Mines (C7)*...2,350
Eden (M7)*..... 150
Edgemere (J3).....6,000
Edmonston (C4)*.....1,190
Eldersburg (G3)..... 300
Eldorado (L6)..... 79
Elk Mills (L2)*..... 300
Elkneck (L2).....
Elkridge (H4)*.....3,000
Elkton (L2)*.....5,245
Ellerslie (D7)*..... 850
Ellerton (D2)..... 41
Ellicott City (G3)*.....1,500
Elliott (L7)*..... 130
Emmitsburg (E2)*.....1,261
Essex (J3)*.....35,000
Ewell (K9)*..... 400
Fair Hill (L2)..... 150
Fairbank (J6)..... 300
Fairland (G4).....
Fairlee (K4)..... 240
Fairmount (L8)*..... 600
Fairmount Heights (C5) 2,097
Fallston (J2)*..... 300
Farmington (K2)..... 50
Fearer (A7)..... 50
Federalsburg (L6)*.....1,878
Ferndale (H4)*.....2,500
Finchville (M6)..... 3
Finksburg (G3)*..... 500
Fishing Creek (J7)*..... 700
Flint Stone (A2)*..... 170
Forest Glen (B4).....1,500
Forest Heights (B5).....1,125
Forest Hill (J2)*..... 300
Forestville (C5).....1,500
Fort Foote (B6)..... 75
Ft. Howard (J4)*.....1,000
Ft. Washington (G6)..... 210
Foxville (E2)..... 150
Frederick (E3)*.....18,142
Freeland (H2)*..... 200
Friendship (H6)*..... 300
Friendship Heights (A4) 315
Friendsville (A7)*..... 607
Frizellburg (F2)..... 193
Frostburg (C7)*.....6,876
Fruitland (M7)*.....1,028
Fullerton (J3)*.....2,500
Funkstown (D2)*..... 879
Gaithersburg (F4)*.....1,755
Galena (L3)*..... 259
Galestown (L6)..... 100
Galesville (H5)*..... 900
Gamber (G3)..... 600
Gambrills (H4)*..... 500
Garrett Park (A3)*..... 524
Garrison (G3)*.....1,000
Germantown (E4)*..... 200
Girdletree (N8)*..... 200
Glen Burnie (H4)*.....8,000
Glen Echo (A4)*..... 356
Glen Echo Heights (A4) 600
Glenarden (C4)*..... 492
Glenarm (J3)*..... 350
Glenelg (G3)*..... 40
Glenn Dale (C4)*..... 625
Glyndon (G3)*..... 500
Golden Hill (K7).....
Goldsboro (L4)*..... 198
Golts (L3)*..... 100
Graceham (E2)*..... 225
Granite (G3)*..... 600
Grantsville (B7)*..... 461
Grasonville (K5)*.....1,200
Greenbelt (C4)*.....7,074
Greenmount (G2)*..... 200
Greensboro (L5)*.....1,181
Hagerstown (C2)*.....36,260
Halethorpe (H4)*.....5,000
Hall (G5)*..... 195
Hampstead (G2)*..... 677
Hancock (B2)*..... 963
Hanover (G4)*.....1,000
Harmans (H4)*..... 200
Harney (F2)..... 142
Havre de Grace (K2)*..7,809
Hebbville (G3)..... 150
Hebron (M7)*..... 723
Helen (H7)*..... 125
Henderson (L4)*..... 106
Henryton (G3)*..... 600
Hereford (E2)*..... 310
Highfield (E2)*.....1,000
Highland Beach ‡(J6)*. 5
Hillsboro (L5)*..... 179
Hillside (C5).....3,000
Hobbs (L5)*..... 95
Hollywood (H7)*..... 800
Hood (B2)..... 11
Hoopersville (K7)*..... 300
Hopewell (L8)..... 200
Howardville (G3).....
Hudson (J6)..... 200
Hughsville (G6)*..... 550
Huntingtown (H6)*..... 438
Hurlock (L6)*..... 944
Hutton (A8)*..... 350
Hyattstown (E3)*..... 135
Hyattsville (B4)*.....12,308
Ijamsville (E3)*.....
Ilchester (G4)*..... 200
Indian Head (F6)*..... 491
Ingleside (L4)*..... 150
Ironshire (O7)..... 100
Ironshire Station (N7).. 25
Island Creek (H7)*..... 250
Issue (G7)*..... 160
Jacksonville (H2)..... 75
Jarrettsville (H2)*..... 250
Jefferson (E3)*..... 275
Jennings (B7)*..... 300
Jesterville (L7)*..... 175
Johnsonville (F2)..... 200
Keedysville (D3)*..... 417
Kempton (A9)*..... 260
Kemptown (E3)*..... 200
Kennedyville (L3)*..... 180
Kensington (A4)*.....1,611
Keymar (F2)*.....
Kingston (M8)*..... 50
Kingsville (J3)*.....
Kitzmiller (B8)*..... 652
Knoxville (D3)*..... 750
Koontz (B7).....
La Plata (G6)*..... 780
Ladiesburg (E2)*..... 126
Lakesville (K7)*..... 37
Landover (C4)*.....1,175
Landover Hills (C4)*.....1,661
Lanham (C4)*.....1,133
Lansdowne (H3)*.....7,500
Lantz (E2)*..... 75
Largo (C5)..... 100
Lauraville (H3).....
Laurel (G4)*.....4,482
Lawsonia (L9)..... 800
Laytonsville (F4)*..... 132
Le Gore (E2)*..... 400
Leeds (L2)..... 40
Leitersburg (D2)..... 250
Leonardtown (H7)*.....1,017
Leslie (L2).....
Level (K2)..... 450
Lewistown (E2)*..... 350
Lexington Park (J7)*.....6,000
Liberty Grove (K2)*..... 210
Libertytown (E3)*..... 600
Lime Kiln (E3)*..... 185
Linden (A4).....1,000
Lineboro (G2)*..... 200
Linkwood (L6)*..... 125
Linthicum Heights(H4)*3,500
Linwood (F2)*.....
Lisbon (F3)*..... 150
Little Orleans (A2)*..... 300
Loch Lynn Heights (A8)..... 415
Lonaconing (C7)*.....2,289
Long Green (H3)*..... 500
Lothian (H5)*.....
Love Point (J4)..... 120
Loveville (H7)*..... 500
Lower Marlboro (H6)*.. 135
Luke (B8)*..... 820
Lusby (J7)*..... 225
Lutherville (H3)*.....2,800
Lynch (K3)*..... 97
Mackall (H7)*.....
Madison (K6)*.....
Madonna (H2)..... 25
Magnolia (J3)*..... 500
Manchester (G2)*.....1,027
Manokin (L8)*..... 400
Mapleville (D2)*..... 175
Marbury (F6)*.....
Mardela Springs (L7)*.. 428
Marion Station (M8)*.. 475
Marshall Hall (F6)..... 50
Marydel (L4)*..... 110
Maryland Line (H2)*..... 202
Maryland Park (C5).....1,500
Mason Springs (F6)..... 50
Massey (L3)*..... 125
Maugansville (D2)*..... 725
Mayberry (F2)..... 108
Mayo (H5)*..... 583
Mc Daniel (J5)*..... 197
Meadows (C5)..... 350
Mechanicsville (H7)*..... 500
Medford (F2)*..... 125
Melitota (K4)..... 100
Melrose (G2)..... 150
Middle River (J3)*.....27,500
Middleburg (F2)*..... 150
Middletown (E3)*..... 936
Midland (C7)*..... 889
Milestown (H7)..... 400
Millers (G2)*..... 225
Millersville (H4)*..... 250
Millington (L3)*..... 356
Monie (L8)*..... 250
Monkton (H2)*..... 105
Monrovia (E3)*..... 112
Montrose (A3)..... 200
Morningside (C5).....1,520
Moscow Mills (B7)..... 300
Mount Airy (F3)*.....1,061
Mt. Lena (D2)..... 150
Mt. Pleasant (E3).....
Mt. Rainier (B4)*.....10,989
Mt. Savage (C7)*.....2,094
Mt. Vernon (L8)..... 400
Mt. Washington (H3)*..4,153
Mountain Lake Park(A8)*
Mountaindale (E2)..... 175
Muirkirk (G4)*..... 400
Mullinix Mill (F3)..... 25
Myersville (D3)*..... 250
Nanjemoy (F7)*..... 264
Nanticoke (L7)*..... 650
National (C7)..... 348
Neavitt (J6)*.....
New Glatz (B6)..... 50
New Market (E3)*..... 301
New Windsor (F2)*..... 707
Newark (N7)*..... 500
Newport (G7)*.....
Nikep (C7)*..... 275
Norbeck (F4)..... 500
Norrisville (J2)..... 100
North Beach (J6)*..... 314
N. Branch (D7)..... 280
N. Brentwood (B4)..... 833
N. East (L2)*.....1,517
Oakland (A8)*.....1,640
Ocean City (O7)*.....1,234
Odenton (H4)*.....1,059
Oella (G3)*.....1,500
Oldtown (D7)*..... 500
Olivet (J7)*..... 250
Olney (F4)*.....1,000
Orangeville (H3)..... 300
Oraville (H7)*..... 300
Oriole (L8)*..... 268
Owings (H6)*..... 230
Owings Mills (G3)*.....1,500
Oxford (K6)*..... 757
Oxon Hill (B6)..... 280
Palmers (H8)*..... 300
Park Hall (J8)*..... 400
Parkton (H2)*..... 500
Parkville (H3)*.....6,500
Parole (H5)*.....1,032
Parran (H6)*.....
Parsonsburg (M7)*..... 350
Pasadena (H4)*.....1,500
Patapsco (G2)*.....
Perry Hall (H3).....1,000
Perryman (K3)*..... 300
Perryville (K2)*..... 679
Petersville (D3)..... 250
Phoenix (H2)*..... 150
Pikesville (G3)*.....15,000
Piney Point (H8)*.....1,000
Pinto (C7)*..... 275
Piscataway (G6)..... 77
Pisgah (F6)*..... 450
Pittsville (N7)*..... 497
Pleasant Valley (G2)..... 170
Plum Point (J6)*.....
Pocomoke City (M8)*...3,191
Point of Rocks (E3)*..... 361
Pomfret (G6)*..... 500
Pomona (K4)..... 35
Pomonkey (F6)..... 200
Poolesville (E4)*..... 161
Popes Creek (G7)*..... 75
Port Deposit (K2)*.....1,139
Port Republic (J6)*..... 50
Port Tobacco (F6)*..... 125
Port Tobacco Station (Springhill*) (G7)..... 150
Potomac (F4)..... 250
Powellville (N7)*..... 350
Preston (L6)*..... 353
Price (L4)*..... 245
Prince Frederick (H6)*. 500
Princess Anne (L8)*.....1,407
Principio Furnace (L2)*. 250
Providence (L2)..... 300
Purdum (E3)..... 175
Quantico (M7)*..... 250
Queen Anne (K5)*..... 396
Queenstown (K5)*..... 316
Randallstown (G3)*.....1,550
Rawlings (C7)*..... 500
Reid (D2)..... 50
Reids Grove (L6)..... 45
Reisterstown (G3)*.....1,500
Relay (H4)*.....1,000
Reliance (L6)..... 30
Revell (J4)..... 100
Rhodes Point (K9)*..... 150
Riderwood (H3)*.....
Ridge (J8)*.....
Ridgely (L5)*..... 834
Ridgeville (F3)..... 150
Ringgold (D2)..... 212
Rising Sun (K2)*..... 668
Ritchie (C5)..... 200
River Springs (G8)..... 300
Riverdale (B4)*.....5,530
Riverside (F7)..... 150
Rock Hall (K4)*..... 786
Rock Point (G7)*..... 200
Rocks (J2)*.....
Rockville (F4)*.....6,934
Rogers Heights (C4).....2,000
Rohrersville (D3)*..... 165
Roland Park (H3)*.....12,000
Rosaryville (G5)..... 100
Rosedale (H3).....3,000
Rowlandsville (K2).....
Royal Oak (K6)*.....
Rumbley (L8)*..... 113
Ruthsberg (L4)..... 25
Rutland (H5)..... 300
Ruxton (H3)*.....
Sabillasville (E2)*..... 300
Saint Augustine (L3)..... 50
St. Inigoes (J8)*..... 400
St. James (C2)*..... 100
St. Leonard (J7)*.....
St. Martin's (O7).....
St. Michaels (J5)*.....1,470
Salem (L7)*..... 42
Salisbury (M7)*.....15,141
Sandy Spring (F4)*..... 650
Sassafras (L3)..... 100
Savage (G4)*.....1,238
Savage Station (G4)..... 25
Scotland (J8)*..... 300
Seabrook (C4)*.....2,500
Seat Pleasant (C5)*.....2,255
Secretary (L6)*..... 344
Security (D2)*..... 350
Severn (H4)*..... 250
Severna Park (H4)*.....1,000
Sharpsburg (C3)*..... 866
Sharptown (M6)*..... 680
Shawsville (H2)..... 50
Shelltown (M9)*..... 28
Shipley (H4).....1,500
Showell (O7)*..... 100
Silver Hill (B5).....1,000
Silver Run (F2)..... 325
Silver Spring (B4)*.....75,000
Smallwood (F2)..... 160
Smithsburg (D2)*..... 641
Snow Hill (N8)*.....2,091
Solomons (J7)*..... 270
Somerset (A4)..... 430
Sparrows Point (J4)*..12,000
Spickler (C2)..... 85
Spielman (C2)..... 202
Springhill (G7)*..... 150
Stemmers Run (H3).....1,260
Stevensville (J5)*..... 350
Steyer (A8)*..... 55
Still Pond (K3)*..... 290
Still Pond Station (K3) 4
Stockton (N8)*..... 500
Street (J2)*..... 200
Sudlersville (L4)*..... 347
Sudley (H5).....
Suitland (C5)*.....2,500
Swanton (A8)*..... 242
Sweetair (H2)..... 35
Sykesville (F3)*..... 941
T. B. (G6)..... 100
Takoma Park (B4).....13,341
Taneytown (F2)*.....1,420
Taylors Island (J7)*..... 300
Taylorsville (F3)..... 125
Templeville (L4)*..... 82
Texas (H3)*.....
Thomas (J6)..... 200
Thurmont (E2)*.....1,676
Tilghman (J6)*.....1,250
Timonium (H3)*.....1,300
Toddville (K7)*..... 330
Tolchester Beach (J4)..... 4
Tompkinsville (G7)*..... 510
Town Creek (A2)..... 50
Town Point (L3)..... 25
Towson (H3)*.....11,000
Trappe (K6)*..... 325
Trappe Station (K6)..... 35
Trenton (G2)..... 100
Tunis Mills (K5)..... 100
Tuxedo (C5)*.....1,000
Tyaskin (L7)*..... 150
Union Bridge (F2)*..... 840
Union Mills (F2)*..... 300
Uniontown (F2)*..... 265
Unionville (F3)*..... 150
Unity (F4)..... 82
University Park (B4).....2,205
Upper Fairmount (L8)*. 824
Upper Falls (J3)*..... 200
Upper Marlboro (H5)*.. 702
Upperco (G2)*..... 150
Urbana (E3).....
Vale Summit (C7)..... 450
Valley Lee (H8)*..... 300
Venton (M8)*..... 100
Vienna (L7)*..... 414
Vindex (B8)*..... 175
Waldorf (G6)*.....1,100
Walkersville (E3)*..... 761
Warwick (L3)*.....
Washington Grove (F4)* 400
Waterview (L8)..... 50
Welcome (F7)*..... 200
Wenona (L8)*..... 300
West Annapolis (H4)*..
W. Lanham Hills (C4)*..1,200
W. River (H5)*.....
Western Port (B8)*.....3,431
Westminster (G2)*.....6,140
Westover (M8)*..... 400
Wetipquin (L7)..... 500
Weverton (D3)*..... 150
Whaleysville (N7)*..... 350
Wheaton (A3)*.....20,000
White Hall (H2)*..... 300
White Marsh (J3)*..... 500
White Oak (B3)..... 50
White Plains (G6)..... 700
Whiteford (J2)*..... 300
Whitehaven (L7)*..... 95
Wicomico (G7)*..... 225
Willards (N7)*..... 464
Williamsburg (L6)*..... 150
Williamsport (C2)*.....1,890
Williston (L5)..... 100
Willows (H6)*.....
Winfield (F3).....
Wingate (K7)*.....
Wittman (J5)*.....
Wolfsville (D2)..... 96
Woodbine (F3)*.....
Woodlawn (H3).....5,000
Woodmoor (B4)*..... 500
Woodsboro (E2)*..... 427
Woodside (B4).....3,500
Woodstock (G3)*..... 100
Woolford (K7)*..... 150
Worton (K3)*..... 150
Wye Mills (K5)*..... 125
Wye Mills Station (K5) 100
Wynne (J8)..... 300
Yellow Springs (D3).....
Zion (L2).....

DISTRICT OF COLUMBIA

Anacostia (B5)*.....
Benning (B5)*.....
Brightwood (B4)*.....
Brookland (B4)*.....
Cleveland Park (A4)*.....
Congress Heights (B5)*
Georgetown (A5)*.....
Petworth (B4)*.....
Tenleytown (A4).....
WASHINGTON, D. C. (B5)*.....802,178
Washington (urban area).....1,281,572

Map on Page 66

MASSACHUSETTS

Total Population 4,690,514

14 COUNTIES

Barnstable (N6)........46,805
Berkshire (B3)........132,966
Bristol (K5)........381,569
Dukes (M7)........ 5,633
Essex (L2)........522,384
Franklin (D2)........52,747
Hampden (D4)........367,971
Hampshire (D3)........87,594
Middlesex (J3)........1,064,569
Nantucket (O7)........ 3,484
Norfolk (K4)........392,308
Plymouth (L5)........189,468
Suffolk (K3)........896,615
Worcester (G3)........546,401

CITIES and TOWNS

Abington (L4)*........△7,152
Accord (E8)*........ 150
Acoaxet (K7)*........ 130
Acton (J3)*........△3,510
Acushnet (L6)*........△4,401
Adams (B2)*........△12,034
Agawam (D4)*........△10,166
Allerton (E7)*........ 500
Amesbury (L1)*........△10,851
Amherst (E3)*........△10,856
Andover (K2)*........△12,437
Annisquam (M2)*........
Arlington (C6)*........△44,353
Ashburnham (G2)*........△2,603
Ashby (G2)*........△1,464
Ashfield (C2)*........△ 977
Ashland (J3)*........△3,500
Ashley Falls (A4)*........ 500
Assinippi (E8)*........ 500
Assonet (K5)*........ 1,002
Athol (F2)*........△11,554
Attleboro (J5)*........23,809
Attleboro Falls (J5)*.. 2,500
Auburn (G4)*........△8,840
Auburndale (B7)*........ 6,218
Avon (K4)*........△2,666
Ayer (H2)*........△5,740
Baldwinville (F2)*........ 1,407
Ballard Vale (K2)*........ 1,200
Barnstable (N6)*........△10,480
Barre (F3)*........△3,406
Barre Plains (F3)*........ 144
Barrowsville (K5)*........ 700
Becket (B3)*........△ 755
Bedford (B6)*........△5,234
Beechwood (F8)*........ 200
Belchertown (E3)*........△4,487
Bellingham (J4)*........△4,100
Belmont (C6)*........△27,381
Berkley (K5)........△1,284
Berlin (H3)*........△1,349
Bernardston (D2)*........△1,117
Beverly (E5)*........28,884
Beverly Farms (E5)*.. 2,500
Billerica (J2)*........△11,101
Blackinton (B2)*........ 440
Blackstone (H4)*........△4,968
Blandford (C4)*........△ 597
Bolton (H3)*........△ 956
Bondsville (E4)*........ 1,200
BOSTON (D7)*........801,444
Boston (urban area)........2,218,893
Bourne (M6)*........△4,720
Bournedale (M5)........
Boxford (K2)*........△ 926
Boylston Center (H3)*........
Braintree (D8)*........△23,161
Brant Rock (M4)*........ 350
Brewster (O5)*........△ 987
Bridgewater (K5)*........△9,512
Brimfield (F4)*........△1,182
Brockton (K4)*........62,860
Brockton (urban area)92,086
Brookfield (F4)*........△1,567
Brookline (C7)*........△57,589
Brookville (K4)*........ 1,300
Bryantville (L4)*........
Buckland (C2)*........△1,605
Burlington (C5)........△3,250
Buzzards Bay (M5)*.. 1,459
Byfield (L1)*........ 950
Cambridge (C6)*........120,740
Canton (C8)*........△7,465
Canton Jct. (C8)........
Carlisle (J2)*........△ 846
Carver (M5)*........△1,530
Caryville (J4)*........ 300
Cataumet (M6)*........ 100
Centerville (N6)*........1,100
Central Village (K6)*.. 350
Charlemont (C2)*........△ 855
Charlton (F4)*........△3,136
Charlton City (F4)*........ 1,200
Charlton Depot (F4)*. 150
Chartley (K5)*........ 600
Chatham (P6)*........△2,457
Chathamport (P6)........ 150
Chelmsford (J2)*........△9,407
Chelsea (D6)*........38,912
Cherry Valley (G3)*........ 1,300
Cheshire (B2)*........△2,022
Chester (C3)*........△1,292
Chesterfield (C3)*........△ 496
Chicopee (D4)*........49,211
Chicopee Falls (D4)*..12,915
Chilmark (M7)*........△ 183
Chiltonville (M5)........
City Mills (J4)*........ 500
Clifton (E6)*........ 5,000
Clinton (H3)*........△12,287
Cochituate (A7)*........ 2,500
Cohasset (F7)*........△3,731
Collinsville (J2)*........ 1,500
Colrain (D2)*........△1,546
Concord (A6)*........△8,623
Conway (D2)*........△ 873
Cordaville (H3)*........ 250
Cotuit (N6)*........ 700
Crescent Beach (M6)*
Cummaquid (N6)*........ 200
Cummington (C3)*........△ 620
Cushing (L1)*........ 398
Cushman (D3)*........ 250
Cuttyhunk (L7)*........ 40
Dalton (B3)*........△4,772
Danvers (D5)*........△15,720
Danversport (E5)........ 2,500
Dartmouth (K6)*........△11,115
Dedham (C7)*........△18,487
Deerfield (D2)*........△3,086
Dennis (O5)*........△2,499
Dennis Port (O6)*........ 1,200
Dighton (K5)*........△2,950
Dodge (G4)*........ 835
Dodgeville (K5)*........ 1,500
Dorchester (D7)*........
Douglas (H4)........△2,624
Dover (B7)*........△1,722
Dracut (J2)........△8,666
Dudley (G4)*........△5,261
Dunstable (J2)*........△ 522
Duxbury (M4)*........△3,167
E. Blackstone (H4)........
E. Braintree (D8)........ 7,000
E. Brewster (O5)*........ 500
E. Bridgewater (L4)*..△4,412
E. Brookfield (G4)*........△1,243
E. Dedham (C8)*........ 5,000
E. Dennis (O5)*........ 275
E. Douglas (G4)*........ 1,846
E. Falmouth (M6)*........ 1,405
E. Foxboro (K4)*........ 500
E. Freetown (L5)*........ 1,200
E. Harwich (O6)*........ 500
E. Lee (B3)*........ 350
E. Longmeadow (E4)*.△4,881
E. Milton (D7)........ 7,500
E. Northfield (E2)*........ 950
E. Norton (K5)........ 800
E. Orleans (P5)*........ 383
E. Otis (B4)*........ 95
E. Pembroke (M4)*........ 200
E. Pepperell (H2)*........ 2,500
E. Sandwich (N6)*........ 325
E. Saugus (D6)........
E. Taunton (K5)*........ 5,000
E. Templeton (G2)*........ 1,200
E. Village (G4)........
E. Walpole (C8)*........ 2,000
E. Wareham (M5)*........ 500
E. Weymouth (E8)*........10,000
E. Whately (D3)........
Eastham (O5)*........△ 860
Easthampton (D3)*...△10,694
Easton (K4)*........△6,244
Eastondale (K4)*........ 600
Edgartown (M7)*........△1,508
Egypt (F8)*........ 600
Elmwood (L4)*........ 350
Erving (E2)*........△1,322
Essex (L2)*........△1,794
Everett (D6)*........45,982
Fairhaven (L6)*........12,764
Fairview (D4)*........ 2,108
Fail River (K6)*........111,963
Fall River (urban area)........117,881
Falmouth (M6)*........△8,662
Farnams (B2)*........ 200
Farnumsville (H4)*........ 1,427
Fayville (H3)*........ 1,000
Feeding Hills (D4)*........ 3,500
Fisherville (H4)*........ 1,167
Fiskdale (F4)*........
Fitchburg (G2)*........42,691
Florence (D3)*........ 4,500
Forest Hills (C7)........10,000
Forge Village (H2)*........ 1,115
Foxboro (J4)*........△7,030
Framingham (A7)*....△28,086
Framingham Center (J3)*........ 4,500
Franklin (J4)*........△8,037
Furnace (F3)*........ 150
Gardner (G2)*........19,581
Gay Head (L7)........△ 88
Georgetown (L2)*........△2,411
Gilbertville (F3)*........ 1,039
Gill (D2)........△1,070
Gleasondale (J3)*........
Glendale (A3)*........ 350
Gloucester (M2)*........25,167
Goshen (C3)*........△ 321
Grafton (H4)*........△8,281
Granby (E3)*........△1,861
Graniteville (J2)*........ 1,000
Granville (C4)*........△ 740
Great Barrington (A4)*........△6,712
Green Harbor (M4)*........ 300
Greenbush (F8)*........ 650
Greenfield (D2)*........△17,349
Greenwood (D6)*........ 5,500
Griswoldville (D2)*........ 590
Groton (H2)*........△2,889
Groveland (L1)*........△2,340
Hadley (D3)*........△2,639
Halifax (L5)*........△ 944
Hamilton (L2)*........△2,764
Hampden (E4)*........△1,322
Hancock (A2)*........△ 445
Hanover (L4)*........△3,389
Hanson (L4)*........△3,264
Hardwick (F3)*........△2,348
Hartsville (B4)........
Harvard (H2)*........△3,983
Harwich (O6)*........△2,649
Harwich Port (O6)*........ 1,350
Hatfield (D3)*........△2,179
Haverhill (K1)*........47,280
Haydenville (C3)*........ 1,009
Heath (C2)*........△ 305
Hebronville (J5)*........ 754
Hingham (E8)*........△10,665
Hingham Center (E8)..
Hinsdale (B3)*........△1,560
Holbrook (D8)*........△4,004
Holden (G3)*........△5,975
Holland (F4)........△ 377
Holliston (A8)*........△3,753
Holyoke (D4)*........54,661
Holyoke-Springfield (urban area)........356,471
Hoosac Tunnel (C2)*... 150
Hopedale (H4)*........△3,479
Hopkinton (J4)*........△3,486
Hortonville (K5)........
Housatonic (A3)*........ 1,601
Hubbardston (F3)*........△1,134
Hubbardston Station (F3)........ 120
Hudson (H3)*........△8,211
Hull (E7)*........△3,379
Humarock (M4)*........ 50
Huntington (C4)*........△1,257
Hyannis (N6)*........ 4,235
Hyannis Port (N6)*........ 300
Hyde Park (C7)*........
Indian Orchard (E4)*.10,000
Interlaken (A3)*........ 60
Ipswich (L2)*........△6,985
Islington (C8)*........2,300
Jamaica Plain (C7)*........
Jefferson (G3)*........
Kendal Green (B6)........
Kingston (M5)*........△3,461
Lakeville (L5)........△2,066
Lancaster (H3)*........△3,601
Lanesboro (A2)*........△2,069
Lanesville (M2)*........ 1,046
Lawrence (K2)*........80,536
Lawrence (urban area)........111,937
Lee (B3)*........△4.820
Leeds (D3)*........ 1,700
Leicester (G4)*........△6,029
Lenox (A3)*........△3,627
Lenox Dale (B3)*........ 500
Leominster (G2)*........24,075
Leverett (E3)*........△ 791
Lexington (B6)*........△17,335
Leyden (D2)........△ 306
Lincoln (B6)*........△2,427
Linwood (H4)*........ 981
Littleton (H2)*........△2,349
Littleton Common (J2)*........ 1,017
Longmeadow (D4)*........△6,508
Lowell (J2)*........97,249
Lowell (urban area)..105,783
Ludlow (E4)*........△8,660
Ludlow Center (E4)... 500
Lunenburg (H2)*........△3,906
Lynn (D6)*........99,738
Lynnfield (D5)*........△3,927
Lynnfield Center (C5)* 2,600
Magnolia (M2)*........
Malden (D6)*........59,804
Manchaug (G4)*........ 790
Manchester (F5)*........△2,868
Manomet (M5)*........ 350
Mansfield (J4)*........△7,184
Marblehead (E5)*........△13,765
Marion (L6)*........△2,250
Marlboro (H3)*........15,756
Marshfield (M4)*........△3,267
Marshfield Hills(M4)*. 500
Marstons Mills (N6)*. 600
Mashpee (M6)*........△ 438
Mattapan (C7)*........
Mattapoisett (L6)*........△2,265
Maynard (J3)*........△6,978
Medfield (B8)*........△4,549
Medfield Jct. (B8)........ 500
Medford (C6)*........66,113
Medway (J4)*........△3,744
Melrose (D6)*........26,988
Melrose Highlds.(D6)*..7,713
Mendon (H4)*........△1,619
Menemsha (L7)*........
Merrimac (L1)*........△2,804
Merrimacport (L1)........ 210
Methuen (K2)*........△24,477
Middleboro (L5)*........△10,164
Middlefield (B3)*........△ 295
Middleton (K2)*........△2,916
Milford (H4)*........△15,442
Mill River (A4)........△ 300
Millbrook (M4)*........ 200
Millbury (H4)*........△8,347
Millers Falls (E2)*........ 1,134
Millis (A8)*........△2,551
Millville (H4)*........△1,692
Milton (D7)*........△22,395
Minot (F8)*........ 150
Monroe Bridge (C2)*.. 150
Monson (E4)*........△6,125
Montague (E2)*........△7,812
Montague City (D2)*.. 668
Monterey (B4)*........△ 367
Montvale (C6)........
Montville (B4)*........
Monument Beach (M6)*........ 650
Moores Corner (E2)*..
Mt. Hermon (D2)*........ 750
Mt. Hope (C7)........ 5,000
Mt. Tom (D3)*........ 230
Mt. Washington (A4)△ 34
Myricks (K5)........ 210
Nabnasset (J2)*........ 500
Nahant (E6)*........△2,679
Nantasket Beach (E7)*........ 1,900
Nantucket (O7)*........△3,484
Natick (A7)*........△19,838
Needham (B7)*........△16,313
Needham Hts. (B7)*.. 5,500
Neponset (D7)........

New Bedford (K6)*...109,185
New Bedford (urban area)........125,354
New Boston (B4)*........
New Braintree (F3)*..△ 478
New Lenox (B3)........
New Marlboro (B4)*..△ 989
New Salem (E2)........△ 392
Newbury (L1)........△1,994
Newburyport (L1)*........14,111
Newton (C7)*........81,994
Newton Center (C7)*..15,214
Newton Highlands (C7)*........11,480
Newton Lower Falls (B7)*........1,215
Newton Upper Falls (C7)*........ 3,451
Newtonville (C7)*........13,689
Nonquitt (L6)*........ 18
Norfolk (J4)*........△2,704
N. Abington (L4)*........3,906
N. Acton (J2)........ 300
N. Adams (B2)*........21,567
N. Amherst (E3)*........ 750
N. Andover (K2)*........△8,485
N. Attleboro (J5)*........△12,146
N. Bellingham (J4)*... 300
N. Billerica (J2)*........ 3,300
N. Brewster (O5)........
N. Brookfield (F3)*........△3,444
N. Carver (L5)*........
N. Chatham (O6)*........ 200
N. Chelmsford (J2)*... 3,249
N. Cohasset (F7)*........
N. Dartmouth (K6)*........
N. Dighton (K5)*........ 1,000
N. Eastham (O5)*........ 270
N. Easton (K4)*........ 4,000
N. Egremont (A4)*........ 215
N. Falmouth (M6)*........ 800
N. Grafton (H4)*........ 2,000
N. Hadley (D3)*........ 1,000
N. Hanover (L4)*........ 800
N. Harwich (O6)*........ 210
N. Hatfield (D3)*........ 300
N. Leominster (G2)........
N. Marshfield (M4)*... 450
N. Middleboro (L5)........ 500
N. Oxford (G4)*........ 1,250
N. Pembroke (M4)*........ 400
N. Plymouth (L5)*........ 4,000
N. Reading (C5)*........△4,402
N. Rutland (G3)........ 125
N. Scituate (F8)*........ 1,100
N. Swansea (K5)........
N. Truro (O4)*........ 250
N. Uxbridge (H4)*........ 2,100
N. Westport (K6)*........ 3,000
N. Weymouth (D8)*........ 700
N. Wilbraham (E4)*........
Northampton (D3)*....29,063
Northboro (H3)*........△3,122
Northbridge (H4)*....△10,476
Northfield (E2)*........△2,246
Northfield Farms (E2) 500
Norton (K5)*........△4,401
Norwell (F8)*........△2,515
Norwood (B8)*........△16,636
Oak Bluffs (M7)*........△1,521
Oakdale (G3)*........
Oakham (F3)*........△ 455
Ocean Bluff (M4)*........ 300
Ocean Grove (K6)*........ 1,000
Old Sturbridge Village (F4)........
Onset (M6)*........ 1,674
Onset Station (M5)........
Orange (E2)*........△5,894
Orleans (O5)*........△1,759
Osterville (N6)*........ 1,003
Otis (B4)*........△ 359
Otter River (F2)........
Oxford (G4)*........△5,841
Palmer (E4)*........△9,533
Paxton (G3)*........△1,066
Peabody (E5)*........22,645
Pembroke (L4)*........△2,579
Pepperell (H2)*........△3,460
Petersham (F3)*........△ 814
Phillipston (F2)........△ 638
Pigeon Cove (M2)*........ 1,011
Pinehurst (B5)*........ 2,905
Pittsfield (A3)*........55,348
Plainfield (C2)*........△ 228
Plainville (J4)*........△2,088
Pleasant Lake (O6)*.. 125
Plymouth (M5)*........△13,608
Plympton (L5)*........△ 697
Pocasset (M6)*........ 500
Pottersville (K6)........ 2,700
Prides Crossing (E5)*.. 450
Princeton (G3)*........△1,032
Princeton Depot (G3).
Provincetown (O4)*....△3,795
Quincy (D7)*........83,835
Quissett (M6)........ 300
Randolph (D8)*........△9,982
Raynham (K5)*........△2,426
Raynham Center (K5)* 1,800
Reading (C5)*........△14,006
Readville (C8)*........ 6,000
Rehoboth (K5)*........△3,700
Renfrew (B2)........
Revere (D6)*........36,763
Richmond (A3)*........△ 737
Richmond Furnace (A3)........ 250
Riverside (D2)........
Riverside (B7)........ 400
Rochdale (G4)*........1,800
Rochester (L6)*........△1,328
Rock (L5)........ 600
Rockland (L4)*........△8,960
Rockport (M2)*........△4,231
Rockville (A8)........ 500
Rowe (C2)*........△ 199
Rowley (L2)*........△1,768
Roxbury (C7)*........
Royalston (F2)*........△ 838
Russell (C4)*........△1,298
Rutland (G3)*........△3,056
Sagamore (M5)*........ 1,500
Salem (E5)*........41,880
Salisbury (L1)*........△2,695
Sandwich (N5)*........△2,418
Santuit (N6)*........ 400
Saugus (D6)*........△17,162
Saundersville (G4)*........ 380
Savoy (B2)*........△ 291
Saxonville (A7)*........ 3,200
Scituate (F8)*........△5,993
Scotland (L5)........
Seekonk (J5)*........△6,104
Segreganset (K5)*........ 300
Sharon (K4)*........△4,847
Shattuckville (D2)*........ 225
Shawsheen Village (K2)*........ 2,100
Sheffield (A4)*........△2,150
Shelburne Falls (D2)*. 2,364
Sheldonville (J4)*........ 300
Sherborn (A8)*........△1,245
Shirley (H2)*........△4,271
Shirley Center (H2)*.. 1,082
Shrewsbury (H3)*........△10,594
Shutesbury (E3)*........△ 213
Siasconset (P7)*........ 225
Silver Lake (L5)*........ 2,024
Somerset (K5)*........△8,566
Somerville (C6)*........102,351
S. Acton (J3)*........ 1,200
S. Amherst (E3)........ 750
S. Ashburnham (G2)*.. 1,000
S. Athol (F2)*........ 100
S. Attleboro (J5)*........
S. Barre (F3)*........ 1,800
S. Berlin (H3)*........ 200
S. Braintree (D8)*........ 5,600
S. Bridgewater (L5)*..
S. Carver (M5)*........ 300
S. Chatham (O6)*........ 450
S. Dartmouth (L6)*........ 6,300
S. Deerfield (D3)*........ 1,418
S. Dennis (O6)*........ 300
S. Duxbury (M4)*........ 800
S. Easton (K4)*........ 1,500
S. Egremont (A4)*........ 415
S. Essex (L2)*........
S. Groveland (L2)........ 900
S. Hadley (D4)*........△10,145
S. Hadley Falls (D4)* 4,000
S. Hanover (L4)*........ 600
S. Harwich (O6)*........ 400
S. Hingham (E8)........ 650
S. Lancaster (H3)*........ 1,462
S. Lawrence (K2)........25,000
S. Lee (A3)*........ 325
S. Lincoln (J3)*........
S. Middleboro (L5)........ 600
S. Middleton (D5)........
S. Natick (A7)*........ 1,500
S. Orleans (O5)*........ 89
S. Royalston (F2)*........ 415
S. Sandisfield (B4)*........
S. Sudbury (J3)*........ 900
S. Vernon (D2)*........ 225
S. Walpole (K4)*........ 750
S. Wareham (L5)........
S. Wellfleet (P5)*........ 450
S. Westport (K6)*........ 200
S. Weymouth (E8)*........ 8,500
S. Worthington (C3)... 50
S. Yarmouth (O6)*........ 1,185
Southampton (C4)*........△1,387
Southboro (H3)*........△2,760
Southbridge (G4)*........△17,519
Southfield (B4)........ 100
Southville (H3)*........ 300
Southwick (C4)*........△2,850
Spencer (F3)*........△7,027
Springfield (D4)*........162,399
Springfield-Holyoke (urban area)........356,471
State Line (A3)*........ 200
Sterling (G3)*........△2,166
Still River (H3)*........ 150
Stockbridge (A3)*........△2,311
Stoneham (C6)*........△13,229
Stoughton (K4)*........△11,146
Stow (H3)*........△1,700
Straits Pond (F7)*........ 250
Sturbridge (F4)*........△2,805
Sudbury (A6)*........△2,596
Sunderland (D3)*........△ 905
Sutton (G4)........△3,102
Swampscott (E6)*........△11,580
Swansea (K5)*........△6,121
Swansea Center (K5)..
Taunton (K5)*........40,109
Teaticket (M6)*........ 600
Templeton (F2)*........△4,757
Tewkesbury (K2)*........△7,505
Thorndike (E4)*........ 1,650
Three Rivers (E4)*........ 2,359
Tolland (B4)........△ 107
Topsfield (L2)*........△1,412
Townsend (H2)*........△2,817
Townsend Harbor (G2)*........ 197
Truro (O5)*........△ 661
Tully (E2)........
Turners Falls (D2)*........ 5,179
Tyngsboro (J2)*........△2,059
Tyringham (A4)*........△ 235
Unionville (J4)........ 150
Upton (H4)*........△2,656
Uxbridge (H4)*........△7,007
Vineyard Haven (M7)* 1,864
Waban (B7)*........ 6,000
Wakefield (C5)*........△19,633
Wales (F4)*........△ 497
Walpole (B8)*........△9,109
Waltham (B6)*........47,187
Waquoit (M6)*........ 400
Ward Hill (K2)*........ 580
Ware (E3)*........△7,517
Wareham (L5)*........△7,569
Warren (F4)*........△3,406
Warwick (E2)*........△ 429
Washington (B3)........△ 281
Watertown (C6)*........△37,329
Waterville (F2)*........ 450
Waverly (B6)*........10,000
Wayland (A7)*........△4,407
Webster (G4)*........△13,194
Wellesley (B7)*........△20,549
Wellesley Hills (B7)*..18,000
Wellfleet (O5)*........△1,123
Wendell (E2)*........△ 342
Wendell Depot (E2)*..
Wenham (L2)*........△1,644
W. Acton (H3)*........ 1,300
W. Auburn (G4)........
W. Barnstable (N6)*... 750
W. Berlin (H3)*........ 325
W. Boxford (K2)*........ 400
W. Boylston (G3)*........△2,570
W. Brewster (O5)........
W. Bridgewater (K4)*........△4,059
W. Brookfield (F4)*........△1,674
W. Chatham (O6)*........ 300
W. Chelmsford (J2)*... 300
W. Chesterfield (C3)*. 200
W. Concord (A6)*........ 1,285
W. Cummington (B3)* 180
W. Dennis (O6)*........ 600
W. Dudley (F4)........ 200
W. Falmouth (M6)*........ 700
W. Granville (C4)........ 200
W. Groton (H2)*........
W. Hanover (L4)*........ 1,200
W. Harwich (O6)*........ 400
W. Hawley (C2)*........ 56
W. Mansfield (K5)*........ 900
W. Medway (J4)*........ 1,625
W. Millbury (G4)*........ 300
W. Newbury (L1)*........△1,598
W. Newton (B7)*........15,000
W. Peabody (D5)*........ 1,100
W. Pittsfield (A3)........ 2,000
W. Rutland (F3)........
W. Springfield (D4)*.△20,438
W. Stockbridge (A3)*△ 1,165
W. Tisbury (M7)*........△ 347
W. Townsend (H2)*........ 900
W. Upton (H4)*........ 1,400
W. Wareham (L5)*........ 800
W. Warren (F4)*........ 1,244
W. Yarmouth (N6)*........ 1,355
Westboro (H3)*........△7,378
Westfield (D4)*........20,962
Westford (J2)*........△4,262
Westford Station (J2). 300

Westhampton (C3).....△ 452
Westminster (G2)*.....△2,768
Weston (B6)*.....△5,026
Westport (K6)*.....△4,989
Westport Point (K6)*. 500
Westwood (B8)*.....△5,837
Weymouth (D8)*.....△32,690
Whately (D3)*.....△ 939
Wheelwright (F3)*..... 270
Whitinsville (H4)*..... 5,662
Whitman (L4)*.....△8,413
Wilbraham (E4)*.....△4,003
Wilkinsonville (G4)*.....
Williamsburg (C3)*.....△2,056
Williamstown (B2)*.....△6,194
Williamstown Station (B2)..... 5,000
Willimansett (D4)*..... 9,474
Wilmington (C5)*.....△7,039
Winchendon (F2)*.....△6,585
Winchendon Spgs. (G2)* 500
Winchester (C6)*.....△15,509
Windsor (B2)*.....△ 372
Winthrop (D6)*.....△19,496
Woburn (C6)*.....20,492
Woods Hole (M6)*..... 750
Woodville (H4)*..... 350
Worcester (H3)*.....203,486
Worcester (urban area).....217,705
Woronoco (C4)*..... 501
Worthington (C3)*.....△ 462
Wrentham (J4)*.....△5,341
Yarmouth (O6)*.....△3,297
Yarmouth Port (N6)*. 330

Map on Page 67

MICHIGAN

Total Population 6,371,766

83 COUNTIES

Alcona (F4).....5,856
Alger (C2).....10,007
Allegan (D6).....47,493
Alpena (F4).....22,189
Antrim (D3).....10,721
Arenac (F4).....9,644
Baraga (A2).....8,037
Barry (D6).....26,183
Bay (E5).....88,461
Benzie (C4).....8,306
Berrien (C7).....115,702
Branch (D7).....30,202
Calhoun (D6).....120,813
Cass (C7).....28,185
Charlevoix (D3).....13,475
Cheboygan (E3).....13,731
Chippewa (E2).....29,206
Clare (E5).....10,253
Clinton (E6).....31,195
Crawford (E4).....4,151
Delta (C2).....32,913
Dickinson (B2).....24,844
Eaton (E6).....40,023
Emmet (E3).....16,534
Genesee (F5).....270,963
Gladwin (E4).....9,451
Gogebic (F2).....27,053
Grand Traverse (D4).....28,598
Gratiot (E5).....33,429
Hillsdale (E7).....31,916
Houghton (G1).....39,771
Huron (F5).....33,149
Ingham (E6).....172,941
Ionia (D6).....38,158
Iosco (F4).....10,906
Iron (G2).....17,692
Isabella (E5).....28,964
Jackson (E6).....107,925
Kalamazoo (D6).....126,707
Kalkaska (D4).....4,597
Kent (D5).....288,292
Keweenaw (A1).....2,918
Lake (D5).....5,257
Lapeer (F5).....35,794
Leelanau (D4).....8,647
Lenawee (E7).....64,629
Livingston (F6).....26,725
Luce (D2).....8,147
Mackinac (D2).....9,287
Macomb (G6).....184,961
Manistee (C4).....18,524
Marquette (B2).....47,654
Mason (C4).....20,474
Mecosta (D5).....18,968
Menominee (B3).....25,299
Midland (E5).....35,662
Missaukee (D4).....7,458
Monroe (F7).....75,666
Montcalm (D5).....31,013
Montmorency (E3).....4,125
Muskegon (C5).....121,545
Newaygo (D5).....21,567
Oakland (F6).....396,001
Oceana (C5).....16,105
Ogemaw (E4).....9,345
Ontonagon (F1).....10,282
Osceola (D5).....13,797
Oscoda (E4).....3,134
Otsego (E3).....6,435
Ottawa (C6).....73,751
Presque Isle (F3).....11,996
Roscommon (E4).....5,916
Saginaw (E5).....153,515
Saint Clair (G6).....91,591
St. Joseph (D7).....35,071
Sanilac (G5).....30,837
Schoolcraft (C2).....9,148
Shiawassee (E6).....45,967
Tuscola (F5).....38,258
Van Buren (C6).....39,184
Washtenaw (F6).....134,606
Wayne (F6).....2,435,235
Wexford (D4).....18,628

CITIES and TOWNS

Acme (D4)..... 300
Ada (D6)*..... 500
Addison (E7)*..... 488
Adrian (F7)*.....18,393
Advance (D3)..... 50
Afton (E3)*..... 450
Ahmeek (A1)*..... 360
Akron (F5)*..... 431
Alabaster (F4)*..... 125
Alanson (E3)*..... 319
Alaska (D6)..... 335
Alba (E4)*..... 500
Albion (E6)*.....10,406
Alden (D4)*..... 350
Alger (E4)*..... 445
Algonac (G6)*.....2,639
Allegan (D6)*.....4,801
Allen (E7)*..... 340
Allen Park (B7)*.....12,329
Allenville (E3)*..... 200
Allouez (A1)*..... 310
Alma (E5)*.....8,341
Almont (F6)*.....1,035
Alpena (F3)*.....13,135
Alpha (A2)*..... 378
Alpine (D5)..... 100
Alston (G1)*..... 150
Alto (D6)*..... 400
Altona (D5)..... 85
Amasa (G2)*..... 700
Amble (D5)*..... 51
Amelith (F5)..... 150
Anchorville (G6)*..... 950
Ann Arbor (F6)*.....48,251
Antrim (D4)..... 300
Applegate (G5)*..... 244
Arcadia (C4)*..... 450
Argyle (G5)*..... 400
Arlene (D4)..... 86
Armada (G6)*..... 961
Arnheim (G1)*..... 100
Arnold (B2)*.....
Ashley (E5)*..... 449
Ashton (D5)*..... 178
Assyria (D6)..... 200
Athens (D6)*..... 768
Atlanta (E3)*..... 350
Atlantic Mine (G1)*..... 800
Attica (F5)*.....
Atwood (D3)..... 60
Au Gres (F4)*..... 442
Au Sable (F4)..... 300
Au Train (C2)*..... 106
Auburn (F5)*..... 869
Auburn Heights (F6)*.....2,500
Augusta (D6)*..... 898
Aura (A2)*..... 295
Averill (E5)..... 100
Avoca (G5)*..... 300
Avondale (D4)..... 50
Azalia (F6)*..... 110
Bach (F5)*..... 125
Bad Axe (G5)*.....2,973
Bagley (B3)..... 60
Baie de Wasai (E2)..... 100
Bailey (D5)*..... 300
Baldwin (D5)*..... 835
Baltic (G1)*..... 500
Bancroft (E6)*..... 615
Bangor (C6)*.....1,694
Bannister (E5)*..... 300
Baraga (G1)*..... 942
Barbeau (E2)*..... 50
Bark River (B3)*..... 500
Baroda (C7)*..... 344
Barryton (D5)*..... 445
Barton City (F4)*..... 100
Batavia (D7)*..... 124
Bates (D4)..... 75
Bath (E6)*..... 600
Battle Creek (D6)*.....48,666
Bay City (F5)*.....52,523
Bay Port (F5)*..... 557
Bay View (E3)*..... 25
Bayshore (D3)*..... 200
Beacon (B2)*..... 300
Beal City (D5)..... 338
Bear Lake (C4)*..... 364
Beaverton (E5)*..... 794
Bedford (D6)*.....
Belding (D5)*.....4,436
Bellaire (D4)*..... 693
Belleville (F6)*.....1,722
Bellevue (E6)*.....1,168
Belmont (D5)*..... 200
Bendon (D4)*..... 79
Benson (D4)..... 22
Bentley (E5)*..... 150
Benton Harbor (C6)*...18,769
Benton Heights (C6).....6,160
Benzonia (D4)*..... 407
Bergland (F1)*..... 800
Berkley (B6)*.....17,931
Berrien Springs (C7)*...1,761
Bessemer (F2)*.....3,509
Beulah (C4)*..... 458
Big Bay (B2)*..... 670
Big Rapids (D5)*.....6,736
Birch (B2)..... 8
Birch Run (F5)*..... 800
Birmingham (B6)*.....15,467
Bishop (D5)..... 100
Bitely (D5)*..... 200
Blackriver (F4)*..... 259
Blaine (G5)*..... 108
Blanchard (D5)*..... 300
Blaney Park (D2)*..... 30
Bliss (E3)..... 75
Blissfield (F7)*.....2,365
Bloomfield Hills (B6)*.1,468
Bloomingdale (C6)*..... 465
Bolton (F3)*..... 25
Boon (D4)*..... 260
Boyne City (E3)*.....3,028
Boyne Falls (E3)*..... 236
Brampton (B3)*..... 300
Branch (D5)*..... 150
Brant (E5)*..... 95
Brassar (E2)..... 75
Breckenridge (E5)*..... 985
Breedsville (C6)*..... 239
Brethren (D4)*..... 500
Brevort (E2)*..... 80
Bridgeport (F5)*.....1,200
Bridgeton (D5)..... 100
Bridgman (C7)*..... 977
Brighton (F6)*.....1,861
Brimley (E2)*..... 500
Bristol (D4)..... 40
Britton (F6)*..... 517
Brohman (D5)*..... 150
Bronson (D7)*.....2,106
Brooklyn (E6)*..... 862
Brown City (G5)*..... 878
Bruce Crossing (G2)*..... 200
Brutus (E3)*..... 200
Buchanan (C7)*.....5,224
Buckley (D4)*..... 194
Burlington (D6)*..... 329
Burnips (D6)*..... 170
Burr Oak (D7)*..... 814
Burt (F5)*..... 200
Burt Lake (E3)*..... 60
Butternut (E5)*..... 128
Byron (E6)*..... 439
Byron Center (D6)*..... 650
Cadillac (D4)*.....10,425
Caledonia (D6)*..... 619
Calumet (A1)*.....1,256
Cambria (E7)..... 210
Camden (E7)*..... 380
Capac (G5)*.....1,104
Carleton (F6)*.....1,039
Carlshend (B2)*..... 100
Carney (B3)*..... 325
Caro (F5)*.....3,464
Carp Lake (E3)*..... 200
Carrollton (E5)*.....2,000
Carson City (E5)*.....1,168
Carsonville (G5)*..... 487
Caseville (F5)*..... 482
Casnovia (D5)*..... 312
Caspian (G2)*.....1,608
Cass City (F5)*.....1,762
Cassopolis (C7)*.....1,527
Castle Park (C6)*..... 9
Cathro (F3)*..... 100
Cedar (D4)*..... 249
Cedar River (B3)*..... 75
Cedar Springs (D5)*....1,378
Cedarville (E2)*..... 250
Cement City (E6)*..... 500
Center Line (B6)*.....7,659
Central Lake (D3)*..... 692
Centreville (D7)*..... 879
Ceresco (D6)*.....
Champion (B2)*..... 567
Channing (B2)*..... 497
Charleston (G5)..... 85
Charlevoix (D3)*.....2,695
Charlotte (E6)*.....6,606
Chase (D5)*..... 300
Chatham (B2)*..... 650
Cheboygan (E3)*.....5,687
Chelsea (E6)*.....2,580
Chesaning (E5)*.....2,264
Chester (D6)..... 50
Chippewa Lake (D5)*..... 125
Clare (E5)*.....2,440
Clarion (E3)..... 84
Clarklake (E6)*..... 500
Clarkston (F6)*..... 722
Clarksville (D6)*..... 339
Clawson (B6)*.....5,196
Clayton (E7)*..... 467
Clifford (F5)*..... 330
Climax (D6)*..... 524
Clinton (F6)*.....1,344
Clio (F5)*.....1,963
Cohoctah (F6)*..... 150
Coldwater (D7)*.....8,594
Coleman (E5)*.....1,024
Coloma (C6)*.....1,041
Colon (D7)*.....1,000
Columbiaville (F5)*..... 789
Comins (E4)*..... 87
Comstock (D6)*.....8,314
Concord (E6)*..... 730
Conklin (D5)*..... 350
Connorville (F1)..... 50
Constantine (D7)*.....1,514
Conway (E3)*..... 100
Cooks (C3)*..... 300
Coopersville (C5)*.....1,371
Copemish (D4)*..... 255
Copper City (A1)*..... 336
Copper Harbor (B1)*..... 30
Coral (D5)*..... 300
Cornell (B3)*..... 20
Corunna (E6)*.....2,358
Covert (C6)*..... 450
Covington (G2)*..... 260
Cross Village (D3)*..... 200
Croswell (G5)*.....1,775
Crump (E5)*..... 75
Crystal (E5)*..... 450
Crystal Falls (A2)*.....2,316
Crystal Valley (C5)*..... 250
Curran (F4)*..... 50
Curtis (D2)*..... 300
Curtisville (F4)*..... 25
Cusino (C2)..... 50
Custer (C5)*..... 260
Dafter (E2)*..... 125
Daggett (B3)*..... 341
Dalton (C5)..... 500
Dansville (E6)*..... 433
Darragh (E4)..... 20
Davison (F5)*.....1,745
Dayton (C7)*..... 125
De Witt (E6)*..... 824
Dearborn (B7)*.....94,994
Decatur (C6)*.....1,664
Decker (F5)*..... 100
Deckerville (G5)*..... 719
Deerfield (F7)*..... 725
Deerton (B2)*..... 225
Deford (F5)*..... 200
Delton (D6)*..... 700
Delwin (E5)..... 100
Detour (F3)*..... 611
Detroit (B7)*.....1,849,568
Detroit (urban area) 2,644,476
Dewings (D4)..... 6
Dexter (F6)*.....1,307
Dighton (D4)*..... 100
Dimondale (E6)*..... 774
Dollar Bay (G1)*..... 600
Dollarville (D2)..... 100
Dorr (D6)*..... 428
Douglas (C6)*..... 447
Dover (E5)..... 20
Dowagiac (D6)*.....6,542
Dowling (D6)*..... 126
Drayton Plains (F6)*....3,500
Drummond (F3)*..... 443
Dryden (F6)*..... 476
Dublin (D4)..... 25
Dukes (B2)*..... 150
Dundee (F7)*.....1,975
Durand (E6)*.....3,194
Dutton (D6)*..... 150
Eagle (E6)*..... 145
Eagle Harbor (A1)*..... 75
Eagle River (A1)*..... 65
East Ann Arbor (F6)....1,826
E. Detroit (B6)*.....21,461
E. Grand Rapids (D6).....6,403
E. Jordan (D3)*.....1,779
E. Lansing (E6)*.....20,325
E. Tawas (F4)*.....2,040
Eastlake (C4)*..... 376
Eastport (D3)*..... 125
Eaton Rapids (E6)*.....3,509
Eau Claire (C6)*..... 480
Eben Junction (B2)*..... 400
Eckerman (E2)*..... 300
Ecorse (B7)*.....17,948
Edenville (E5)*..... 140
Edgerton (D5)..... 200
Edgewood (E5)..... 50
Edmore (E5)*..... 971
Edwardsburg (C7)..... 616
Elba (F5).....
Elberta (C4)*..... 597
Eldorado (E4)*..... 31
Elk Rapids (D4)*..... 889
Elkton (F5)*..... 854
Ellsworth (D3)*..... 369
Elmira (E3)*..... 230
Elmwood (F5)..... 100
Elo (G1)*..... 35
Eloise (F6)*.....5,000
Elsie (E5)*..... 911
Elwell (E5)*..... 150
Emerson (F3).....
Emmett (G6)*..... 230
Empire (C4)*..... 251
Engadine (D2)*..... 500
Ensign (C3)*..... 446
Epoufette (D2)*..... 50
Erie (F7)*..... 800
Escanaba (C3)*.....15,170
Essexville (F5)*.....3,167
Estey (E5)..... 50
Estral Beach (F7)..... 188
Eureka (E5)*.....
Evart (D5)*.....1,578
Ewen (F2)*..... 817
Fair Haven (G6)*.....1,200
Fairgrove (F5)*..... 570
Fairview (F4)*..... 300
Faithorn (B3)*..... 233
Falmouth (E4)*..... 300
Fargo (G5)*..... 200
Farmington (F6)*.....2,325
Farwell (E5)*..... 694
Felch (B3)*..... 200
Fennville (C6)*..... 639
Fenton (F6)*.....4,226
Fenwick (D5)*..... 150
Ferndale (B6)*.....29,675
Ferry (C5)*..... 200
Ferrysburg (C5)*.....1,454
Fife Lake (D4)*..... 347
Filer City (C4)*..... 340
Filion (G5)*..... 200
Flat Rock (F6)*.....1,931
Flint (F6)*.....163,143
Flint (urban area)....197,151
Flushing (F5)*.....2,226
Forest Lake (C2)*..... 110
Forester (G5)..... 100
Forestville (G5)*..... 124
Forsyth (B2)*..... 400
Foster City (B3)*..... 300
Fosters (F5)*..... 130
Fostoria (F5)*..... 275
Fountain (C4)*..... 247
Fowler (E5)*..... 675
Fowlerville (F6)*.....1,466
Fox (B3)*..... 20
Frankenmuth (F5)*.....1,208
Frankfort (C4)*.....1,858
Franklin Mine (G1)*..... 90
Fraser (B6)*.....1,379
Frederic (E4)*..... 250
Free Soil (C4)*..... 208
Freeland (E5)*.....1,000
Freeport (D6)*..... 452
Fremont (D5)*.....3,056
Frontier (E7)*..... 265
Fruitport (C5)*..... 638
Fulton (D6)*..... 200
Gaastra (G2)*..... 575
Gagetown (F5)*..... 401
Gaines (F6)*..... 352
Galesburg (D6)*.....1,200
Galien (C7)*..... 610
Ganges (C6)*..... 150
Garden (C3)*..... 399
Garden City (B7)*.....9,012
Garnet (D2)*..... 75
Gay (A1)*..... 156
Gaylord (E3)*.....2,271
Genesee (F5)*..... 600
Germfask (C2)*..... 300
Gibbs City (G2)*..... 200
Gilford (F5)*..... 200
Gilmore (E5).....
Girard (E6)..... 275
Gladstone (C3)*.....4,831
Gladwin (E5)*.....1,878
Glen Arbor (C4)*..... 100
Glen Haven (C4)..... 25
Glenn (C6)*..... 180
Glennie (F4)*..... 250
Glenwood (C6)*..... 110
Gobles (D6)*..... 622
Goetzville (E2)*..... 150
Good Hart (D3)*..... 50
Goodells (G5)*..... 600
Goodrich (F6)*..... 525
Gotts (F5)..... 50
Gould City (D2)*..... 350
Gowen (D5)*..... 200
Grace (E3)..... 50
Grand Beach (C7)*..... 105
Grand Blanc (F6)*..... 998
Grand Haven (C5)*.....9,536
Grand Junction (C6)*..... 350
Grand Ledge (E6)*.....4,506
Grand Marais (D2)*..... 600
Grand Rapids (D5)*..176,515
Grand Rapids (urban area).....225,427
Grandville (D6)*.....2,022
Grant (D5)*..... 646
Grass Lake (E6)*..... 878
Grawn (D4)*..... 175
Grayling (E4)*.....2,066
Green (F1).....
Greenbush (F4)*..... 100
Greenland (G1)*..... 600
Greenville (D5)*.....6,668
Gregory (E6)*..... 300
Grind Stone City (G4)*.
Grosse Ile (B7)*.....2,500
Grosse Pointe (B7)*.....6,283
Grosse Pointe Farms (B6).....9,410
Grosse Pointe Park (B7).....13,075
Grosse Pointe Shores (B6).....1,032
Grosse Pointe Woods (B6).....10,381
Gulliver (D2)*..... 300
Gwinn (B2)*..... 900
Hadley (F6)*..... 275
Hagensville (F3)..... 100
Hale (F4)*..... 500
Hamburg (F6)*..... 350
Hamilton (C6)*..... 600
Hamtramck (B6)*.....43,355
Hancock (G1)*.....5,223
Hanover (E6)*..... 377
Harbor Beach (G5)*.....2,349
Harbor Springs (D3)*....1,626
Harper Woods (B6).....9,148
Harrietta (D4)*..... 152
Harris (B3)*..... 150
Harrison (E4)*..... 884
Harrisville (F4)*..... 485
Hart (C5)*.....2,172
Hartford (C6)*.....1,838
Hartland (F6)*.....
Haslett (E6)*.....1,000
Hastings (D6)*.....6,096
Hawkins (D5)..... 50
Hawks (F3)*..... 250
Hazel Park (B6)*.....17,770
Helena (G5)..... 75
Helmer (D2)..... 35
Hemlock (E5)*..... 700
Henderson (E5)*..... 300
Herman (A2)*..... 155
Hermansville (B3)*..... 800
Herron (F3)*.....
Hersey (D5)*..... 239
Hesperia (D5)*..... 760
Hessel (E2)*..... 200
Hiawatha (C2)..... 150
Hickory Corners (D6)*..... 180
Highland Park (B6)*.....46,393
Hillman (F3)*..... 442
Hillsdale (E7)*.....7,297
Hockaday (E4)..... 5
Holland (C6)*.....15,858
Holly (F6)*.....2,663
Holt (E6)*.....6,500
Holton (C5)*..... 350
Home Acres (D6).....20,000
Homer (E6)*.....1,301
Honor (D4)*..... 269
Hope (E5)*..... 100
Hopkins (D6)*..... 531
Horton (E6)*..... 350
Horton Bay (D3)..... 50
Houghton (G1)*.....3,829
Houghton Lake (E4)*.....
Houghton Point (E4)*..
Howard City (D5)*..... 791
Howell (E6)*.....4,353
Hoxeyville (D4)*..... 128
Hubbard Lake (F4)*..... 150
Hubbardston (E5)*..... 335
Hubbell (A1)*.....1,690
Hudson (E7)*.....2,773
Hudsonville (D6)*.....1,101
Hulbert (D2)*..... 400
Huntington Woods (F6)*.....4,949
Huron City (G4)..... 55
Huron Mountain (B2)*.. 20
Ida (F7)*..... 950
Idlewild (D5)*..... 450
Imlay City (F5)*.....1,654
Ina (D4)..... 30
Indian River (E3)*..... 600
Ingalls (B3)*..... 150
Ingallston (B3)*..... 50
Inkster (B7)*.....16,728
Interlochen (D4)*..... 150
Ionia (D6)*.....6,412
Iron Mountain (B3)*.....9,679
Iron River (G2)*.....4,048
Irons (D4)*..... 30
Ironwood (F2)*.....11,466
Isabella (C3)..... 2
Ishpeming (B2)*.....8,962
Ithaca (E5)*.....2,377
Ivanhoe (F5).....
Jackson (E6)*.....51,088
Jacobsville (A1)*..... 145
Jamestown (D6)*..... 300
Jasper (E7)*..... 300
Jeddo (G5)*..... 150
Jenison (D6)*..... 300
Jennings (D4)*..... 250
Johannesburg (E4)*..... 250
Jones (D7)*..... 300
Jonesville (E6)*.....1,594
Kalamazoo (D6)*.....57,704
Kalamazoo (urban area).....82,859
Kalamo (D6)..... 135
Kaleva (C4)*..... 346
Kalkaska (D4)*.....1,250
Kawkawlin (F5)*..... 500
Keego Harbor (F6)*.....7,700
Kent City (D5)*..... 506
Kenton (G2)*..... 400
Keweenaw Bay (G1)*..... 300
Kilmanagh (F5).....
Kinde (G5)*..... 571
Kingsford (A3)*.....5,038
Kingsley (D4)*..... 425
Kingston (F5)*..... 371
Kipling (B3)..... 335
Kneeland (E4)..... 60
La Salle (F7)*..... 74
Labranche (B3)..... 25
Lachine (F3)*..... 90
Laingsburg (E6)*..... 942
Lake (E5)*..... 300
Lake Angelus ‡(F6)..... 123
Lake Ann (D4)*..... 99
Lake City (D4)*..... 719
Lake George (E5)*..... 145
Lake Leelanau (D4)*..... 400
Lake Linden (A1)*.....1,462
Lake Odessa (D6)*.....1,596
Lake Orion (F6)*.....2,385
Lakeland (F6)*..... 300
Lakeview (D5)*..... 975
Lamont (D6)*..... 350
L'Anse (G1)*.....2,376
LANSING (E6)*.....92,129
Lansing (urban area).....133,625
Lapeer (F5)*.....6,143
Laporte (E5)..... 300
Larkin (E5)..... 50
Lathrop (B2)..... 46
Laurium (A1)*.....3,211
Lawrence (C6)*..... 679
Lawton (D6)*.....1,206
Le Roy (D4)*..... 243
Leer (F3)..... 20
Leetsville (D4)*..... 35
Leland (D3)*..... 536
Lenox (G6)*..... 975
Leonard (F6)*..... 391
Leonidas (D6)*..... 225
Leslie (E6)*.....1,543
Levering (E3)*..... 387
Lewiston (E4)*..... 700
Lexington (G5)*..... 594
Lincoln (F4)*..... 409
Lincoln Park (B7)*.....29,310
Linden (F6)*..... 933
Linkville (F5).....
Livonia (F6).....17,534
Linwood (F5)*..... 425
Lisbon ‡(D5).....
Liske (F3)..... 6
Litchfield (E6)*..... 882
Long Lake (F4)*..... 100
Long Rapids (F3)..... 50
Loretto (B3)*..... 350
Lovells (E4)..... 100
Lowell (D6)*.....2,191
Lucas (D4)*..... 120
Ludington (C5)*.....9,506
Lum (F5)*..... 300
Lupton (E4)*..... 200
Luther (D4)*..... 314
Luzerne (E4)*..... 150
Lyon Manor (E4)*..... 87
Lyons (E6)*..... 683
Mackinac Island (E3)*.. 572
Mackinaw City (E3)*.. 970
Mancelona (E4)*.....1,000
Manchester (E6)*.....1,388
Manistee (C4)*.....8,642
Manistique (C3)*.....5,086
Manton (D4)*.....1,085
Maple City (D4)*..... 190
Maple Rapids (E5)*..... 645
Maple Ridge (F4)..... 75
Mapleton (D4)..... 60
Marcellus (D6)*.....1,014
Marenisco (F2)*.....1,300
Marilla (D4)..... 80
Marine City (G6)*.....4,270
Marion (D4)*..... 879
Marlette (G5)*.....1,489
Marne (D5)*..... 600

Map on Page 68

MINNESOTA

Total Population 2,982,483

Dumont (B5)* 223
Dunbar (D3) 76
Dundas (E6)* 469
Dundee (C7)* 179
Dunnell (D7)* 242
Dunvilla (B4) 4
Duquette (F4)* 65
Eagle Bend (C4)* 691
Eagle Lake (E6)* 310
East Chain (D7) 80
East Grand Forks(B3)* 5,049
East Gull Lake (D4) 238
East Lake (E4)* 65
Easton (E7)* 379
Ebro (C3)* 70
Echo (C6)* 490
Eden Prairie (G6) 100
Eden Valley (D5)* 792
Edgerton (B7)* 961
Edina (E6)* 9,744
Effie (E3)* 202
Eitzen (G7)* 151
Elba (F6)* 147
Elbow Lake (B4)* 1,398
Eldred (B3)* 44
Elgin (F6)* 438
Elizabeth (B4)* 168
Elk River (E5)* 1,399
Elko (E6)* 111
Elkton (F7)* 141
Ellendale (E7)* 476
Ellsworth (C7)* 630
Elmdale (D5) 119
Elmer (F3)* 216
Elmore (D7)* 1,074
Elrosa (C5)* 173
Ely (G3)* 5,474
Elysian (E6)* 402
Embarrass (F3)* 450
Emily (E4)* 200
Emmons (E7)* 356
Enfield (E5)* 26
Englund (B2) 6
Erdahl (C5)* 120
Erhard (B4)* 145
Ericsburg (E2)* 210
Erie (C2) 20
Erskine (B3)* 608
Esko (F4)* 300
Essig (D6)* 88
Etter (F6)* 100
Euclid (B3)* 120
Eureka (F5) 50
Evan (D6)* 141
Evansville (C4)* 478
Eveleth (F3)* 5,872
Everdell (B4) 10
Evergreen (C4) 10
Excelsior (E6)* 1,763
Eyota (F7)* 495
Fairbanks (G3)* 12
Fairfax (D6)* 1,143
Fairhaven (D5)* 200
Fairmont (D7)* 8,193
Faith (B3) 29
Falcon Heights (G5) 3,884
Faribault (E6)* 16,028
Farmington (E6)* 1,916
Farwell (C5)* 112
Federal Dam (D3)* 225
Felton (B3)* 258
Fergus Falls (B4)* 12,917
Fernando (D6) 25
Fertile (B3)* 890
Fifty Lakes (D4)*
Fillmore (F7)
Finland (G3)* 175
Finlayson (F4)* 195
Fisher (B3)* 302
Flensburg (D5)* 281
Fletcher (F5) 70
Flom (B3)* 75
Floodwood (E4)* 667
Florence (B6)* 137
Florenton (F3)* 95
Foley (D5)* 1,089
Fond du Lac (F4)* 500
Forada (C5)* 89
Forbes (F3)* 125
Forest Center (G3) 100
Forest City (D5) 50
Forest Lake (F5)* 1,766
Foreston (E5)* 301
Fort Ripley (D4)* 88
Fort Snelling (G5)* 1,096
Fosston (C3)* 1,614
Fountain (F7)* 312
Four Town (C2) 6
Foxhome (B4)* 217
Franklin (D6)* 546
Franklin (F3) 115
Fraser (F3) 134
Frazee (C4)* 1,021
Freeborn (E7)* 300
Freeburg (G7) 58
Freedhem (D4) 30
Freeport (D5)* 558
French River (G4)
Fridley (G5) 3,796
Friesland (F4) 25
Frontenac (F6)* 151
Frost (D7)* 326
Fulda (C7)* 1,149
Funkley (D3)* 28
Garden City (D6)* 273
Garfield (C5)* 244
Garrison (E4)* 150
Garvin (C6)* 264
Gary (B3)* 278
Gatzke (C2)* 36
Gaylord (D6)* 1,229
Gemmell (D3)* 150
Geneva (E7)* 332
Genola (D5)* 79
Gentilly (B3)* 100
Georgetown (B3)* 192
Georgeville (C5)* 50
Gheen (F3)* 67
Ghent (C6)* 336
Gibbon (D6)* 830
Giese (E4)* 50
Gilbert (F3)* 2,247
Gilchrist (C5) 80
Gilman (E5)* 150
Glen (E4)* 30
Glencoe (D6)* 2,801
Glendorado (E5) 11
Glenville (E7)* 672
Glenwood (C5)* 2,666
Glory (E4) 2
Gluek (C6)* 72
Glyndon (B4)* 411
Godahl (D6) 40
Golden Valley (G5) 5,551
Gonvick (C3)* 375
Good Thunder (D6)* 476
Goodhue (F6)* 489
Goodland (E3)* 450
Goodridge (C2)* 144
Goodview (G6) 777
Gordonsville (E7)* 100
Gowan (F4)*
Graceton (D2)* 38
Graceville (B5)* 962
Graff (D4) 125
Granada (D7)* 403
Grand Marais (G2)* 1,078
Grand Meadow (F7)* 766
Grand Portage (G2)* 150
Grand Rapids (E3)* 6,019
Grandy (E5)* 175
Granger (F7)* 158
Granite Falls (C6)* 2,511
Grasston (E5)* 154
Grattan (D3) 100
Greaney (F3)* 100
Greeley (E5) 12
Green Isle (E6)* 332
Green Valley (C6)* 121
Greenbush (B2)* 713
Greenleaf (D6) 28
Greenleafton (F7) 54
Greenwald (D5)* 207
Grey Eagle (D5)* 400
Groningen (F4)* 27
Grove City (D5)* 481
Grovelake (C5) 60
Grygla (C2)* 216
Guckeen (D7)* 116
Gully (C3)* 183
Gunflint Trail (H2)
Guthrie (D3)* 60
Hackensack (D4)* 272
Hader (F6) 30
Hadler (B3) 10
Hadley (C7)* 139
Hallock (A2)* 1,552
Halma (B2)* 177
Halstad (B3)* 635
Hamburg (D6)* 184
Hamel (F5)* 200
Hammond (F6)* 192
Hampton (E6)* 275
Hancock (C5)* 852
Hanley Falls (C6)* 320
Hanover (E5)* 228
Hanska (D6)* 473
Harding (E4)* 124
Hardwick (B7)* 297
Harmony (F7)* 1,022
Harney (F4)* 75
Harris (F5)* 569
Hart (G7) 18
Hartland (E7)* 300
Hassan (E5) 50
Hastings (F6)* 6,560
Hatfield (B7)* 110
Haug (B2) 14
Havana (E6) 25
Hawick (D5)* 63
Hawley (B4)* 1,196
Haydenville (B5) 10
Hayfield (F7)* 805
Hayward (E7)* 241
Hazel (B2)* 20
Hazel Run (C6)* 129
Hector (D6)* 1,196
Heidelberg (E6) 61
Heinola (C4) 9
Henderson (E6)* 762
Hendricks (B6)* 781
Hendrum (B3)* 352
Henning (C4)* 1,004
Henriette (E5)* 57
Herman (B5)* 752
Heron Lake (C7)* 837
Hewitt (C4)* 312
Hibbing (F3)* 16,276
High Landing (C2) 7
Hill City (E4)* 501
Hillman (E4)* 85
Hills (B7)* 520
Hillview (C4) 45
Hinckley (F4)* 902
Hines (D3)* 100
Hitterdal (B4)* 262
Hoffman (C5)* 575
Hokah (G7)* 643
Holdingford (D5)* 458
Holland (B6)* 263
Hollandale (E7)* 360
Holloway (C5)* 264
Holmes City (C5)* 116
Holt (B2)* 172
Holyoke (F4)* 75
Homer (G6)* 200
Hope (E7)* 148
Hopkins (G5)* 7,595
Hopper (F3)* 175
Houston (G7)* 973
Hovland (G2)* 300
Howard Lake (D5)* 931
Hubbard (C4)* 140
Hugo (E5)* 440
Humboldt (A2)* 143
Huntersville (D4) 25
Huntley (D7)* 118
Huot (B3) 12
Hutchinson (D6)* 4,690
Ihlen (B7)* 135
Illgen City (G3) 7
Independence (F4)* 20
Indus (E2)* 55
Inger (D3)* 100
International Falls (E2)* 6,269
Inver Grove (E6)* 667

Iona (C7)* 355
Iron (F3)* 128
Ironton (D4)* 828
Isabella (G3)*
Isanti (E5)* 422
Island Park (F5)* 1,357
Island View (E2) 18
Isle (E4)* 674
Ivanhoe (B6)* 682
Jackson (C7)* 3,313
Jacobson (E4)* 106
Janesville (E6)* 1,287
Jasper (B7)* 840
Jeffers (C6)* 516
Jenkins (D4)* 170
Jesse Lake (E3)* 97
Johnsburg (F7) 31
Johnson (B5)* 54
Jordan (E6)* 1,494
Judson (D6)* 153
Kabetogama (F2)* 28
Kanaranzi (B7)* 100
Kandiyohi (D5)* 293
Karlstad (B2)* 804
Kasota (D6)* 600
Kasson (F6)* 1,353
Keewatin (E3)* 1,807
Kelliher (D3)* 336
Kellogg (G6)* 409
Kelly Lake (F3)* 700
Kelsey (F3)* 15
Kennedy (B2)* 480
Kenneth (B7)* 119
Kensington (C5)* 354
Kent (B4)* 178
Kenyon (E6)* 1,651
Kerkhoven (C5)* 664
Kerrick (F4)* 81
Kettle River (E4)* 223
Kiester (E7)* 541
Kilkenny (E6)* 174
Kimball (D5)* 479
Kimberly (E4)* 35
Kinbrae (C7)* 85
Kingsdale (F4)* 72
Kingston (D5) 140
Kinmount (F2)
Kinney (F3)* 336
Klossner (D6)* 88
Knapp (D5) 6
Knife River (G4)* 375
Kragnes (B3) 25
Kroschel (E4) 25
La Crescent (G7)* 1,229
La Prairie ‡(E3) 88
La Salle (D6)* 144
Lac qui Parle (B5) 100
Lafayette (D6)* 438
Lake Benton (B6)* 863
Lake Bronson (B2)* 438
Lake City (F6)* 3,457
Lake Crystal (D6)* 1,430
Lake Elmo (F6)* 386
Lake Fremont (Zimmerman*) (E5) 169
Lake George (D3)* 95
Lake Henry (D5) 97
Lake Hubert (D4)* 125
Lake Itasca (C3)* 50
Lake Lillian (C6)* 358
Lake Netta (E5)
Lake Park (B4)* 689
Lake Shore (D4) 326
Lake Wilson (B7)* 434
Lakefield (C7)* 1,651
Lakeland (F6)* 43
Lakeside (D6) 23
Lakeville (E6)* 628
Lakewood (G4) 917
Lamberton (C6)* 1,208
Lamoille (G6)* 50
Lamson (D5) 20
Lancaster (B2)* 536
Lanesboro (G7)* 1,100
Lansing (F7)* 240
Laporte (D3)* 189
Larsmont (G4)* 185
Lastrup (D4)* 158
Lauderdale (G5) 1,033
Lawler (E4)* 75
Lawndale (B4)* 25
Le Center (E6)* 1,314
Le Roy (F7)* 959
Le Sueur (E6)* 2,713
Leader (D4)* 20
Leaf Valley (C4)* 50
Lemond (E7) 8
Lengby (C3)* 206
Lenora (G7) 50
Leonard (C3)* 88
Leoneth (Leonidas) (F3)* 88
Leota (C7)* 250
Lerdal (E7) 26
Lester Prairie (D6)* 663
Lewiston (G7)* 786
Lewisville (D7)* 362
Libby (E4)* 17
Lime Creek (C7)* 54
Lincoln (D4)* 30
Linden (D6) 13
Lindstrom (F5)* 729
Lismore (B7)* 317
Litchfield (D5)* 4,608
Little Falls (D5)* 6,717
Little Marais (G3)* 50
Little Rock (D5) 28
Little Sauk (D5)* 100
Littlefork (E2)* 671
Lockhart (B3)* 60
Loman (E2)* 80
London (E7)* 100
Long Beach (C5) 181
Long Lake (F5)* 399
Long Prairie (D5)* 2,443
Long Siding (E5)* 48
Longville (D4)* 116
Lonsdale (E6)* 510
Loretto (F5)* 179
Louisburg (B5)* 93
Lowry (C5)* 285
Lucan (C6)* 246
Luce (C4) 32
Lutsen (F2)* 75
Luverne (B7)* 3,650
Luxemburg (D5) 66
Lydia (E6) 93
Lyle (F7)* 609
Lyman (C4) 10
Lynd (C6)* 275
Lyndale (F5)
Mabel (G7)* 788
Madelia (D6)* 1,790
Madison (B5)* 2,303
Madison Lake (E6)* 357
Magnolia (B7)* 260
Mahkonce (C3) 6
Mahnomen (C3)* 1,464
Mahtomedi (F5)* 1,375
Mahtowa (F4)* 150
Maine (C4) 14
Makinen (F3)* 255
Malmo (E4)* 58
Malung (C2)* 5
Manannah (D5) 50
Manchester (E7)* 113
Manganese ‡(D4) 41
Manhattan Beach (E4)* 72
Manitou (D2)* 50
Mankato (E6)* 18,809
Mansfield (E7) 20
Mantorville (F6)* 477
Maple Bay (B3) 110
Maple Island (E7) 175
Maple Lake (D5)* 780
Maple Plain (F5)* 479
Mapleton (E7)* 1,083
Mapleview ‡(F7) 435
Marble (E3)* 867
Marcell (E3)* 60
March (B2) 15
Marcy (G3) 18
Margie (E2)* 100
Marietta (B5)* 380
Marine on Saint Croix (F5)* 334
Markham (F3) 310
Markville (F4)* 100
Marshall (C6)* 5,923
Matawan (E7)* 59
Mavie (B2) 10
Max (D3)* 45
Mayer (E6)* 153
Mayhew Lake (D5) 24
Maynard (C6)* 507
Mazeppa (F6)* 523
McGrath (E4)* 135
McGregor (E4)* 322
McIntosh (C3)* 881
McKinley (F3)* 196
Meadow Brook (F3)* 21
Meadowlands (F3)* 134
Medford (E6)* 409
Medicine Lake (G5) 284
Meire Grove (C5) 128
Melby (C4)* 75
Melrose (D5)* 2,106
Melrude (F3)* 109
Melvin (B3) 25
Menahga (C4)* 849
Mendota (G5)* 243
Mentor (B3)* 321
Meriden (E6)* 131
Merrifield (D4)* 78
Mesaba (F3)
Middle River (B2)* 356
Milaca (E5)* 1,917
Milan (C5)* 561
Mildred (D4)* 25
Millerville (C4) 173
Millville (F6)* 168
Milroy (C6)* 268
Miltona (C4)* 150
Mineral Center (G2) 6
Minneapolis (E5)* 521,718
Minneapolis-St. Paul (urban area) 977,931
Minneska (G6)* 134
Minneota (C6)* 1,274
Minnesota City (G6)* 201
Minnesota Falls (C6) 150
Minnesota Lake (E7)* 609
Minnetonka Beach ‡(F5)* 376
Mizpah (D3)* 166
Moland (E6) 23
Money Creek (G7) 150
Monterey (D7)* 315
Montevideo (C6)* 5,459
Montgomery (E6)* 1,913
Monticello (E5)* 1,231
Montrose (E5)* 300
Moorhead (B4)* 14,870
Moose Lake (E4)* 1,603
Mora (E5)* 2,018
Morgan (D6)* 949
Morningside (G5) 1,699
Morrill (E5) 40
Morris (C5)* 3,811
Morristown (E6)* 533
Morton (C6)* 794
Moscow (E7) 25
Motley (D4)* 435
Mound (E6)* 2,061
Mound Prairie (G7) 8
Mountain Iron (F3)* 1,377
Mountain Lake (D7)* 1,733
Murdock (C5)* 393
Myrtle (E7)* 136
Nary (D3) 7
Nashua (B4)* 181
Nashwauk (E3)* 2,029
Nassau (B5)* 205
Naytahwaush (C3)* 220
Nebish (D3)* 35
Nelson (C5)* 160
Nemadji (F4)* 25
Nerstrand (E6)* 228
Nett Lake (E2)*
Nevis (D4)* 332
New Auburn (D6)* 290
New Brighton (G5)* 2,218
New Germany (E6)* 286
New London (C5)* 726
New Market (E6)* 193
New Munich (D5)* 277
New Prague (E6)* 1,915
New Richland (E7) 908
New Trier (F6) 73
New Ulm (D6)* 9,348
New York Mills (C4)* 977
Newburg (G7)
Newfolden (B2)* 367
Newhouse (G7) 15
Newport (F6)* 1,672
Newry (E7) 7
Nichols (E4) 3
Nickerson (F4)* 48
Nicollet (D6)* 493
Nielsville (B3)* 189
Nimrod (D4)* 112
Nisswa (D4)* 578
Nodine (G7) 50
Nopeming (F4)* 474
Noracres (B2)
Norcross (B5)* 179
Norland (B2) 5
Norseland (D6) 75
North Branch (F5)* 769
North Mankato (D6)* 4,788
North Redwood (D6)* 215
North Saint Paul (E5)* 4,248
Northcote (A2)* 35
Northfield (E6)* 7,487
Northome (D3)* 349
Northrop (D7)* 157
Norway Lake (C5) 30
Norwood (E6)* 749
Nowthen (E5) 18
Noyes (A2)* 93
Oak Center (F6) 30
Oak Island (D1)* 40
Oak Park (E5)* 100
Oakland (E7)* 110
Odessa (B5)* 283
Odin (D7)* 208
Ogema (C3)* 249
Ogilvie (E5)* 362
Okabena (C7)* 236
Oklee (C3)* 494
Olga (C3) 7
Olivia (C6)* 2,012
Onamia (E4)* 704
Opole (D5)* 100
Opstead (E4) 18
Orchard Lake (E6) 150
Org (C7) 25
Orleans (B2)* 53
Ormsby (D7)* 190
Oronoco (F6)* 200
Orr (F2)* 309
Orrock (E5) 9
Ortonville (B5)* 2,577
Osage (C4)* 184
Osakis (C5)* 1,488
Oshawo (D4) 6
Oslo (A2)* 440
Osseo (G5)* 1,167
Ostrander (F7)* 191
Otisco (E7)* 100
Ottawa (E6)* 110
Ottertail (C4)* 237
Outing (E4)* 150
Owatonna (E6)* 10,191
Oylen (D4) 35
Padua (C5) 40
Page (E5) 22
Palisade (E4)* 212
Palmdale (F5) 12
Palmers (G4) 15
Palo (F3) 700
Parent (D5) 9
Park Rapids (D4)* 3,027
Parkers Prairie (C4)* 900
Parkville (F3)* 500
Payne (F3)* 110
Paynesville (D5)* 1,503
Pease (E5)* 179
Pelan (B2) 30
Pelican Lakes (D4) 154
Pelican Rapids (B4)* 1,676
Pemberton (E7)* 152
Penasse (C1)* 3
Pencer (C2)* 11
Pengilly (E3)* 75
Pennington (D3)* 100
Pennock (C5)* 238
Pequot Lakes (D4)* 552
Perham (C4)* 1,926
Perley (B3)* 204
Petersburg (C7) 100
Peterson (G7)* 318
Peyla (F3)*
Phelps (C4) 15
Philbrook (D4)* 100
Pickwick (G7) 122
Pierz (D5)* 856
Pillager (D4)* 362
Pilot Grove (D7) 24
Pilot Mound (F7) 18
Pine City (F5)* 1,937
Pine Island (F6)* 1,298
Pine River (D4)* 835
Pinecreek (C2)* 32
Pinewood (C3)* 8
Pipestone (B7)* 5,269
Pitt (D2)* 12
Plainview (F6)* 1,524
Plato (D6)* 263
Pleasant Lake (D5) 53
Plummer (B3)* 340
Ponemah (D2)* 200
Ponsford (C2)* 250
Pontoria (D4) 60
Poplar (D4)* 12
Porter (B6)* 291
Potsdam (F6) 50
Powderhorn (G6)* 11,118
Pratt (E6)* 43
Predmore (F7) 30
Preston (F7)* 1,399
Priam (C5) 14
Princeton (E5)* 2,108
Prinsburg (C6)* 390
Prior Lake (E6)* 536
Proctor (F4)* 2,693
Prosit (F4)* 227
Prosper (G7)* 65
Providence (B6) 8
Puposky (C3)* 100
Quamba (E5)* 100
Rabey (E4) 30
Racine (F7)* 175
Radium (B2)* 40
Rako (D2) 9
Ramey (E5) 75
Randall (D4)* 425
Randolph (E6)* 259
Ranier (E2)* 227
Ranum (B3) 2
Rapidan (D6)*
Rauch (E3)* 95
Ray (E2)* 95
Raymond (C5)* 580
Reading (C7)* 160
Reads Landing (F6)* 201
Red Lake Falls (B3)* 1,733
Red Wing (F6)* 10,645
Redby (D3)* 210
Redlake (C3)* 350
Redtop (E4)* 26
Redwood Falls (C6)* 3,813
Regal (D5)* 64
Remer (E3)* 412
Renville (C6)* 1,323
Revere (C6)* 198
Rice (D5)* 328
Rice Lake (E5) 100
Richfield (E6)* 17,502
Richmond (D5)* 700
Richville (C4)* 141
Richwood (C4)* 65
Ridgeway (G7) 50
River (C2)
Riverton (D4)* 148
Robbin (A2) 40
Robbinsdale (G5)* 11,289
Roberts (B4) 5
Rochert (C4)* 120
Rochester (F6)* 29,885
Rock Creek (F5)* 100
Rock Dell (F7) 41
Rockford (F5)* 369
Rockville (D5)* 288
Rogers (E5)* 268
Rollag (B4) 27
Rollingstone (G6)* 315
Ronneby (E5)* 72
Roosevelt (C2)* 228
Roscoe (D5)* 182
Roscoe (F6) 20
Rose Creek (F7)* 314
Roseau (C2)* 2,231
Roseland (C6)* 100
Rosemount (E6)* 567
Rosen (B5) 50
Rosendale (D5) 40
Roseville (G5) 6,437
Rosewood (B2)*
Ross (C2)* 20
Rothsay (B4)* 537
Round Lake (C7)* 435
Round Prairie (D5)* 35
Royalton (D5)* 500
Rush City (F5)* 1,175
Rush River (D6) 15
Rushford (G7)* 1,270
Rushford (Village) ‡(G7) 612
Rushmore (C7)* 368
Russell (C6)* 508
Rustad (B4)* 32
Ruthton (B6)* 534
Rutledge (F4)* 163
Sabin (B4)* 211
Sacred Heart (C6)* 745
Saginaw (F4)* 51
Saint Anna (D5) 12
St. Anthony (D5) 66
St. Anthony Falls(G5)* 1,406
St. Bonifacius (F5)* 438
St. Charles (F7)* 1,548
St. Clair (E6)* 324
St. Cloud (D5)* 28,410
St. Francis (E5)* 125
St. George (D6) 74
St. Hilaire (B2)* 276
St. James (D7)* 3,861
St. Joseph (D5)* 1,246
St. Kilian (C7)
St. Leo (C6)* 128
St. Louis Park (G5)* 22,644
St. Martin (D5)* 195
St. Michael (E5)* 487
SAINT PAUL (E6)* 311,349
St. Paul-Minneapolis (urban area) 977,931
St. Paul Park (F6)* 2,438
St. Peter (E6)* 7,754
St. Rosa (D5) 69
St. Stephen (D5) 234
St. Vincent (A2)* 272
Salol (C2)* 55
Sanborn (C6)* 613
Sandstone (F4)* 1,097
Santiago (E5)* 68
Sargeant (F7)* 121
Sartell (D5)* 662
Sauk Centre (C5)* 3,140
Sauk Rapids (D5)* 3,410
Saum (D3)* 40
Savage (E6)* 389
Sawbill Landing (G3) 25
Sawyer (F4)* 183
Scandia (F5)* 200
Scanlon (F4)* 572
Schley (D3)* 3
Schroeder (G3)* 200
Seaforth (C6)* 136
Searles (D6)* 102

Sebeka (C4)* 802
Sedan (C5)* 134
Shafer (F5)* 127
Shakopee (E6)* 3,185
Shaw (F3)* 82
Sheldon (G7) 45
Shelly (B3)* 329
Sherack (B2) 14
Sherburn (D7)* 1,221
Shevlin (C3)* 242
Shieldsville (E6) 28
Shirley (B3) 7
Shooks (D3)* 30
Shoreham (C4)* 91
Shotley (D2) 35
Shovel Lake (E4)* 10
Side Lake (E3)* 120
Silver Creek (D5)* 104
Silver Lake (D6)* 603
Silverdale (E3) 90
Simpson (F7)* 92
Sioux Valley (C7) 200
Skime (C2)*
Skyberg (F6)* 25
Slayton (C7)* 1,887
Sleepy Eye (D6)* 3,278
Sobieski (D5) 189
Solana (E4) 12
Solway (C3)* 124
Soudan (F3)* 1,190
South Branch (D7) 698
South Haven (D5)* 305
South International Falls (E2)* 1,840
South St. Paul (F6)* 15,909
Spafford (C7) 10
Spicer (C5)* 566
Spooner (D2)* 420
Spring Grove (G7)* 1,093
Spring Hill (D5) 91
Spring Lake (E3)* 24
Spring Lake (E5) 18
Spring Park (F5)* 500
Spring Vale (E5) 25
Spring Valley (F7)* 2,467
Springfield (C6)* 2,574
Squaw Lake (D3)* 132
Stacy (E5)* 150
Stanchfield (E5)* 100
Stanton (E6)* 60
Staples (D4)* 2,782
Star Lake (B4) 125
Starbuck (C5)* 1,143
Stark (E5) 39
Steen (B7)* 228
Stephen (A2)* 877
Sterling Center (D7) 22
Stewart (D6)* 695
Stewartville (F7)* 1,193
Stillwater (F5)* 7,674
Stockton (G6)* 235
Storden (C6)* 398
Strandquist (B2)* 208
Strathcona (B2)* 143
Strout (D5) 10
Sturgeon Lake (F4)* 189
Sumter (D6) 17
Sunburg (C5)* 151
Sundahl (B3) 10
Sunrise (F5)* 80
Svea (C6)* 97
Swan River (E3)* 30
Swanville (D5)* 373
Swatara (E4)* 100
Swift (C2)* 40
Swift Falls (C5) 120
Syre (B3) 10
Tabor (B2) 60
Taconite (E3)* 322
Talmoon (E3)* 25
Tamarack (E4)* 132
Taopi (F7)* 118
Taunton (B6)* 217
Taylors Falls (F5)* 520
Tenney (B4)* 62
Tenstrike (D3)* 206
Terrace (C5)* 80
Terrebonne (B3) 50
Theilman (F6)* 95
Thief River Falls (B2)* 6,926
Thomson (F4)* 170
Thorpe (D6) 7
Tintah (B5)* 235
Tobique (E3)*
Tofte (H3)* 100
Togo (E3)* 7
Toimi (G3) 100
Toivola (F3)* 312
Tonka Bay (F5) 899
Tower (F3)* 773
Tracy (C6)* 3,020
Trail (C3)* 123
Traverse (D6) 15
Triumph (D7)* 561
Trommald (D4)* 117
Trosky (B7)* 140
Truman (D7)* 1,106
Turtle River (D3) 57
Twig (F4)* 100
Twin Lakes (E7)* 124
Twin Valley (B3)* 899
Two Harbors (G3)* 4,400
Tyler (B6)* 1,121
Ulen (B3)* 525
Underwood (C4)* 336
Upsala (D5)* 366
Urbank (C4) 162
Utica (G7)* 194
Vasa (F6)* 60
Vawter (D5)
Verdi (B6)* 101
Vergas (C4)* 301
Vermillion (F6)* 112
Verndale (C4)* 576
Verndon (E4) 40
Vernon Center (D7)* 344
Veseli (E6)* 132
Vesta (C6)* 340
Victoria (E6)* 302
Viking (B2)* 130
Villard (C5)* 288
Vining (C4)* 180
Viola (F6)* 80
Virginia (F3)* 12,486
Wabasha (F6)* 2,468
Wabasso (C6)* 693
Waconia (E6)* 1,569
Wadena (C4)* 3,958
Wahkon (E4)* 202
Waite Park (D5)* 1,639
Waldorf (E7)* 266
Wales (G3)* 35
Walker (D3)* 1,192
Walnut Grove (C6)* 890
Walters (E7)* 139
Waltham (F7)* 212
Wanamingo (F6)* 496
Wanda (C6)* 178
Wannaska (C2)* 66
Warba (E3)* 125
Ward Springs (D5)* 45
Warren (B2)* 1,779
Warroad (C2)* 1,276
Warsaw (E6)* 150
Waseca (E6)* 4,927
Wasioja (F6) 150
Waskish (C2)* 40
Waterford (E6) 65
Watertown (E6)* 837
Waterville (E6)* 1,627
Watkins (D5)* 659
Watson (C5)* 284
Waubun (C3)* 426
Waverly (E5)* 493
Wawina (E3)*
Wayzata (E6)* 1,791
Weaver (G6)* 105
Webster (E6)*
Wegdahl (C6)* 51
Welch (F6)* 70
Welcome (D7)* 712
Wells (E7)* 2,475
Weme (C3)
Wendell (B4)* 284
West Concord (F6)* 770
W. Saint Paul (G5) 7,955
W. Union (C5)* 100
Westbrook (C6)* 1,017
Westbury (C4) 25
Westport (C5)* 96
Whalan (G7)* 176
Wheaton (B5)* 1,948
Whipholt (D3)* 100
White Bear Lake (G5)* 3,646
White Earth (C3)* 800
White Rock (F6) 100
Wig Wam Bay (E4) 50
Wilbert (D7) 30
Wilder (C7)* 118
Wildwood (E3) 40
Wilkinson (D3)* 200
Willernie (H5)* 592
Williams (D2)* 414
Willmar (C5)* 9,410
Willow Creek (D7) 12
Willow River (F4)* 294
Wilmington (G7) 15
Wilmont (C7)* 473
Wilson (G7)
Wilton (C3)* 108
Windom (C7)* 3,165
Winger (B3)* 283
Winnebago (D7)* 2,127
Winona (G6)* 25,031
Winsted (D6)* 941
Winthrop (D6)* 1,251
Winton (G3)* 184
Wirock (C7) 20
Wirt (E3)* 138
Witoka (G7)
Wolf Lake (C4)* 109
Wolverton (B4)* 198
Wood Lake (C6)* 504
Woodland ‡(G5) 411
Woodstock (B7)* 277
Worthington (C7)* 7,923
Wrenshall (F4)* 148
Wright (E4)* 199
Wrightstown (C4) 23
Wyattville (G7) 26
Wykoff (F7)* 509
Wylie (B3) 10
Wyoming (F5)* 325
York (F7) 6
Young America (E6)* 365
Yucatan (G7) 15
Zemple ‡(E3) 87
Zim (F3)* 110
Zimmerman (E5)* 258
Zumbro Falls (F6)* 172
Zumbrota (F6)* 1,686

Map on Page 69

MISSISSIPPI

Total Population 2,178,914

82 COUNTIES

Adams (B8) 32,256
Alcorn (G1) 27,158
Amite (C8) 19,261
Attala (E4) 26,652
Benton (F1) 8,793
Bolivar (C3) 63,004
Calhoun (F3) 18,369
Carroll (E4) 15,499
Chickasaw (G3) 18,951
Choctaw (F4) 11,009
Claiborne (C7) 11,944
Clarke (G6) 19,362
Clay (G3) 17,757
Coahoma (C2) 49,361
Copiah (D7) 30,493
Covington (E7) 16,036
De Soto (E1) 24,599
Forrest (F8) 45,055
Franklin (C8) 10,929
George (G9) 10,012
Greene (G8) 8,215
Grenada (E3) 18,830
Hancock (E10) 11,891
Harrison (F10) 84,073
Hinds (D6) 142,164
Holmes (D4) 33,301
Humphreys (C4) 23,115
Issaquena (B5) 4,966
Itawamba (H2) 17,216
Jackson (G9) 31,401
Jasper (F6) 18,912
Jefferson (B7) 11,306
Jefferson Davis (E7) 15,500
Jones (F7) 57,235
Kemper (G5) 15,893
Lafayette (E2) 22,798
Lamar (E8) 13,225
Lauderdale (G6) 64,171
Lawrence (D7) 12,639
Leake (E5) 21,610
Lee (G2) 38,237
Leflore (D3) 51,813
Lincoln (D8) 27,899
Lowndes (H4) 37,852
Madison (D5) 33,860
Marion (E8) 23,967
Marshall (E1) 25,106
Monroe (H3) 36,543
Montgomery (E4) 14,470
Neshoba (F5) 25,730
Newton (F6) 22,681
Noxubee (G4) 20,022
Oktibbeha (G4) 24,569
Panola (E2) 31,271
Pearl River (E9) 20,641
Perry (G8) 9,108
Pike (D8) 35,137
Pontotoc (F2) 19,994
Prentiss (G1) 19,810
Quitman (D2) 25,885
Rankin (E6) 28,881
Scott (E6) 21,681
Sharkey (C5) 12,903
Simpson (E7) 21,819
Smith (E6) 16,740
Stone (F9) 6,264
Sunflower (C3) 56,031
Tallahatchie (D3) 30,486
Tate (E1) 18,011
Tippah (G1) 17,522
Tishomingo (H1) 15,544
Tunica (D1) 21,664
Union (F2) 20,262
Walthall (D8) 15,563
Warren (C6) 39,616
Washington (C4) 70,504
Wayne (G7) 17,010
Webster (F3) 11,607
Wilkinson (B8) 14,116
Winston (F4) 22,231
Yalobusha (E2) 15,191
Yazoo (D5) 35,712

CITIES and TOWNS

Abbeville (F2)*
Abbott (G3)
Aberdeen (H3)* 5,290
Aberdeen Jct. (E4)
Ackerman (F4)* 1,463
Acona (D4) 250
Adair (D4)
Adams (C6)* 40
Agricola (G9)* 200
Alcorn (B7)* 500
Algoma (G2)*
Allen (C7)
Alligator (C2)* 214
Alva (F3)
Amory (H3)* 4,990
Anding (D5)* 140
Anguilla (C5)* 601
Ansley (E10) 65
Arcola (C4)* 413
Ariel (C8) 19
Arkabutla (D1)* 207
Arm (D8)* 135
Artesia (G4)* 594
Ashland (F1)* 328
Askew (D1)*
Auburn (C8)* 200
Auter (C4) 25
Avalon (D3)*
Avent (G8)
Avera (G8)*
Bailey (G6)* 35
Baird (C4)* 193
Baldwyn (G2)* 1,567
Ballardsville (H2) 30
Ballground (C5) 300
Baltzer (C3)* 250
Banks (D1)*
Banner (F2)* 125
Barbara (G9) 50
Barland (C7) 10
Barlow (C7)* 60
Barnett (G7)* 250
Barr (E1)* 275
Barto (D8) 25
Basic (G6)
Bassfield (E8)* 320
Batesville (E2)* 2,463
Battle (H8)
Baxter (F6)
Baxterville (E8)*
Bay Saint Louis (F10)* 4,621
Bay Springs (F7)* 1,302
Bayland (C5)
Bear Creek (D6)
Beatty (E4) 50
Beaumont (G8)* 1,200
Beauregard (D7)* 231
Becker (G3)* 300
Bee Lake (D4)
Belden (G2)* 360
Belen (D2)*
Bellefontaine (F3)*
Bellewood (C4) 75
Belmont (H1)* 814
Belzoni (C4)* 4,071
Benndale (G9)*
Benoit (C3)* 444
Benton (D5)* 225
Bentonia (D5)* 496
Berclair (D4) 100
Bethany (G2)*
Beulah (B3)* 342
Bewelcome (C8)
Bexley (G9)*
Big Creek (F3)* 147
Big Point (H9) 300
Bigbee Valley (H4)* 51
Biloxi (G10)* 37,425
Binnsville (H5) 50
Black Hawk (E4)* 100
Blaine (C3)* 200
Blanton (C5)*
Blodgett (F8) 5
Blue Mountain (G1)* 875
Blue Springs (G2)* 125
Bobo (C2)*
Bogue Chitto (D8)*
Bolatusha (E5) 50
Bolton (D6)* 741
Bond (F9)* 500
Bonhomie (F8)
Bonita (G6)*
Booneville (G1)* 3,295
Bothwell (G8)
Bourbon (C4)*
Bovina (C6)* 82
Bowling Green (E4) 28
Boyle (C3)* 799
Bradley (G4)
Brandon (E6)* 1,827
Braxton (D6)* 206
Brewer (G7) 50
Briers (B8)
Brody (F1)
Brookhaven (C7)* 7,801
Brooklyn (F8)* 500
Brooksville (G4)* 819
Brownfield (G1)* 300
Brownsville (D6) 50
Brozville (D4) 25
Bruce (F3)* 1,719
Brunswick (C5) 150
Bryant (E3)* 150
Buckatunna (G7)* 500
Bude (C8)* 1,195
Buena Vista (G3)* 50
Burgess (E2)
Burnell (C7)* 30
Burns (E6)* 213
Burnside (F5)* 75
Burnsville (H1)* 525
Byhalia (E1)* 581
Byram (D6)*
Byrd (G8)
Caesar (E9) 50
Caile (C4) 150
Caledonia (H3)* 252
Calhoun City (F3)* 1,319
Calyx (G5)* 150
Camden (E5)* 350
Cameta (C4)* 89
Canaan (F1)*
Cannonsburg (B7)*
Canton (D5)* 7,048
Carlisle (C7)* 350
Carmichael (G7)*
Carnes (F8)
Carpenter (C6)* 150
Carriere (E9)* 500
Carrollton (E4)* 475
Carson (E7)* 206
Carter (D5)*
Carthage (E5)* 1,925
Cary (C5)* 390
Cascilla (D3)* 108
Cato (E6)
Cayuga (C6)
Cedar Hill (E3)
Cedarbluff (G3)*
Cedars (C6) 65
Center (F5)*
Centreville (B8)* 2,025
Chalybeate (G1)*
Charleston (D2)* 2,629
Chatawa (D8)* 240
Chatham (B4)* 30
Cheraw (E8) 100
Chester (F4)*
Chesterville (G2) 40
Chicora (G7)* 500
Choctaw (C3)
Chotard (C5)
Chunky (G6)* 258
Church Hill (B7)*
Clara (G7)* 450
Clarksdale (D2)* 16,539
Clarkson (F3) 150
Clayton (D1)* 350
Clermont Harbor (F10)* 175
Cleveland (C3)* 6,747
Cliftonville (H4) 300
Clinton (D6)* 2,255
Cloverhill (C2)
Clyde (E8)
Coahoma (C2)* 300
Cockrum (E1)*
Coffeeville (E3)* 739
Cohay (E6)
Coila (E4)*
Coldwater (E1)* 949
Coles (C8)*
College Hill (E2)
Collins (E7)* 1,293
Collinsville (G6)*
Colony Town (D4)
Columbia (E8)* 6,124
Columbus (H3)* 17,172
Como (E1)* 703
Conehatta (F6)* 50
Conway (E5)*
Cooksville (H5)*
Corinth (G1)* 9,785
Cornersville (F1)
Cotton Plant (G1)* 125
Courtland (E2)* 275
Coxburg (D5)
Crandall (G7)* 145
Cranfield (B7) 20
Crawford (G4)* 374
Crenshaw (D2)* 740
Crosby (B8)* 1,152
Crowder (D2)* 476
Cruger (D4)* 494
Crupp (D5) 150
Crystal Springs (D7)* 3,676
Cuevas (F10)* 150
Cumberland (F3)*
Curtis Station (D2)
Cybur (E9)
Cynthia (D6)
Daleville (G5)* 125
Dancy (F3)
Darbun (D8)
Darling (D2)*
Davenport (C2) 75
De Kalb (G5)* 953
De Lay (F2)* 200
De Lisle (F10)* 600
De Soto (G7)*
Deasonville (D5) 50
Decatur (F6)* 1,225
Deemer (F5)*
Deerbrook (G4)
Deeson (C2)*
Delta City (C4)* 250
Denmark (F2)* 50
Dennis (H1)* 158
Dentville (C7)
Derby (E9)
Derma (F3)* 494
D'Iberville (G10) 1,429
Dickerson (C2) 100
Dixon (F5)* 100
D'Lo (E7)* 516
Dockery (C3) 25
Doddsville (C3)* 201
Doloroso (B8)*
Dorsey (H2)* 58
Dossville (E5)* 150
Drew (C3)* 1,681
Dry Creek (E7)
Dry Grove (D6)
Dubard (E3)*
Dubbs (D1)
Dublin (C2)*
Duck Hill (E3)* 537
Duffee (G6)* 65
Dumas (G1)* 187
Duncan (C2)* 436
Dundee (D1)* 250
Dunleith (C4)
Durant (E4)* 2,311
Eaglebend (C5) 38
East Side (H10) 1,215
Ebenezer (D5)* 95
Ecru (F2)* 494
Eddiceton (C8)*
Eden (D5)* 306
Edgewater Park (G10)* 500
Edinburg (F5)* 900
Edwards (C6)* 1,002
Egremont (C5)* 43
Egypt (G3)*
El Dorado (C5) 50
Electric Mills (G5)*
Elizabeth (C4)* 200
Elliott (E3)* 250
Ellisville (F7)* 3,579
Embry (F3) 300
Enid (E2)* 94
Enondale (G5) 61
Enterprise (G6)* 691
Errata (F7) 50
Erwin (B4)
Escatawpa (G10)*
Essex (D2) 25
Estabutchie (F8)* 150
Estes (F4)
Estesmill (F5) 150
Estill (C4)* 500
Ethel (F4)* 723
Etta (F2)* 75
Eucutta (G7) 50
Eudora (D1) 200
Eupora (F3)* 1,338
Eutaw (B3)*
Evansville (D1) 15
Fair River (D7)
Falcon (D2)* 200
Falkner (G1)* 600
Fannin (E6)*
Farmhaven (E5)*
Farrell (C2)*
Fayette (B7)* 1,498
Fearns Springs (G4)
Fenton (F10) 25
Fentress (F4)
Fernwood (D8)* 600
Fitler (B5)* 300
Flora (D5)* 655
Florence (D6)* 313
Foote (C4) 100
Forest (F6)* 2,874
Forkville (E6)* 145
Fort Adams (B8)* 105
Foxworth (E8)* 750
French Camp (F4)* 162
Friars Point (C2)* 916
Fruitland Park (F9)* 63
Fulton (H2)* 1,343
Gainesville (E10) 50
Gallman (D7)* 170
Garlandville (F6)* 180
Gatesville (D6)*
Gattman (H3)* 150
Gautier (G10)*
Geneill (C4)
Georgetown (D7)* 327
Geren (D3)*
Germania (C5)*
Gholson (G5)* 25
Gibson (G3)* 275
Gillsburg (C8) 50
Gitano (F7)
Glancy (C7)*
Glen (H1)*
Glen Allan (B4)* 400
Glendora (D3)* 178
Gloster (B8)* 1,467
Glover (D1)
Gluckstadt (D5)
Golden (H2)* 206
Good Hope (E5) 200
Goodman (E5)* 878
Goodyear (E9)
Goshen Springs (E6)*
Goss (E8)* 250
Grace (C5)*
Grand Gulf (B6) 25
Grapeland (B3)
Greenville (B4)* 29,936
Greenwood (D4)* 18,061
Greenwood Spgs. (H3)* 65
Grenada (E3)* 7,388
Gulfport (F10)* 22,659
Gunnison (C3)* 453
Guntown (G2)* 299
Halstead (C3)
Hamburg (B7)*
Hamilton (H3)*
Hampton (B4) 10
Handsboro (F10)* 1,275
Hankinson (C6) 10
Hardee (C5)
Hardy (E3)
Harperville (E6)*
Harriston (C7)* 150
Harrisville (D7)*
Hathorn (E8)* 350
Hatley (H3) 100
Hattiesburg (F8)* 29,474
Hazlehurst (D7)* 3,397
Heads (C4) 100
Heidelberg (F7)* 863
Helm (C4) 100
Hermanville (C7)* 255
Hernando (E1)* 1,206
Hesterville (E4)
Hickory (F6)* 614
Hickory Flat (F1)* 345
Highlandale (D3) 100
Highpoint (F4)* 300
Hillhouse (C2)* 100
Hillsboro (E6)*
Hillsdale (F9)
Hinchcliff (D2)* 50
Hintonville (F8) 150
Hinze (F4)*
Hiwannee (G7)* 300
Hohenlinden (F3) 200
Holcomb (D3)* 229
Holcut (H1)* 300
Hollandale (C4)* 2,346
Holly Bluff (C5)*
Holly Ridge (C4)* 518
Holly Springs (E1)* 3,276
Hollyknowe (C4)
Hollywood (D1)* 117
Holmesville (D8)* 70
Homewood (E6)*
Honey Island (D4)
Hopewell (D7)* 350
Horn Lake (D1)* 1,000
Houlka (G2)* 545
Houston (G3)* 1,664
Howard (D4) 25
Howison (F9)* 75
Hub (E8)* 280
Hudsonville (F1) 50
Hurley (H9)*
Hushpuckena (C2)* 200
Increase (G6) 40
Independence (E1)*
Indianola (C4)* 4,369
Ingomar (F2)*
Inverness (C4)* 1,010
Irene (D8) 100
Isola (C4)* 450
Itta Bena (D4)* 1,725
Iuka (H1)* 1,527
Jacinto (H1) 140
JACKSON (D6)* 98,271
Jackson (urban area) 99,677
James (B4)* 500
Jamestown (E8) 25
Jayess (D8)* 50
Jeffries (C2)
Johns (E6)* 800
Johnstons Station (D8)*
Jonestown (D2)* 741
Keirn (D4)*
Kendrick (H1)
Keownville (G1) 15
Kewanee (H6)* 200
Kienstra (B8)*
Kilmichael (E4)* 511
Kiln (F10)*
Kipling (G5)
Kirby (C7) 98
Kirkville (H2) 125
Kittrell (G8) 100
Klein (F6) 10
Knoxville (B8)*
Kokomo (E8)* 300

Kolola Springs (H3)* 81
Kosciusko (E4)* 6,753
Kossuth (G1)* 242
Kreole (H10)* 1,106
Lafayette Spgs. (F2)*
Lake (F6)* 345
Lake Como (F7)* 150
Lake Cormorant (D1)*
Lake View (D1) 100
Lakeshore (F10)* 107
Lamar (F1)*
Lambert (D2)* 1,023
Lamkin (D4)* 100
Lamont (B3)* 250
Landon (F10) 500
Laneheart (B8)*
Langford (E6)
Langsdale (G7)* 100
Lauderdale (G5)* 648
Laurel (F7)* 25,038
Lawrence (F6)* 300
La Flore (D3)* 75
Leaf (G8)*
Leakesville (G8)* 893
Learned (C6)* 126
Leedo (C7)*
Leedy (H1)
Leesburg (E6)
Leesdale (B7) 20
Leland (C4)* 4,736
Lemon (E6)
Lena (E5)* 353
Leota Landing (B4) 20
Lessley (B8)*
Lexie (D8)
Lexington (D4)* 3,198
Liberty (C8)* 683
Little Rock (F5)*
Lobdell (B3) 50
Lockhart (G6) 50
Lodi (E3)* 50
Logtown (E10)* 300
Lombardy (C3) 300
Long (C4) 100
Long Beach (F10)* 2,703
Longtown (D1) 82
Longview (G4)*
Longwood (C4)* 65
Looxahoma (E1)* 50
Lorena (F6)
Lorenzen (C5)*
Lorman (B7)*
Louin (F6)* 478
Louise (C5)* 479
Louisville (G4)* 5,282
Love (D1)* 75
Luce Farms (H9) 85
Lucedale (G9)* 1,631
Lucien (C7)*
Ludlow (E5)* 500
Lula (C2)* 488
Lumberton (E8)* 1,803
Lux (F8)
Lyman (F10)*
Lynn Creek (G4)
Lyon (D2)* 386
Maben (F3)* 616
Macel (D3)* 50
Macon (G4)* 2,241
Madden (F5)* 350
Madison (D6)* 540
Magee (E7)* 1,738
Magnolia (D8)* 1,984
Mahned (F8) 100
Malone (E1) 25
Malvina (C3)*
Mantachie (H2)* 178
Mantee (F3)* 189
Marietta (H2)* 125
Marion (G6)*
Marks (D2)* 2,209
Martinsville (D7)*
Marydell (F5) 200
Mashulaville (G4)* 150
Matagorda (D2)
Matherville (G7)*
Mathiston (F3)* 584
Mattson (C2)*
Maud (D1)* 102
Maxie (F9)* 80
Mayersville (B5)*
Mayhew (G4)*
Mc Adams (E4)*
Mc Bride (C7)* 35
Mc Call Creek (C7)* 300
Mc Carley (E3)* 300
Mc Comb (D8)* 10,401
Mc Condy (G3) 100
Mc Cool (F4)* 305
Mc Crary (H4) 10
Mc Donald (F5)*
Mc Henry (F9)*
Mc Lain (G8)*
Mc Laurin (F8)*
Mc Leod (H4)*
Mc Nair (C7)* 200
Mc Neill (E9)* 500
Mc Ville (E5)
Meadville (C8)* 524
Mechanicsburg (D5)* 15
Meehan (G6)* 107
Meltonia (C3)*
Mendenhall (E7)* 1,539
Meridian (G6)* 41,893
Merigold (C3)* 682
Merit (E7) 25
Merrill (G9)*
Mesa (D8)
Metcalfe (B4)* 100
Michigan City (F1)* 38
Midnight (C4)* 400
Mileston (D4)* 47
Millard (E9)
Miller (E1)* 200
Millville (E5)
Mineral Wells (E1)* 275
Minter City (D3)* 400
Mississippi City (F10)* 2,125
Misterton (E3)
Mize (E7)* 430
Money (D3)*
Monroe (C8)* 100
Monticello (D7)* 1,382
Montpelier (G3)*
Montrose (F6)* 222
Mooreville (G2)*
Moorhead (C4)* 1,749
Morgan City (D4)*
Morgantown (E8)* 300
Morton (E6)* 1,664
Moscow (G5)
Moselle (F8)* 500
Moss (F7)*
Moss Point (G10)* 3,782
Mound Bayou (C3)* 1,328
Mount Carmel (E7) 50
Mount Helena (C5)
Mount Olive (E7)* 827
Mount Pleasant (E1)* 300
Muldon (G3)* 60
Murphy (C4)* 200
Myles (C7) 50
Myrleville (D5)
Myrtle (F1)* 331
Nanachehaw (B6) 19
Natchez (B7)* 22,740
Neely (G8)* 300
Nesbit (D1)* 250
Neshoba (F5)* 300
Nettleton (G2)* 1,204
New Albany (G2)* 3,680
New Augusta (F8)* 500
New Site (H1)* 24
Newhebron (D7)* 303
Newman (C6) 12
Newton (F6)* 2,912
Nicholson (E10)* 500
Nitta Yuma (C4)*
Nod (D5) 20
Nola (D7) 120
Norfield (C8)* 123
Norris (F6)
Northcarrollton (E3)* 506
Noxapater (F5)* 615
Nugent (F10)
Oak Ridge (C6) 200
Oak Vale (E8)* 136
Oakland (E2)* 551
Oakley (D6) 205
Ocean Springs (G10)* 3,058
Ofahoma (E5)* 50
Okolona (G2)* 2,167
Oldenburg (C7)*
Olive Branch (E1)*
Oloh (E8) 50
Oma (D7)* 50
Onward (C5)*
Ora (E7)
Orange Grove (H10) 150
Orvisburg (E9)
Osborn (G3)
Osyka (D8)* 724
Ovett (F8)* 357
Owens Wells (E4)
Oxford (F2)* 3,956
Pace (C3)* 422
Pachuta (G6)* 273
Paden (H1)* 158
Palmers Crossing (F8)*
Panther Burn (C4)* 30
Parchman (D3)*
Paris (F2)* 84
Pascagoula (G10)* 10,805
Pass Christian (F10)* 3,383
Pattison (C7)* 300
Paulding (F6)* 400
Paulette (H4)* 126
Paynes (D3)*
Pearlington (E10)* 150
Pearson (D6)*
Pecan (H10) 100
Pelahatchie (E6)* 867
Penton (D1)
Peoria (C8)*
Percy (C4)*
Perkinston (F9)* 400
Perthshire (C3)*
Petal (F8)* 2,148
Pettit (C4)* 175
Peyton (C7)* 25
Pheba (G3)*
Philadelphia (F5)* 4,472
Philipp (D3)* 350
Phoenix (C5)*
Piave (G8)*
Picayune (E9)* 6,707
Pickens (E5)* 638
Pinckneyville (B8)*
Pine Ridge (B7)*
Pine Valley (E2)*
Pineville (F6)*
Piney Woods (D6)* 750
Pinola (E7)* 143
Pittsboro (F3)* 246
Plain (D6)* 500
Plantersville (G2) 479
Plattsburg (F5)
Pleasant Grove (D2)*
Pleasant Hill (E1) 200
Plumpoint (E1)
Pocahontas (D6)* 500
Polkville (E6)* 150
Pond (B8)*
Pontotoc (G2)* 1,596
Pope (E2)* 246
Poplar Creek (E4)* 350
Poplarville (E9)* 1,852
Port Gibson (B7)* 2,920
Porterville (G5)* 88
Potts Camp (F1)* 432
Powell (D2)* 80
Prairie (G3)* 654
Prairie Point (H4)*
Prentiss (E7)* 1,212
Preston (G5)* 375
Pricedale (D8)* 300
Prichard (D1)*
Priscilla (C3)* 75
Puckett (E6)* 300
Pulaski (E6)* 1,000
Purvis (F8)* 1,270
Pyland (F3) 125
Quentin (C8)* 300
Quincy (H3)*
Quitman (G6)* 1,817
Raleigh (F6)* 580
Randolph (F2)* 243
Rara Avis (H2)
Ratliff (H2) 60
Ravine (H4)
Raymond (D6)* 1,259
Red Banks (F1)* 450
Red Lick (B7)*
Redwood (C6)*
Reform (F4)* 400
Rena Lara (C2)* 50
Renfro (F5)
Renova (C3) 250
Riceville (F9) 40
Rich (D2)* 61
Richey (C4)* 86
Richton (G8)* 1,158
Ridgeland (D6)* 526
Rienzi (G1)* 468
Rio (G5)*
Ripley (G1)* 2,383
Roberts (F6)
Robinsonville (D1)* 100
Rockport (D7)*
Rodney (B7)* 209
Rolling Fork (C5)* 1,229
Rome (C3)* 189
Rose Hill (F6)* 500
Rosedale (B3)* 2,197
Rosetta (B8)*
Roundaway (C2) 150
Roundlake (C2)* 230
Rounsaville (G8) 19
Roxie (B7)* 521
Rudyard (C2)* 110
Ruleville (C3)* 1,521
Runnelstown (F8)
Rural Hill (F4) 3
Russell (G6)* 275
Russum (B7)* 350
Ruth (D8)*
Sabougla (F3) 100
Sallis (E4)* 228
Saltillo (G2)* 501
Sanatorium (E7)*
Sandersville (F7)* 681
Sandhill (E5)*
Sandy Hook (E8)*
Sanford (F8)*
Sapa (F3)
Sarah (D1)* 93
Saratoga (E7) 65
Sardis (E2)* 1,913
Sarepta (F2)* 90
Satartia (C5)* 105
Saucier (F9)*
Savage (D1)*
Schlater (D3)*
Scobey (E3)* 112
Scooba (G5)* 734
Scott (B3)* 2,000
Sebastopol (F5)* 330
Selma (B7) 2
Seminary (E7)* 345
Senatobia (E1)* 2,108
Seneca (F8) 12
Sessums (G4)*
Shannon (G2)* 520
Sharon (E5)*
Shaw (C3)* 1,892
Shelby (C3)* 2,148
Sherard (C2)* 75
Sherman (G2)* 386
Shipman (G9) 7
Shivers (E7)* 100
Shoccoe (E5)
Shubuta (G7)* 782
Shuqualak (G5)* 714
Sibley (D8)* 25
Sidon (D4)* 361
Signal (C6) 360
Silver City (C4)* 381
Silver Creek (D7)* 275
Skene (C3)* 250
Slate Spring (F3)* 134
Slayden (F1) 45
Sledge (D2)* 383
Smedes (C5)
Smithdale (C8)*
Smiths (C6)
Smithville (H2)* 419
Soegaard (D7)
Sontag (D7)*
Soso (F7)* 171
Spanish Fort (C5)* 120
Springville (F2)* 400
Stafford Springs (F7)* 200
Stallo (F5)* 500
Stampley (B7)* 23
Stanton (B7)*
Star (D6)* 300
Starkville (G4)* 7,107
State College (G4)* 4,000
State Line (G8)* 492
Steel (F6)
Steens (H3)* 95
Stewart (F4)* 311
Stokes (D5)
Stoneville (C4)* 1,015
Stonewall (G6)*
Stovall (C2)*
Stover (D2)*
Stratton (F6)*
Strayhorn (D1) 125
Street (C8) 50
Stringer (F7)* 150
Stringtown (C3)* 500
Strong (G3)* 500
Sturgis (G4)* 402
Sucarnochee (H5)*
Summerland (F7)* 112
Summit (D8)* 1,558
Sumner (D3)* 550
Sumrall (E8)* 853
Sun (F6)
Sunflower (C3)* 639
Swan Lake (D3)* 50
Sweatman (E3)*
Swiftown (D4)*
Swiftwater (B4) 10
Sylvarena (F6)* 112
Symonds (C3)*
Tallula (B5)*
Tamola (G5) 55
Taylor (E2)* 125
Taylorsville (F7)* 1,116
Tchula (D4)* 927
Terry (D6)* 497
Thaxton (F2)* 300
Theadville (G7) 75
Thomastown (E5)* 250
Thomasville (E6) 25
Thorn (F3)* 60
Thornton (D4)* 50
Thrasher (G1)* 200
Thyatira (E1)*
Tibbee Station (G3) 35
Tie Plant (E3)* 400
Tilden (H2) 150
Tillatoba (E3)* 127
Tillman (C7)* 150
Tiplersville (G1)* 110
Tippo (D3)* 80
Tishomingo (H1)* 335
Toccopola (F2)* 262
Tomnolen (F4)* 150
Toomsuba (G6)* 500
Topton (G6) 15
Tougaloo (D6)*
Tralake (C4)* 250
Traxler (E6) 75
Trebloc (G3)* 300
Tremont (H2)*
Trenton (E6)*
Tribbett (C4)* 100
Troy (G2)*
Tula (F2)*
Tunica (D1)* 1,354
Tupelo (G2)* 11,527
Turnbull (B8)*
Tuscola (E5)* 250
Tutwiler (D2)* 939
Tylertown (D8)* 1,331
Tyro (E1)* 750
Union (F5)* 1,559
Union Church (C7)* 275
University (E2)* 1,200
Utica (C6)* 824
Utica Institute (C6)*
Vaiden (E4)* 583
Valley (D5)* 125
Valley Park (C5)*
Value (D6)* 300
Van Vleet (G3)* 300
Vance (D2)*
Vancleave (G9)*
Vardaman (F3)* 686
Vaughan (D5)* 350
Velma (E2)
Verba (F6)
Verna (D8) 12
Vernal (G8)*
Verona (G2)* 589
Vicksburg (C6)* 27,948
Victoria (E1)*
Vidalia (F10) 25
Vimville (H6)*
Vossburg (F7)* 500
Wade (G9)* 300
Wahalak (G5)*
Waldrup (F7)*
Wallerville (G2)* 100
Wallfield (F2)
Walls (D1)* 318
Walnut (G1)* 481
Walnut Grove (F5)* 517
Waltersville (C6) 250
Walthall (F3)* 149
Wanilla (D7)*
Washington (B7)*
Water Valley (E2)* 3,113
Waterford (E1)* 125
Waveland (F10)* 793
Waxhaw (C3)*
Way (E5)*
Waynesboro (G7)* 3,442
Wayside (C4)*
Weathersby (E7)* 145
Webb (D3)* 680
Weir (F4)* 570
Wanasoga (G1)* 150
Wesson (D7)* 1,235
West (E4)* 354
West Enterprise (G6)*
West Point (G3)* 6,432
Whaley (D3) 15
Wheeler (G1)* 300
White Apple (B8) 25
White Bluff (E8) 25
Whitfield (E6)*
Whitfield (D3)
Whiteoak (E6) 50
Whynot (G6) 60
Wicker (E6)
Wiggins (F9)* 1,436
Wilkinson (B8)* 300
Williamsville (F4)
Willows (C6) 30
Winborn (F1)*
Winchester (G7)*
Wingate (G8) 150
Winona (E4)* 3,441
Winstonville (C3)* 322
Winterville (B4)*
Woodland (F3)* 133
Woodville (B8)* 1,609
Wren (G3) 250
Wyatte (E1)* 100
Yazoo City (D5)* 9,746
Yokena (C6)* 25
Youngs (E3) 25
Zama (F5)*
Zion Hill (C8) 50

MISSOURI

Map on Page 70

Total Population 3,954,653

115 COUNTIES

Adair (G2) 19,689
Andrew (C3) 11,727
Atchison (B2) 11,127
Audrain (J4) 23,829
Barry (E9) 21,755
Barton (D7) 12,678
Bates (D6) 17,534
Benton (F6) 9,080
Bollinger (M8) 11,019
Boone (H4) 48,432
Buchanan (C3) 96,826
Butler (M9) 37,707
Caldwell (E3) 9,929
Callaway (J5) 23,316
Camden (G6) 7,861
Cape Girardeau (N8) 38,397
Carroll (F4) 15,589
Carter (L9) 4,777
Cass (D5) 19,325
Cedar (E7) 10,663
Chariton (G3) 14,944
Christian (F9) 12,412
Clark (J2) 9,003
Clay (D4) 45,221
Clinton (D3) 11,726
Cole (H6) 35,464
Cooper (G5) 16,608
Crawford (K7) 11,615
Dade (E8) 9,324
Dallas (F7) 10,392
Daviess (E3) 11,180
De Kalb (D3) 8,047
Dent (J7) 10,936
Douglas (G9) 12,638
Dunklin (M10) 45,329
Franklin (K6) 36,046
Gasconade (J6) 12,342
Gentry (D2) 11,036
Greene (F8) 104,823
Grundy (E2) 13,220
Harrison (E2) 14,107
Henry (E6) 20,043
Hickory (F7) 5,387
Holt (B2) 9,833
Howard (G4) 11,857
Howell (J9) 22,725
Iron (L7) 9,458
Jackson (D5) 541,035
Jasper (D8) 79,106
Jefferson (L6) 38,007
Johnson (E5) 20,716
Knox (H2) 7,617
Laclede (G7) 19,010
Lafayette (E4) 25,272
Lawrence (E8) 23,420
Lewis (J2) 10,733
Lincoln (L4) 13,478
Linn (F3) 18,865
Livingston (E3) 16,532
Macon (G3) 18,332
Madison (M8) 10,380
Maries (J6) 7,423
Marion (J3) 29,765
Mc Donald (D9) 14,144
Mercer (E2) 7,235
Miller (H6) 13,734
Mississippi (O9) 22,551
Moniteau (G5) 10,840
Monroe (H3) 11,314
Montgomery (K5) 11,555
Morgan (G6) 10,207
New Madrid (N9) 39,444
Newton (D9) 28,240
Nodaway (C2) 24,033
Oregon (K9) 11,978
Osage (J6) 11,301
Ozark (H9) 8,856
Pemiscot (N10) 45,624
Perry (N7) 14,890
Pettis (F5) 31,577
Phelps (J7) 21,504
Pike (K4) 16,844
Platte (C4) 14,973
Polk (F7) 16,062
Pulaski (H7) 10,392
Putnam (F2) 9,166
Ralls (J3) 8,686
Randolph (G3) 22,918
Ray (E4) 15,932
Reynolds (L8) 6,918
Ripley (L9) 11,414
St. Charles (L5) 29,834
St. Clair (E6) 10,482
St. Francois (M7) 35,276
St. Louis (M5) 406,349
St. Louis City (M5) 856,796
Ste. Genevieve (M7) 11,237
Saline (F4) 26,694
Schuyler (G2) 5,760
Scotland (H2) 7,332
Scott (N8) 32,842
Shannon (K8) 8,377
Shelby (H3) 9,730
Stoddard (N9) 33,463
Stone (F9) 9,748
Sullivan (F2) 11,299
Taney (F9) 9,863
Texas (J8) 18,992
Vernon (D7) 22,685
Warren (K5) 7,666
Washington (L7) 14,689
Wayne (L8) 10,514
Webster (G8) 15,072
Worth (D2) 5,120
Wright (H8) 15,834

CITIES and TOWNS

Aaron (D6) 15
Abo (H7)
Acorn (L9)
Adrian (D6)* 905
Advance (N8)* 733
Affton (P3)* 5,000
Agency (C3)* 234
Aholt (G4)
Aid (M9) 55
Airport Drive ‡(D8) 225
Alanthus Grove (D2) 45
Alba (D8)* 352
Albany (D2)* 1,850
Aldrich (F7)* 198
Alexandria (K2)* 465
Allbright (M8)
Allendale (D2)* 142
Allenton (N3)*
Allenville (N8)* 125
Alley Spring (K8)*
Alma (E4)* 357
Almartha (H9)*
Alpha (F3) 25
Altamont (D3)* 178
Altenburg (O7)* 272
Alton (K9)* 571
Altona (D6) 13
Amazonia (C3)* 308
Americus (J5)*
Amity (D3)* 128
Amoret (C6)* 255
Amsterdam (C6)*
Anabel (H3)* 25
Ancell (N8)* 295
Anderson (D9)* 1,073
Andover (E1) 18
Annada (L4)* 93
Annapolis (L8)* 490
Anniston (O9)* 377
Anthonies Mill (K6)*
Anutt (J7)* 250
Apex (L4)
Appleton (Old Appleton*) (N7) 120
Appleton City (E6)* 1,150
Aquilla (N9) 50
Arab (M8)*
Arbela (H2)* 87
Arbor Terrace ‡(P3) 1,150
Arbyrd (M10)* 679
Arcadia (L7)* 414
Archie (D5)* 300
Arcola (E7)* 125
Ardmore (H3) 25
Argyle (J6)* 162
Arkoe (C2)* 48
Arlington (H7)*
Armstrong (G4)* 424
Arnica (E7) 4
Arno (G9)
Arrow Rock (F4)* 170
Asbury (C8)* 210
Ash Grove (E8)* 970
Ashburn (K3)* 153
Ashland (H5)* 416
Ashley (K4)* 205
Ashton (J2)*
Atherton (R5)* 375
Atlanta (H3)* 438
Augusta (M3)* 218
Aullville (E4)* 123
Aurora (E9)* 4,153
Austin (D5) 40
Auxvasse (J4)* 507
Ava (G9)* 1,611
Avalon (F3)* 200
Avert (N9) 45
Avilla (D8)* 142
Avondale (P5)* 532
Azen (H1)
Bachelor (J5)* 20
Bado (H8)* 15
Bagnell (G6) 74
Bakersfield (H9)*
Ballard (D6) 49
Ballwin (O3)* 600
Banner (L7)*
Bardley (K9)* 75
Baring (H2)* 274
Barnard (C2)* 275
Barnesville (G3) 12
Barnett (G6)* 200
Barry (P5) 30
Bartlett (K8) 15
Bates City (E5)* 87
Battlefield (F8)
Bay (J5)*
Beaman (F5)* 45
Bearcreek (E7)* 41
Beaufort (K6)* 250
Beck (P4)
Bedford (F3) 50
Bedison (C2) 13
Bel-Nor ‡(P3)* 1,290
Bel-Ridge ‡(P3) 1,116
Belgique (N7)* 66
Belgrade (L7)*
Bell City (N8)* 482
Bella Villa ‡(P3) 557
Bellamy (D7) 25
Belle (J6)* 906
Bellefontaine (O3)
Bellerive ‡(P3) 180
Belleview (L7)*
Bellflower (K4)* 226
Belton (C5)* 1,233
Bem (K6) 18
Bennett (L9)* 3
Benton (O8)* 546
Benton City (J4)* 141
Bentonville (F6)* 11
Berdell Hills ‡(P3) 583
Berger (K5)* 210
Berkeley (P2)* 5,268
Bernie (M9)* 1,308
Bertha (H9)* 80
Bertrand (O9)* 390
Bessville (N8)*
Bethany (E2)* 2,714
Bethel (J3)* 194
Beulah (J7)* 110
Beverly (O4)* 29
Beverly Hills ‡(P3) 938
Bevier (G3)* 838
Big Piney (H7)* 80
Bigelow (B2)* 132
Billings (F8)* 597
Billingsville (G5) 10
Billmore (K9)
Birch Tree (K9)* 409
Birdspoint (O9)
Birmingham (P5)* 236
Bismarck (L7)* 1,244
Bixby (K7)* 20
Black (L7)*
Black Jack (P2) 700
Blackburn (F4)* 306
Black Walnut (P2) 20
Blackwater (G5)* 313
Blairstown (E5)* 199
Bland (J6)* 596
Bliss (L6) 20
Blodgett (O8)* 218
Bloomfield (M9)* 1,382
Bloomington (H3) 18
Bloomsdale (M6)*
Blue Lick (F4)
Blue Ridge (D2) 27
Blue Springs (R6)* 1,068
Blythedale (E2)* 238
Boaz (F8) 26
Bogard (E4)* 285
Bois D'Arc (F8)*
Bolckow (C2)* 250
Boles (M3)
Bolivar (F7)* 3,482
Bona (E7) 12
Bonfils (O2) 125
Bonne Terre (L7)* 3,533
Bonnots Mill (J5)* 150
Boomer (F3)* 30
Boonesboro (G4)* 46
Boonville (G5)* 6,686
Boss (K7)* 108
Boston (D8)* 52
Bosworth (F4)* 503
Bourbon (K6)* 543
Bowen (E5) 30
Bowers Mill (E8) 29
Bowling Green (K4)* 2,396
Bradleyville (F9)* 69
Bragg City (N10)* 294
Braggadocio (N10)* 350
Branch (G7)*
Brandsville (J9)* 204
Branson (F9)* 1,314
Brashear (H2)* 119
Brasher (N10) 152
Braymer (E3)* 955
Brays (H6)
Brazil (K7)* 25
Brazito (H6) 25
Breckenridge (E3)* 617
Breckenridge Hills‡(P3) 4,063
Brentwood (P3)* 7,504
Brewer (N7)
Brickeys (M6)*
Bridgeton (P8)* 202
Bridgeton Terrace‡(P3) 578
Brighton (F8)* 84
Brimson (E2)* 139
Brinktown (J6)* 48
Bronaugh (C7)* 214
Brookfield (F3)* 5,810
Brooklyn (D2) 30
Brookline (F8)*
Broseley (M9)* 177
Brownbranch (G9)* 13
Browning (F2)* 492
Brownington (E6)* 179
Browns Spring (F9)
Browns Station (H4)* 75
Brumley (H6)* 78
Bruner (F8)* 85
Brunot (M8)* 31
Brunswick (F4)* 1,653
Brush Creek (G7)* 91
Brushy (K8) 14
Brushyknob (G9)*
Bryant (G8) 6
Bryson (F5) 25
Buckhart (H9)* 18
Buckhorn (M8)*
Bucklin (G3)* 783
Buckner (R5)* 639
Bucoda (M10) 20
Bucyrus (H8)* 25
Buell (K4)* 69
Buffalo (F7)* 1,213
Buick (K7)* 101
Bunceton (G5)* 556
Bunker (K8)*
Burch (M8)
Burfordville (N8)* 88
Burgess (C7) 123
Burlington Jct. (B2)* 746
Burnham (J9) 74
Burton (G4) 11
Burtville (E5) 75
Busch (K3) 3
Bute (G2)
Butler (D6)* 3,333
Butterfield (E9)* 136

Melrose (N3) 15
Memphis (H2)* 2,035
Mendon (F3)* 349
Mendota (G1) 2
Menfro (N7)* 80
Mercer (F2)* 377
Merwin (C6)* 88
Meta (H6)* 353
Metz (C6)* 178
Mexico (J4)* 11,623
Miami (F4)* 217
Middle Grove (H4) 48
Middletown (J4)* 240
Midridge (K8)* 75
Milan (F2)* 1,972
Milford (D7)* 100
Mill Grove (E2)*
Mill Spring (L8)*
Millard (G2) 100
Millcreek (M7)* 75
Miller (E8)* 615
Millersburg (H5)* 40
Millville (E4) 150
Milo (D7)* 124
Mincy (F9)* 6
Mindenmines (D8)* 425
Mine La Motte (M7)*
Mineola (J5)* 75
Mineral Point (L7)* 304
Mingo (M9)* 200
Minnith (M7)*
Mirabile (D3) 60
Missouri City (R5)* 344
Moberly (G4)* 13,115
Modena (E2)* 95
Mokane (J5)* 477
Moline Acres ‡(R2) 99
Molino (J4)* 31
Monett (E9)* 4,771
Monroe City (J3)* 2,093
Montauk (J8)* 20
Monterey (L7)*
Montevallo (D7)* 53
Montgomery City(K5)* 1,679
Monticello (J2)* 154
Montier (J8)* 55
Montreal (G7)* 83
Montrose (E6)* 518
Montserrat (E5)* 130
Moody (J9)* 100
Mooresville (E3)* 134
Mora (F5)* 75
Morehouse (N9)* 1,635
Morgan (G7)* 55
Morley (N8)* 494
Morrellton (K6)*
Morrison (J5)* 291
Morrisville (F8)* 296
Morse Mill (L6)*
Morton (E4) 16
Mosby (R4)* 213
Moscow Mills (M1)* 350
Moselle (M4)* 130
Mound City (B2)* 1,412
Moundville (C7)* 168
Mount Leonard (F4)* 142
Mount Moriah (E2)* 260
Mount Vernon (E8)* 2,057
Mountain Grove (H8)* 3,106
Mountain View (J8)* 892
Mount Washington (R5)
Munger (L7)
Murphy (O4) 160
Musselfork (G3) 19
Myrtle (K9)* 95
Napier (B2)
Napoleon (E4)* 143
Napton (F4)* 80
Nashua (P4)*
Nashville (D8)* 50
Nauvoo (F9) 4
Naylor (L9)* 520
Nebo (H7)* 30
Neck (C8)* 117
Neelys Landing (O7)*
Neelyville (M9)* 457
Nelson (F4)* 297
Nelsonville (J3)
Nemo (F7)
Neola (E7) 3
Neosho (D9)* 5,790
Netherlands (N10)* 72
Nevada (D7)* 8,009
New Bloomfield (J5)* 400
New Boston (G3)* 86
New Cambria (G3)* 295
New Florence (K5)* 522
New Frankfort (F4) 50
New Franklin (G4)* 1,060
New Hamburg (O8)* 156
New Hampton (D2)* 375
New Hartford (K4)* 38
New Haven (K5)* 1,009
New Hope (L4) 175
New Liberty (K9) 10
New London (K3)* 858
New Madrid (O9)* 2,726
New Market (C4)*
New Melle (M2)* 150
New Offenburg (M7)* 111
New Point (B2)* 80
New Wells (N7)* 48
Newark (H2)* 156
Newburg (J7)* 949
Newland (F5) 11
Newtonia (D9)* 190
Newtown (F2)* 231
Niangua (G8)* 344
Nind (G2) 25
Nishnabotna (B2)* 21
Nixa (F8)* 509
Noble (G9)*
Nodaway (C3)* 65
Noel (D9)* 685
Norborne (E4)* 1,114
Normandy (P3)* 2,306
North Fork (H3) 10
N. Kansas City (P5)* 3,886
North Salem (G3)*
Northmoor (P5)
Northview (G8)* 200
Northwoods ‡(P3) 1,602
Northwye (J7) 99
Norton (F4)*
Norwood (H8)*
Norwood Court ‡(P9) 72
Nottinghill (G9)* 11
Novellty (H2)* 188
Novinger (G2)* 734
Oak (C3)
Oak Grove (S6)* 761
Oak Hill (K6)
Oak Ridge (N7)* 202
Oakland (G7)* 15
Oakland (P3) 1,041
Oakside (J8)
Oakton (D8) 14
Oakville (P4)
Oakwood (K3)*
Oasis (F9)
Ocie (G9)*
Octa (M10) 20
Odessa (E5)* 1,969
Oermann (L6)*
O'Fallon (N2)* 789
Ohio (E6) 10
Olathe (H8) 20
Old Appleton (N7)* 120
Old Monroe (N1)* 268
Old Mines (L6)*
Olden (J9) 61
Olean (G6)* 165
Olivette ‡(P3) 1,761
Olney (K4)* 93
Omaha (G1) 10
Ongo (G9)
Oran (N8)* 1,156
Orchardfarm (O2)* 50
Oregon (B2)* 870
Orla (G7)* 9
Oronogo (D8)* 519
Orrick (O5)* 675
Osa (E9) 15
Osage Beach (G6) 237
Osage City (H5)* 250
Osborn (D3)* 237
Osceola (E6)* 1,082
Osgood (F2)* 173
Oskaloosa (D7)* 72
Otterville (G5)* 414
Overland (P3)* 11,566
Owensville (K6)* 1,946
Owls Bend (K8)* 75
Oxly (L9)* 150
Oyer (E7) 12
Ozark (F8)* 1,087
Pacific (N4)* 1,985
Pagedale (P3) 3,866
Palmer (L7)* 60
Palmyra (J3)* 2,295
Panama (D6)
Papinsville (D6) 55
Paradise (D4) 120
Paris (J4)* 1,407
Parker (C2)
Parkville (O5)* 1,186
Parma (N9)* 1,163
Parnell (C2)* 362
Pasadena Hills ‡(P2) 1,102
Pasadena Park ‡(P2) 682
Pascola (N10)* 242
Passaic (D6)* 75
Patterson (L8)* 125
Patton (M7)* 162
Pattonsburg (D2)* 883
Pattonville (P2)*
Paynesville (L4)*
Peace Valley (J9)* 68
Peach Orchard ‡(N10)* 59
Peculiar (D5)* 267
Peerless Park (O3) 119
Peers (K5)* 25
Pennsboro (E8) 17
Pennville (F2) 18
Perkins (N8)* 164
Perrin (D3)*
Perry (J4)* 813
Perryville (N7)* 4,591
Pershing (J5)* 36
Peruque (O2)* 85
Pevely (M6)* 416
Phelps City (A2)* 139
Phenix (F8)
Philadelphia (J3)* 200
Phillipsburg (G7)* 170
Pickering (C2)* 213
Piedmont (L8)* 1,548
Pierce City (E8)* 1,156
Pilot Grove (G5)* 635
Pilot Knob (L7)* 582
Pine (K9)* 100
Pine Lawn (P3)* 6,425
Pineville (D9)* 464
Piney Park ‡(L6) 21
Pioneer (E9) 45
Piper (D6) 25
Pittsburg (F7)* 56
Pittsville (E5)* 56
Plad (G7)* 30
Plato (H8)* 100
Platte City (C4)* 742
Platte Woods ‡(C4) 159
Plattsburg (D3)* 1,655
Pleasant Gap (D6) 15
Pleasant Green (F5)* 24
Pleasant Hill (D5)* 2,200
Pleasant Hope (F8)* 174
Plevna (H3)* 120
Plymouth (E3) 35
Pocahontas (N8)* 130
Point Pleasant (O10)* 101
Polk (F7)*
Pollock (F2)*
Polo (D3)* 549
Pomona (J9)* 300
Pond (N3) 260
Ponder (L9)* 9
Pontiac (G9)* 37
Poplar Bluff (L9)* 15,064
Portageville (N10)* 2,662
Portage Des Sioux(P2)* 264
Portia (D7) 5
Portland (J5)* 200
Postoak (E5)* 52
Potosi (L7)* 2,359
Pottersville (H9)* 25
Powe (M9) 95
Powersville (F1)* 227
Poynor (L9)* 40
Prairie Hill (G3)* 124
Prairie Home (G5)* 208
Prescott (J8)*
Preston (F7)* 109
Priceland ‡(E6) 124
Princeton (E2)* 1,506
Prior (H8) 4
Proctor (G6) 2
Prosperine (G7)* 7
Prospect Hill (R2)
Protem (G9)* 60
Purcell (D8)* 334
Purdin (F3)* 255
Purdy (E9)* 437
Pure Air (G2) 10
Purvis (G6)
Puxico (M9)* 749
Quaker (L7)*
Quarles (E6) 10
Queen City (H2)* 554
Quincy (F6)* 36
Quitman (C2)* 135
Qulin (M9)* 426
Racine (C9)* 150
Racket (F6) 27
Racola (L6)
Rader (G8)
Rainey (E7)
Randles (N8)* 169
Rat (K8)* 3
Ravanna (E2)* 132
Ravenwood (C2)* 319
Rayborn (H8)*
Raymondville (J8)* 175
Raymore (D5)* 208
Raytown (P6)*
Rayville (E4)* 193
Rea (C2)* 110
Readsville (J5)* 21
Red Bird (J6)
Red Oak (D8) 30
Redford (L8)* 60
Redtop (F7)* 50
Reeds (D8)* 136
Reeds Spring (F9)* 313
Reger (F2)* 103
Renick (H4)* 157
Rensselaer (J3)* 63
Republic (E8)* 965
Revere (J2)* 180
Reynolds (K8)*
Rhineland (J5)* 198
Rhyse (J7)* 25
Rich Fountain (J6)*
Rich Hill (D6)* 1,820
Richards (D7)* 190
Richland (H7)* 1,133
Richmond (D4)* 4,299
Richmond Hts. (P3)* 15,045
Richwoods (L6)* 250
Ridgedale (F9)*
Ridgeway (D2)* 560
Rinehart (D7)
Risco (N9)* 495
Ritchey (D9)* 137
Rivermines (L7)* 485
Rives (M10)* 166
Roanoke (G4)* 65
Robertson (P2)* 1,200
Robertsville (N4)* 117
Roby (H7)* 28
Rocheport (H5)* 376
Rock Creek (O4) 35
Rock Hill (P3)* 3,847
Rockbridge (H9)*
Rockport (B2)* 1,511
Rockville (D6)* 372
Rocky Comfort (D9)* 230
Rocky Mount (G6)* 4
Rogersville (G8)* 321
Rolla (J7)* 9,354
Rombauer (M9)*
Rome (G9)* 25
Rosati (J6)* 650
Roscoe (E7)* 128
Rosebud (K6)* 254
Rosendale (C2)* 245
Rothville (F3)* 152
Round Spring (J8)*
Rover (J9)
Ruble (L8)* 75
Ruegg (P2) 200
Rueter (G9)*
Rush Hill (J4)* 127
Rushville (B3)* 319
Russ (G7) 50
Russellville (H6)* 336
Rutledge (H2)* 217
Sabula (L8)* 60
Saco (M8)* 75
Safe (J6)* 25
Saginaw (C8)*
Sagrada (F6)
St. Albans (N3)* 30
St. Ann (P3) 4,557
St. Anthony (H6)* 30
St. Catharine (G3)* 80
St. Charles (O2)* 14,314
St. Clair (L6)* 1,779
St. Elizabeth (H6)* 59
St. Francisville (J2) 275
St. Francois (M7)* 295
St. George (H8)* 642
St. James (J6)* 1,811
St. Johns (P2)* 2,499
St. Joseph (C3)* 78,588
St. Joseph (urban area) 79,280
St. Louis (P3)* 856,796
St. Louis (urban area) 1,394,051
St. Marys (M7)* 635
St. Patrick (J2)* 53
St. Paul (N2)* 102
St. Peters (N2)* 377
Ste. Genevieve (M6)* 3,992
Salem (J7)* 3,611
Salem (Coffey*) (D2) 253
Saline (E1) 25
Salisbury (G4)* 1,676
Sammylane (F9)
Sampson (G8) 5
Sands (O2)
Sandstone (D7)
Sandyhook (G5)* 57
Sank (N8)* 6
Santa Fe (J4)* 83
Santa Rosa (D3)*
Santiago (F6)
Sappington (P3)*
Sarcoxie (D8)* 1,042
Sargent (H8)
Savannah (C3)* 2,332
Severton (K3)* 150
Schell City (D6)* 400
Schluersburg (N3) 30
Schuermann Hts.‡(P3) 306
Scopus (N8)*
Seckman (P4)
Sedalia (F5)* 20,354
Sedgewickville (N7)* 92
Seligman (D9)*
Senath (M10)* 1,528
Seneca (C9)* 1,195
Seventysix (N7)* 14
Seymour (G8)* 1,015
Shackleford (F4)* 55
Shafter (F3) 10
Shamrock (J4)* 23
Shelbina (H3)* 2,113
Shelby (F3) 32
Shelbyville (H3)* 635
Sheldon (D7)* 427
Shell Knob (E9)* 25
Sheridan (C1)* 370
Sherman (O3)* 225
Shirley (L7)*
Shook (M8)* 5
Shrewsbury (P3) 3,382
Sibley (O5)* 200
Sidney (G2) 6
Sikeston (N9)* 11,640
Silex (K4)* 188
Siloam Springs (H9)*
Silva (M8)* 66
Silver Lake (M7)* 53
Simmons (H8)* 50
Skidmore (B2)* 485
Slater (G4)* 2,836
Sleeper (G7)* 131
Sligo (K7)* 35
Smallett (G9)* 12
Smithfield (C8) 150
Smithton (F5)* 339
Smithville (D4)* 947
Sni Mills (S6) 25
Snyder (F3)* 150
Solo (J8)*
South Fork (J9)* 20
South Gifford (G3)* 128
South Gorin (H2) 303
South Greenfield (E8)* 186
South Lineville (E1) 92
South West City (D9)* 595
Spalding (J3) 25
Spanish Lake (P2)
Sparta (F9)* 244
Spencerburg (K4) 35
Spickard (F2)* 517
Splitlog (D9) 50
Spokane (F9)* 55
Spooneville (M9) 500
Sprague (D6) 29
Spring City (C9) 140
Spring Creek (J7) 85
Spring Fork (F5)* 120
Spring Garden (H6) 46
Springfield (F8)* 66,731
Springfield (urban area) 75,117
Springhill (E3) 28
Spruce (D6)* 38
Spurgeon (C9) 25
Squires (G9)*
Stahl (G2) 5
Stanberry (C2)* 1,651
Standish (F4)* 24
Stanton (K6)* 250
Stark City (D9)* 154
Steele (N10)* 2,360
Steelville (K7)* 1,157
Steffenville (J3)* 75
Stella (D9)* 177
Stet (E4)*
Stewartsville (C3)* 414
Stickney (J6)*
Stockton (E7)* 811
Stone Hill (K7)*
Stotesbury (C7)* 71
Stotts City (E8)* 285
Stoutland (G7)* 192
Stoutsville (J3)* 146
Stover (G6)* 693
Strafford (F8)* 300
Strasburg (D5)* 180
Strother (J4)
Sturdivant (M8)* 103
Sturgeon (H4)* 544
Sturges (E3)
Sublette (G2)
Success (H8)* 45
Sudheimer (H6)
Sue City (H3)
Sugar Creek (R5)* 1,858
Sugar Tree (E4) 16
Sullivan (K6)* 3,019
Sulphur Springs (M6)* 135
Summerfield (J6)* 75
Summersville (J8)* 306
Sumner (F3)* 309
Sunnyvale ‡(D9) 28
Swart (C7) 1
Swedeborg (H7)* 150
Sweden (H9)*
Sweet Springs (F5)* 1,439
Swinton (M8)* 65
Swiss (K5) 21
Sycamore (H9)* 44
Sycamore Hills ‡(P3) 989
Syracuse (G5)* 221
Taberville (E6)* 100
Taitsville (E4) 5
Tallapoosa (N9)*
Taneyville (F9)* 132
Tarkio (B2)* 2,221
Tarsney (S6)
Tauria (F9) 25
Taylor (J3)* 60
Tea (K6) 15
Tebbetts (J5)* 150
Tecumseh (H9)* 36
Ten Brook (P4)
Teresita (J9)* 6
Thayer (J9)* 1,639
Thomasville (J9)* 70
Thompson (J4)* 70
Thornfield (G9)* 30
Tiff (L6)* 75
Tiff City (C9)*
Tiffin (E7)* 100
Tigris (G8) 15
Tilsit (N8) 53
Timber (K8)* 15
Tina (F3)* 224
Tindall (E2)* 102
Tipton (G5)* 1,234
Tolona (J2)
Topaz (H9) 4
Torch (L9)* 15
Toronto (G6)
Town and Country ‡(P3) 162
Townley (M9) 50
Tracy (C4)* 201
Trenton (E2)* 6,157
Trimble (D4)* 141
Triplett (F4)* 301
Troy (L5)* 1,738
Truesdail (K5)* 235
Truxton (K4)* 125
Tunas (F7)*
Turley (H8)
Turners (F8)*
Turney (D3)* 152
Turtle (K7)* 28
Tuscumbia (H6)* 221
Twin Bridges (H9)* 22
Twin Oaks ‡(P3) 81
Tyler (N10)* 150
Tyrone (J8)* 45
Ulman (H6)* 75
Union (L6)* 2,917
Union Star (C2)* 373
Uniontown (N7)*
Unionville (G2) 2,050
University City (P3)* 39,892
Uplands Park ‡(P3) 563
Upton (H8)*
Urbana (F7)* 359
Urbandale (G4) 35
Urich (E6)* 400
Utica (E3)* 475
Vale (R6)
Valles Mines (L6)* 225
Valley City (E5) 30
Valley Park (O3)* 2,956
Van (F7) 11
Van Buren (L8)* 708
Vancleve (H6)
Vandalia (J4)* 2,624
Vanduser (N9)* 281
Vanzant (H9)* 20
Velda ‡(P3) 480
Velda Village Hills ‡(P3) 1,527
Verona (E9)* 396
Versailles (G6)* 1,929
Vibbard (D4) 83
Viburnum (K7)* 53
Vichy (J6)* 150
Victoria (M6)* 250
Vida (J7)* 50
Vienna (H6)* 471
Vigus (O2)* 400
Villa Ridge (M4)* 142
Vineland (L6)*
Vinita Park ‡(P3) 1,801
Vinita Terrace ‡(P3) 389
Viola (E9)* 20
Virginia (G6) 23
Vista (E7)*
Vulcan (L8)* 200
Waco (C8)* 177
Wakenda (F4)* 255
Waldron (O5)* 95
Walker (D7)* 204
Wallace (C3)*
Walnut Grove (F8)* 347
Wappapello (M9)* 210
Wardell (N10)* 454
Warren (J3)* 25
Warrensburg (E5)* 6,857
Warrenton (K5)* 1,584
Warsaw (F6)* 936
Warson Woods ‡(P3) 529
Washburn (E9)* 250
Washington (K5)* 6,850
Watkins (H6) 2
Watson (A1)* 199
Waverly (E4)* 809
Wayland (J2)* 350
Wayne (E9)* 84
Waynesville (H7)* 1,010
Weatherby (D3)* 156
Weaubleau (F7)* 432
Webb City (C8)* 6,919
Webster Groves (P3)* 23,390
Weldon Spring (O2)*
Wellington (E4)* 649
Wellston (P3)* 9,396
Wellsville (K4)* 1,519
Wentworth (D8)* 212
Wentzville (M2)* 1,227
Wesco (K7)* 100
West Line (C5)* 68
West Eminence (J8)* 144
West Fork (K8)* 20
West Plains (J9)* 4,918
Westalton (R2)* 400
Westboro (B1)* 297
Weston (C4)* 1,067
Westphalia (J6)* 319
Westville (G3)
Wheatland (F7)* 299
Wheaton (E9)* 394
Wheeling (F3)*
Whiteoak (M10)* 91
Whiteside (K4)* 93
Whitesville (C2)*
Whitewater (N8)* 187
Whiting (O9) 125
Wilbur Park ‡(P3) 743
Wilcox (C2)* 100
Wilderness (K9)* 155
Willard (F8)* 300
Willhoit (H9)*
Williamsburg (J5)* 95
Williamstown (J2)* 158
Williamsville (L9)* 492
Willmathsville (G2)* 31
Willow Springs (H9)* 1,914
Winchester (J2)
Winchester ‡(O3) 176
Windsor (E5)* 2,429
Windyville (F7)* 30
Winfield (L5)* 474
Winigan (G2)* 110
Winkler (J7) 11
Winnipeg (H7)* 12
Winona (K8)* 473
Winston (D3)* 278
Wisdom (F6)*
Wishart (F7)* 90
Wittenberg (O7)* 54
Wolf Island (O9)*
Womack (M7)* 40
Woodland (J3) 25
Woodlawn (H3) 50
Woodson Terrace ‡(P3) 616
Wooldridge (G5)* 137
Worland (C6)* 40
Worth (C2)* 141
Worthington (G2)* 186
Wright City (K5)* 543
Wyaconda (J2)* 483
Wyatt (O9)* 345
Yancy Mills (J7)* 6
Yarrow (G2)* 45
Yates (G4)* 39
Youngers (H4)
Yount (M7)*
Yukon (J8)* 15
Zalma (N8)* 137
Zanoni (H9)*
Zeta (N9) 35
Zion (M8)*

Map on Page 71

MONTANA

Total Population 591,024

57 COUNTIES

Beaverhead (C5) 6,671
Big Horn (J5) 9,824
Blaine (G2) 8,516
Broadwater (E4) 2,922
Carbon (G5) 10,241
Carter (M5) 2,798
Cascade (E3) 53,027
Chouteau (F3) 6,974
Custer (L4) 12,661
Daniels (L2) 3,946
Dawson (M3) 9,092
Deer Lodge (C5) 16,553
Fallon (M4) 3,660
Fergus (G3) 14,015
Flathead (B2) 31,495
Gallatin (E5) 21,902
Garfield (J3) 2,172
Glacier (C2) 9,645
Golden Valley (G4) 1,337
Granite (C4) 2,773
Hill (F2) 14,285
Jefferson (D4) 4,014
Judith Basin (F4) 3,200
Lake (B3) 13,835
Lewis and Clark (D3) 24,540
Liberty (E2) 2,180
Lincoln (A2) 8,693
Madison (D5) 5,998
Mc Cone (L3) 3,258
Meagher (F4) 2,079
Mineral (B3) 2,081
Missoula (C3) 35,493
Musselshell (H4) 5,408
Park (F5) 11,999
Petroleum (H3) 1,026
Phillips (J2) 6,334
Pondera (D2) 6,392
Powder River (L5) 2,693
Powell (D4) 6,301
Prairie (L4) 2,377
Ravalli (B4) 13,101
Richland (M3) 10,366
Roosevelt (L2) 9,580
Rosebud (K4) 6,570
Sanders (A3) 6,983
Sheridan (M2) 6,674
Silver Bow (D5) 48,422
Stillwater (G5) 5,416
Sweet Grass (G5) 3,621
Teton (D3) 7,232
Toole (E2) 6,867
Treasure (J4) 1,402
Valley (K2) 11,353
Wheatland (G4) 3,187
Wibaux (M4) 1,907
Yellowstone (H4) 55,875
Yellowstone Nat'l. Park† (F6) 58

† Population for Montana part only. See Wyoming and Idaho.

CITIES and TOWNS

Abe (E5)
Aberdeen (J5) 8
Absarokee (G5)* 423
Accola (E5)
Acton (H5)* 14
Agawam (D2)* 17
Alberton (B3)* 326
Albion (M5)* 6
Alder (D5)* 100
Alhambra (E4) 45
Alice (J4)
Aloe (D2)
Alpine (G5)*
Alta (B5)
Alzada (M5)* 75
Amazon (E4) 1
Amsterdam (E5) 65
Anaconda (C4)* 11,254
Anceney (E5) 10
Andes (M3)* 32
Angela (K4)* 7
Antelope (M2)* 125
Apex (D5)
Apgar (C2) 76
Archer (M2)* 5
Arlee (B3)* 300
Armells (G3) 3
Armington (F3)* 120
Armstead (D6)* 207
Arrow Creek (F3) 25
Ashland (K5)* 150
Ashuelot (E3)
Augusta (D3)* 475
Austin (D4)* 50
Avon (D4)* 200
Avondale (K2) 5
Axtell (L3) 50
Babb (C2)* 25
Bainville (M2)* 356
Baker (M4)* 1,772
Ballantine (J5)* 298
Bannack (C5)
Barber (G4)* 60
Bascom (J4)
Basin (D4)* 300
Battrick (H4) 3
Bay Horse (L5)* 39
Bear Spring (G3) 50
Bearcreek (G5)* 162
Bearmouth (C4) 15
Beaverton (J2) 20
Becket (G4) 3
Beehive (G5)* 12
Belfry (H5)* 200
Belgrade (E5)* 663
Belknap (A3)* 72
Belltower (M5)*
Belmont (G4)* 25
Belt (E3)* 702
Benchland (F3)* 57
Benrud (L2)
Bercail (G4) 2
Bernice (D4) 2
Biddle (L5)* 5
Big Arm (B3)* 100
Big Sag (F3) 6
Big Sandy (G2)* 743
Big Timber (G5)* 1,679
Bigfork (C2)* 450
Bighorn (J4)* 21
Billings (H5)* 31,834
Birney (K5)* 35
Black Eagle (E3)* 1,449
Blackfoot (D2)* 200
Blackleaf (D2)
Blatchford (L4) 8
Bloomfield (M3)* 40
Blossburg (D4)* 35
Bole (D3)
Bonita (C4) 150
Bonner (C4)* 250
Boulder (E4)* 1,017
Bowdoin (J2)
Bowers (L5)* 26
Bowler (H5) 8
Box Elder (F2)* 284
Boyd (G5)* 32
Boyes (M5)* 25
Bozeman (F5)* 11,325
Brady (E2)* 435
Brandenberg (K5)* 49
Bredette (L2)
Brenner (C6)
Bridger (H5)* 854
Brinkman (F2) 15
Broadus (L5)* 517
Broadview (H4)* 164
Brockton (M2)* 350
Brockway (L3)* 103
Brooks (G3)* 11
Brookside (H2) 25
Browning (C2)* 1,691
Brunelda (J4) 13
Brusett (J3)* 20
Buelow (E2)
Buffalo (G4)* 150
Bundy (H4)

Burnham (G2)	26
Burns (M3)	8
Busby (J5)*	20
Butte (D5)*	33,251
Butte Creek (J3)	
Bynum (D3)*	52
Cabin Creek (M4)	6
Calkins (F4)	
Calvert (E3)	
Camas (B3)*	125
Camas Prairie (B3)	5
Cameron (E5)*	138
Camps Pass (L5)*	
Campsite (E3)	3
Canton (E4)	10
Canyon Creek (D4)*	76
Canyon Ferry (E4)*	150
Capitol (M5)*	4
Carbella (F5)	5
Carbert (L2)	
Cardwell (E5)*	98
Carlyle (M4)*	
Carter (E3)*	100
Cartersville (K4)*	
Cascade (E3)*	447
Cat Creek (H3)*	65
Ceekay (H3)	
Centerville (D4)	1,800
Central Park (E5)	
Chadbourn (F5)	7
Chalk Buttes (M5)	41
Chance (H5)	7
Chapman (J2)*	35
Charlo (B3)*	260
Chester (E2)*	733
Chestnut (F5)	12
Chico (F5)	20
Chinook (G2)*	2,307
Choteau (D3)*	1,618
Christina (G3)*	20
Circle (L3)*	856
Clancey (E4)*	161
Clarkston (E4)*	20
Clasoil (E4)	8
Cleiv (E3)	
Cleveland (G2)*	17
Cliff Lake (E6)*	21
Clinton (C4)*	150
Clyde Park (F5)*	280
Coalridge (M2)*	49
Coalwood (L5)*	2
Coburg (H2)	
Coffee Creek (F3)*	50
Cohagen (K3)*	36
Cole (J2)	
Collins (E3)*	26
Colony Bay (F2)	
Colstrip (K5)*	300
Columbia Falls (B2)*	1,232
Columbus (G5)*	1,097
Comanche (H4)	12
Comertown (M2)*	50
Conner (B5)*	150
Conrad (D2)*	1,865
Content (J3)	
Cooke (G5)*	45
Coolidge (C5)	2
Coram (C2)*	500
Corbin (D4)	50
Cordova (E3)	175
Corinth (J5)*	16
Corvallis (C4)*	350
Corwin Springs (F5)*	2
Corwine Center (J2)	
Cottonwood (G2)	40
Cottonwood (C3)	
Craig (D3)*	80
Crane (M3)*	50
Creston (C2)*	200
Crow Agency (J5)*	500
Crow Rock (L4)	
Culbertson (M2)*	779
Cushman (H4)*	17
Custer (J4)*	300
Cut Bank (D2)*	3,721
Dagmar (M2)*	46
Dailey (F5)	
Daleview (M2)	
Danvers (G3)*	32
Darby (B4)*	415
Dayton (B3)*	95
De Smet (C4)	10
Dean (G5)*	92
Deborgia (A3)*	75
Decker (K5)*	21
Deer Lodge (D4)*	3,779
Dell (D6)*	150
Delphia (H4)*	14
Delphine (F4)	
Dempsey (D4)	10
Denton (G3)*	435
Devon (E2)*	50
Dillon (D5)*	3,268
Divide (D5)*	116
Dixon (B3)*	350
Dodson (H2)*	330
Dooley (M2)*	17
Dover (F3)	20
Dovetail (H3)	35
Dowd (M2)	
Drexel (A3)*	9
Drummond (D4)*	531
Dryhead (H5)	4
Duderanch (F5)	3
Dunkirk (E2)*	13
Dupuyer (D2)*	125
Dutton (E3)*	431
Eagle Butte (F3)	72
Eagleton (G3)	
East Glacier Park (C2)*	300
E. Helena (E4)*	1,216
Eddy (A3)*	25
Eden (E3)*	5
Edgar (H5)*	160
Ekalaka (M5)*	904
Electric (F5)	20
Elgin (M5)	15
Elk Park (D4)	80
Elliston (D4)*	
Elmdale (M3)	25
Elmer (J4)	10
Elmo (B3)*	104
Emigrant (F5)*	25
Emory (G4)	
Enid (M3)*	8
Ennis (E5)*	600
Epsie (L5)*	65
Essex (C2)*	75
Ethridge (D2)*	45
Eureka (B2)*	929
Evans (E3)	
Evaro (C3)*	92
Fairchild (F2)	20
Fairfield (D3)*	693
Fairview (M3)*	942
Fallon (L4)*	251
Family (D2)	150
Farmington (D3)	30
Ferdig (E2)*	15
Fergus (H3)*	4
Finch (K4)	
Findon (F4)	
Finn (D4)	50
First Creek (J3)	
Fishtail (G5)*	50
Fishtrap (C5)	10
Flaxville (L2)*	220
Florence (B4)*	350
Floweree (E3)*	60
Forestgrove (H3)*	25
Forks (J2)*	3
Forsyth (K4)*	1,906
Fort Belknap (H2)	
Ft. Benton (F3)*	1,522
Ft. Browning (D2)	1,674
Ft. Logan (E4)	
Ft. Maginnis (H3)	4
Ft. Peck (K2)*	1,214
Ft. Shaw (E3)*	180
Ft. Union (M2)	
Fortine (A2)*	100
Foundation (L4)	
Four Buttes (L2)*	50
Fourchette (H3)	
Fowler (E2)	
Fox (G5)	15
Francis (F4)*	10
Franklin (G4)*	7
Frazer (K2)*	575
Frenchtown (B3)*	100
Fresno (G2)	10
Froid (M2)*	555
Fromberg (H5)*	442
Gage (H4)	8
Galata (E2)*	63
Galen (D4)	220
Gallatin Gateway (E5)*	200
Gardiner (F5)*	
Garland (L4)	3
Garneill (G4)*	33
Garnet (C4)	20
Garrison (D4)*	150
Garryowen (J5)*	28
Gateway (A2)	50
Genou (E2)*	25
Geraldine (F3)*	374
Geyser (F3)*	150
Gibson (G4)	
Giffen (E3)	12
Gildford (F2)*	340
Gilman (D3)	15
Giltedge (G3)	8
Girard (M3)	7
Glasgow (K2)*	3,821
Glen (D5)*	100
Glendive (M3)*	5,254
Glengarry (G3)	7
Glentana (K2)*	65
Gold Stone (F2)*	9
Goldbutte (E2)	
Goldcreek (D4)*	190
Golden (G5)	
Grant (C5)*	25
Grantsdale (B4)*	50
Grass Valley (B4)	
Grassrange (H3)*	234
Grayling (E6)*	20
Great Falls (E3)*	39,214
Greenough (C4)*	50
Gregson (D4)	35
Greycliff (G5)*	125
Grisdella (J3)	2
Gunsight (D2)	
Hall (C4)*	100
Hamilton (B4)*	2,678
Hammond (M5)*	10
Hanover (G3)*	100
Hardin (J5)*	2,306
Hardy (E3)	
Harlem (H2)*	1,107
Harlowton (F4)*	1,733
Harrison (E5)*	305
Hathaway (K4)*	25
Haugan (A3)*	70
Havre (G2)*	8,086
Haxby (K3)*	25
Hay Coulee (F2)	12
Hays (H2)*	150
Hazel (L3)	
Heart Butte (C2)*	50
Heath (G3)*	16
Hedgesville (G4)*	25
HELENA (E4)*	17,581
Helmville (C4)*	50
Henderson (A3)	
Heron (A2)*	200
Hesper (H5)	27
Hibbard (J4)	
Highwood (F3)*	272
Hilger (G3)*	42
Hill (E2)*	
Hillsboro (H5)	4
Hillside (K4)	
Hingham (F2)*	214
Hinsdale (K2)*	350
Hobson (G4)*	205
Hodges (M4)*	40
Hogeland (H2)*	75
Holland (E5)	
Homestake (D5)*	15
Homestead (M2)*	87
Hoosac (G3)	4
Horton (L4)	
Hot Springs (B3)*	733
Howard (K4)	
Hughesville (F3)	18
Hungry Horse (B2)*	
Hunters Hotsprings (F5)	7
Huntley (H5)*	268
Huson (B3)*	75
Hysham (J4)*	410
Inga (F2)	
Ingomar (J4)*	100
Intake (M3)*	8
Inverness (F2)*	360
Iron Mountain (A3)	3
Ismay (M4)*	182
Ivanell (J4)	
Jackson (C5)*	82
Jardine (F5)*	40
Jeffers (E5)*	60
Jefferson City (E4)*	100
Jefferson Island (E5)*	50
Jennings (A2)*	10
Jens (D4)*	25
Joliet (G5)*	410
Joplin (F2)*	368
Jordan (J3)*	800
Judith Gap (G4)*	175
Kalispell (B2)*	9,737
Kenilworth (F2)	
Kevin (D2)*	351
Kila (B2)*	100
Kinsey (L4)*	8
Kintla (B2)	
Kirby (J5)*	14
Klein (H4)*	400
Knobs (M5)	33
Knowlton (L4)	
Kolin (G3)*	12
Korner (D2)	50
Koyl (D3)	
Kremlin (F2)*	160
Lake Mc Donald (B2)*	1
Lakeview (E6)	18
Lambert (M3)*	359
Lame Deer (K5)*	400
Lanark (M2)	3
Landusky (H3)*	65
Lane (M3)	25
Laredo (G2)*	38
Larslan (K2)*	159
Laurel (H5)*	3,663
Laurin (D5)*	110
Lavina (H4)*	195
Lebo (F4)	
Ledger (E2)*	20
Lee (K5)	
Legg (J3)	
Lehigh (F3)	5
Lennep (F4)*	25
Leroy (G3)*	10
Lewistown (G3)*	6,573
Libby (A2)*	2,401
Lima (D6)*	483
Limestone (F5)*	43
Lincoln (D4)*	250
Lindsay (L3)*	57
Lingshire (E4)	
Little Crooked (H3)	3
Living Springs (G4)*	7
Livingston (F5)*	7,683
Lloyd (G2)*	5
Locate (L4)*	4
Lockwood (H5)	200
Lodge Grass (J5)*	536
Lodgepole (H2)	50
Loesch (L5)	10
Logan (E5)*	172
Lohman (G2)*	
Lolo (B4)*	210
Lolo Hot Springs (B4)	25
Loma (F3)	200
Lombard (E4)*	26
Lonepine (B3)*	9
Loring (J2)*	50
Lost Lake (H2)	25
Lothair (E2)*	72
Lothrop (B4)	
Loweth (F4)	20
Lowry (D3)	
Lozeau (B3)*	12
Lupfer (B2)	8
Lustre (K2)*	4
Luther (G5)*	22
Madoc (L2)*	33
Malta (J2)*	2,095
Manhattan (E5)*	716
Manicke (A2)	30
Manson (E2)	
Marias (E2)	10
Marion (B2)*	47
Marsh (M4)*	100
Martinsdale (F4)*	130
Marysville (D4)*	
Maschetah (J5)	25
Maudlow (E4)*	50
Maxville (C4)*	40
Mc Allister (E5)*	21
Mc Cabe (M2)*	55
Mc Elroy (M2)	2
Mc Leod (G5)*	10
Mc Rae (J5)*	5
Meaderville (D4)	250
Mecaha (J3)	
Medicine Lake (M2)*	454
Meharry (J2)	4
Melrose (D5)*	130
Melstone (H4)*	195
Melville (F4)*	29
Menard (E5)	
Merino (F3)*	5
Midby (M2)	7
Mike Horse (D4)*	200
Mildred (M4)*	75
Miles City (L4)*	9,243
Mill Iron (M5)*	75
Millegan (E3)	
Milltown (C4)*	750
Miner (E5)*	53
Mink (L3)	30
Mission (F5)	
Missoula (C4)*	22,485
Mizpah (L4)	
Moccasin (F3)*	300
Mock (Radnor) (B2)	8
Moiese (B3)*	8
Molt (H5)*	25
Mona (M3)	25
Monarch (F3)*	53
Monida (D6)*	50
Montague (F3)*	20
Moon Creek (L4)	
Moore (G4)*	224
Moorhead (K5)*	15
Mosby (J4)*	3
Mossmain (H5)	12
Moulton (G3)*	50
Musselshell (H4)*	250
Myers (J4)*	37
Nashua (K2)*	691
Natal (G4)	3
Navajo (M2)*	7
Neihart (F4)*	289
Nelson (E3)	
New Chicago (C4)	20
Niarada (B3)*	4
Nibbe (H4)*	20
Nickwall (L2)	
Nihill (G4)	2
Nimrod (C4)*	45
Ninemile (B4)*	
Nohly (M3)*	57
Norris (E5)*	100
Noxon (A3)*	113
Nyack (C2)	40
Nye (G5)*	3
Oilmont (E2)*	250
Oka (G4)	
Olanda (L3)	
Olive (L5)*	6
Ollie (M4)*	
Olney (B2)*	147
Oneill (L4)	
Opheim (K2)*	383
Osborn (H5)	
Ossette (L2)	
Oswego (L2)*	100
Otter (K5)*	57
Outlook (M2)*	235
Ovando (D3)*	100
Oxford (G4)	10
Pablo (B3)*	150
Paola (C2)	
Paradise (B3)*	300
Paragon (K4)	
Park City (H5)*	450
Paxton (L3)	20
Peerless (L2)*	125
Pendroy (D2)*	80
Perma (B3)*	60
Philipsburg (C4)*	1,048
Phillips (H2)	
Piedmont (D5)	21
Pineview (J4)	
Piniele (M5)	10
Pioneer (D4)	
Piper (G4)	6
Pipestone Hot Springs (D5)	12
Placer (E4)	
Plains (B3)*	714
Plentywood (M2)*	1,862
Plevna (M4)*	247
Polaris (C5)*	25
Polebridge (B2)*	56
Polson (B3)*	2,280
Polytechnic (H5)*	250
Pompeys Pillar (J5)*	200
Pony (E5)*	185
Poplar (L2)*	1,169
Portage (E3)	22
Post Creek (C3)	
Potomac (C4)*	65
Powderville (L5)*	4
Power (E3)*	75
Pray (F5)*	14
Proctor (B3)*	125
Pryor (H5)*	70
Quartz (B3)	4
Quietus (K5)*	3
Race Track (D4)	20
Radersburg (E4)*	
Radio (B3)	
Radnor (Mock) (B2)	8
Ramsay (D5)*	131
Ranchcreek (L5)*	
Rapelje (G5)*	150
Rapids (G5)	
Ravalli (B3)*	190
Rayfield (G4)	11
Raymond (M2)*	50
Raymond (M2)*	50
Raynesford (F3)*	45
Red Lodge (G5)*	2,730
Redstone (M2)*	105
Redwater (L3)	
Reedpoint (G5)*	150
Regina (J3)*	
Renova (D5)	6
Reserve (M2)*	215
Rexford (A2)*	200
Richey (L3)*	595
Richland (K2)*	
Ridge (M5)*	50
Ridgway (M5)*	3
Riebeling (D3)	
Rimini (D4)	
Rimroad (L3)	20
Rimrock (H5)	
Ringling (F4)*	135
Riverdale (E3)	50
Rivulet (B4)*	47
Roanwood (K2)	3
Roberts (G5)*	200
Rock Springs (K4)*	1
Rockvale (H5)	10
Rocky Boy (G2)	50
Rollins (B3)*	200
Ronan (C3)*	1,251
Roscoe (G5)*	75
Rosebud (K4)*	125
Ross Fork (G3)*	
Rothiemay (G4)*	55
Round Butte (B3)*	
Roundup (H4)*	2,856
Roy (H3)*	175
Rudyard (F2)*	521
Rumble Creek (C3)	30
Ryegate (G4)*	339
Saco (J2)*	539
Saint Ignatius (C3)*	781
St. Pauls (H3)	70
St. Peter (E3)	
St. Phillips (M4)	6
St. Regis (A3)*	500
St. Xavier (J5)*	150
Salem (E3)	
Saltese (A3)*	95
Sand Creek (L3)	
Sand Springs (J3)*	12
Sandcoulee (E3)*	500
Sanders (J4)*	40
Santa Rita (D2)*	145
Sappington (E5)*	34
Sarpy (J5)	5
Savage (M3)*	300
Savoy (H2)*	15
Sayle (L5)*	10
Scobey (L2)*	1,628
Sedan (F4)	6
Seeley Lake (C3)*	250
Selma (E2)	7
Selmes (G5)	6
Selway (K5)	4
Shambo (G2)*	
Shawmut (G4)*	122
Sheffield (K4)	
Shelby (E2)*	3,058
Shepherd (H5)*	100
Sheridan (D5)*	572
Shirley (L4)	
Shonkin (F3)*	6
Shriver (H5)	10
Sidney (M3)*	3,987
Silesia (H5)*	50
Silver Star (D5)*	55
Silverbow (D5)*	50
Simms (E3)*	250
Simpson (F2)*	
Sioux Pass (M3)*	40
Sipple (G4)	
Sixteen (F4)	10
Sloan (B3)	
Snowden (M2)	16
Somers (B2)*	750
Sonnette (L5)*	5
Soo (L2)	
Southern Cross (C4)	50
Spion Kop (F3)	10
Springdale (F5)*	75
Springhill (F5)	
Square Butte (F3)*	75
Stacey (L5)*	7
Stanford (F3)*	542
Stark (B3)*	25
Stevensville (C4)*	772
Stipek (M3)	50
Stockett (E3)*	300
Stone (C4)	
Stonehill (A2)	5
Strater (J2)	
Straw (G4)*	25
Stryker (B2)*	60
Suffolk (G3)*	14
Sula (B5)*	112
Sumatra (J4)*	
Sun Prairie (J3)	
Sun River (E3)*	115
Sunburst (E2)*	845
Superior (B3)*	626
Sutherland (L4)	
Swan Lake (C3)*	100
Sweetgrass (E2)*	
Swingley (F5)	
Taft (A3)	2
Tampico (K2)*	80
Tarkio (B4)*	75
Teigen (H3)*	
Telegraph Creek (J3)*	5
Terry (L4)*	1,191
Teton (F3)	
Thoeny (K2)*	10
Thompson Falls (A3)*	851
Three Forks (E5)*	1,114
Thurlow (K4)	
Tonquin (M4)	
Toston (E4)*	100
Townsend (E4)*	1,316
Trailcreek (B2)*	10
Trego (B2)*	48
Trident (E5)*	150
Trine (H3)	
Trout Creek (A3)*	52
Troy (A2)*	770
Tunis (F3)	6
Turner (H2)*	200
Tuscor (A3)*	4
Twin Bridges (D5)*	497
Twodot (F4)*	150
Tyler (H4)	3
Ulm (E3)*	150
Union (L3)	50
Ural (A2)*	37
Utical (F4)*	60
Valentine (H3)	3
Valier (D2)*	710
Van Norman (K3)*	4
Vananda (K4)*	100
Vandalia (J2)*	25
Vanstel (K4)	
Varney (E5)	12
Vaughn (E3)*	190
Verona (F2)	
Victor (B4)*	350
Vida (L3)*	58
Virgelle (F2)*	20
Virginia City (E5)*	323
Volborg (L5)*	7
Volt (L2)	
Wagner (H2)*	
Waleston (J2)	
Walkerville (D4)*	1,631
Wallum (G4)	
Waltham (E3)*	25
Ware (G3)*	4
Warland (A2)*	90
Warmsprings (D4)*	2,000
Warren (H5)*	40
Warrick (G2)*	3
Washoe (G5)*	
Waterloo (D5)*	95
Watkins (K3)*	10
Webster (M4)*	2
Weldon (K3)*	2
West Fork (L2)	
W. Gallatin (E5)	
W. Glacier (C2)*	440
W. Yellowstone (E6)*	500
Westby (M2)*	396
Westmore (M4)	16
Wheat Basin (G5)	10
Wheeler (K2)*	
White Sulphur Springs (E4)*	1,025
Whitefish (B2)*	3,268
Whitehall (D5)*	929
Whitepine (A3)*	175
Whitetail (L2)*	240
Whitewater (J2)*	85
Whitlash (E2)*	18
Wibaux (M3)*	739
Wickes (D4)*	70
Wickett (H5)	
Wilborn (D4)	
Willard (M4)*	3
Williams (D2)*	10
Willow Creek (E5)*	300
Wilsall (F5)*	300
Windham (F3)*	116
Winifred (G3)*	217
Winnett (H4)*	407
Winston (E4)*	53
Wisdom (C5)*	125
Wise River (C5)*	50
Wolf Creek (D3)*	156
Wolf Point (L2)*	2,557
Woodside (B4)	100
Woodworth (C3)	45
Worden (H5)*	375
Wyola (J5)*	110
Yaak (A2)*	
Yakt (B2)	28
Yates (M4)	
Yegen (H5)	10
Youngs Point (G5)	
Zero (L4)*	22
Zortman (H3)*	
Zurich (G2)*	85

Map on Page 72

NEBRASKA

Total Population 1,325,510

93 COUNTIES

Adams (F4)	28,855
Antelope (F2)	11,624
Arthur (C3)	803
Banner (A3)	1,325
Blaine (E3)	1,203
Boone (F3)	10,721
Box Butte (A2)	12,279
Boyd (F2)	4,911
Brown (E2)	5,164
Buffalo (E4)	25,134
Burt (H3)	11,536
Butler (G3)	11,432
Cass (H4)	16,361
Cedar (G2)	13,843
Chase (C4)	5,176
Cherry (C2)	8,397
Cheyenne (A3)	12,081
Clay (F4)	8,700
Colfax (G3)	10,010
Cuming (H3)	12,994
Custer (E3)	19,170
Dakota (H2)	10,401
Dawes (A2)	9,708
Dawson (E4)	19,393
Deuel (B3)	3,330
Dixon (H2)	9,129
Dodge (H3)	26,265
Douglas (H3)	281,020
Dundy (C4)	4,354
Fillmore (G4)	9,610
Franklin (F4)	7,096
Frontier (D4)	5,282
Furnas (E4)	9,385
Gage (H4)	28,052
Garden (B3)	4,114
Garfield (F3)	2,912
Gosper (E4)	2,734
Grant (C3)	1,057
Greeley (F3)	5,575
Hall (F4)	32,186
Hamilton (F4)	8,778
Harlan (E4)	7,189
Hayes (C4)	2,404
Hitchcock (C4)	5,867
Holt (F2)	14,859
Hooker (C3)	1,061
Howard (F3)	7,226

NEVADA

Map on Page 73 — *Total Population 160,083*

17 COUNTIES

Churchill (C3)......6,161
Clark (F6)......48,289
Douglas (B4)......2,029
Elco (F1)......11,654
Esmeralda (D5)...... 614
Eureka (E3)...... 896
Humboldt (C1)......4,838
Lander (D3)......1,850
Lincoln (F5)......3,837
Lyon (B3)......3,679
Mineral (C4)......5,560
Nye (E5)......3,101
Ormsby (B3)......4,172
Pershing (C2)......3,103
Storey (B3)...... 671
Washoe (B2)......50,205
White Pine (F3)......9,424

CITIES and TOWNS

Adaven (F4)*...... 25
Alamo (F5)*...... 384
Arden (F6)*...... 43
Arthur (F2)*...... 3
Austin (E3)*...... 300
Babbitt (C4)*......2,464
Baker (G3)*...... 50
Battle Mountain (E2)*. 850
Beatty (E6)*...... 485
Beowawe (E2)*...... 175
Black Springs (B3)*...... 100
Blue Diamonds (F6)...... 210
Bonne Springs (G2)...... 12
Boulder City (G7)*......3,903
Bristol Silver (G4)...... 25
Bunkerville (G6)*...... 180
Caliente (G5)*...... 970
Carlin (E2)*......1,203
Carp (G5)*...... 120
CARSON CITY (B3)*......3,082
Charleston (F1)*......
Cherry Creek (G3)*...... 75
Coaldale (D4)...... 16
Cobre (G1)*...... 51
Contact (G1)*...... 20
Cortez (E2)...... 7
Crystal Bay (A3)*...... 150
Currant (F4)......
Currie (G2)*...... 52
Dayton (B3)...... 300
Deeth (F1)*...... 75
Denio (C1)......
Dry Lake (G6)*...... 48
Duckwater (F4)*...... 5
Dunphy (E2)...... 6
Dyer (C5)*...... 87
East Ely (G3)*......1,000
East Gate (D3)...... 10
Elgin (G5)*...... 50
Elko (F2)*......5,393
Ely (G3)*......3,558
Eureka (E3)*...... 500
Fallon (C3)*......2,400
Fernley (B3)*...... 650
Flanigan (B2)*...... 44
Gabbs (D4)*...... 278
Gardnerville (B4)*...... 600
Genoa (B4)*...... 75
Gerlach (B2)*...... 200
Glenbrook (B3)*...... 30
Glendale (G6)...... 20
Golconda (D2)*...... 350
Gold Hill (B3)...... 68
Gold Point (D5)*...... 100
Goldfield (D5)*...... 275
Goodsprings (F7)*...... 175
Halleck (F2)*......
Hawthorne (C4)*......1,861
Hazen (C3)*...... 70
Henderson (G6)*......3,643
Hiko (F5)*...... 23
Hudson (B4)...... 2
Humboldt (C2)...... 30
Imlay (C2)*...... 250
Indian Springs (F6)...... 50
Ione (D4)*......
Jarbidge (F1)*...... 46
Jean (F7)*...... 52
Jiggs (F2)*...... 100
Jungo (C2)*...... 30
Kimberly (F3)*...... 300
Lamoille (F2)*...... 200
Las Vegas (F6)*......24,624
Lee (F2)*...... 135
Logandale (G6)*...... 300
Lovelock (C2)*......1,604
Lower Rochester (C2)...... 5
Lund (F4)*...... 365
Luning (C4)*...... 52
Manhattan (E4)*...... 125
Mason (B4)*...... 89
Mc Dermitt (D1)*...... 100
Mc Gill (G3)*......2,297
Mesquite (G6)*...... 540
Metropolis (G1)...... 15
Midas (E1)...... 100
Mill City (D2)...... 35
Mina (C4)*...... 274
Minden (B4)*...... 250
Moapa (G6)*...... 18
Montello (G1)*...... 350
Mt. Montgomery (C5)...... 19
Mountain City (F1)*...... 180
Nelson (G7)...... 67
Nivloc (D5)...... 4
Nixon (B3)*...... 450
North Fork (F1)...... 31
North Las Vegas (F6)*.3,875
Oasis (G1)...... 25
Oreana (C2)...... 24
Orovada (D1)*...... 150
Overton (G6)*...... 750
Owyhee (F1)......
Pahrump (E6)*...... 120
Palisade (E2)*...... 53
Panaca (G5)*...... 499
Paradise Valley (D1)*.. 95
Pioche (G5)*......1,392
Pittman (F6)*...... 150
Potts (E3)...... 35
Preston (G4)*...... 45
Pyramid (B2)*...... 27
Rawhide (C4)...... 10
Rebel Creek (D1)...... 10
Red House (D2)*......
Reese River (D4)*...... 184
Reno (B3)*......32,497
Rio Tinto (E1)...... 1
Riverside (G6)...... 25
Round Mountain (E4)*. 305
Rowland (F1)...... 11
Rox (G6)...... 20
Ruby Valley (F2)*...... 200
Ruth (F3)*......1,244
San Jacinto (G1)...... 6
Schurz (C4)*...... 150
Searchlight (F7)*...... 229
Shafter (G2)*...... 91
Shoshone (G4)*...... 25
Silver City (B3)*...... 200
Silverpeak (D5)*...... 63
Sloan (F7)*...... 200
Smith (B4)*...... 28
Sparks (B3)*......8,203
Steamboat (B3)*...... 94
Stillwater (C3)*...... 9
Sulphur (C2)*...... 33
Tippett (G3)...... 50
Tobar (G2)...... 10
Tonopah (D4)*......1,375
Tungsten (C2)*...... 300

Tuscarora (E1)*...... 30
Unionville (C2)*...... 15
Ursine (G5)*...... 60
Valmy (D2)*...... 75
Verdi (B3)*...... 350
Virginia City (B3)*...... 800
Vya (B1)...... 30
Wabuska (B3)*...... 50
Wadsworth (B3)*...... 275
Weeks (B3)...... 200
Wellington (B4)*...... 60
Wells (G1)*...... 947
White Rock (E1)...... 26
Whitney (F6)*...... 200
Wilkins (G1)*...... 60
Winnemucca (D2)*......2,847
Yerington (B4)*......1,157
Zephyr Cove (A3)*...... 50

NEW HAMPSHIRE

Map on Page 74 — *Total Population 533,242*

10 COUNTIES

Belknap (D4)......26,632
Carroll (D4)......15,868
Cheshire (B6)......38,811
Coos (D2)......35,932
Grafton (C4)......47,923
Hillsboro (C6)......156,987
Merrimack (C5)......63,022
Rockingham (D5)......70,059
Strafford (D5)......51,567
Sullivan (B5)......26,441

CITIES and TOWNS

Acworth (B5)*......Δ 418
Alexandria (C4)*......Δ 402
Allenstown (D5)......Δ1,540
Alstead (B5)*......Δ 851
Alton (D5)*......Δ1,189
Alton Bay (D5)*...... 200
Amherst (C6)*......Δ1,461
Andover (C5)*......Δ1,057
Antrim (C5)*......Δ1,030
Apthorp (C3)......
Ashland (C4)*......Δ1,599
Ashuelot (B6)*...... 500
Atkinson (D6)......Δ 492
Atkinson Depot (D6)*.
Auburn (D5)*......Δ1,158
Barnstead (D5)*......Δ 846
Barrington (E5)......Δ1,052
Bartlett (D3)*......Δ1,074
Bath (C3)*......Δ 706
Bear Island (D4)*......
Bedford (C6)......Δ2,176
Beebe River (C4)*...... 275
Belmont (D5)*......Δ1,611
Bennington (C5)*......Δ 593
Benton (C3)......Δ 247
Berlin (D3)*......16,615
Berlin Mills (D3)......
Bethlehem (C3)*......Δ 882
Blodgett (D5)......
Blodgett Landing (C5)*
Boscawen (C5)*......Δ1,857
Bow (C5)......Δ1,062
Bradford (C5)*......Δ 606
Brentwood (D6)......Δ 819
Bretton Woods (D3)*.. 14
Bridgewater (C4)......Δ 222
Bristol (C4)*......Δ1,586
Brookfield (D4)......Δ 159
Brookline (C6)*......Δ 671
Campton (C4)*......Δ1,149
Canaan (B4)*......Δ14,065
Canaan Center (B4)*.. 179
Candia (D5)*......Δ1,243
Canobie Lake (D6)*...... 778
Canterbury (C5)*......Δ 627
Carroll (D3)......Δ 359
Cascade (D3)*...... 1,000
CenterBarnstead (D5)* 550
Ctr. Conway (D4)*...... 400
Ctr. Harbor (D4)*......Δ 451
Ctr. Ossipee (D4)*...... 750
Ctr. Sandwich (C4)*... 725
Ctr. Strafford (D5)*...
Ctr. Tuftonboro (D4)*. 500
Charlestown (B5)*......Δ2,077
Chatham (D3)......Δ 177
Chesham (B6)*......
Chester (D6)*......Δ 807
Chesterfield (B6)*......Δ 970
Chichester (D5)......Δ 735
Chocorua (D4)*...... 375
Claremont (B5)*......12,811
Colebrook (D2)*......Δ2,116
CONCORD (C5)*......27,988
Contoocook (C5)*...... 1,000
Conway (D4)*......Δ4,109
Coos Junction (C2)......
Cornish Flat (B5)*...... 200
Crawford House (D3)* 6
Croydon (B5)*......Δ 349
Crystal (D2)...... 50
Dalton (C3)......Δ 557
Danbury (C4)*......Δ 496
Danville (D6)*......Δ 508
Deerfield (D5)*......Δ 706
Deering (C5)......Δ 392
Derry (D6)*......Δ5,826
Dixville Notch (D2)*..Δ 13
Dorchester (C4)......Δ 133
Dover (E5)*......15,874
Drewsville (B5)*...... 150
Dublin (B6)*......Δ 675
Dummer (D2)......Δ 229
Dunbarton (C5)*......Δ 533
Durham (E5)*......Δ4,770
East Andover (C5)*......
E. Barrington (E5)*......
E. Candia (D5)*...... 250
E. Canterbury (D5)......
E. Concord (D5)*......
E. Derry (D6)*...... 300
E. Grafton (C4)...... 100
E. Hampstead (D6)*...... 920
E. Haverhill (C3)*...... 150
E. Hebron (C4)*......
E. Jaffrey (B6)*...... 1,866
E. Kingston (E6)*......Δ 449
E. Lempster (B5)*......
E. Madison (D4)*...... 80
E. Milford (C6)......
E. Rochester (E5)*...... 1,100
E. Rindge (C6)*...... 200
E. Sullivan (B6)*...... 150
E. Swanzey (B6)*...... 700
E. Tilton (D5)......
E. Wakefield (E4)*......
E. Weare (C5)*...... 260
E. Westmoreland (B6)* 200
E. Wolfeboro (D4)*...... 301
Easton (C3)......Δ 94
Eaton Center (D4)*....Δ 221
Effingham Falls (D4)..Δ 341
Elkins (C5)*...... 200
Ellsworth (C4)......Δ 24
Elmwood (C6)*......
Emerson (West Henniker) (C5)......
Enfield (B4)*......Δ1,612
Enfield Center (B4)*...
Epping (D5)*......Δ1,796
Epsom (D5)*......Δ 756
Errol (D2)*......Δ 224
Etna (B4)*......
Exeter (E6)*......Δ5,664
Fabyan House (D3)*...... 300
Fairview (C3)......
Farmington (D5)*......Δ3,454
Fitzwilliam (B6)*......Δ 872
Fitzwilliam Depot (B6)*...... 250
Francestown (C6)*......Δ 405
Franconia (C3)*...... 549
Franklin (C5)*...... 6,552
Freedom (E4)*......Δ 315
Fremont (D6)*......Δ 698
Gaza (C4)......
Georges Mills (B5)*...... 170
Gerrish (C5)*...... 275
Gilford (D4)......Δ1,251
Gilmanton (D5)*......Δ 754
Gilmanton Iron Works (D5)*......
Gilsum (B5)*......Δ 578
Glen (D3)*......
Glencliff (C4)*...... 200
Glendale (D4)......
Goffs Falls (D6)*...... 800
Goffstown (C5)*......Δ5,638
Gonic (E5)*...... 1,000
Gorham (D3)*......Δ2,639
Goshen (B5)*......Δ 356
Gossville (D5)*...... 300
Grafton (C4)*......Δ 442
Grafton Center (C4)*.. 93
Grange (D3)...... 80
Grantham (B5)*......Δ 359
Grasmere (D5)*...... 1,545
Greenfield (C6)*......Δ 430
Greenland (E5)*......Δ 719
Greenville (C6)*......Δ1,280
Groton (C4)......Δ 105
Groveton (C2)*...... 1,918
Guild (B5)*...... 200
Hampstead (D6)*......Δ 902
Hampton (E6)*......Δ2,847
Hampton Beach (E6)*
Hampton Falls (E6)*..Δ 629
Hancock (B6)*......Δ 612
Hanover (B4)*......Δ6,259
Harrisville (B6)*......Δ 519
Haverhill (B3)*......Δ3,357
Hedding (E5)*......
Henniker (C5)*......Δ1,675
Hill (C4)*......Δ 310
Hillsboro (C5)*......Δ2,179
Hillsboro Lower Village (C5)...... 400
Hillsboro Upper Village (C5)...... 500
Hinsdale (A6)*......Δ1,950
Holderness (C4)*......Δ 731
Hollis (C6)*......Δ1,196
Hollis Depot (C6)*...... 380
Hooksett (D5)*......Δ2,792
Hopkinton (C5)*......Δ1,831
Hudson (D6)*......Δ4,183
Intervale (D3)*...... 600
Jackson (D3)*......Δ 344
Jaffrey (B6)*......Δ2,911
Jefferson (C3)*......Δ 728
Kearsarge (D3)*......
Keene (B6)*......15,638
Kingston (D6)*......Δ1,283
Laconia (D4)*......14,745
Lakeport (C4)*...... 3,600
Lancaster (C3)*......Δ3,113
Landaff (C3)......Δ 342
Langdon (B5)...... 378
Leavitts Hill (D5)*......
Lebanon (B4)*......Δ8,495
Lee (E5)......Δ 575
Lempster (B5)*......Δ 309
Lincoln (C3)*......Δ1,415
Lisbon (C3)*......Δ2,009
Litchfield (D6)......Δ 427
Little Boars Head (E6)
Littleton (C3)*......Δ4,817
Livermore Falls (C4)...
Londonderry (D6)*......Δ1,640
Loudon (D5)*......Δ1,012
Lyme (B4)*......Δ 924
Lyme Center (B4)*...... 350
Lyndeboro (C6)......Δ 552
Madbury (E5)*......Δ 489
Madison (D4)*......Δ 486
Manchester (C6)*......82,732
Manchester (urban area)......84,768
Maplewood (C3)*......
Marleboro (B6)*......Δ1,561
Marlow (B5)*......Δ 330
Martins (D5)......
Mascoma (B4)*...... 100
Meadows (C3)*...... 89
Melvin Mills (C5)*...... 65
Melvin Village (D4)*...
Meredith (C4)*......Δ2,222
Meredith Ctr. (C4)*...... 150
Meriden (B4)*...... 500
Merrimack (C6)*......Δ1,908
Middleton (D5)......Δ 255
Milan (D2)*......Δ 743
Milford (C6)*......Δ4,159
Milton (E5)*...... 1,510
Milton Mills (E5)*...... 280
Mirror Lake (D4)*...... 135
Monroe (B3)*......Δ 410
Mont Vernon (C6)*......Δ 405
Moultonboro (D4)*......Δ 880
Moultonville (D4)*...... 200
Mount Sunapee (B5)*. 125
Munsonville (B5)*......
Nashua (C6)*......34,669
Nelson (B5)......Δ 231
New Boston (C6)*......Δ 865
New Castle (E5)*......Δ 583
New Durham (D5)*......Δ 463
New Hampton (C4)*......Δ 723
New Ipswich (C6)*......Δ1,147
New London (C5)*......Δ1,484
Newbury (C5)*......Δ 320
Newfields (E5)*......Δ 469
Newington (E5)......Δ 494
Newmarket (D5)*......Δ2,709
Newport (B5)*......Δ5,131
Newton (E6)*......Δ1,173
Newton Jct. (D6)*......
North Branch (C5)......
N. Charlestown (B5)*.. 200
N. Chatham (D3)*...... 177
N. Chichester (D5)*...... 740
N. Conway (D3)*...... 1,200
N. End (C4)*......
N. Groton (C4)...... 30
N. Hampton (E6)*......Δ1,104
N. Haverhill (C3)*...... 500
N. Holderness (C4)......
N. Monroe (C3)...... 160
N. Newport (B5)*...... 200
N. Rochester (E5)*......
N. Salem (D6)*...... 400
N. Sandwich (D4)*......
N. Stratford (C2)*......
N. Sutton (C5)*......
N. Wakefield (D4)......
N. Walpole (B5)...... 1,000
N. Weare (C5)*......
N. Woodstock (C3)*...... 675
Northfield (C5)......Δ1,561
Northumberland (D2)*......Δ2,779
Northwoou (D5)*......Δ 966
Northwood Ctr. (D5)* 120
Northwood Narrows (D5)*...... 325
Nottingham (D5)*......Δ 566
Orange (C4)......Δ 82
Orford (B4)*......Δ 726
Orfordville (B4)*......
Ossipee (D4)*......Δ1,412
Parkhill (B6)...... 45
Pelham (D6)*......Δ1,317
Pembroke (D5)......Δ3,094
Penacook (C5)*...... 3,100
Percy (D2)*...... 48
Peterborough (C6)*......Δ2,556
Piermont (B4)*......Δ 511
Pike (B3)*...... 175
Pittsburg (D1)*......Δ 697
Pittsfield (D5)*......Δ2,321
Plainfield (B4)*......Δ1,011
Plaistow (D6)*......Δ2,082
Plymouth (C4)*......Δ3,039
Ponemah (C6)......
Portsmouth (E5)*......18,830
Powwow River (D6)...... 75
Province Lake (E4)......
Quincy (C4)*...... 125
Randolph (D3)*......Δ 158
Raymond (D5)*......Δ1,428
Redstone (D3)*...... 250
Reeds Ferry (C6)*...... 500
Richmond (B6)......Δ 259
Rindge (B6)*......Δ 707
Riverdale (C5)......
Rochester (D5)*......13,776
Rockingham (E5)......
Roxbury (B6)......Δ 117
Rumney (C4)*......Δ 859
Rumney Depot (C4)*... 165
Rye (E5)*......Δ1,982
Rye Beach (E6)*...... 1,000
Rye North Beach (E5)
Saint Paul's School (C5)*
Salem (D6)*......Δ4,805
Salem Depot (D6)*...... 1,637
Salisbury (C5)*......Δ 423
Salmon Falls (E5)*...... 1,290
Sanbornton (C5)*......Δ 755
Sanbornville (E4)*...... 460
Sandown (D6)*......Δ 315
Sandwich (D4)*......Δ 615
Seabrook (E6)*......Δ1,788
Sharon (C6)......Δ 62
Shelburne (D3)*......Δ 184
Short Falls (D5)*...... 100
Silver Lake (D4)*...... 500
Smithtown (E6)*...... 100
Somersworth (E5)*...... 6,927
Snowville (D4)*...... 100
Soo Nipi (C5)...... 25
South Acworth (B5)*..
S. Alexandria (C4)...... 100
S. Chatham (E3)*...... 54
S. Danbury (C5)*......
S. Danville (D6)*...... 125
S. Deerfield (D5)*......
S. Effingham (E4)*......
S. Hampton (E6)......Δ 314
S. Keene (B6)...... 200
S. Lee (D5)...... 70
S. Lyndeboro (C6)*...... 552
S. Merrimack (C6)*...... 250
S. Newbury (C5)*...... 88
S. Pittsfield (D5)......
S. Seabrook (E6)...... 1,000
S. Stoddard (B5)......
S. Sutton (C5)*...... 139
S. Tamworth (D4)*......
S. Wolfeboro (D4)...... 248
S. Weare (C5)......
Spofford (B6)*...... 350
Springfield (B4)*......Δ 324
Stark (D2)......Δ 373
State Line (B6)*...... 125
Stewartstown (D2)......Δ 970
Stinson Lake (C4)*......
Stoddard (B5)*......Δ 200
Strafford (D5)*......Δ 770
Stratford (C2)*......Δ 973
Stratham (E5)*......Δ 759
Sugar Hill (C3)*...... 250
Sullivan (B5)*......Δ 272
Sunapee (B5)*......Δ1,108
Suncook (C5)*......
Surry (B5)*......Δ 291
Sutton (C5)*......Δ 554
Swanzey (B6)......Δ2,806
Swiftwater (C3)......
Tamworth (D4)*......Δ1,025
Temple (C6)*......Δ 330
The Weirs (D4)*......
Thornton (C4)......Δ 460
Tilton (C5)*......Δ2,085
Troy (B6)*......Δ1,360
Tuftonboro (D4)......Δ 697
Twin Mountain (C3)*. 352
Union (D5)*...... 550
Unity (B5)*......Δ 653
Village (D6)*......
Wakefield (E4)*......Δ1,267
Walpole (B5)*......Δ2,536
Warner (C5)*......Δ1,080
Warren (C4)*......Δ 581
Washington (B5)*......Δ 168
Waterville Valley (C4)......Δ 11
Weare (C4)......Δ1,345
Webster (C5)......Δ 386
Wendell (B5)*...... 200
Wentworth (C4)*......Δ 413
Wentworth Location (D2)*......Δ 48
West Alton (D4)*......
W. Andover (C5)*......
W. Brentwood (D6)......
W. Campton (C4)*...... 125
W. Canaan (B4)*......
W. Chesterfield (A6)*...... 250
W. Claremont (B5)*...... 100
W. Epping (D5)......
W. Hampstead (D6)*...
W. Henniker (Emerson) (C5)......
W. Hopkinton (C5)*...... 100
W. Lebanon (B4)*...... 1,737
W. Manchester (C6)....
W. Milan (D2)*...... 250
W. Nottingham (D5)*...... 80
W. Ossipee (D4)*...... 175
W. Peterborough (B6)* 350
W. Rindge (C6)*...... 230
W. Rumney (C4)*...... 200
W. Rye (E6)*...... 55
W. Springfield (B5)*... 100
W. Stewartstown (C2)* 385
W. Swanzey (B6)*...... 1,400
W. Thornton (C4)*...... 450
W. Windham (D6)......
Westmoreland (B6)*Δ... 789
Westmoreland Depot (A6)*......
Westport (B6)...... 328
Westville (D6)*...... 300
Whiteface (D4)......
Whitefield (C3)*......Δ1,677
Willey House (D3)*...... 10
Wilmot (C5)*......Δ 370
Wilmot Flat (C5)*......
Wilton (C6)*......Δ1,952
Winchester (B6)*......Δ2,388
Windham (D6)......Δ 964
Windham Depot (D6)*.
Winnipesaukee (D4)*..
Winnisquam (D5)*...... 400
Wolfeboro (D4)*......Δ2,581
Wolfeboro Falls (D4)*...... 600
Wonalancet (D4)*...... 36
Woodstock (C4)*...... 894
Woodsville (B3)*...... 1,542

NEW JERSEY

Map on Page 75 — *Total Population 4,835,329*

21 COUNTIES

Atlantic (D5)......132,399
Bergen (E2)......539,139
Burlington (D4)......135,910
Camden (D4)......300,743
Cape May (D5)......37,131
Cumberland (C5)......88,597
Essex (E2)......905,949
Gloucester (C4)......91,727
Hudson (E2)......647,437
Hunterdon (D2)......42,736
Mercer (D3)......229,781
Middlesex (E3)......264,872
Monmouth (E3)......225,327
Morris (D2)......164,371
Ocean (E4)......56,622
Passaic (E1)......337,093
Salem (C4)......49,508
Somerset (D2)......99,052
Sussex (D1)......34,423
Union (E2)......398,138
Warren (C2)......54,374

CITIES and TOWNS

Absecon (D5)*......2,355
Adamston (E3)*...... 450
Adelphia (E3)*...... 300
Allamuchy (D2)*...... 600
Allendale (B1)*......2,409
Allenhurst (F3)*...... 758
Allentown (D3)*...... 931
Allenwood (E3)*......
Alloway (C4)*...... 700
Almonesson (B4)*......
Alpha (C2)*......2,117
Alpine (C1)*...... 644
Ampere (B2)*......10,000
Andover (D2)*...... 560
Annandale (D2)*......
Arlington (B2)*......16,000
Asbury (C2)*...... 300
Asbury Park (F3)*......17,094
Ashland (D4)*......1,240
Atco (D4)*......2,500
Atlantic City (E5)*......61,657
Atlantic City (urban area)......105,326
Atlantic Highlands (F3)*......3,083
Audubon (C4)*......9,531
Audubon Park (B3)......1,859
Augusta (D1)*...... 80
Aura (C4)...... 100
Avalon (D5)*...... 428
Avenel (E2)*......8,700
Avon by the Sea (F3)*..1,650
Awosting (E1)......
Baptistown (D2)*...... 350
Barber (E2)*......
Barnegat (E4)*......1,150
Barnegat Light (E4)*...... 227
Barrington (B3)*......2,651
Bartley (D2)*...... 500
Basking Ridge (D2)*......1,899
Bay Head (E3)*...... 808
Bayonne (B2)*......77,203
Bayville (E4)*......2,000
Beach Haven (E4)*......1,050
Beach Haven Crest (E4)*......
Beach Haven Terrace (E4)*...... 350
Beachwood (E4)*......1,251
Beaver Lake (D1)*...... 175

Map on Page 76 — NEW MEXICO — Total Population 681,187

32 COUNTIES

County	Pop.	County	Pop.
Bernalillo (C3)	145,673	Mora (E3)	8,720
Catron (A4)	3,533	Otero (D6)	14,909
Chaves (E5)	40,605	Ouay (F3)	13,971
Colfax (E2)	16,761	Rio Arriba (B2)	24,997
Curry (F4)	23,351	Roosevelt (F4)	16,409
De Baca (E4)	3,464	San Juan (A2)	18,292
Dona Ana (C6)	39,557	San Miguel (D3)	26,512
Eddy (E6)	40,640	Sandoval (C3)	12,438
Grant (A5)	21,649	Santa Fe (C3)	38,153
Guadalupe (E4)	6,772	Sierra (B5)	7,186
Harding (F3)	3,013	Socorro (C5)	9,670
Hidalgo (A7)	5,095	Taos (D2)	17,146
Lea (F6)	30,717	Torrance (D4)	8,012
Lincoln (D5)	7,409	Union (F2)	7,372
Los Alamos (C3)	10,476	Valencia (A4)	22,481
Luna (B6)	8,753		
Mc Kinley (A3)	27,451		

CITIES and TOWNS

Place	Pop.
Abbott (E2)*	
Abeytas (C4)*	
Abiquiu (C2)*	
Abo (C4)*	
Acme (E5)	
Acomita (B3)*	
Adams Diggings (A4)*	
Afton (B6)	15
Agua Fria (D2)*	
Akela (B6)	40
Alameda (C3)*	1,792
Alamogordo (C6)*	6,783
Albert (F3)*	35
Albuquerque (C3)*	96,815
Alcalde (C2)*	
Algodones (C3)*	250
Alma (A5)	50
Alto (D5)*	50
Amalia (D2)*	
Amistad (F3)*	33
Anapra (C7)*	
Ancho (D5)*	100
Animas (A7)*	
Anthony (C6)*	800
Anton Chico (D3)*	600
Apache Creek (A5)*	85
Arabela (D5)	60
Aragon (A5)*	89
Arch (F4)*	35
Arrey (B6)*	350
Arroyo Hondo (D2)*	500
Arroyoseco (D2)*	400
Artesia (E6)*	8,244
Atarque (A4)*	100
Atoka (E6)	64
Augustine (B4)*	
Aztec (B2)*	885
Bard (F3)*	45
Bayard (A6)*	2,119
Beaverhead (A5)	
Belen (C4)*	4,495
Bell Ranch (E3)*	20
Bellview (F4)*	150
Bent (D5)*	250
Berino (C6)*	300
Bernalillo (C3)*	1,922
Bernardo (C4)	30
Bibo (B3)	
Bingham (C5)*	7
Blanco (B2)*	135
Bloomfield (A2)*	500
Bluewater (A3)*	350
Bluit (F5)	
Boaz (F5)*	30
Bosque (C4)*	400
Brilliant (E2)*	225
Broadview (F4)*	80
Buchanan (E4)*	
Buckeye (F6)*	227
Buckhorn (A5)*	500
Buena Vista (D3)*	265
Bueyeros (F3)*	38
Caballo (B6)*	
Cabezon (B3)*	
Cambray (B6)*	8
Cameron (F4)*	18
Canjilon (C2)*	900
Canones (C2)*	140
Canoncito (C3)	
Capitan (D5)*	575
Caprock (F5)*	12
Capulin (F2)*	200
Carlsbad (E6)*	17,975
Carrizozo (D5)*	1,389
Carson (D2)*	25
Carthage (C5)	
Casa Blanca (B4)*	493
Causey (F5)*	50
Cebolla (C2)*	1,000
Cedar Crest (C3)*	1,000
Cedar Hill (B2)*	130
Cedarvale (D4)*	50
Central (A6)*	1,511
Cerrillos (D3)*	
Cerro (D2)*	600
Chacon (D2)*	
Chama (C2)*	1,300
Chama (C6)*	1,000
Chamberino (C6)*	1,000
Chamisal (D2)*	500
Chapelle (D3)	25
Chaperito (E3)*	125
Chico (E2)*	6
Chilili (C4)	
Chimayo (D3)*	1,550
Chloride (B5)*	56
Cienega (D6)	2
Cimarron (E2)*	855
Clapham (F2)*	
Claunch (C4)*	
Clayton (F2)*	3,515
Cleveland (D2)*	700
Cliff (A6)*	250
Closson (A3)	
Cloudcroft (C6)*	251
Cloverdale (A7)	
Clovis (F4)*	17,318
Cochiti (C3)*	250
Colfax (E2)	
Colmor (E2)*	80
Colonias (E3)*	150
Columbus (B7)*	251
Conchas Dam (E3)*	100
Contreras (C4)	
Coolidge (A3)*	8
Cooper (F6)	6
Cordova (D2)*	
Corona (D4)*	530
Correo (B4)*	8
Costilla (D2)*	300
Cowles (D3)*	200
Coyote (C2)*	
Coyote Canyon (A3)	
Crossroads (F5)*	60
Crownpoint (A3)*	125
Crystal (A2)*	125
Cuba (B2)*	850
Cubero (B3)*	
Cuchillo (B5)*	105
Cuervo (E3)*	100
Cundiyo (D3)*	160
Cunico (E2)	60
Cutter (B5)*	55
Dahlia (B3)*	100
Datil (B4)*	500
Dawson (E2)*	1,206
Dayton (E6)	
Delphos (F4)*	2
Deming (B6)*	5,672
Derry (B6)*	300
Des Moines (F2)*	282
Dexter (E5)*	784
Dilia (D3)*	250
Dixon (D2)*	1,250
Domingo (C3)*	120
Dona Ana (C6)*	400
Dora (F5)*	120
Dulce (B2)*	500
Dunlap (E4)*	90
Duoro (D4)*	
Duran (D4)*	300
Dusty (B5)*	15
Dwyer (B6)	
Eagle Nest (D2)*	200
East Vaughn (D4)*	1,800
Edgewood (C3)*	45
El Morro (A3)*	300
El Paso Gap (E6)*	12
El Porvenir (D3)*	350
El Prado (D2)*	
El Pueblo (D3)*	175
El Rito (C2)*	1,200
El Vado Dam (C2)	18
Elephant Butte (B5)*	150
Elida (F5)*	430
Elizabethtown (D2)	
Elk (D6)*	35
Elkins (E5)*	26
Embudo (C2)*	
Encino (D4)*	408
Endee (F3)*	50
Engle (B5)*	65
Ensenada (C2)*	400
Escabosa (C4)	
Espanola (C3)*	1,446
Espuella (E6)	50
Estancia (D4)*	916
Eunice (F6)*	2,352
Fairacres (C6)*	350
Farley (E2)*	111
Farmington (A2)*	3,637
Faywood (B6)*	
Fence Lake (A4)*	250
Field (B4)	300
Fierro (A6)*	500
Fillmore (C6)*	
Flora Vista (A2)*	150
Florida (B6)	15
Florida (C4)*	350
Floyd (F4)*	50
Flying H (E5)*	55
Folsom (F2)*	206
Forrest (F4)*	130
Fort Bayard (A6)*	483
Fort Stanton (D5)*	500
Ft. Sumner (E4)*	1,978
Ft. Wingate (A3)*	250
Frazier (E5)*	12
French (F3)*	10
Frisco (A5)	
Fruitland (A2)*	200
Gage (A6)*	100
Galisteo (D3)*	150
Gallegos (F3)*	
Gallina (C2)*	31
Gallup (A3)*	9,133
Gamerco (A3)*	200
Gardiner (E2)*	50
Garfield (B6)*	300
Garita (E3)*	200
Gila (A6)*	700
Gilman (C3)*	119
Gladiola (F5)*	99
Gladstone (F2)*	61
Glencoe (D5)*	200
Glenrio (F3)*	60
Glenwood (A5)*	300
Glorieta (D3)*	500
Golden (C3)*	75
Governador (B2)*	45
Grady (F4)*	130
Gran Quivira (D4)*	50
Grants (C3)*	2,251
Green Tree (D5)*	363
Greens Gap (A4)	25
Grenville (F2)*	102
Grier (E3)*	200
Guadalupita (D2)*	475
Guy (F2)	
Hachita (A7)*	200
Hagerman (E5)*	1,024
Hanover (A6)*	1,200
Hatch (B6)*	1,064
Hayden (F3)*	
Heck Canyon (D2)*	
Hernandez (C2)*	400
Hickman (B4)*	17
High Rolls (D5)*	175
Hill (C6)*	100
Hillsboro (B6)*	300
Hilton Lodge (D3)*	2
Hobbs (E6)*	13,875
Hollene (F4)*	20
Hollywood (D5)*	
Holman (D2)*	
Hondo (D5)*	250
Hope (E6)*	186
Horse Springs (A5)*	100
House (F4)*	295
Humble City (F6)*	42
Hurley (A6)*	2,079
Ilfeld (D3)*	
Ima (E4)*	4
Ione (F3)*	3
Isleta (C4)*	1,400
Jal (F6)*	2,047
Jarales (C4)*	1,199
Jemez Pueblo (C3)*	878
Jemez Springs (C3)*	135
Jicarilla (D5)	20
Jordan (F4)*	93
Kelly (B4)*	55
Kenna (F5)*	100
Kingston (B6)*	50
Kirtland (A2)*	
Knowles (F6)	10
Koehler (E2)*	385
La Cueva (D3)	
La Jara (B2)*	2,500
La Lande (E4)*	35
La Liendre (E3)	12
La Luz (C6)*	200
La Madera (C2)*	
La Mesa (C6)*	650
La Puente (C2)	300
La Union (C7)	475
La Ventana (B3)	
Laguna (B3)*	3,004
Lajoya (C4)*	
Lake Arthur (E5)*	380
Lake Valley (B6)*	9
Lakewood (E6)*	
Lamy (C3)*	105
Laplata (A2)*	
Las Cruces (C6)*	12,325
Las Padillas (C3)*	487
Las Palomas (B5)*	60
Las Tablas (C2)*	100
Las Vegas (city) (D3)*	7,494
Las Vegas (town) (D3)	6,269
Ledoux (D3)*	800
Lemitar (B4)*	500
Levy (E2)*	15
Leyba (D3)*	
Lincoln (D5)*	80
Lindrith (C2)*	300
Lingo (F5)*	20
Llano (D2)*	550
Loco Hills (F6)*	300
Logan (F3)*	500
Lon (D4)	
Lordsburg (A6)*	3,525
Los Alamos (C3)*	9,934
Los Griegos (C3)*	3,025
Los Lunas (C4)*	889
Lour..es (D3)*	
Loving (E6)*	1,487
Lovington (F6)*	3,134
Lucy (D4)*	10
Lumberton (C2)*	
Luna (A5)*	300
Lyden (C2)*	
Madrid (C3)*	477
Maes (E3)*	50
Magdalena (B4)*	1,297
Malaga (E6)*	250
Mangas (A4)	25
Manuelito (A3)*	
Manzano (C4)*	250
Marquez (B3)*	60
Maxwell (E2)*	404
Mayhill (D6)*	
Mc Alister (F4)*	
Mc Donald (F5)*	100
Mc Gaffey (A3)*	50
Mc Intosh (D4)*	25
Melrose (F4)*	936
Mentmore (A3)*	100
Mescalero (D5)*	
Mesilla (C6)*	1,264
Mesilla Park (C6)*	2,000
Mesquite (C6)*	400
Mexican Springs (A3)*	
Miami (E2)*	
Mills (E2)*	
Milnesand (F5)*	
Mimbres (B6)*	36
Mogollon (A5)*	26
Monero (C2)*	207
Montezuma (D3)*	1,200
Monticello (B5)*	400
Montoya (F3)*	75
Monument (F6)*	
Mora (D3)*	1,750
Moriarty (D4)*	
Moses (F2)*	70
Mosquero (F3)*	583
Mount Dora (F2)*	100
Mountain Park (D6)*	60
Mountainair (C4)*	1,418
Mule Creek (A5)*	16
Nambe (D3)*	500
Nara Visa (F3)*	350
New Laguna (B3)*	150
Newcomb (A2)*	200
Newkirk (E3)*	250
Nogal (D5)*	25
Nolan (E2)*	11
Norton (F4)*	7
Obar (F3)*	5
Ocate (E2)*	105
Oil Center (F6)*	70
Ojo Caliente (D2)*	
Ojo Feliz (E2)*	365
Ojo Sarco (D2)*	150
Old Albuquerque (C3)*	
Old Tapicitoes (C2)*	
Olive (E5)*	12
Omega (A4)*	30
Onava (C3)	
Optimo (C3)	
Organ (C6)*	50
Orogrande (D6)*	45
Oscura (C5)	
Otis (E6)*	150
Paguate (B3)*	500
Palma (B3)*	
Park View (C2)*	300
Pasamonte (F2)	12
Pastura (E4)*	120
Pecos (D3)*	1,241
Pedernal (D4)*	30
Penablanca (C3)*	350
Penasco (D2)*	700
Penistaja (B3)	
Pep (F5)*	30
Peralta (C4)*	300
Perea (C3)	
Petaca (C2)*	
Picacho (D5)*	175
Pie Town (A4)*	135
Pinehaven (A3)	
Pinon (D6)*	100
Pinos Altos (A6)*	250
Pintada (D4)*	
Placitas (C3)*	350
Pleasanton (A5)*	48
Pojoaque (C3)*	200
Polvadera (B4)*	
Ponderosa (C3)*	100
Portales (C3)*	8,112
Prewitt (B3)*	65
Puerto de Luna (E4)*	600
Quarai (C4)*	55
Quay (F4)*	120
Quemado (A4)*	400
Questa (D2)*	1,400
Radium Springs (B6)*	
Ragland (F4)*	12
Rainsville (D2)*	350
Ramah (A3)*	300
Ramon (D4)	
Ranches of Taos (D2)*	1,386
Raton (E2)*	8,241
Rayo (C4)	
Red Hill (A4)*	
Red River (D2)*	150
Redrock (A6)*	17
Regina (C3)*	100
Rehoboth (A3)*	90
Rencona (D3)*	32
Reserve (A5)*	
Ribera (D3)*	400
Ricardo (E4)*	25
Rincon (C6)*	500
Riverside (C2)	
Rociada (D3)*	40
Rodarte (D2)*	750
Rodeo (A7)*	250
Rodey (B6)*	250
Rogers (F5)*	71
Romeroville (D3)*	18
Rosa (D2)*	100
Rosebud (F3)	
Roswell (E5)*	25,738
Rowe (D3)*	365
Roy (E3)*	1,074
Ruidoso (D5)*	806
Rutheron (C2)*	25
Sabinoso (E3)*	125
Sacramento (D6)*	
Saint Vrain (F4)*	48
Sais (C4)*	
Salem (B6)*	350
San Acacia (B4)*	200
San Antonio (B5)*	900
San Cristobal (D2)*	215
San Felipe (C3)*	500
San Fidel (B3)*	89
San Ildefonzo (C3)*	400
San Jon (F3)*	362
San Jose (D3)*	
San Juan	
San Juan Puebio (C2)*	1,200
San Lorenzo (B6)*	350
San Marcial (C5)	
San Mateo (B3)*	150
San Miguel (C6)*	300
San Patricio (D5)*	300
San Rafael (A3)*	500
San Ysidro (C3)*	
Sandia Park (C3)*	100
Sandoval (C3)*	
Santa Clara (C3)	
Santa Cruz (D3)*	
SANTA FE (C3)*	27,998
Santa Rita (B6)*	2,135
Santa Rosa (E4)*	2,199
Sapello (D3)*	80
Scholle (C4)*	
Seboyeta (B3)*	
Sedan (F2)*	100
Sena (D3)*	190
Seneca (F2)*	20
Separ (A6)*	50
Serafina (D3)*	100
Servilleta (D2)*	15
Sherman (B6)*	
Shiprock (A2)*	250
Shoemaker (E3)*	200
Silver City (A6)*	7,022
Skarda (D3)*	25
Socorro (C4)*	4,334
Soham (D3)*	250
Solano (E3)*	40
Springer (E2)*	1,558
Spur Lake (A5)*	3
Stanley (D3)*	75
State College (C6)*	1,200
Stead (E4)*	11
Steins (A6)	
Stong (C3)	
Strauss (C7)*	
Sugarite (E2)*	20
Sunshine Valley (D2)*	
Tafoya (E2)*	325
Taiban (F4)*	
Tajique (C4)*	250
Talpa (D2)*	
Taos (D2)*	1,815
Tapicitoes (B2)*	
Tatum (F5)*	688
Taylor Springs (E2)*	25
Tecolotenos (D3)*	95
Tererro (D3)*	40
Tesuque (C3)*	
Texico (F4)*	691
Thoreau (A3)*	150
Three Rivers (C5)*	350
Tierra Amarilla (C2)*	800
Tijeras (C3)*	
Tinnie (D5)*	80
Toadlena (A2)*	500
Tohatchi (A3)*	350
Tolar (F4)	
Tome (C4)*	400
Torrance (D4)	10
Torreon (C4)*	100
Trampas (D2)*	
Trementina (E3)*	
Tres Lagunas (B4)*	14
Tres Piedras (D2)*	75
Tres Ritos (D2)*	50
Truchas (D2)*	750
Trujillo (E3)*	500
Truth or Consequences (B5)*	4,563
Tsaya (A2)*	50
Tucumcari (F3)*	8,419
Tularosa (C5)*	1,642
Turley (B2)*	
Two Wells (A3)	
Tyrone (A6)*	
Ute Park (D2)*	
Vadito (D2)*	500
Vado (C6)*	350
Valdez (D2)*	360
Valencia (C4)*	818
Vallecitos (C2)*	400
Valley Ranch (D3)*	
Valmora (D3)*	100
Van Houten (E2)*	
Vanadium (A6)*	450
Vaughn (D4)*	1,356
Veguita (C4)*	
Velarde (C2)*	600
Vermejo Park (D2)*	300
Villanueva (D3)*	
Virden (A6)*	146
Wagon Mound (E2)*	1,120
Waterflow (A2)*	150
Watrous (D3)*	250
Weed (D6)*	100
White Oaks (D5)*	61
White Signal (A6)	
Whitewater (A6)*	40
Willard (D4)*	296
Wilna (A6)*	8
Winston (B5)*	150
Witt (D4)	12
Yeso (E4)*	500
Youngsville (C2)*	120
Zamora (C3)	
Zuni (A3)*	2,563

Map on Page 77 — NEW YORK — Total Population 14,830,192

62 COUNTIES

County	Pop.	County	Pop.
Albany (M5)	239,386	Ontario (F5)	60,172
Allegany (D6)	43,784	Orange (C1)	152,255
Bronx (C2)	1,451,277	Orleans (D4)	29,832
Broome (J6)	184,698	Oswego (H4)	77,181
Cattaraugus (C6)	77,901	Otsego (K5)	50,763
Cayuga (G4)	70,136	Putnam (D1)	20,307
Chautauqua (B6)	135,189	Queens (D2)	1,550,849
Chemung (G6)	86,827	Rensselaer (O5)	132,607
Chenango (J6)	39,138	Richmond (C3)	191,555
Clinton (N1)	53,622	Rockland (C1)	89,276
Columbia (N6)	43,182	St. Lawrence (K2)	98,897
Cortland (H5)	37,158	Saratoga (N4)	74,869
Delaware (K6)	44,420	Schenectady (M5)	142,497
Dutchess (N7)	136,781	Schoharie (M5)	22,703
Erie (C5)	899,238	Schuyler (G5)	14,182
Essex (N2)	35,086	Seneca (G5)	29,253
Franklin (M1)	44,830	Steuben (F6)	91,439
Fulton (M4)	51,021	Suffolk (F2)	276,129
Genesee (D4)	47,584	Sullivan (L7)	40,731
Greene (M6)	28,745	Tioga (H6)	30,166
Hamilton (L3)	4,105	Tompkins (H6)	59,122
Herkimer (L4)	61,407	Ulster (M7)	92,621
Jefferson (J2)	85,521	Warren (N3)	39,205
Kings (C3)	2,738,175	Washington (O4)	47,144
Lewis (K3)	22,521	Wayne (F4)	57,323
Livingston (E5)	40,257	Westchester (D1)	625,816
Madison (J5)	46,214	Wyoming (D5)	32,822
Monroe (E4)	487,632	Yates (F5)	17,615
Montgomery (M5)	59,594		
Nassau (D2)	672,765		
New York (C3)	1,960,101		
Niagara (C4)	189,992		
Oneida (J4)	222,855		
Onondaga (H5)	341,719		

CITIES and TOWNS

Place	Pop.
Accord (M7)*	500
Adams (J3)*	1,762
Adams Center (H3)*	850
Addison (F6)*	1,920
Adirondack (N3)*	150
Afton (J6)*	875
Akron (C4)*	2,481
ALBANY (N5)*	134,995
Albany-Troy (urban area)	290,209
Albion (D4)*	4,850
Alden (C5)*	1,252
Alder Creek (K4)*	50
Alexander (D5)*	304
Alexandria Bay (J2)*	1,688
Alfred (E6)*	2,053
Allegany (E6)*	1,738
Allentown (E6)*	500
Almond (E6)*	659
Alpine (G6)*	194
Altamont (M5)*	1,127
Altmar (J3)*	299
Alton (G4)*	350
Altona (N1)*	500
Amagansett (G2)*	1,000
Amber (H5)*	130
Amenia (N7)*	1,300
Ames (L5)*	193
Amityville (E3)*	6,164
Amsterdam (M5)*	32,240
Ancram (N6)*	200
Andes (L6)*	430
Andover (E6)*	1,351
Angelica (E6)*	928
Angola (C5)*	1,936
Annandale-on-Hudson (N6)*	405
Antwerp (J2)*	846
Apalachin (H6)*	900
Appleton (C4)*	100
Apulia Station (H5)*	220
Arcade (D5)*	1,818
Ardsley (H1)*	1,744
Argyle (O4)*	351
Arkport (E6)*	701
Arkville (L6)*	600
Asharoken ‡(E2)*	116
Ashland (M6)*	275
Ashokan (M7)*	
Ashwood (D4)*	110
Athens (N6)*	1,545
Athol (N4)*	60
Atlanta (F5)*	500
Atlantic Beach (D3)*	2,000
Attica (D5)*	2,676
Au Sable Forks (N2)*	1,643
Auburn (G5)*	36,722
Aurora (G5)*	711
Ava (K4)*	
Averill Park (O5)*	
Avoca (F6)*	952
Avon (E5)*	2,102
Babylon (D2)*	6,015
Bainbridge (J6)*	1,505
Baldwin (B3)*	22,000
Baldwinsville (H4)*	4,495
Ballston (N5)*	5,374
Ballston Spa (N5)*	4,937
Bangor (M1)*	300
Barker (D4)*	523
Barnes Corners (J3)*	105
Barneveld (K4)*	331

Barre Center (D4)........ 350
Barryville (L7)*........... 550
Bosom (D4)*............... 80
Batavia (D5)*............17,799
Bath (F6)*....................5,416
Baxter Estates ‡(D2).. 862
Bay Shore (E2)*..........9,665
Bayport (E2)*............1,463
Bayville (B2)*............1,981
Beach Ridge (C4)........ 500
Beacon (N7)*............14,012
Beaver Dams (F6)*....... 230
Beaver Falls (K3)*....... 618
Beaver River (L3)*....... 20
Bedford Hills (D1)*......
Belfast (D6)*............... 750
Belle Terre ‡(E2)........ 120
Bellerose (A2)*...........1,134
Belleville (H3)*........... 305
Bellmore (B2)*...........12,000
Bellport (F2)*............1,449
Belmont (E6)*............1,211
Bemus Point (B6)*...... 424
Benson Mines (L2)....... 400
Bergen (E4)*............... 786
Berkshire (H6)*........... 350
Berlin (O5)*................ 900
Berne (M5)*................ 225
Bernhards Bay (J4)*.... 764
Bethel (L7)*............... 500
Big Flats (G6)*........... 523
Big Indian (M6)*.......... 175
Big Moose (L3)*.......... 105
Binghamton (J6)*......80,674
Binghamton (urban area) 144,570
Black River (J3)*.........1,062
Blasdell (C5)*.............3,127
Bliss (D5)*.................. 678
Bloomingburg (L7)*...... 263
Bloomingdale (M2)*..... 476
Bloomville (L6)*.......... 350
Blue Mountain Lake (M3)* 275
Bolivar (D6)*..............1,490
Bolton Landing (N3)*..1,200
Bombay (M1)*............. 500
Boonville (K4)*............2,329
Boston (C5)*...............1,500
Bouckville (J5)*.......... 195
Branchport (F5)*.........1,000
Brant (B5)*................. 500
Brant Lake (N3)*........ 200
Brasher Falls (L1)*...... 800
Breakabeen (M5)*........ 165
Breesport (G6)*........... 500
Brentwood (E2)*.........2,803
Brewerton (H4)*.......... 800
Brewster (D1)*............1,810
Briarcliff Manor‡(D1)*2,494
Bridgehampton (G2)*...
Bridgeport (J4)*..........1,800
Bridgewater (K5)*........ 309
Brier Hill (J1)*........... 200
Brightwaters ‡(E2)*....2,336
Broadalbin (M4)*.........1,400
Brockport (D4)*..........4,748
Brocton (B6)*.............1,380
Bronx, The (D2)*....1,451,277
Bronxville (J1)*............6,778
Brookfield (K5)*.......... 400
Brooklyn (C2)*.......2,738,175
Brooktondale (H6)*..... 300
Brookville ‡(D2).......... 337
Brownville (H3)*..........1,013
Brushton (L1)*............ 516
Buchanan (D1)*............1,820
Buffalo (B5)*............580,132
Buffalo (urban area).794,747
Burdett (G6)*.............. 432
Burke (M1)*................ 316
Burlington Flats (K5)*. 185
Burt (C4)*................... 300
Busti (B6).................. 210
Byron (D4)*................ 300
Cadyville (N1)*........... 697
Cairo (M6)*................ 600
Caledonia (E5)*...........1,683
Callicoon (K7)*........... 800
Callicoon Center (L7)*. 405
Cambridge (O4)*...........1,692
Camden (J4)*..............2,407
Cameron (F6)*............ 200
Camillus (H4)*.............1,225
Campbell (F6)*............ 600
Campbell Hall (C1)*..... 251
Canaan (O6)*...............
Canajoharie (L5)*........2,761

Canadaigua (F5)*.........8,332
Canaseraga (E6)*......... 693
Canastota (J4)*...........4,458
Candor (H6)*............... 802
Caneadea (D6)*............ 400
Canisteo (E6)*............2,625
Canton (K1)*...............4,379
Cape Vincent (H2)*...... 812
Carlisle (L5)*.............. 200
Carlton (D4)................ 250
Carmel (D1)*...............1,526
Caroga Lake (L4)*........ 325
Caroline (H6)............... 35
Carthage (J3)*.............4,420
Cassadaga (B6)*.......... 676
Castile (D5)*...............1,072
Castleton-on-Hudson (N5)* 1,751
Castorland (J3)*.......... 308
Cato (G4)*.................. 431
Catskill (N6)*..............5,392
Cattaraugus (C6)*........1,190
Cayuga (G5)*.............. 534
Cayuga Hts. ‡(G5).......1,131
Cazenovia (J5)*...........1,946
Cedarhurst (B3)*..........6,051
Cedarville (K5)............ 149
Celoron (B6)*...............1,555
Center Moriches (F2)*..1,761
Central Bridge (M5)*.. 500
Central Square (H4)*... 665
Central Valley (C1)*....1,300
Centre Island (B2)........ 199
Ceres (D6)*................. 350
Chadwicks (K4)*...........2,500
Chafee (C5)*............... 350
Champlain (N1)*..........1,505
Charlotteville (L5)*...... 200
Chase Mills (K1)*....... 250
Chateaugay (N1)*........1,234
Chatham (N6)*............2,304
Chatham Center (N6)*. 378
Chaumont (H2)*.......... 513
Chautauqua (A6)*......... 500
Chazy (N1)*................ 600
Cheektowaga (C5)........
Chemung (G6)*............ 400
Chenango Bridge (J6)*.2,500
Chenango Forks (J6)*.. 400
Chepachet (K5)*.......... 84
Cherry Creek (B6)*....... 631
Cherry Valley (L5)*...... 760
Chester (B1)*...............1,215
Chestertown (N3)*....... 350
Chichester (M6)*.......... 225
Childwold (L2)*............ 200
Chittenango (J4)*........1,307
Churchville (E4)*......... 755
Churubusco (N1)*......... 200
Cicero (H4)*.................1,000
Cincinnatus (H5)*......... 900
Clarence (C5)*.............1,018
Clarkson (E4)*............. 382
Clarksville (M5)*.......... 600
Claverack (N6)*.......... 500
Clayton (H2)*...............1,981
Clayville (K5)*............. 719
Clermont (N6)*............ 500
Cleveland (J4)*........... 555
Clifton Springs (F4)*...1,838
Clinton (K4)*................1,630
Clinton Corners (N7)*.. 300
Clintondale (M7)*......... 800
Clyde (G4)*..................2,492
Clymer (A6)*................ 500
Cobleskill (L5)*............3,208
Cochecton (K7)*........... 150
Coeymans (N6)*...........1,250
Cohocton (F5)*............ 943
Cohoes (N5)*...............21,272
Cold Brook (L4)*.......... 342
Cold Spring (C1)*.........1,788
Cold Spring Harbor (E2)* 1,500
Colden (C5)*................ 700
Collins (C6)*................ 500
Collins Center (C6)*..... 450
Colonie ‡(N5)*............2,068
Colton (L1)*................. 250
Comstock (O4)*............2,250
Conesus (E5)*.............. 200
Conewango (C6)*.........
Connelly (M7)*............. 350
Constable (M1)*........... 200
Constableville (J3)*...... 378
Constantia (H4)*..........1,250
Cooks Falls (K7)*......... 200
Coopers Plains (F6)*.... 304

Cooperstown (L5)*........2,727
Copake (N6)*............... 600
Copake Falls (N6)*.......
Copenhagen (J3)*......... 690
Corfu (D5)*................. 542
Corinth (N4)*...............3,161
Corning (F6)*.............17,684
Cornwall (C1)*.............2,211
Cortland (H5)*............18,152
Cove Neck ‡(D2).......... 200
Cranberry Lake (L2)*.. 232
Croghan (K3)*............. 772
Cowlesville (D5)*......... 232
Coxsackie (N6)*...........2,722
Croton Falls (D1)*.......1,000
Croton-on-Hudson (C1)* 4,837
Crown Point (N3)*....... 800
Cuba (D6)*...................1,783
Cutchogue (F2)*...........1,500
Cuylerville (E5)*.......... 350
Dalton (E5)*................ 500
Dannemora (N7)*.........4,122
Dansville (E5)*.............5,253
Darien (D5).................. 90
Darien Center (D5)*..... 303
Davenport (L6)*........... 250
Dayton (C6)*................ 300
De Kalb Junction (K2)* 500
De Peyster (K1)*.......... 200
De Ruyter (J5)*............ 561
Deer River (J3)*........... 166
Deerland (M3)*............ 40
Deferiet (J2)*.............. 616
Degrasse (L2)*............. 250
Delanson (M5)*............ 430
Delevan (D6)*.............. 611
Delhi (L6)*...................2,223
Delmar (N5)*...............
Demster (H3)............... 200
Depauville (H2)*.......... 350
Depew (C5)*.................7,217
Deposit (K6)*...............2,016
Derby (B5)*.................
Dering Harbor ‡(G2).... 4
Dexter (H2)*................1,038
Diamond Point (N4)*.... 278
Dickinson Center (M1)* 200
Dobbs Ferry (H1)*........6,268
Dolgerville (L4)*...........3,204
Dover Plains (O7)*........ 800
Downsville (L6)*.......... 720
Dresden (F5)*.............. 373
Dresden Station (O3)*.. 76
Dryden (H6)*................ 976
Duanesburg (M5)*........ 287
Dundee (F5)*................1,165
Dunkirk (B5)*.............18,007
Durhamville (J4)*......... 700
Eagle Bay (L3)*............ 150
Eagle Bridge (O5)*.......
Earlyville (J5)*............. 945
E. Aurora (C5)*............5,962
E. Bethany (D5)*......... 150
E. Bloomfield (E5)*...... 425
E. Branch (K7)*............ 300
E. Durham (M6)*.......... 300
E. Greenbush (N5)*......1,100
E. Hampton (G2)*.........1,737
E. Hills ‡(D2)...............2,547
E. Islip (E2)*................2,834
E. Meredith (L6)*........ 132
E. Moriches (F2)*........1,500
E. Northport (E2)*.......3,842
E. Otto (C6)*............... 742
E. Pembroke (D5)*....... 650
E. Randolph (C6)*........ 628
E. Rochester (F4)*.......7,022
E. Rockaway ‡(D2)*....7,970
E. Springfield (L5)*..... 350
E. Syracuse (H4)*........4,766
E. Williamson (F4)*..... 300
E. Williston ‡(D2)*......1,734
E. Worcester (L5)*...... 456
Eastport (F2)*............. 600
Eaton (J5)*.................. 250
Ebenezer (C5).............
Eden (C5)*...................1,394
Edmeston (K5)*............ 500
Edwards (K2)*.............. 584
Elba (D4)*................... 569
Elbridge ‡(H4)*............ 586
Elizabethtown (N2)*.... 665
Ellenburg Center (N1)* 350
Ellenburg Depot (N1)*. 400
Ellenville (M7)*...........4,225
Ellicottville (C6)*.........1,073
Ellington (B6)*............ 925

Ellisburg (H3)*............ 285
Elmira (G6)*..............49,716
Elmira Heights (G6)*...5,009
Elmont (B2)*..............21,125
Elmsford (J1)*.............3,147
Elnora (N5)*............... 100
Endicott (H6)*............20,050
Ephratah (L4).............. 250
Erieville (J5)*.............. 300
Esperance (M5)*.......... 322
Essex (O2)*................. 525
Evans (B5)...................
Evans Mills (J2)*.......... 518
Fabius (J5)*................ 369
Fair Haven (G4)*......... 628
Fairport (F4)*..............5,267
Falconer (B6)*.............3,292
Farmingdale (D2)*.......4,492
Farnham (B5)*............ 396
Faust (M2)*.................
Fayetteville (J4)*.........2,624
Felts Mills (J3)*.......... 300
Fernwood (H4)*........... 200
Fillmore (D6)*.............. 527
Findley Lake (A6)*....... 500
Fine (K2)*................... 350
Fishers Island (G1)*..... 536
Fishkill (N7)*.............. 841
Fishs Eddy (K7)*.......... 300
Fleischmann's (L6)*..... 469
Floral Park (A2)*.......14,582
Florence (J4)*............. 75
Florida (B1)*................1,376
Flower Hill ‡(D2).........1,948
Fly Creek (K5)*............ 350
Fonda (M5)*................1,026
Forestport (K4)*.......... 730
Forestville (B6)*.......... 786
Fort Ann (N4)*............ 463
Fort Covington (M1)*... 891
Fort Edward (O4)*........3,797
Fort Jackson (L1)*...... 138
Fort Johnson (M5)*...... 930
Fort Plain (L5)*............2,935
Fort Ticonderoga (O3)* 46
Frankfort (K4)*............3,844
Franklin (K6)*............. 558
Franklinville (D6)*........2,092
Fredonia (B6)*.............7,095
Freehold (N6)*............ 300
Freeport (B3)*............24,680
Freeville (H5)*............. 373
Frewsburg (B6)*...........1,383
Friendship (D6)*...........1,344
Fulton (H4)*...............13,922
Fultonville (M5)*......... 840
Gainesville (D5)*.......... 314
Galway (N4)*............... 188
Gansevoort (N4)*......... 300
Garden City (B2)*......14,486
Gardenville (C5)...........
Garrison (C1)*..............1,600
Gasport (C4)*.............. 880
Geneseo (E5)*..............2,838
Geneva (G5)*..............17,144
Genoa (G5)*................
Germantown (N6)*.......
Gerry (B6)*.................. 475
Ghent (N6)*................. 600
Gilbertsville (K6)*........ 456
Gilboa (M6)*................ 125
Glasco (M6)*................1,300
Glen Cove (B2)*..........15,130
Glen Park (J3)............. 516
Glenfield (K3)*............. 450
Glens Falls (N4)*........19,610
Gloversville (M4)*.......23,634
Golden's Bridge (D1)*.. 800
Gorham (F5)*............... 650
Goshen (B1)*................3,311
Gouverneur (K2)*..........4,916
Gowanda (B6)*.............3,289
Grafton (N5)*...............
Grahamsville (L7)*....... 450
Grand Gorge (L6)*........ 500
Grand Island (B5)*.......
Grand View-on-Hudson ‡(C2) 302
Granville (O4)*.............2,826
Great Bend (J2)*.......... 500
Great Neck (A2)*..........7,759
Great Neck Estates (A2) 2,464
Great Neck Plaza (A2).4,246
Great Valley (C6)*........
Green Island (N5)*.......4,016
Greene (J6)*.................1,628
Greenport (F1)*............3,028
Greenville (N6)*........... 376
Greenwich (O4)*...........2,212
Greenwood (E6)*.......... 700
Greenwood Lake (B1)*. 819
Groton (H5)*................2,150
Groveland (E5)*............ 500
Guilford (J6)*............... 557
Hadley (N4)*................ 500
Hagaman (M5)*.............1,114
Hague (N3)*................. 400
Hailesboro (K2)*........... 268
Hamburg (C5)*..............6,938
Hamden (K6)*.............. 250
Hamilton (J5)*..............3,507
Hamlet (B6)*................ 100
Hamlin (E4)*................ 400
Hammond (J2)*............ 329
Hammondsport (F6)*....1,190
Hampton (O3)*............ 150
Hampton Bays (F2)*....1,269
Hancock (K7)*..............1,560
Hannawa Falls (L1)*.... 245
Hannibal (G4)*............. 501
Harford (H6)*..............
Harpursville (J6)*........ 520
Harriman (C1)*............ 676
Harrison (J1)*..............
Harrisonville (K2)*....... 868
Hartford (O4)*............. 150
Hartwick (K5)*............. 625
Hastings on Hudson (J1)* 7,565

Haverstraw (C1)*.........5,818
Hawthorne (H1)*..........
Head of the Harbor ‡(E2) 334
Hector (G5)*................ 65
Helena (L1)*................
Hemlock (E5)*............. 400
Hempstead (A2)*.......29,135
Henderson (H3)*.......... 260
Henrietta (E4)*............
Herkimer (L4)*............9,400
Hermitage (D5)............ 100
Hermon (K2)*.............. 547
Herrings (J2)*............. 192
Heuvelton (K1)*........... 712
Hewlett Bay Park ‡(D2) 466
Hewlett Harbor ‡(D2). 411
Hewlett Neck ‡(D2)..... 369
Hicksville (B2)*..........13,000
High Falls (M7)*..........1,000
Highland (M7)*...........3,035
Highland Falls (C1)*....3,930
Hillburn (C2)*..............1,212
Hillsdale (O6)*............ 400
Hilton (E4)*.................1,036
Himrod (G5)*.............. 225
Hinckley (K4)*............ 198
Hinsdale (D6)*............ 350
Hobart (L6)*............... 618
Hogansburg (L1)*........ 300
Holcomb (F5)*............ 313
Holland (C5)*............. 980
Holland Patent (K4)*.. 400
Holley (D4)*.................1,551
Homer (H5)*................3,244
Honeoye (F5)*............ 200
Honeoye Falls (F5)*.....1,460
Hoosick Falls (O5)*......4,297
Hopkinton (L1)*........... 300
Hornell (E6)*..............15,049
Horseheads (G6)*.........3,606
Houghton (D6)*............ 500
Howes Cave (M5)*........
Hubbardsville (J5)*...... 300
Hudson (N6)*..............11,629
Hudson Falls (O4)*......7,236
Hughsonville (N7)*....... 250
Hulberton (D4)*............ 500
Hume (D5)*................. 250
Hunter (M6)*............... 526
Huntington (E2)*.........9,324
Huntington Bay ‡(E2). 585
Hurleyville (L7)*.......... 800
Hyde Park (N7)*..........1,059
Ilion (K5)*...................9,363
Indian Lake (M3)*.......
Inlet (L3)*.................... 250
Interlaken (G5)*.......... 770
Inwood (A3)*...............9,200
Ira (G4)*..................... 100
Irondequoit (E4)........^34,417
Irving (B5)*................. 350
Irvington (H1)*.............3,657
Ischua (D6)*................ 170
Island Park (B3)*........2,031
Islip (E2)*....................5,254
Ithaca (G6)*...............29,257
Jamaica (D2)*...........100,000
Jamestown (B6)*........43,354
Jamesville (H5)*..........1,200
Jasper (F6)*................ 600
Jay (N2)*..................... 425
Jefferson (L6)*............ 300
Jeffersonville (L7)*...... 450
Jericho (B2)*............... 500
Johnsburg (M3)*........... 200
Johnson City (J6)*.....19,249
Johnsonville (O5)*........ 520
Johnstown (M4)*.........10,923
Jordan (H4)*.................1,295
Kanona (F6)*............... 400
Katonah (D1)*..............
Keene (N2)*................. 550
Keene Valley (N2)*......1,000
Keeseville (O2)*............1,977
Kendall (E4)*............... 325
Kenmore (C5)*............20,066
Kennedy (B6)*.............. 508
Kensington ‡(D2)*....... 978
Kerhonkson (M7)*........1,000
Kill Buck (C6)*............ 304
Kinderhook (N6)*......... 853
King Ferry (G5)*.......... 400
Kings Park (E2)*........10,960
Kings Point ‡(E2)*.....2,445
Kingston (M7)*...........28,817
Kirkwood (J6)*............. 343
Knapp Creek (C6)*....... 215
Knowlesville (D4)*........ 300
Knoxboro (J5)*............ 315
La Fargeville (J2)*...... 425
La Fayette (H5)*.......... 260
Lackawanna (B5)*......27,658
Lacona (J3)*............... 540
Lake Clear Junction (M2)* 250
Lake George (N4)*.......1,005
Lake Huntington (L7)*. 300
Lake Katrine (M7)*...... 750
Lake Kushaqua (M2)*.. 300
Lake Luzerne (N4)*..... 750
Lake Placid (N2)*.........2,999
Lake Pleasant (M4)*.... 200
Lake Success (A2)........1,264
Lake View (B5)*...........
Lakeville (E5)*............. 384
Lakewood (B6)*.............3,013
Lancaster (C5)*............8,665
Larchmont (J1)*............6,330
Lattingtown ‡(D2)....... 745
Laurel Hollow ‡(D2).... 169
Laurens (K5)*.............. 261
Lawrence (A3)*.............4,681
Lawrenceville (L1)*..... 236
Le Roy (E5)*.................4,721
Lebanon Springs · (O6)* 520
Lee Center (K4)*..........
Leeds (N6)*.................. 750

Leicester (D5)*............ 364
Leon (C6)*.................. 740
Leonardsville (K5)*....... 500
Levittown (B2)*..........40,000
Lewis (N2)*................. 350
Lewiston (B4)*.............1,626
Lexington (M6)*......... 500
Liberty (L7)*................4,658
Lily Dale (B6)*............ 275
Lima (E5)*...................1,147
Limestone (C6)*........... 601
Lincklaen (J5)*............ 110
Lindenhurst (E2)*.........8,644
Lindley (F6)*................ 250
Lisbon (K1)*................. 300
Lisle (H6)*.................. 221
Little Falls (L4)*..........9,541
Little Genesee (D6)*.... 300
Little Valley (C6)*........1,287
Liverpool (H4)*............2,933
Livingston Manor (L7)*
Livingstonville (M6)..... 80
Livonia (E5)*................ 837
Lloyd Harbor ‡(D2)..... 945
Locke (H5)*................. 275
Lockport (C4)*............25,133
Lodi (G5)*.................... 362
Long Beach (B3)*.......15,586
Long Eddy (K7)*.......... 350
Long Lake (L3)*...........1,000
Loon Lake (N1)*.......... 100
Lorraine (J3)*.............. 250
Lowville (J3)*...............3,671
Lycoming (H3)*............ 200
Lynbrook (A3)*...........17,314
Lyndonville (D4)*......... 777
Lyon Mountain (N1)*...1,053
Lyons (G4)*..................4,217
Lyons Falls (K3)*........ 864
Lysander (H4)*............ 250
Macedon (F4)*............. 614
Machias (D6)*.............. 850
Madison (J5)*.............. 335
Madrid (K1)*...............
Mahopac (D1)*.............
Maine (H6)*................. 600
Mallory (H4)*............... 150
Malone (M1)*................9,501
Malverne (A2)*.............8,086
Mamaroneck (J1)*......15,016
Manchester (F5)*........1,262
Manhasset (B2)*..........
Manhattan (C2).....1,960,101
Manlius (J5)*................1,742
Mannsville (H3)*.......... 378
Manorhaven ‡(D2)........1,819
Manorville (F2)*........... 900
Marathon (J6)*.............1,057
Marcellus (H5)*.............1,382
Margaretville (L6)*...... 905
Marilla (C5)*................ 350
Marion (F4)*................ 800
Marlboro (M7)*............1,709
Martinsburg (J3)*........ 343
Maryland (L5)*............ 300
Masonville (K6)*.......... 370
Massapequa Park‡ (D2)* 2,334
Massena (L1)*............13,137
Matinecock (B2)........... 507
Mattituck (F2)*.............1,089
Maybrook (B1)*............1,316
Mayfield (M4)*............ 761
Mayville (A6)*...............1,492
McConnellsville (J4)*.... 300
Mc Donough (J5)*........ 179
Mc Graw (H5)*.............1,197
Mc Keever (K3)*........... 55
Mc Lean (H5)*............. 250
Mechanicville (N5)*.....7,385
Mecklenburg (G6)*....... 300
Medina (D4)*................6,179
Menands ‡(N5)*...........2,453
Mendon (E4)*............... 327
Meridian (G4)*............ 334
Merrill (N1)*................ 200
Mexico (H4)*................1,398
Middle Falls (O4)*........ 500
Middle Granville (O4)*.. 800
Middleburg (M5)*........1,298
Middleport (C4)*..........1,641
Middlesex (F5)*........... 300
Middletown (B1)*.......22,586
Middleville (K4)*.......... 647
Milford (K5)*............... 502
Mill Neck ‡(D2)*.......... 505
Millbrook (N7)*............1,568
Millerton (O7)*.............1,048
Millport (G6)*.............. 362
Milton (M7)*................
Mineola (B2)*.............14,831
Minerva (N3)*.............. 364
Minetto (H4)*...............
Mineville (O2)*............. 996
Minoa (J4)*..................1,008
Mohawk (L4)*...............3,196
Moira (M1)*................. 750
Monroe (C1)*................1,753
Montauk (G2)*............. 700
Montgomery (B1)*.......1,063
Monticello (L7)*...........4,223
Montour Falls (G6)*.....1,457
Mooers (N1)*................ 496
Moravia (H5)*..............1,480
Moriah (N2)*................ 700
Moriah Center (N2)*.... 400
Morley (K1)*................ 226
Morris (K5)*................ 641
Morrisonville (N1)*...... 600
Morristown (J1)*.......... 546
Morrisville (J5)*...........1,250
Mt. Kisco (D1)*............5,907
Mt. Morris (E5)*..........3,450
Mt. Upton (K6)*........... 400
Mt. Vernon (H1)*.......71,899
Mountain Dale (L7)*.... 700
Mumford (E4)*............. 687
Munnsville (J4)*........... 412
Munsey Park ‡(D2)......2,048
Muttontown ‡(D2)....... 382

Napanoch (M7)*...........1,094
Naples (F5)*.................1,141
Narrowsburg (L7)*....... 614
Nassau (N5)*............... 952
Natural Bridge (K2)*... 600
Natural Dam (J2)......... 200
Nelliston (L5)*............. 693
Nelsonville (C1)*.......... 522
New Baltimore (N6)*.... 550
New Berlin (K5)*.........1,178
New Bremen (K3)*....... 150
New City (C2)*............. 962
New Hamburg (N7)*.... 350
New Hartford (K4)*.....1,947
New Haven (H4)*......... 800
New Hyde Park (A2)*...7,349
New Lebanon (O6)*......
New Paltz (M7)*..........2,285
New Rochelle (J1)*.....59,725
New Windsor (C1)........2,754
New Woodstock (J5)*... 500
New York (5 Boroughs) (C2)* 7,891,957
New York-Northeastern New Jersey (urban area) 12,222,963
New York Mills (K4)*...3,366
Newark (G4)*..............10,295
Newark Valley (H6)*....1,027
Newburgh (C1)*..........31,956
Newcomb (M3)*........... 425
Newfane (C4)*..............1,578
Newfield (G6)*............ 500
Newport (K4)*............. 752
Newton Falls (K2)*...... 700
Niagara Falls (C4)*....90,872
Niagara Falls (urban area) 97,648
Nichols (H6)*.............. 578
Nicholville (L1)*.......... 300
Nineveh (J6)*.............. 182
Niobe (B6)*.................
Nissequogue ‡(E2)....... 219
Norfolk (K1)*...............1,252
N. Bangor (M1)*.......... 500
N. Bay (J4)*................ 500
N. Chili (E4)*...............1,000
N. Collins (C5)*............1,325
N. Creek (M3)*............ 942
N. Haven ‡(F1)............ 153
N. Hills ‡(D2).............. 330
N. Hornell (E6)............ 605
N Hudson (N3)*........... 250
N. Java (D5)*.............. 500
N. Lawrence (L1)*........ 500
N. Pelham (H1)............5,046
N. River (M3)*............ 253
N. Rose (G4)*.............. 708
N. Syracuse (H4)*........3,356
N. Tarrytown (H1)*......8,740
N. Tonawanda (C4)*...24,731
Northport (E2)*............3,859
Northville (M4)*...........1,114
Norwich (J5)*................8,816
Norwood (L1)*..............1,995
Number Four (K3)........ 50
Nunda (E5)*.................1,224
Nyack (C2)*..................5,889
Oakfield (D4)*..............1,781
Ocean Beach (E2)*....... 73
Oceanside (B3)*..........15,000
Odessa (G6)*............... 526
Ogdensburg (K1)*.......16,166
Olcott (C4)*................. 875
Old Brookville ‡(D2)..... 644
Old Field ‡(E2)............ 238
Old Forge (L3)*........... 900
Old Westbury (B2)*.....1,160
Olean (D6)*................22,884
Olmstedville (N3)*........ 300
Oneida (J4)*...............11,325
Oneida Castle ‡(J4)..... 596
Oneonta (K6)*............13,564
Onoville (B6)*.............. 400
Ontario (F4)*............... 800
Orchard Park (C5)*......2,054
Orient (G1)*................ 500
Oriskany (K4)*.............1,346
Oriskany Falls (J5)*..... 893
Orwell (J3)*................. 425
Osceola (J3)*............... 241
Ossining (D1)*............16,098
Oswegatchie (K2)*........ 500
Oswego (G4)*..............22,647
Otego (K6)*................. 699
Otisco Lake (H5)..........
Otisville (B1)*.............. 911
Otto (C6)*.................... 350
Ovid (G5)*................... 646
Owasco (G5)*............... 300
Owego (H6)*.................5,350
Oxford (J6)*..................1,811
Oyster Bay (B2)*..........5,215
Oyster Bay Cove ‡(D2). 561
Painted Post (F6)*.......2,405
Palatine Bridge ‡(L5)* 592
Palenville (M6)*........... 350
Palmer (N4)*................ 800
Palmyra(F4)* 3,034
Panama (A6)*.............. 456
Parish (H4)*................ 574
Parishville (L1)*........... 450
Parksville (L7)*............ 400
Patchogue (E2)*...........7,361
Patterson (D1)*............ 400
Pattersonville (M5)*..... 259
Paul Smiths (M2)*....... 375
Pavilion (D5)*.............. 615
Pawling (N7)*...............1,430
Pearl River (C2)*..........
Peasleeville (N1)*......... 200
Peconic (F2)*............... 850
Peekskill (D1)*............17,731
Pelham ‡(H1)*.............1,843
Pelham Manor (H1)......5,306
Pendleton (C4)............
Penfield (F4)*...............1,013
Penn Yan (F5)*.............5,481
Pennellville (H4)*......... 250
Perkinsville (E5)*......... 421

NORTH CAROLINA

Map on Page 78   **NORTH CAROLINA**   *Total Population 4,061,929*

E. Lake (N3)* 100
E. Laport (D8)* 240
E. Laurinburg (G5)* 745
E. Lumberton (H5)* 1,106
E. Spencer (E3)* 2,444
Edenton (M2)* 4,468
Edgemont (D7)* 85
Edneyville (F8)* 500
Edward (M4)* 155
Efland (G2)* 500
Elams (K1)* 10
Elberon (J2)* 75
Eldorado (F4)*
Eldreth (D5) 50
Eleazer (F3)* 60
Elizabeth City (N2)* 12,685
Elizabethtown (H5)* 1,611
Elk Park (C7)* 545
Elkin (D2)* 2,842
Elkton (H6)*
Ellenboro (B4)* 537
Ellerbe (F4)* 773
Elliott (J5) 25
Elm City (K3)* 839
Elmwood (D3)* 300
Elon College (G2)* 1,109
Elrod (G5)* 135
Emerson (H6)* 85
Enfield (K2)* 2,361
Engelhard (O3)* 500
Enka (E8)* 1,792
Ernul (L4)* 150
Erwin (H4)* 3,344
Essex (J2)* 35
Estatoe (C7) 300
Ether (F4)* 50
Etowah (E8)* 400
Eufola (D3) 150
Eure (M2)* 200
Eureka (K3)* 192
Everetts (L3)* 244
Evergreen (H6)* 245
Ewart (B7)*
Fair Bluff (H6)* 1,056
Fairfield (N3)* 250
Fairmount (G6)* 2,319
Fairview (E8)* 300
Faison (J4)* 768
Faith (E3)* 490
Falcon (H4)* 245
Falkland (K3)* 174
Fallston (B4)* 500
Farmer (F3)* 125
Farmington (D3)* 300
Farmville (K3)* 2,942
Faro (K4) 140
Faust (E7) 100
Fayetteville (H4)* 34,715
Ferguson (C2)* 50
Fig (D6)* 75
Finley (D7) 100
Flat Rock (E9)* 1,000
Flats (C8)* 150
Fleetwood (D6)* 50
Fletcher (E8)* 500
Florence (M4)* 500
Folkstone (K5)* 100
Forbes (B7)* 253
Forest City (B4)* 4,971
Fork (E3)* 300
Fort Bragg (H4)* 16,000
Fountain (K3)* 451
Four Oaks (H4)* 942
Francisco (E2)*
Frank (C7)* 25
Franklin (C9)* 1,975
Franklinton (J2)* 1,414
Franklinville (F3)* 778
Freeland (J6)* 300
Fremont (J3)* 1,395
Frisco (O4)* 100
Fuquay Springs (H3)* 1,992
Furches (E6)* 150
Garland (J5)* 539
Garner (H3)* 1,180
Garysburg (K2)* 344
Gaston (K1)* 1,218
Gastonia (C4)* 23,069
Gates (M2)* 150
Gatesville (M2)* 323
Germanton (E2)* 118
Ghio (F5)* 104
Gibson (F5)* 609
Gibsonville (F2)* 1,866
Gilkey (B4)*
Glade Valley (C2)* 75
Glen Alpine (B3)* 695
Glen Raven (G2) 750
Glendale Springs (D6)* 200
Glendon (G4)* 110
Glenola (F3) 100
Glenville (D9)* 200
Glenwood (A3)*
Globe (D7)* 200
Gloucester (N5)* 130
Gneiss (D9)* 250
Godwin (H4)* 145
Gold Hill (E3)*
Gold Point (L3) 132
Goldsboro (K4)* 21,454
Goldston (G3)* 372
Graham (G2)* 5,026
Grainger (K4) 168
Grandview (B9) 75
Grandy (O2)* 500
Granite Falls (C3)* 2,286
Granite Quarry (D3) 591
Grantsboro (M4)* 1,500
Grassy Creek (E5)* 500
Greenmountain (B7)* 600
Greensboro (F2)* 74,389
Greensboro,
(urban area) 82,719
Greenville (L3)* 16,724
Grifton (L4)* 510
Grimesland (L3)* 414
Grover (C4)* 535
Guilford (F2)* 500
Guilford College (F2)* 500
Gulf (G3)* 300
Gulrock (O4)* 51
Gupton (J2) 75
Halifax (K2)* 346
Halls Mills (E6) 300
Hallsboro (H6)* 300
Hamilton (L3)* 514
Hamilton Lakes ‡(F2) 882
Hamlet (F5)* 5,061
Hampstead (K6)*
Hamptonville (D2)* 150
Hanes (E2)* 1,000
Harbinger (O2)* 250
Harkers Island (M5)* 1,244
Harmony (D3)* 374
Harrellsville (M2)* 167
Harrell Store ‡(J5) 147
Harris (G9)* 110
Harrisburg (D4)* 300
Hassell (L3)* 137
Hasty (G5) 125
Hatteras (O4)* 700
Havelock (M5)* 4,500
Haw River (G2)* 1,175
Hawk (C7)*
Hayesville (C9)* 356
Hayne (H5) 40
Hays (C2)* 400
Haywood (G3) 169
Hazelwood (D8)* 1,769
Heathsville (K2) 150
Heaton (C6)* 50
Helton (D5)* 192
Hemlock (D5) 750
Henderson (J2)* 10,996
Hendersonville (F8)* 6,103
Hendrix (E7)* 150
Henrietta (B4)* 1,013
Hertford (N2)* 2,096
Hester (H2) 110
Hickory (C3)* 14,755
Hiddenite (C3)* 600
Higgins (B7)*
High Point (E3)* 39,973
High Rock (E3) 75
Highfalls (F4)* 310
Highlands (D9)* 515
Highshoals (C4)* 875
Hildebran ‡(B3)* 529
Hillsboro (G2)* 1,329
Hobbsville (M2)* 75
Hobgood (L2)* 603
Hobucken (N4)*
Hoffman (F4)* 398
Hollifield (A3) 200
Hollis (B4)* 65
Hollister (K2)* 200
Holly Springs (H3)* 406
Hollyridge (L6)* 1,082
Hookerton (K4)* 253
Hope Mills (H5)* 1,077
Hot Springs (E7)* 721
Houstonville (D2)* 150
Hubert (L5)* 40
Hudson (C3)* 922
Huntdale (B7)*
Huntersville (D4)* 916
Hurdle Mills (G2)* 200
Husk (D5)* 78
Icard (C3)* 1,100
Icemorlee (D5)
Idlewild (E6)* 175
Indian Trail (D4)* 308
Inez (J2)* 40
Ingalls (C7)* 75
Ingold (J5)* 350
Iron Station (C4)* 232
Ivanhoe (J5)* 200
Jackson (L2)* 843
Jackson Springs (F4)* 246
Jacksons Creek (F3)* 100
Jacksonville (K5)* 3,960
James City (M4)* 750
Jamestown (F3)* 748
Jamesville (M3)* 529
Jarvisburg (O2)*
Jefferson (E6)* 359
Joe (E7)* 251
Johns (F5)* 300
Jonas Ridge (C7)*
Jonesville (D2)* 1,768
Joynes (C2)* 240
Julian (F3)* 300
Jupiter (E8) 136
Kannapolis (D4)* 28,448
Kelford (L2)* 405
Kelly (J6)* 100
Kenansville (K5)* 674
Kenly (J3)* 1,129
Kernersville (E2)* 2,396
Kerr (J5)* 40
Kill Devil Hills (O3)* 125
Kimesville (G3) 100
King (E2)* 1,000
Kings Creek (C3)* 300
Kings Mountain (C4)* 7,206
Kinston (K4)* 18,336
Kipling (H4)* 101
Kittrell (H2)* 189
Kitty Hawk (O2)* 300
Knightdale (J3)* 461
Knotts Island (O2)* 400
Kure Beach (K6)* 228
La Grange (K4) 1,852
Lagoon (J5)* 233
Lake Landing (O4)*
Lake Lure (A4)* 174
Lake Toxaway (E9)* 270
Lake Waccamaw (J6)* 575
Lakedale (H4) 4,000
Lakeview (G4)* 300
Landis (D3)* 1,827
Lansing (D5)*
Lasker (L2)* 177
Lassiter (J3) 35
Lattimore ‡(B4)* 286
Laurel Hill (F5)* 400
Laurel Park (E8) 302
Laurel Springs (E6)* 250
Laurinburg (F5)* 7,134
Lawndale (B4)* 964
Lawsonville (E2)* 200
Laxon (D6)* 61
Leaksville (F2)* 4,045
Leaman (F4)* 21
Leasburg (G2)* 400
Leechville (M3)* 200
Legerwood (B2)* 85
Leggett (K3) 200
Leicester (E7)* 750
Leland (J6)*
Lemon Springs (G4)* 200
Lenoir (C3)* 7,888
Letitia (B9)* 35
Lewarae (F5) 479
Lewiston (L2)* 339
Lexington (E3)* 13,571
Liberty (F3)* 1,342
Lilesville (F5)* 605
Lillington (H4)* 1,061
Lincolnton (C4)* 5,423
Linden (H4)* 194
Linville (C7)* 500
Linville Falls (A3)*
Linwood (E3)* 350
Little Switzerland (A3)* 400
Littleton (K2)* 1,173
Locust (E4) 216
Lola (N5)* 150
Longhurst (G2)* 1,539
Longisland (D3)* 350
Longview (C3)* 2,291
Longwood (J6)* 800
Loray (C3)* 115
Louisburg (J2)* 2,545
Lovill (D6)
Lowe (G5) 73
Lowell (C4)* 2,313
Lowgap (D1)* 500
Lowland (N4)* 200
Lucama (J3)* 405
Lumber Bridge (G5)* 154
Lumberton (G5)* 9,186
Lynn (F9)* 600
Mabel (C6)* 200
Macclesfield (K3)* 370
Mackeys (M3)* 250
Macon (J2)* 238
Madison (F2)* 1,789
Maggie (D8)*
Magnolia (K5)* 585
Maiden (C3)* 1,952
Mamers (G4)* 200
Mamie (O2)* 250
Manly (G4)* 280
Manns Harbor (O3)* 325
Manson (J2)* 40
Manteo (O3)* 635
Maple Hill (K5)* 75
Mapleton (L2)
Mapleville (J2) 50
Marble (C9)*
Margarettsville (L1)* 113
Marietta (G6)* 94
Marion (A3)* 2,740
Mars Hill (E7) 1,404
Marshall (E8)* 983
Marshallberg (N5)* 784
Marshville (E4)* 1,258
Marston (F5)* 159
Mashoes (O3)*
Matthews (D4)* 589
Maury (K4)* 251
Maxton (G5)* 1,974
Mayodan (F2)* 2,246
Maysville (L5)* 818
Mc Adenville (D4)* 1,060
Mc Cain (G4)* 900
Mc Cullers (H3) 89
Mc Donalds (G5)* 78
Mc Farlan (E5)* 136
Mc Grady (E6)* 175
Mebane (G2)* 2,068
Melvin Hill (A4)* 188
Merrimon (M5)* 250
Merry Hill (M2)* 200
Merry Oaks (G3)* 160
Mesic (M4)* 425
Method (H3)* 350
Micaville (B7)* 200
Micro (J3)* 310
Middleburg (J2)* 217
Middlesex (J3)* 446
Middletown (O4)* 200
Midland (E4)* 250
Midway Park (L5)* 3,703
Milam (D6)* 50
Mill Spring (A4)*
Millbrook (H3)* 100
Millers Creek (E6)* 500
Milton (G1)* 317
Milwaukee (L2)* 302
Mineral Springs (D5)* 135
Minneapolis (C7)* 100
Mint Hill (D4)
Mocksville (D3)* 1,909
Momeyer (J3) 200
Moncure (G3)* 500
Monroe (E5)* 10,140
Montague (K6) 100
Montezuma (C7)* 75
Mooresboro (B4)*
Mooresville (D3)* 7,121
Moravian Falls (C2)* 375
Morehead City (M5)* 5,144
Morganton (B3)* 8,311
Morrisville (H3)* 221
Mortimer (B2)* 13
Morven (E5)* 601
Mount Airy (D1)* 7,192
Mt. Gilead (F4)* 1,201
Mt. Holly (D4)* 2,241
Mt. Mourne (D3)* 232
Mt. Olive (K4)* 3,732
Mt. Pleasant (E4)* 1,019
Mt. Vernon Springs (G3)* 90
Mount Zion (D7)* 100
Moyock (N1)*
Murfreesboro (M2)* 2,140
Murphy (C9)* 2,433
Nags Head (O3)*
Nakina (H6)* 350
Nantahala (C8)* 125
Nashville (K3)* 1,302
Nathans Creek (E6)* 75
Navassa (J6)* 500
Nebo (B3)*
Needmore (C8)* 200
Neuse (H3)*
New Bern (L4)* 15,812
New Holland (N4)* 50
New London (E4)* 285
Newhill (H3)* 232
Newhope (C2)* 25
Newland (C7)* 425
Newport (M5)* 676
Newsom (E3)
Newton (C3)* 6,039
Newton Grove (J4)* 374
Norlina (J2)* 874
Norman (F4)* 300
North Cove (B3)* 500
N. Harlowe (M5)* 300
N. Lumberton (H5) 423
N. Wilkesboro (C2)* 4,379
Northside (H2)* 100
Norwood (E4)* 1,735
Oak City (L3)* 518
Oak Ridge (F2)* 500
Oakboro (E4)* 631
Oakland (E9)* 200
Oakley (L3) 58
Ocracoke (O4)* 600
Old Dock (H6) 300
Old Fort (A3)* 771
Old Trap (O2)* 380
Olin (D3)* 60
Olivia (G4)* 450
Olyphic (H7) 50
Orange (H4) 50
Oriental (M4)* 590
Orrum (G6)* 162
Oteen (E8) 1,000
Otto (C9)* 100
Overhills (G4)* 535
Oxford (H2)* 6,685
Pactolus (L3)* 265
Paint Gap (B7)* 200
Palmyra (L3)* 67
Pantego (M3)* 275
Parker (D6)* 50
Parkersburg (J5)* 114
Parkton (H5)* 527
Parmele (L3)* 406
Parsonville (E6)* 250
Paschall (J1) 75
Passion (F9) 196
Patterson (B3)* 195
Peachland (E5)* 485
Pee Dee (F5)* 200
Peletier (L5)*
Pelham (G1)* 200
Pembroke (G5)* 1,212
Pendleton (L2)* 88
Penrose (E8)* 350
Pensacola (B8)* 150
Peoria (C6) 300
Phoenix (J6)
Pike Road (M3)* 250
Pikeville (J4)* 464
Pilot Mountain (D2)* 1,092
Pine Hall (F2)* 575
Pine Level (J4)* 602
Pinebluff (F4) 575
Pinehurst (F4) 1,016
Pineola (C7)* 350
Pinetops (K3)* 1,031
Pinetown (M3)* 301
Pineview (G4) 175
Pineville (D4)* 1,373
Piney Creek (E5)* 35
Pink Hill (K4)* 386
Pinnacle (E2)* 450
Pisgah (F3)* 60
Pisgah Forest (E9)* 900
Pittsboro (G3)* 1,094
Pleasant Hill (K1)* 200
Plumtree (C7)* 300
Plymouth (M3)* 4,486
Point Harbor (O2)* 110
Polkton (E4)* 459
Pollocksville (L5)* 420
Pomona (F2)* 1,500
Ponzer (N3)* 110
Poplar (B7)* 575
Poplar Branch (O2)* 325
Pores Knob (C2)* 150
Portsmouth (N4)* 15
Postell (B9) 120
Powells Point (O2)* 375
Powellsville (M2)* 250
Prentiss (D9)* 100
Price (F1)* 175
Princeton (J4)* 608
Princeville (L3) 919
Proctorville (H6)* 232
Prospect Hill (G2)* 110
Pungo (M3)* 200
Purlear (E6)* 60
Purvis (G5)*
Quitsna (L3) 210
Radical (E6) 50
Raeford (G5)* 2,030
RALEIGH (H3)* 65,679
Raleigh (urban area) 68,190
Ramsaytown (B7)* 100
Ramseur (F3)* 1,134
Randleman (F3)* 2,066
Ranger (B9)* 150
Ransomville (M4)* 170
Raynham (G5) 30
Red Oak (J2)* 250
Red Springs (G5)* 2,245
Reddies River (E6) 175
Reese (C6)* 1,450
Reidsville (F2)* 11,708
Relief (B7)* 129
Rennert (G5)*
Rex (H5)* 180
Reynolda (E2)* 300
Rhodhiss ‡(B3)* 923
Rich Square (L2)* 971
Richfield (E4)* 237
Richlands (K5)* 877
Ridgeville (G2) 45
Ridgeway (J2)* 250
Ringwood (K2) 60
Roanoke Rapids (K2)* 8,156
Roaring Gap (D2)*
Roaring River (C2)* 350
Robbins (F4)* 1,158
Robbinsville (C8)* 515
Roberdell (F5)* 451
Robersonville (L3)* 1,414
Rockfish (G5)* 150
Rockford (D2)* 225
Rockingham (F5)* 3,356
Rockwell (E3)* 852
Rocky Mount (K3)* 27,697
Rocky Point (K6)*
Rodanthe (P3)* 86
Roe (N5)* 215
Rolesville (J3)* 288
Rominger (C6)* 200
Ronda (D2)* 545
Roper (M3)* 793
Roseboro (J5)* 1,241
Rosehill (K5)* 896
Rosindale (J6) 35
Rosman (E9)* 535
Rougemont (G2)* 300
Rowland (G5)* 1,293
Roxboro (H2)* 4,321
Roxobel (L2)* 394
Royal (M4)* 250
Royall Cotton Mills (H2) 250
Ruffin (F2)* 530
Rufus (B3) 80
Rural Hall (E2)* 1,200
Ruth (A4)* 324
Rutherford College (B3)* 750
Rutherfordton (A4)* 3,146
Ryland (H2)* 50
Saint Pauls (H5)* 2,251
Salemburg (J4)* 435
Salisbury (D3)* 20,102
Salter Path (M5)* 300
Saluda (F9)* 547
Salvo (P3)* 77
Sandy Ridge (E1)* 200
Sanford (G4)* 10,013
Sapphire (E9)* 50
Saratoga ‡(K3)* 366
Saxapahaw (G3)* 660
Scaly (D9)* 200
Scotland Neck (L2)* 2,730
Scotts (D3)* 50
Scotts Hill (K6) 150
Scottville (E5)* 180
Scranton (N4)* 125
Seaboard (K1)* 745
Seagrove (F3)* 319
Sealevel (N5)*
Selma (J3)* 2,639
Semora (G3)* 250
Senia (C7)* 25
Seven Springs (K4)* 197
Severn (L2)* 340
Sevier (A3) 130
Shallotte (J7)* 493
Shannon (G5)* 150
Sharpsburg (K3)* 415
Shawboro (N2)* 150
Shelby (C4)* 15,508
Shelmerdine (L4) 32
Sherwood (D6)* 350
Shoals (E2) 250
Shooting Creek (C9)* 260
Shulls Mills (D7)* 175
Siler City (G3)* 2,501
Siloam (D2)* 250
Silverdale (L5)*
Simpson (Chicod*) (L3) 278
Sims (J3)* 207
Skyland (E8)* 1,200
Sly (D6)*
Smithfield (J3)* 5,574
Smithtown (E2) 182
Smyrna (M5)* 200
Sneads Ferry (L5)* 125
Snow Camp (G3)* 90
Snow Hill (K4)* 946
Snowden (N2)* 85
Sophia (F3)* 200
South Creek (M4)* 108
S. Mills (N2)*
S. Wadesboro (E5) 390
S. Pines (G4)* 4,272
Southmont (E3)* 500
Southport (J7)* 1,748
Southside (C4)* 250
Sparta (C1)* 820
Spear (C7)* 445
Speed (L3)* 103
Spencer (D3)* 3,242
Spies (F4)* 100
Spindale (B4)* 3,891
Spray (F1)* 5,542
Spring Hope (K3)* 1,275
Spring Lake (H4)* 3,500
Springfield (E6)* 50
Spruce Pine (C7)* 2,280
Stacy (N5)* 302
Staley (F3)* 236
Stanfield (E4)* 350
Stanley (C4)* 1,644
Stantonsburg (K3)* 627
Star (F4)* 677
State Road (D2)* 475
Statesville (D3)* 16,901
Stecoah (C8)* 160
Stedman (H4)* 424
Steeds (F4)* 50
Stella (L5)* 100
Stem (H2)* 217
Stokes (L3)* 217
Stokesdale (F2)* 400
Stoneville (F2)* 786
Stonewall (M4)* 272
Stony Point (C3)* 1,020
Stovall (H2)* 410
Straits (M5)* 100
Stratford (E5)* 16
Stumpy Point (O3)* 300
Sturgills (D5)*
Sugar Grove (C6)* 225
Suit (B9)* 150
Summerfield (F2)* 923
Summit (E6)* 50
Sunbury (M2)* 350
Supply (J6)* 207
Surf City (L6)
Swannanoa (F8)* 1,800
Swanns (G4) 30
Swanquarter (N4)* 212
Swansboro (L5)* 559
Sylva (D8)* 1,382
Tabor City (H6)* 2,033
Tamarack (D6)* 150
Tapoco (B8)* 100
Tarboro (K3)* 8,120
Tarheel (H5)* 200
Taylorsville (C3)* 1,310
Teacheys (J5)* 226
Terrell (C3)* 200
Thomasville (E3)* 11,154
Thurmond (D2)* 77
Tillery (K2)* 250
Timberlake (H2)* 200
Timberland (G4) 11
Toast (D2)* 1,401
Todd (D6)* 89
Toecane (B7)* 250
Toliver (D6)*
Tomahawk (J5)* 30
Topia (E5)* 69
Topton (C9)* 125
Townsville (J1)* 219
Traphill (D2)* 150
Trenton (L4)* 469
Trinity (F3)* 764
Triplett (D6)* 120
Troutmans (D3)* 613
Troy (F4)* 2,213
Tryon (A4)* 1,985
Tunis (M2) 200
Turkey (J4)* 223
Turnersburg (D3)* 75
Tyner (M2)* 150
Ulah (F3)*
Unaka (B9)*
Union (L2)
Union Grove (D2)* 125
Union Mills (B3)* 200
Unionville (E4) 124
University (G2)*
Upton (D7)* 93
Uree (A4) 100
Vade Mecum (E2)*
Valdese (B3)* 2,730
Vale (C3)* 200
Valle Crucis (C6)* 200
Vanceboro (L4)* 753
Vandemere (M4)* 475
Vannoy (E6)* 25
Varina (H3)* 593
Vass (G4)* 757
Vaughan (J2)* 181
Vein Mountain (A3) 75
Verona (K5)* 125
Vilas (C6)* 60
Waco ‡(C4)* 310
Wade (H4)*
Wadesboro (E5)* 3,408
Wadeville (E4)*
Wagoner (E6)* 200
Wagram (G5)* 397
Wake Forest (H3)* 3,704
Walkertown (E2)* 1,000
Wallace (J5)* 1,622
Wallburg (E3)* 165
Walnut (E7)* 450
Walnut Cove (E2)* 1,132
Walstonburg (K3)* 177
Wanchese (O3)* 1,000
Warne (C9)* 200
Warren Plains (J2)* 100
Warrensville (E6)* 120
Warrenton (J2)* 1,166
Warsaw (J4)* 1,598
Washington (M3)* 9,698
Washington Park
(M3) 421
Watha (J5)* 222
Waves (P3)* 65
Waxhaw (D5)* 818
Waynesville (E8)* 5,295
Weaverville (E8)* 1,111
Webster (D8)* 142
Weeksville (N2)*
Welcome (E3)* 600
Weldon (K2)* 2,295
Wendell (J3)* 1,253
Wenona (M3)*
Wentworth (F2)* 100
West End (F4)* 850
W. Jefferson (D6)* 871
Westfield (D2)* 300
Wests Mill (D9)* 50
Whitakers (K2)* 962
White Lake (H5)* 400
White Oak (H5)* 125
White Plains (D2)* 500
Whitehall (Seven
Springs*) (K4) 197
Whitehead (E6)* 250
Whiterock (E7) 100
Whiteville (H6)* 4,238
Whitnel (B3)* 1,405
Whittier (D8)* 400
Wilkesboro (C2)* 1,370
Willard (J5)*
Williamston (M3)* 4,975
Wilmington (J6)* 45,043
Wilson (K3)* 23,010
Wilsons Mills (H3)* 349
Windom (B7)* 100
Windsor (L2)* 1,781
Winfall (N2)* 421
Wingate (E5)* 793
Winnabow (J6)* 250
Winston-Salem (E2)* 87,811
Winston-Salem,
(urban area) 91,493
Winterville (L3) 870
Winton (L2)* 834
Wise (J2)* 300
Wolf Mountain (D9)* 25
Wood (J2)* 128
Woodard (M3)* 325
Woodland (L2)* 590
Woodleaf (D3)* 500
Woodsdale (H2)* 200
Woodville (L2)* 387
Worthville (F3)* 550
Wrightsville Beach (K6)* 711
Wrightsville Sound (K6)* 500
Yadkin College (E3)* 82
Yadkin Valley (C2)* 12
Yadkinville (D2)* 820
Yanceyville (G2)* 1,391
Yellowcreek (B8)* 4
Youngsville (J2)* 619
Zebulon (J3)* 1,378
Zionville (D6)* 250
Zirconia (E9)*

Map on Page 79

NORTH DAKOTA

Total Population 619,636

53 COUNTIES

Adams (F7) 4,910
Barnes (O5) 16,864
Benson (M3) 10,675
Billings (D5) 1,777
Bottineau (J2) 12,140
Bowman (C7) 4,001
Burke (E2) 6,621
Burleigh (J6) 25,673
Cass (R5) 58,877
Cavalier (N2) 11,840
Dickey (N7) 9,121
Divide (C2) 5,967
Dunn (E5) 7,212
Eddy (N4) 5,372
Emmons (K7) 9,715
Foster (N5) 5,337
Golden Valley (C5) 3,499
Grand Forks (P3) 39,443
Grant (G6) 7,114
Griggs (O5) 5,460
Hettinger (E7) 7,100
Kidder (L6) 6,168
La Moure (N7) 9,498
Logan (L7) 6,357
Mc Henry (J3) 12,556
Mc Intosh (L7) 7,590
Mc Kenzie (D4) 6,849
Mc Lean (G4) 18,824
Mercer (G5) 8,686
Morton (H6) 19,295
Mountrail (E3) 9,418
Nelson (O4) 8,090
Oliver (H5) 3,091
Pembina (P2) 13,990
Pierce (K3) 8,326
Ramsey (N3) 14,373
Ransom (P7) 8,876
Renville (G2) 5,405
Richland (R7) 19,865
Rolette (L2) 11,102
Sargent (P7) 7,616
Sheridan (K4) 5,253
Sioux (H7) 3,696
Slope (C7) 2,315
Stark (E6) 16,137
Steele (P4) 5,145
Stutsman (M5) 24,158
Towner (M2) 6,360
Traill (R5) 11,359
Walsh (P3) 18,859
Ward (G3) 34,782
Wells (L4) 10,417
Williams (C3) 16,442

CITIES and TOWNS

Abercrombie (S7)* 244
Absaraka (P6)* 45
Adams (O3)* 411
Adrain (O6)* 55
Agate (L2)* 14
Akra (P2)* 25
Alamo (D2)* 192
Alexander (C4)* 302
Alfred (N6)* 150
Alice (P6)* 162
Alkabo (C2)* 70
Almont (H6)* 190
Alsen (N2)* 114
Alta (J5) 6
Ambrose (D2)* 286
Amenia (R6)* 127
Amidon (D7)* 82
Anamoose (K4)* 542
Aneta (P4)* 469
Anselm (R6) 22
Antelope (F6)* 23

OHIO

Total Population 7,946,627

Map on Page 80

OKLAHOMA

Map on Page 81   **OKLAHOMA**   Total Population 2,233,351

Spiro (N4)* 1,365
Springer (H6)* 325
Stafford (D3)* 60
Stanley (M5)* 50
Stapp (N5)
Stecker (F5)* 60
Steedman (J5) 75
Sterling (F5)* 447
Stidham (L4)* 46
Stigler (M4)* 2,125
Stillwater (J2)* 20,238
Stilwell (N3)* 1,813
Stonebluff (L3)* 300
Stonewall (K5)* 634
Strang (M2)* 201
Stratford (H5)* 1,065
Stringtown (L6)* 499
Strong City (C3)* 107
Stroud (J3)* 2,450
Stuart (K5)* 303
Sugden (G6)* 105
Sulphur (J5)* 4,389
Summerfield (N5)* 300
Sumner (H2)* 46
Sunkist (L6)* 15
Sweetwater (C4)* 60
Swink (M6)* 96
Tabler (G4)*
Taft (M3)* 541
Tahlequah (M3)* 4,750
Tahona (N4)* 45
Talala (L1)* 210
Talihina (N5)* 965
Tallant (K1)* 130
Taloga (E2)* 430
Tamaha (N4)* 117
Tangier (C2) 25
Tatums (H6)* 210
Tecumseh (J4)* 2,275
Tegarden (E1)* 14
Temple (F6)* 1,442
Teresita (N2)* 50
Terlton (K2)* 122
Terral (G7)* 616
Texanna (M4) 25
Texhoma (D8)* 1,464
Texola (C4)* 265
Thackerville (H7)* 178
Thomas (E3)* 1,171
Three Sands (H1)* 50
Ti (L5)* 23
Tiawah (L2) 100
Tip (M2)* 25
Tipton (D6)* 1,172
Tishomingo (J6)* 2,325
Tom (N7)*
Tomy Town (N3) 75
Tonkawa (H1)* 3,643
Tribbey (H4)* 100
Trousdale (H4)* 50
Troy (J6)*
Tryon (J3)* 285
Tullahassee (L3)* 209
Tulsa (K2)* 182,740
Tulsa (urban area) 203,968
Tupelo (K5)* 376
Turkey Ford (N1)* 100
Turley (L2)* 200
Turpin (A1)* 175
Tushka (K6)*
Tuskahoma (M5)* 325
Tuskegee (K3)* 84
Tussy (G6)* 96
Tuttle (G4)* 715
Tuxedo Park (L1) 1,179
Tyrone (E7)* 261
Ulan (L4)* 30
Uncas (H1)* 100
Union (G4)* 301
Utica (K7)* 100
Valliant (M6)* 661
Vanoss (J5)* 118
Velma (G6)* 1,034
Vera (L2)* 164
Verden (F4)* 508
Verdigris (L2)* 150
Vernon (L4)* 450
Veterans Village ‡(H2) 3,355
Vian (N4)* 927
Vici (D2)* 620
Vinco (H3) 25
Vinita (M1)* 5,518
Vinson (C5)* 125
Virgil (M6) 55
Vivian (L4) 75
Wade (K7)* 150
Wagoner (M3)* 4,395
Wainwright (M3)* 138
Wakita (G1)* 440
Walters (F6)* 2,743
Wanette (H5)* 594
Wann (L1)* 99
Wapanucka (J6)* 592
Wardville (L5)* 89
Warner (M4)* 382
Warr Acres (G3)* 2,378
Warwick (H3)* 132
Washington (H4)* 292
Washita (F4)* 45
Washunga (J1) 91
Watonga (F3)* 3,249
Watova (L1)* 250
Watson (N6)* 100
Watts (N2)* 267
Wauhillau (N3) 48
Waukomis (F2)* 537
Waurika (G6)* 2,327
Wayne (H5)* 501
Waynoka (E1)* 2,018
Weatherford (E4)* 3,529
Weathers (L5) 200
Webb (D3)* 33
Webb City (J1)* 284
Webbers Falls (M3)* 489
Welch (M1)* 483
Weleetka (K4)* 1,548
Welling (N3)* 77
Wellston (H3)* 643
Welty (K3)* 50
Wesley (L5)* 35
Westville (N2)* 781
Wetumka (K4)* 2,025
Wewoka (K4)* 6,747
Wheatland (G4)* 300
Wheeless (B8)* 15
Whitefield (M4)* 350
Whiteoak (M1)* 100
Whitesboro (N5)*
Wilburton (M5)* 1,939
Wildcat (L3) 147
Willard (C1) 2
Williams (O4)* 200
Willis (J7)* 115
Willow (C4)* 223
Wilson (H6)* 1,832
Wirt (G6)* 700
Wister (N5)* 729
Wolco (K1)* 100
Woodford (H6)* 105
Woodville (J7)* 78
Woodward (D2)* 5,915
Wright City (M6)* 1,121
Wyandotte (N1)* 242
Wybark (M3) 50
Wynne Wood (H5)* 2,423
Wynona (K1)* 678
Yahola (L3) 65
Yale (J2)* 1,359
Yanush (M5) 156
Yarnaby (K7)* 200
Yeager (K4)* 180
Yewed (F1)* 100
Yonkers (M2)* 20
Yuba (K7)* 108
Yukon (G3)* 1,990
Zena (N2)* 25
Zincville (N1)*
Zoe (N5)* 80

Map on Page 82

OREGON

Total Population 1,521,341

36 COUNTIES

Baker (K3) 16,175
Benton (D3) 31,570
Clackamas (E2) 86,716
Clatsop (D1) 30,776
Columbia (D2) 22,967
Coos (C4) 42,265
Crook (G3) 8,991
Curry (C5) 6,048
Deschutes (F4) 21,812
Douglas (E4) 54,549
Gilliam (G2) 2,817
Grant (J3) 8,329
Harney (H4) 6,113
Hood River (F2) 12,740
Jackson (E5) 58,510
Jefferson (F3) 5,536
Josephine (D5) 26,542
Klamath (F5) 42,150
Lake (G5) 6,649
Lane (E4) 125,776
Lincoln (D3) 21,308
Linn (E3) 54,317
Malheur (K4) 23,223
Marion (E3) 101,401
Morrow (H2) 4,783
Multnomah (E2) 471,537
Polk (D3) 26,317
Sherman (G2) 2,271
Tillamook (D2) 18,606
Umatilla (J2) 41,703
Union (J2) 17,962
Wallowa (K2) 7,264
Wasco (F2) 15,552
Washington (D2) 61,269
Wheeler (G3) 3,313
Yamhill (D2) 33,484

CITIES and TOWNS

Ada (D4)* 100
Adams (J2)* 154
Adel (H5)* 83
Adrian (K4)* 170
Agate Beach (C3)* 379
Agness (D5)* 48
Airlie (D3) 30
Albany (D3)* 10,115
Albee (J2) 7
Alfalfa (F3) 25
Algoma (F5) 50
Alicel (J2)* 30
Allegany (D4)* 220
Aloha (A2)* 50
Alpine (D3)* 325
Alsea (D3)* 130
Altamont (F5) 9,419
Alvadore (D3)* 130
Amity (D2)* 672
Andrews (J5)* 8
Anlauf (D4) 50
Antelope (G3)* 60
Antone (H3)
Applegate (D5)* 75
Arago (C4)* 117
Arcadia (K4)
Arlington (G2)* 686
Arock (K5)* 100
Ash (D4) 120
Ashland (E5)* 7,739
Ashwood (G3)* 19
Astoria (D1)* 12,331
Athena (J2)* 750
Aumsville (E3)* 281
Aurora (A2)* 242
Austin (J3) 39
Azalea (D5)* 50
Baker (K3)* 9,471
Ballston (D2)* 100
Bancroft (D5) 75
Bandon (C4)* 1,251
Banks (A1)* 376
Bar View (C2)* 200
Barlow (B2)* 75
Bartlett (K2)
Barton (B2)
Bates (J3)* 500
Bay City (D2)* 761
Bayocean (C2)* 70
Bayview (C3) 15
Beatty (F5)* 50
Beaver (D2)* 567
Beavercreek (B2)* 60
Beaverton (A2)* 2,512
Beech Creek (H3)* 2
Belknap Springs (F3)* 12
Bellfountain (D3) 50
Bend (F3)* 11,409
Berlin (E3)
Bethany (A2) 20
Beulah (J4) 10
Big Eddy (F2) 36
Biggs (G2)* 15
Birkenfeld (D1)* 100
Blachly (D3)* 24
Black Rock (D3) 17
Blackbutte (E4)* 50
Blaine (D2)* 75
Blalock (G2)* 21
Blitzen (H5) 7
Blodgett (D3)* 200
Blue River (E3)* 200
Bly (F5)* 800
Boardman (H2)* 120
Bonanza (F5)* 259
Bonita (A2) 50
Bonneville (F2)* 250
Booth (C4)
Boring (E2)*
Bourne (J3)
Boyd (F2)* 38
Breitenbush (F3)* 6
Bridal Veil (E2)* 120
Bridge (D4) 200
Bridgeport (K3)* 63
Brighton (C2)* 107
Brightwood (E2)* 150
Broadacres (A3) 30
Broadbent (C4)* 50
Brockway (D4)* 61
Brogan (K3)* 75
Brookings (C5)* 1,000
Brooks (A3)* 350
Brothers (G4) 15
Brownlee (L3)
Brownsboro (E5)* 100
Brownsville (E3)* 1,175
Buena Vista (D3) 160
Bullards (C4)* 25
Burlington (A1) 200
Burns (H4)* 3,093
Burnt Ranch (G3)
Butte Falls (E5)* 372
Butteville (A2) 50
Buxton (D2)* 150
Cairo (K4) 50
Camas Valley (D4)* 60
Camp Namanu (E2)* 2
Camp Sherman (F3)* 50
Canary (D4) 50
Canby (B2)* 1,671
Cannon Beach (D2)*
Canyon City (J3)* 508
Canyonville (D5)* 861
Carlton (D2)* 1,081
Carnation (A2) 100
Carpenterville (C5) 30
Carson (K3)* 100
Carver (B2) 200
Cascade Locks (F2)* 733
Cascade Summit (F4)* 50
Cascadia (E3)* 200
Cave Junction (D5)* 283
Cayuse (J2)* 48
Cecil (H2)* 20
Cedar Mill (A2) 300
Celilo (G2) 300
Central Point (D5)* 1,667
Chapman (D2) 100
Charleston (C4)* 576
Chelsea (F5) 300
Chemawa (A3)* 850
Chemult (F4)* 115
Cherry Grove (D2)* 375
Cherryville (E2)* 160
Cheshire (D3)* 73
Chiloquin (F5)* 668
Clackamas (B2)* 550
Clarno (G3)
Clatskanie (D1)* 901
Claxtar (A3) 100
Clem (G2) 12
Clifton (D1)* 68
Cloverdale (D2)* 280
Coaledo (C4) 125
Coburg (D3)* 693
Cochran (D2) 50
Colestin (E5) 7
Colton (B3)* 167
Columbia City (E2)* 405
Condon (G2)* 968
Coos Bay (C4)* 6,223
Copperfield (K3) 13
Coquille (C4)* 3,523
Cornelius (A2)* 998
Cornucopia (K3)
Corvallis (D3)* 16,207
Cottage Grove (D4)* 3,536
Courtrock (H3)* 60
Cove (K2)* 282
Cove Orchard (D2)* 140
Cow Creek (D5)
Crabtree (E3)* 350
Crane (J4)* 99
Crater Lake (E5)* 47
Crawfordsville (E3)* 250
Crescent (F4)* 300
Crescent Lake (F4)* 50
Creston (K4) 4
Creswell (D4)* 662
Crow (D4) 100
Crowley (K4) 5
Crystal (E5) 15
Culp Creek (E4)* 260
Culver (F3)* 301
Curry (J3) 4
Curtin (D4)* 70
Cushman (D4)* 150
Dairy (F5)* 50
Dale (J3)* 10
Dallas (D3)* 4,793
Danner (K5) 20
Dawson (D3) 40
Days Creek (D5)* 40
Dayton (A3)* 719
Dayville (H3)* 286
Dee (F2)* 250
Deer Island (E2)* 79
Delake (C3) 644
Denmark (C5)* 13
Denzer (D3)
Depoe Bay (C3)* 750
Deschutes (F3) 20
Deter (E5) 15
Detroit (E3)*
Dexter (E4)* 400
Diamond (J4)* 8
Diamond Lake (E4)*
Dillard (D4)* 300
Dilley (A2)* 200
Disston (E4)* 300
Divide (D4)
Dixonville (D4) 30
Dolph (D2) 50
Donald (A3)* 187
Dora (D4) 80
Dorena (E4)* 300
Drain (D4)* 1,150
Draperville (D3) 201
Drew (E5)* 265
Drewsey (J4)* 64
Dryden (D5)* 25
Drylake (G4) 18
Dufur (F2)* 422
Duncan (J2)* 18
Dundee (A2)* 308
Durham (A2) 250
Durkee (K3)* 50
Eagle Creek (E2)* 75
Eagle Point (E5)* 607
Eastside (C4)* 890
Echo (H2)* 457
Eddyville (D3)*
Eightmile (H2)
Elgarose (D4) 12
Elgin (K2)* 1,223
Elk City (D3)* 50
Elk Lake (F4)*
Elkton (D4)* 201
Elmira (D3)* 500
Elmonica (A2) 50
Elsie (D2)
Empire (C4)* 2,261
Enright (D2) 5
Enterprise (K2)* 1,718
Erskine (G2) 7
Estacada (E2)* 950
Eugene (D3)* 35,879
Eula (E4) 20
Evans (K2) 47
Fair Grounds (A3)
Fairview (B2)* 438
Fall Creek (E4)* 144
Falls City (D3)* 853
Faloma (B2) 600
Fargo (A3) 18
Farmington (A2) 20
Faubion (F2) 30
Ferndale (J2) 225
Fields (J5)* 12
Fife (G4)
Fisher (D3)
Flora (K2)* 190
Florence (C4)* 1,026
Foleysprings (E3) 4
Follyfarm (J4) 5
Forest Grove (A2)* 4,343
Fort Klamath (E5)* 350
Ft. Rock (G4)* 18
Ft. Stevens (C1) 60
Foss (D2) 50
Fossil (G2)* 645
Foster (E3)* 350
Fox (H3)* 65
Freewater (J2)* 1,489
Frenchglen (H5)* 46
Friend (F2)* 15
Fruita (L2)
Galena (J3) 1
Gales Creek (D2)* 200
Galice (D5) 40
Garden Home (A2)* 750
Gardiner (C4)* 600
Garibaldi (D2)* 1,249
Gaston (D2)* 368
Gates (E3)* 445
Gateway (F3)* 75
Gaylord (C5)* 135
Gearhart (C1)* 568
Gervais (A3)* 457
Gibbon (J2)* 52
Gladstone (B2)* 2,434
Glenada (C4) 110
Glencoe (A1) 10
Glendale (D5)* 871
Gleneden Beach (C3)* 185
Glenwood (D2)* 20
Glide (D4)* 100
Goble (E1)* 73
Gold Beach (C5)* 677
Gold Hill (D5)* 619
Gooch (E3) 25
Goshen (D4)* 250
Government Camp (F2)* 100
Grand Ronde (D2)* 800
Granite (J3)* 40
Grant (G2) 25
Grants Pass (D5)* 8,116
Grass Valley (G2)* 195
Green (D4) 60
Greenburg (A2) 20
Greenhorn (J3)
Greenleaf (D3)* 111
Gresham (B2)* 3,049
Grizzly (G3) 25
Gunter (D4) 25
Gurdane (J2) 18
Gwendolen (G2) 6
Gypsum (K3)
Haines (J3)* 321
Halfway (K3)* 312
Halsey (D3)* 388
Hamilton (H3)* 58
Hamlet (D2)* 20
Hammond (C1)* 522
Hampton (G4)* 22
Harbor (C5)* 600
Hardman (H2)* 58
Harlan (D3)* 240
Harney (J4) 6
Harper (K4)* 200
Harriman (E5)* 42
Harrisburg (D3)* 862
Hauser (C4)* 158
Hay Creek (G3) 15
Hayesville (A3) 2,697
Hebo (D2)* 250
Helix (J2)* 182
Hemlock (D2) 20
Heppner (H2)* 1,648
Hereford (K3)* 66
Hermiston (H2)* 3,804
Hershal (K3) 4
Hildebrand (F5)
Hilgard (J2) 40
Hillsboro (A2)* 5,142
Hillsdale (B2)*
Hines (H4)* 918
Holbrook (A1) 100
Holdman (J2) 30
Holland (D5)* 100
Holley (E3)* 225
Home (K3)* 10
Homestead (L2) 25
Hood River (F2)* 3,701
Hopewell (D2) 125
Hopmere (A3) 75
Horton (D3)* 168
Hot Lake (K2) 25
Hubbard (A3)* 493
Huber (A2)* 250
Hugo (D5)* 100
Hullt (B3)
Huntington (K3)* 733
Idanha (E3)* 442
Idaville (D2) 150
Idleyld Park (D4)* 100
Illahe (C5)
Imbler (J2)* 149
Imnaha (L2)* 30
Independence (D3)* 1,987
Ione (H2)* 262
Ironside (K3) 150
Irrigon (H2)* 75
Irving (D3) 300
Island City (K2)* 138
Izee (H3)* 4
Jacksonville (D5)* 1,193
Jamieson (K3)* 300
Jasper (E3)* 200
Jefferson (D3)* 636
Jennings Lodge (B2)* 3,500
Jewell (D2)*
John Day (J3)* 1,597
Jordan Valley (K5)* 236
Joseph (K2)* 666
Junction City (D3)* 1,475
Juntura (K4)* 107
Kamela (J2) 25
Keasey (D2)* 8
Keating (K3)* 10
Keno (F5)* 300
Kent (G2)* 60
Kerby (D5)* 150
Kernville (D3)* 105
Kerry (D1) 30
Kimberly (H3)* 60
Kings Valley (D3)* 210
Kinzua (H3)* 900
Kirk (F5) 25
Klamath Agency (F5)* 150
Klamath Falls (F5)* 15,875
Klondike (G2)* 6
Knappa (D1) 100
La Grande (J2)* 8,635
La Pine (F4)* 250
Lacomb (E3)* 100
Lafayette (A2)* 662
Lake Grove (B2)* 4,000
Lakecreek (E5)* 30
Lakeside (C4)*
Lakeview (G5)* 2,831
Langlois (C5)* 65
Latourell Falls (E2)* 72
Laurel (A2) 30
Lawen (J4)* 15
Leaburg (E3)* 106
Lebanon (E3)* 5,873
Leland (D5) 71
Leona (D4) 50
Lewis (K2) 2
Lexington (H2)* 237
Liberal (B3) 40
Liberty (A3)
Lime (K3)* 100
Lincoln Beach (C3)* 100
Linneman (B2) 550
Linnton (A2)
Linslaw (D4)* 75
Logan (B2) 50
Logdell (H3) 4
Logsden (D3)* 340
London (D4)
Lonerock (H2)* 38
Long Creek (H3)* 288
Lookingglass (D4) 100
Lostine (K2)* 178
Lowell (E4)* 700
Lyons (E3)* 600
Mabel (E3)* 85
Macksburg (B3) 50
Macleay (A3) 25
Madras (F3)* 1,258
Malheur (K3) 25
Malin (F5)* 592
Manhattan Beach (D2)*
Manning (D2)* 100
Manzanita (C2)* 339
Mapleton (C3)* 1,016
Marcola (E3)* 800
Marial (D5)* 45
Marion (D3)* 200
Marquam (B3)* 70
Marshland (D1)* 120
Maupin (F2)* 312
Maxville (K2)
Mayger (D1)* 95
Mayville (G2)* 102
Mc Coy (D2)* 75
Mc Credie Springs (E4)* 87
Mc Ewen (J3) 25
Mc Kee (A3) 75
Mc Kenzie Bridge (E3)* 195
Mc Kinley (D4)* 155
Mc Minnville (D2)* 6,635
Mc Nary (H2)*
Meacham (J2)*
Medford (E5)* 17,305
Medical Springs (K2)* 15
Mehama (E3)* 200
Melrose (D4) 150
Merlin (D5)* 225
Merrill (F5)* 835
Metolius (F3)* 157
Metzger (A2)* 2,000
Middleton (A2) 150
Midland (F5)* 85
Mikkalo (G2)* 150
Mill City (E3)* 1,792
Miller (G2)* 75
Millican (F4)* 5
Millington (C4) 300
Milo (E5)* 300
Milton (J2)* 2,362
Milwaukie (B2)* 5,253
Minam (K2)
Minerva (C3) 25
Mission (J2) 200
Mist (D1)* 269
Mitchell (G3)* 415
Modoc Point (F5)* 100
Mohawk (E3)* 20
Mohler (D2)* 100
Molalla (B3)* 1,497
Monitor (B3)* 50
Monmouth (D3)* 1,956
Monroe (D3)* 362
Monument (H3)* 228
Morgan (H2)* 10
Moro (G2)* 359
Mosier (F2)* 259
Mount Angel (B3)* 1,315
Mt. Hood (F2)* 59
Mt. Vernon (H3)* 451
Mountaindale (A1) 50
Mowich (F4) 20
Mulino (B2)* 275
Multnomah (B2)* 5,000
Murphy (D5)* 50
Myrtle Creek (D4)* 1,781
Myrtle Point (C4)* 2,033
Narrows (H4) 7
Nashville (D3)* 25
Needy (B3) 50
Nehalem (D2)* 270
Nelscott (D3)* 400
Neotsu (C2)* 300
Neskowin (D2)* 120
Netarts (C2)* 500
New Bridge (K3)* 51
New Era (B2) 100
New Pine Creek (G5)* 200
Newberg (A2)* 3,946
Newport (C3)* 3,241
North Bend (C4)* 6,099
N. Junction (G3) 2
N. Plains (A2)* 600
N. Portland (B1)* 340
N. Powder (K2)* 403
Norway (C4)* 250
Nyssa (K4)* 2,525
Oak Grove (B2)* 2,000
Oakland (D4)* 829
Oakridge (E4)* 1,562
O'Brien (D5)* 265
Oceanlake (C3)* 700
Oceanside (C2)* 150
Odell (F2)* 350
Odell Lake (F4) 50
Olene (F5)* 35
Olex (G2)* 168
Olney (D1)
Ontario (K3)* 4,465
Opal City (F3)
Ophir (C5)*
Ordnance (H2)*
Oregon Caves (D5)* 2
Oregon City (B2)* 7,682
Orenco (A2)* 313
Oretown (D2)* 60
Oswego (B2)* 3,316
Otis (D2)* 200
Otter Rock (C3)* 100
Owyhee Corner (K4)
Pacific City (C2)* 200
Paisley (G5)* 214
Palmer Junction (K2) 3
Paradise (K2) 42
Park Place (B2)* 500
Parkdale (F2)* 300
Parkers Mill (H2)
Parkrose (B2)* 3,800
Paulina (G3)*
Pedee (D3) 125
Pendleton (J2)* 11,774
Pengra (E4)
Peoria (D3) 76
Perry (J2) 125
Perrydale (D2)* 75
Phillips (A2) 3
Philomath (D3)* 1,289
Phoenix (E5)* 746
Pilot Rock (J2)* 847
Pine (K3)* 73
Pinehurst (E5) 6
Pistol River (C5)* 100
Placer (D5) 48
Plainview (D3) 20
Pleasant Valley (K3)* 30
Plush (H5)* 110
Pondosa (K2)* 150
Port Orford (C5)* 674
Portland (B2)* 373,628
Portland (urban area) 509,120
Post (G3)*
Powell Butte (G3)* 661
Powell Valley (B2) 725
Powers (D5)* 895
Prairie City (J3)* 822
Pratum (A3)* 44
Prescott (D1) 119
Princeton (J4)* 6
Prineville (G3)* 3,233
Pringle (A3) 250
Promise (K2)
Prospect (E5)* 500
Prosper (C4) 55
Provolt (D5)* 200
Quartz Mountain (G5) 12
Quinaby (A3) 100
Quincy (D1)* 400
Rainbow (E3) 65
Rainier (E1)* 1,285
Rainrock (C3)
Redland (B2) 50

Redmond (F3)*....2,956
Reed (D3)....
Reedsport (C4)*....2,288
Reedville (A2)*.... 250
Remote (D5)*.... 60
Rex (A2).... 5
Richland (K3)*.... 220
Richmond (H3)*....
Rickreall (D3)*.... 150
Riddle (D5)*.... 634
Rieth (J2)*.... 325
Riley (H4)*.... 5
Ritter (H3)*.... 107
Riverside (J4)*.... 38
Riverton (C4)*.... 125
Roberts (G3)....
Robinette (L3)*.... 20
Rockaway (C2)*....1,027
Rockcreek (G2).... 19
Rockton (A2).... 150
Rockville (K4).... 31
Rocky Point (A1)....
Rogue River (D5)*.... 590
Rome (K5).... 50
Roosevelt Beach (C3)....
Rose Lodge (D3)*.... 150
Roseburg (D4)*....8,390
Rowena (F2).... 75
Rowland (D3).... 15
Roy (A2)*.... 48
Ruch (E5).... 50
Rufus (G2)*.... 50
Rye Valley (K3).... 25
Saginaw (E4)*....
Saint Benedict (B3)*.... 230
St. Helens (E2)*....4,711
St. Louis (A3).... 30
Saint Paul (A3)*.... 226
Saloda (D3).... 12
SALEM (A3)*....43,140
Sams Valley (E5)*....
Sandlake (C2)*.... 300
Sandy (E2)*....1,003
Scappoose (E2)*.... 654
Scholls (A2).... 70
Scio (E3)*.... 448
Scofield (D2).... 75
Scotts Mills (B3)*.... 217
Scottsburg (D4)*.... 100
Seal Rock (C3)*.... 330
Seaside (D2)*....3,886
Selma (D5)*.... 125
Seneca (J3)*.... 760
Service Creek (G3)*.... 13
Shaniko (G3)*.... 61
Shaw (A3).... 150
Sheaville (K4)*.... 64
Shedd (D3)*.... 165
Shelburn (E3).... 20
Sheridan (D2)*....1,922
Sherwood (A2)*.... 575
Shevlin (F4).... 600
Siletz (D3)*.... 570
Siltcoos (C4)*.... 28
Silver Lake (F4)*....
Silverton (A3)*....3,146
Silvies (H3)*....
Simnasho (F3)*.... 40
Siskiyou (E5).... 50
Sisters (F3)*.... 723
Sitkum (D4)*.... 50
Sixes (C5)*.... 250
Sodaville (E3).... 157
South Junction (G3)*.... 10
Southbeach (C3)*.... 300
Sparta (K3)*.... 25
Sprague River (F5)*.... 350
Spray (H3)*.... 375
Springbrook (A2)*.... 500
Springfield (E3)*....10,807
Springwater (E2).... 300
Stanfield (H2)*.... 845
Star (E4)....
Starkey (J2).... 30
Stauffer (G4).... 2
Stayton (E3)*....1,507
Sublimity (E3)*.... 367
Summer Lake (G5)*.... 3
Summerville (K2)*.... 73
Summit (D3)*.... 250
Sumner (C4)*.... 141
Sumpter (J3)*.... 146
Sunny Valley (D5)*.... 79
Susanville (J3)*.... 9
Sutherlin (D4)*....2,230
Svensen (D1).... 100
Sweet Home (E3)*....3,603
Swisshome (D3)*.... 500
Sycamore (B2)....
Sylvan (B2)....1,500
Table Rock (E5).... 200
Taft (C3)*.... 450
Takilma (D5)*.... 50
Talent (E5)*.... 739
Tallman (E3).... 25
Tangent (D3)*.... 200
Telocaset (K2)*.... 80
Tenmile (D4)*.... 40
Terrebonne (F3)*.... 198
The Dalles (F2)*....7,676
Thompson (K3).... 3
Thurston (E3)*.... 66
Tidewater (D3)*.... 100
Tiernan (C3)*.... 200
Tigard (A2)*.... 800
Tillamook (D2)*....3,685
Tiller (E5)*.... 150
Timber (D2)*.... 300
Toledo (D3)*....2,323
Tolovana Park (C2)*....
Top (H3)*.... 27
Trail (E5)*.... 45
Trent (E4)*.... 300
Troutdale (E2)*.... 541
Troy (K2)*.... 150
Tualatin (A2)*.... 248
Tumalo (F3).... 50
Turner (E3)*.... 610
Twin Rocks (C2)*.... 300
Tygh Valley (F2)*.... 449
Ukiah (J2)*.... 300
Umapine (J2)*.... 50
Umatilla (H2)*.... 883
Umpqua (D4)*.... 20
Union (K2)*....1,307
Union Creek (E5).... 100
Unity (J3)*.... 212
Vale (K4)*....1,518
Valley Falls (G5).... 14
Valsetz (D3)*.... 60
Van (J4)*.... 5
Vaughn (D3).... 200
Venator (J4).... 28
Veneta (D3)*.... 750
Verboort (A2).... 125
Vernonia (D2)*....1,521
Vida (E3)*.... 250
Viento (F2).... 50
Viola (B2).... 50
Waconda (A3).... 50
Wagontire (H4).... 3
Waldport (C3)*.... 689
Walker (D4).... 100
Wallowa (K2)*....1,055
Walterville (E3)*.... 100
Walton (D3)*.... 70
Wamic (F2)*.... 125
Wapinitia (F2).... 20
Warm Springs (F3)*.... 350
Warren (E2)*.... 81
Warrendale (F2).... 50
Warrenton (C1)*....1,896
Wasco (G2)*.... 305
Waterloo (E3)*.... 180
Waterman (H3)....
Wauna (D1)*.... 325
Weatherby (K3).... 25
Wecoma Beach (C3)*.... 350
Wedderburn (C5)*.... 250
Welches (E2)*.... 119
Wemme (E2)*.... 109
Wendling (E3)*.... 124
West Linn (B2)*....2,945
West Portland (B2)....3,000
W. Salem (A3)....
W. Side (G5).... 16
W. Woodburn (A3).... 150
Westfall (K3)*.... 3
Westfir (E4)*....1,200
Westlake (C4)*.... 180
Weston (J2)*.... 679
Westport (D1)*.... 600
Wheeler (D2)*.... 291
Wheeler Heights (C2).... 125
Whiteson (D2)*.... 200
Whitney (J3).... 3
Wilark (D2).... 10
Wilbur (D4)*.... 150
Wilderville (D5)*.... 300
Wilhoit (B3).... 5
Wilkesboro (A2).... 45
Willamette (B2)*....
Willamina (D2)*....1,082
Williams (D5)*.... 100
Willowcreek (K3)*.... 300
Willowdale (G3).... 35
Willows (G2).... 100
Wilsonville (A2)*.... 162
Wimer (D5).... 100
Winchester (D4)*.... 300
Winchester Bay (C4)*.... 500
Wing (K3)....
Winlock (H3).... 12
Wolf Creek (D5)*.... 250
Wonder (D5)*.... 300
Woodburn (A3)*....2,395
Woods (C2).... 110
Worden (F5)*....
Wyeth (F2).... 15
Yachats (C3)*.... 300
Yamhill (D2)*.... 539
Yamsay Station (F4)....
Yaquina (C3)*.... 76
Yoder (B3).... 150
Yoncalla (D4)*.... 626
Zigzag (F2)*.... 150
Zumwalt (L2).... 2

Map on Page 83

PENNSYLVANIA

Total Population 10,498,012

67 COUNTIES

Adams (H6)....44,197
Allegheny (B5)....1,515,237
Armstrong (D4)....80,842
Beaver (B4)....175,192
Bedford (E6)....40,775
Berks (K5)....255,740
Blair (F4)....139,514
Bradford (J2)....51,722
Bucks (M5)....144,620
Butler (C4)....97,320
Cambria (E4)....209,541
Cameron (F3)....7,023
Carbon (L4)....57,558
Centre (G4)....65,922
Chester (L6)....159,141
Clarion (D3)....38,344
Clearfield (F3)....85,957
Clinton (G3)....36,532
Columbia (K3)....53,460
Crawford (B2)....78,948
Cumberland (H5)....94,457
Dauphin (J5)....197,784
Delaware (M6)....414,234
Elk (E3)....34,503
Erie (B2)....219,388
Fayette (C6)....189,899
Forest (D2)....4,944
Franklin (G6)....75,927
Fulton (F6)....10,387
Greene (B6)....45,394
Huntingdon (F5)....40,872
Indiana (D4)....77,106
Jefferson (D3)....49,147
Juniata (H4)....15,243
Lackawanna (L3)....257,396
Lancaster (K5)....234,717
Lawrence (B4)....105,120
Lebanon (K5)....81,683
Lehigh (L4)....198,207
Luzerne (L3)....392,241
Lycoming (H3)....101,249
Mc Kean (E2)....56,607
Mercer (B3)....111,954
Mifflin (G4)....43,691
Monroe (M3)....33,773
Montgomery (M5)....353,068
Montour (J3)....16,001
Northampton (M4)....185,243
Northumberland (J4)....117,115
Perry (H5)....24,782
Philadelphia (M6)....2,071,605
Pike (M3)....8,425
Potter (G2)....16,810
Schuylkill (K4)....200,577
Snyder (H4)....22,912
Somerset (D6)....81,813
Sullivan (J3)....6,745
Susquehanna (L2)....31,970
Tioga (H2)....35,474
Union (H4)....23,150
Venango (C3)....65,328
Warren (D2)....42,698
Washington (B5)....209,628
Wayne (M2)....28,478
Westmoreland (D5)....313,179
Wyoming (K2)....16,766
York (J6)....202,737

CITIES and TOWNS

Aaronsburg (H4)*.... 350
Abbottstown (J6)*.... 538
Adamsburg ‡(C5)*.... 238
Adamstown (K5)*....1,020
Adamsville (B2)*.... 200
Addison (D6)*.... 237
Adrian (D4)*.... 130
Airville (K6)*.... 125
Aitch (F5)*.... 219
Akeley (D2)*.... 50
Akron (K5)*....1,028
Alba (J2)*.... 190
Albion (B2)*....1,729
Albrightsville (L3)*.... 150
Alburtis (L5)*.... 979
Aldan (M7)*....3,430
Aldenville (M2)*.... 100
Alexandria (F4)*.... 443
Aliquippa (B4)*....26,132
Allen (H5)*.... 395
Allenport ‡(C5)*.... 923
Allensville (G4)*.... 300
Allentown (L4)*....106,756
Allentown-Bethlehem (urban area)....225,155
Allenwood (H3)*.... 367
Allison Park (C4)*....2,000
Altoona (F4)*....77,177
Altoona (urban area)....86,249
Alum Bank (E5)*.... 342
Amberson (G5)*....
Ambler (M5)*....4,565
Ambridge (B4)*....16,429
Amity (B5)*.... 240
Andalusia (N5)*....1,800
Anita (D3)*.... 350
Annville (J5)*....3,564
Ansonville (E4)*.... 158
Antes Fort (H3)*.... 300
Antrim (H2)*.... 300
Apollo (D4)*....3,015
Applewold ‡(C4)*.... 500
Ararat (L2)*.... 72
Arbuckle (C1).... 25
Arcadia (E4)*.... 500
Archbald (M2)*....6,304
Ardmore (M6)*....20,000
Arendtsville (H6)*.... 409
Argentine (C3)*.... 150
Armagh ‡(E4)*.... 176
Arnold (C4)*....10,263
Arnot (H2)*.... 300
Arona ‡(C5)*.... 482
Artemas (E6)*.... 19
Ashland (K4)*....6,192
Ashley (L3)*....5,243
Ashville (F4)*.... 441
Aspers (H6)*.... 220
Aspinwall (C6)*....4,084
Atglen (K6)*.... 668
Athens (K2)*....4,430
Athol (L5)*.... 200
Atlantic ....(B3)*.... 157
Atlas (K4)*....3,090
Atwood ‡(D4).... 110
Auburn (K4)*.... 994
Aultman (D4)*.... 600
Austin (F2)*.... 804
Avalon (B6)*....6,463
Avella (B5)*....1,356
Avis (H3)*....1,193
Avoca (L3)*....4,040
Avondale (L6)*.... 941
Avonmore (C4)*....1,367
Baden (B4)*....3,732
Bainbridge (J5)*.... 500
Bakers Summit (F5)*.... 70
Bakersville (D5).... 170
Bala-Cynwyd (N6)*....
Bally (L5)*.... 753
Bangor (M4)*....6,050
Barnesboro (E4)*....3,442
Barto (L5)*.... 151
Bartonsville (M4)*.... 150
Bath (M4)*....1,824
Baxter (D3)*.... 87
Beach Haven (K3)*.... 500
Beachlake (M2)*.... 250
Beadling (B7)*.... 500
Beallsville (C5)*.... 598
Bear Creek (L3)*.... 150
Bear Lake (C1)*.... 239
Beaver (B4)*....6,360
Beaver Falls (B4)*....17,375
Beaver Meadows (L4)*....1,723
Beaver Spgs. (H4)*.... 750
Beaverdale (E5)*....2,200
Beavertown (H4)*.... 700
Bechtelsville ‡(L5)*.... 603
Bedford (F5)*....3,521
Bedford Valley (E6).... 300
Bedminster (M5)*.... 500
Beech Creek (G3)*.... 574
Belle Vernon (C5)*....2,271
Bellefonte (G4)*....5,651
Belleville (G4)*....1,304
Bellevue (B6)*....11,604
Bellwood (F4)*....2,559
Ben Avon (B6)*....2,465
Ben Avon Hts. ‡(B5).... 394
Bendersville (H6)*.... 409
Benezett (F3)*.... 400
Benson (Hollsopple*) (E5).... 377
Bentleyville (B5)*....3,295
Benton (K3)*.... 890
Berlin (E6)*....1,507
Bermudian (J5).... 50
Bernharts (K5).... 760
Bernville (K5)*.... 363
Berrysburg (J4)*.... 386
Berwick (K3)*....14,010
Berwyn (L5)*....3,000
Bessemer (B4)*....1,461
Bethany (M2).... 148
Bethel (K5)*.... 500
Bethel (B7)....11,324
Bethlehem (M4)*....66,340
Bethlehem-Allentown (urban area)....225,155
Betula (F2)*.... 90
Big Cove Tannery (F6)* 25
Big Run (E4)*.... 896
Bigler (F4)*.... 500
Biglerville (H6)*.... 870
Birchardville (L2)*.... 35
Birdsboro (L5)*....3,158
Birmingham (F4)*.... 178
Black Lick (D4)*....1,000
Blain (H5)*.... 315
Blairs Mills (G5)*.... 150
Blairsville (D5)*....5,000
Blakely ‡(L3)....6,828
Blakeslee (L3)*.... 50
Blanchard (G3)*.... 550
Blandburg (F4)*....1,200
Blawnox (C6)*....2,165
Bloomfield (New Bloomfield*) (H5)....1,098
Blooming Grove (M3)*.. 113
Blooming Valley (B2).. 256
Bloomsburg (J3)*....10,633
Blossburg (H2)*....1,954
Blue Ridge Summit (G6)*.... 650
Blythedale (C5)*.... 890
Boalsburg (G4)*.... 500
Bobtown (B6)*....1,553
Bodines (H3)*.... 110
Boiling Spgs. (H5)*.... 900
Bolivar (D5)*.... 828
Boltz (E5)*.... 250
Boothwyn (L7)*....4,500
Boston (C7)*....1,700
Boswell (E5)*....1,679
Bowmansdale (J5)*.... 200
Bowmanstown (L4)*.... 878
Bowmansville (L5)*.... 350
Boyers (C3)*.... 800
Boyertown (L5)*....4,074
Brackenridge (C4)*....6,178
Brackney (K2)*.... 75
Braddock (C7)*....16,488
Braddock Hills (C7)....1,965
Bradford (E2)*....17,354
Bradfordwoods ‡(B4)*.. 458
Braeburn (C4)*.... 800
Branch Dale (K4)*....1,500
Branchton (C3)*.... 130
Brave (B6)*.... 200
Brentwood (B7)*....12,535
Briar Creek (K3)*.... 348
Brickerville (K5).... 150
Bridgeport (M5)*....5,827
Bridgeville (B5)*....5,650
Bridgewater (W. Bridgewater*) (B4)....1,316
Brisbin (F4)*.... 463
Bristol (N5)*....12,710
Broad Ford (C5)*.... 112
Broad Top (F5)*.... 483
Brockport (E3)*.... 450
Brockway (E3)*....2,650
Brodbecks (J6)*.... 50
Brodheadsville (M4)*.... 550
Brogueville (J6)*.... 55
Brookhaven (M7)....1,042
Brooklyn (L2)*.... 500
Brookville (D3)*....4,274
Broomall (M6)*....6,000
Broughton (B7)*....2,500
Brownfield (C6)*....
Brownstown (K5).... 700
Brownstown ‡(E5)....1,508
Brownsville (C5)*....7,643
Bruceton (B7)*.... 250
Bruin (C3)*.... 717
Bryn Athyn (M5)*.... 913
Bryn Mawr (M5)*....12,000
Bucksville (M5)*.... 200
Buffalo Mills (E6)*.... 105
Bulger (B5)*.... 800
Burgettstown (A5)*....2,379
Burlington (J2)*.... 148
Burnham (H4)*....2,954
Burnside (E4)*.... 400
Burnt Cabins (G5)*.... 125
Burrows (G2).... 15
Bushkill (M3)*.... 500
Butler (C4)*....23,482
Byrnedale (E3)*.... 500
Cadogan (C4)*.... 727
Cairnbrook (E5)*....1,504
Caledonia (F3).... 300
California (C5)*....2,831
Callensburg (D3)*.... 261
Callery (C4)*.... 407
Cambra (K3)*.... 100
Cambridge Spgs. (C2)*.2,246
Cameron (F3)*.... 114
Cammal (H3)*.... 120
Camp Hill (H5)*....5,934
Camptown (K2)*.... 300
Canadensis (M3)*.... 400
Cannelton (A4)*.... 100
Canonsburg (B5)*....12,072
Canton (J2)*....2,118
Carbondale (L2)*....16,296
Carlisle (H5)*....16,812
Carlton (C3)*.... 50
Carmichaels (C6)*.... 895
Carnegie (B7)*....12,105
Carrolltown (E4)*....1,452
Cashtown (H6)*.... 270
Cassandra (E5)*.... 381
Casselman (D6).... 130
Cassville (G5)*.... 158
Castle Shannon (B7)*..5,459
Catasauqua (M4)*....4,923
Catawissa (K4)*....2,000
Cecil (B5)*....1,200
Cedar Run (H2)*.... 62
Center Moreland (K3)*.. 100
Center Road (A2).... 35
Centerport ‡(K5)*.... 226
Centerville (C2)*.... 245
Centerville (B6)....5,845
Central City (E5)*....1,935
Centralia (K4)*....1,986
Centre Hall (G4)*.... 834
Cessna (F5).... 50
Chalfant ‡(C7)....1,381
Chalfont (M5)*.... 828
Chambersburg (G6)*....17,212
Chambersville (D4)*.... 300
Chandlers Valley (D2)* 170
Chaneysville (F6).... 80
Chapman ‡(M4).... 285
Charleroi (C5)*....9,872
Cheltenham (M5)*....▵22,854
Cherry Tree (E4)*.... 517
Cherry Valley (C3).... 94
Chest Springs (E4)*.... 232
Chester (L7)*....66,039
Chester Hts. (L7)*.... 474
Chester Hill ‡(F4).... 954
Cheswick (C6)*....1,534
Cheyney (M6)*.... 289
Chicora (C4)*....1,172
Choconut (K2).... 50
Christiana (K6)*....1,043
Churchill ‡(C7)....1,733
Churchtown (L5)*.... 250
Clairton (C7)*....19,652
Clarence (G3)*....1,700
Clarendon (D2)*.... 748
Clarington (D3)*.... 125
Clarion (D3)*....4,409
Clark (B3)*.... 345
Clarks Green ‡(L3)*.... 824
Clarks Mills (B3)*.... 100
Clarks Summit (L3)....2,940
Clarksville (B6)*.... 428
Clarksville (Clark*) (B3).... 345
Claysburg (F5)*....1,355
Claysville (B5)*.... 963
Claytonia (B3).... 50
Clear Ridge (F5)*.... 31
Clearfield (F3)*....9,357
Clearville (F6)*.... 200
Cleona ‡(K5)*....1,483
Clermont (E2)*.... 175
Clifford (L2)*.... 300
Clifton Heights (M7)*..7,549
Climax (D4)*.... 300
Clinton (B5)*.... 575
Clintondale (H3).... 120
Clintonville (C3)*.... 307
Cloe (E4)*.... 275
Clune (D4)*.... 500
Clymer (E4)*....2,500
Coal Center ‡(C5)*.... 584
Coal Valley (C7)*.... 700
Coaldale (L4)*....5,318
Coaldale ‡(F5).... 231
Coalmont ‡(F5)*.... 207
Coalport (E4)*....1,052
Coatesville (L5)*....13,826
Coburn (H4)*.... 280
Cochranton (B2)*....1,092
Cochranville (L6)*.... 350
Cocolamus (H4)*....
Codorus (J6)*.... 449
Cogan Station (H3)*.... 39
Cokeburg (B5)*....1,170
Cokeville (D5)*.... 600
Colegrove (F2)*.... 50
Collegeville (M5)*....1,900
Colley (K2)*.... 100
Collingdale (N7)*....8,443
Colmar (M5).... 600
Columbia (K5)*....11,993
Columbus (C2)*....
Colver (E4)*....1,708
Colwyn ‡(M7)....2,143
Commodore (D4)*.... 450
Concord (G5)*.... 190
Concordville (M6)*.... 126
Conemaugh (E5)*....5,000
Conestoga (K6)*.... 480
Confluence (D6)*....1,037
Conneaut Lake (B2)*.... 676
Conneaut Lake Park (B2).... 225
Conneautville (A2)*....1,177
Connellsville (D5)*....13,293
Conoquenessing (B4)*.... 441
Conrad (G2).... 15
Conshohocken (M5)*....10,922
Conway (B4)*....1,570
Conyngham (K3)*.... 935
Cooksburg (D3)*.... 50
Coopersburg (M5)*....1,462
Cooperstown (C2).... 271
Coplay (L4)*....2,994
Coral (D5)*.... 675
Coraopolis (B4)*....10,498
Cornwall (K5)*....1,760
Corry (C2)*....7,911
Corsica (D3)*.... 421
Corydon (D2)*.... 250
Coryville (F2)*.... 320
Costello (G2).... 100
Coudersport (G2)*....3,210
Courtdale ‡(L3).... 982
Covington (J2)*.... 725
Cowan (H4).... 105
Cowanesque (H2)*.... 200
Cowansville (C4)*.... 306
Crafton (B7)*....8,066
Cranberry (C3)*.... 450
Cranesville (B2)*.... 602
Creekside (D4)*.... 525
Creighton (C4)*....
Crenshaw (E3)*....
Cresco (M3)*.... 150
Cresson (E5)*....2,569
Cressona (K4)*....1,758
Crosby (F2)*.... 400
Cross Fork (G3)*.... 85
Cross Roads ‡(J6).... 178
Crum Lynne (M7)*....3,500
Cuddy (B5)*....2,500
Curllsville (D3)*.... 156
Curryville (F5)*.... 150
Curwensville (E4)*....3,332
Custer City (E2)*.... 500
Cyclone (E2)*.... 700
Dagus Mines (E3)*.... 500
Daguscahonda (E3)*.... 190
Daisytown ‡(E5).... 442
Dale ‡(E5)....3,310
Dallas (K3)*....1,674
Dallastown (J6)*....3,304
Dalmatia (J4)*.... 517

Philadelphia (N6)*..2,071,605
Philadelphia (urban area) 2,913,516
Philipsburg (F4)*.........3,988
Phoenixville (L5)*.......12,932
Picture Rocks (J3)*...... 569
Pillow (J4)*.............. 369
Pine Bank (B6)*............ 25
Pine Grove (K4)*.........2,237
Pine Grove Furnace (H5)............ 40
Pine Grove Mills (G4)*.1,200
Pipersville (M5)*........ 125
Pitcairn (C5)*..............5,857
Pittock (B7)*...............2,600
Pittsburgh (B7)*.......676,806
Pittsburgh (urban area) 1,525,966
Pittsfield (D2)*...............
Pittston (L3)*.............15,012
Plains (L3)*..............^12,541
Platea (B2)*.............. 290
Pleasant Gap (G4)*.......1,312
Pleasant Hills (B7).......3,808
Pleasant Mount (M2)*.. 438
Pleasantville (C2)*...... 704
Pleasantville ‡(E5)....... 242
Plumsteadville (M5)*.... 312
Plumville (D4)*............ 452
Plymouth (K3)*............13,021
Pocono Lake (L3)*......... 225
Pocono Pines (M3)*...... 475
Point Marion (C6)*......2,197
Point Pleasant (N5)*.... 400
Poland Mines (B6)*......
Polk (C3)*...................4,004
Pond Eddy (N3)*...........
Port Allegany (F2)*......2,519
Port Carbon (K4)*.........3,024
Port Clinton (K4)*......... 451
Port Matilda (F4)*........ 685
Port Royal (H4)*........... 800
Port Trevorton (J4)*..... 280
Port Vue (C7)...............4,756
Portage (E5)*................4,371
Portersville (B4)*........ 294
Portland (M4)*............. 551
Pottersdale (F3)*......... 325
Potterville (K2).............. 63
Pottstown (L5)*...........22,589
Pottsville (K4)*...........23,640
Powell (J2)*.................. 300
Powelton (F4)*.............. 315
President (C3)............... 100
Primos (M7)*................. 500
Pringle ‡(L3)................1,727
Proctor (J3)*................. 100
Prompton (M2)*............. 197
Prospect (B4)*.............. 726
Prospect Park (M7)*.....5,834
Pulaski (B3)*................ 350
Punxsutawney (E4)*.....8,969
Quakertown (M5)*.........5,673
Quarryville (K6)*...........1,187
Quecreek (D5)*.............. 550
Queen (E5)*.................. 200
Racine (B4)*.................. 500
Railroad (J6)*................ 300
Rainsburg (F6)............... 189
Ralphton (D5)*.............. 225
Ralston (H2)*................ 700
Ramey (F4)*.................. 696
Rankin (C7)*.................6,941
Ravine (K4)*.................. 600
Reading (L5)*............109,320
Reading (urban area) 154,571
Reamstown (K5)*........... 950
Rebersburg (H4)*.......... 600
Red Hill ‡(M5)*.............. 914
Red Lion (J6)*...............5,119
Reedsville (G4)*............1,238
Refton (K6)*.................. 235
Rehrersburg (K5)*......... 365
Renfrew (C4)*................ 400
Reno (C3)*...................1,000
Renovo (G3)*.................3,751
Rew (F2)*...................... 500
Reynoldsville (D3)*........3,569
Rices Landing (C6)*...... 796
Riceville (C2)*................ 200
Richfield (H4)*................ 350
Richland (K5)*...............1,090
Richlandtown (M5)*........ 762
Riddlesburg (F5)*........... 700
Ridgway (E3)*................6,244
Ridley Park (M7)*..........4,921
Riegelsville (M4)*.......... 871
Rillton (C5)*.................. 875
Rimer (C4)*...................... 80
Rimersburg (D3)*...........1,398
Ringtown (K4)*............... 835
Riverside (J4)*................ 524
Rixford (F2)*.................. 650
Roaring Branch (J2)*...... 375
Roaring Creek (K4).......... 40
Roaring Spring (F5)*....2,771
Robertsdale (F5)*............
Robesonia (K5)*.............1,590
Robinson (D5)*................
Rochester (B4)*..............7,197
Rochester Mills (D4)*.. 230
Rock Glen (K4)*.............. 250
Rockhill ‡(G5)................. 567
Rockledge ‡(M5)............2,261
Rockwood (D6)*..............1,237
Rogersville (B6)*............ 300
Rome (K2)*...................... 257
Roscoe (C5)*..................1,396
Rose Valley (L7).............. 498
Rosemont (M5)*..............2,000
Roseto (M4)*...................1,676
Roseville (Rutland*) (J2) 126
Rossiter (E4)*.................1,078
Rosslyn Farms ‡(B7)........ 448
Rothsville (K5)*...............1,000
Roulette (F2)*.................. 800
Rouseville (C3)*..............1,009
Rouzerville (G6)*.............1,000
Roxbury (G5)*.................. 400
Royalton (J5)*.................1,175
Royersford (L5)*..............3,862
Rummerfield (K2)*............ 100
Rural Valley (D4)*........... 857
Rush (K2)*.........................
Russell (D2)*.................... 800
Russellton (C4)*..............1,670
Rutland (J2)*..................... 126
Rutledge (M7)*................. 919
Sabinsville (G2)*.............. 300
Sabula (E3)...................... 275
Saegerstown (B2)*............ 836
Sagamore (D4)*................1,128
Saint Benedict (E4)*........ 500
St. Clair (K4)*..................5,856
St. Clairsville ‡(E5)*....... 127
St. Lawrence ‡(E4)*......... 810
St. Marys (E3)*.................7,846
St. Petersburg (C3)*......... 451
St. Thomas (G6)*.............. 534
Salisbury (D6)*................ 865
Salladasburg (H3)*........... 250
Salona (H3)*..................... 500
Saltillo (G5)*..................... 435
Saltsburg (D4)*.................1,156
Sand Patch (E6)*................ 56
Sandy Lake (B3)*.............. 767
Sandy Ridge (F4)*............. 700
Sankertown ‡(E5).............. 865
Sarver (C4)*....................... 410
Sawyer City (E2)................ 500
Saxonburg (C4)*................ 602
Saxton (F5)*.....................1,093
Saybrook (D2)*.................. 137
Saylorsburg (M4)*.............. 513
Sayre (K2)*........................7,735
Scalp Level (E5)*...............1,756
Schaefferstown (K5)*.......1,000
Schellsburg (E5)*............... 305
Schnecksville (L4)*............ 375
Schuylkill Haven (K4)*.6,597
Schwenksville (L5)*............ 563
Sciota (M4)*...................... 300
Scotland (G6)*................... 500
Scottdale (C5)*...................6,249
Scranton (L3)*.............125,536
Scranton (urban area) 235,122
Secane (M7)*.....................1,500
Seelyville (M2)*................... 600
Selinsgrove (J4)*.................3,514
Sellersville (M5)*.................2,373
Seminole (D4)*..................... 250
Seneca (C3)*........................ 700
Sergeant (E2)*...................... 150
Seven Valleys (J6)*.............. 437
Seward (E5)*......................... 852
Sewickley (B4)*....................5,836
Sewickley Heights ‡(B4) 679
Shade Gap (G5)*.................. 157
Shadygrove (G6)*................. 500
Shamokin (J4)*.................16,879
Shamokin Dam (J4)*........... 730
Shanksville (E5)*.................. 342
Sharon (B3)*....................26,454
Sharon Hill (N7)*................5,464
Sharpsburg (B6)*................7,296
Sharpsville (A3)*.................5,414
Shawanese (K3)*................... 200
Shawmut (E3)...........................
Shawnee on Delaware (N3)*............. 200
Sheakleyville (B3)*............... 141
Sheffield (D2)*.....................2,087
Shelocta ‡(D4)*....................... 105
Shenandoah (K4)*..............15,704
Shenango (A3)*..................... 200
Sheppton (K4)*..........................
Shermans Dale (H5)*................ 83
Shickshinny (K3)*..................2,156
Shillington (K5)*.....................5,059
Shinglehouse (F2)*................1,201
Shippensburg (H5)*................5,722
Shippenville (D3)*.................... 522
Shippingport ‡(B4)*................. 408
Shiremanstown ‡(H5)*.............. 887
Shirleysburg (G5)*.................... 241
Shoemakersville (K4)*..1,066
Shohola (N3)*........................... 600
Shohola Falls (N3)*..................... 70
Shrewsbury (J6)*........................ 787
Shunk (J2)*................................... 60
Sidman (E5)*............................... 490
Sigel (D3)*.................................. 600
Silverdale ‡(M5)*........................ 384
Simpson (M2)*.........................2,800
Sinking Spring (K5)*.............1,982
Sinnamahoning (G3)*.................. 450
Six Mile Run (F5)*....................... 400
Skinners Eddy (K2)*.................... 225
Skippack (M5)*............................ 425
Skytop (M3)*................................. 25
Slate Run (H3)*..............................
Slatedale (L4)*............................... 800
Slatington (L4)*..........................4,343
Slickville (C5)*............................1,266
Sligo (C3)*....................................... 913
Slippery Rock (B3)*..................2,294
Smethport (F2)*.............................1,797
Smicksburg (D4)*............................. 92
Smithfield (C6)*..............................1,066
Smithmill (F4)*................................1,500
Smithton (C5)*................................ 690
Snow Shoe (G3)*............................. 670
Snydertown (J4)*.............................. 314
Soldier (E3)... 300
Somerfield ‡(D6)..................................
Somerset (D6)*..............................5,936
Sonestown (K3)*................................ 275
Souderton (M5)*..............................4,521
South Bend (D4)*................................ 100
S. Bethlehem ‡(D4)............................ 489
S. Coatesville ‡(L6).........................1,996
S. Connellsville (D6)*.....................2,610
S. Fork (E5)*.....................................2,616
S. Greensburg ‡(C5).........................2,980
S. Heights (B4)*..................................... 691
S. Mountain (H6)*...............................1,300
S. New Castle ‡(B4)............................... 993
S. Philipsburg ‡(F4)................................ 512
S. Renovo (G3).. 862
S. Waverly (J2).....................................1,298
S. Williamsport (J3)............................6,364
Southmont ‡(E5)...................................2,278
Southwest (C5)*.. 800
Southwest Greensburg ‡(C5) 3,144
Spangler (E4)*...3,013
Spartansburg (C2)*................................... 482
Speers ‡(C5)...1,089
Spinnerstown (M5)*.................................... 400
Spring City (L5)*......................................3,258
Spring Creek (D2)*..................................... 160
Spring Grove (J6)*...................................1,238
Spring Mills (G4)*.. 720
Springboro (B2)*... 611
Springdale (C4)*..4,939
Springfield (M7)*..8,000
Springtown (M4)*.. 600
Springville (L2)*.. 250
Spruce Creek (F4)*... 150
Starrucca (M2)*... 326
State College (G4)*.....................................17,227
State Line (G6)*... 375
Steelton (J5)*...12,574
Sterling (M3)*.. 40
Sterling Run (F3)*... 225
Stewartstown (K6)*..1,133
Stillwater (K3)*.. 189
Stockdale ‡(C5)*... 870
Stockertown (M4)*.. 757
Stoneboro (B3)*..1,294
Stowe (L5)*...2,524
Stowe (B7)...^12,210
Stoystown (E5)*.. 517
Strasburg (K6)*..1,109
Strattanville (D3)*.. 562
Strausstown (K5)*.. 368
Stroudsburg (M4)*...6,361
Stump Creek (E3)*.. 675
Sturgeon (B5)*..1,150
Sugar Notch (L3)*..2,002
Sugargrove (D1)*.. 520
Summer Hill (E5)*.. 849
Summerville (D3)*.. 933
Summit Hill (L4)*...4,294
Sunbury (J4)*..15,570
Surveyor (F3)*.. 53
Susquehanna (L2)*...2,646
Sutersville ‡(C5)*.. 854
Swarthmore (M7)*...4,825
Sweet Valley (K3)*.. 200
Swissvale (C7)*..16,488
Swoyersville ‡(L3)..7,795
Sycamore (B6)*.. 22
Sykesville (E3)*..1,652
Sylvan (G6)*.. 22
Sylvania (J2)*.. 211
Tamaqua (L4)*..11,508
Tamarack (G3).. 60
Tannersville (M3)*.. 500
Tarentum (C4)*...9,540
Tatamy (M4)*.. 681
Taylor (L3)*...7,176
Taylorstown (A5)*.. 400
Telford ‡(M5)*...2,042
Temple (L5)*...1,460
Templeton (C4)*..1,000
Terre Hill (L5)*...1,000
Thomasville (J6)*.. 320
Thompson (L2)*........... 320
Thompsontown (H4)*..... 486
Thornburg ‡(B7)........... 335
Thornhurst (L3)*........... 100
Three Springs (G5)*..... 417
Throop (L3)*.................5,861
Tidioute (D2)*................ 998
Timblin (D4)*................ 327
Tioga (H2)*................... 544
Tiona (D2)*................... 350
Tionesta (C2)*............... 728
Tipton (F4)*................... 425
Tire Hill (E5)*............... 700
Titusville (C2)*..............8,923
Tobyhanna (M3)*............ 825
Topton (L5)*..................1,572
Torpedo (D2)*................... 65
Torrance (D5)*................ 500
Toughkenamon (L6)*........ 500
Towanda (J2)*................4,069
Tower City (J4)*.............2,054
Townville (C2)*................ 351
Trafford (C5)*................3,965
Trainer (L7)...................2,001
Transfer (A3)*................. 400
Trappe ‡(M5)................... 773
Tremont (K4)*................2,102
Trevorton (J4)*...............2,545
Trexlertown (L4*).............. 500
Trough Creek (F5)................ 60
Trout Run (H3)*................. 325
Troutville ‡(E3)*................. 223
Troxelville (H4)*.................. 130
Troy (J2)*..........................1,371
Truemans (D2)*..................... 80
Trumbauersville (M5)*.. 838
Tryonville (C2)*...................... 134
Tullytown (N5)*...................... 648
Tunkhannock (L2)*................2,170
Tunnelhill ‡(E5)....................... 535
Turbotville (J3)*....................... 518
Turtle Creek (C7)*.................12,363
Turtlepoint (F2)*........................ 150
Twilight ‡(C5).............................. 318
Twin Rocks (E4)*......................1,850
Tyler (F3)*................................... 250
Tylersburg (D3)*.......................... 215
Tylersville (G4)*.......................... 200
Tyrone (F4)*..............................8,214
Ulster (J2)*................................... 400
Ulysses (G2)*................................ 495
Union City (C2)*.......................3,911
Union Dale (M2)*.......................... 350
Union Deposit (J5)*....................... 550
Uniontown (C6)*.....................20,471
Uniontown ‡(J4).........................1,280
Unionville ‡(H4)*.............................. 341
Unity (C4)*.. 700
Unityville (K3)*.................................... 55
Universal (C7)*.................................3,200
Upland (L7)*.....................................4,081
Upper Black Eddy (N4)*.... 550
Upper Darby (M6)*..^84,951
Upper Strasburg (G5)*.. 262
Urban (J4)*.. 100
Ursina (D6)*.. 334
Utica (C3)*.. 264
Uwchland (L5)*...................................... 300
Valencia (C4)*... 298
Valier (D4)*.. 600
Valley Forge (L5)*..................................... 475
Valley View (J4)*......................................1,618
Van (C3)*.. 75
Vanderbilt (C5)*... 937
Vandergrift (D4)*......................................9,524
Vandling (M2)*.. 722
Vanport (B4)*...2,500
Venango (B2)*... 359
Venus (C3)*... 150
Verona (C6)*..4,235
Versailles (C7)...2,484
Villanova (M6)*...1,500
Vintage (K5)... 150
Vintondale (E5)*.........1,185
Volant (B3)*................... 229
Wall (C5)*......................1,850
Wallaceton (F4)*............ 440
Wallingford (L7)*...........6,000
Walnut (G4)*...................... 85
Walnut Bottom (H5)*.. 325
Walnutport (L4)*...........1,427
Walston (D4)*.................. 330
Wampum (B4)*..............1,090
Wanamie (L3)*..............1,092
Wapwallopen (K3)*....... 377
Warfordsburg (F6)*........ 105
Warren (D2)*................14,849
Warren Center (K2)*...... 275
Warrendale (B4)*............ 600
Warrensville (J3)*........... 175
Warrior Run ‡(L3)..........1,056
Warriors Mark (F4)*........ 225
Washington (B5)*........26,280
Washington Boro ‡(K6)* 483
Washington Crossing (N5)* 300
Washingtonville (J3)*...... 194
Waterford (B2)*...............1,195
Watsontown (J3)*.............2,327
Wattsburg (C1)*................ 343
Wawa (L7)*...................... 600
Waymart (M2).................1,068
Wayne (M6)*..................6,000
Waynesboro (G6)*..........10,334
Waynesburg (B6)*............5,514
Weatherly (L4)*................2,622
Webster (C5)*.......................
Webster Mills (F6)*............. 95
Weedville (F3)*..................... 700
Weissport ‡(L4)*.................. 674
Wellersburg (E6)*.................. 369
Wellsboro (H2)*...................4,215
Wellscreek (E5)...................... 100
Wellsville (J5)*....................... 309
Wernersville (K5)*...............1,280
Wesley (C3)................................ 80
Wesleyville (C1)*..................3,411
West Alexander (B5)*.. 466
W. Bridgewater (B4)*..1,316
W. Brownsville (C5)*....1,610
W. Chester (L6)*........15,168
W. Conshohocken ‡(M5)* 2,482
W. Easton ‡(M4)................1,368
W. Elizabeth (C5)*..............1,137
W. Fairview ‡(J5)*..............1,896
West Finley (B5)*..................... 93
W. Grove (L6)*......................1,521
W. Hazleton (K4)*................6,988
W. Hickory (C2)*..................... 400
W. Homestead ‡(B7)....3,257
W. Kittanning ‡(C4)............... 910
W. Lawn (K5)*.......................2,144
W. Leechburg ‡(C4).............1,113
W. Leesport ‡(L5)*.................. 535
W. Liberty ‡(C5)....................... 245
W. Mayfield ‡(B4).................1,768
W. Middlesex (B3)*...............1,217
W. Middletown (A5)*............... 268
W. Mifflin (C7)*....................17,985
W. Milton (J3)*.......................... 700
W. Monterey (C3)*..................... 125
W. Nanticoke (K3)*................1,780
W. Newton (C5)*....................3,619
W. Pittsburg (B4)*...................... 900
W. Pittston ‡(L3)*..................7,230
W. Reading ‡(L5)....................5,072
W. Salisbury (D6)*...................... 300
W. Springfield (B2)*.....................
W. Sunbury (B4)*........................ 262
W. Union (B6)................................ 25
W. View (B6)*............................7,581
W. Winfield (C4)*......................... 600
W. Wyoming ‡(L3).....................2,863
W. York ‡(J6)............................5,756
Westfield (H2)*............1,357
Westford (A2)*..................... 47
Westland (B5)*................1,025
Westline (E2)*...................... 150
Westmont ‡(C5)...............4,410
Weston (K4)*...................... 602
Westover (E4)*.................... 605
Westport (G3)*.................... 221
Westtown (L6)*................... 258
Westville (E3)*.................... 250
Wharton (G2)......................... 50
Wheatland (B3)*..............1,402
Wheelerville (J2)*................. 34
Whitaker (C7)*.................2,149
White Haven (L3)*...........1,461
White Mills (M2)*................ 600
White Oak (C7).................6,159
Whitedeer (J3)*.................... 300
Whitehall (B7)....................7,342
Whitney (D5)*...................... 875
Wiconisco (J4)*.................1,549
Widnoon (D4)*..................... 350
Wilawana (J2)*..................... 100
Wilcox (E2)*......................1,000
Wilkes-Barre (L3)*........76,826
Wilkes-Barre (urban area) 270,978
Wilkinsburg (C7)*..........31,418
Williamsburg (F5)*..........1,792
Williamsport (H3)*.......45,047
Williamstown (J4)*..........2,332
Willock (B7)*........................ 275
Willow Grove (M5)*.........7,000
Willow Hill (G5)*................ 440
Wilmerding (C7)*..............5,325
Wilmore (E5)*...................... 390
Wilpen (D5)*..........................
Wilson (M4)*......................8,159
Winburne (F4)*..................... 785
Windber (E5)*.....................8,010
Windgap (M4)*....................1,577
Windsor (J6)*.......................1,126
Winfield (J4)*........................ 320
Wingate (G4)*........................ 216
Winterdale (M2)........................ 50
Winterstown ‡(J6).................. 298
Winton (M3)...........................6,280
Wolfdale (B5)*......................... 800
Wolfsburg (F5)........................... 125
Womelsdorf (K5)*..................1,549
Woodbury (F5)*........................ 254
Woodcock (C2)........................... 130
Woodland (F4)*.....................1,000
Woodlyn (M7)*......................5,000
Woodruff (B6).............................. 25
Woodville (B7)*......................3,775
Woolrich (H3)*......................... 450
Wormleysburg ‡(J5)*.....1,511
Worthington (C4)*................... 800
Worthville (D3)*........................ 73
Wrights (F2)*............................ 250
Wrightsville (J5)*....................2,104
Wyalusing (K2)*........................ 612
Wyoming (L3)*.......................4,511
Wyomissing (K5)*...................4,187
Wyomissing Hills ‡(K5) 646
Wysox (K2)*.............................. 250
Yardley (N5)*..........................1,916
Yatesboro (D4)*......................1,264
Yatesville ‡(L3)......................... 565
Yeadon (N7)*........................11,068
Yeagertown (G4)*....................1,628
Yoe ‡(J6)*................................... 681
York (J6)*...............................59,953
York (urban area).................78,495
York Haven (J5)*........................ 743
York Springs (H6)*..................... 413
Yorkana ‡(J6)*........................... 229
Youngstown (D5)*....................... 577
Youngsville (D2)*....................1,944
Youngwood (D5)*....................2,720
Yukon (C5)*...........................1,099
Zelienople (B4)*.....................2,981

Map on Page 66 **RHODE ISLAND** *Total Population 791,896*

5 COUNTIES

Bristol (J6)..................29,079
Kent (H6)......................77,763
Newport (K6)..................61,539
Providence (H5)..........574,973
Washington (H7)..........48,542

CITIES and TOWNS

Adamsville (K6)*........ 250
Albion (H5)*............... 800
Allenton (H6)*............ 250
Alton (G7)*................. 300
Anthony (H6)*............ 2,000
Arcadia (H6)............... 100
Arctic (J6).................. 3,000
Arnold Mills (J5)......... 300
Ashaway (G7)*............1,022
Ashton (J5)*...............1,000
Barrington (J6)*.........^8,246
Block Island (H8)*....... 848
Bradford (H7)*............1,024
Bridgeton (G5)............. 661
Bristol (J6)*..............^12,320
Canonchet (H7)............. 150
Carolina (H7)*............... 200
Centerdale (H5)*.......... 2,500
Central Falls (J5)*......23,550
Charlestown (H7)*.......^1,598
Chepachet (H5)*..........1,200
Clayville (H5)*.............. 300
Conimicut (J6)*..................
Coventry (H6)*............^9,869
Cranston (J5)*............55,060
Crompton (J6).............1,500
Davisville (H6)............ 1,400
East Greenwich (H6)*...........................^4,923
E. Providence (J5)*..^35,871
Esmond (H5)*............. 2,000
Exeter (H6)*...............^1,870
Farmingdale (H5).......
Fiskeville (H6)*...........
Foster (H5).................^1,630
Foster Center (H5)*...... 225
Georgiaville (H5)*........1,247
Glendale (H5)*.............. 243
Greene (G6)*.................. 71
Greenville (H5)*...........2,000
Hamilton (J6)*................ 950
Harmony (H5)*................ 500
Harrisville (H5)*...........1,055
Hillsgrove (J6)*..................
Hope (H6)*..................... 800
Hope Valley (H6)*.........1,000
Hopkinton (H7)*..........^3,676
Howard (J5)*...............6,000
Jamestown (J6)*..........^2,068
Kenyon (H7)*.................. 100
Kingston (J7)*...............2,156
La Fayette (H6)*.............. 550
Little Compton (K6)*.^1,556
Lonsdale (J5)*...............2,500
Lymansville (J5)..................
Manton (J5)................. 2,500
Manville (H5)*...............3,429
Mapleville (H5)*.............1,015
Middletown (J6)..........^7,382
Narragansett (J7)*.....^2,288
Nasonville (H5)................ 677
Natick (H6)*.................. 2,000
Newport (J7)*...............37,564
North Scituate (H5)*. 1,000
N. Tiverton (K6)............ 4,000
Norwood (J5)................. 2,300
Oak Lawn (H5)*................ 600
Oakland (H5)*.................. 226
Oakland Beach (J6)*..10,000
Pascoag (H5)*................1,760
Pawtucket (J5)*............81,436
Peace Dale (J7)*............ 2,177
Phenix (H6)*................... 1,500
Phillipsdale (J5)............. 1,500
Pontiac (J6)*.........................
Portsmouth (J6)*........^6,578
Potter Hill (H7)*.............. 400
PROVIDENCE (H5)*.248,674
Providence (urban area) 581,607
Prudence (J6)......................
Prudence Island (J6)* 80
River Point (H6)........... 1,000
Riverside (J5)*............10,000
Rockville (G6)*................ 175
Rumford (J5)*.............10,000
Saunderstown (J6)*.... 450
Saylesville (J5)*........... 3,500
Shannock (H7)*................ 300
Shawomet (J6).............. 1,500
Slatersville (H4)*.......... 1,780
Slocum (H6)*.................... 100
South Foster (H5)...............
Stillwater (H5)....................
Summit (H6)...................... 110
Tarkiln (H5)....................... 191
Thornton (H5)......................
Tiverton (K6)*..............^5,659
Tiverton Four Corners (K6).......................... 12
Usquepaug (H6)................. 142
Valley Falls (J5)*.............2,500
Wakefield (H7)*.............. 3,047
Warren (J6).....................^8,513
Warwick (J6)*................43,028
Warwick Neck (J6)*.............
Washington (H6)*............ 2,800
Watch Hill (G7)*................. 750
Weekapaug (G7)*................ 200
West Barrington (J5)* 4,250
W. Glocester (G5)................. 100
W. Greenwich (H6)........^ 847
W. Kingston (H7)*.............. 500
Westerly (G7)*..............^12,380
Wickford (J6)*................. 2,437
Wood River Jct. (H7)* 103
Woonsocket (J4)*...........50,211
Wyoming (H6)*.................... 315

Map on Page 84

SOUTH CAROLINA

Total Population 2,117,027

46 COUNTIES

Abbeville (B3)...22,456
Aiken (D4)...53,137
Allendale (E6)...11,773
Anderson (B2)...90,664
Bamberg (F5)...17,533
Barnwell (E5)...17,266
Beaufort (F7)...26,993
Berkeley (G5)...30,251
Calhoun (F4)...14,753
Charleston (H6)...164,856
Cherokee (D1)...34,992
Chester (E2)...32,597
Chesterfield (G2)...36,236
Clarendon (G4)...32,215
Colleton (F6)...28,242
Darlington (H3)...50,016
Dillon (J3)...30,930
Dorchester (G5)...22,601
Edgefield (D4)...16,591
Fairfield (E3)...21,780
Florence (H3)...79,710
Georgetown (J5)...31,762
Greenville (C2)...168,152
Greenwood (C3)...41,628
Hampton (E6)...18,027
Horry (J4)...59,820
Jasper (E6)...10,995
Kershaw (F3)...32,287
Lancaster (F2)...37,071
Laurens (D2)...46,974
Lee (G3)...23,173
Lexington (E4)...44,297
Marion (J3)...33,110
Marlboro (H2)...31,766
McCormick (C4)...9,577
Newberry (D3)...31,771
Oconee (A2)...39,050
Orangeburg (F5)...68,726
Pickens (B2)...40,058
Richland (F3)...142,565
Saluda (D3)...15,924
Spartanburg (D2)...150,349
Sumter (G4)...57,634
Union (D2)...31,334
Williamsburg (H4)...43,807
York (E2)...71,596

CITIES and TOWNS

Abbeville (C3)*...5,395
Adams Run (G6)*...250
Adamsburg (D2)*...150
Adrian (J4)*...150
Aiken (D4)*...7,083
Alcolu (G4)*...800
Allendale (E5)*...2,474
Allsbrook (K3)...200
Anderson (B2)*...19,770
Andrews (H5)*...2,702
Angelus (G2)*...50
Antioch (F3)...350
Antreville (B3)...300
Appleton (E5)*...
Aragon Mills (E2)...
Arcadia (C2)*...2,554
Ariail (B2)*...1,098
Arthur (E3)...50
Ashepoo (G6)*...150
Ashton (E5)*...
Atkins (G3)*...50
Awendaw (H5)*...75
Aynor (J3)*...551
Badham (F5)...118
Baldock (E5)*...80
Baldwin Mills (E2)*...1,440
Ballentine (E3)*...150
Bamberg (E5)*...2,954
Barnwell (E5)*...2,005
Batesburg (D4)*...3,169
Bath (D5)*...1,232
Beaufort (F7)*...5,081
Belton (C2)*...3,371
Belton Mills (B2)...1,500
Bennetts Point (G6)*...73
Bennettsville (H2)*...5,140
Bethera (H5)*...
Bethune (G3)*...639
Bingham (H3)...169
Bishopville (G3)*...3,076
Blacksburg (D1)*...2,056
Blackstock (E2)*...
Blackville (E5)*...1,294
Blair (E3)*...74
Blaney (F3)*...183
Blenheim (H2)*...153
Blue Brick (J3)*...
Bluffton (F7)*...474
Blythewood (E3)*...400
Bonneau (H5)*...408
Bordeaux (B4)...75
Borden (G3)*...50
Bowling Green (E1)*...
Bowman (F5)*...857
Boykin (F3)*...13
Bradley (C3)*...100
Branchville (F5)*...1,353
Bristow (H3)...50
Brogdon (G4)...25
Brookgreen (K4)...
Brunson (E6)*...607
Bucksport (J4)*...800
Bucksville (J4)*...
Buffalo (D2)*...1,580
Burgess (J4)*...200
Burnettown ‡(D5)...578
Burton (F7)*...275
Cades (H4)*...150
Caesars Head (B1)*...16
Calhoun (B2)*...
Calhoun Falls (B3)*...2,396
Callison (C3)*...50
Camden (F3)*...6,986
Cameron (F4)*...630
Campobello (C1)*...394
Canadys (F5)*...150
Carlisle (D2)*...405
Cartersville (H3)*...96
Cashville (C2)...58
Cassatt (G3)*...125
Catawba (F2)*...150
Cateechee (B2)*...650
Cayce (E4)*...3,294
Cedar Springs (D2)*...1,500
Centenary (J3)*...
Central (B2)*...1,263
Chapin (E3)*...327
Chappells (D3)*...199
Charleston (G6)*...70,174
Charleston (urban area)...116,441
Cheraw (H2)*...4,836
Cherokee Falls (D1)*...
Chesnee (D1)*...1,051
Chester (E2)*...6,893
Chesterfield (G2)*...1,530
Chisolm (F6)...5
Claremont (G4)...
Clarks Hill (C4)*...
Claussen (H3)*...
Clearwater (D4)*...800
Clemson (B2)*...1,204
Cleveland (C1)*...250
Clifton (D2)*...1,707
Clinton (D3)*...7,168
Clio (H2)*...837
Clover (E1)*...3,276
Colliers (C4)...175
COLUMBIA (F4)*...86,914
Columbia (urban area)...119,747
Conestee (C2)*...750
Congaree Field (F4)...50
Converse (D2)*...1,200
Conway (J4)*...6,073
Cooper (H4)*...200
Coosawhatchie (F6)*...
Cope (E5)*...209
Cordesville (H5)*...450
Cordova (F5)*...175
Coronaca (C3)*...
Cottageville (G6)*...553
Coward (H4)*...500
Cowpens (D1)*...1,879
Crescent Beach (K4)*...540
Creston (F4)...75
Crete (B2)...
Crocketville (E6)*...120
Cross (G5)*...85
Cross Anchor (D2)*...350
Cross Hill (D3)*...543
Cross Keys (D2)...250
Crow Creek (B2)...40
Cummings (E6)...
Dacusville (B2)*...95
Dale (F6)*...300
Dalzell (G3)*...209
Darlington (H3)*...6,619
Daufuskie Island (F7)*...270
Davis Station (G4)*...200
Denmark (E5)*...2,814
Dents (F3)...1,000
Dillon (J3)*...5,171
Donalds (C3)*...332
Dorchester (G5)*...250
Dovesville (H3)*...250
Drake (H3)*...200
Drayton (D2)*...1,228
Due West (C3)*...1,033
Dunbar (H2)*...200
Duncan (C2)*...599
Eadytown (G5)...250
Early Branch (F6)*...250
Easley (B2)*...6,316
Eastover (F4)*...564
Eau Claire (E3)*...9,238
Ebenezer (E2)...680
Edgefield (C4)*...2,518
Edgemoor (E2)*...258
Edisto Island (G6)*...2,500
Effingham (H3)*...200
Ehrhardt (E5)*...510
Elko (E5)*...142
Elliott (G3)*...
Elloree (F4)*...1,127
Enoree (D2)*...1,045
Estill (E6)*...1,659
Eureka (D4)...50
Eureka Mills (E2)...1,990
Eutawville (G5)*...478
Fair Play (A2)*...250
Fairfax (E6)*...1,567
Fairforest (C2)*...800
Fairmont (D2)*...250
Filbert (E1)*...200
Fingerville (D1)*...400
Florence (H3)*...22,513
Floyd Dale (J3)*...100
Folly Beach (H6)*...800
Forest Acres (F3)...3,240
Foreston (G4)*...
Fork (J3)*...115
Fork Shoals (C2)...250
Fort Lawn (F2)*...216
Fort Mill (F1)*...3,204
Fort Motte (F4)*...350
Fountain Inn (C2)*...1,325
Four Holes (G5)*...200
Frogmore (F7)*...200
Furman (E6)*...293
Gable (G4)*...90
Gadsden (F4)*...
Gaffney (D1)*...8,123
Galivants Ferry (J3)*...150
Garnett (E6)*...100
Gaston (E4)*...250
Georgetown (J5)*...6,004
Giant (G5)...
Gifford (E6)*...
Gilbert (E4)*...172
Gillisonville (E6)...25
Givhans (G5)...100
Glendale (D2)*...1,244
Glenn Springs (D2)*...
Gluck (B3)*...1,634
Goldville (Joanna*) (D3)...1,730
Goose Creek (H6)*...600
Gossett Mills (B2)...
Govan (E5)*...109
Gowensville (C1)...100
Gramling (C1)*...200
Graniteville (D4)*...3,362
Gray Court (C2)*...479
Grays (E6)...50
Great Falls (F2)*...3,533
Greeleyville (H4)*...600
Green Pond (F6)*...
Green Sea (J3)*...500
Greenville (C2)*...58,161
Greenwood (C3)*...13,806
Greer (C2)*...5,050
Gresham (J4)*...150
Grover (F5)*...145
Gurley (J3)*...300
Hagood (F3)*...4
Hamburg (D5)...
Hamer (J3)*...500
Hampton (E6)*...2,007
Hardeeville (E7)*...546
Harleyville (G5)*...483
Hartsville (G3)*...5,658
Heath Springs (F2)*...694
Helena (D3)*...
Hemingway (J4)*...821
Hendersonville (F6)...
Henry (J4)...100
Herbert (E2)...25
Hickory Grove (E2)*...275
Hilda (E5)*...304
Hiltonhead (F7)*...1,600
Hodges (C3)*...275
Holly Hill (G5)*...1,116
Hollywood (G6)*...246
Honea Path (C3)*...2,840
Honey Hill (H5)*...69
Hopkins (F4)*...125
Horatio (G3)*...50
Huger (H5)*...500
Hyman (H4)*...150
Industrial Mills (E2)...1,868
Inman (C1)*...1,514
Irmo (E3)*...281
Islandton (F6)*...25
Isle of Palms (H6)*...1,379
Iva (B3)*...1,164
Jackson (D5)*...500
Jacksonboro (G6)*...150
Jalapa (D3)...50
Jamestown (H5)*...1,100
Jamison (F4)...75
Jedburg (G5)*...500
Jefferson (G2)*...556
Jenkinsville (E3)*...
Joanna (D3)*...1,730
Jocassee (A2)...25
Johns Island (G6)*...5,000
Johnsonville (J4)*...616
Johnston (D4)*...1,426
Jonesville (D2)*...1,345
Jordan (G4)...15
Jordanville (J4)...150
Kathwood (D5)*...30
Kelton (D2)*...90
Kershaw (G2)*...1,376
Killian (F3)...50
Kinards (D3)*...
Kings Creek (E1)*...140
Kingsburg (H4)...50
Kingstree (H4)*...3,621
Kingville (F4)...100
Kirksey (C3)...
Kline (E5)*...230
La France (B2)*...
Ladson (G6)*...500
Lake City (H4)*...5,112
Lake View (J3)*...653
Lamar (G3)*...958
Lancaster (F2)*...7,159
Lancaster Mills (F2)...4,313
Lando (E2)*...500
Landrum (C1)*...1,333
Lane (H5)*...580
Lanford (C2)*...250
Langley (D4)*...3,000
Latta (J3)*...1,602
Laurens (C3)*...8,658
Leeds (E2)*...150
Lees (E5)...25
Leesville (E4)*...1,453
Lena (E6)*...71
Leo (H4)*...350
Lesslie (E2)*...275
Level Land (C3)...230
Levys (E7)*...50
Lewis Turnout (E2)...
Lexington (E4)*...1,081
Liberty (B2)*...2,291
Liberty Hill (F3)*...200
Lincolnville (G6)...278
Little Mountain (E3)*...213
Little River (K4)*...108
Little Rock (J3)*...150
Livingston (E4)*...210
Lobeco (F6)*...137
Lockhart (D2)*...1,685
Lodge (F5)*...316
Lone Star (F4)*...50
Long Creek (A2)*...35
Longs (K4)*...300
Longtown (F3)...
Loris (K3)*...1,614
Lowndesville (B3)*...252
Lowrys (E2)*...368
Lugoff (F3)*...
Luray (E6)*...102
Lydia (G3)*...
Lydia Mills (D3)*...1,212
Lykesland (F4)*...300
Lyman (C2)*...1,365
Lynchburg (G3)*...506
Macbeth (H5)*...100
Madison (A2)*...450
Manning (G4)*...2,775
Marietta (C1)*...1,000
Marion (J3)*...6,834
Mars Bluff (H3)*...
Martin (D5)*...
Mauldin (C2)*...300
Mayesville (G4)*...706
Mayo (D1)*...500
McBee (G3)*...420
McClellanville (H5)*...417
McColl (H2)*...2,688
McConnells (E2)*...255
McCormick (C4)*...1,744
Meggett (G6)*...224
Meriwether (C4)...
Miley (E6)*...300
Millettville (D5)*...
Minturn (J2)*...47
Modoc (C4)*...150
Monarch Mills (D2)...2,158
Moncks Corner (G5)*...1,818
Monetta (D4)*...
Mont Clare (H3)*...150
Monticello (E3)*...100
Montmorenci (D4)*...425
Moore (D2)*...300
Morgana (D4)...50
Moselle (E6)...30
Mount Carmel (B3)*...84
Mount Croghan (G2)*...209
Mount Holly (H5)*...
Mount Pleasant (H6)*...1,857
Mountain Rest (A2)*...
Mountville (C3)*...
Mullins (J3)*...4,916
Murrells Inlet (K4)*...50
Myers (H6)*...
Myrtle Beach (K4)*...3,345
Naval Base (G6)*...
Neeses (E4)*...328
Nesmith (H4)*...72
New Ellenton (D5)...
New Town Village (J3)...650
New Zion (H4)*...140
Newberry (D3)*...7,546
Newry (B2)*...1,000
Nichols (J3)*...380
Nimmons (B1)*...130
Nine Times (B2)...
Ninety Six (D3)*...1,556
Nixonville (K4)*...
Norris (B2)*...325
North (E4)*...954
North Augusta (C5)*...3,659
North Charleston (G6)*...18,000
North Mullins (J3)...297
Norway (E5)*...476
Oakland Mill (D3)...621
Oakley (G5)*...150
Oakway (A2)...99
Ocean Drive Beach (K4)*...255
Oceda (H5)...300
Ogden (E2)...12
Olanta (H4)*...586
Olar (E5)*...414
Ora (D2)*...185
Orangeburg (F4)*...15,322
Orr (B3)*...2,625
Osborn (G6)*...100
Oswego (G3)*...300
Owings (C2)*...200
Pacolet (D2)*...455
Pacolet Mills (D2)*...2,170
Padgetts (F5)...35
Pageland (G2)*...1,925
Pamplico (H4)*...728
Paris (C2)*...200
Parksville (C4)*...198
Parr (E3)*...100
Paris Island (F7)*...
Patrick (G2)*...310
Pauline (D2)*...200
Pawleys Island (J5)*...2,000
Paxville (G4)*...208
Peak (E3)*...134
Peedee (H3)*...150
Pelham (C2)*...750
Pelion (E4)*...196
Pelzer (B2)*...2,692
Pendleton (B2)*...1,432
Perry (E4)*...133
Pickens (B2)*...1,961
Pickens Mill (B2)...1,000
Piedmont (C2)*...2,673
Pineland (E6)*...
Pineville (H5)*...500
Pinewood (G4)*...578
Pinopolis (G5)*...300
Plantersville (J4)*...100
Pleasant Hill (F2)...200
Pleasant Lane (D4)...102
Plum Branch (C4)*...158
Pomaria (E3)*...251
Pontiac (F3)...45
Port Royal (F7)*...793
Poston (J4)*...100
Pregnall (G5)...200
Princeton (C2)*...
Pritchardville (E7)*...200
Prosperity (D3)*...699
Rains (J3)*...50
Ravenel (G6)*...337
Red River (F2)...346
Reevesville (F5)*...285
Reidville (C2)*...236
Rembert (G3)*...300
Renno (D2)*...100
Rhems (H4)...
Richburg (E2)*...238
Richland (A2)*...75
Richtex (E3)*...85
Ridge Spring (D4)*...598
Ridgeland (E7)*...1,078
Ridgeville (G5)*...507
Ridgeway (F3)*...414
Rimini (G4)*...250
Rion (E3)*...500
Ritter (F6)*...
Riverside (E2)...30
Rock Hill (E2)*...24,502
Rocky Bottom (B1)...100
Rodman (E2)*...750
Round O (F6)*...103
Rowesville (F5)*...363
Ruby (G2)*...315
Ruffin (F6)*...500
Russellville (H5)*...300
Saint Andrews (G6)*...20,000
Saint Charles (G3)*...100
Saint George (F5)*...1,938
Saint Matthews (F4)*...2,351
Saint Paul (G4)...125
Saint Stephen (H5)*...1,341
Salem (A2)*...504
Salley (E4)*...407
Salters (H4)*...
Saluda (D4)*...1,594
Samaria (E4)*...100
Sandy Springs (B2)*...500
Santee (F5)*...107
Santuck (D2)*...300
Sardinia (G4)*...150
Scotia (E6)*...226
Scranton (H4)*...602
Seabrook (F6)*...500
Sedalia (D2)*...300
Seiglingville (E5)...
Sellers (H3)*...530
Seneca (A2)*...3,649
Sharon (E2)*...365
Sheldon (F6)*...300
Shelton (E3)*...50
Shiloh (G4)...
Shoals Junction (C3)*...85
Shulerville (H5)*...400
Silver (G4)...15
Silverstreet (D3)*...201
Simpsonville (C2)*...1,529
Six Mile (B2)*...157
Slater (C1)*...1,000
Smith (E2)*...55
Smithboro (J3)...53
Smoaks (F5)*...130
Smyrna (E1)*...105
Snelling (E5)...34
Society Hill (H2)*...645
South Greenwood (C3)*...3,712
Spartanburg (C1)*...36,795
Springfield (E4)*...782
Starr (B3)*...282
Startex (C2)*...1,638
State Park (F3)*...
Steedman (E4)...50
Stokes (F6)...80
Stoneboro (F2)...100
Strangeville (F5)...626
Strawberry (G5)...
Strother (E3)*...25
Sullivans Island (H6)*...898
Summerton (G4)*...1,419
Summerville (G5)*...3,312
Summit (E4)*...105
Sumter (G4)*...20,185
Sunset (B1)*...40
Swansea (E4)*...762
Switzer (C2)*...64
Switzerland (E7)*...74
Sycamore (E5)*...383
Syracuse (G3)...50
Tamassee (A2)*...300
Tatum (H2)*...119
Taxahaw (F2)...40
Taylors (C2)*...1,518
Tigerville (C1)*...
Tillman (E7)*...500
Timmonsville (H3)*...2,001
Tirzah (E2)...75
Toddville (J4)*...200
Townville (B2)*...250
Tradesville (F2)...125
Travelers Rest (C2)*...1,200
Trenton (D4)*...296
Trio (H5)*...187
Troy (C3)*...242
Turbeville (G4)*...271
Ulmers (E5)*...139
Union (D2)*...9,730
Van Wyck (F2)*...100
Vance (G5)*...106
Varnville (E6)*...1,180
Vaucluse (D4)*...750
Verdery (C3)*...119
Wadmalaw Island (G6)*...2,500
Wagener (E4)*...584
Walhalla (A2)*...3,104
Wallace (H2)*...
Walterboro (F6)*...4,616
Wampee (K4)*...162
Wando (H6)*...114
Ward (D4)*...122
Ware Shoals (C3)*...3,032
Warrenville (D4)*...1,604
Wateree (F4)*...100
Waterloo (C3)*...162
Wattsville (D3)*...1,649
Wedgefield (F4)*...450
Wellford (C2)*...721
West Columbia (E4)*...4,373
West Marion (J3)...175
West Pelzer (B2)...578
West Springs (D2)...300
West Union (B2)*...429
Westminster (A2)*...2,219
Westville (F3)*...350
White Hall (F6)*...
White Oak (E3)*...200
White Pond (D5)*...275
White Rock (E3)*...250
Whitmire (D3)*...3,006
Whitney (D1)*...1,611
Wiggins (F6)*...50
Wilkins (F7)*...150
Williams (F5)*...254
Williamston (B2)*...2,782
Willington (B4)*...75
Williston (E5)*...896
Wilson (G4)*...300
Windsor (D5)*...
Winnsboro (E3)*...3,267
Winnsboro Mills (E3)...2,936
Wisacky (G3)*...135
Wolfton (E4)*...40
Woodford (E4)*...179
Woodruff (D2)*...3,831
Woodward (E2)*...150
Yemassee (F6)*...712
Yonges Island (G6)*...
York (E1)*...4,181
Zion (J3)...

Map on Page 85

SOUTH DAKOTA

Total Population 652,740

67 COUNTIES

Aurora (M6)...5,020
Beadle (N5)...21,082
Bennett (F7)...3,396
Bon Homme (O7)...9,440
Brookings (R5)...17,851
Brown (N2)...32,617
Brule (L6)...6,076
Buffalo (L5)...1,615
Butte (B4)...8,161
Campbell (J2)...4,046
Charles Mix (M7)...15,558
Clark (O4)...8,369
Clay (P8)...10,993
Codington (P4)...18,944
Corson (G2)...6,168
Custer (B6)...5,517
Davison (N6)...16,522
Day (O3)...12,294
Deuel (R4)...7,689
Dewey (G3)...4,968
Douglas (N7)...5,636
Edmunds (L3)...7,275
Fall River (B7)...10,439
Faulk (L3)...4,752
Grant (R3)...10,233
Gregory (L7)...8,556
Haakon (F5)...3,167
Hamlin (P4)...7,058
Hand (L4)...7,149
Hanson (O6)...4,896
Harding (B2)...2,289
Hughes (J5)...8,111
Hutchinson (O7)...11,423
Hyde (K4)...2,811
Jackson (F6)...1,768
Jerauld (M5)...4,476
Jones (H6)...2,281
Kingsbury (O5)...9,962
Lake (P5)...11,792
Lawrence (B5)...16,648
Lincoln (R7)...12,767
Lyman (J6)...4,572
Marshall (O2)...7,835
McCook (P6)...8,828
McPherson (L2)...7,071
Meade (D5)...11,516
Mellette (H6)...3,046
Miner (O5)...6,268
Minnehaha (R6)...70,910
Moody (R5)...9,252
Pennington (C6)...34,053
Perkins (D3)...6,776
Potter (J3)...4,688
Roberts (P2)...14,929
Sanborn (N5)...5,142
Shannon (D7)...5,669
Spink (N4)...12,204
Stanley (H5)...2,055
Sully (J4)...2,713
Todd (H7)...4,758
Tripp (K7)...9,139
Turner (P7)...12,100
Union (R8)...10,792
Walworth (J3)...7,648
Washabaugh (F6)...1,551
Yankton (P7)...16,804
Ziebach (F4)...2,606

CITIES and TOWNS

Map on Page 86

TENNESSEE   Total Population 3,291,718

95 COUNTIES

Madison (D3)............60,128
Marion (K4)...............20,520
Marshall (H4)..............17,768
Maury (G3)..................40,368
Mc Minn (M4)..............32,024
Mc Nairy (D4)..............20,390
Meigs (M3)...................6,080
Monroe (N4)................24,513
Montgomery (G2)........44,186
Moore (J4).....................3,948
Morgan (M2)................15,727
Obion (C2)..................29,056
Overton (L2)................17,566
Perry (F3).......................6,462
Pickett (M1)....................5,093
Polk (N4)......................14,074
Putnam (K2).................29,869
Rhea (M3)....................16,041
Roane (M3)...................31,665
Robertson (H1).............27,024
Rutherford (J3).............40,696
Scott (M2)....................17,362
Sequatchie (L4)...............5,685
Sevier (O3)...................23,375
Shelby (B4)................482,393
Smith (K2)....................14,098
Stewart (F1).....................9,175
Sullivan (R1).................95,063
Sumner (J2)...................33,533
Tipton (B3)....................29,782
Trousdale (J2)..................5,520
Unicoi (R2)....................15,886
Union (O2)........................8,670
Van Buren (L3)..................3,985
Warren (K3)....................22,271
Washington (Q2).............59,971
Wayne (F4).....................13,864
Weakley (D2)..................27,962
White (L3)......................16,204
Williamson (H3)..............24,307
Wilson (J2).....................26,318

CITIES and TOWNS

Abiff (G3)........................ 12
Adams (G1)*................ 525
Adamsville (E4)*.......... 927
Addison (M4)................. 40
Aetna (G3)*.................. 100
Afton (Q2)*.................. 150
Alamo (C3)*................1,501
Alcoa (N3)*................6,355
Alexandria (J2)*.......... 372
Algood (K2)*............... 729
Allardt (M2)*............... 800
Allens (C3).......................
Allisona (H3)*................ 75
Allons (L2)*.................. 270
Allred (L2)*.................. 300
Alpine (L2)*.................. 200
Altamont (K4)*............ 296
Alto (K4)........................ 125
Anderson (K4)*............ 375
Andersonville (O2)*...... 525
Anes (H3)........................ 35
Annadel (M2).................. 25
Anthras (N1)................. 100
Antioch (H2)*............... 298
Apison (L5)*......................
Archville (N4)*............. 150
Ardmore (H4)*.............. 157
Arlington (B4)*............ 463
Armathwaite (M2)*........ 350
Arrington (H3)*............ 250
Arthur (O1)*................. 450
Ashland City (G2)*.......1,024
Ashport (B3)*......................
Ashwood (G3)*................ 80
Aspen Hill (G4)*........... 225
Athens (M4)*..............8,618
Atoka (B4)*.................. 334
Atwood (D3)*..............1,000
Auburntown (J3)*.......... 273
Bailey (B4)*.................. 207
Baileyton (Q2)*............ 224
Bakerville (F3)*............... 68
Bakewell (L4)*.............. 250
Banner Springs (M2)*.. 406
Barr (B3)*.............................
Barren Plains (H1)....... 100
Bartlett (B4)*................ 489
Bath Springs (E4)*.......... 50
Baugh (H4)...................... 25
Baxter (K2)*................. 861
Beacon (E3)*................. 200
Bean Station (P2)*..............
Beans Creek (J4)*........... 50
Bear Spring (F2).......... 100
Bearden (N3)..............1,600
Beardstown (F3)*.......... 100
Beech Bluff (D3)*.......... 180
Beechgrove (J3)*........... 250
Beersheba Springs (K4)* 300
Belfast (H4)*................ 150
Bell Buckle (J3)*.......... 341
Belle Meade (H2).........2,831
Belleview (H2)*............ 250
Bells (C3)*.................1,225
Belltown (N4)............... 100
Belvidere (J4)*............. 250
Bemis (D3)*...............3,248
Benton (M4)*................ 650
Berry Hill ‡(H2)*........1,248
Bethel (G4)*................. 150
Bethel Springs (D4)*.... 623
Bethpage (J1)*.............. 280
Big Lick (L3)*.............. 150
Big Rock (F1)*.............. 250
Big Sandy (E2)*............ 621
Big Spring (M4)*............ 68
Birchwood (M4)*........... 800
Blaine (O2)*................. 225
Blanche (H4)*............... 250
Block (N2)*.................. 160
Bloomington Springs
(K2)* 200
Blountville (R1)*.......... 500
Bluff City (R2)*..........1,074

Bogota (C2)*................. 300
Bolivar (C4)*..............2,429
Bon Air (L3)*............... 300
Bon Aqua (G3)*............ 120
Boom (L1)*................... 121
Boonshill (H4)................ 35
Boothspoint (B2)*......... 200
Boston (G3).................. 100
Boyds Creek (O3)*........ 485
Braden (B4)*................. 250
Bradford (D2)*.............. 599
Bradyville (J3)*............... 98
Brazil (C3).................... 140
Brentwood (H2)*...................
Briceville (N2)*...........2,500
Bridgeport (P3)*..................
Brighton (B4)*............... 306
Bristol (R1)*..............16,771
Brockdell (L3)*....................
Brotherton (L2)*............ 600
Brownsville (C3)*.........4,711
Bruceton (E2)*............1,204
Brunswick (B4)*............ 500
Brush Creek (J2)*.......... 200
Buchanan (E2)*............. 100
Buena Vista (E3)*............ 60
Buffalo (F3)*.................... 25
Buffalo Valley (K2)*.... 300
Buford (G4).........................
Bullsgap (P2)*............... 558
Bumpus Mills (F1)*....... 225
Bunker Hill (H4)........... 100
Burlison (B3)*................. 75
Burns (G2)*..........................
Burrville (M2)*.............. 230
Bybee (P2)*................... 250
Byington (N3)*.............. 125
Byrdstown (L1)*............ 379
Cades (D3)*..................... 68
Cades Cove (O3).............. 40
Cagle (L4)..................... 165
Cainsville (J3).....................
Calderwood (N3)*.......... 245
Calhoun (M4)*............... 450
Cambria (M4)................ 100
Camden (E2)*..............2,029
Campaign (K3)*............. 100
Caneyspring (H3)............. 55
Capleville (B4)*............. 950
Carderview (S2)*..................
Carter (R2).................... 600
Carters Creek (G3)*...... 250
Carthage (K2)*............1,604
Caryville (N2)*............1,234
Castalian Springs
(J2)* 129
Cedar Grove (D3)*.......... 25
Cedar Hill (H1)*............ 872
Cedarcreek (Q2)*........... 175
Celina (K1)*................1,136
Centerville (G3)*.........1,532
Cerro Gordo (E4)*........... 10
Chalybeate (K3)....................
Chanute (L1).................. 450
Chapel Hill (H3)*........... 603
Chapmansboro (G2)*...... 25
Charleston (M4)*..................
Charlotte (G2)*.............. 478
Chaska (N1)*................. 121
Chattanooga (K4)....131,041
Chattanooga (urban
area) 167,031
Cherry (B3)..........................
Chesterfield (E3)*.......... 150
Chestnut Mound (K2)*.. 150
Chewalla (D4)*.............. 150
Chilhowee (O3)*............ 150
Christiana (J3)*............. 300
Chuckey (Q2)*............... 300
Church Hill (Q1)*........1,741
Clairfield (O1)*............2,000
Clarkrange (L2)*..................
Clarksburg (E3)*............ 350
Clarksville (G1)*.........16,246
Clayton (C2).................... 30
Clementsville (K1)........... 25
Cleveland (M4)*..........12,605
Clifton (F4)*.................. 818
Clifty (L3)*....................... 51
Clinchmore (N2)*..................
Clinton (N2)*...............3,712
Clouds (O2)*.................... 50
Coalfield (M2)*....................
Coalmont (K4)*.............. 800
Coble (F3)..................... 100
Cokercreek (N4)*........... 366
Coldwater (H4)................ 85
Colesburg (G2).............. 150
College Grove (H3)*...... 300
Collegedale (M4)*........1,200
Collierville (B4)*..........1,153
Collinwood (F4)*............ 589
Columbia (G3)*............10,911
Como (E2)*.................... 120
Conasauga (M4)*........... 475
Concord (N3)*............... 294
Cookeville (L2)*...........6,924
Copperhill (N4)*............ 924
Cordova (B4)*................ 250
Cornersville (H4)*......... 358
Coryton (O2)*..............1,275
Cortner (J4)..................... 63
Cosby (P3)*..........................
Cottagegrove (E2)*........ 126
Cottontown (H2)*........... 250
Cotula (O2).................... 250
Counce (E4)*........................
Covington (B3)*...........4,379
Cowan (J4)*................1,835
Crab Orchard (M3)*...... 315
Crawford (L2)*.............. 100
Creston (L2)................... 125
Crestview (G4).............. 356
Crockett Mills (C3)*..... 148
Cross Plains (H1)*......... 200
Crossville (L3)*............2,291
Crump (E4)*.................. 500
Culleoka (G4)*............... 300
Cumberland City (F2)*.. 500

Cumberland Furnace
(G2)* 350
Cumberland Gap (O1)*.. 403
Cummingsville (L3)......... 50
Cunningham (G2)*......... 250
Curve (B3).............................
Cypress Inn (F4)*.........1,000
Daisy (L4)*..................1,336
Dale Hollow ‡(K1)............. 5
Dancyville (C4)................ 80
Dandridge (O2)*............ 690
Danville (F2)........................
Darden (E3)*................. 250
Daus (L4)*............................
Davidson (L2)........................
Daylight (K8)*............... 250
Dayton (L3)*................3,191
De Rossett (L3)*........... 250
Dean (N2)*.................... 130
Decatur (M3)*............... 235
Decaturville (E3)*......... 514
Decherd (J4)*...............1,435
Deer Lodge (M2)*.......... 275
Del Rio (P3)*................ 300
Delano (M4)*................. 350
Dellrose (H4)*............... 350
Denmark (D3)*.................. 69
Densons Landing (F3)...
Denver (F2)*.................. 130
Devonia (N2)*................ 250
Diana (H4)*..........................
Dickson (G2)*...............3,348
Difficult (K2)*............... 500
Dixon Springs (J2)*...... 200
Dodson (L3).................... 98
Doeville (S2)*................ 125
Donelson (H2)*............1,765
Double Springs (K2)*.... 200
Dover (F2)*................... 800
Dowelltown (K2)*........... 262
Doyle (K3)*.................... 500
Dresden (D2)*...............1,509
Drummonds (A4)*.......... 160
Duck River (G3)*..................
Ducktown (N4)*............1,064
Duff (N2)*.............................
Dukedom (D2)*............... 115
Dunlap (L4)*.................. 873
Dyer (D2)*...................1,864
Dyersburg (C2)*..........10,885
Eads (B4)*.................... 250
Eagan (O1)*.................. 300
Eagle Creek (E3)*................
Eagleville (H3)*............. 378
East Jamestown (M2)* 100
East Ridge (L5)*...........9,645
Eastland (L3)*......................
Eaton (C3)*..........................
Edenwold (H2)*............. 500
Eidson (P1)*.................. 300
Elbridge (C2)*................. 89
Elgin (M2)*.................... 350
Elizabethton (R2)*......10,754
Elk Valley (N1)*............. 300
Elkmont (O3)................... 35
Elkton (H4)*.................. 168
Ellendale (B4)*.............. 700
Elora (J4)*..................... 225
Elva (M1)......................... 15
Embreeville (Q2)*........1,273
Emory Gap (M3)*........... 350
Englewood (M4)*..........1,545
Enville (E4)*.................. 350
Erie (M3)*........................ 25
Erin (F2)*...................... 858
Erwin (R2)*..................3,387
Estill Springs (J4)*....... 496
Ethridge (G4)*............... 500
Etowah (M4)*...............3,261
Eva (E2)*....................... 250
Evensville (M3)*............ 450
Fairfield (J3)................ 100
Fairview (G3)*......................
Fall Branch (Q2)*.......... 300
Fall Mills (J4)................. 34
Fall River (G4)................ 50
Farmers Exchange (F3)* 134
Farmington (H3)............ 200
Farner (N4)*................... 200
Faxon (E2)*.................... 120
Fayetteville (H4)*........5,447
Finger (D4)*.................. 130
Finley (B2)*.................1,000
Five Points (G4)*.......... 125
Flag Pond (Q2)*............. 300
Flat Woods (F4)*........... 275
Flatcreek (J4).......................
Flintville (J4)*.............. 300
Florence (H3)................ 125
Flynns Lick (K2)............. 50
Forbus (M1)*................. 200
Fordtown (Q2)*.....................
Forest Hill (B4)*............ 200
Fork Mountain (N2)*...... 900
Fort Henry (E1)*.............. 10
Fort Pillow (B3)*........... 150
Fosterville (J3)*............ 200
Fountain City (O2)*....15,000
Fountain Head (J1)*...... 252
Fowlkes (C3)*................ 150
Frankewing (H4)*............ 90
Frankfort (M2)......................
Franklin (H3)*..............5,475
Frayser (A4)*........................
French Broad (P3)*........ 154
Friendship (C3)*............ 452
Friendsville (N3)*.......... 625
Fruitland (D3)*......................
Fruitvale (C3)*................. 50
Fulton (B3)*.................. 150
Gadsden (D3)*............... 255
Gainesboro (K2)*........... 992
Gallatin (H2)*...............5,107
Gallaway (B4)*............... 200
Gardner (D2)..........................
Garland (B3).................. 157
Gassaway (K3)*................ 80
Gates (C3)*.................... 234
Gatlinburg (O3)*..........1,301

Gennett (N2).................... 25
Georgetown (L4)*.......... 100
Germantown (B4)*......... 408
Gibbs (D2)..................... 100
Gibson (D3)*.................. 308
Gillises Mills (E4)...............
Gladeville (J2)*............. 114
Glass (C2)........................ 75
Gleason (D2)*..............1,063
Glen Alice (M3)............. 300
Glendale (G3)................ 130
Glenmary (M2)*............. 300
Goin (O2)*..................... 300
Golddust (B3)*................ 50
Goodlettsville (H2)*.....1,590
Goodspring (G4)*............ 31
Gordonsburg (F3)..................
Gordonsville (K2)*........ 304
Gorman (F2)..................... 80
Graham (G3)*.................. 25
Grand Junction (C4)*.. 477
Grandview (M3)*............ 250
Granville (K2)*.............. 130
Gravel Hill (D4)............... 42
Graysville (L4)*............. 820
Green Brier (H2)*.......... 890
Greenback (N3)*...........1,200
Greeneville (Q2)*.........8,721
Greenfield (D2)*...........1,706
Greenwood (J2).............. 200
Groveland (G3)................ 25
Gruetli (K4)*.................. 600
Guys (D4)*..................... 100
Habersham (N2)*........... 500
Hales Point (B3).............. 25
Haley (J4)*.................... 150
Halls (C3)*..................1,808
Hamburg (E4)................ 350
Hampshire (G3)*............ 200
Hampton (R2)*.............1,164
Harms (H4)...................... 75
Harriman (M3)*............6,389
Harris (C2)...................... 75
Harrison (L4)*............... 500
Harrogate (O1)*....................
Hartford (P3)*............... 200
Hartsville (J2)*............1,130
Hartsville Junction (J2) 40
Haydenburg (K2)*......... 100
Hebbertsburg (M2)........ 110
Heiskell (O2)*............... 130
Helenwood (M2)*........... 500
Henderson (D4)*...........2,532
Hendersonville (J2)*...1,000
Hendon (L4)*................. 125
Henning (B3)*................ 493
Henry (E2)*.................... 200
Henryville (G4)*............ 150
Hermitage (H2)*............. 800
Hermitage Springs (K1) 200
Hickman (K2)*............... 175
Hickory Point (G2)*...... 100
Hickory Valley (C4)*..... 400
Hickory Withe (C4)*....... 50
Highland Park (R1)......3,500
Hilham (L2)*.................. 177
Hillsboro (K4)*.............. 200
Hillsdale (J2)*......................
Hillside (D2).................. 160
Hitchcox (L3)*................. 98
Hixon (L4)*..................2,100
Hohenwald (F3)*...........1,703
Holladay (E3)*............... 200
Hollow Rock (E2)*......... 397
Holston Valley (R1)....... 125
Holtland (H3)*............... 400
Hopson (R2)................... 300
Horn Springs (J2)........... 200
Hornbeak (C2)*.............. 309
Hornsby (D4)*................ 280
Howell (H4)*.................. 150
Humboldt (D3)*............7,426
Huntingdon (E2)*..........2,043
Huntland (J4)*............... 285
Huntsville (N2)*...........1,400
Huron (E3)*...................... 70
Hurricane Mills (F3)*..... 35
Idlewild (D2)*................ 200
Indian Mound (F1)*....... 375
Indian Springs (R1)*..... 300
Inskip (N2)..................5,000
Iron City (F4)*............... 750
Ironsburg (N4).............. 100
Isabella (N4)*................ 400
Isham (N1)....................... 75
Isoline (L2)................... 275
Ivyton (L2)*..........................
Jacks Creek (D4)*............ 75
Jacksboro (N2)*...........1,500
Jackson (D3)*.............30,207
Jamestown (M2)*..........2,115
Jasper (K4)*................1,198
Jefferson City (P2)*......3,633
Jellico (N1)*................1,556
Joelton (H2)*................2,500
Johnson City (R2)*......27,864
Johnsonville (F2)*......... 100
Jones (C3)*.................... 140
Jonesboro (Q2)*...........1,126
Joppa (O2)...................... 85
Juno (E3)*........................ 80
Keeling (C4).................. 100
Kelso (J4)*....................... 85
Kenton (C2)*.................. 899
Kerrville (B4)*............... 300
Kimberlin Heights (O3)* 120
Kimmins (F3)*.................. 78
Kingsport (Q1)*...........19,571
Kingston (N3)*.............1,627
Kingston Springs (G2)* 390
Kinzel Springs (O3)....... 100
Kirkland (H3)................. 225
Knoxville (O3)*..........124,769
Knoxville (urban
area) 148,174
Kodak (O3)*.................1,670
Kyles Ford (P1)*.............. 75
La Follette (N2)*..........5,797
La Grange (C4)*............ 241

La Vergne (H2)*............ 500
Laager (K4)*.................. 650
Laconia (C4)*.................. 75
Lafayette (J1)*.............1,195
Lake City (N2)*............1,827
Lancing (M2)*................ 250
Lane (C2)*...................... 150
Lascassas (J3)*.............. 250
Latham (D2)..................... 85
Laurel Bloomery (S1)*.. 208
Laurel Hill (K2)*...................
Laurelburg (L3)*...................
Lavinia (D3)*................... 88
Lawrenceburg (G4)*.....5,442
Leach (E3)*...................... 15
Leapwood (E4)*.............. 110
Lebanon (J2)*...............7,913
Ledbetter (D3)................. 25
Lee Valley (P2)*............ 200
Leinarts (N2)*.................. 32
Leipers Fork (G3).......... 325
Lenoir City (N3)*..........5,159
Lenox (C2)*................... 500
Leoma (G4)*.................. 398
Lewisburg (H4)*...........5,164
Lexington (E3)*............3,566
Liberty (K2)*................. 314
Liberty Hill (O2)*..................
Limestone (Q2)*............ 450
Linary (L3)*................... 160
Linden (F3)*.................. 854
Littlecrab (L2)*............. 100
Littlelot (G3)*................ 150
Litton (L3)*...................... 25
Livingston (L2)*...........2,082
Lobelville (F3)*............. 600
Lodge (K4)*..........................
Lone Mountain (O2)*.... 175
Lonely (F2)...................... 76
Lookout Mountain
(L5)* 1,675
Loretto (G4)*................. 706
Loudon (N3)*...............3,567
Louisville (N3)*............ 130
Lucy (B4)*..................... 600
Lula (E4)*.............................
Lupton City (L4)*.........1,250
Luray (D3)*................... 300
Luther (P2)*.........................
Luttrell (O2)*................ 382
Lutts (F4)*..................... 250
Lyles (G3)*.................... 500
Lynchburg (J4)*............. 401
Lynnville (G4)*............. 356
Macon (B4)*................... 215
Madison (H2)*..............7,000
Madisonville (N3)*.......1,487
Malesus (D3)*................ 500
Manchester (J4)*..........2,341
Mansfield (E2)*.............. 110
Manson (L2)*.......................
Martel (N3)*..................... 95
Martha (J2)*..................... 25
Martin (D2)*.................4,082
Martin Springs (K4)....... 200
Martins Mills (F4)........... 33
Maryville (O3)*.............7,742
Mascot (O2)*................2,500
Mason (B4)*................... 414
Masonhall (C2).............. 175
Maury City (C3)*........... 553
Maxwell (J4)*................... 85
Mayland (L2)*............... 175
Maynardville (O2)*...............

Mc Cloud (Q2)*.............. 100
Mc Connell (D2).....................
Mc Daniel (H3)............... 100
Mc Donald (M4)*............ 150
Mc Ewen (F2)*............... 710
Mc Ghee (N3)................... 75
Mc Kenzie (E2)*...........3,774
Mc Kinnon (F2)*............ 250
Mc Lemoresville (D3)*.. 242
Mc Minnville (K3)*.......7,577
Mc Nairy (D4)*................ 90
Medina (D3)*................. 690
Medon (D4)*.................. 115
Memorial (K1)*.............. 300
Memphis (B4)*...........396,000
Memphis(urban area)404,033
Mengelwood (B2)........... 200
Mentor (O3)*.................. 425
Mercer (D4)*.................. 400
Michie (E4)*..........................
Middleton (D4)*............. 362
Midway (P2)*................. 200
Mifflin (D3).................... 250
Milan (D3)*..................4,938
Milledgeville (E4)*......... 300
Milligan College (R2)*. 213
Millington (B4)*............4,696
Milo (L3)*...................... 300
Milton (J3)*...................... 75
Minor Hill (G4)*............ 292
Miston (B2)*.................. 350
Mitchell (H1)........................
Mitchellville (J1)*.......... 202
Model (F1)*................... 140
Mohawk (P2)*................. 200
Monoville (K2)*................ 75
Monroe (L2)*.........................
Monteagle (K4)*............. 865
Monterey (L2)*.............2,043
Montezuma (D4)*........... 130
Moodyville (L1)*............. 400
Mooresburg (P2)*........... 250
Morley (O1)*.................. 300
Morris Chapel (E4)*..............
Morrison (K3)*............... 301
Morristown (P2)*.........13,019
Moscow (C4)*................ 394
Mosheim (Q2)*.............. 350
Moss (K1)*.................... 200
Mount Juliet (H2)*................
Mount Pleasant (G3)*..2,931
Mount Vernon (N4)*....... 250
Mountain City (S2)*.....1,405
Mountainy (L4)*............. 140
Mulberry (H4)*............... 220
Munford (B4)*................ 976
Murfreesboro (J3)*.......13,052
Napier (F4)....................... 75
NASHVILLE (H2)*....174,307
Nashville (urban
area) 257,898
Nemo (M2)......................... 8
Neptune (G2)*................ 125
Neubert (O3)*..............2,800
Neva (S2)*........................ 50
New Market (O2)*........... 600
New Middleton (J2)*...... 150
New Providence (G1)...1,825
New River (M2)*............. 650
New Tazewell (O2)*.....1,400
Newbern (C2)*.............1,734
Newcomb (N1)*......................
Newport (P3)*...............3,892
Niota (M3)*.................... 956

Noah (J3)........................ 100
Nolensville (H3)*...................
Norene (J2)*.................. 250
Norma (N2)*..........................
Normandy (J4)*.............. 159
Norris (N2)*.................1,134
Nunnelly (G3)*......................
Oak Ridge (N2)*..........30,229
Oakdale (M3)*................ 718
Oakfield (D3)*................ 125
Oakland (B4)*................. 236
Oakley (L2)....................... 50
Oakville (A4)................1,500
Obey City (L2).......................
Obion (C2)*..................1,212
Ocoee (M4)*.................. 225
Old Hickory (H2)*.......10,000
Oldfort (M4)*................. 133
Olivehill (E4)*................ 140
Olive Springs (N2)*......1,089
Oneida (N1)*................1,304
Only (F3)*.............................
Ooltewah (M4)*............. 900
Orlinda (H1)*................. 275
Orme (K4)*.................... 230
Overall (J3)*.................. 135
Ozone (M3)*................... 140
Pall Mall (M1)*.............. 100
Palmer (K4)*.................. 871
Palmersville (D2)*......... 100
Palmyra (G2)*................ 200
Paris (E2)*...................8,826
Parrottsville (P2)*......... 115
Parsons (E3)*...............1,640
Peakland (M3)*.....................
Peavine (M2)..................... 35
Pegram (H2)*................. 325
Pelham (K4)*.........................
Perry (D3)....................... 100
Perryville (F3)*.............. 150
Persia (P2)*..................... 50
Peters Landing (F4)*...... 40
Petersburg (H4)*............ 497
Petros (M2)*.................. 800
Philadelphia (M3)*........ 600
Phillippy (C2)*............... 375
Pickwick Dam (E4)*....... 250
Pierce Station (C2)*....... 50
Pigeon Forge (O3)*......1,500
Pikeville (L3)*............... 882
Pine Top (D4).................. 15
Pinewood (F3)..................... 5
Piney Flats (R2)*........... 300
Pinson (D4)*.................. 300
Pioneer (N2)*........................
Pittsburg Landing (E4)* 114
Plant (F3)....................... 250
Pleasant Hill (L3)*........ 152
Pleasant Shade (K2)*.... 125
Pleasant View (G2)*...... 300
Pleasantville (F3)*................
Pocahontas (D4)*........... 250
Polk (C2)*........................ 50
Pope (F3)*........................ 30
Port Royal (G1).....................
Portland (H1)*..............1,660
Postelle (N4)*................ 232
Powder Springs (O2)*... 110
Powell (N2)*.................. 400
Primm Springs (G3)*........ 4
Prospect Station (G4)* 350
Pruden (O1)*................. 250
Pulaski (G4)*................5,762
Puryear (E2)*................ 430

Quebeck (K3)*... 200
Rader (Q2)... 72
Raines (A4)...
Raleigh (B4)*...1,100
Ralston (D2)*... 78
Ramer (D4)*... 400
Rankin (P2)...
Rasar (O3)*... 200
Ravenscroft (L3)*... 96
Readyville (J3)*... 250
Reagan (E3)*... 250
Red Bank (L4)*...
Red Boiling Springs (K1)* ...1,000
Reliance (N4)*...
Reverie (A3)*... 250
Rheatown (Q2)*... 107
Riceville (M4)*... 450
Richard City (K5)*... 300
Richardsons (B4)... 50
Rickman (L2)*... 500
Riddleton (J2)*... 150
Ridgely (B2)*...1,504
Ridgeside (L4)... 337
Ridgetop (H2)*... 354
Ridley (G3)... 150
Ripley (B3)*...3,318
Riverside (F4)... 80
Rives (C2)*... 413
Roan Mountain (R2)*...1,000
Robbins (M2)*... 900
Rock Creek (M1)... 20
Rock Island (K3)*... 150
Rockdale (G4)... 25
Rockford (O3)*...1,500
Rockvale (J3)*... 139
Rockwood (M3)*...4,272
Roddy (M3)... 200
Rogers Springs (D4)*... 100
Rogersville (P2)*...2,545
Rome (J2)... 125
Rosedale (N2)*...
Rosemark (B4)... 300
Roslin (M2)*... 300
Rossville (B4)*... 175
Routon (E2)... 150
Rowland (K3)... 35
Rucker (J3)... 78
Rugby (M2)*...
Ruskin (F2)... 26
Russellville (P2)*... 608
Rutherford (C2)*... 994
Ruthville (D2)...
Rutledge (P2)*... 600
Sadlersville (G1)*... 100
Saint Andrews (K4)*...
St. Bethlehem (G1)*... 275
St. Joseph (G4)*... 550
Sale Creek (L4)*... 650
Saltillo (E4)*... 400
Samburg (C2)*... 378
Sanford (M4)...
Santa Fe (G3)*... 250
Sardis (E4)*... 299
Saulsbury (C4)*... 143
Saundersville (J2)... 200
Savannah (E4)*...1,698
Scotts Hill (E4)*... 299
Selmer (D4)*...1,759
Sequatchie (K4)*...
Serles (D4)*... 50
Servilla (M4)*... 100
Sevierville (P3)*...1,620
Sewanee (K4)*...1,407
Seymour (O3)*... 120
Shady Valley (S1)*...2,238
Sharon (D2)*... 880
Sharps Chapel (O2)*... 50
Shawanee (O1)*... 350
Shea (N2)... 150
Shelbyville (H4)*...9,456
Shell Creek (R2)*... 200
Shepherd (L4)*...1,000
Shepp (C4)*...
Sherwood (K4)*...
Shirley (M2)*... 171
Shop Spring (J2)*... 150
Shouns (S2)*... 350
Sidonia (D2)*... 175
Signal Mountain (L4)*.1,786
Silerton (D4)*... 121
Silver Point (K2)*... 150
Slayden (G2)*... 90
Smartt (K3)*... 300
Smithville (K3)*...1,558
Smokey Junction (N2)* 200
Smyrna (H3)*...1,544
Sneedville (P1)*... 500
Soddy (L4)*...2,157
Somerville (C4)*...1,760
South Dyersburg (C2)...
S. Fulton (D2)...2,119
S. Harriman (M3)...2,761
S. Pittsburg (K4)*...2,573
S. Tunnel (H2)*... 500
Southside (G2)*... 200
Sparta (K3)*...4,299
Speedwell (O2)*...
Spencer (L3)*... 721
Spring City (M3)*...1,725
Spring Hill (H3)*... 541
Springcreek (D3)*...
Springfield (H2)*...6,506
Springville (E2)*... 30
Stainville (N2)*... 800
Stanton (C4)*... 503
Stantonville (E4)*... 300
Statesville (J2)*... 150
Static (L1)*... 40
Stewart (F2)*...
Stonypoint (Q1)*...
Strawberry Plains (O2)*
Sugar Grove (J1)... 25
Sugar Tree (E3)*...
Summertown (G4)*... 300
Summitville (K3)*... 400
Sunbright (M2)*... 600
Surgoinsville (Q2)*... 800
Sweetwater (N3)*...4,199
Sycamore Landing (F3)* 53
Sylvia (G2)*... 186
Taft (H4)*... 225
Talbott (P2)*... 250
Tarlton (K3)... 75
Tasso (M4)*... 150
Tazewell (P2)*...1,000
Telford (R2)*... 300
Tellico Plains (N4)*... 833
Temperance Hall (K2).. 100
Ten Mile (M3)*...
Tennessee City (F2)*... 180
Tennessee Ridge (F2)*.. 275
Terrell (D2)*... 70
Tharpe (F1)... 30
Theta (G3)... 250
Thomasville (G2)... 27
Thompsons Station (H3)* ... 150
Thorn Hill (P2)*... 35
Tidwell (G2)... 50
Tigrett (C3)*... 175
Timothy (L2)*...
Tipton (B4)*... 35
Tiptonville (B2)*...1,953
Tobaccoport (F1)... 30
Toone (D4)*... 231
Townsend (O3)*... 328
Tracy City (K4)*...1,414
Trade (S2)*... 75
Treadway (P2)*...
Trenton (D3)*...3,868
Trezevant (D2)*... 765
Trimble (C2)*... 674
Triune (H3)... 225
Troy (C2)*... 593
Tullahoma (J4)*...7,562
Turley (N2)... 40
Turtletown (N4)*... 200
Tusculum (Q2)... 250
Twinton (L2)... 75
Tyner (L4)*...1,000
Una (H2)... 500
Unicoi (R2)*...1,500
Union City (C2)*...7,665
Unionville (H3)*... 176
Vale (E2)*... 50
Vanleer (G2)*... 243
Vasper (N2)*...
Vernon (F3)*... 150
Victoria (K4)*...
Vildo (C4)*... 75
Viola (K3)*... 223
Vonore (N3)*... 478
Wales (G4)*... 50
Walland (O3)*... 300
Walling (K3)*... 200
Walnut Grove (E4)...
Walterhill (J3)*... 200
Warren (C4)*... 75
Warrensburg (P2)... 75
Wartburg (M2)*... 400
Wartrace (J3)*... 545
Washburn (O2)*... 170
Watauga (R2)*... 500
Watauga Valley (R2)... 200
Watertown (J2)*... 933
Watts Bar Dam (M3)*.. 110
Waverly (F2)*...1,892
Waynesboro (F4)*...1,147
Weavers Store (F1)...
West Harpeth (H3)... 30
Westbourne (O1)*... 600
Western State Hospital (C4)* ...3,000
Westmoreland (J1)*... 895
Westpoint (G4)*... 350
Westport (E3)*... 175
Wetmore (N4)... 125
Wheelerton (H4)*... 65
White (B4)...
White Bluff (G2)*... 506
White Horn (Q2)...
White House (H2)*...
White Pine (P2)*... 780
Whitehaven (A4)*...1,311
Whites Creek (H2)*... 100
Whitesburg (P2)*... 500
Whiteside (K5)*... 500
Whiteville (C4)*... 794
Whitleyville (K2)*... 75
Whitlock (E2)*... 142
Whitthorne (D3)... 15
Whitwell (K4)*...1,586
Wilder (L2)*... 300
Wildersville (E3)*... 275
Willette (K2)... 100
Williamsport (G3)*... 140
Williston (C4)*... 175
Winchester (J4)*...3,974
Windrock (N2)*... 337
Winesap (L3)*... 80
Winfield (M1)*... 350
Winona (N2)*...
Woodbine (H2)*...
Woodbury (J3)*...1,000
Woodland Mills (C2)*... 175
Woodlawn (G1)*... 35
Woodstock (A4)... 300
Wooldridge (N1)*...
Wrigley (G3)*...
Wynnburg (C2)*... 200
Yorkville (C2)*... 500
Yuma (E3)*...
Zach (E2)... 100
Zenith (M2)... 40

Map on Page 87

TEXAS

Total Population 7,711,194

254 COUNTIES

Anderson (J6)...31,875
Andrews (B5)...5,002
Angelina (K6)...36,032
Aransas (H10)...4,252
Archer (F4)...6,816
Armstrong (C3)...2,215
Atascosa (F9)...20,048
Austin (H8)...14,663
Bailey (B3)...7,592
Bandera (E8)...4,410
Bastrop (G7)...19,622
Baylor (E4)...6,875
Bee (G9)...18,174
Bell (G6)...73,824
Bexar (F8)...500,460
Blanco (F7)...3,780
Borden (C5)...1,106
Bosque (G6)...11,836
Bowie (K4)...61,966
Brazoria (J3)...46,549
Brazos (H7)...38,390
Brewster (D12)...7,309
Briscoe (C3)...3,528
Brooks (F11)...9,195
Brown (F6)...28,607
Burleson (H7)...13,000
Burnet (F7)...10,356
Caldwell (G8)...19,350
Calhoun (H9)...9,222
Callahan (E5)...9,087
Cameron (G11)...125,170
Camp (K5)...8,740
Carson (C2)...6,852
Cass (K4)...26,732
Castro (B3)...5,417
Chambers (L1)...7,871
Cherokee (J6)...38,694
Childress (D3)...12,123
Clay (F4)...9,896
Cochran (B4)...5,928
Coke (D6)...4,045
Coleman (E6)...15,503
Collin (H4)...41,692
Collingsworth (D3)...9,139
Colorado (H8)...17,576
Comal (F8)...16,357
Comanche (F5)...15,516
Concho (E6)...5,078
Cooke (G4)...22,146
Coryell (G6)...16,284
Cottle (D3)...6,099
Crane (B6)...3,965
Crockett (C7)...3,981
Crosby (C4)...9,582
Culberson (C11)...1,825
Dallam (B1)...7,640
Dallas (G2)...614,799
Dawson (C5)...19,113
De Witt (G9)...22,973
Deaf Smith (B3) ...9,111
Delta (J4)...8,964
Denton (G4)...41,365
Dickens (D4)...7,177
Dimmit (E9)...10,654
Donley (D2)...6,216
Duval (F10)...15,643
Eastland (F5)...23,942
Ector (B6)...42,102
Edwards (D7)...2,908
El Paso (A10)...194,968
Ellis (H5)...45,645
Erath (F5)...18,434
Falls (H6)...26,724
Fannin (H4)...31,253
Fayette (H8)...24,176
Fisher (D5)...11,023
Floyd (C3)...10,535
Foard (E3)...4,216
Fort Bend (J2)...31,056
Franklin (J4)...6,257
Freestone (H6)...15,696
Frio (E9)...10,357
Gaines (B5)...8,909
Galveston (K3)...113,066
Garza (C4)...6,281
Gillespie (F7)...10,520
Glasscock (C6)...1,089
Goliad (G9)...6,219
Gonzales (G8)...21,164
Gray (D2)...24,728
Grayson (H4)...70,467
Gregg (K5)...61,258
Grimes (J7)...15,135
Guadalupe (G8)...25,392
Hale (C3)...28,211
Hall (D3)...10,930
Hamilton (F6)...10,660
Hansford (C1)...4,202
Hardeman (E3)...10,212
Hardin (K7)...19,535
Harris (J1)...806,701
Harrison (K5)...47,745
Hartley (B2)...1,913
Haskell (E4)...13,736
Hays (F7)...17,840
Hemphill (D2)...4,123
Henderson (J5)...23,405
Hidalgo (F11)...160,446
Hill (G5)...31,282
Hockley (B4)...20,407
Hood (G5)...5,287
Hopkins (J4)...23,490
Houston (J6)...22,825
Howard (C5)...26,722
Hudspeth (B10)...4,298
Hunt (H4)...42,731
Hutchinson (C2)...31,580
Irion (C6)...1,590
Jack (F4)...7,755
Jackson (H9)...12,916
Jasper (K7)...20,049
Jeff Davis (C11)...2,090
Jefferson (K8)...195,083
Jim Hogg (F11)...5,389
Jim Wells (F10)...27,991
Johnson (G5)...31,390
Jones (E5)...22,147
Karnes (G9)...17,139
Kaufman (H5)...31,170
Kendall (F8)...5,423
Kenedy (G11)... 632
Kent (D4)...2,249
Kerr (E7)...14,022
Kimble (E7)...4,619
King (D4)... 870
Kinney (D8)...2,668
Kleberg (G10)...21,991
Knox (E4)...10,082
La Salle (E9)...7,485
Lamar (J4)...43,033
Lamb (B3)...20,015
Lampasas (F6)...9,929
Lavaca (H8)...22,159
Lee (H7)...10,144
Leon (J6)...12,024
Liberty (K7)...26,729
Limestone (H6)...25,251
Lipscomb (D1)...3,658
Live Oak (F9)...9,054
Llano (F7)...5,377
Loving (D10)... 227
Lubbock (C4)...101,048
Lynn (C4)...11,030
Madison (J6)...7,996
Marion (K5)...10,172
Martin (C5)...5,541
Mason (E7)...4,945
Matagorda (H9)...21,559
Maverick (D9)...12,292
Mc Culloch (E6)...11,701
Mc Lennan (G6)...130,194
Mc Mullen (F9)...1,187
Medina (E8)...17,013
Menard (E7)...4,175
Midland (B6)...25,785
Milam (H7)...23,585
Mills (F6)...5,999
Mitchell (D5)...14,357
Montague (G4)...17,070
Montgomery (J7)...24,504
Moore (C2)...13,349
Morris (K4)...9,433
Motley (D3)...3,963
Nacogdoches (K6)...30,326
Navarro (H5)...39,916
Newton (L7)...10,832
Nolan (D5)...19,808
Nueces (G10)...165,471
Ochiltree (D1)...6,024
Oldham (B2)...1,672
Orange (L7)...40,567
Palo Pinto (F5)...17,154
Panola (K5)...19,250
Parker (G5)...21,528
Parmer (B3)...5,787
Pecos (B7)...9,939
Polk (K7)...16,194
Potter (C2)...73,366
Presidio (C12)...7,354
Rains (J5)...4,266
Randall (C2)...13,774
Reagan (C6)...3,127
Real (E8)...2,479
Red River (J4)...21,851
Reeves (D11)...11,745
Refugio (G9)...10,113
Roberts (D2)...1,031
Robertson (H6)...19,908
Rockwall (H5)...6,156
Runnels (E6)...16,771
Rusk (K5)...42,348
Sabine (L6)...8,568
San Augustine (K6)...8,837
San Jacinto (J7)...7,172
San Patricio (G10)...35,842
San Saba (F6)...8,666
Schleicher (D7)...2,852
Scurry (D5)...22,779
Shackelford (E5)...5,001
Shelby (K6)...23,479
Sherman (C1)...2,443
Smith (J5)...74,701
Somervell (G5)...2,542
Starr (F11)...13,948
Stephens (F5)...10,597
Sterling (C6)...1,282
Stonewall (D4)...3,679
Sutton (D7)...3,746
Swisher (C3)...8,249
Tarrant (F2)...361,253
Taylor (E5)...63,370
Terrell (B7)...3,189
Terry (B4)...13,107
Throckmorton (E4)...3,618
Titus (K4)...17,302
Tom Green (D6)...58,929
Travis (G7)...160,980
Trinity (J6)...10,040
Tyler (K7)...11,292
Upshur (K5)...20,822
Upton (B6)...5,307
Uvalde (E8)...16,015
Val Verde (C8)...16,635
Van Zandt (J5)...22,593
Victoria (H9)...31,241
Walker (J7)...20,163
Waller (J8)...11,961
Ward (A6)...13,346
Washington (H7)...20,542
Webb (E10)...56,141
Wharton (H8)...36,077
Wheeler (D2)...10,317
Wichita (F3)...98,493
Wilbarger (E3)...20,552
Willacy (G11)...20,920
Williamson (G7)...38,853
Wilson (F8)...14,672
Winkler (A6)...10,064
Wise (G4)...16,141
Wood (J5)...21,308
Yoakum (B4)...4,339
Young (F4)...16,810
Zapata (E11)...4,405
Zavala (E9)...11,201

CITIES and TOWNS

Abbott (H6)*... 345
Abernathy (B4)*...1,692
Abilene (E5)*...45,570
Acala (B10)*... 150
Ackerly (C5)*... 550
Acme (E3)*... 200
Adamsville (F6)*... 300
Addison (G1)*... 258
Adkins (F8)*... 20
Adrian (B2)*... 205
Afton (D4)*... 115
Agua Dulce (F10)*... 660
Alamo (F11)*...3,017
Alamo Hts. ‡(F8)*...8,000
Alanreed (D2)*... 200
Alba (J5)*... 547
Albany (E5)*...2,241
Aledo (G5)*... 260
Alexander (F5)*... 96
Algoa (K3)*... 250
Alice (F10)*...16,449
Allamoore (C11)*... 50
Allison (D2)*... 150
Allred (B4)*... 30
Almeda (J2)*...1,800
Alpine (D11)*...5,261
Alta Loma (K3)*...1,400
Alto (J6)*...1,021
Alvarado (G5)*...1,656
Alvin (J3)*...3,701
Alvord (G4)*... 735
Amarillo (C2)*...74,246
Amarillo (urban area).74,450
Amherst (B4)*... 922
Anahuac (K8)*...1,284
Anderson (J7)*... 500
Andrews (B5)*...3,294
Angeles (C10)...
Angleton (J8)*...3,399
Anna (H4)*... 525
Annona (K4)*... 392
Anson (E5)*...2,708
Antelope (F4)*... 125
Anthony (A10)*...1,200
Anton (B4)*... 934
Aquilla (G6)*... 450
Aransas Pass (G10)*...5,396
Arcadia (K3)*... 865
Archer City (K4)*...1,901
Arlington (F2)*...7,692
Armstrong (G11)*... 97
Arp (J5)*... 909
Artesia Wells (E9)*... 200
Asherton (E9)*...2,425
Aspermont (D4)*...1,062
Athens (J5)*...5,194
Atlanta (K4)*...3,782
Aubrey ‡(H4)*... 491
AUSTIN (G7)*...132,459
Austin (urban area)..135,465
Austonio (J6)*...
Austwell (H9)*... 228
Avalon (H5)*... 400
Avery (K4)*... 442
Avinger (K5)*... 546
Avoca (E5)*... 210
Azle (E1)*...1,700
Bagwell (J4)*... 400
Bailey ‡(H4)*... 198
Baileyboro (B3)*... 50
Baird (E5)*...1,821
Bakersfield (B7)*... 150
Balcones Hts. ‡(F8)... 376
Ballinger (E6)*...5,302
Balmorhea (D11)*... 500
Bandera (F8)*...1,036
Bangs (E6)*... 935
Bardwell ‡(H5)*... 229
Barksdale (D8)*... 300
Barnhart (C6)*... 357
Barstow (A6)*... 683
Bartlett (G7)*...1,727
Bastrop (G7)*...3,176
Batesville (E9)*... 500
Batson (K7)*... 800
Bay City (H9)*...9,427
Bayside (G9)*... 300
Baytown (L2)*...22,983
Beaumont (K7)*...94,014
Beaumont (urban area) ...94,050
Beckville (K5)*... 550
Becton (C4)... 50
Bedford (F2)*... 150
Bedias (J7)*... 575
Beeville (G9)*...9,348
Belcherville ‡(G4)*... 31
Bellaire (J2)*...10,173
Bellevue (F4)*... 418
Bells (H4)*... 614
Bellville (H8)*...2,112
Belton (G7)*...6,246
Ben Wheeler (J5)*... 400
Benavides (F10)*...3,016
Benbrook (E2)*... 617
Bend (F7)*... 228
Benjamin (E4)*... 530
Berclair (G9)*... 300
Bertram (F7)*... 900
Bessmay (L7)*...1,800
Best (C6)*... 26
Beverly Hills ‡(G6)*... 701
Big Bend National Park (A8)*...
Big Lake (C6)*...2,152
Big Sandy (J5)*... 689
Big Spring (C5)*...17,286
Big Foot (F9)... 150
Big Wells (E9)*...1,077
Bishop (G10)*...2,731
Blackwell (D5)*... 600
Blanco (F7)*... 718
Blanket (F6)*... 361
Bledsoe (A4)*... 105
Blessing (H9)*... 600
Blewett (D8)*... 200
Bloomburg (L4)*... 477
Blooming Grove (H5)*.. 736
Bloomington (H9)*...1,500
Blossom (J4)*... 780
Blue Ridge (H4)*... 306
Bluff Dale (F5)*...
Blum (G5)*... 368
Boerne (F8)*...1,802
Bogata (J4)*... 936
Boling (H8)*...1,200
Bomarton (E4)*... 300
Bon Wier (L7)*...1,200
Bonham (H4)*...7,049
Booker (D1)*... 619
Borger (C2)*...18,059
Boston (K4)*... 200
Bovina (A3)*... 612
Bowie (G4)*...4,544
Boyd (G4)*... 550
Brackettville (D8)*...1,858
Bradshaw (E5)*... 105
Brady (E6)*...5,944
Brandon ‡(H5)*... 180
Brazoria (J9)*... 776
Breckenridge (F5)*...6,610
Bremond (H6)*...1,141
Brenham (H7)*...6,941
Bridgeport (G4)*...2,049
Briggs (F7)*...
Briscoe (D2)*... 100
Britton (F3)*... 138
Broaddus (K6)*... 150
Bronco (B4)*... 42
Bronson (L6)*... 250
Bronte (D6)*...1,020
Brookeland (L6)*... 350
Brookshire (J8)*...1,015
Brownfield (B4)*...6,161
Brownsboro (J5)*... 518
Brownsville (G12)*...36,066
Brownwood (F6)*...20,181
Bruni (F10)*... 700
Bryan (H7)*...18,102
Bryson (F4)*... 588
Buckholts (H7)*... 700
Buda (G7)*... 483
Buenavista (B6)*...
Buffalo (J6)*... 970
Bula (B4)*...
Bullard (J5)*... 317
Buna (L7)*...
Burkburnett (F3)*...4,555
Burke (K6)*... 500
Burkett (E5)*... 225
Burkeville (L7)*... 500
Burleson ‡(G5)*... 791
Burnet (F7)*...2,394
Burton (H7)*... 510
Bushland (B2)*... 80
Byers (F3)*... 542
Bynum (H6)*... 325
Caddo (F5)*...
Caddo Mills ‡(H4)*... 509
Cain City (E7)*... 32
Caldwell (H7)*...2,109
Call (L7)*...1,500
Calliham (F9)*... 160
Calvert (H7)*...2,548
Cameron (H7)*...5,052
Camp Allison (D7)*...
Camp Ruby (K7)*... 100
Camp Wood (D8)*... 785
Campbellton (F9)*... 368
Canadian (D2)*...2,700
Candelaria (C12)*... 250
Canton (J5)*... 881
Canutillo (A10)*...1,326
Canyon (C3)*...4,364
Carbon (F5)*... 444
Carlsbad (D6)*...
Carlton (F6)*... 250
Carmine (H7)*... 495
Carmona (K6)*... 300
Caro (K6)*... 220
Carrizo Spgs. (E9)*...4,316
Carrollton (G1)*...1,610

Shallowater (B4)*........ 500
Shamrock (D2)*........3,322
Sheffield (B7)*........ 350
Shelbyville (L6)*........
Sheldon (K1)*........ 200
Shepherd (K7)*........
Sherman (H4)*........20,150
Sherwood (D6)*........ 247
Shiner (G8)*........1,778
Shiro (J7)*........ 300
Shore Acres ‡(J8)........ 783
Sierra Blanca (B11)*.... 900
Silsbee (K7)*........3,179
Silverton (C3)*........ 857
Sinton (G9)*........4,254
Skellytown (C2)*........ 700
Skidmore (G9)*........ 800
Slaton (C4)*........5,036
Slocum (J6)*........ 200
Smeltertown (A10)*......3,500
Smiley (G8)*........ 503
Smithfield (F1)*........ 500
Smithville (G7)*........3,379
Snyder (D5)*........12,010
Socorro (A10)*........
Somerset (F8)*........ 920
Somerville (H7)*........1,425
Sonoma ‡(H5)........ 210
Sonora (D7)*........2,633
Sourlake (K7)*........1,630
South Bend (F5)*........ 325
South Groveton (J7).....
South Houston (J2)*.....4,126
South Plains (C3)........ 100
Southland (C4)*........ 210
Southside Place (J2)....1,436
South Texarkana ‡(K4) 317
Spanish Fort (G4)*........ 203
Sparenberg (B5)*........
Spearman (C1)*........1,852
Spicewood (F7)*........
Spofford (D8)*........ 246
Spring (J7)*........ 500
Springlake (B3)*........
Springtown (G5)*........ 650
Spur (D4)*........2,183
Stamford (E5)*........5,819
Stanton (C5)*........1,603
Star (F6)*........
Stephenville (F5)*........7,155
Sterley (C3)*........ 96
Sterling City (D6)*.... 846
Stinnett (C2)*........1,170
Stockdale (G8)*........1,105
Stonewall (F7)*........ 135
Stratford (C1)*........1,385
Strawn (F5)*........ 922
Streeter (E7)*........ 26
Streetman (H6)*........ 419
Sudan (B3)*........1,348
Sugar Land (J8)*........2,285
Surphur Spgs. (J4)*.....8,991
Summerfield (B3)*........
Sundown (B4)*........1,492
Sunray (C1)*........1,530
Sunset (G4)*........
Swearingen (D3)*........ 45
Sweeny (J8)*........1,393
Sweet Home (H8)*........ 500
Sweetwater (D5)*........13,619
Swenson (D4)*........ 175
Sylvester (D5)*........
Taft (G9)*........2,978
Tahoka (C4)*........2,848
Talco (K4)*........ 917
Talpa (E6)*........ 234
Tarzan (B5)*........ 79
Tascosa (B2)*........ 125
Tatum (K5)*........ 599
Taylor (G7)*........9,071
Teague (H6)*........2,925
Tehuacana ‡(H6)*........ 389
Telegraph (E7)*........ 17
Telephone (J4)*........ 275
Tell (D3)*........ 100
Temple (G6)*........25,467
Tenaha (K6)*........ 715
Tennyson (D6)*........
Terlingua (D12)*........ 20
Terrell (H5)*........11,544
Terrell Hills ‡(F8)........2,708
Tesnus (B7)*........ 8
Texarkana (L4)*........24,753
Texas City (K3)*........16,620
Texhoma (C1)........ 299
Texline (B1)*........ 437
Texon (C6)*........ 500
Thalia (E4)*........ 223
Thomas (J5)*........ 200
Thorndale (G7)*........ 855
Thornton (H6)*........ 623
Thorp Spring (F5)*........ 200
Thrall ‡(G7)*........ 585
Three Rivers (F9)*........2,026
Throckmorton (F4)*........1,320
Tilden (F9)*........ 425
Timpson (K6)*........1,455
Tioga (H4)*........ 529
Tivoli (H9)*........ 300
Tokio ((B4)*........ 200
Tolar (G5)*........ 338
Tom Bean ‡(H4)*........ 286
Tomball (J7)*........1,065
Tornillo (A10)*........ 400
Toyah (D11)*........ 409
Toyahvale (D11)*........ 16
Trent (D5)*........ 296
Trenton (H4)*........ 603
Trinidad (J5)*........ 950
Trinity (J7)*........2,054
Troup (J5)*........1,539
Truscott (E4)*........ 255
Tulia (C3)*........3,222
Turkey (D3)*........1,005
Turnersville (G6)*........ 150
Tuscola (E5)*........ 497
Twin Sisters (F7)........ 50
Tyler (J5)*........38,968
Tynan (G9)*........ 70
Umbarger (B3)*........ 465
University Park (H2)*.24,275
Utopia (E8)*........ 350
Uvalde (E8)*........8,674
Valentine (C11)*........ 510
Valera (E6)*........ 300
Valley Mills (G6)*........1,037
Valley Spg. (F7)*........
Valley View (H4)*........ 500
Van (J5)*........ 610
Van Alstyne (H4)*........1,649
Van Horn (C11)*........1,161
Vance (E8)*........ 100
Vancourt (D6)*........ 11
Vanderbilt (H9)*........ 400
Vanderpool (E8)*........ 150
Vealmoor (C5)*........ 35
Vega (B2)*........ 620
Velasco (J9)*........2,260
Venus ‡(H5)*........ 357
Vera (E4)*........ 270
Veribest (D6)*........ 33
Vernon (E3)*........12,651
Victoria (H9)*........16,126
Vigo Park (C3)*........
Village Mills (K7)*........ 267
Voca (E7)*........ 100
Voth (K7)*........1,200
Waco (G6)*........84,706
Waco (urban area)........92,299
Wadsworth (J9)*........ 250
Waelder (G8)*........1,275
Waka (D1)*........ 100
Wake ‡(K4)*........1,066
Wall (D6)*........ 200
Waller (J7)*........ 715
Wallis (H8)*........1,500
Wallisville (L1)*........ 300
Walnut Spgs. (G5)*........ 626
Waring (F8)*........ 176
Washington (J7)*........ 300
Waskom (L5)*........ 719
Watauga (F1)........ 150
Water Valley (C6)*........ 300
Waxahachie (H5)*........11,204
Wayside (C3)*........ 43
Weatherford (G5)*........8,093
Webb (E10)*........ 17
Webb (F2)........ 45
Webster (K2)*........
Weesatche (G9)*........ 250
Weimar (H8)*........1,663
Weinert (E4)*........ 288
Welch (B5)*........
Weldon (J6)*........ 250
Wellington (D3)*........3,676
Wellman (B5)*........ 165
Wells (J6)*........ 718
Weslaco (G11)*........7,514
West (G6)*........2,130
W. Columbia (J8)*........2,100
W. University Pl. (J2).17,074
W. Vernon (E3)........
W. Worth (E2)........ 529
Westbrook (C5)*........ 220
Westhoff (G8)*........ 610
Westminster ‡(H4)*........ 192
Westover Hills (E2)........ 266
Wharton (J8)*........4,450
Wheeler (D2)*........ 904
White Deer (C2)*........ 629
White Settlement (E2)10,827
Whiteface (B4)*........ 579
Whiteflat (D3)*........ 100
Whitesboro (H4)*........1,854
Whitewright (H4)*........1,372
Whitharral (B4)*........ 275
Whitney (G6)*........1,383
Whitsett (F9)*........ 100
Whitt (G5)*........ 150
Wichita Falls (F4)*....68,042
Wickett (B6)*........
Wiergate (L6)*........1,000
Wildorado (B2)*........ 150
Willis (J7)*........1,164
Willow City (F7)*........ 75
Wills Point (J5)*........2,030
Wilmer (H2)*........ 465
Wilson (C4)*........ 300
Winchell (E6)*........ 100
Winchester (H7)*........ 275
Windom ‡(H4)*........ 297
Windthorst (F4)*........ 400
Winfield (K4)*........ 319
Winfree (L1)........ 50
Wingate (D5)*........ 262
Wink (A6)*........1,521
Winnie (K8)*........ 800
Winnsboro (J5)*........2,512
Winona (J5)*........ 450
Winters (E6)*........2,676
Wolfe City (J4)*........1,345
Wolfforth (C4)*........ 300
Woodsboro (G9)*........1,836
Woodson (E5)*........ 483
Woodville (K7)*........1,863
Wooster (K2)........2,500
Wortham (H6)*........1,170
Wylie (H5)*........1,295
Yantis (J5)*........ 300
Yoakum (G8)*........5,231
Yorktown (G9)*........2,596
Ysleta (A10)*........4,782
Zapata (E11)*........1,409
Zavalla (K6)*........ 956
Zephyr (F6)*........

Map on Page 88

UTAH

Total Population 688,862

29 COUNTIES

Beaver (A5)........4,856
Box Elder (A2)........19,734
Cache (C2)........33,536
Carbon (D4)........24,901
Daggett (E3)........ 364
Davis (B3)........30,867
Duchesne (D3)........8,134
Emery (D4)........6,304
Garfield (C6)........4,151
Grand (E5)........1,903
Iron (A6)........9,642
Juab (A4)........5,981
Kane (B6)........2,299
Millard (A4)........9,387
Morgan (C2)........2,519
Piute (B5)........1,911
Rich (C2)........1,673
Salt Lake (B3)........274,895
San Juan (E6)........5,315
Sanpete (C4)........13,891
Sevier (C5)........12,072
Summit (D3)........6,745
Tooele (A3)........14,636
Uintah (E3)........10,300
Utah (C3)........81,912
Wasatch (C3)........5,574
Washington (A6)........9,836
Wayne (C5)........2,205
Weber (B2)........83,319

CITIES and TOWNS

Abraham (B4)*........ 100
Adamsville (B5)*........ 50
Alpine (C3)........ 571
Alton (B6)*........ 154
Altonah (D3)*........ 363
Amalga (C2)........ 225
American Fork (C3)*........5,126
Angle (C5)........ 30
Annabella (C5)*........ 263
Antimony (C5)*........ 187
Arcadia (D3)*........ 168
Aurora (B5)*........ 614
Axtell (C4)*........ 155
Bacchus (B3)*........ 94
Bear River City (B2)*........ 438
Beaver (B5)*........1,685
Benjamin (C3)........ 450
Beryl (A6)*........ 26
Bicknell (C5)*........ 373
Bingham Canyon (B3)*........2,569
Birdseye (C4)*........ 75
Black Rock (B5)*........ 19
Blanding (E6)*........1,177
Blue Creek (B2)........ 43
Bluebell (D3)*........ 218
Bluff (E6)*........ 100
Bonanza (E4)*........
Boneta (D3)*........ 134
Bothwell‡ (B2)........ 317
Boulder (C6)*........ 185
Bountiful (C3)*........6,004
Bridgeland (D3)*........ 240
Bridgeport (E3)........ 6
Brigham City (C2)*........6,790
Brighton (C3)*........
Bryce Canyon (B6)*........ 200
Burrville (C5)........ 35
Cache Junction (C2)*........ 80
Caineville (D5)........ 12
Callao (A4)*........ 65
Cannonville (C6)*........ 205
Castle Dale (D4)*........ 715
Castle Gate (D4)*........ 701
Castle Rock (C2)........ 20
Cedar City (A6)*........6,106
Cedar Fort (B3)........ 213
Cedar Valley (B3)*........ 82
Centerfield (C4)*........ 601
Centerville (C3)*........1,262
Central (A6)*........ 49
Central (B5)........ 100
Charleston (C3)........ 201
Chester (C4)*........ 153
Circleville (B5)*........ 603
Cisco (E5)*........ 41
Clarkston (B2)*........ 526
Clawson (C4)*........ 136
Clearcreek (C4)*........ 168
Clearfield (B2)*........4,723
Cleveland (D4)*........ 343
Clinton ‡(B2)........ 670
Clive (A3)........ 10
Clover (B3)........ 110
Coalville (C3)*........ 850
Collinston (B2)*........ 145
Colton (C4)........ 21
Columbia (D4)*........ 412
Corinne (B2)*........ 427
Cornish (B2)*........ 181
Cove Fort (B5)........ 10
Croydon (C2)*........ 90
Delle (B3)*........ 35
Delta (B4)*........1,703
Deseret (B4)*........ 332
Devils Slide (C2)*........ 200
Deweyville (B2)*........ 233
Dividend (C4)*........ 30
Dragerton (D4)*........3,453
Dragon (E4)........
Draper (C3)*........2,000
Duchesne (D3)*........ 804
East Layton‡ (C2)........ 217
Echo (C3)*........ 175
Eden (C2)*........ 235
Elberta (B4)*........ 138
Elmo (D4)*........ 170
Elsinore (B5)*........ 657
Elwood ‡(B2)........ 393
Emery (C5)*........ 488
Enterprise (A6)*........ 790
Ephraim (C4)*........1,987
Escalante (C6)*........ 773
Etna (A2)........ 22
Eureka (B4)*........1,318
Fairfield (B3)........ 37
Fairview (C4)*........ 974
Farmington (C3)*........1,468
Fayette (C4)*........ 200
Ferron (C4)*........ 478
Fielding (B2)*........ 249
Fillmore (B5)*........1,890
Five Mile Pass (B3)........
Fort Duchesne (E3)*........ 200
Fountain Green (C4)*........ 767
Francis (C3)........ 276
Fremont (C5)*........ 224
Frisco (A5)........
Fruit Heights (C2)........ 124
Fruitland (D3)*........ 127
Gandy (A4)........ 48
Garden City (C2)*........ 164
Garfield (B3)*........2,079
Garland (B2)*........1,008
Garrison (A5)*........ 34
Geneva (C3)........
Genola (C4)........ 314
Glendale (B6)*........ 226
Glenwood (C5)*........ 338
Gold Hill (A3)........ 4
Goshen (C4)*........ 525
Grantsville (B3)*........1,537
Green River (D4)*........ 583
Greenville (B5)*........ 128
Greenwich (B5)*........ 50
Grouse Creek (A2)*........ 167
Grover (C5)*........ 53
Gunlock (A6)*........ 89
Gunnison (C4)*........1,144
Gusher (E3)*........ 125
Hanksville (D5)*........ 100
Hanna (D3)*........ 175
Hatch (B6)*........ 244
Hatton (B5)........ 9
Hayden (D3)*........ 52
Heber (C3)*........2,936
Helper (D4)*........2,850
Henefer (C2)*........ 346
Henrieville (C6)*........ 114
Hiawatha (D4)*........1,421
Hinckley (B4)*........ 589
Hite (D6)........
Holden (B4)*........ 476
Holladay (C3)........3,100
Honeyville (B2)*........ 599
Hooper (B2)*........1,243
Howell (B2)*........ 176
Hoytsville (C3)........ 330
Huntington (C4)*........1,029
Huntsville (C2)*........ 494
Hurricane (A6)*........1,271
Hyde Park (C2)*........ 644
Hyrum (C2)*........1,704
Ibapah (A3)*........ 150
Indianola (C4)........ 50
International (B3)........
Ioka (D3)........ 238
Iron Mountain (A6)........
Iron Springs (A6)........ 20
Ivins (A6)*........ 95
Jensen (E3)*........
Joseph (B5)*........ 208
Junction (B5)*........ 285
Kamas (C3)*........ 721
Kanab (B6)*........1,287
Kanarraville (A6)*........ 263
Kanosh (B5)*........ 476
Kaysville (B2)*........1,898
Keetley (C3)*........
Kelton (A2)........
Kenilworth (D4)*........ 932
Kingston (B5)*........ 138
Knolls (A3)........ 12
Koosharem (C5)*........ 300
La Sal (E5)*........ 75
La Verkin (A6)*........ 387
Lakeside (B2)........ 25
Laketown (C2)*........ 217
Lapoint (E3)*........ 400
Lark (B3)*........ 750
Latuda (C4)*........ 200
Layton (C2)*........3,456
Laytona ‡(C2)........ 405
Leamington (B4)*........ 214
Leeds (A6)*........ 160
Leeton (D3)........ 50
Lehi (C3)*........3,627
Leland (C3)........ 175
Leota (E3)........ 124
Levan (C4)*........ 521
Lewiston (C2)*........1,533
Liberty (C2)........ 196
Lindon (C3)........ 801
Linwood (E3)*........ 22
Loa (C5)*........ 437
Lofgreen (B3)*........ 20
Logan (C2)*........16,832
Lucin (A2)*........ 51
Lund (A5)*........ 42
Lyman (C5)*........ 276
Lynn (A2)*........ 50
Lynndyl (B4)*........ 241
Maeser (E3)........ 643
Magna (B3)*........3,502
Mammoth (B4)*........ 137
Manila (E3)*........ 147
Manti (C4)*........2,051
Mantua (C2)........ 271
Mapleton (C3)........1,175
Marysvale (B5)*........ 520
Mayfield (C4)*........ 390
Meadow (B5)*........ 378
Mendon (B2)*........ 369
Mercur (B3)........ 2
Mexican Hat (E6)........
Midvale (B3)*........3,996
Midway (C3)*........ 711
Milford (A5)*........1,673
Mills, (B4)........ 42
Millville (C2)*........ 401
Minersville (A5)*........ 593
Moab (E5)*........1,274
Modena (A6)*........ 130
Mohrland (D4)........
Mona (C4)*........ 328
Monroe (B5)*........1,214
Monticello (E6)*........1,172
Moore (C5)*........ 41
Morgan (C2)*........1,064
Moroni (C4)*........1,076
Motoqua (A6)........ 25
Mounds (D4)........ 15
Mount Carmel (B6)*........ 158
Mount Emmons (D3)*........ 276
Mount Pleasant (C4)*........2,030
Mountain Home (D3)*........ 300
Murray (C3)*........9,006
Myton (D3)*........ 435
Nada (A5)........
National (C4)*........
Neola (D3)*........ 400
Nephi (C4)*........2,990
New Harmony (A6)*........ 126
Newcastle (A6)*........ 229
Newton (C2)*........ 497
Nibley (C2)........ 304
North Logan (C2)........ 535
North Ogden (C2)........1,105
North Salt Lake (C3)*........ 255
Oak City (B4)*........ 334
Oakley (C3)*........ 264
Oasis (B4)*........ 190
Ogden (C2)*........57,112
Onaqui ‡(B3)........ 333
Ophir (B3)*........ 199
Orangeville (C4)*........ 589
Orderville (B6)*........ 371
Orem (C3)*........8,351
Ouray (E3)*........ 111
Panguitch (B6)*........1,501
Paradise (C2)*........ 401
Paragonah (B6)........ 404
Park City (C3)*........2,254
Park Valley (A2)*........ 142
Parowan (B6)*........1,455
Payson (C3)*........3,998
Peoa (C3)*........ 210
Perry (C2)........ 449
Peterson (C2)........ 275
Pickleville (C2)........ 96
Pine Valley (A6)........ 16
Pinto (A6)........
Pintura (A6)*........ 40
Plain City (B2)........ 899
Pleasant Grove (C3)*........3,195
Pleasant View (B2)........ 420
Plymouth (B2)*........ 228
Portage (B2)*........ 254
Price (D4)*........6,010
Promontory (B2)........ 72
Providence (C2)*........1,055
Provo (C3)*........28,937
Randlett (E3)*........ 400
Randolph (C2)*........ 562
Redmond (C4)*........ 600
Richfield (B5)*........4,212
Richmond (C2)*........1,091
River Heights ‡(C2)........ 468
Riverdale (C2)........ 871
Riverside (B2)*........ 281
Riverton (B3)*........1,666
Rockville (A6)*........ 180
Roosevelt (D3)*........1,628
Rosette (A2)........ 68
Roy (B2)*........3,723
Royal (D4)*........ 195
Rubys Inn (B6)*........
Saint George (A6)*........4,562
St. John (B3)*........ 130
Salem (C3)*........ 781
Salina (C5)*........1,789
SALT LAKE CITY (C3)*........182,121
Salt Lake City (urban area)........226,880
Saltair (B3)*........ 75
Sandy (C3)*........2,095
Santa Clara (A6)*........ 319
Santaquin (C4)*........1,214
Scipio (B4)*........ 491
Scofield (C4)*........ 236
Sego (E4)*........ 50
Sevier (B5)*........ 104
Sigurd (B5)*........ 431
Silver City (B4)*........ 30
Smithfield (C2)*........2,383
Snowville (B2)*........ 199
Soldier Summit (C4)*........ 93
South Jordan (C3)........1,048
S. Ogden (C2)........3,763
S. Salt Lake (C3)*........7,704
S. Weber (C2)........ 244
Spanish Fork (C3)*........5,230
Spring Canyon (C4)*........ 458
Spring City (C4)*........ 703
Springdale (B6)*........ 174
Springville (C3)*........6,475
Spry (B5)*........ 56
Standardville (C4)*........ 307
Sterling (C4)*........ 188
Stockton (B3)*........ 414
Sulphurdale (B5)........ 2
Summit (B6)*........ 145
Summit Point (E5)*........ 42
Sunnyside (D4)*........1,881
Sunset (B2)........ 993
Syracuse (B2)........ 837
Tabiona (D3)*........ 160
Talmage (D3)*........ 174
Taylorsville (B3)........
Teasdale (C5)*........ 237
Thatcher (B2)........ 268
Thistle (C4)*........ 200
Thompson (E5)*........ 100
Tooele (B3)*........7,269
Toquerville (A6)*........ 219
Torrey (C5)*........ 241
Tremonton (B2)*........1,662
Trenton (B2)*........ 451
Tridell (E3)*........ 347
Tropic (B6)*........ 483
Trout Creek (A4)*........ 65
Uintah (C2)........ 317
Upalco, (D3)*........ 175
Venice (C5)*........ 238
Vernal (E3)*........2,845
Vernon (B3)*........ 175
Veyo (A6)*........ 84
Vineyard (C3)........ 113
Virgin (A6)*........ 147
Wahsatch (C2)*........ 35
Wales (C4)*........ 179
Wallsburg (C3)*........ 207
Wanship (C3)........ 173
Washington (A6)*........ 435
Watson (E4)........
Wattis (C4)*........ 283
Wellington (D4)*........ 845
Wellsville (C2)*........1,241
Wendover (A3)*........ 250
West Bountiful (C3)........ 682
W. Jordan (C3)*........2,107
W. Point ‡(B2)........ 433
W. Weber (B2)........ 276
Westwater (E4)*........ 50
Whiterocks (E3)*........ 395
Widtsoe (C6)........ 25
Willard (C2)*........ 548
Woodland (C3)........ 200
Woodruff (C2)*........ 175
Woods Cross (B3)*........ 273
Woodside (D4)*........ 14
Yost (A2)*........ 107
Zion Nat'l. Park (B6)*........ 63

Map on Page 89

VERMONT

Total Population 377,747

14 COUNTIES

Addison (A2)........19,442
Bennington (A4)........24,115
Caledonia (C1)........24,049
Chittenden (A2)........62,570
Essex (D1)........6,257
Franklin (B1)........29,894
Grand Isle (A1)........3,406
Lamoille (B1)........11,388
Orange (C3)........17,027
Orleans (C1)........21,190
Rutland (A3)........45,905
Washington (B2)........42,870
Windham (B5)........28,749
Windsor (B4)........40,885

CITIES and TOWNS

Addison (A2)........△ 628
Albany (C1)*........ 196
Alburg (A1)*........ 563
Andover (B4)........△ 185
Arlington (A4)*........△1,463
Ascutney (C4)*........ 200
Averill (D1)*........△ 20
Bakersfield (B1)*........△ 779
Barnard (B3)*........△ 439
Barnet (D2)*........△1,425
Barre (C2)*........10,922
Barton (C1)*........1,267
Bartonsville (B4)*........ 200
Beebe Plain (C1)*........ 173
Beecher Falls (D1)*........ 500
Bellows Falls (C4)*........ 3,881
Belvidere (B1)........ 207
Belvidere Center (B1)*........ 50
Bennington (A5)*........ 8,002
Benson (A3)*........△ 573
Benson Landing (A3)........ 2
Berkshire (B1)*........△1,063
Bethel (B3)*........△1,534
Bolton (B2)........△ 301
Boltonville (C2)*........ 50
Bomoseen (A3)*........ 275
Bondville (B4)*........ 229
Bradford (C3)*........ 725
Braintree (B3)*........△ 626
Brandon (A3)*........△3,304
Brattleboro (C5)*........△11,522
Bread Loaf (B3)*........ 11
Bridgewater (B3)*........△ 903
Bridgewater Corners* (B3)........ 173
Bridport (A3)*........△ 663
Briggs (B3)........ 125
Bristol (A2)*........ 1,308

Map on Page 90   VIRGINIA   Total Population 3,318,680

Map on Page 91

WASHINGTON

Total Population 2,378,963

39 COUNTIES

Adams (G3) 6,584
Asotin (H4) 10,878
Benton (F4) 51,370
Chelan (E3) 39,301
Clallam (B2) 26,396
Clark (C5) 85,307
Columbia (H4) 4,860
Cowlitz (C4) 53,369
Douglas (F3) 10,817
Ferry (G2) 4,096
Franklin (G4) 13,563
Garfield (H4) 3,204
Grant (F3) 24,346
Grays Harbor (B3) 53,644
Island (C2) 11,079
Jefferson (B3) 11,618
King (D3) 732,992
Kitsap (C3) 75,724
Kittitas (E3) 22,235
Klickitat (E5) 12,049
Lewis (C4) 43,755
Lincoln (G3) 10,970
Mason (B3) 15,022
Okanogan (F2) 29,131
Pacific (B4) 16,558
Pend Oreille (H2) 7,413
Pierce (C3) 275,876
San Juan (C2) 3,245
Skagit (D2) 43,273
Skamania (D5) 4,788
Snohomish (D2) 111,580
Spokane (H3) 221,561
Stevens (H2) 18,580
Thurston (C4) 44,884
Wahkiakum (B4) 3,835
Walla Walla (G4) 40,135
Whatcom (D2) 66,733
Whitman (H4) 32,469
Yakima (E4) 135,723

CITIES and TOWNS

Aberdeen (B3)* 19,653
Acme (C2)* 300
Addy (H2)* 387
Adna (B4)* 110
Adrian (F3)* 33
Aeneas (F2)* 5
Ahtanum (E4) 45
Ajlune (C4)* 6
Albion (H4)* 256
Alder (C4)*
Alderdale (E5)* 20
Alderton (C3)* 300
Alderwood Manor (C3)* 250
Algona (C3)* 1,400
Allyn (C3)* 275
Almira (G3)* 395
Almota (H4)* 33
Aloha (A3)* 150
Alpha (C4)*
Alstown (F3)
Altoona (B4)* 81
Amanda Park (A3)* 150
Amber (H3)* 20
Amboy (C5)* 225
American River (D4) 10
Anacortes (C2)* 6,919
Anatone (H4)* 60
Annapolis (A2) 800
Appleton (D5)* 50
Appleyard (South Wenatchee*) (E3) 1,479
Arden (H2) 25
Ardenvoir (E3)* 350
Ariel (C5)* 95
Arlington (C2)* 1,635
Ashford (C4)* 350
Asotin (H4)* 740
Attalia (G4)* 75
Auburn (C3)* 6,497
Austin (C3) 12
Avon (C2) 150
Azwell (F3)* 105
Baldi (D3) 5
Bangor (A1) 124
Baring (D3)* 150
Battle Ground (C5)* 750
Batum (G3)
Bay Center (A4)* 200
Bay City (B4)
Bay View (C2)* 200
Beaver (A2)* 125
Beebe (F3)
Belfair (C3)* 450
Bellevue (B2)* 14,182
Bellingham (C2)* 34,112
Belmont (H3)* 72
Benge (G4)* 50
Benton City (F4)* 863
Berrian (F5)
Beverly (F4)* 75
Beverly Park (C3)*
Biarly (H2) 5
Bickleton (E5)* 125
Biglake (C2) 120
Bingen (D5)* 736
Black Diamond (D3)* 1,500
Blaine (C2)* 1,693
Blanchard (C2)* 150
Blockhouse (E5) 8
Bluecreek (H2)* 62
Bluestem (G3)* 23
Blyn (B3) 200
Bonney Lake (C3) 275
Bossburg (H2)
Bothell (B1)* 1,019
Boundary (H2)* 3
Bow (C2)* 100
Boyds (G2)* 61
Bremerton (A2)* 27,678
Brewster (F2)* 851
Bridgeport (F3)* 802
Brief (E3) 20
Brinnon (B3)* 150
Brookfield (B4)* 13
Brooklyn (B4)* 85
Brownstown (E4)* 80
Brownsville (A2) 75
Brush Prairie (C5)* 60
Bryant (C2)*
Bryn Mawr (B2)* 4,781
Buckley (D3)* 2,705
Bucoda (C4)* 473
Buena (E4)* 600
Burbank (G4)* 150
Burien (A2)* 4,387
Burley (C3)* 350
Burlington (C2)* 2,350
Burton (C3)* 1,400
Byron (F4)* 50
Camas (C5)* 4,725
Camden (H2)* 12
Cape Horn (C5)
Carbonado (D3)* 412
Carlsborg (B2)* 350
Carlton (F2)* 200
Carnation (D3)* 446
Carrolls (C4)* 400
Carson (D5)* 450
Casey (G4)* 75
Cashmere (E3)* 1,768
Castle Rock (B4)* 1,255
Cathlamet (B4)* 501
Cedar Falls (D3)* 300
Cedonia (G2)* 26
Centerville (D5)* 125
Central Ferry (H4) 10
Centralia (C4)* 8,657
Chattaroy (H3)* 141
Chehalis (C4)* 5,639
Chelan (E3)* 2,157
Chelan Falls (E3)* 350
Cheney (H3)* 2,797
Chesaw (G2)* 45
Chewelah (H2)* 1,683
Chico (A2) 1,151
Chimacum (C3)*
Chinook (B4)* 390
Chopaka (F2)
Cinebar (C4)* 160
Clallam Bay (A2)* 350
Clarkston (H4)* 5,617
Clayton (H3)* 280
Cle Elum (E3)* 2,206
Clearlake (C2)* 400
Clearwater (A3)* 100
Cliffdell (E4) 10
Cliffs (E5) 16
Clinton (C3)* 1,623
Clipper (C2)* 70
Cloverland (H4) 10
Clyde (G4) 10
Coalfield (B2) 150
Colbert (H3)* 52
Colby (A2)* 200
Cold Creek (F4)
Colfax (H4)* 3,057
College Place (G4)* 3,174
Colton (H4)* 207
Colville (H2)* 3,033
Conconully (F2)* 141
Concrete (D2)* 760
Connell (G4)* 465
Conway (C2)* 150
Cook (D5)* 20
Copalis Beach (A3)* 500
Copalis Crossing (B3)* 100
Corfu (F4) 11
Cosmopolis (B4)* 1,164
Cougar (C4)* 70
Coulee City (F3)* 977
Coulee Dam (F2)*
Coupeville (C2)* 379
Covada (G2)* 31
Cove (A2)* 150
Cowiche (E4)* 200
Craige (H4) 40
Creosote (A2)* 225
Creston (G3)* 268
Cumberland (D3)* 175
Cunningham (G4)* 23
Curlew (G2)* 100
Curtis (B4)* 46
Cusick (H2)* 360
Custer (C2)* 250
Dabob (C3)* 102
Daisey (G2)* 180
Dalkena (H2) 25
Dallesport (D5)* 25
Danville (G2)* 155
Darrington (D2)* 921
Davenport (G3)* 1,417
Dayton (H4)* 2,979
Deep Creek (H3)* 95
Deep River (B4)* 45
Deer Harbor (B2)* 145
Deer Park (H3)* 1,167
Deming (C2)* 500
Denison (H3)* 26
Des Moines (B2)* 2,694
Diamond (H4)* 98
Disautel (F2)* 121
Dishman (H3)* 1,500
Dixie (G4)* 250
Doebay (C2)* 60
Donald (E4) 100
Doty (B4)* 350
Douglas (F3)* 50
Dryad (B4)* 400
Dryden (E3)* 300
Dungeness (B2) 300
Dusty (H4) 65
Duvall (D3)* 236
Duwamish (B2) 900
Earlington (B2) 175
East Olympia (B4)* 300
E. Stanwood (C2)* 378
E. Wenatchee (E3)* 389
Easton (D3)* 300
Eastsound (B2)* 125
Eatonville (C4)* 1,048
Edgecomb (C2)* 75
Edison (C2)* 150
Edmonds (C3)* 2,057
Edwall (H3)* 143
Elbe (C4)* 250
Elberton (H4)* 145
Eldon (B3) 50
Eleanor (G3)
Electric City (F3)* 1,484
Electron (C4)
Elk (H2)* 97
Ellensburg (E3)* 8,430
Elma (B4)* 1,543
Elmer City (G2)* 513
Eltopia (G4)* 61
Endicott (H4)* 397
Entiat (E3)* 420
Enumclaw (D3)* 2,789
Ephrata (F3)* 4,589
Espanola (H3)* 35
Ethel (C4)*
Eureka (G4)* 25
Evans (H2)* 326
Everett (C3)* 33,849
Everson (C2)* 345
Ewan (H3)* 100
Fairchild (H3) 10,000
Fairfax (C4) 70
Fairfield (H3)* 369
Fall City (D3)* 850
Farmer (F3)* 125
Farmington (H3)* 239
Ferndale (C2)* 979
Ferry (G2)
Finley (F4) 25
Fircrest ‡(C3) 1,459
Fletcher Bay (A2)
Florence (C2) 20
Ford (H3)* 20
Forest (C4) 62
Forest City (A2)* 300
Forks (A3)* 1,120
Fort Lewis (C3)* 35,000
Fortson (D2)*
Foster (B2) 400
Four Lakes (H3)* 200
Fragaria (A2)* 20
Frances (B4)* 250
Freeland (C2)*
Freeman (H3)* 100
Friday Harbor (B2)* 783
Fruitland (G2)* 75
Fruitvale (E4) 3,654
Furport (H2) 40
Galvin (B4)* 250
Gardiner (B2)* 150
Garfield (H3)* 674
Gate (B4)*
Getchell (C2) 35
Gifford (G2)* 74
Gig Harbor (C3)* 803
Glacier (D2)* 114
Glenoma (C4)*
Glenwood (D4)*
Gold Bar (D3)* 305
Goldendale (E5)* 1,907
Goodnoe Hills (E5)* 114
Gooseprairie (D4)* 20
Gorst (A2)* 550
Govan (G3)* 22
Graham (C3)* 95
Grand Coulee (G3)* 2,741
Grand Mound (C4)* 55
Grandview (F4)* 2,503
Granger (E4)* 1,164
Granite Falls (D2)* 635
Grant Orchards (F3)* 102
Grapeview (C3)* 150
Grayland (A4)* 600
Grays River (B4)* 300
Greenacres (J3)* 1,287
Greenbank (C2)* 200
Grotto (D3)* 90
Guler (D4) 87
Haas (G4)*
Hadlock (C2)* 250
Hamilton (D2)* 294
Hanford (F4)
Hansville (C3)* 127
Harper (A2)* 478
Harrah (E4)* 297
Harrington (G3)* 620
Hartline (F3)* 205
Hatton (G4)* 42
Havillah (F2) 20
Hay (H4)* 130
Heisson (C5)* 50
Hellgate (G3) 15
Hillyard (H3)*
Hobart (D3)* 350
Holcomb (B4) 150
Holden (E2)* 601
Holly (C3) 60
Home Valley (D5)* 175
Hoodsport (B3)* 500
Hooper (G4)* 200
Hoquiam (A3)* 11,123
Hot Springs (D3)
Houghton (B2)* 1,005
Humptulips (A3)* 100
Hunters (G2)* 350
Huntsville (G4)* 113
Husum (D5)* 75
Hyak (D3)* 20
Ilwaco (A4)* 628
Impach (G2)* 30
Inchelium (G2)* 97
Independence (B4)
Index (D3)* 211
Ione (H2)* 714
Irby (G3)* 30
Issaquah (C3)* 955
Johnson (H4)* 200
Joyce (B2)* 350
Juanita (B1) 900
Junction City (B4)* 176
Kahlotus (G4)* 151
Kalaloch (A3)* 24
Kalama (C4)* 1,121
Kapowsin (C4)*
Kartar (F2)
Keller (G2)* 75
Kelso (C4)* 7,345
Kendall (C2) 72
Kenmore (B1)* 2,500
Kennewick (F4)* 10,106
Kennydale (B2)* 2,200
Kent (C3)* 3,278
Kettle Falls (H2)* 714
Kewa (G2)* 5
Keyport (A2)* 500
Kingston (C3)* 500
Kiona (F4)* 102
Kirkland (B2)* 4,713
Kitsap (A1)* 200
Kittitas (E4)* 586
Klaber (B4)*
Klickitat (D5)* 800
Knappton (B4) 20
Kosmos (C4)
Krupp (Marlin*) (F3) 98
La Center (C5)* 204
La Conner (C2)* 594
La Grande (C4)* 102
Lacey (C3)* 1,952
Lacrosse (H4)* 457
Lafleur (F2) 28
Lake City (B1)* 2,800
Lake Forest Park (B1) 3,500
Lake Stevens (D3)* 2,586
Lakebay (C3)* 250
Lakeside (E3)* 288
Lakewood (C2)* 40
Lamona (G3)* 44
Lamont (H3)* 101
Lancaster (H3)* 65
Langley (C2)* 427
Lapush (A3)* 248
Latah (H3)* 244
Laurel (D5)* 200
Laurier (G2)* 29
Leadpoint (H2) 10
Leavenworth (E3)* 1,503
Lebam (B4)* 400
Leland (C3)* 115
Lester (D3)* 150
Liberty (E3) 30
Liberty Bond (D5) 6
Liberty Lake (J3)* 600
Lilliwaup (B3)* 200
Lincoln (G3)* 200
Lind (G4)* 796
Littell (B4) 68
Littlerock (B4)* 250
Locke (H2)* 6
Long Beach (A4)* 783
Longbranch (C3)* 495
Longmire (D4)* 85
Longview (B4)* 20,385
Loomis (F2)* 210
Loon Lake (H2)* 300
Lopez (C2)* 33
Lost Creek (H2) 20
Lowden (G4)* 30
Lowell (C3)* 1,754
Lucerne (E2)* 142
Lummi Island (C2)* 232
Lyle (D5)* 250
Lyman (D2)* 378
Lynden (C2)* 2,161
Lynnwood (C3)* 650
Mabton (E4)* 831
Macall (G3)
Mae (F3)* 14
Malaga (E3)* 70
Malden (H3)* 332
Malo (G2)* 27
Malone (B4)* 340
Malott (F2)* 250
Maltby (C3)* 385
Manchester (A2)* 500
Mansfield (F3)* 414
Manson (E3)* 2,000
Maple Falls (D2)* 105
Maple Valley (C3)* 1,800
Marble (H2) 25
Marblemount (D2)* 80
Marcellus (G3) 15
Marcus (H2)* 149
Marengo (G3)* 35
Marietta (C2)* 200
Markham (B4)
Marlin (F3)* 98
Marshall (H3)* 115
Maryhill (E5)* 120
Marysville (C2)* 2,259
Mason City (G3) 2,606
Matlock (B3)* 100
May View (H4)* 16
Mayfield (C4)* 70
Mazama (E2)* 4
Mc Cleary (B3)* 1,175
Mc Kenna (C4)* 95
Mc Loughlin Heights (C5)* 14,500
Mc Millin (C3)* 100
Mc Murray (C2) 70
Mead (H3)* 200
Medical Lake (H3)* 4,488
Medina (B2)* 500
Melbourne (B4) 100
Menlo (B4)*
Mercer Island (B2)* 6,000
Merritt (E3) 25
Mesa (G4)* 105
Metaline (H2)* 547
Metaline Falls (H2)*
Methow (E2)*
Mica (H3)* 155
Midlakes (B2) 20
Midvale (E4)
Midway (F4)* 500
Milan (H3)* 95
Miles (G3)* 25
Millwood (H3)* 1,240
Milton (C3)* 1,374
Mineral (C4)* 600
Moclips (A3)* 425
Mohler (G3)* 30
Mold (F3)* 6
Molson (F2)*
Mondovi (G3)* 150
Monitor (E3)* 308
Monroe (D3)* 1,556
Monse (F2)* 62
Montborne (C2) 66
Montesano (B4)* 2,328
Moore (E2)* 40
Morton (C4)* 1,140
Moses Lake (F3)* 2,679
Mossyrock (C4)* 356
Mottinger (F5) 12
Mount Hope (H3)* 28
Mt. Vernon (C2)* 5,230
Mountain View (H4)* 31
Moxee City (E4)* 543
Mukilteo (C3)* 826
Naches (E4)* 633
Nagrom (D3)
Nahcotta (A4)* 250
Napavine (C4)* 242
Naselle (B4)* 750
National (D4)* 750
Neah Bay (A2)* 1,000
Neilton (B3)* 100
Nesika (C4)
Nespelem (G2)* 425
Newman Lake (J3)* 64
Newport (H2)* 1,385
Nighthawk (F2)* 36
Nine Mile Falls (H3)* 130
Nisqually (C3)* 250
Nooksack (C2)* 323
Nordland (C2)* 500
North Bend (D3)* 787
N. Bonneville (C5)* 564
N. Cove (A4)
N. Richland (F4)* 3,067
Northport (H2)* 487
Oak Harbor (C2)* 1,193
Oak Point (B4)
Oakesdale (H3)* 576
Oakville (B4)* 372
O'Brien (B2) 350
Ocean City (A3)*
Ocean Park (A4)* 550
Ocosta (B4)
Odessa (G3)* 1,127
Ohop (C4)*
Okanogan (F2)* 2,013
Olalla (A2)* 800
Olequa (C4)
Olga (C2)* 100
OLYMPIA (C3)* 15,819
Omak (F2)* 3,791
Onalaska (C4)* 280
Opportunity (H3)* 10,000
Orchards (C5)* 600
Orient (G2)* 200
Orillia (B2)* 135
Orin (H2) 37
Orondo (E3)* 250
Oroville (F2)* 1,500
Orting (C3)* 1,299
Osborne (G3) 100
Oso (D2)* 250
Ostrander (C4)
Othello (F4)* 526
Otis Orchards (H3)* 1,500
Outlook (F4)* 308
Ovington (B2) 10
Oysterville (A4)* 140
Ozette (A2) 21
Pacific ‡(C3)* 755
Pacific Beach (A3)* 600
Packard (G3)
Packwood (D4)* 650
Page (G4)* 31
Paha (G3) 12
Palisades (E3)* 120
Palmer (D3)* 80
Palouse (H4)* 1,036
Paradise Inn (D4)*
Park Rapids (H2) 11
Parker (E4)* 200
Parkland (C3)* 3,000
Parkwater (H3)* 1,000
Parkway (D3) 25
Pasco (F4)* 10,288
Pataha City (H4) 60
Pateros (E2)* 866
Paterson (F5)* 100
Pe Ell (B4)* 787
Pearl (F2)
Pearson (A2) 50
Peshastin (E3)* 675
Pillar Rock (B4) 31
Pine City (H3)* 75
Pinehurst (C3)* 4,260
Plain (E3) 30
Plaza (H3)* 55
Plymouth (F5)* 325
Point Roberts (B2)* 230
Pomeroy (H4)* 1,775
Port Angeles (B2)* 11,233
Port Blakely (A2)*
Port Gamble (C3)* 500
Port Ludlow (C3)* 275
Port Madison (A1)
Port Orchard (A2)* 2,320
Port Townsend (C2)* 6,888
Portage (A2)* 200
Porter (B4)* 200
Potlatch (B3)* 150
Poulsbo (A1)* 1,014
Prescott (G4)* 244
Preston (D3)* 500
Prevost (B2)* 8
Prosser (F4)* 2,636
Puget Island (B4) 735
Pullman (H4)* 12,022
Puyallup (C3)* 10,010
Pysht (A2) 15
Queets (A3) 250
Quilcene (B3)* 600
Quillayute (A3) 10
Quinault (B3)* 450
Quincy (F3)* 804
Rainier (C4)* 331
Ralston (G4)* 27
Randle (D4)* 500
Ravensdale (D3)* 300
Raymond (B4)* 4,110
Reardan (H3)* 410
Redmond (B1)* 573
Redondo (C3)* 540
Renton (B2)* 16,039
Republic (G2)* 895
Retsil (A2)* 738
Rice (G2)* 40
Richardson (B2)* 10
Richland (F4)* 21,809
Richmond Beach (A1)* 1,900
Richmond Highlands (A1)* 11,081
Ridgefield (C5)* 762
Riffe (C4)* 750
Riparia (G4)* 37
Ritzville (G3)* 2,145
Riverside (F2)* 149
Riverton (A2)* 2,000
Riverton Heights (B2) 3,060
Robe (D2)* 55
Roche Harbor (B2)* 98
Rochester (C4)* 325
Rock Island (E3)* 152
Rockdale (D3) 12
Rockford (H3)* 360
Rocklyn (G3)* 24
Rockport (D2)* 100
Rogersburg (H4) 3
Rollingbay (A2)* 800
Ronald (E3)*
Roosevelt (E5)* 75
Rosalia (H3)* 660
Rosburg (B4)* 300
Roslyn (E3)* 1,537
Roxboro (G4)* 9
Roy (C4)* 263
Ruby (H2) 10
Ruff (F3)* 75
Ruston ‡(C3) 838
Ryderwood (B4)*
Saint Andrews (F3)* 120
St. John (H3)* 542
Salkum (C4)* 360
San de Fuca (C2)* 90
Sappho (A2)* 250
Satsop (B3)* 125
Sauk (D2) 75
Saxon (C2) 149
Scandia (A1) 50
Scenic (D3) 25
Schrag (G3) 5
Scotia (H2) 2
Seabeck (C3)* 300
Seabold (A1) 250
Seahurst (A2)* 2,305
Seattle (A2)* 467,591
Seattle (urban area) 616,047
Seaview (A4)* 600
Sedro Woolley (C2)* 3,299
Sekiu (A2)* 211
Selah (E4)* 2,489
Selleck (D3)* 250
Sequim (B2)* 1,044
Sharon (H3) 95
Shaw Island (B2)* 80
Shelton (B3)* 5,045
Silvana (C2)* 300
Silver Creek (C4)* 312
Silverdale (A2)* 750
Silverlake (C4)* 1,500
Silverton (D2) 16
Skamania (C5)*
Skamokawa (B4)* 562
Skykomish (D3)* 497
Smyrna (F4)* 21
Snake River (G4)* 35
Snohomish (D3)* 3,094
Snoqualmie (D3)* 806
Snoqualmie Falls (D3)*
Soap Lake (F3)* 2,091
South Bellingham (C2)*
S. Bend (B4)* 1,857
S. Cle Elum (D3)* 442
S. Colby (A2)* 280
S. Prairie (D3)* 207
S. Wenatchee (E3)* 1,479
Southworth (A2)* 250
Spanaway (C3)* 600
Spangle (H3)* 242
Spirit Lake (C4) 20
Spokane (H3)* 161,721
Spokane (urban area) 174,853
Spokane Bridge (J3)* 50
Sprague (G3)* 598
Spring Valley (H3)
Springdale (H2)* 268
Stanwood (C2)* 710
Starbuck (G4)* 194
Startup (D3)* 386

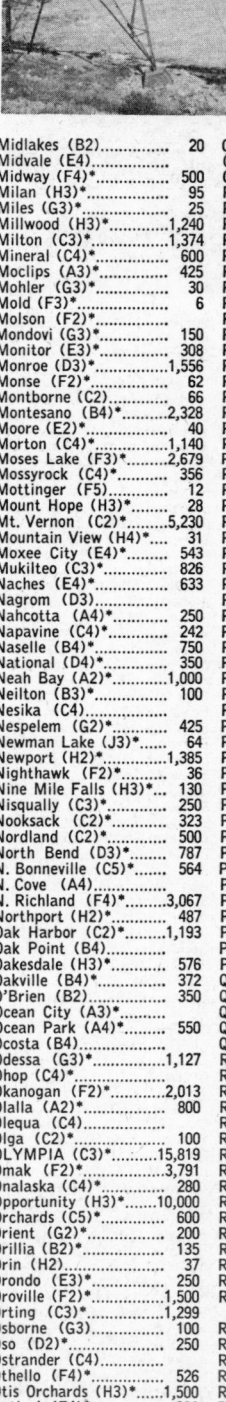

Stehekin (E2)*... 37
Steilacoom (C3)*...1,233
Stella (B4)...
Steptoe (H3)*... 110
Stevenson (C5)*... 584
Stillwater (D3)...
Stratford (F3)*... 112
Sultan (D3)*... 814
Sumas (C2)*... 658
Sumner (C3)*...2,816
Sundale (E5)... 72
Sunnydale (B2)...1,296
Sunnyside (F4)*...4,194
Sunset (H3)*... 65
Supplee (F3)...
Suquamish (A1)*...1,000
Synarep (F2)*... 3
Tacoma (C3)*...143,673
Tacoma (urban area).166,910
Tahola (A3)*... 380
Tahuya (B3)*... 60
Tampico (E4)... 50
Tatoosh (A2)... 30
Tekoa (H3)*...1,189
Telma (E3)... 12
Tenino (C4)*... 969
Thatcher (C2)... 4
Thornton (H3)*... 225
Thorp (E3)*... 350
Tieton (E4)*... 620
Tiger (H2)*... 79
Tillicum (C3)*...3,000
Timentwa (F2)...
Tokeland (A4)*... 150
Toledo (C4)*... 602
Tolt (Carnation*) (D3). 446
Tonasket (F2)*... 957
Tono (C4)... 1
Toppenish (E4)*...5,265
Touchet (G4)*... 350
Toutle (C4)*...
Tracy (G4)...
Tracyton (A2)*... 500
Trinidad (F3)*... 25
Troutlake (D5)*... 350
Tukwila (B2)*... 800
Tulalip (C2)*...
Tumtum (H3)*... 100
Tumwater (B3)*...2,725
Turner (H4)... 25
Twisp (E2)*... 776
Tyler (H3)*... 25
Underwood (D5)*... 370
Union (B3)*... 350
Union Gap (E4)*...1,766
Uniontown (H4)*... 254
Urban (C2)*... 11
Usk (H2)*... 300
Vader (B4)*... 426
Vail (C4)*... 175
Valley (H2)*... 250
Valleyford (H3)*... 213
Van Zandt (C2)*... 62
Vancouver (C5)*...41,664
Vantage (E4)*... 67
Vashon (A2)*... 550
Vaughn (C3)*... 280
Veradale (H3)*...1,700
Wahkiacus (D5)*... 40
Waitsburg (G4)*...1,015
Waldron (B2)*... 40
Walla Walla (G4)*...24,102
Wallula (G4)*... 400
Walville (B4)... 15
Wapato (E4)*...3,185
Warden (F4)*... 322
Warm Beach (C2)*...
Washougal (C5)*...1,577
Washtucna (G4)*... 316
Waterville (E3)*...1,013
Wauconda (F2)*... 3
Waukon (H3)*... 40
Wauna (C3)*... 100
Waverly (H3)*... 120
Wawawai (H4)*... 6
Wellpinit (G3)*... 60
Wenatchee (E3)*...13,072
West Wenatchee (E3)...2,690
Western (B4)...
Westport (A4)*... 731
Wheeler (F3)*... 30
White Center (A2)*...30,000
White Salmon (D5)*...1,353
White Swan (E4)*... 200
Whites (B3)... 75
Wickersham (C2)*... 135
Wilbur (G3)*...1,043
Wiley (E4)... 450
Wilkeson (D3)*... 386
Willapa (B4)*... 230
Willard (D5)... 245
Wilson Creek (F3)*... 337
Winchester (F3)*... 30
Winesap (E3)...
Winlock (C4)*... 878
Winona (H4)*... 75
Winslow (A2)*... 637
Winthrop (E2)*... 396
Winton (E3)... 23
Wishram (D5)*... 678
Withrow (F3)*... 53
Woodinville (B1)*...1,500
Woodland (C5)*...1,292
Yacolt (C5)*... 411
Yakima (E4)*...38,486
Yardley (H3)*... 500
Yelm (C4)*... 470
Zenith (C3)*... 600
Zillah (E4)*... 911

WEST VIRGINIA

Map on Page 92

Total Population 2,005,552

55 COUNTIES

Barbour (F2)...19,745
Berkeley (K2)...30,359
Boone (C4)...33,173
Braxton (E3)...18,082
Brooke (K5)...26,904
Cabell (B4)...108,035
Calhoun (D3)...10,259
Clay (D4)...14,961
Doddridge (E2)...9,026
Fayette (D4)...82,443
Gilmer (E3)...9,746
Grant (H2)...8,756
Greenbrier (F5)...39,295
Hampshire (J2)...12,577
Hancock (K4)...34,388
Hardy (J2)...10,032
Harrison (F2)...85,296
Jackson (C3)...15,299
Jefferson (L2)...17,184
Kanawha (C4)...239,629
Lewis (E2)...21,074
Lincoln (B4)...22,466
Logan (C5)...77,391
Marion (F2)...71,521
Marshall (K6)...36,893
Mason (B3)...23,537
Mc Dowell (C6)...98,887
Mercer (D6)...75,013
Mineral (J2)...22,333
Mingo (B5)...47,409
Monongalia (F1)...60,797
Monroe (E5)...13,123
Morgan (K1)...8,276
Nicholas (E4)...27,696
Ohio (K5)...71,672
Pendleton (H3)...9,313
Pleasants (D2)...6,369
Pocahontas (F4)...12,480
Preston (G1)...31,399
Putnam (C4)...21,021
Raleigh (D5)...96,273
Randolph (G3)...30,558
Ritchie (D2)...12,535
Roane (D3)...18,408
Summers (E5)...19,183
Taylor (F2)...18,422
Tucker (G2)...10,600
Tyler (E2)...10,535
Upshur (F3)...19,242
Wayne (B4)...38,696
Webster (F4)...17,888
Wetzel (E1)...20,154
Wirt (D2)...5,119
Wood (C2)...66,540
Wyoming (C5)...37,540

CITIES and TOWNS

Accoville (C5)*...1,400
Acme (D4)*... 200
Ada (D6)*... 300
Addison (Webster Springs*) (F4)...1,313
Adolph (F3)*... 85
Adrian (F3)*... 400
Advent (C3)*... 100
Albert (G2)*...
Albion (D4)...
Albright (G1)... 396
Alderson (E5)*...1,489
Alexander (F3)*... 250
Algoma (D6)*...
Alkol (C4)*... 125
Allen (B4)*...
Allingdale (E4)...
Alma (E2)*...
Alpena (G3)*... 125
Alpoca (D5)*... 550
Alton (F3)*... 156
Alum Bridge (E2)... 125
Alum Creek (C4)*... 249
Alvon (F5)*... 100
Alvy (E2)*... 155
Amblersburg (G2)... 4
Amboy (G2)*... 75
Ambrosia (C3)... 100
Ameagle (D5)*...
Amherstdale (C5)...
Amma (D3)*... 500
Anawalt (D6)*...1,383
Angerona (C3)... 10
Anmoore (F2)*...1,388
Ansted (D4)*...1,543
Anthony (F5)*... 82
Antioch (H2)*... 50
Apple Grove (B3)*... 22
Arbovale (G4)*... 80
Arbuckle (C3)*... 50
Arcola (F4)*... 125
Ardel (A4)... 200
Arden (G2)*... 250
Arlee (B3)*... 100
Arnett (D5)*...
Arnoldsburg (D3)*... 130
Arthur (H2)*... 30
Arthurdale (G1)*... 900
Asbury (E5)*... 320
Asco (C6)*... 200
Ashford (C4)*... 350
Ashley (E2)*... 90
Ashton (B3)*... 66
Athens (E6)*... 935
Auburn (E2)*... 149
Augusta (J2)*... 250
Aurora (G2)*... 337
Avon (E2)... 50
Avondale (C6)*... 975
Backus (E5)... 200
Baileysville (C5)*...1,127
Baisden (C5)*...
Baker (J2)*... 75
Bakerton (L2)*... 300
Bald Knob (C5)*... 500
Baldwin (E3)*... 95
Ballard (E6)*... 300
Ballengee (E5)*...
Bamboo (E4)... 25
Bancroft (C3)*... 700
Barboursville (B4)*...1,943
Bardane (L2)... 120
Barnabus (C5)*...1,500
Barnum (H2)*... 95
Barrackville (F1)*...2,500
Barrett (C5)*...
Bartley (C6)*...1,275
Bartow (G3)*... 200
Bass (J3)... 25
Bath (Berkeley Sprs.*) (K1)...1,213
Bayard (H2)*... 589
Bays (E3)*...
Beard (F4)*... 50
Beards Fork (D4)*... 750
Bearsville (E2)... 30
Beaver (Glen Hedrick) (D5)*...1,484
Bebee (E1)*... 200
Beckley (D5)*...19,397
Bedington (L1)*... 150
Beech (D3)*... 41
Beechbottom (K5)*...1,100
Beechwood (G1)...
Beeson (D6)*...
Belfont (E3)... 25
Belgrove (C3)*...
Belington (F2)*...1,699
Belle (C4)*...2,350
Belleville (C2)*... 101
Belmont (D2)*... 215
Belo (B5)... 150
Belva (D4)*... 301
Bemis (G3)*... 75
Benbush (G2)*... 135
Bens Run (D2)*... 135
Benwood (K5)*...3,485
Berea (E2)*... 66
Bergoo (F4)*... 800
Berkeley Springs (K1)*1,213
Berkeley Station (L2)... 75
Berlin (F2)... 66
Bernie (C4)*...
Berryburg (F2)... 200
Berwind (C6)*...1,354
Beryl (H2)*... 150
Bethany (L5)*...1,063
Bethlehem (K5)...1,146
Beverly (G3)*... 515
Bias (B5)...
Bickmore (D4)*...
Big Chimney (C4)*... 500
Big Creek (B5)*... 500
Big Four (C6)... 200
Big Isaac (E2)*... 30
Big Otter (D3)*... 200
Big Springs (D3)*... 150
Bigbend (D3)*... 100
Bim (C5)*... 750
Bingham (E4)... 90
Birch River (E4)*... 200
Bismarck (H2)*...
Blacksville (F1)*... 241
Blaine (H2)... 300
Blair (C5)*... 624
Blakeley (D4)*...
Blaker Mills (E5)*... 115
Bloomery (K2)*...
Blue Creek (D4)*... 140
Blue Spring (F3)...
Blue Sulphur Springs (E5)*... 400
Bluefield (D6)*...21,506
Board Tree (L6)... 25
Boaz (D2)... 50
Boggs (E4)*... 211
Bolair (F4)*... 300
Bomont (D4)*... 206
Booher (E2)...
Boomer (D4)*...
Boothsville (F2)... 200
Borderland (B5)*... 270
Bowden (G3)*... 150
Bower (E3)... 35
Bownemont (C4)... 400
Boyer (G3)*... 150
Bradshaw (C6)*...1,062
Bramwell (D6)*...1,587
Brandonville (G1)*... 100
Brandywine (H3)*... 150
Braxton (E3)*... 67
Breeden (B5)*... 300
Bridgeport (F2)*...2,414
Bristol (F2)*... 300
Brohard (D2)*... 400
Brood (H3)...
Brooklyn (E1)*... 500
Brooks (E5)*...
Brounland (C4)*... 50
Brown (F2)*... 250
Brownton (F2)*... 928
Bruce (E4)*... 175
Bruceton Mills (G1)*... 165
Brushy Run (H3)*... 300
Buck (E5)... 50
Buckeye (F4)*... 40
Buckhannon (F3)*...6,016
Bud (D5)*... 500
Buffalo (C3)*... 333
Bunker Hill (K2)*... 350
Burlington (J2)*... 300
Burning Springs (D3)*
Burnsville (E3)*... 731
Burnt House (D2)*... 40
Burnwell (D4)*...1,000
Burton (F1)*... 219
Byrnside (C4)...
Cabell (C4)...
Cabins (H2)*... 120
Cairo (D2)*... 500
Caldwell (F5)*... 600
Caloric (D5)... 320
Calvin (E4)*...
Camden (E2)*... 150
Camden on Gauley(E4)* 373
Cameron (L6)*...1,736
Camp Creek (D5)*... 150
Canebrake (C6)*... 568
Canfield (E3)*... 65
Canton (E2)...
Canvas (E4)*... 500
Capehart (C3)... 15
Capon Bridge (K2)*... 223
Capon Springs (K2)*... 220
Captina (K6)*... 200
Carbon (D4)*... 500
Cascade (G1)*... 200
Cashmere (E6)*... 100
Cass (G4)*... 417
Cassie (B5)*... 350
Cassity (G3)*... 250
Cassville (F1)*...
Catawba (F1)*...
Cave (H3)*... 50
Cedar Grove (D4)*...1,738
Cedarville (E3)*... 103
Center Point (E2)*... 200
Central Station (E2)*... 350
Centralia (E3)*...
Century (F2)*... 500
Ceredo (B4)*...1,399
Chapel (E3)*... 50
Chapmanville (B5)*...1,349
Charles Town (L2)*...3,035
CHARLESTON (D4)*..73,501
Charleston (urban area)...130,122
Charmco (E4)*... 700
Chattaroy (B5)*...1,484
Chelyan (C4)*...
Cherry Run (L1)*... 150
Chesapeake (D4)*...2,566
Chester (L4)*...3,758
Christian (C5)*...
Churchville (E2)... 125
Cicerone (D3)*...
Cinco (D4)*...
Cinderella (B5)*... 600
Circleville (H3)*... 250
Clarksburg (F2)*...32,014
Clay (D4)*... 500
Clayton (E5)... 135
Clear Creek (D5)*...
Clearco (F4)*... 120
Clendenin (D3)*...1,475
Cleveland (F3)*... 150
Clifftop (E4)*... 400
Clifton (B3)*... 355
Clifton Mills (G1)*... 51
Clifty (E4)*...
Clinton (K5)...
Clintonville (E5)*...
Clio (D3)*...
Clothier (C5)*... 636
Clover (D3)*...
Clover Lick (F4)*... 324
Coal City (D5)*...1,000
Coal Fork (D4)*...1,185
Coalton (G3)*... 407
Coalwood (C6)*...1,310
Coburn (F1)*...
Coco (D4)*... 200
Coe (F4)...
Coketon (G2)*... 200
Colcord (D5)*...1,800
Cold Stream (J2)*... 50
Coldwater (E2)*... 27
Colliers (L5)*... 425
Conaway (E2)... 10
Congo (K4)... 100
Copen (E3)*... 309
Corinne (D5)*...
Corinth (H2)*... 175
Corley (E3)*... 15
Cornwallis (D2)*... 124
Costa (C4)*... 168
Cottageville (C3)*... 250
Countsville (C3)*... 6
Cove Gap (B4)*... 125
Cowen (E4)*... 632
Coxs Mills (E2)*... 50
Craigsville (E4)*...
Cranberry (D5)*... 750
Craneco (C5)... 596
Cranesville (G1)... 25
Crawford (F3)*... 100
Crawley (E5)*... 150
Creekvale (K2)... 30
Cressmont (E4)...
Creston (D3)*...
Crow Summit (C3)... 25
Crum (B5)*... 350
Crystal (D6)*... 400
Cucumber (C6)*... 350
Culloden (B4)*... 250
Curry (C5)*...
Custis (E3)...
Cuzzart (H1)*... 75
Cuzzie (B4)*... 100
Cyclone (C5)*... 265
Czar (F3)*...
Dahmer (H3)... 125
Dallas (K5)*... 110
Daniels (D5)*... 800
Danville (C4)*... 544
Darkesville (L2)... 275
Davis (H2)*...1,271
Davisville (C2)*... 45
Davy (C6)*...1,650
Dawes (D4)*... 700
Dawson (E5)*... 100
Dean (E1)... 15
Decota (D4)*...1,300
Deer Run (H3)*...
Deer Walk (D2)... 75
Delbarton (B5)*...1,353
Dellslow (G1)*...
Denver (K6)... 50
Diamond (C4)*...
Diana (F3)*...
Dickson (B4)...
Dille (E4)*... 500
Dingess (B5)*... 400
Dixie (D4)*... 50
Dola (F2)*... 110
Doman (J2)... 50
Donohue (D2)... 75
Dorcas (H3)*... 60
Dorfee (D4)... 19
Dorothy (D5)*... 3,000
Dott (D6)*... 400
Douglas (D3)... 25
Dry Creek (D5)*... 489
Dryfork (H3)*... 200
Duck (E3)*...
Duffy (F3)*... 40
Dulin (D2)... 3
Dunbar (C4)*...8,032
Duncan (C3)*... 50
Dundon (D4)*... 125
Dunlow (B4)*... 125
Dunmore (G4)*... 65
Dunns (D5)*... 35
Duo (E4)*...
Durbin (G3)*... 540
Durgon (J3)... 50
Dyer (F4)... 25
East Lynn (B4)*... 300
E. Rainelle (E5)*...1,695
Eastbank (D4)*... 735
Eatons (D2)*...
Eccles (D5)*...1,885
Eckman (C6)*...1,574
Edgarton (B5)*... 500
Edray (F4)... 32
Edwight (C5)*...
Egeria (D5)*... 300
Eglon (G2)*... 110
Elana (D3)*... 145
Elbert (C6)*...1,565
Elgood (E6)*... 75
Elizabeth (D2)*... 755
Elk Garden (H2)*... 318
Elkhorn (D6)*...1,035
Elkhurst (D4)*... 66
Elkins (G3)*...9,121
Elkridge (D4)*... 475
Elkview (C4)*... 400
Elkwater (G3)*... 75
Ellamore (F3)*... 600
Ellenboro (D2)*... 307
Elm Grove (K5)*...8,000
Elmira (E3)*... 200
Elton (E5)*... 200
Emoryville (H2)*... 100
English (C6)*... 890
Enoch (E4)*... 282
Enon (E4)...
Enterprise (F2)*...1,200
Erbacon (E3)*... 210
Eskdale (C4)*...
Ethel (C5)*...1,032
Eureka (D2)*... 125
Evans (C3)*... 150
Evansville (G2)... 45
Evenwood (G3)... 25
Everettville (F1)*... 750
Everson (F2)... 50
Exchange (E3)*... 25
Fabius (J2)*... 30
Fairmont (F2)*...29,346
Fairplain (C3)*...
Fairview (F1)*... 775
Falling Springs (Renick*) (F4)... 307
Failing Waters (L1)*... 75
Fallsmill (E3)*... 50
Fame (H3)... 15
Far (E1)... 20
Farmington (F1)*... 824
Farmington (F1)*... 824
Fayetteville (D4)*...1,952
Fellowsville (G2)... 120
Fenwick (E4)*... 500
Ferguson (B4)*...
Ferrellsburg (B4)*... 275
Fink (E2)... 8
Fire Creek (E5)... 30
Fireco (D5)*...
Fisher (H2)*... 20
Flat Top (D5)*... 150
Flat Woods (E3)*... 288
Flemington (F2)*... 572
Fletcher (C3)...
Flint (G3)...
Follansbee (K5)*...4,435
Folsom (E2)*... 485
Forest Hill (E5)*... 45
Fort Ashby (J2)*... 800
Ft. Branch (C5)...
Ft. Gay (A4)*... 714
Ft. Seybert (H3)*... 200
Ft. Spring (E5)*... 225
Foster (C4)*...
Four States (F2)*... 470
Frame (C3)*... 98
Frametown (E3)*... 500
Frankford (F5)*... 185
Franklin (H3)*... 777
Fraziers Bottom (B3)* 75
Freed (D2)*...
Freeman (D6)*... 400
Freemansburg (F2)... 21
French Creek (F3)*... 175
Frenchton (F3)*... 221
Friendly (D1)*... 216
Frost (G4)*... 99
Gallipolis Ferry (B3)*... 100
Galloway (F2)*...1,000
Gandeeville (D3)*... 328
Ganotown (K2)... 75
Gap Mills (F5)*...
Garretts Bend (C4)*... 125
Gary (C6)*...1,600
Gassaway (E3)*...1,306
Gauley Bridge (D4)*...1,134
Gauley Mills (E4)*... 200
Gay (C3)*...
Gem (E3)*... 22
Genoa (B4)*...
Gerrardstown (K2)*... 205
Ghent (D5)*... 488
Giatto (D6)*... 550
Gilbert (C5)*... 722
Gilboa (E4)*... 275
Gill (B4)*... 50
Gilmer (E3)*... 250
Given (C3)*... 250
Glade Farms (G1)...
Gladesville (G2)... 100
Gladwin (G2)... 30
Glady (G3)*... 300
Glasgow ‡(D4)*... 881
Gleason (H2)... 40
Glebe (J2)... 50
Glen (D4)*... 200
Glen Dale (K5)*...1,467
Glen Daniel (D5)*...
Glen Easton (K6)*... 200
Glen Ferris (D4)*... 500
Glen Jean (D5)*...1,800
Glen Hedrick (Beaver*) (D5)...1,484
Glen Rodgers (D5)*...1,593
Glen White (D5)*... 300
Glenalum (C5)*... 600
Glengary (K2)*... 50
Glenhayes (A4)*... 300
Glenray (E5)... 75
Glenville (E3)*...1,789
Glenwood (B3)*... 150
Glovergap (F1)*... 150
Good (K2)... 100
Goodwill (D6)*... 800
Goose Creek (D2)... 100
Gordon (C5)*... 800
Gormania (H2)*... 185
Grace (D3)... 3
Grafton (G2)*...7,365
Grandview (D5)*... 175
Grant Town (F1)*...1,273
Grantsville (D3)*... 959
Granville (Mona*)(G3)..1,004
Grassy (B4)*...
Grassy Meadows (E5)*.. 100
Great Cacapon (K1)*... 550
Green Bank (G4)*... 200
Green Hill (E1)... 175
Green Sulphur Springs (E5)*...
Greenland (H2)*... 14
Greenview (C4)*... 400
Greenville (E5)*... 65
Greenwood (E2)*... 366
Greer (G1)*...
Griffithsville (B4)*... 500
Grimms Landing (B3)*. 420
Grove (E2)...
Guardian (F3)*... 600
Guyan (C5)*... 300
Hacker Valley (F3)*... 150
Hall (F2)*... 43
Halltown (L2)*... 250
Hambleton (G2)*... 283
Hamlin (B4)*... 841
Hammond (F2)*... 102
Hampden (C5)*... 50
Hancock (K1)*... 131
Handley (D4)*...1,007
Hanging Rock (J2)*... 75
Hanover (C5)*... 500
Hany (B4)... 350
Harding (G3)*... 250
Harman (G3)*... 146
Harmony (D3)*... 13
Harper (D5)*...1,700
Harpers Ferry (L2)*... 822
Harris Ferry (C2)... 25
Harrisville (E2)*...1,387
Hartford (C2)*... 366
Hartland (D4)... 50
Harts (B4)*... 160
Harvey (D5)*... 503
Havaco (C6)*...
Hazelton (G1)*... 80
Headsville (J2)*... 240
Heaters (E3)*...
Hebron (D2)*... 50
Hedgesville (K1)*... 419
Heights (B3)*... 300
Helvetia (F3)*... 94
Hemphill (C6)*...2,300
Henderson (B3)*... 483
Hendricks (G2)*... 492
Henlawson (B5)*...1,750
Henry (H2)... 5
Hepzibah (F2)*...1,800
Herndon (D5)*... 500
Hewlet (A4)... 75
Higginsville (J2)... 150
Hico (D4)*... 300
High View (K2)*... 50
Highcoal (C5)*... 500
Highland (D2)*... 100
Hillsboro (F4)*... 241
Hilltop (D5)*... 615
Hinton (E5)*...5,780
Hoard (G1)... 6
Hodgeville (F2)... 100
Hogsett (B3)*... 25
Holcomb (E4)*... 50
Holden (B5)*...
Hollidays Cove (K5)...
Hollywood (F5)*... 75
Hominy Falls (E4)*... 310
Hookersville (E4)*...
Horner (F3)*... 97
Horse Shoe Run (G2)*.. 125
Horton (G3)...
Hosterman (G4)... 25
Howard (K6)... 25
Howesville (G2)*... 250
Hubball (B4)... 200
Hubbardstown (A4)... 400
Hudson (G1)... 40
Hundred (E1)*... 587
Huntersville (G4)*... 80
Hunting Ground (H3)... 75

Map on Page 93

WISCONSIN

Total Population 3,434,575

71 COUNTIES

CITIES and TOWNS

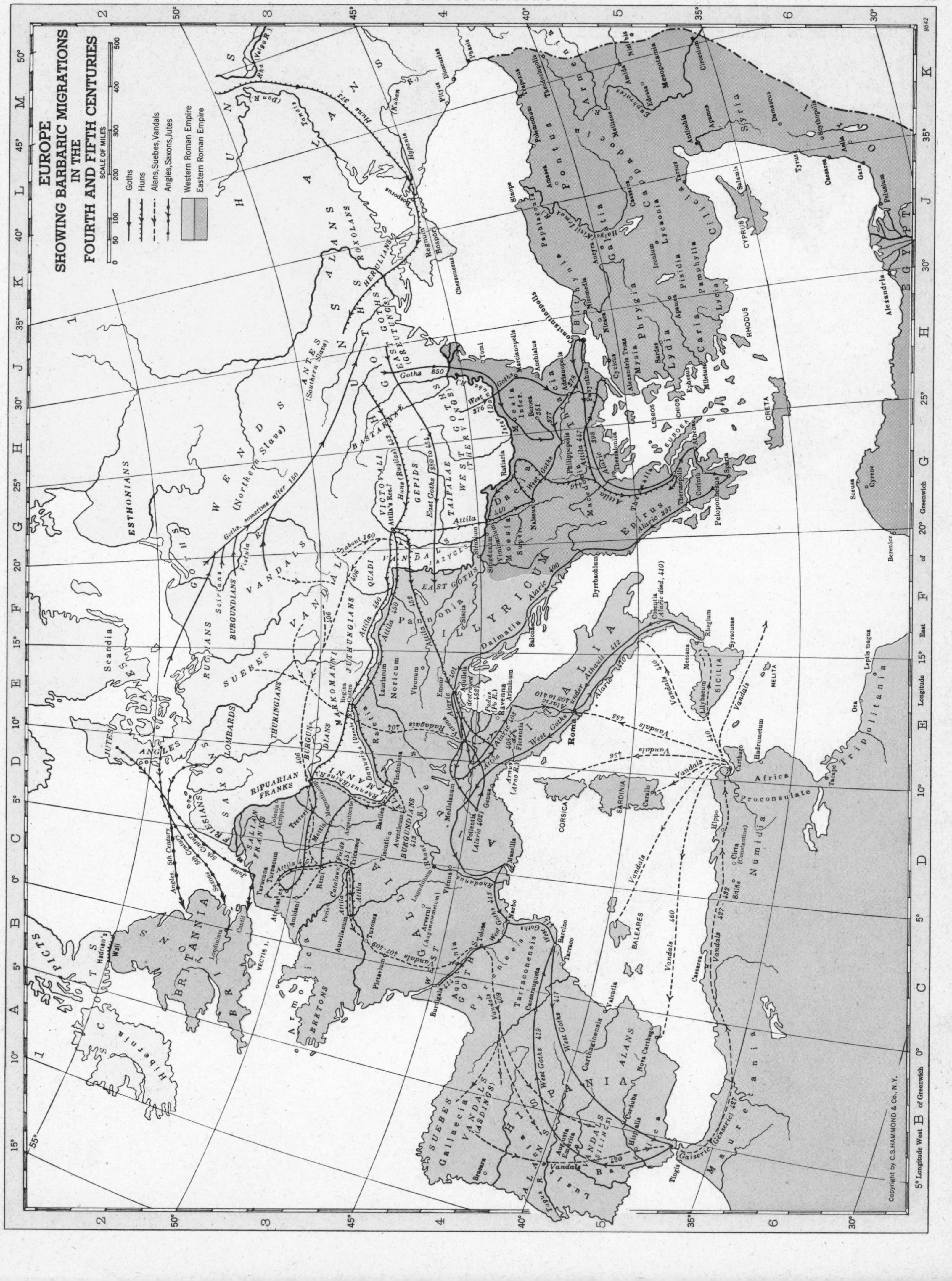

EUROPE
SHOWING BARBARIC MIGRATIONS
IN THE
FOURTH AND FIFTH CENTURIES
SCALE OF MILES
0 50 100 200 300 400 500
Goths
Huns
Alans, Suebes, Vandals
Angles, Saxons, Jutes
Western Roman Empire
Eastern Roman Empire
Copyright by C.S. HAMMOND & Co., N.Y.

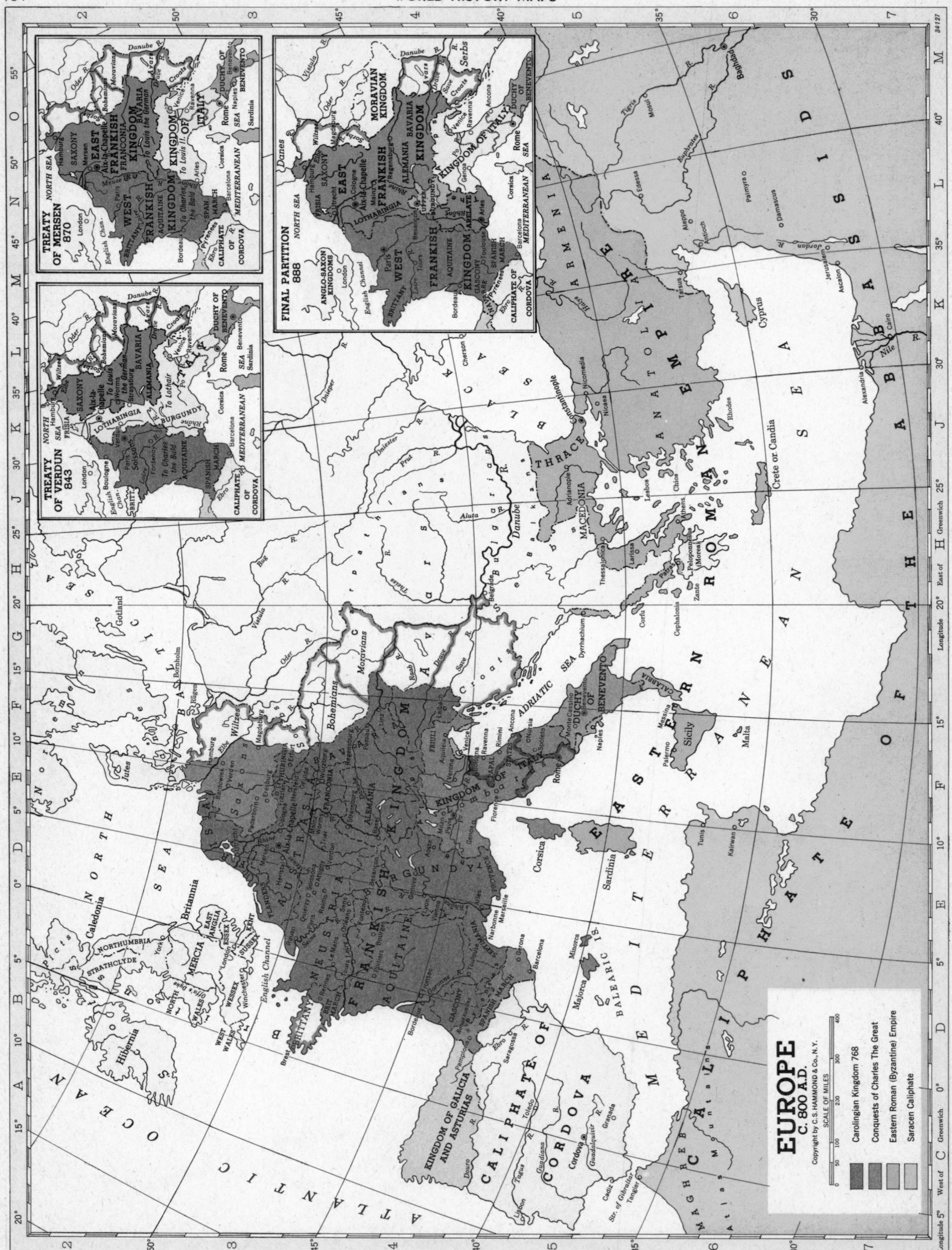

TREATY OF MERSEN 870

TREATY OF VERDUN 843

FINAL PARTITION 888

EUROPE
C. 800 A.D.

Copyright by C. S. HAMMOND & Co., N.Y.

SCALE OF MILES

Carolingian Kingdom 768
Conquests of Charles The Great
Eastern Roman (Byzantine) Empire
Saracen Caliphate

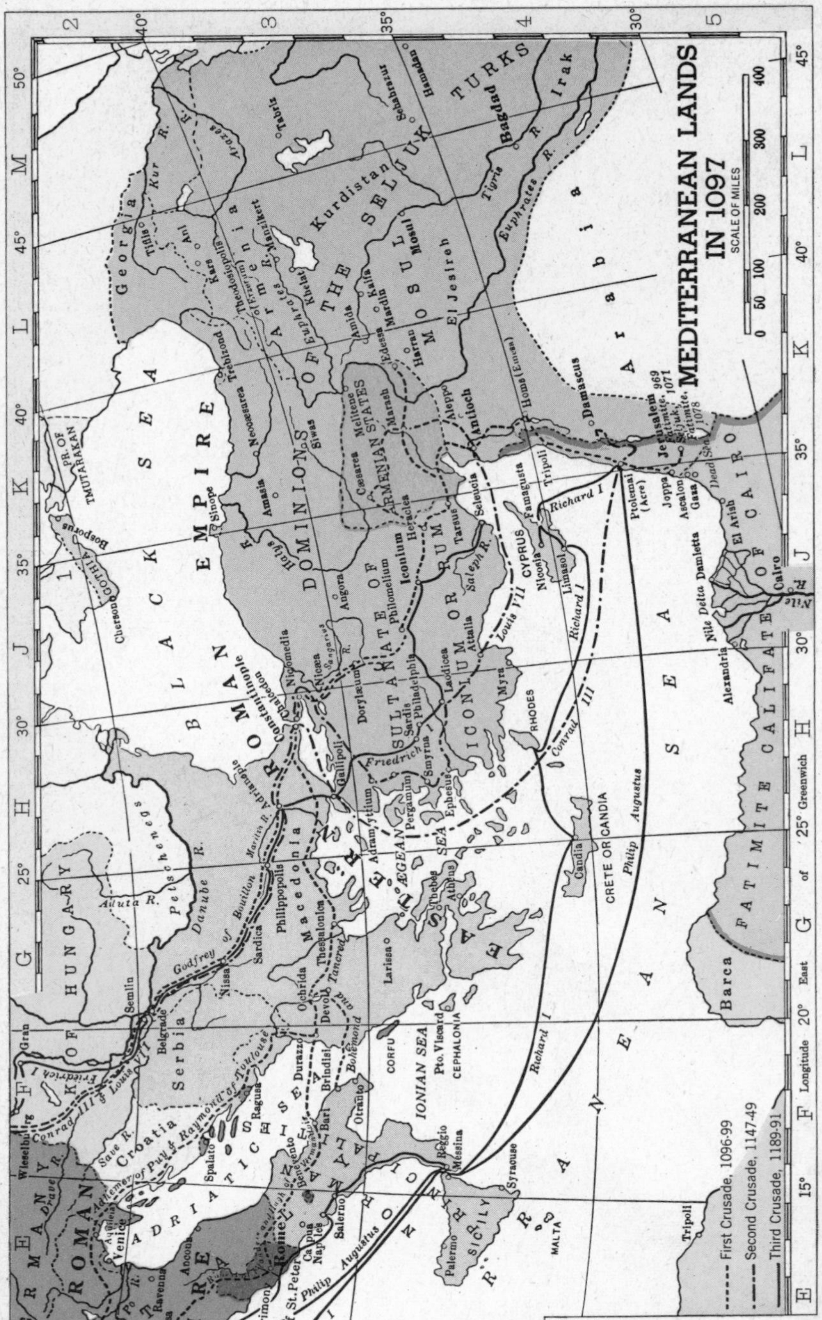

MEDITERRANEAN LANDS IN 1097

SCALE OF MILES
0 50 100 200 300 400

First Crusade, 1096-99
Second Crusade, 1147-49
Third Crusade, 1189-91

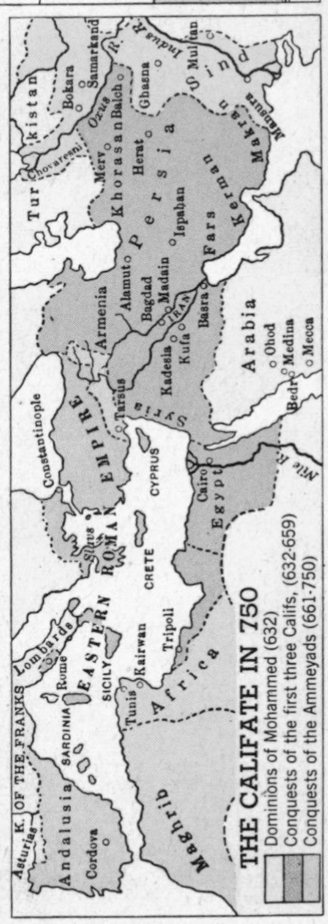

THE CALIFATE IN 750

Dominions of Mohammed (632)
Conquests of the first three Califs, (632-659)
Conquests of the Ommeyads (661-750)

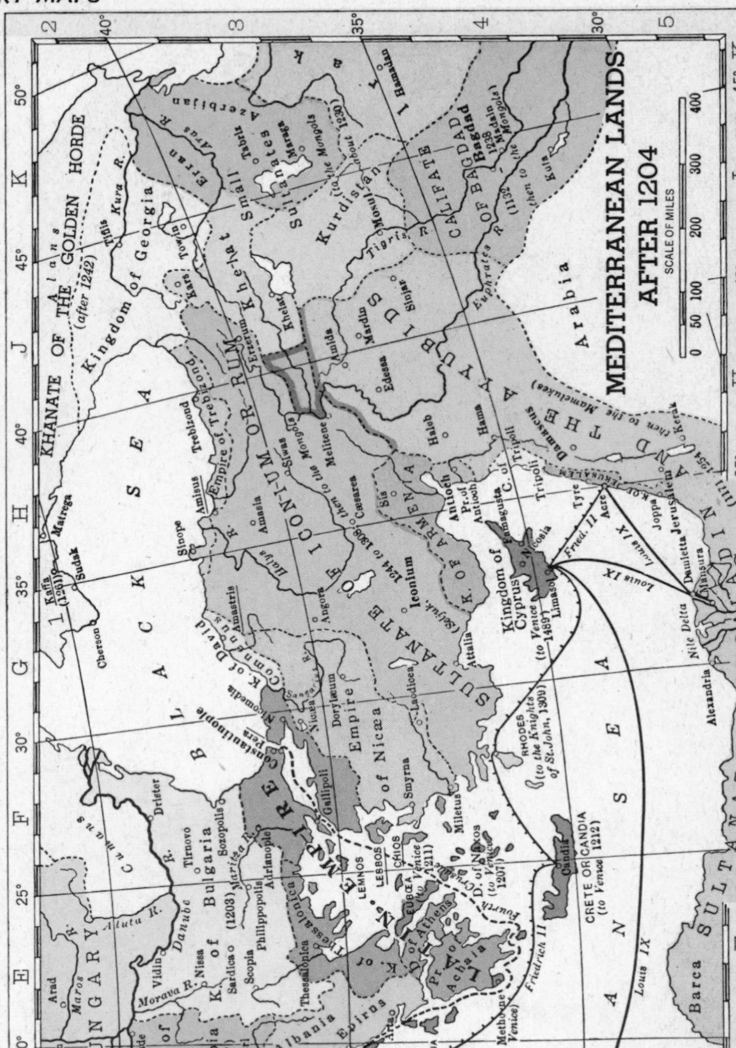

MEDITERRANEAN LANDS AFTER 1204

SCALE OF MILES
0 50 100 200 300 400

Fourth Crusade, 1202-04
Crusade of Friedrich II, 1228-29
Crusades of Louis IX, 1248-54 and in 1270
Venetian possessions
Genoese acquisitions after 1261 underlined: Pera

Kingdom of Jerusalem as fixed by the Treaty of 1229

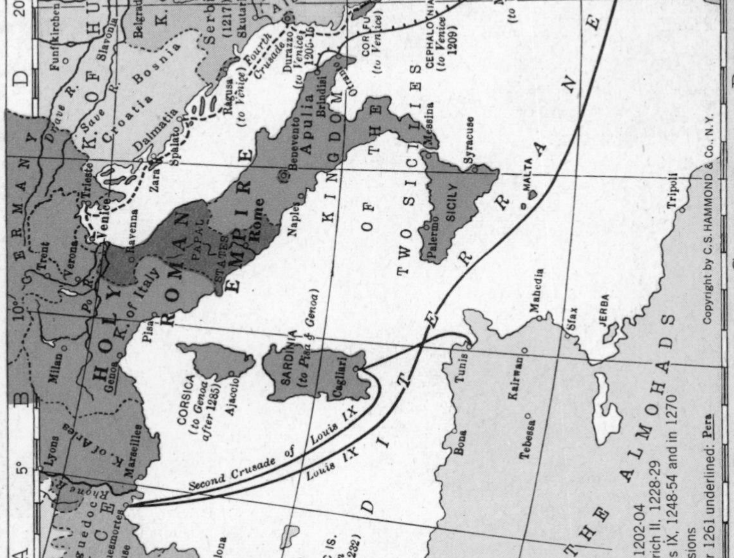

LATIN STATES IN SYRIA
After the 1st Crusade

SCALE OF MILES
0 20 40 60 80 100

Dates are those of conquests by the Crusaders; years of losses in italics.

Copyright by C. S. Hammond & Co. N.Y.

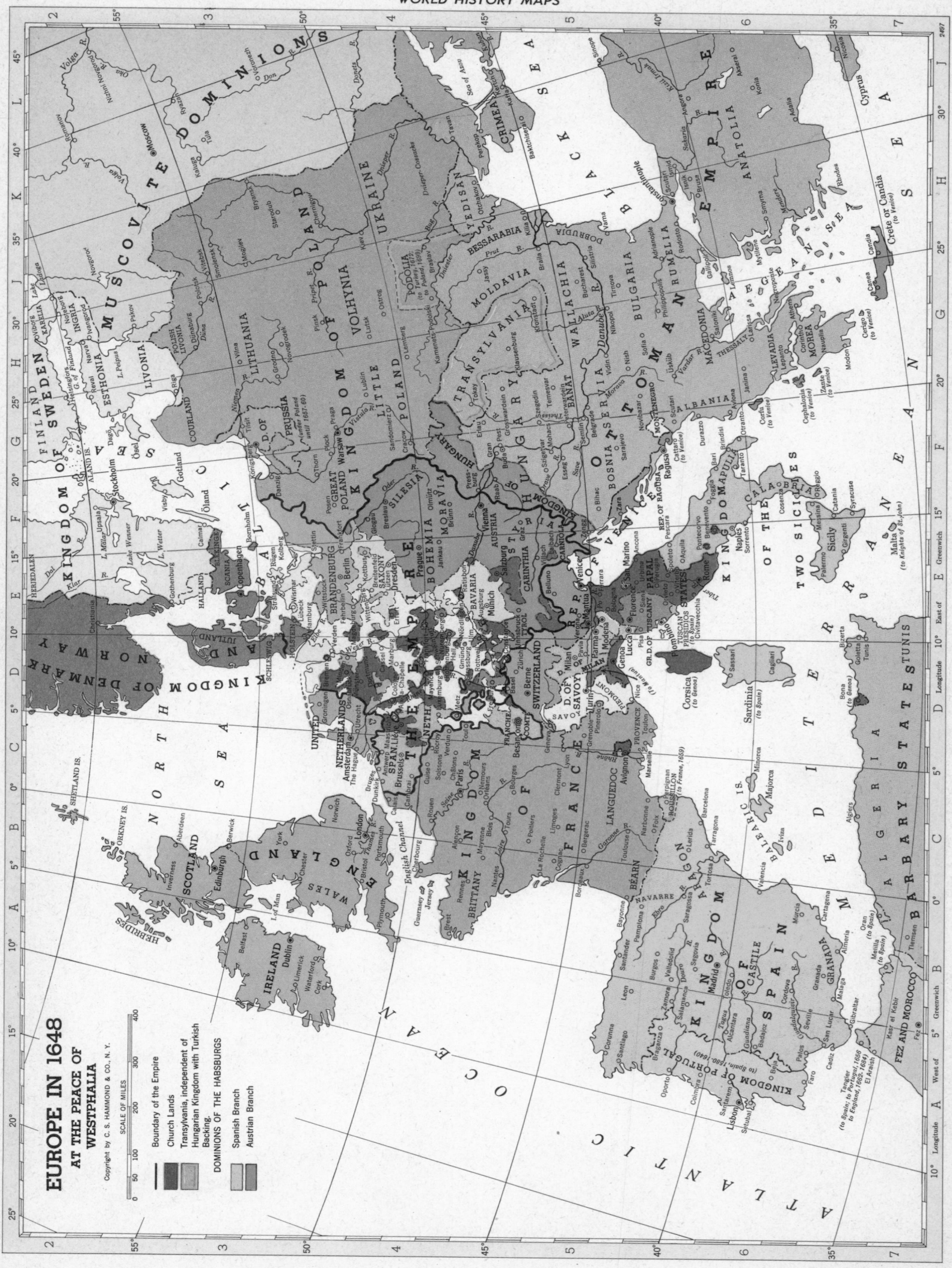

EUROPE IN 1648
AT THE PEACE OF WESTPHALIA

Copyright by C. S. HAMMOND & CO., N.Y.

SCALE OF MILES

Boundary of the Empire
Church Lands
Transylvania, independent of
Hungarian Kingdom with Turkish
Backing.
DOMINIONS OF THE HABSBURGS
Spanish Branch   Austrian Branch

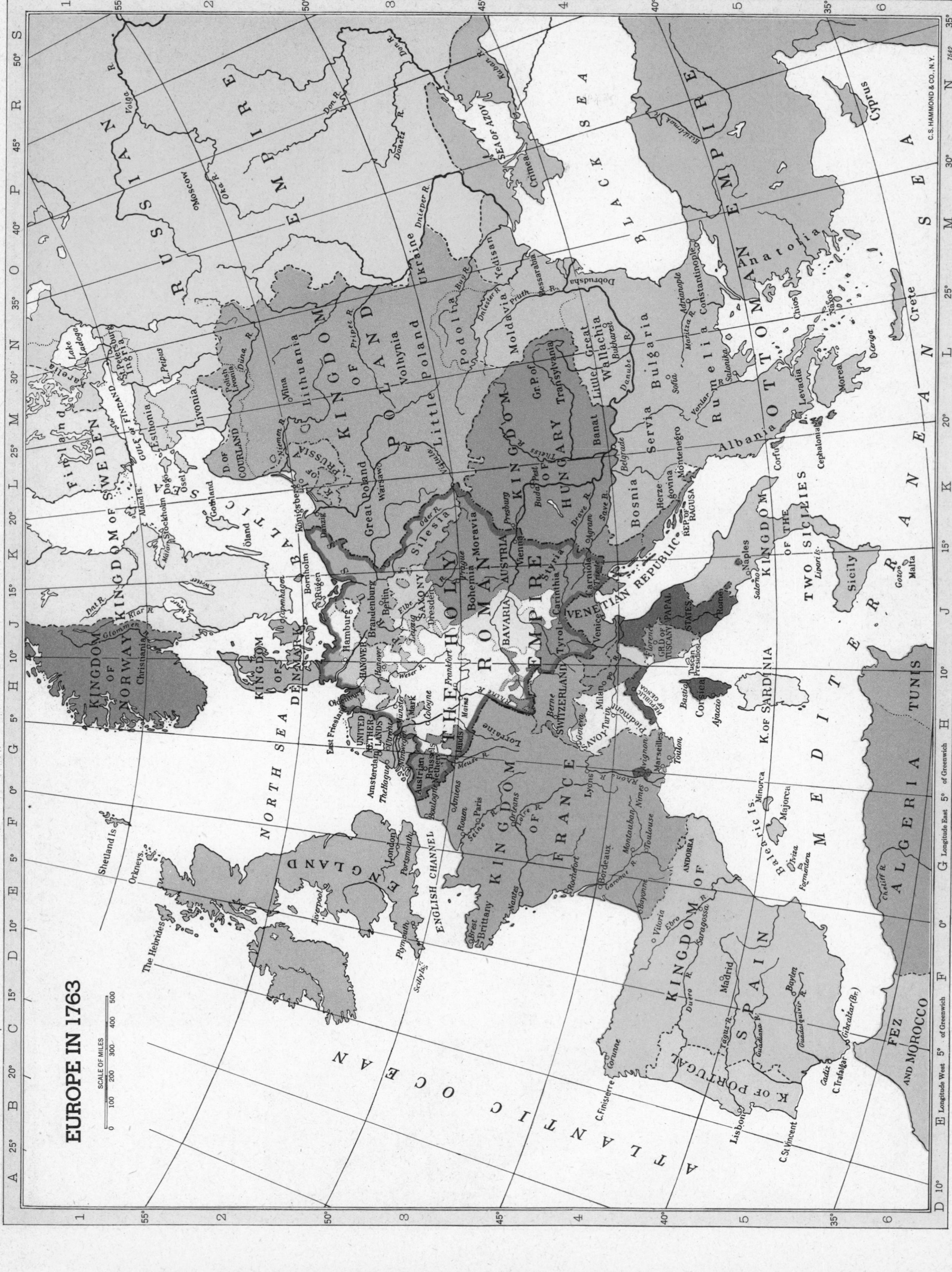

EUROPE IN 1763

SCALE OF MILES
0 100 200 300 400 500

C.S. HAMMOND & CO., N.Y.

RUSSIAN EMPIRE

KINGDOM OF SWEDEN

KINGDOM OF NORWAY

KINGDOM OF DENMARK

Finland
GULF OF FINLAND
Lake Ladoga
St. Petersburg
Ingria
Moscow
Volga R.
Oka R.
Don R.
Donetz R.
Dnieper R.
Dniester R.
Bug R.

KINGDOM OF POLAND
Lithuania
Great Poland
Little Poland
Volhynia
Podolia
Ukraine
Warsaw
Vilna
Livonia
Courland
D. OF COURLAND
Esthonia
Polish Livonia
Düna R.
Niemen R.
Pripet R.

PRUSSIA
Königsberg
Danzig
Gothland
Öland
Stockholm
Copenhagen
Bornholm
Rügen
Hamburg

BALTIC SEA
NORTH SEA

ENGLAND
London
Liverpool
Plymouth
Portsmouth
The Hebrides
Orkneys
Shetland Is.
Scilly Is.

ENGLISH CHANNEL

KINGDOM OF FRANCE
Paris
Rouen
Amiens
Orleans
Nantes
Brittany
Bordeaux
Toulouse
Montauban
Nîmes
Marseilles
Toulon
Lyons
Rochefort
Bayonne
Seine R.
Loire R.
Garonne R.
Rhone R.

UNITED NETHERLANDS
Amsterdam
The Hague
Brussels
Austrian Netherlands
East Friesland
Meuse R.
Rhine R.

THE HOLY ROMAN EMPIRE
Hanover
Brandenburg
Berlin
Saxony
Bohemia
Moravia
Bavaria
Silesia
Cologne
Frankfort
Mayence
Munster
Mark
Oldenburg
Dresden
Prague
Elbe R.
Oder R.
Weser R.
Main R.

AUSTRIA
Vienna
Tyrol
Carinthia
Carniola
Styria
Lorraine
SWITZERLAND
Berne
Geneva
Savoy
Turin
Piedmont
Milan
Genoa
REPUBLIC OF GENOA
Corsica
Bastia
Ajaccio

KINGDOM OF HUNGARY
Buda
Pest
Presburg
Transylvania
Banat
Temesvar
Drave R.
Save R.
Belgrade

VENETIAN REPUBLIC
Venice
Trieste

PAPAL STATES
Rome
GR. D. OF TUSCANY
Florence

KINGDOM OF SARDINIA

KINGDOM OF THE TWO SICILIES
Naples
Sicily
Salerno
Lipari Is.
Gozo
Malta

MEDITERRANEAN SEA

KINGDOM OF SPAIN
Madrid
Barcelona
Saragossa
Valencia
Bilbao
Vitoria
Coruña
C. Finisterre
Gibraltar (Br.)
Cadiz
C. Trafalgar
C. St. Vincent
Ebro R.
Duero R.
Guadiana R.
Guadalquivir R.

K. OF PORTUGAL
Lisbon

Balearic Is.
Minorca
Majorca
Iviza
Formentera
ANDORRA

ATLANTIC OCEAN

FEZ AND MOROCCO
ALGERIA
TUNIS

OTTOMAN EMPIRE
Rumelia
Servia
Bosnia
Bulgaria
Moldavia
Great Wallachia
Little Wallachia
Dobrudsha
Bessarabia
Montenegro
Herzegovina
REP. OF RAGUSA
Albania
Anatolia
Constantinople
Adrianople
Sofia
Salonika
Morea
Crete
Cyprus
Chios
Naxos

BLACK SEA
SEA OF AZOV
Crimea

Danube R.
Pruth R.
Dniester R.

D. Longitude West of Greenwich 0° Longitude East of Greenwich

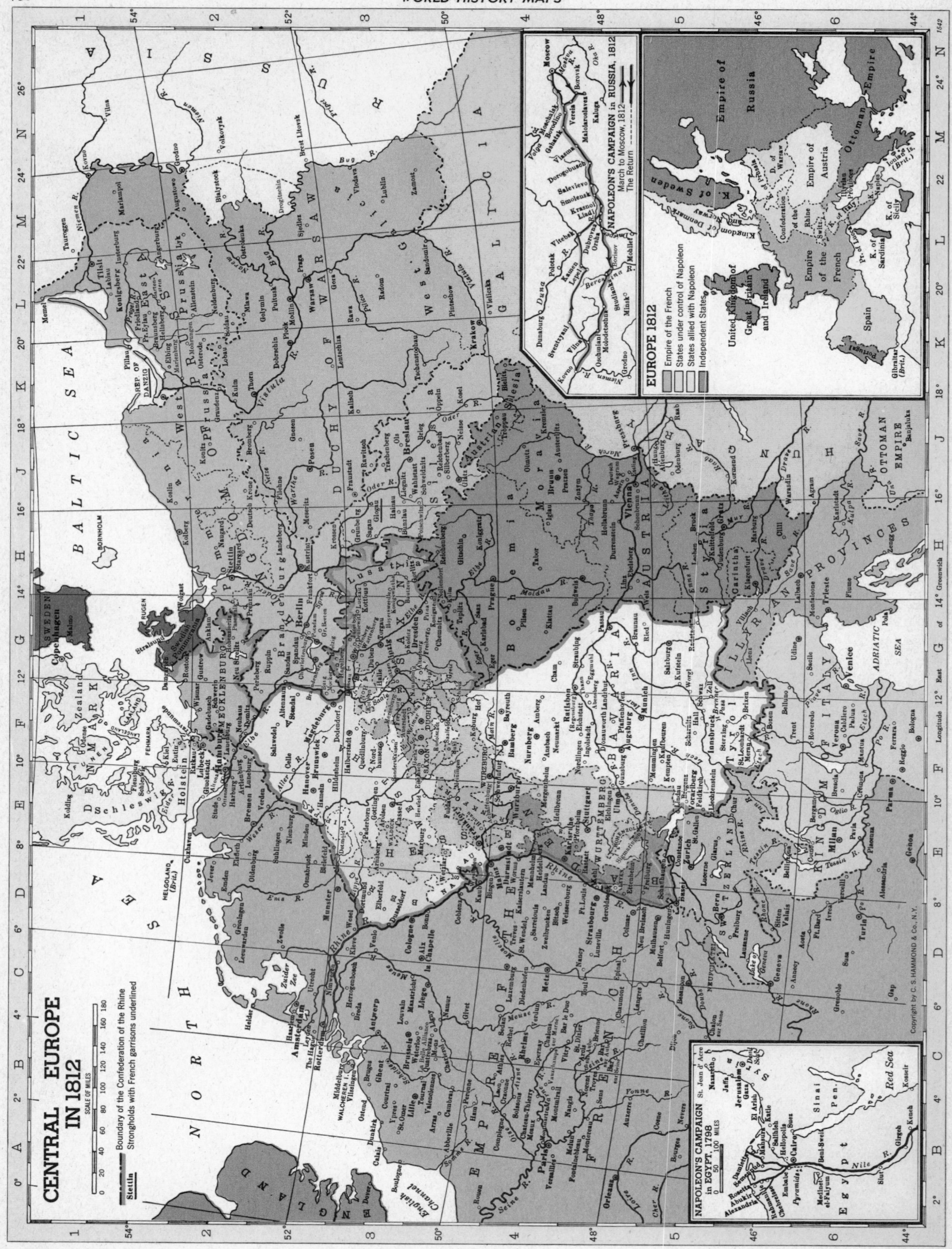

CENTRAL EUROPE
IN 1812

SCALE OF MILES
0 20 40 60 80 100 120 140 160 180

Stettin   Boundary of the Confederation of the Rhine
           Strongholds with French garrisons underlined

Copyright by C. S. HAMMOND & Co., N.Y.

NAPOLEON'S CAMPAIGN in RUSSIA, 1812
March to Moscow, 1812
The Return

EUROPE 1812
Empire of the French
States under control of Napoleon
States allied with Napoleon
Independent States
United Kingdom of
Great Britain
and Ireland

NAPOLEON'S CAMPAIGN
in EGYPT, 1798
0 50 100 MILES

EUROPE IN 1914
Copyright by C. S. HAMMOND & CO., N.Y.
SCALE OF MILES
SCALE OF KILOMETRES
Capitals of Countries
International Boundaries
Canals
Longitude West D of Greenwich
Longitude East E of Greenwich
ATLANTIC OCEAN
BARENTS SEA
NORTH SEA
BALTIC SEA
BLACK SEA
CASPIAN SEA
MEDITERRANEAN SEA
TYRRHENIAN SEA
IONIAN SEA
Bay of Biscay
URAL MOUNTAINS
RUSSIAN EMPIRE
OTTOMAN EMPIRE
GREAT BRITAIN
BRITISH ISLES
FRANCE
SPAIN
PORTUGAL
ITALY
GERMAN EMPIRE
AUSTRIA-HUNGARY
SWITZERLAND
DENMARK
NORWAY
SWEDEN
FINLAND
POLAND
RUMANIA
BULGARIA
SERBIA
ALBANIA
GREECE
IRELAND
ICELAND
TUNISIA
ALGERIA
MOROCCO
ST. PETERSBURG
MOSCOW
CONSTANTINOPLE
BERLIN
VIENNA
PARIS
LONDON
ROME
MADRID
Caucasus
Pyrenees
Carpathian Mts.
Alps

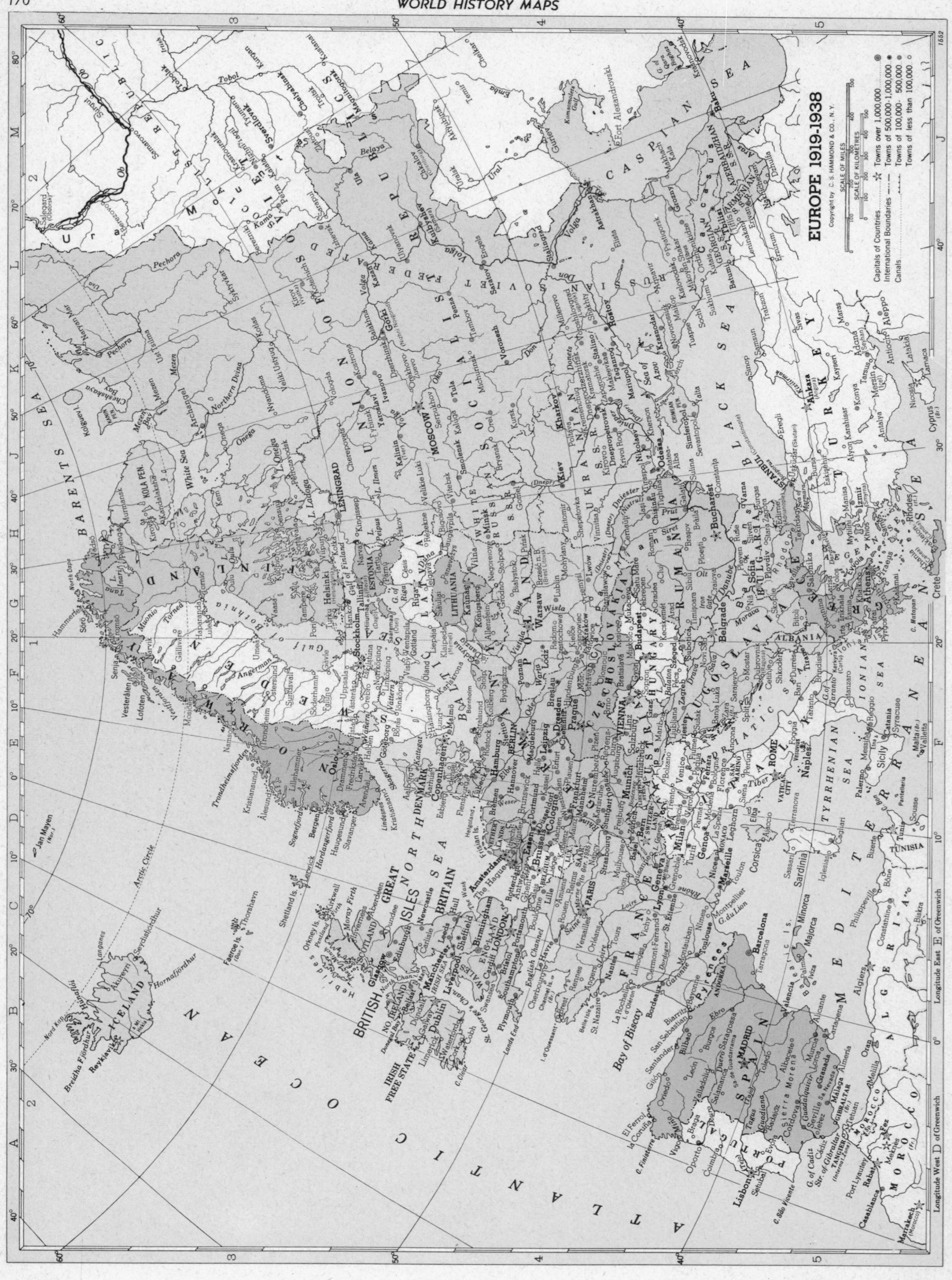

EUROPE 1919-1938

Copyright by C. S. HAMMOND & CO., N.Y.

SCALE OF KILOMETERS

Capitals of Countries .... ★
International Boundaries .... ----
Canals .... ----

Towns over 1,000,000 ⊛
Towns of 500,000-1,000,000 ●
Towns of 100,000-500,000 ◉
Towns of less than 100,000 ○

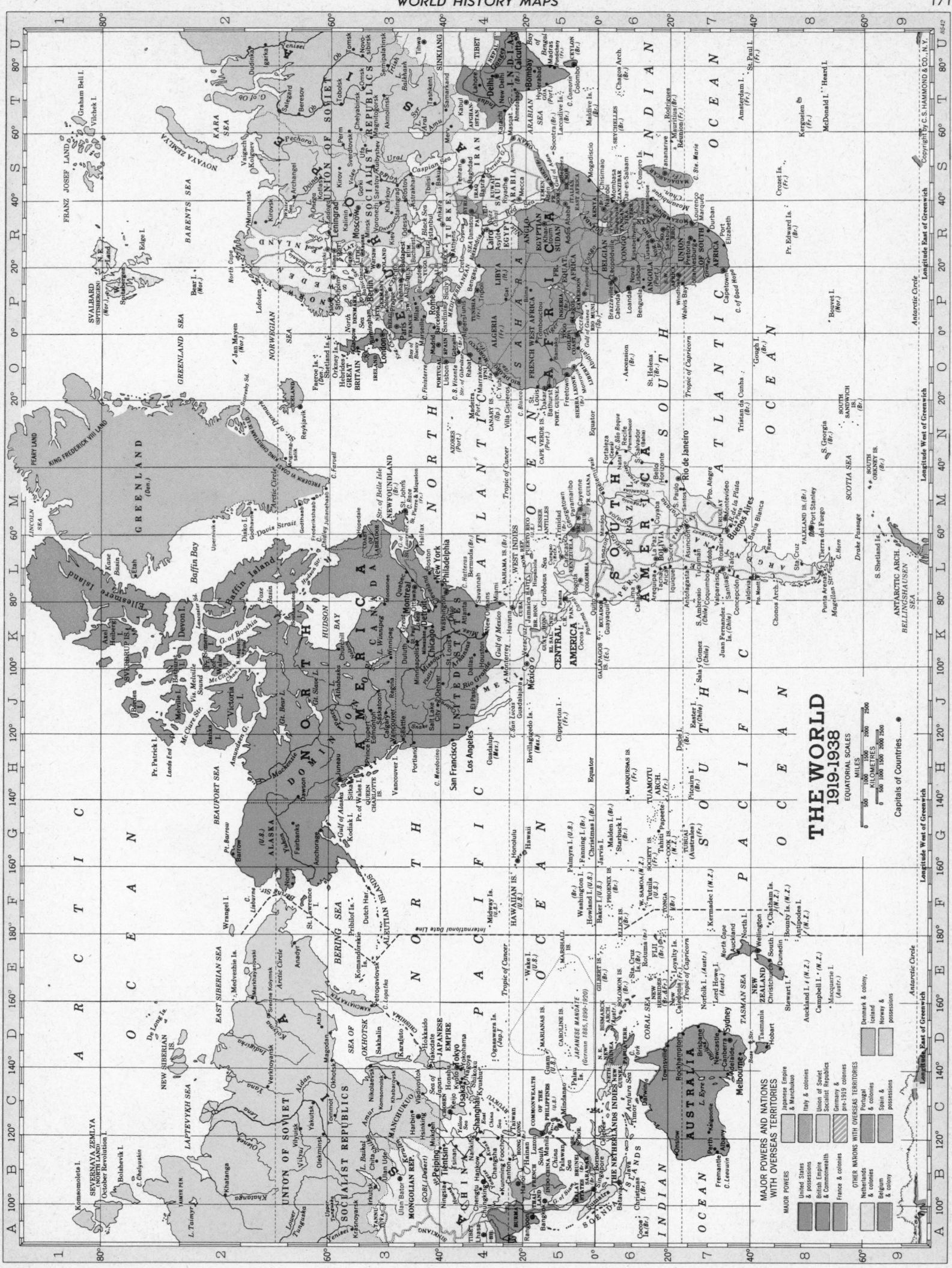

THE WORLD
1919-1938

EQUATORIAL SCALES

MILES

KILOMETRES

Capitals of Countries........ •

MAJOR POWERS AND NATIONS
WITH OVERSEAS TERRITORIES

MAJOR POWERS

United States
& possessions

British Empire
& Commonwealth

France & colonies

OTHER NATIONS WITH OVERSEAS TERRITORIES

Netherlands
The Netherlands Indies

Belgium
& colony

Japanese Empire & Manchukuo

Italy & colonies

Union of Soviet
Socialist Republics

Germany
pre-1919 colonies

Portugal
& colonies

Spain &
possessions

Denmark & colony
Iceland

Norway &
possessions

Copyright by C. S. HAMMOND & CO., N.Y.

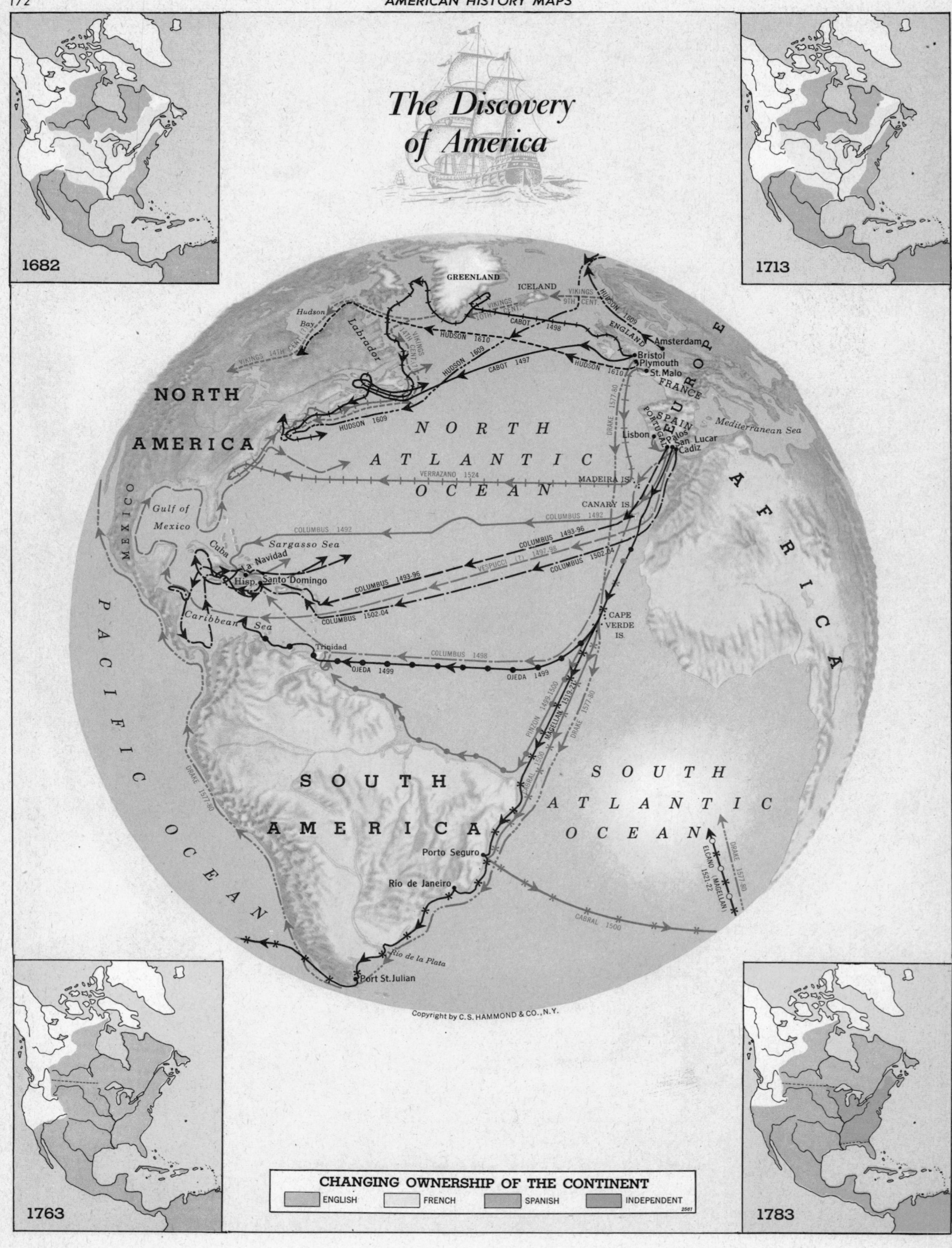

The Discovery of America

1682

1713

GREENLAND

ICELAND

VIKINGS 9TH CENT.

HUDSON 1609

VIKINGS 10TH CENT.

CABOT 1498

Hudson Bay

Labrador

VIKINGS 11TH CENT.

VIKINGS 14TH CENT.

HUDSON 1610

HUDSON 1609

CABOT 1497

HUDSON 1610

ENGLAND

Amsterdam

Bristol
Plymouth
St. Malo

NORTH AMERICA

EUROPE

FRANCE

DRAKE 1577-80

SPAIN

PORTUGAL

Lisbon

Palos
San Lucar
Cadiz

Mediterranean Sea

NORTH ATLANTIC OCEAN

VERRAZANO 1524

MADEIRA IS.

CANARY IS.

COLUMBUS 1492

Gulf of Mexico

MEXICO

COLUMBUS 1492

Sargasso Sea

Cuba

La Navidad
Hisp. Santo Domingo

COLUMBUS 1493-96

VESPUCCI (?) 1497-98

COLUMBUS 1493-96

COLUMBUS 1502-04

A F R I C A

Caribbean Sea

COLUMBUS 1502-04

Trinidad

COLUMBUS 1498

CAPE VERDE IS.

OJEDA 1499

OJEDA 1499

PACIFIC OCEAN

DRAKE 1577-80

SOUTH AMERICA

PINZON 1499-1500

MAGELLAN 1519-21

DRAKE 1577-80

SOUTH ATLANTIC OCEAN

Porto Seguro

Rio de Janeiro

CABRAL 1500

ELCANO 1521-22
MAGELLAN

DRAKE 1577-80

Rio de la Plata

Port St. Julian

1763

1783

CHANGING OWNERSHIP OF THE CONTINENT

ENGLISH   FRENCH   SPANISH   INDEPENDENT

2561

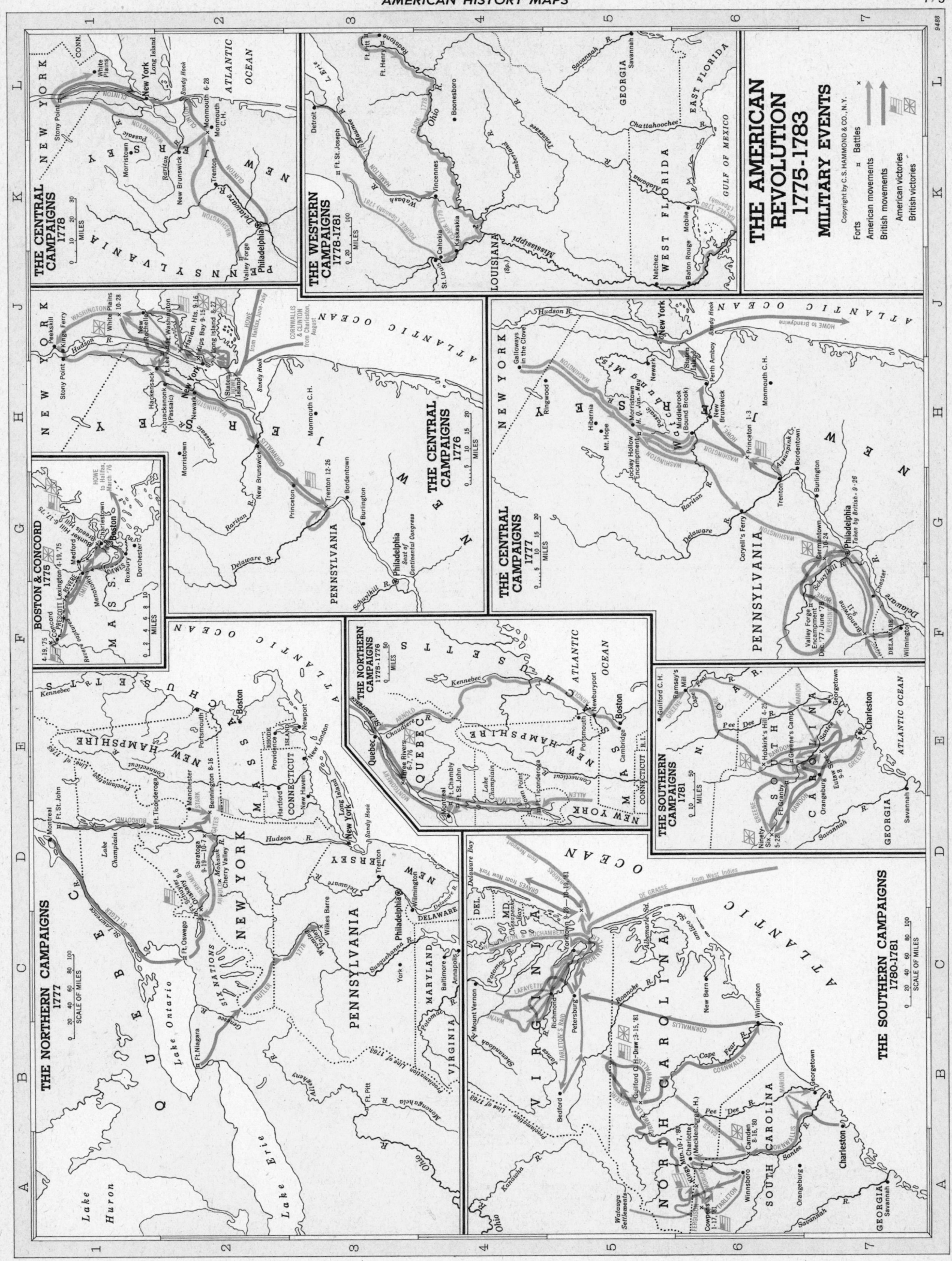

THE CENTRAL CAMPAIGNS 1778

THE WESTERN CAMPAIGNS 1778-1781

THE AMERICAN REVOLUTION 1775-1783 MILITARY EVENTS

Copyright by C. S. HAMMOND & CO., N.Y.

Forts × Battles
American movements
British movements
American victories
British victories

BOSTON & CONCORD 1775

THE CENTRAL CAMPAIGNS 1776

THE CENTRAL CAMPAIGNS 1777

THE NORTHERN CAMPAIGNS 1775-1776

THE SOUTHERN CAMPAIGNS 1781

THE NORTHERN CAMPAIGNS 1777

THE SOUTHERN CAMPAIGNS 1780-1781

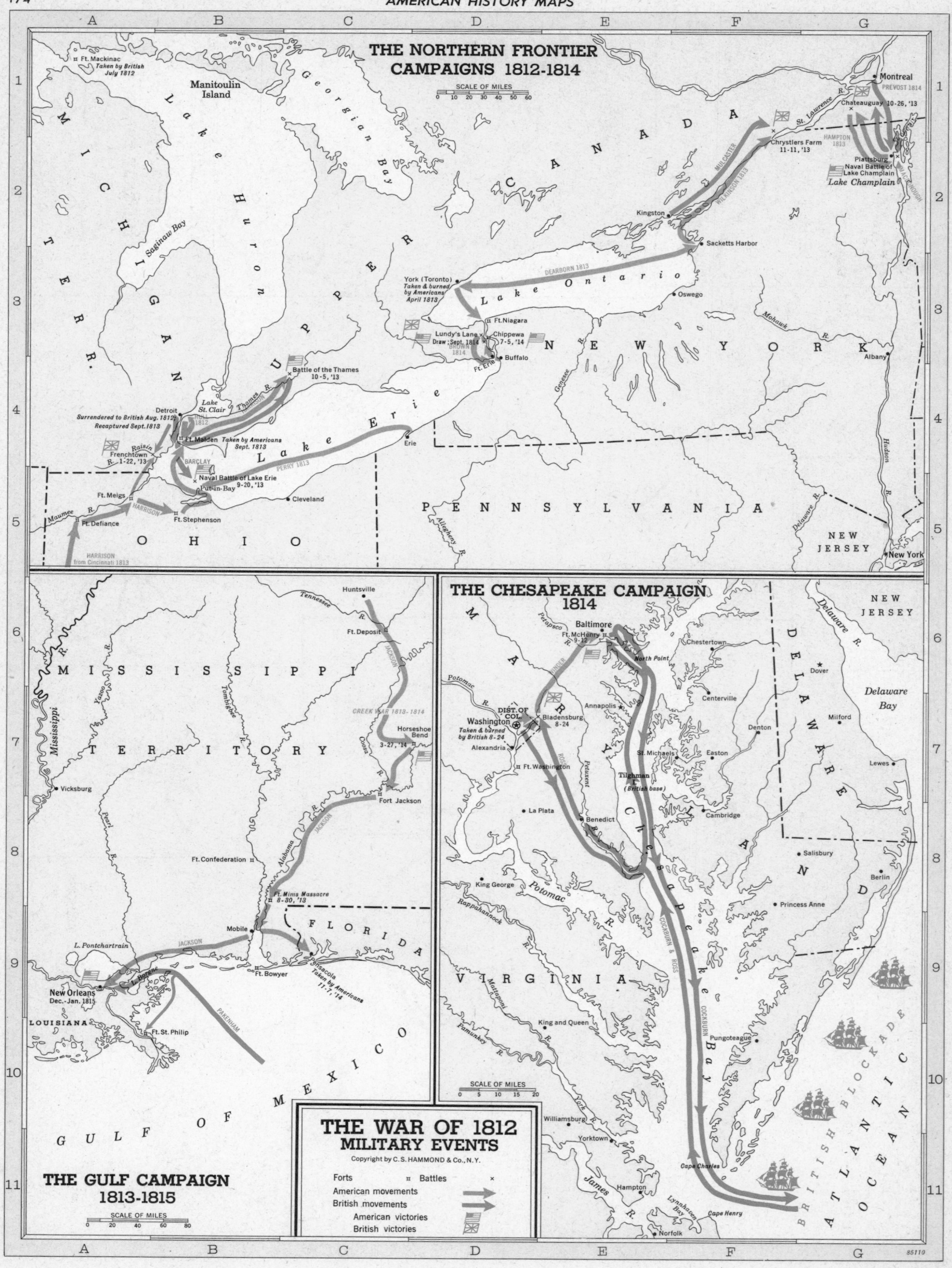

THE NORTHERN FRONTIER CAMPAIGNS 1812-1814

SCALE OF MILES
0 10 20 30 40 50 60

¤ Ft. Mackinac
Taken by British
July 1812

Manitoulin Island

Georgian Bay

Lake Huron

M I C H I G A N   T E R R.

Saginaw Bay

Lake St. Clair

Detroit
Surrendered to British Aug. 1812
Recaptured Sept. 1813

Raisin R.
Frenchtown
R-1-22, '13

Ft. Malden Taken by Americans Sept. 1813

Battle of the Thames
10-5, '13

Lake Erie

BARCLAY
Naval Battle of Lake Erie
Put-in-Bay 9-20, '13

PERRY 1813

Ft. Meigs
HARRISON
Ft. Stephenson

Maumee R.
Ft. Defiance

HARRISON
from Cincinnati 1813

O H I O

Cleveland

Erie

U P P E R   C A N A D A

Lake Ontario
DEARBORN 1813

York (Toronto)
Taken & burned
by Americans
April 1813

Ft. Niagara
Lundy's Lane
Draw; Sept. 1814
Chippewa
7-5, '14
BROWN
1814
Ft. Erie
Buffalo

Kingston

Sacketts Harbor

Oswego

Genesee R.

N E W   Y O R K

Mohawk R.

Albany

Hudson R.

Delaware R.

P E N N S Y L V A N I A

Allegheny R.

NEW
JERSEY

New York

Montreal
PREVOST 1814
Chateauguay 10-26, '13
St. Lawrence R.
Chrystlers Farm
11-11, '13
WILKINSON 1813
HAMPTON 1813
Plattsburg
Naval Battle of
Lake Champlain
Lake Champlain

THE CHESAPEAKE CAMPAIGN 1814

NEW
JERSEY

Delaware R.

Patapsco R.
Baltimore
Ft. McHenry
R-9-12
North Point

M A R Y L A N D

Potomac R.

Washington
DIST. OF COL.
Taken & burned by British 8-24
Alexandria
Bladensburg
8-24
Ft. Washington

Annapolis
Chesterton
Centerville

Dover

Delaware Bay

Milford

Denton

Easton
St. Michaels
Tilghman
(British base)
Cambridge

Patuxent R.

La Plata

King George

Benedict

Rappahannock R.

V I R G I N I A

Mattaponi R.

King and Queen

Pamunkey R.

Williamsburg

Yorktown

Hampton
Norfolk

James R.
Lynnhaven Bay
Cape Henry

Cape Charles

COCKBURN & ROSS

COCKBURN & ROSS

Chesapeake Bay

Salisbury

Berlin

Princess Anne

Pungoteague

Lewes

B R I T I S H   B L O C K A D E

A T L A N T I C   O C E A N

SCALE OF MILES
0 5 10 15 20

THE GULF CAMPAIGN 1813-1815

Huntsville

Tennessee R.

Ft. Deposit

M I S S I S S I P P I   T E R R I T O R Y

Mississippi R.
Yazoo R.

Vicksburg

Tombigbee R.

Pearl R.

Alabama R.

JACKSON

CREEK WAR 1813-1814

Coosa R.

Horseshoe Bend
3-27, '14

Fort Jackson

Ft. Confederation ¤

Ft. Mims Massacre
8-30, '13

Mobile

Ft. Bowyer

F L O R I D A

Pensacola
Taken by Americans
11-1, '14

L. Pontchartrain
JACKSON
L. Borgne
New Orleans
Dec.-Jan. 1815

L O U I S I A N A

Ft. St. Philip

PAKENHAM

G U L F   O F   M E X I C O

SCALE OF MILES
0 20 40 60 80

THE WAR OF 1812
MILITARY EVENTS
Copyright by C.S. HAMMOND & Co., N.Y.

Forts ¤	Battles ×
American movements ➤	
British movements ➤	
American victories	
British victories	

85110

THE GROWTH of the UNITED STATES From 1776 to 1867

MILES
0 50 100 200

The acquisitions made by the United States from 1776 to 1867 are shown by different colors.

The boundaries of the States and Territories at the close of 1867 are outlined by solid blue lines:

The Capitals of the States and Territories in 1867 are shown on map by: ⊙

Copyright by C.S. HAMMOND & CO., N.Y.

WASHINGTON TERRITORY
Olympia
OREGON COUNTRY
Acquired by Treaty with Great Britain in 1846
OREGON 1859
Salem
MONTANA TERRITORY
Virginia City
IDAHO TERRITORY
DAKOTA TERRITORY
Yankton
MINNESOTA 1858
St. Paul
WISCONSIN 1848
MICHIGAN 1837
Lansing
Lake of the Woods
MAINE 1820
Augusta
VERMONT 1791
Montpelier
NEW HAMPSHIRE 1788 Concord
MASS. Boston
Providence
CONN. Hartford
New Haven
NEW YORK
Albany
Trenton
NEVADA 1864
Carson City
UTAH TERRITORY
Salt Lake City
THE MEXICAN CESSION OF 1848
COLORADO TERRITORY
Golden City
NEBRASKA 1867
Des Moines
IOWA 1846
ILLINOIS 1818
Springfield
Lincoln
Topeka
KANSAS 1861
INDIANA 1816
Indianapolis
OHIO 1803
Columbus
MISSOURI 1821
Jefferson City
KENTUCKY 1792
Frankfort
PENNSYLVANIA 1787
Harrisburg
WEST VIRGINIA 1863
Wheeling
VIRGINIA
Richmond
Washington
MD.
DEL.
CALIFORNIA 1850
Sacramento
ARIZONA TERRITORY
NEW MEXICO TERRITORY
Santa Fe
INDIAN TERRITORY
ARKANSAS 1836
Little Rock
TENNESSEE 1796
Nashville
NORTH CAROLINA
Raleigh
SOUTH CAROLINA
Columbia
GEORGIA
Milledgeville
THE GADSDEN PURCHASE 1853
Tucson
TEXAS Annexed in 1845
Austin
1845
MISSISSIPPI 1817
Jackson
ALABAMA 1819
Montgomery
LOUISIANA 1812
Baton Rouge
FLORIDA 1845
Tallahassee
Acquired by Treaty with Spain in 1819
GULF OF MEXICO
MEXICO
PACIFIC OCEAN
ATLANTIC OCEAN
Purchased from France in 1803
Acquired by Conquest and by Treaty in 1783
DURING THE REVOLUTION
BOUNDARY OF ADAMS-ONIS TREATY 1819

ARCTIC OCEAN
ALASKA Purchased from Russia in 1867
CANADA
BERING SEA
PRIBILOF Is.
ALEUTIAN ISLANDS
PACIFIC
Scale of Miles
0 100 200 300 400 500

Copyright by C.S. HAMMOND & CO., N.Y.

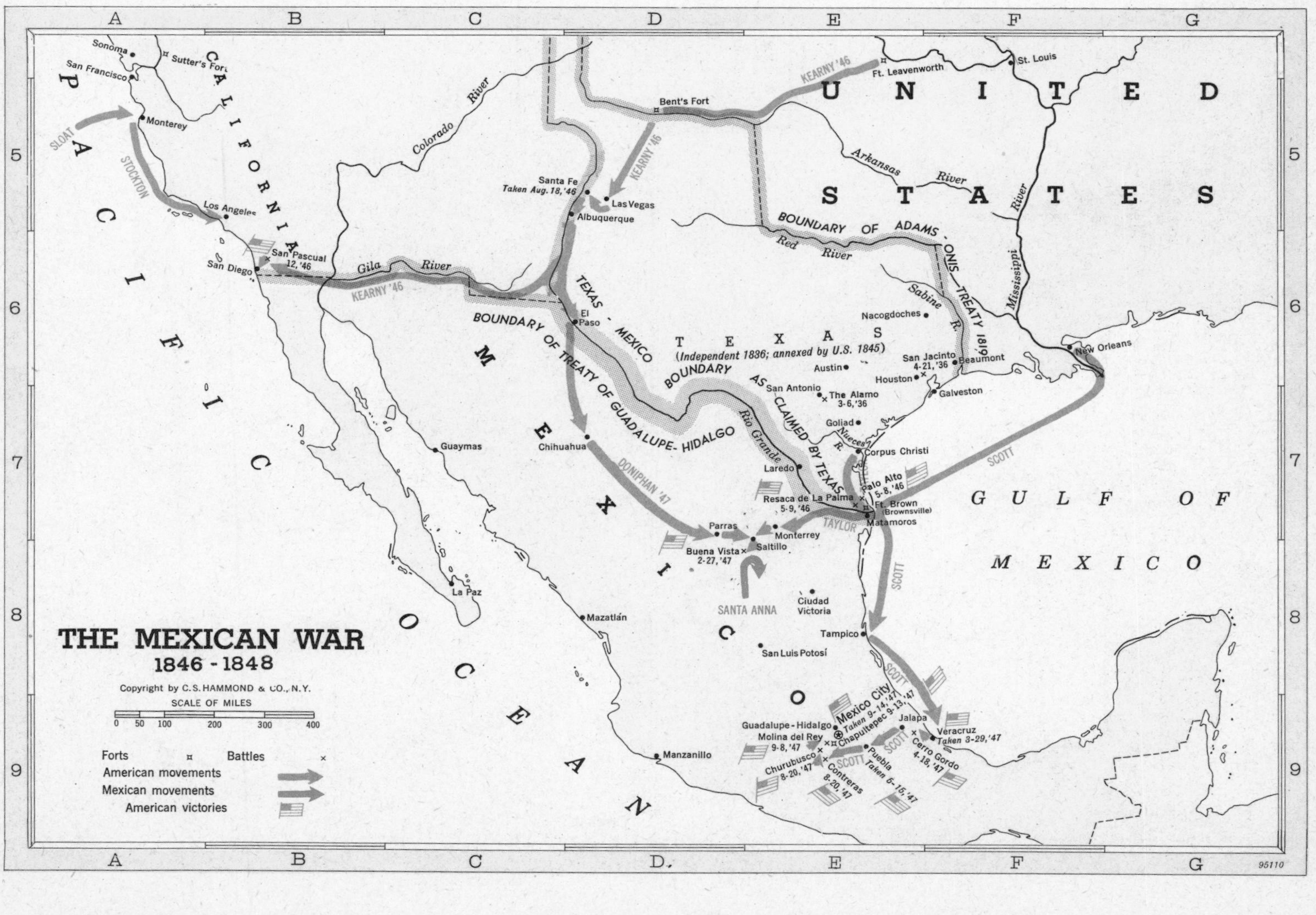

THE MEXICAN WAR 1846-1848

Copyright by C.S. HAMMOND & CO., N.Y.

SCALE OF MILES
0 50 100 200 300 400

Forts ⊓
Battles ×
American movements →
Mexican movements ⇒
American victories ▨

UNITED STATES
PACIFIC OCEAN
GULF OF MEXICO
MEXICO
CALIFORNIA

Sonoma
Sutter's Fort
San Francisco
Monterey
SLOAT
STOCKTON
Los Angeles
San Pascual 12, '46
San Diego
Ft. Leavenworth
St. Louis
KEARNY '46
Bent's Fort
Santa Fe Taken Aug. 18, '46
Las Vegas
Albuquerque
KEARNY '46
Colorado River
Gila River
El Paso
Chihuahua
DONIPHAN '47
Guaymas
La Paz
Mazatlán
Manzanillo
BOUNDARY OF TREATY OF GUADALUPE-HIDALGO
TEXAS-MEXICO BOUNDARY AS CLAIMED BY TEXAS
Rio Grande
Parras
Buena Vista 2-27, '47
Saltillo
Monterrey
Laredo
SANTA ANNA
Ciudad Victoria
San Luis Potosí
Tampico
Arkansas River
Red River
BOUNDARY OF ADAMS-ONIS TREATY 1819
Sabine R.
Nacogdoches
San Jacinto 4-21, '36
Beaumont
Austin
Houston
San Antonio
The Alamo 3-6, '36
Goliad
Galveston
Corpus Christi
Nueces R.
Palo Alto 5-8, '46
Resaca de La Palma 5-9, '46
Ft. Brown (Brownsville)
Matamoros
TAYLOR
New Orleans
Mississippi R.
SCOTT
GULF OF MEXICO
TEXAS (Independent 1836; annexed by U.S. 1845)
Mexico City Taken 9-14, '47
Chapultepec 9-13, '47
Molina del Rey 9-8, '47
Guadalupe-Hidalgo
Churubusco 8-20, '47
Contreras 8-20, '47
Puebla Taken 6-15, '47
Jalapa
Cerro Gordo 4-18, '47
Veracruz Taken 3-29, '47
SCOTT

95110

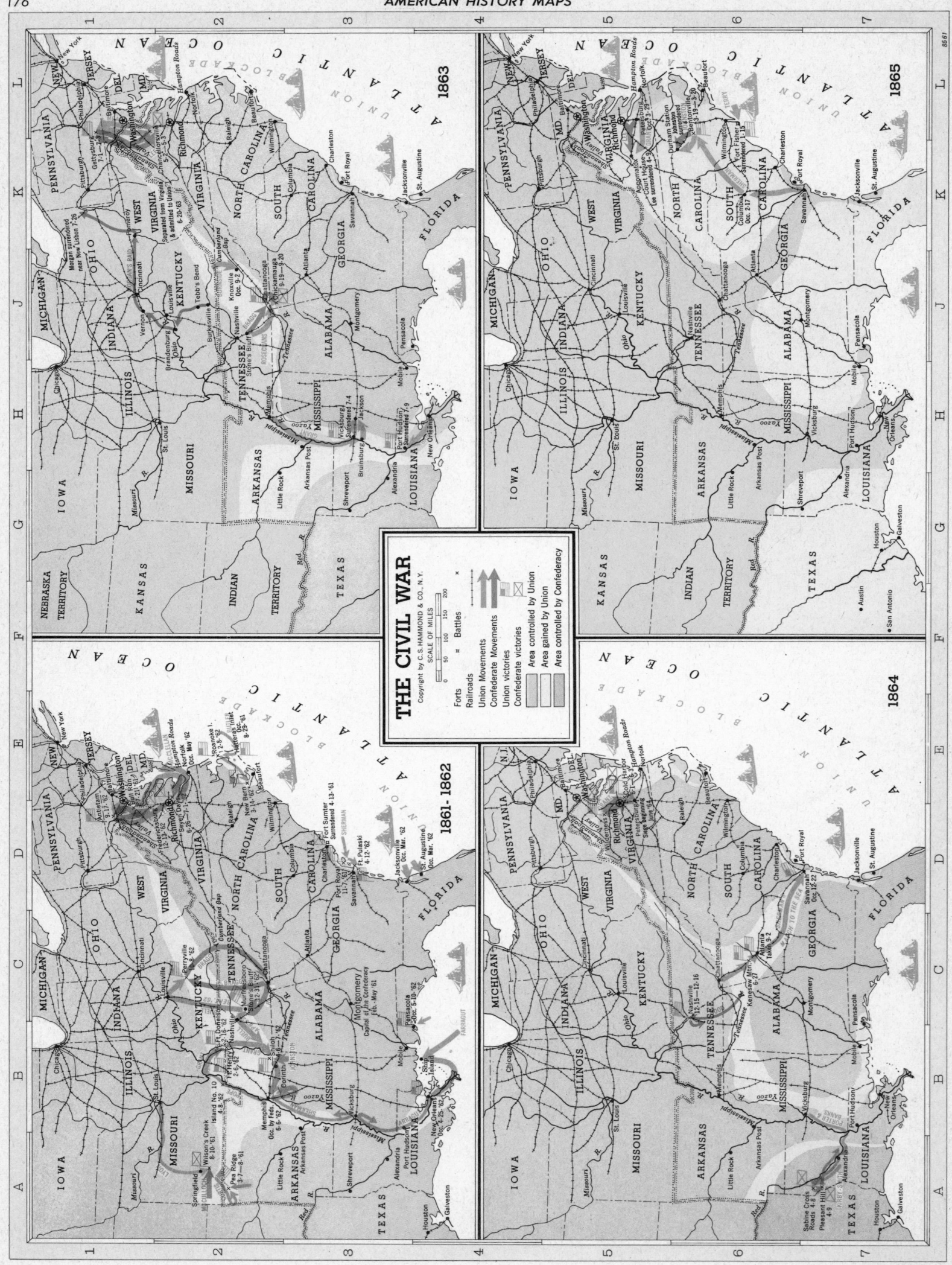

THE CIVIL WAR

Copyright by C.S. HAMMOND & CO., N.Y.

SCALE OF MILES

Forts
Railroads
Union Movements
Confederate Movements
Union victories
Confederate victories
Battles

Area controlled by Union
Area gained by Union
Area controlled by Confederacy